T0391204

The Right to Health

Brigit Toebes · Rhonda Ferguson
Milan M. Markovic · Obiajulu Nnamuchi
Editors

Zlatka Koleva
Assistant Editor

The Right to Health

A Multi-Country Study of Law, Policy and Practice

Editors
Brigit Toebes
Faculty of Law, Constitutional and
 International Law
University of Groningen
Groningen
The Netherlands

Rhonda Ferguson
Law
Irish Centre for Human Rights
Galway
Ireland

Milan M. Markovic
Institute of International Law
University of Graz
Graz
Austria

and

Institute of Social Sciences
Belgrade
Serbia

Obiajulu Nnamuchi
Faculty of Law, Dept. of Public
 and Private Law
University of Nigeria, Enugu Campus
Enugu
Nigeria

ISBN 978-94-6265-013-8   ISBN 978-94-6265-014-5   (eBook)
DOI 10.1007/978-94-6265-014-5

Library of Congress Control Number: 2014942052

© T.M.C. ASSER PRESS and the authors 2014

Published by T.M.C. ASSER PRESS, The Hague, The Netherlands www.asserpress.nl
Produced and distributed for T.M.C. ASSER PRESS by Springer-Verlag Berlin Heidelberg

No part of this work may be reproduced, stored in a retrieval system, or transmitted in any form or by
any means, electronic, mechanical, photocopying, microfilming, recording or otherwise, without written
permission from the Publisher, with the exception of any material supplied specifically for the purpose
of being entered and executed on a computer system, for exclusive use by the purchaser of the work.
The use of general descriptive names, registered names, trademarks, etc. in this publication does not
imply, even in the absence of a specific statement, that such names are exempt from the relevant
protective laws and regulations and therefore free for general use.

Printed on acid-free paper

Springer is part of Springer Science+Business Media (www.springer.com)

Foreword

The key challenge confronting the health and human rights movement is the translation of international and national human rights law into operational policies, programmes and other health-related interventions. Nowhere is this more challenging—and more important—than within countries.

How can the right to the highest attainable standard of health ('the right to health') shape national policies? Does the right to health require that a national hospital—or a district health system—be organized differently? If so, what changes are needed? Does this human right demand that a country give more attention to community-level health promotion, for example via radio messages, poster campaigns, street theatre or primary education? Does it mean that the government has an obligation to regulate the sugar content of children's beverages? Does the right to health require the government to improve access to safe drinking water and adequate sanitation for rural communities and, if so, how can this be done within a finite budget?

This is just a tiny sample of the challenging questions facing those who wish to operationalise the right to health—and other health-related rights—in communities, districts and at national level.

One of the problems is context. What works well in one country might not work at all in another. It might not even work in a country of the same size and same stage of economic development. However, despite the enormous challenge of context, lessons can be learnt from the rich experiences of others. Indeed, it is crucial that we learn how different countries implement (or not) health-related rights.

That is why this book is so useful and important. It opens a right-to-health window onto different countries and continents. With a particular focus on eleven countries and five regions, it provides studies on the realization of the right to health (or dimensions of the right to health) from all regions of the world. It introduces research from a diverse group of authors operating through different disciplinary and cultural lenses, and demonstrates how scholars use the right to health framework and how they understand its strengths and weaknesses in relation to a particular country or region. In this way, we learn how the right to health framework is (and is not) being implemented in practice, and also how the authors envision the possibilities and limits of the framework for promoting health and well-being.

Some of the authors are representatives of a new generation of health and human rights academic-activists in the field of health-rights. They deserve—demand—our attention.

Each contribution focuses on a theme that is of specific relevance to the country in question, varying from access to health care for vulnerable groups (e.g., Aboriginal peoples in Canada and migrant workers in Saudi Arabia), to the use of indicators (in Brazil) and healthcare privatization (in the US and the Netherlands). Many of these themes overlap across countries and regions; for example, vulnerable populations exist in every country and region and are the focus of multiple chapters.

How many books on health-rights include contributions on the right to health in China, Japan, Saudi Arabia, Jordan and Peru? In this sense, this collection breaks new ground while emphasizing the need for deeper analysis and more studies.

Crucially, the contributors' examination of context-specific laws, policies and practices contributes to cross-cultural dialogue on the best practices and shortcomings, and provides insights that will be useful in a wide-range of countries.

So I warmly recommend this excellent volume to everyone interested in the great challenge of operationalising health-rights for all.

Paul Hunt
UN Special Rapporteur on the Right to
Health (2002–2008)
University of Essex

Contents

Part I Africa

1 Health and Millennium Development Goals in Africa: Deconstructing the Thorny Path to Success 3
Obiajulu Nnamuchi

2 Ensuring the Realization of the Right to Health Through the African Union (AU) System: A Review of Its Normative, Policy and Institutional Frameworks 43
Getahun A. Mosissa

Part II Asia

3 Equality and the Right to Health: A Preliminary Assessment of China 97
Shengnan Qiu

4 The Right to Health in Japan: Its Implications and Challenges 121
Tokuko Munesue

Part III Middle East

5 Codification and Implementation of the 'Right to Health' in the Arab World 135
Salman Rawaf and Sondus Hassounah

6 The Right to Health and Access to Health Care in Saudi Arabia with a Particular Focus on the Women and Migrants 165
Lara Walker

vii

viii

7 The Realization of the Right to Health for Refugees in Jordan ... 193
Katharine Heus and Thamer Sartawi

Part IV The Americas

8 The Right to Health: The Next American Dream ... 233
Dabney P. Evans

9 The Brazilian Human Rights Indicators System:
The Case of the Right to Health ... 259
Aline Albuquerque

10 Aboriginal-Specific Health Initiatives and Accessible Health Care
in Canada; Are Goodwill Initiatives Enough ... 281
Rhonda Ferguson

11 The Right to Health in Peru: Persistent Vulnerabilities
in the Context of HIV/AIDS ... 313
Ruth Iguiñiz, Nancy Palomino and Marco Barboza

Part V Europe

12 The Right to Health for Vulnerable and Marginalised Groups:
Russia as a Case Study ... 341
Natalya Pestova

13 The Challenges to Realising the Right to Health in Ireland ... 373
Adam McAuley

14 Dutch Realities: Evaluating Health Care Reform
in the Netherlands from a Human Rights Perspective ... 403
Brigit Toebes and Maite San Giorgi

Part VI Conclusions

15 Conclusions ... 439
Rhonda Ferguson, Obiajulu Nnamuchi and Milan M. Markovic

About the Authors ... 445

Abbreviations

AAAQ	Availability, Accessibility, Acceptability and Quality
ACA	Affordable Care Act
ACHPR	African Charter on Human and People's Rights
AHWS	Aboriginal Healing and Wellness Strategy (Canada)
AU	Africal Union
AWBZ	Exceptional Medical Expenses Act (the Netherlands)
BIG	Dutch Health Care Professionals Act
CAT	Convention against Torture and Other Cruel, Inhuman or Degrading Treatment or Punishment (UN, 1984)
CEDAW	Convention on the Elimination of All forms of Discrimination Against Women (UN, 1979)
CHA	Canada Health Act
CHIP	Comprehensive Health Insurance Plan (USA)
CHRA	Canadian Human Rights Act
CIE	Committee of Independent Experts (ESC, CoE)
CoE	Council of Europe
CONAMUSA	National Multisectoral HIV-Related Coordination Mechanism (Peru)
CPT	European Convention for the Prevention of Torture (CoE, 1987)
CRPD	UN Convention on the Rights of Persons with Disabilities
CRC	Convention on the Rights of the Child (UN, 1989)
CRPD	Convention on the Rights of Persons with Disabilities (UN, 2006)
CSDH	Committee on the Social Determinants of Health (WHO)
CVZ	Dutch Health Care Insurance Board
DRCSC	Development Research Centre of the State Council (China)
ECHR	Convention for the Protection of Human Rights and Fundamental Freedoms (CoE, 1950)
EComHR	European Commission of Human Rights
ECtHR	European Court of Human Rights (CoE)
EC Treaty	Treaty establishing the European Community (EU, 1993)
ECSR	European Committee of Social Rights (ESC, CoE)

ECFR	Charter of Fundamental Rights of the European Union (EU, 2000)
ECJ	European Court of Justice
ESC	European Social Charter (CoE, 1961)
EU	European Union
EUCFR	EU Charter of Fundamental Rights
FLACSO	Facultad Latinoamericana de Ciencias Sociales
General Comment 14	General Comment 14 to the ICESCR (on the right to health) (UN, 2000)
GHWA	Global Health Workforce Atlas
GHO	Global Health Observatory
GMS	General Medical Services Scheme (Ireland)
GOJ	Government of Jordan
GP	General Practitioner
GPPHP	Global public-private health partnerships
GTE Health	Technical-Executive Group on Health (Brazil)
HIA	Health Insurance Authority (Ireland)
HIV	Human immunodeficiency virus
HIQA	Health Information and Quality Authority
HRW	Human Rights Watch
HS	Health System
HSE	Health Services Executive (Ireland)
IACHR	Inter-American Commission on Human Rights
IBGE	Brazilian Institute for Geography and Statistics
ICCPR	International Convention on Civil and Political Rights (UN, 1966)
ICERD, CERD	International Convention on the Elimination of All Forms of Racial Discrimination (UN, 1965)
ICESCR	International Covenant on Economic, Social and Cultural Rights (UN, 1966)
ICF	International Classification of Functioning, Disability and Health
IFHHRO	International Federation on Health and Human Rights Organizations
IGZ	Dutch Health Care Inspectorate
ILO	International Labour Organization
IPEA	Applied Economic Research Institute (Brazil)
JHS	Jordanian Health System
KZi	Dutch Qualities of Health Facilities Act
MDGs	Millennium Development Goals
MENA	Middle East and Northern Africa
MMR	Maternal Mortality Ratio
MWC	International Convention on the Protection of the Rights of All Migrant Workers and Members of their Families (UN, 1990)

NAFDAC	National Agency for Food and Drug Administration and Control of Nigeria
NAHO	National Aboriginal Health Organization (Canada)
NCCAH	National Collaborating Centre for Aboriginal Health (Canada)
NEPAD	New Partnership for Africa's Development
NHAD	National Health Accounts Directory
NHRI	National Health Rights Indicators (Brazil)
NHRP	National Human Rights Program (Brazil)
NHS	National Health Service
NIHB	Non-Insured Health Benefits (Canada)
NRCMIS	New Rural Cooperative Medical Insurance Scheme
NZA	Dutch Health Authority
OCAP	Ownership, Control, Acces and Possession Principles
OECD	Organisation for Economic Co-Operation and Development
OHCHR	Office of the High Commissioner for Human Rights
OHIP	Ontario Health Insurance Plan
OOP	Out-of-pocket Payment
PAHO	Pan-American Health Organization
PHC	Primary health care
PLWHA	People Living with HIV or AIDS
PQP	Prequalification of Medicines Program
(Revised) ESC	Revised European Social Charter (CoE, 1996)
RMS	Royal Medical Services (Jordan)
SCOTUS	Supreme Court of the USA
SERAC	Social and Economic Rights Action Center (Nigeria)
SHP	Skilled Health Personnel
TB	Tuberculosis
TEPCO	Tokyo Electric Power Company
THSTP	Traditional Healer Services Travel Policy (Canada)
UAE	United Arab Emirates
UDHR	Universal Declaration of Human Rights (UN, 1948)
UHC	Universal Health Coverage
UN	United Nations
UNAIDS	UN Programme on HIV and AIDS
UNCRC	United Nations Committee on the Rights of the Child
UNDP	United Nations Development Program
UNESCO	UN Educational, Scientific and Cultural Organization
UNICEF	United Nations International Children's Emergency Fund
UNPAN	UN Public Administration Network
UNRWA	UN Relief and Works Agency
ULMIS	The Urban Labour Medical Insurance Scheme (China)
VHI	Voluntary Health Insurance
WB	World Bank

WDI	World Development Indicator
WGBO	Dutch Medical Treatment Agreement Act
WHO	World Health Organization
WIPO	World Intellectual Property Organization
WMCZ	Dutch Client Representation Act
WMA	World Medical Association
WMO	Dutch Social Support Act

Introduction

The 'right to the highest attainable standard of health' (or right to health) is by now firmly embedded in international law. Over the past 20 years there has been a steady stream of documents, reports and other publications clarifying the meaning and contents of the right to health. The most important explanatory source is General Comment 14 of the UN Committee on Economic, Social and Cultural Rights (CESCR), which gives an authoritative explanation of the right to health in Article 12 ICESCR. As a result of this clarification process the right to health is by now a norm under international law which has a considerable legal weight and which has the potential to impact on the health and well-being of individuals all over the world.

As we now have a fairly clear picture of the normative content of the right to health, the next step is to find out more about how these standards are to be applied in practice. We should assess their content in the light of national realities and current findings in the public health arena, social medicine, health economics and related fields. In other words, if we want to obtain a proper understanding of this norm, we should also look beyond its international definition and doctrinal foundation. We must not look at human rights norms in a vacuum, rather we must reconsider them consistently in the light of national and regional realities and particularities, new trends and developments, and for this we must also look beyond our own disciplinary borders. Examples of such developments are the increasing health inequalities between and within nations, continued health problems such as HIV/AIDS and maternal mortality, the lack of medicines in the developing world, as well as the way in which health systems are organized, such as the increasing worldwide trend of healthcare privatization, and the magnitude of health sector corruption.

This study focuses on the implementation of the right to health at regional and national levels. This project brings together a set of experts from thirteen different countries in the world, with each of them analyzing the implementation of the right to health in his or her country or region. The foundations for this project were laid during a modest project that we ran at the University of Aberdeen School of Law, where I worked as a Lecturer between 2006 and 2009. The project enabled advanced students to write a report about the implementation of the right to health in their country, or another country of their choice. Some of the issues that the reports addressed were the legal status of the right to health, the way health systems are organized, healthcare commercialization trends, the position of vulnerable groups and the underlying determinants of health.

Gradually, we were able to entice more experienced scholars for this project, and it grew into a more substantial research project. The project was moved to the Right to Health Wiki of the International Federation of Health and Human Rights Organisations (IFHHRO).[1] Some of the reports placed on this website had a considerable impact in the country under scrutiny. For example, the report on the right to health in Nigeria was adopted by the Association of Commissioners for Health as an authoritative statement on the state of health in that country.[2] The report about Brazil was published in Portuguese by the Brazilian government and was thus made available to a wider public in Brazil. Other reports that were made available included reports on Canada, Iran, Russia and Serbia.

The current follow-up project builds on the country reports by publishing a number of theme-oriented country studies in connection with the right to health. With theme-oriented country reports we mean reports that do not give a mere assessment of the implementation of the right to health in general, but that focus on a particular theme. For example, while the Millennium Development Goals are an important issue in relation to the implementation of the right to health in Africa, important issues in Europe are the social determinants of health, and the identification of vulnerable groups when it comes to accessing healthcare services. This approach enables us to focus on those issues that are of particular relevance to a certain country or region, so as to gain a greater understanding of these themes, and their applicability in a particular national or regional context. In addition, as a collection of tangentially connected themes, it helps to enrich our understanding of the right in practice. As mentioned, this project brings together experts from 13 different countries in the world, with each of them analysing the implementation of the right to health in his or her country or region. The authors are all scholars with considerable expertise in the right to health (see attached bibliography). As they all write about their own country or region, they can build a bridge between their expertise on the right to health with their specific backgrounds and expertise in his or her country or region. By covering countries from every region, the project can truly be called a global project which at the same time has relevance for every particular region in the world.

In the conclusions to this book, Rhonda Ferguson, Milan Markovic and Obi Nnamuchi distill the most important findings from the contributions and draw some conclusions in relation to the national implementation of the right to health. This may inspire scholars, policy makers and civil society to set the stage for a more effective implementation of the right to health at a national level.

---

[1] See http://righttohealthifhhro.pbworks.com—Health and Human rights by Country. Last visited 16 June 2014.

[2] In addition, an abridged version of the report was published (in Dutch) as "The Right to Health in Nigeria: A Challenge for a Young Democracy". See *Dutch Physicians for Human Rights, Newsletter* 14–17 (2007). See http://www.johannes-wier.nl/userfiles/file/Nieuwsbrief%20nr10_JWS.pdf.

Compiling this work has meant collaborating with scholars from all over the world and has, therefore, been a complicated process. I am entirely grateful to editors Rhonda, Obi and Milan, for their ongoing dedication to this project. Without them this book would never have materialized. We have never met in person, but after the many emails and Skype conversations I feel I know them well, which is both a huge pleasure and a tremendous honour. I also thank Zlatka Koleva, student at the University of Groningen, for her fantastic editorial work, and Asser Press for turning our work into an appealing book. Last but not least: a big thank you to all the authors in the book for their wonderful submissions and for providing us with inspiration. We trust their contributions will lead to interesting discussions regarding the implementation of the right to health in their country, their region and beyond.

Brigit Toebes
Associate Professor and Rosalind Franklin Fellow
in International Law, University of Groningen

Part I
Africa

Chapter 1
Health and Millennium Development Goals in Africa: Deconstructing the Thorny Path to Success

Obiajulu Nnamuchi

Abstract This chapter seeks to detangle the complex web of challenges paralyzing health in Africa and militating against the attainment of the various benchmarks of the Millennium Development Goals (MDGs), particularly the ones that are health-related (health MDGS). By relying on the health MDGs as a proxy for interrogating the right to health in the region, the chapter makes a case that the process which would eventuate in meeting the required benchmarks precariously perches on the threshold of being stifled by seemingly insuperable challenges. It projects surmounting these challenges as holding the key to rescuing the various health systems in the region from their current paralytic stupor. Adopting a human rights approach, the chapter identifies critical interventions both within and outside the health sector that must ground and propel national initiatives aimed at reversing the status quo and repositioning the region on a sustainable path to achieving the health MDGs and realizing the right to health.

Contents

1.1	Introduction	4
1.2	Background to the Study	6
1.3	Major Challenges to Achieving the Health MDGs	9
	1.3.1 Shortage of Health Professionals	10
	1.3.2 Shortage of Essential Drugs and Medicine	11
	1.3.3 Inadequate Resources	14
	1.3.4 Misalignment of Priorities	15

The author is Assistant Professor, Faculty of Law, Dept. of Public and Private Law, University of Nigeria, Enugu Campus, Enugu, Nigeria; President and Chief Consultant, Centre for Health, Bioethics and Human Rights (CHBHR), Enugu, Nigeria.

O. Nnamuchi (✉)
Faculty of Law, Dept. of Public and Private Law, University of Nigeria, Enugu, Nigeria
e-mail: obi.nnamuchi@yahoo.com

B. Toebes et al. (eds.), *The Right to Health*, DOI: 10.1007/978-94-6265-014-5_1,
© T.M.C. ASSER PRESS and the authors 2014

	1.3.5 Corruption and Bad Governance	18
1.4	Interventions for Change	21
	1.4.1 Poverty Reduction	22
	1.4.2 Addressing Underlying Determinants of Health	27
	1.4.3 Integrating Human Rights into Health Systems	29
	1.4.4 Individual Empowerment	30
	1.4.5 Civil Society Empowerment	32
1.5	Conclusion	36
References		39

1.1 Introduction

Desirous of repositioning and strengthening the United Nations (U.N.) to more effectively deal with the challenges of the twenty-first century, the General Assembly adopted resolution 53/202, convening the Millennium Summit as a key part of the Millennium Assembly of the organization.[1] The Summit, which was held at the U.N. headquarters in New York in September 2000, was attended by the largest cohort of world leaders ever. Its distinctive highlight was the ratification by all 189 U.N. member countries in attendance of the Millennium Declaration—a set of objectives upon which the Millennium Development Goals (MDGs or Goals) are based.[2] The MDGs commit countries to pursue a series of specific, monitorable, and quantifiable targets (Targets), with 2015 as the deadline for achieving most of them. Numbering 21, each of the Targets has corresponding indicators designed to guide countries in setting their national policies, priorities, and strategic initiatives as well as measuring progress toward the various Goals.[3]

There are eight Goals to which each country aspires to attain within the specified period. Of these Goals, three are directly related to health (health MDGs), namely, to: (i) reduce child mortality, (ii) improve maternal health, and (iii) combat HIV/AIDS, malaria, and other diseases. To this list may be added a fourth, (iv) to eradicate poverty.[4] Although the term "health MDGs" is most

---

[1] See G.A. Res. 53/202, U.N. GAOR, 53rd Sess., Agenda Item 30, U.N. Doc. A/Res/53/202 (1999).

[2] The Millennium Declaration is an expression of global commitment to peace, security and disarmament; development and poverty eradication; protecting the environment; promoting human rights, democracy and good governance; protecting the vulnerable; meeting the special needs of Africa; and, strengthening the U.N. See G.A. Res. 55/2, U.N. GAOR, 55th Sess., Supp. No. 49, at 4, U.N. Doc. A/55/49 (2000).

[3] See U.N. Statistics Div., 'Official List of MDG Indicators', 15 January 2008, available at http://unstats.un.org/unsd/mdg/Resources/Attach/Indicators/OfficialList2008.pdf (accessed 18 February 2013).

[4] The remaining MDGs are to: achieve universal primary education, promote gender equality and empower women, ensure environmental sustainability and develop a global partnership for development. See Ibid.

commonly associated with the first three, there is no legitimate reason for excluding poverty reduction. A more expansive interpretation is justified by the close link between poverty and ill-health. Poverty is both a cause and a consequence of ill-health and vice versa; the two are mutually reinforcing.[5] Moreover— and, for this discourse, perhaps most important—progress (or lack thereof) toward the first three Goals crucially hinges on the extent to which the fourth (poverty reduction) is being (or has been) actualized. That is, the latter makes the former possible. In fact, a consequential discourse on the MDGs must proceed on the premise that all the "goals and targets are interrelated" and, as such, deserving of no less than a holistic approach.[6]

Nevertheless, as the 2015 deadline draws nigh, it is becoming increasingly clear that Africa is not on target to meet the MDGs. A recent admission by the African Union Conference of Health Ministers is quite striking: "Africa is still not on track to meet the health Millennium Declaration targets and the prevailing population trends could undermine progress made."[7] Why Africa is not on track to meet the MDGs, particularly those related to health, as well as suggestions on the path that would crystallize to success constitute the major task of this chapter.

The chapter consists of five sections. Following the Introduction, Part II lays the background to the study. In Sect. 1.3 the chapter discusses the major obstacles to attaining the health MDGs in Africa. Though legion, the section focuses on health system deficiencies, with particular attention to dearth of health professionals, shortage of essential drugs and medicine, resource constraints, and misalignment of health priorities. In addition, the section considers the devastating challenge posed by corruption and bad governance. Having situated the challenges, Sect. 1.4 suggests major interventions that could turn things around, namely addressing underlying health determinants, remediating poverty, integrating human rights into health systems and empowerment of individuals as well as civil society. The conclusion— Sect. 1.5—is that although the present state of health in Africa gives little room for optimism, it is possible for countries in the region to make significant headway by being innovative and incorporating reform initiatives identified in this discourse.

---

[5] Referring to this link as a "vicious cycle," the African Union Conference of Health Ministers explained: just as "poverty and its determinants drive up the burden of disease," so too "ill-health contributes to poverty." See The African Health Strategy: 2007–215, Third Session of the African Union Conference of Ministers of Health, Johannesburg, South Africa, April 9–13, 2007, CAMH/MIN/5(III), 4, available at http://www.africa-union.org/root/UA/Conferences/2007/avril/ SA/9-13%20avr/doc/en/SA/AFRICA_HEALTH_STRATEGY.pdf (accessed 28 August 2013) [hereinafter African Health Strategy]. See also WHO 2005 (acknowledging that "emphasis on health reflects a global consensus that ill-health is an important dimension of poverty in its own right. Ill-health contributes to poverty. Improving health is a condition for poverty alleviation and for development. Sustainable improvement of health depends on successful poverty alleviation and reduction of inequalities").

[6] U.N. Dev. Group, Indicators for Monitoring the Millennium Development Goals: Definitions, Rationale, Concepts and Sources, U.N. Doc. ST/ESA/STAT/SER.F/95, U.N. Sales No. E.03.XVII. 18 (2003).

[7] African Health Strategy p. 3.

1.2 Background to the Study

The Goals and Targets relating to health provide a yardstick, a concrete barometer for measuring the outcome of socioeconomic and political investments in health by all member nations of the U.N. They serve, in a sense, as human rights tools for assessing the degree of commitment of governments to the health and wellbeing of individuals within their respective jurisdictions. For stakeholders, being apprised of such information (knowledge of specific policies, including implementation strategies) positions them on a firm footing to demand accountability on the part of responsible authorities in their various countries. And this, in itself, is a crucial driver of health sector development.

The specific Targets attached to each Goal are as follows: Goal 4 (reduce by two-thirds, between 1990 and 2015, the under-five mortality rate); Goal 5 (reduce by three quarters, between 1990 and 2015, the maternal mortality rate); Goal 6 (to have halted by 2015 and begun to reverse the spread of HIV/AIDS and achieve, by 2010, universal access to treatment for HIV/AIDS for all those who need it; to have halted and begun to reverse the incidence of malaria by 2015; and to have halted and begun to reverse the incidence of tuberculosis by 2015); and, Goal 1 (to halve, between 1990 and 2015, the proportion of people whose income is less than $1 (reversed to $1.25 in 2005) or suffering from hunger). While not denying the importance or relevance of these Goals and associated Targets to the objective of this chapter, space constraint forecloses an in-depth discussion. This is not a discourse on specificities of a particular MDG or Target. Instead—and this is critical—the chapter's objective is very cosmopolitan. Its focus is on the big picture. It adopts a broader approach, by concentrating on the major obstacles in the path to meeting MDG obligations in the region and incorporating specific interventions that would dramatically turn things around.

This chapter, inspired by the African Health Strategy: 2007–2015,[8] the objective of which is to "strengthen health systems in order to reduce ill-health and accelerate progress towards attainment of the [MDGs] in Africa,"[9] is essentially a critical analysis of the state of health in Africa. The chapter argues that the poor state of health in Africa is a product not only of deficiency of access to health care but, more fundamentally, other socioeconomic and environmental health determinants (positively defined) and related problems. This deficiency is most apparent in data showing stagnating or downward spiraling of key health indices in most countries

---

[8] Ibid. Additional inspiration is provided by the New Partnership for Africa's Development (NEPAD) Health Strategy, the second leading policy document on health in Africa. Its vision and goal is to rid Africa of "the heavy burden of avoidable ill-health, disability and premature death" by "[dramatically reducing] the burden of disease, especially for the poorest in Africa." The NEPAD Health Strategy was adopted at the first African Union Conference of Health Ministers held in Tripoli in April 2003 and endorsed by the African Union in Maputo in July 2003, http://www.sarpn.org.za/documents/d0000612/NEPAD_Health_Strategy.pdf (accessed 12 March 2013). Ibid., p. 14.

[9] African Health Strategy, p. 7.

in the region. While not denying the monstrous reality of resource constraints (particularly on an individual level), the paper blames the status quo on irresponsible governance, which is sustained by docility on the part of the citizenry, in terms of not using the democratic process to demand and force necessary changes. It identifies crucial interventions both within and outside the health sector that must ground regional and national initiatives aimed at achieving the desired outcome.

Four critical facts shape the thrust of this chapter. First, the MDGs are not exactly novel obligations. Juxtaposed against previous international agreements, they are far-reaching and embody more specific obligations. But they are, on a more in-depth analysis, restatements of previous unmet commitments. For instance, WHO's "Global Strategy Health for All by the Year 2000," which was launched in 1979, had as its goal, the attainment by all people of the world by the year 2000 of a level of health that would permit them to lead socially and economically productive lives.[10] This goal, sweeping as it is, clearly encompasses all the health MDGs and had the goal been met as envisaged, there would certainly have been no need for the MDGs. Even more specific to Africa, Target 6.C (to "[h]ave halted by 2015 and begun to reverse the incidence of malaria ...") is substantially similar to an earlier pledge (in April 2000, 4 months before the Millennium Declaration) by African countries (to "[h]alve the malaria mortality for Africa's people by 2010..."),[11] the only material difference being a five-year interval between the cutoff dates for meeting the obligations. Moreover, as the Millennium Development Project acknowledges, "human rights (economic, social, and cultural rights) already encompass many of the Goals, such as those for poverty, hunger, education, health, and the environment."[12] What all these signify is that the Millennium Declaration, despite its omnibus reach, does not hold a magic wand in terms of radically improving the health of Africans, or anyone else for that matter, versus earlier international initiatives. The key would be whether the political leadership in Africa is prepared, this time around, to extirpate the obstacles retarding progress toward achieving health for all in the region, thereby positioning the region on a fast track to meet its MDGs obligations.

The second point worthy of note is whether countries in the region are on pace to meet the obligations imposed by the health MDGs? Aside from the statement of the African Union Conference of Health Ministers, referenced previously, New York University professor of economics William Easterly recently documented

---

[10] The Global Strategy was launched in 1979 at the 32nd World Health Assembly by adopting resolution WHA32.30, although the original idea for global pursuit of health for all by the year 2000 was conceived at the 30th World Health Assembly in 1977 (WHA 30.43). See WHO 1981, p. 7, 15. On the link between the Global Strategy and the MDGs, see Franco 2009, p. 63. The author describes the MDGs as a "sequel to one of the most ambitious commitments of the twentieth century to health through the objectives outlined in Health for All by the Year 2000".

[11] African Union, 2000, available at http://www.usaid.gov/our_work/global_health/id/malaria/publications/docs/abuja.pdf (accessed 12 March 2013).

[12] U.N. Millennium Project 2005, p. 119.

several instances of skepticism[13] including, inter alia, a statement by the U.N. Department of Public Information, "[a]t the midway point between their adoption in 2000 and the 2015 target date for achieving the [MDGs], sub-Saharan Africa is not on track to achieve any of the goals," including those that are health-related.[14] Take MDG 4 as an illustration. Its Target is to reduce by two-thirds, between 1990 and 2015, the under-5 mortality rate (U5MR). In this key area, sub-Sahara Africa is seriously lagging behind other regions, as evident in the following devastating statistics. Out of every eight children born in Africa, one dies before his or her fifth birthday.[15] The U5MR, at 142 deaths per 1,000 live births, is abysmal in comparison to other regions (the rates in America and Europe are 18 and 14 deaths per 1,000 live births respectively.)[16] More specifically, there are 31 countries with U5MR exceeding 100, all of which are African, except one (Afghanistan).[17] And in 2008, sub-Sahara Africa accounted for half of the 8.8 million under-five deaths in the world.[18] Quite a bleak picture indeed, which raises the question whether Africa is on pace to reduce its U5MR by 66 % in 2015, relative to 1990 level as called for by MDG 4. All available data suggest that this is very unlikely. Since the U5MR in 1990 was 182,[19] meeting the Target would require reducing the number to 62. This is a very difficult feat to accomplish, especially considering that the current figure is 127, a couple of years before the deadline.[20]

Third, it has to be noted, as mentioned in the Abstract, that the MDG project is used in this chapter as a proxy, sort of shorthand, for analyzing broader human right to health issues. The various benchmarks and indicators of the health MDGs are relevant markers for assessing also the commitment of countries to actualizing the right to health in their respective jurisdictions. In other words, advancement toward the health MDGs is tantamount to progress toward realizing the right to health or vice versa. The two are intimately related. Underlying this chapter, therefore, is concern about the right of the people of Africa to health and how to concretize it in their lives.

The final issue (and closely related to the first) is the place of corruption in the overall scheme of attaining the Goals. What proportion of disbursed aid would translate to concrete programs and completed projects in the region? What accountability measures are in place to guarantee the desired result? Remarkably, despite the hue and cry about making aid dependent on good governance, there is, thus far, very minimal evidence of international practice denying aid to countries for

---

[13] Easterly 2009, p. 26.

[14] U.N., Africa, and the Millennium Development Goals 2007 Update, p. 1, available at unstats.un.org/unsd/mdg/resources/.../Africa/Africa-MDGs07.pdf (accessed 9 January 2013).

[15] U.N. 2011, The Millennium Development Goals Report 2011, p. 25.

[16] WHO 2010, p. 24.

[17] U.N. 2011, The Millennium Development Goals Report 2011, p. 25.

[18] U.N. 2010a, The Millennium Development Goals Report 2010, p. 27.

[19] WHO 2010, pp. 56–57, UNICEF 2009, p. 121.

[20] WHO 2011, pp. 54–55.

insufficient commitment to good governance and corruption eradication measures.[21] This is of critical importance as a central claim of this chapter is that the current state of health in Africa, contrary to extant orthodoxy, is not explicable on the basis of finitude of resources. The roots, as the next section clearly shows, are much more ominous.

1.3 Major Challenges to Achieving the Health MDGs

One can sum up the major obstacles to achieving the health MDGs in Africa as systemic deficiencies—that is, gaps, inefficiencies, and other drawbacks that negatively impact health system capability to respond to the needs of the people dependent on it.[22] A health system consists of "all the activities whose primary purpose is to promote, restore or maintain health."[23] Merging these two definitions yields the proposition that "health system deficiencies" amount to failure of health-related activities to effectively contribute to health promotion, restoration or maintenance. This failure is gauged by the responsiveness of the health system to the demand placed upon it by its users, and the response curve itself is influenced by the availability or otherwise of several factors, particularly health personnel, essential drugs, equipment, infrastructure, and whether equity is built into the system in terms of access and health outcomes. The pendulum swings up and down in tandem with the response curve. That is, the availability and equitable access to these goods pushes the response curve up and vice versa. Decrepit and dilapidated infrastructure, poorly staffed hospitals and clinics, drought of essential medicines, and escalating cost of services—all too common in most African nations—combine to perennially hold the pendulum down. The depressing health data animated in the various sections of this discourse is directly linked to health system deficiencies throughout the region.

Each year, WHO publishes two authoritative reports on global state of health, namely the World Health Statistics and the World Health Report. Common to both reports is the consistency of atrocious health indices in sub-Sahara Africa. Indeed, in the 2000 edition of the World Health Report, which analyzed health system

---

[21] To the contrary, Alberto Alesina and Beatrice Weder found that "there is no evidence that bilateral or multilateral aid goes disproportionally to less corrupt governments" or that "debt relief programs [another form of foreign aid] have been targeted to less corrupt countries." See Alesina and Weder 2002, p. 1126.

[22] The NEPAD Health Strategy notes, as the reason "Africa is not on track to achieve [the MDGs]," the following: health systems and services are too weak to support targeted reduction in disease burden; disease control programs do not match the scale of the problem; safety in pregnancy and childbirth has not been achieved; people are not sufficiently empowered to improve their health; insufficient resources; widespread poverty, marginalization and displacement on the continent; and, the benefits of health services do not equitably reach those with the greatest disease burden. See NEPAD Health Strategy, pp. 6–13; Africa Health Strategy, pp. 4–5.

[23] WHO 2000, p. 5.

attainment and performance of 191 countries, only two countries in the region (Senegal and Seychelles) were ranked in the top 50 percentile.[24] The dismal state of the rest of the countries' health systems stridently testifies to the multifarious public health challenges facing the region, none of which is really new but now poised, more than ever, to obstruct the attainment of health MDGs in the region.

1.3.1 Shortage of Health Professionals

Foremost among the systemic challenges is accessibility of health professionals. Although there is worldwide shortage, no place is worse hit than Africa. Notwithstanding that the region bears a whopping 24 % of the disease burden in the world, it has only 3 % of the global health workforce compared, for instance, to the Americas which shoulders just 10 % share of the global diseases but is home to 37 % of the world's health workers.[25] The situation in some African countries is so dire that even where urgently needed resources such as drugs and equipments are available, severely limited human capacity constrains rapid and efficient deployment of the resources. There are dual dimensions to this problem. Medical schools in Africa do not graduate sufficient number of physicians, nurses, midwives, and other paramedical professionals to adequately staff available health facilities. And notwithstanding this deficit, a significant portion of the few available hands migrate abroad, most to Western countries, in search of better conditions of service.[26] Having less than adequate hands to deliver critical services does not bode well for health systems in the region. The true impact of this deficiency, however, is dependent on the severity of the circumstances in each country.

WHO projects that for a country to be able to deliver essential health interventions and achieve the MDGs, the availability of its health personnel (doctors, nurses and midwives) must be higher than 2.28 per 1,000 people.[27] Countries not meeting this threshold are said to be suffering critical shortages. There are 57 such countries, 36 of them in Africa.[28] To make up the shortfall, estimated at 817, 992, Africa needs to boost its recruitment (doctors, nurses, and midwives) by 139 %.[29] Regrettably, a 2009 study of the density of physicians and nurses in 12 African countries found that not only is the workforce inadequate to meet current demand,

---

[24] Ibid., pp. 152–155.

[25] WHO 2006, pp. XVIII–XIX.

[26] Other factors responsible for health worker shortage in Africa include early retirement of health workers, morbidity, and mortality. See Kinfu et al. 2009, p. 225, Kumar 2007, pp. 2564–2567, Naicker et al. 2009, pp. S1-60–64.

[27] WHO 2006, pp. 11–12.

[28] Ibid., p. 12.

[29] WHO 2006, p. 13 citing WHO, Global Atlas of the Health Workforce.

1 Health and Millennium Development Goals in Africa

in at least half of the countries surveyed, there is no capacity in existing training programs to produce sufficient number of graduates to maintain existing levels.[30]

Worse still, thousands continue to flee the region's hospitals and clinics. As much as 37 % of South African doctors (29 and 19 %, respectively, in Ghana and Angola) are employed in just eight countries belonging to the Organization for Economic Co-operation and Development (OECD).[31] The level of migration to the United States is even more alarming. The health system of Liberia ranks among the worst globally (186th out of 191 countries surveyed),[32] but 43 % of its physicians work in the United States, with Ghana and Uganda next in line, contributing 30 and 20 %, respectively, of their doctors.[33]

For nascent and fragile health systems in Africa, cushioning the effect of such massive brain drain is quite a daunting task. Consider, for instance, that one of the factors contributing to high number of maternal deaths across Africa is insufficiency of skilled health personnel (SHP). Deaths resulting from this single factor are blamable, in large part, on efflux of the region's nurses and midwives to foreign countries. With 880 deaths per 100,000 live births,[34] Zimbabwe stands afar, as most African nations, from meeting its MDG obligation regarding maternal mortality. Yet, more than one-third of its nurses and midwives (3,183 out of 9,357) are employed in OECD countries, as do 18 %, respectively, from Lesotho and Mauritius, two other countries with equally abysmal MMR.[35]

1.3.2 Shortage of Essential Drugs and Medicine

Since the Declaration of Alma-Ata, countries in Africa, as elsewhere, have been striving to secure universal coverage for everyone in their territories. Even health systems that have succeeded in attracting and retaining ample number of health practitioners will falter unless regular supply of essential drugs is secured. There is, as noted previously, a crunching shortage of health personnel throughout Africa, and the same goes for essential drugs—defined as "those that satisfy the priority health care needs of the population" and "are selected with due regard to public health relevance, evidence on efficacy and safety, and comparative cost-effectiveness."[36] Key attributes of essential medicines is that they address priority

---

[30] Kinfu et al. 2009, p. 227.

[31] WHO 2006, p. 100 citing Trends in international migration.

[32] WHO 2000, p. 53.

[33] Hagopian et al. 2004, p. 2.

[34] WHO 2010, p. 68.

[35] WHO 2006, p. 100.

[36] WHO, 'Essential Medicines', available at http://www.who.int/topics/essential_medicines/en/ (accessed 8 January 2013). Since 1977, WHO has published a list of essential medicines that is updated biennially. The current version, the 16th list, dates from March 2009. See WHO, 'Model

needs, are available at all times, are of acceptable quality and are sold "at a price the individual and the community can afford."[37] Viewed in light of these attributes, it becomes clear that Africa faces difficult hurdles in making essential drugs available to its people.

Owing to the embryonic state of the drug industry in Africa, a sizeable amount of pharmaceutical products dispensed in the region are imported, often at exorbitant prices. Because these drugs are largely unsubsidized and are mostly paid for out-of-pocket, those unable to pay the price are denied the benefit of the drugs. To address this problem, African countries have begun purchasing generics (cheaper than patented drugs) from other developing countries, especially India and China, resulting in substantial price reductions, although for the very poor, access still remains problematic. The most obvious response to this challenge is to develop capacity for local production, as has been explicitly called for by the African Union.[38] A sound idea, but then developing a drug manufacturing base requires huge capital outlay, advanced technology and technical expertise, all of which are in short supply in Africa. This explains the difficulties local production plants are having in meeting the needs of the population they serve.

But the situation is gradually improving. In addition to South Africa, production is rising in several other countries. In Nigeria, for instance, over 30 % of all medicines in the country are produced by local pharmaceutical industries, numbering more than 80.[39] This is certainly an encouraging development; still, a different concern remains—the quality of the finished product. It is striking that other than companies in South Africa, only one other country in sub-Saharan Africa (Uganda) has a plant that has successfully gone through the WHO Prequalification of Medicines Program (PQP)[40]—a process through which WHO determines the quality, safety, and efficacy of drugs based on a comprehensive evaluation of the drugs and manufacturing facilities.[41] Nonetheless, there is no evidence of substandard products being churned out at production facilities in Africa.

Aside from high prices, another problem affecting access to essential medicines in Africa is widespread circulation of counterfeit and adulterated medicines in the region's drug supply chain. The combined forces of poverty, lax rules and regulations, and avarice on the part of vendors combine to ensure that adulterated drugs populate pharmacy store shelves throughout the region. Weak enforcement regime feeds into the greed of unscrupulous vendors who import and distribute fake drugs

---

(Footnote 36 continued)

List of Essential Medicines', available at http://www.who.int/medicines/publications/essentialmedicines/en/ (accessed 8 January 2013).

[37] Ibid.

[38] African Union 2007, CAMH/MIN/8(III) (on file with author).

[39] See Mohammed 2009, p. 42, available at http://www.medicinestransparency.org/fileadmin/uploads/Documents/MeTA-Uganda_AfricaHealth.pdf (accessed 2 March 2013).

[40] Anderson 2010, p. 1597.

[41] WHO 2009, Technical Report Series No. 953, Annex 3 apps.who.int/prequal/info general/documents/.../TRS_953-Annex3.pdf (accessed 8 February 2013).

without regard to adverse impact on users. In 2004, 70 % of pharmaceuticals marketed in Angola were fake, as was the case in Nigeria in 2002.[42] But the situation has shown remarkable improvement in recent years. As of September 2010, the proportion of counterfeit drugs in Nigeria has shrunk to 5 %.[43] How was this feat accomplished?

Sanitizing the chaotic pharmaceutical industry in Nigerian began with the appointment of a woman of integrity, a fearless "warrior," to lead the National Agency for Food and Drug Administration and Control (NAFDAC), the nation's food and drug regulator, in 2001. Within months of assuming office, Dora Akunyili had fired corrupt employees, shut down shady pharmaceutical businesses, and blacklisted several foreign-based manufacturers of counterfeit drugs, mostly in India and China.[44] Both countries are now cooperating with Nigeria in stemming the flow of counterfeits from their countries.[45] NAFDAC officials have assumed a more visible presence and proactive role at the nation's airports, seaports, major markets, and distribution centers, confiscating and burning tons of seized drugs.

Prosecution of crooked dealers is up. In addition, the agency is seeking active cooperation of members of the public in its efforts. There is an ongoing awareness campaign aimed at empowering individuals to detect counterfeits and report offending vendors. In February 2010, NAFDAC launched the Mobile Authentication Service (MAS), an innovation of Sproxil Technology, which allows drug purchasers to use their mobile phones to verify the authenticity of the product.[46] The process is not cumbersome. Purchasers simply text a unique number on a scratch card attached to the medicine to a database in the United States and instantly receive a message confirming authenticity or warning that the product is fake. These bold moves are continuing to drive down counterfeits in Africa's most populous country, and should have an even more dramatic impact on smaller countries facing similar problems.

---

[42] WHO, Around the World: Reports of Counterfeit Medicines, http://www.who.int/medicines/services/counterfeit/impact/ImpactF_S/en/index1.html (accessed 8 February 2013); Abiodun Raufu, 'Influx of Fake Drugs to Nigeria Worries Health Experts', Lancet 324, no. 7339 (2002), p. 698.

[43] Obinna and Duru 2010, available at http://www.vanguardngr.com/2010/09/fake-drugs-down-to-5-says-nafdac/ (accessed 8 February 2013).

[44] For a list of companies on the list, see 'NAFDAC, Blacklisted Companies', http://www.nafdacnigeria.org/drugs.html (accessed 8 February 2013).

[45] Securing Industry, Chinese fake drug traders receive death sentence, 15 December 2009, available at http://www.securingindustry.com/pharmaceuticals/chinese-fake-drug-traders-receive-death-sentence/s40/a333/ (accessed 28 August 2013) (reporting that China imposed death sentence on six of its nationals for exporting substandard drugs to Nigeria).

[46] The Sproxil Blog, NAFDAC Launches Mobile Authentication Service in Nigeria with Sproxil's Technology, available at http://www.sproxil.com/blog/?p=78 (accessed 12 March 2013).

1.3.3 Inadequate Resources

Resource deficit is at the root of challenges facing health systems in Africa and a formidable obstacle to achieving the health MDGs. This is basic economics. Without adequate budgetary allocation, Ministries of Health are forced to scale back spending on health sector needs. Critical interventions such as hiring and retaining health workers, immunization drives, procurement of essential medicines, and public health emergency preparedness are scrapped or curtailed. This is the bane of health sector development in Africa. Inability to match needs with funds is the reason programs and strategies targeting the region's disease burden often end in failure. The WHO Commission on Macroeconomics and Health projects that developing countries need to spend about $34 per person each year to provide a package of essential preventive and curative healthcare services.[47] While per capita health spending in industrialized economies is hundred or more times this sum, the stark reality is that for many African countries, such level of spending is simply unthinkable. Democratic Republic of Congo and Zimbabwe, for instance, were able to spend just $17 and $20 per capita on health in 2007.[48]

The Abuja Declaration, adopted at the conclusion of the African Summit on HIV/AIDS, TB, and Other Related Infectious Diseases in April 2001, aims to plug this hole by committing African countries to allocate at least 15 % of their annual budgets to the health sector.[49] But a decade after adoption, the Declaration has not been matched with action. As of 2010, just six countries—Rwanda, Botswana, Niger, Malawi, Zambia, and Burkina Faso—have met the benchmark.[50] Even Nigeria, on whose shores the Declaration was adopted, is yet to boost its health spending in accordance with the Declaration. But even though the target remains largely unmet, significant strides have been made in several countries. Notable instances include Gabon which has increased its health budget to 14 %, Chad and Tanzania (nearly 14 %) and many others hovering around 10 % or more.[51] For those still to show progress, the temptation is great to demand that they step up efforts in that direction, but such demand glosses over the difficult financial circumstances of many of these countries.

---

[47] WHO 2001, Report of the Commission on Macroeconomics and Health, p. 11.

[48] Kaiser Family Foundation, Health Expenditure Per Capita 2007, available at http://www.globalhealthfacts.org/topic.jsp?i=66 (accessed 12 March 2013).

[49] Abuja Declaration on HIV/AIDS, Tuberculosis and Other Related Infectious Diseases, OAU/SPS/ABUJA/3, para 26.

[50] Africa Public Health Alliance, 2010 Africa Health Financing Scorecard, available at http://resultsuk.files.wordpress.com/2010/05/MDGs-africa-health-financing-scorecard-wha-summary-draft-april-may-2010.pdf (accessed 12 March 2013).

[51] Id.

1.3.4 Misalignment of Priorities

The canonization of primary health care (PHC) as "the central function and main focus" of health systems[52] at the 1978 International Conference on PHC received the imprimatur of 134 governments and 67 representatives of U.N. organizations, specialized agencies and accredited non-governmental organizations (NGOs) in attendance.[53] Participants at the conference affirmed PHC as providing the most effective and cost efficient path for governments to fulfill their responsibility for the health of their peoples, an affirmation that has been strengthened by the Committee on ESCR. In 2000, the ESCR Committee declared that the provision and availability of "minimum essential levels of … [PHC]" is a core obligation incumbent upon States Parties to the ICESCR.[54] A core obligation differs from an ordinary obligation in that whereas resource constraints, for instance, can justify non-compliance with the latter, there are no circumstances that would excuse non-performance of a core obligation.[55] As of September 2010, 46 out of 53 countries in Africa have ratified the Covenant and are therefore bound by its non-derogable provisions.[56]

The essence of PHC approach is its emphasis on deployment of more resources toward basic health care and disease prevention services at PHC centers (in contrast to concentrating primarily on hospitals and sophisticated technologies) as a means to achieving universal coverage.[57] Indeed, the centrality of PHC to achieving universal access and reducing global disease burden was the impetus for its adoption as the key to attaining the target of the Global Strategy for Health for all by the Year 2000,[58] the precursor to the MDGs. As indicated in the introductory section, the health MDGs share similar objective as the Global Strategy for Health, to wit, the attainment by everyone of a level of health that would enable them to

---

[52] WHO/UNICEF 1978, Primary Health Care: Report of the International Conference on Primary Health Care, Alma-Ata, USSR, p. 16, para 15.

[53] Ibid., p. 13, para 5.

[54] U.N. Committee on ESCR (CECSR), General Comment No. 14: The right to the Highest Attainable Standard of Health, para 43, U.N. Doc. E/C.12/2000/4 (11 August 2000), reprinted in Compilation of General Comments and General Recommendations, adopted by Human Rights Treaty Bodies; U.N. Doc. HRI/GEN/1/Rev.6 at 85 (2003); U.N. Econ. & Soc. Council [ECOSOC], U.N. Committee on ESCR, General Comment No. 3: The Nature of States Parties' Obligations, para 10, U.N. Doc. E/1991/23, annex III, p. 86 (1991), reprinted in Compilation of General Comments and General Recommendations Adopted by Human Rights Treaty Bodies, U.N. Doc. HRI/GEN/1/Rev.6 p. 14 (2003).

[55] General Comment No. 14, para 47; Nnamuchi 2008, pp. 32–33.

[56] See U.N., Treaty Collection, Chapter IV, Human Rights, No. 4: ICESCR, Status of Ratification, as of Dec. 20, 2010, available at http://treaties.un.org/Pages/ViewDetails.aspx?src=TREATY&mtdsg_no=IV-3&Chapter=4&lang=en (accessed 12 March 2013).

[57] Pan American Health Organization (PAHO), 44th PAHO Directing Council: Ministers Urge New Push Toward 'Health for All' in the Americas, available at http://www1.paho.org/english/dd/pin/PAHOTodayOctp03.pdf, p. 1 (accessed 12 March 2013).

[58] See WHO 2000, Global Strategy, p. 12, at pp. 17–18.

lead socially and economically productive lives.[59] As such, the 2015 target for attainment of the MDGs can be legitimately construed as an extension of the 2000 deadline of the Global Strategy for Health.

To accelerate efforts toward the Global Strategy for Health, WHO recommends that in national health policies, countries should give priority to PHC.[60] By seeking prioritization of PHC, WHO was reiterating one of the pillars of the Declaration of Alma-Ata.[61] Since the Declaration was adopted, all WHO member countries have incorporated this approach as the cornerstone of their national health systems. But operationalizing this prescription requires that the PHC system of each country receives a lion share of human and material resources available for health. Especially for Africa, sticking to this prescription has enormous benefits in terms of better use of its lean resources. To reap the dividend, however, entry point to the health system must be relocated from higher tiers (specialized clinics, hospitals, and outpatient and emergency services) to generalist primary care in close-to-client settings.[62] The advantages to this relocation include alleviation of suffering, prevention of avoidable illness and death, and health equity improvement.[63] There is also a cost–benefit. Because generalists prescribe fewer invasive interventions,[64] fewer and shorter hospitalizations[65] and are more preventive care oriented,[66] the overall healthcare cost is reduced. Besides, quality of care does not suffer as there is virtually no difference in adherence to clinical practice guidelines between generalists and specialists.[67] Are these benefits being harnessed in Africa?

Evidence abounds that the rhetoric of PHC approach is not aligned with appropriate policy initiatives in most African countries. Declining health indicators in the region present the strongest proof of this misalignment. Paradoxically, most of the region's health problems are diseases of the poor—the so-called

---

[59] Ibid., at p. 15.

[60] Ibid., at pp. 39–40. The African Health Strategy also emphasized this approach: "The basic unit of a well organised health system is the district [PHC system], which needs to be strengthened and adequately resourced, in a balanced manner with the higher levels of health care." See African Health Strategy, 8. Pursuit of PHC prioritization, in other words, should not lead to the neglect of secondary and tertiary tiers, but must be balanced in such a way as not to detrimentally affect the availability or quality of services provided at that level.

[61] Declaration of Alma-Ata, Article V (which states that "A main social target of governments, international organizations and the whole world community in the coming decades should be the attainment by all peoples of the world by the year 2000 of a level of health that will permit them to lead a socially and economically productive life. [PHC] is the key to attaining this target as part of development in the spirit of social justice.").

[62] WHO 2008, p. 53.

[63] Ibid.

[64] Rose et al. 2000, pp. 1103–1118, Krikke and Bell 1989, pp. 637–643, WHO 2008, p. 53.

[65] Abyad and Homsi 1993, pp. 465–470, Heuston et al. 1995, p. 435, pp. 351–435.

[66] Ryan et al. 2001, pp. 184–190.

[67] Beck et al. 2001, pp. 33–40, WHO 2008, p. 53.

1 Health and Millennium Development Goals in Africa   17

"neglected diseases"[68]—which are easy to prevent and cheap to treat, precisely the type of disease burden for which PHC system is best suited. Take malaria, for instance. The disease is inexpensively preventable (mosquito nets cost approximately \$5),[69] easily diagnosable (pyrexia is a common symptom), and treatable for next to nothing (\$1.50–2.40 for adults and \$0.40–0.90 for children).[70] Providing information on preventive methods as well as diagnosing and treating such diseases are the core functions of PHC clinics. Yet, the disease remains a leading cause of outpatient morbidity and a major contributor to high mortality in the region, accounting for 768,070 deaths or 89 % of the global malaria mortality in 2008.[71] This has little or nothing to do with resources. It is simply a question of misallocation and misalignment of resources with need. Most countries in the region devote a greater share of their health budgets to specialized tertiary care which, as observed by the World Bank, is less cost-effective while neglecting the low-cost and highly effective programs handled at PHC centers.[72]

Nigeria presents a remarkable illustration. Although its National Health Policy aims to "provide a comprehensive healthcare system that is based on [PHC]"[73] and declares PHC to be "the basic philosophy and strategy for national health development,"[74] appropriate framework to concretize these pronouncements does not exist. Responsibility for the three tiers of care (primary, secondary, and tertiary) is apportioned among the three levels of government, with the federal government in charge of tertiary care, states responsible for provision of secondary care and primary care assigned to local governments. Rather than allot PHC management to the most resourced unit (federal government), the duty was foisted on the weakest link—local governments, the result being that the federal government pours vast sums of money to tertiary care while PHC facilities flounder. The poor state of health in the country is the most visible, but unintended, consequence of this misalignment and misallocation of resources. So, what to do?

The World Bank estimates that by redirecting about half of what is now spent on less cost-effective specialist care to essential public health programs and clinical services (that is, PHC), developing countries could collectively reduce

---

[68] These are diseases which are typically concentrated amongst poor third world inhabitants and which generally receive little attention (inadequate research and investment) in global health policy. Examples include malaria, tuberculosis, lymphatic filariasis, onchocerciasis, leishmaniasis, schistosomiasis, African trypanosomiasis and Chagas disease. See WHO 2001, pp. 78–80.

[69] See Project Mosquito Net Website, http://www.projectmosquitonet.org/ (accessed 4 April 2013).

[70] Médecins Sans Frontières (Doctors without Borders), Malaria: MSF Facts and Figures, May 2004, p. 3, http://www.msfaccess.org/fileadmin/user_upload/diseases/other_diseases/malariafactsheetjun04.pdf (accessed 22 March 2013).

[71] WHO 2009, p. 27.

[72] World Bank 1993, iii, pp. 3–4.

[73] Federal Ministry of Health (FMH), Revised National Health Policy 2004, at iv, http://www.herfon.org/docs/Nigeria_NationalHealthPolicy_sept_2004.pdf (accessed 16 March 2013).

[74] Ibid., p. 4.

their disease burden by 25 %.[75] In other words, even without infusion of additional resources, substantial improvement in health is possible with prudent utilization of resources already available for health. For countries with dubious distribution of responsibilities among different levels of government, like Nigeria, a solution might be to vest PHC management in the unit of government best positioned to raise, deploy, and maintain adequate resources for its effective operation (the central government). Alternatively, where the state or local government retains responsibility, a system should be put in place, specifying the level of budgetary allocation to primary care, separate and distinct from allocations to other items on the budget. This ensures that the PHC system would be sufficiently resourced regardless of the unit of government charged with its operation.

This latter alternative is preferable as decentralization of health services to the district level, by "bringing health care as close as possible to where people live and work," provides the best formula for optimal performance of PHC systems.[76] Evidence of the benefit of decentralization is seen in Brazil's Unified Health System (*Sistema Único de Saúde*). The Brazilian health system is strongly marching toward universal coverage (75 % currently) in part because of legislation which vests responsibility for health financing and management in states and municipal governments and requires them to allocate at least 12 and 15 % of their respective budgets to health, with the central government providing additional support.[77] Serious commitment of municipal governments (many exceeding the statutory required budgetary allocation) and emphasis on PHC (provided free) are major drivers of health improvement—in terms of greater access to care and better health outcomes—in that country.

Implicit in the Brazilian experience is this lesson: having determined the entity in charge of PHC, each country must specify the level of resources needed to be set aside for that purpose. In some cases, this would mean hiking the general allocation to the unit of government allotted the responsibility. But since general allocations to local governments are barely enough to cover salaries and infrastructure mainte-nance, it is not enough to mandate dedicating a set percentage of their budgets to PHC. Instead, once the decision to entrust them with running the PHC system has been made, their receipt from the general revenue must be commensurably increased and intermittently adjusted to reflect fluctuating operational costs.

1.3.5 Corruption and Bad Governance

More than anything else, the most malevolent factor stunting economic growth and development in Africa is corruption. African leaders gathered at Maputo, Mozambique on 11 July 2003 were quite explicit about the "negative effect of corruption" as well as "its devastating effects on the economic and social

---

[75] World Bank 1993, World Development Report 1993, iii, p. 6.

[76] Declaration of Alma-Ata, Article VI.

[77] Jurberg and Humphreys 2010, p. 646.

1 Health and Millennium Development Goals in Africa

development of the African peoples."[78] The devastating impact of corruption in the region is visible in the dilapidation and waste in all sectors, not just health, and which have combined to wreak havoc in the lives of especially the marginalized and vulnerable populations. As Nuhu Ribadu, erstwhile head of Nigeria's Economic and Financial Crimes Commission explains, in reference to the regimes of three successive military leaders in Nigeria—Babangida, Abacha, and Abdulsalami—which he describes as being responsible for institutionalizing kleptocracy as a permanent fixture of governance in the country[79]:

> The decline we notice in the education sector today also started in that period. The shameless rot in the aviation sector, the absence of an efficient public transport system, the collapse of our public schools, the thievery in the ports and the decay in our healthcare delivery system all of which huge sums had been budgeted and spent are a direct reflection of the poverty of leadership of that era.[80]

While the impact, of course, varies from country to country, none is spared from the fang of this social ill. Consider this particularly striking case. Equatorial Guinea, a sparsely populated country of about half a million people, is the third largest oil exporter in Africa. With annual oil revenue of $3.7 billion,[81] the country undoubtedly deserves a spot among the world's affluent countries, in per capita terms. But its citizens are among the poorest as oil money is deposited into secret bank accounts controlled by the country's ruthless dictator and his coterie.[82] In 2006, the dictator's son, who was earning a monthly salary of $4,000 as the country's Minister for Agriculture and Forestry, was reported to have paid $35 million for a mansion in California,[83] a sum that is more than double what it would take to provide essential medicine for the entire population.[84]

---

[78] See Preamble, African Union Convention on Preventing and Combating Corruption, adopted 11 July 2003, entered into force 5 August 2006.

[79] See Corruption: The Trouble with Nigeria, Speech Delivered at the 3rd Media Trust Annual Dialogue in Abuja, Nigeria, 19 January 2006, http://www.againstbabangida.com/news/2006/0106_IBBcorrupt_ribadu.htm (accessed 4 April 2013).

[80] Ibid., echoing a statement by former President Obasanjo in 2005 that "General Babangida is the main architect of the state in which the nation finds itself today, and that General Abacha was his eminent disciple, faithful supporter, and beneficiary". See Akinbode, OBJ on IBB, The Guardian (Nigeria), 11 August 2005 //againstbabangida.com/articles/2005/akinbode_obj-on-ibb.htm (accessed 4 April 2013).

[81] Global Witness 2009, p. 22, citing IMF, Republic of Equatorial Guinea Article IV Consultation, May 2008, p. 24, http://www.globalwitness.org/sites/default/files/pdfs/undue_diligence_text_only.pdf (accessed 7 March 2013).

[82] Ibid., pp. 26–44.

[83] Ibid., p. 27, citing John Reed, Taking a Cut Acceptable, says African Minister, Financial Times, 25 October 2006; Global Witness, African Minister Buys Multimillion Dollar California Mansion, Press Release, 8 November 2006.

[84] Only $17 million is needed to cover everyone in the country. The calculation is based on the WHO's estimate of $34 per person for essential medical care. See Global Witness, Undue Diligence, ibid., p. 32, citing DFID, Working together for better health, 2007, p. 23, http://www.dfid.gov.uk/Pubs/files/health-strategy07.pdf (accessed 2 April 2013).

Equatorial Guinea is not alone. There are countless examples all over Africa. In the much more prosperous Nigeria, for instance, an average of at least $4 billion to $8 billion per year was lost to corruption during the eight years of Obasanjo administration (1999–2007), the man who took over the reins of power from the military dictators mentioned previously.[85] This figure amounts to between 4.25 and 9.5 % of Nigeria's total GDP in 2006.[86] Yet, Nigeria's health system ranks 187th in the world out of 191 countries surveyed,[87] and in terms of human development index was 142nd out of 169 countries.[88] Even worse, although the proportion of those infected with HIV in the country pales in comparison to countries in Southern and Eastern Africa, its antiretroviral therapy (ART) coverage rate is only 26 %.[89] Inexplicably, this is blamed on resource dearth, notwithstanding that "[b]etween 1960 and 1999, Nigerian officials had stolen or wasted more than $440 billion. That is six times the Marshall Plan".[90]

One way to evaluate this perennial claim that finite resources constrain countries in Africa from being responsive to the health of individuals within their jurisdictions is to subject the claim to a governance framework analysis. The Constitution of Nigeria provides a useful guide. It lays down what could rightly be described as the essential components of good governance, namely national integration, abolition of corruption and abuse of power, and management of the economy for the benefit of all.[91] The term "essential components" suggests that these are core elements that are indispensable to responsible governance and, where operationalized, these elements will act as a catalyst to advancement in the health and overall wellbeing of the population. Botswana exemplifies the virtues and benefits of good governance. At independence in 1960, the country was among the poorest in the world, with a GDP per capita estimated at between $70 and $90, and highly dependent on foreign aid.[92] But by 2004, the GDP per capita had risen to $4,771[93] and the national budget had skyrocketed from less than $3 million to

---

[85] Human Rights Watch 2007 pp. 31–32, http://www.hrw.org/reports/2007/nigeria1007/nigeria1007webwcover.pdf (accessed 18 April 2013).

[86] Ibid.

[87] WHO 2000, p. 154.

[88] UNDP 2010, p. 162.

[89] WHO 2010, p. 93.

[90] Ribadu 2009, p. 4.

[91] Sections 15(3), 15(5), 16(1)(b). For a more robust discussion of good governance as the key to achieving the MDGs (based on the fact that it is one of the prerequisites for receipt of assistance under MDG 8—which calls for increase in aid flowing from the Global North to Global South), see Nnamuchi and Ortuanya 2012, pp. 178–198.

[92] Mogae, Botswana's Development Experience, Lecture by the Former President of Namibia at the Institute of Development Studies, Sussex University, 2 February 2005, http://www.sarpn.org.za/documents/d0001114/index.php (accessed 4 April 2013).

[93] United Nations Conference on Trade and Development (UNCTAD), "Botswana," available at www.unctad.org/sections/ldc_dir/docs//lldc-bot.pdf.

$3 billion,[94] moving the country into the ranks of upper-middle-income economies.[95] This success story has been attributed to "political stability, sound economic management and prudent financial husbandry."[96] Are these not the inevitable result of incorporating the "essential components" identified above into the governance framework of the country? In 2009, Botswana was ranked 37th in Transparency International's Corruption Perception Index, the best record in Africa and a clear testament to its governance credentials.[97] Other countries in the region have not followed suit.

As nation after nation cling unto resource deficit as explicatory of their woes, the gulf between elegant constitutional stipulations on responsible governance and the reality on the ground continues to widen, with the only beneficiaries being worsening health indicators throughout the region. In their 2002 publication, human rights advocates Olisa Agbakoba and Willy Mamah were forceful in their rejection of this state of affairs.[98] The fundamental issue, they argue, "has been corruption ... where individuals, using State power have continued to amass so much wealth" for themselves and their coterie, without regard for the common good.[99] Indeed, the abysmal state of health in Africa, the difficulty confronting health systems en route to meeting their MDG obligations as well as the precipitous plunge in other vital statistics cannot be disassociated from orchestrated plunder and pillage of national treasuries by the region's political leadership.[100]

1.4 Interventions for Change

The complexity and multifarious nature of the factors stymieing health improvement in Africa suggest that remedial measures must be comprehensive, targeted, and sustainable in order to have any meaningful chance of success. Because disease burden differs widely across the region, as do resources, the approach to be adopted will, of necessity, vary according to the particular circumstances of each country. Nevertheless, there are certain interventions that would be productive in virtually

---

[94] Mogae, Botswana's Development Experience, ibid.

[95] World Bank, Country and Lending Groups, http://data.worldbank.org/about/country-classifications/country-and-lending-groups#Lower_middle_income (accessed 4 April 2013).

[96] Mogae, Botswana's Development Experience, ibid.

[97] Transparency International, Corruption Perceptions Index 2009, http://www.transparency.org/policy_research/surveys_indices/cpi/2009/cpi_2009_table (accessed 4 April 2013).

[98] Towards a Peoples' Constitution in Nigeria: A Civic Education Manual for the Legal Community (Lagos: Human Rights Law Service 2002).

[99] Ibid., p. 43.

[100] For a detailed discussion on the link between poor performance of health systems and misappropriation of public funds in the context of delivery of health services in Nigeria, see Nnamuchi, Kleptocracy and its Many Faces, pp. 12–18.

all the countries irrespective of differing circumstances. The NEPAD Health Strategy specifies some of these interventions. The strategy directs countries to strengthen commitment and the stewardship role of government; build secure health systems and services; strengthen programs to reduce the burden of disease; and, provide skilled care for pregnancy and childbirth.[101] Countries are further directed to enable individual action to improve health, mobilize and effectively use sufficient sustainable resources; and, strive for equity for the poor, displaced and marginalized populations.[102] Aside from these and specific suggestions already put forth (on ways of addressing the various challenges previously identified), there are additional interventions each of which has a broad and far-reaching application and must form an integral component of the overall strategy for repositioning Africa on a sustainable path toward the MDGs and improving overall population health.

1.4.1 Poverty Reduction

The fact that a greater proportion of global diseases and illnesses afflict the most impoverished region in the world (Africa) tells quite a fairly straightforward story—and that is, there is a causal link between diseases and poverty. Hence the main target of MDG 1, to reduce by half between 1990 and 2015 the number of people with income of less than \$1.25 per day, is particularly crucial to people in the region. Poverty is both a cause and a consequence of ill-health and vice versa; the two are mutually reinforcing.[103] The sole reason millions of lives are lost each year in Africa to easily preventable and treatable illnesses is no other than poverty, explaining its rather apt description as the world's most lethal diseases.[104] "Poverty ... wields its destructive influence at every stage of human life, from the moment of conception to the grave. It conspires with the most deadly and painful diseases to bring a wretched existence to all who suffer from it."[105] This pernicious dimension of poverty makes it a human rights issue. Strikingly, what exactly constitutes poverty is not defined by any of the major international human rights instruments, but the U.N. Committee on Economic, Social and Cultural Rights (Committee on ESCR), the implementation monitoring body of the International

---

[101] NEPAD Health Strategy, pp. 17–25.

[102] Ibid.

[103] Referring to this link as a "vicious cycle," the African Union Conference of Health Ministers explained: just as "poverty and its determinants drive up the burden of disease," so too "ill-health contributes to poverty." See African Health Strategy, p. 4. See also WHO 2005, p. 8. The report acknowledges that "emphasis on health reflects a global consensus that ill-health is an important dimension of poverty in its own right. Ill-health contributes to poverty. Improving health is a condition for poverty alleviation and for development. Sustainable improvement of health depends on successful poverty alleviation and reduction of inequalities." Ibid.

[104] WHO 1995, p. v.

[105] Ibid.

Covenant on Economic, Social and Cultural Rights (ICESCR) does. The Committee on ESCR defines poverty as "a human condition characterized by sustained or chronic deprivation of the resources, capabilities, choices, security and power necessary for the enjoyment of an adequate standard of living and other civil, cultural, economic, political and social rights."[106]

This expansive definition, a clear departure from the dominant traditional account of poverty as inability to provide basic goods and services for oneself, is compatible with the holistic approach of human rights; that is, in terms of the multidimensional manifestations of poverty and the need for a comprehensive response. These manifestations include lack of income and productive resources sufficient to ensure sustainable livelihoods, hunger and malnutrition, illness, limited or lack of access to education and other basic services as well as increased morbidity and mortality from illness.[107] Other instances of poverty are homelessness, inadequate housing, unsafe environment, social discrimination, and lack of participation in decision-making and in civil, social, and cultural life—all of which contributes to poor health.[108]

Global concern about the destructive impact of poverty on human well-being and the need for its eradication has a long genealogy. The preamble to the Universal Declaration of Human Rights (UDHR)[109] and the common preamble to the International Covenant on Civil and Political Rights (ICCPR)[110] and the ICESCR[111] proclaims "freedom from ... want" as a basic human right. This proclamation entitles everyone to a "standard of living adequate for the health and well-being of himself and his family, including food, clothing, housing and medical care and necessary social services."[112] Because it negates the enjoyment of this right (to a decent standard of life, life with dignity and so forth) "poverty constitutes a denial of human right"[113] or, as the Brazilian theologian Leonardo Boff postulates, "an evil and an injustice" on those laboring under its yoke.[114]

---

[106] U.N. Econ. & Soc. Council [ECOSOC], Committee on ESCR, Report of the Twenty-Fifth Session, 23 April–11 May 2001, Poverty and the International Covenant on Economic, Social and Cultural Rights, E/C.12/2001/10, para 8, http://www.unhchr.ch/tbs/doc.nsf/0/518e88bfb89822c9c1256a4e004df048?Opendocument (accessed 2 February 2013).

[107] U.N., World Summit for Social Development, Programme of Action of the World Summit for Social Development (accessed 4 April 2013) 1995, A/CONF.166/9, Chapter II, para 19, http://www.un-documents.net/poa-wssd.htm (accessed 4 April 2013).

[108] Ibid.

[109] UDHR, G.A. res. 217A (III), U.N. Doc A/810 at 71 (1948), adopted December 10, 1948.

[110] ICCPR, G.A.res.2200A (XXI), 21 U.N. GAOR Supp. (No. 16) at 52, U.N. Doc. A/6316 (1966), 999 U.N.T.S. 171, adopted 16 December 1966, entered into force 23 March 1976.

[111] International Covenant on Economic, Social, and Cultural Rights (ICESR) opened for signature Dec. 16, 1966, G.A. Res. 2200A (XXI), U.N. GAOR, 21st Sess., Supp. No. 16, p. 49, U.N. Doc. A/6316 (1966), 999 U.N.T.S. 3, entered into force 3 January1976.

[112] UDHR, Article 25; ICESCR, Article 11.

[113] ECOSOC, Committee on ESCR, Report of the Twenty-Fifth Session, 23 April–11 May 2001, Poverty and the International Covenant on Economic, Social and Cultural Rights, para 1.

[114] Faith on the Edge: Religion and Marginalized Existence 1989, p. 23.

Subsequent human rights documents have been more explicit as to the nexus between poverty and human wellbeing and the need for concerted action toward its elimination. The Vienna Declaration and Program of Action, for instance, recognizes that "extreme poverty inhibits the full and effective enjoyment of human rights," and therefore "its immediate alleviation and eventual elimination must remain a high priority for the international community."[115] And the Heads of States and Government gathered at the World Summit for Social Development in Copenhagen, in 1995, committed their respective countries to the "goal of eradicating poverty in the world, through decisive national actions and international cooperation, as an ethical, social, political and economic imperative of humankind,"[116] marking the first international commitment to eradicate, not merely alleviate, poverty.[117] But whether it would ever be possible to completely eradicate poverty or create a poverty-free world is beside the point. What is important is that whatever the ultimate goal (alleviation or eradication), it must involve a fundamental restructuring of the socioeconomic order in a way capable of remediating inbuilt inequality of opportunities otherwise the entire process risks becoming an exercise in futility.

That the incidence of poverty is severest in Africa is as notoriously a common knowledge as is the fact that poverty is (on an individual or institutional level) singularly more responsible for the tepid pace of economic growth and development in the region than all other factors combined. Beginning in 1990, the United Nations Development Program (UNDP) has published an annual report which ranks countries according to their respective human development[118] and poverty levels.[119] Least performing countries are described as having "low human

---

[115] Adopted by the World Conference on Human Rights, 14–25 June 1993, A/CONF.157/23, Article 1, para 14 Copenhagen Declaration on Social Development, adopted by the World Summit for Social Development, 12 March 1995, A/CONF.166/9, Chapter 1, Annex 1, see Commitment 2. For other international initiatives at fighting poverty, see "Human Rights and Extreme Poverty," General Assembly Resolution, 17 December 1991, A/RES/46/121; "United Nations Millennium Declaration," General Assembly Resolution, 8 September 2000, A/RES/55/2; and, "2005 World Summit Outcome," General Assembly Resolution, 16 September 2005, A/RES/60/1.

[116] Ibid.

[117] UNDP 1997, Human Development Report 1997: Human Development to Eradicate Poverty, p. 106.

[118] Defined as a "composite index measuring average achievement in three basic dimensions of human development—a long and healthy life, access to knowledge and a decent standard of living." See UNDP, Human Development Report 2009: Overcoming Barriers: Human Mobility and Development, p. 210. A subsequent Report adds three additional criteria (the multidimensional measures of inequality and poverty), namely, (i) Inequality-adjusted HDI (IHDI), a measurement of inequality in health, education and income, (ii) Gender Inequality Index (GII) which assesses gender disparities in reproductive health, empowerment and labor market participation; and, (iii) Multidimensional Poverty Index (MPI), a measurement of overlapping deprivations suffered by households in health, education and living standards. See UNDP 2010, p. 86.

[119] UNDP 2009, p. 210 (which defines human poverty index as a "composite index measuring deprivations in the three basic dimensions captured in the human development index—a long and healthy life, access to knowledge and a decent standard of living").

development."[120] Of countries so designated (listed 128—169) all, except seven, are in Africa.[121] On the ranking on human poverty index, African countries also underperformed countries in other regions. Out of 35 countries with the worst record (ranked 100–135), only seven are not African.[122] The highest proportion of people living in poverty (relative to population), on less than $1.25 a day, is also found in Africa.[123] Understanding these numbers involves asking one basic question: why does poverty rate in Africa consistently exceed that of other parts of the world? The reasons are legion, but one is particularly illuminating: poor governance. Post colonial politicking in Africa has produced vast enclaves of unscrupulous ruling class, leaders with visions of governance that are diametrically opposed to stewardship of national resources and protection of individual liberty and freedom. Decades of unmitigated resource misappropriation and profligate squandermania have left very little for anything else.

But beyond corruption, authorities in the region can be also held culpable for obstructive governance (enacting legislation and policies that obstruct the ability of individuals to create wealth for themselves). Obstructive governance is most commonly manifested in institutionalizing unnecessary bureaucracies and stifling regulations that make it difficult to establish or operate a business. Recently, the World Bank carried out a study to gauge the "ease of doing business" across the globe.[124] It ranked countries (183 in all) according to the following indicators: starting a business, dealing with construction permits, employing workers, registering property, obtaining credit, protecting investors, paying taxes, trading across borders, enforcing contracts, and closing a business. All African countries, except seven, ranked in the bottom 50 percentile.[125] Does this sort of study hold any implication for growth and poverty reduction in the region?

---

[120] This contrasts with "medium," "high," and "very high" human development ascribed to better performing countries. Ibid., pp. 176–178.

[121] UNDP 2010, pp. 145–146, 150–151.

[122] UNDP 2009, p. 179.

[123] Ibid., pp. 176–178 (Tanzania holds the worst record (88.5 percent), followed by Liberia (83.7), Burundi (81.3), Rwanda (76.6), Malawi (73.9) and so forth).

[124] World Bank 2010, p. 97.

[125] Ibid., p. 4. A similar report known as the Economic Freedom of the World has been published annually by the Frasier Institute since 1996. Individuals enjoy economic freedom, according to the maiden edition, "when (a) property they acquire without the use of force, fraud, or theft is protected from physical invasions by others and (b) they are free to use, exchange, or give their property to another as long as their actions do not violate the identical rights of others." See Gwartney et al. 1996, p. 12. Countries are rated on five major areas, considered to indicate the degree to which their policies and institutions are supportive of economic freedom, to wit, (i) size of government, (ii) legal structure and security of property rights, (iii) access to sound money, (iv) freedom to trade internationally, and (v) regulation of credit, labor, and business. In the latest report, only five African countries were in the top 50 percentile in the ranking on these indicators. See Gwartney et al. 2010, p. 7.

Indeed, the regulatory environment under which domestic businesses must operate is a crucial measurement of the existence of conditions conducive for economic growth and escaping poverty in that particular geographic location. Difficulty in establishing or running a business is an important consideration in deciding whether to venture into a business enterprise in the first place. Moreover, the degree of this difficulty is a decisive factor that can make or mar a nation's economic growth as evident in the fact that advanced economies consistently outranked developing (and, not coincidentally, poorer) countries in the study and previous ones. The phrase "life, liberty and pursuit of happiness" in the American Declaration of Independence—regarded by many as the foremost contemporary incarnation of the Magna Carta—is declaratory not just of civil and political liberty; it does have some compelling economic undertone. The Declaration was a solemn repudiation of the British imperial authority, including its burdensome confiscatory taxation policies, which the founding fathers saw as inimical to economic prosperity. They were fully cognizant of the price of rebellion (death) but detested the yoke of imperialism even more. They understood that without liberty (civil and political as well as social and economic) there can be no meaningful pursuit of happiness and therefore a life that is seriously impaired. The patriots were under no illusion that an environment in which government interference in business is kept to the barest minimum is one in which happiness is maximized as individuals are most able to pursue their freely chosen ends. In short, the uniquely rugged individualist ethos in the United States is concretized on this principle. From this prism, therefore, it becomes easy to appreciate the economic might and dominance of the United States as no happenstance. This is a paradigm that commends itself to Africa.

Interestingly, when in a World Bank study, 60,000 poor people around the globe were asked how they hope to escape poverty, their unequivocal response was through income generated from owning their own businesses or wages from employment.[126] Neither of these two income-generating paths is actualizable save in a climate where businesses are allowed to thrive and prosper, suggesting that removing obstacles to forming and operating a business is of paramount importance to the success of antipoverty and health-promotion strategies in the region. Less poverty signals better health—a perspective shared by the World Bank which, in 1993, recommended that for governments to improve health in developing countries, they "need to foster an economic environment that enables households to improve their own health."[127]

---

[126] Narayan et al. 2000, vi–vii.

[127] World Bank 1993, p. iii.

1.4.2 Addressing Underlying Determinants of Health

The Commission on Social Determinants of Health (Commission),[128] in its final report to WHO, tersely describes the interface between poverty and health: "[i]n countries at all levels of income, health and illness follow a social gradient: the lower the socioeconomic position, the worse the health."[129] Put differently, one's station in life (socioeconomic circumstances) is an accurate predictor of the person's health status at any given point in time. This impact of poverty on health is not necessarily the result of poorer peoples' relative difficulty in accessing health services. Beyond access difficulties, there are other factors, the consequences of which can be more deleterious than lack of medical care. These factors, known as "underlying or social determinants of health," consist of the "structural determinants and conditions of daily life;"—that is, "the conditions in which people are born, grow, live, work, and age."[130] These conditions have more direct and enduring impact on the health and quality of life of individuals than access to medical care (though itself also a health determinant).

The more favorable these conditions are in a given community, the better the health of its members or vice versa. There are, of course, certain illnesses (genetic disorders, for instance) that are not the consequences of the failure of any of these conditions. But those are the exceptions, not the rule. For the most part, the less well-off is more susceptible to illnesses and shorter life span than someone with all the advantages, explaining why, as a 1990 study found, the life expectancy of young black men in Harlem (an impoverished black neighborhood in New York City) is less than men in Bangladesh, a country classified by the World Bank as one of the poorest in the world.[131] The reason was that nearly half of the people in Harlem live below the poverty line (41 %)—and with this burden, a disproportionately higher rate of diseases and deaths compared to the general population.[132] This deplorable situation is not explicable by lack of access to treatment, and this is confirmed in a more recent finding in a country with universal health insurance. In Glasgow, Scotland, the life expectancy of poorest males is 54 years, compared to 82 years for affluent males living in the same city.[133] Yet, the two groups have equal access to health care, guaranteed by the National Health Service (NHS).

Social determinants of health include, inter alia, food, housing, access to potable water and adequate sanitation, safe and healthy working conditions, and a

---

[128] The Commission was established to adduce evidence on ways to promote health equity and engineer its global actualization. See Commission on Social Determinants of Health (CSDH), Closing the Gap in a Generation: Health Equity through Action on the Social Determinants of Health, p. 1.

[129] Ibid., see executive summary; Wilkinson and Marmot 2003, p. 7.

[130] CSDH, p. 1.

[131] McCord and Freeman 1990, pp. 173–177.

[132] Ibid.

[133] Wilensky and Satcher 2009 w195; CSDH, p. 32.

healthy environment.[134] These are basic components of a decent life, and one's access to them greatly influences the person's health, quality of life, and life expectancy. That these goods and conditions are not uniformly available to all is responsible for health disparities within and across nations. Disparities, both in health and well-being, generated by maldistribution of basic components of a decent life are not, as a Harvard medical anthropologist so adroitly puts it, "the result of accident or a force majeure," rather, "they are the consequences, direct or indirect, of human agency."[135] They are, indeed, manmade.

Particularly in terms of sensitivity to the plight of the citizenry or being responsive to their needs, enthronement of democracy in Africa has meant very little. Most governments in the region have shown little or no inclination to distance themselves from the kleptocratic and oligarchic tendencies of their predecessors. Avarice, sectionalism and nepotism have hijacked the stewardship role of elected officials—a tragic case of governance gone amok. The demise of dictatorships in the 1990s was thought to usher in a new dawn for the region. But majority rule has not lived up to its billing. The benefits long hoped for by the people are still nowhere in the horizon. The force of this hope, solid as the Gibraltar rock not quite long ago, is gradually dissipating, giving way to despondency as intense suffering and extreme hardship overwhelm the masses. Food remains scarce, as does housing and, in most countries, virtually all other social goods and services. But—quite tragically—not diseases and illnesses.

The proportion of Africans with access to potable water stagnates at 61 %[136] and just 34 % has access to adequate sanitation, a marginal increase from 30 % in 1990.[137] Low access to safe water supplies and adequate sanitation increases exposure to many diseases such as cholera, typhoid, diarrhea, schistosomiasis, and hepatitis[138] as well as trypanosomiasis and dracontiasis—all of which are pervasive in Africa. Confronting these pathologies requires not just the provision of treatment but, more important, improving the living conditions of the people—restructuring the socioeconomic dynamics which triggered the diseases in the first place. The diversity of these conditions calls for diversified action; that is, in terms of organizing human and material resources necessary for ensuring the availability of goods and conditions that promote good health.

While the Ministry of Health, since its primary charge is protecting the health of the population, has a leadership role in this process, it must seek the collaboration of other Ministries (Agriculture, Housing, Education, Commerce etc.) as well as the private sector (individuals, industries, and civil society). The expertise

---

[134] General Comment No. 14, paras 4, 11.

[135] Farmer 2003, p. 40. See also CSDH, p. 31 (the Commission argues that poor health of the masses is a product of unequal distribution of resources—in itself not a natural phenomenon but the consequence of policies which promote the interests "all too often of a rich and powerful minority over" that "of a disempowered majority").

[136] WHO 2010, p. 18.

[137] Ibid., p. 19.

[138] Ibid., p. 99.

1 Health and Millennium Development Goals in Africa

and experiences of non-health institutions should be harnessed and incorporated into strategies aimed at attending to social health determinants throughout the region.[139] This partnership, consisting of diverse sectors (public and private), points to the "multisectoral dimension of health"—meaning that reforming the health sector alone is insufficient to improve overall health. The entire socioeconomic structure of each country must be fully aligned with the trajectory of the health system, the aim being to scale-up the availability of, and access to, each and every good that contributes to health. The necessity of this alignment is borne out by the fact that countries on the upper echelon of health outcomes are also those where education, shelter, safe drinking water, adequate sanitation, health care, jobs, and social protection—in short, the whole armamentarium of social health determinants—are reasonably (if not abundantly) available.

1.4.3 Integrating Human Rights into Health Systems

The adoption of the African Charter on Human and Peoples' Rights in 1981 marked a turning point (or so it was thought) in the protection of human rights in Africa, the Charter being the first human rights instrument to recognize the three genres of human rights—civil and political; economic, social and cultural; and, peoples' rights.[140] Article 16 recognizes the right of every individual "to enjoy the best attainable state of physical and mental health" and obligates States Parties to the Charter to take measures necessary for realizing the right. But even before the adoption of the Charter, many countries in Africa had bound themselves to respect, protect, and promote the right to health. The ICESCR, the first international treaty to recognize the right to health, was ratified by a vast majority of countries in the region (46 out of 53 countries).[141] Have these ratifications resulted in substantial improvement in the health of citizens and residents of ratifying countries? Judging by the health data in these countries, it is difficult to return an affirmative verdict. Evidence of this dissonance (between lofty treaty aspirations and implementation) runs through the length and breadth of health systems in Africa. Yet, erasing the dissonance—by incorporating human rights principles into country health policies—is fundamental to securing the health of the population, thereby advancing the right to health.

Integrating human rights into health systems means positioning human rights as an important component of decisions relating to governance, financing, and

---

[139] See Declaration of Alma-Ata, Article VII, para 4: "... in addition to the health sector, all related sectors and aspects of national and community development, in particular agriculture, animal husbandry, food, industry, education, housing, public works, communications and other sectors" must be coordinated to achieve PHC.

[140] Adopted June 27, 1981, OAU Doc. CAB/LEG/67/3 rev. 5, 21 I.L.M. 58 (1982).

[141] See U.N., Treaty Collection, Chapter IV: Human Rights, No. 4: ICESCR, Status of Ratification, as of Dec. 20, 2010b.

delivery of health services. From policy formulation stages, through allocatory decisions, down to service delivery, priority is given to strategies that has the greatest potential to yield the best possible outcome for everyone, with preference given to the most marginalized and vulnerable recipient of services. It is de facto operationalization of the right to health, putting concrete measures in place to ensure the full realization of the right for everyone, not just a select few.

The value of anchoring national health systems on human rights principles is to direct the attention of policy makers to inequities that could be generated by certain decisions, enabling them to proactively guard against making such decisions in the first place. In this context, the catechism of human rights is to conceive of health inequities as systemic deficiencies that should be expurgated as expeditiously and exhaustively as possible. As it relates to health, human rights is an invisible hand directing decision makers to plans, initiatives, or programs that would efface access and outcome differentials, thereby infusing equity to the entire chain that make up the health system. An equitable health system is one that caters to the interests of the poor as much as the wealthy, in which, inter alia, the voice of the poor is assigned the same (if not more) weight as everyone else's in decision-making processes.

The place of equity in a health system is of paramount importance, for the more equitable a health system is, the better the health of the population it serves. This is reflected in the fact that better performing health systems, evident in WHO's 2000 ranking of global health systems, are also fairer and more equitable.[142] The converse is also true and precisely the reason health systems in Africa (with remarkably few exceptions) are ranked in the bottom 30 % of the countries surveyed.[143] But the policy landscape in the region seems to be improving. African leaders recently dedicated themselves to ensuring that "[e]quity in health care is a foundation for all health systems" in the region.[144] This is a great beginning, but only a beginning. To be meaningful, the rhetoric must be coupled with concrete action in terms of reforming or overhauling health systems, as the case may be, to better serve the needs of vulnerable populations in the region.

1.4.4 Individual Empowerment

The public health aphorism "prevention is better than cure" is a powerful testament to the advantages inherent in preventing the occurrence of illnesses (in terms

---

[142] WHO 2000, pp. 152–154.

[143] Ibid.

[144] Africa Health Strategy, p. 6. See also NEPAD Health Strategy, p. 15 (which states, as values underlining the strategy: "Health and access to quality affordable health care is a human right. Equity in health and health care is beneficial to countries as well as individuals ..." and so forth).

of cost and avoidance of unnecessary pain and suffering) than treatment.[145] The phrase describes the role expected of individuals in protecting their health. Cognizant of the importance of this role, the African Union Conference of Ministers for Health urges that health systems place "strong emphasis on behaviour change" as part of "an integrated approach" to addressing Africa's disease burden.[146] Even for certain conditions whose etiology is genetic, there are precautions or lifestyle changes that can mitigate an individual's risk.[147] Beyond this, for a great many diseases and illnesses, individual exposure to risks depends on the extent to which appropriate preventive measures have been incorporated into one's daily life. Another term that has been used to describe individual empowerment is "health promotion"—defined as a "process of enabling people to increase control over, and to improve, their health;"[148] that is, putting individuals in charge of their own health. This is preventive care in action—a core principle of a PHC system—and consists of, at the barest minimum, education concerning prevailing health problems (including methods of preventing and controlling them), promotion of food supply and proper nutrition, an adequate supply of safe water and basic sanitation, family planning, immunization against infectious diseases, prevention and control of locally endemic diseases, and provision of essential drugs.[149]

While the advantages stemming from empowering individuals to be proactively involved in their health cut across regional boundaries, resource-poor settings in Africa stand to reap greater benefit. That much is incontrovertible. Why? First, there is, as already discussed, dearth of appropriately trained health personnel in most countries in the region. And, second, even where availability is not a problem, access might still be constrained due to inability to pay for services. In these circumstances, the kernel of individual empowerment is that it reduces exposure to these problems, saving the individual from the pain, suffering, and expenses to which he could have otherwise been exposed. But there are two challenges that must be overcome to harness this benefit, namely educating individuals about health promotion or preventive care, and creating access to resources that would make it possible for them to put the knowledge to productive use.

---

[145] Preventive health services are generally more cost-effective than curative care, although a recent study disputes whether the difference is really significant. See Cohen et al. 2008, pp. 661–663.

[146] Africa Health Strategy, p. 20. But such "behaviour change" is only possible when the individual has attained a certain level of health literacy—that is, acquired "basic knowledge and skills to enhance [his] health." See NEPAD Health Strategy, p. 23.

[147] See Opara and Jiburum 2010, http://wjso.com/content/8/1/73 (accessed 14 April 2013). The authors found that individuals suffering from albinism (a genetic disorder which makes the body unable to produce or distribute melanin) are more susceptible to skin cancer than the general population and that certain precautionary measures can reduce the risk: limited exposure to the sun, wearing protective clothing and avoidance of outdoor activities.

[148] Ottawa Charter for Health Promotion, First International Conference on Health Promotion, Ottawa, 2 November 1986, WHO/HPR/HEP/95.1.

[149] Declaration of Alma-Ata, Article VII, para 3.

Cholera has been known for centuries to be deadly but, at the same time, easily preventable by proper sanitation and avoidance of contaminated water sources. It is striking that the Torah does not record any incident of cholera outbreak among the Jews during their 40-year sojourn in the wilderness en route to Israel, even though the living arrangement (camping in tents in close quarters) was a fertile ground for such outbreaks. The reason was that the Jews followed a simple instruction:

> Set up a place outside the camp to be used as a toilet area. And make sure that you have a small shovel in your equipment. When you go out to the toilet area, use the shovel to dig a hole. Then, after you relieve yourself, bury the waste in the hole.[150]

Because human waste was disposed outside their living quarters, the Israelites were spared from cholera and similar outbreaks.

This antediluvian adjuration is expressive of public health at its most archaic form but the principle remains valid today, and straying from it often has disastrous consequences, as a recent experience in Zimbabwe demonstrates. In 2008, seepage of sewage into the Limpopo River (a major source of drinking water) triggered a cholera epidemic in the country, resulting in 3,000 deaths and 60,000 cases.[151] The high casualty is not in the least surprising given that many Zimbabweans, especially the poor and residents of rural communities, lack access to safe drinking water sources. Discernible from this experience is a lesson that the success of individual empowerment goes beyond knowledge transfer to include material resources needed for attending to underlying health determinants. Knowing how to protect oneself from cholera, for instance, is a good start but, to be an effective public health tool, the knowledge must be coupled with access to potable water and sanitation facilities, and the state must be prepared to protect the entire public sewage system.

1.4.5 Civil Society Empowerment

In her opening address at the International Conference on Health for Development in 2007, Margaret Chan, Director-General of WHO, remarked that global efforts at achieving the MDGs will be fruitless "unless we return to the values, principles, and approaches of [PHC]."[152] Her statement translates to saying that these values and principles are crucial drivers of health system development and sustainability, and therefore indispensable to attaining the health MDGs. In other words,

---

[150] Deuteronomy 23: 12, 13, The Bible (Contemporary English Version).

[151] Bateman 2009, p. 138. See also Mason 2009, p. 148.

[152] Chan, The contribution of [PHC] to the Millennium Development Goals, Opening Address at the International Conference on Health for Development Buenos Aires, Argentina, August 16, 2007, http://www.who.int/dg/speeches/2007/20070816_argentina/en/index.html (accessed 4 April 2013).

anchoring the operation of health systems—initiatives, programs, and strategies—on the basic principles of PHC is a surefire way to generate positive outcomes for the population dependent on them.

One of the building blocks—indeed, a requirement of a PHC system—is that "[t]he people have the right and duty to participate individually and collectively in the planning and implementation of their health care."[153] The obvious advantage of this requirement is the element of democracy it embodies. But this sort of democracy has a somewhat different appeal in the sense that the interest of those on the higher end of socioeconomic ladder is not, as often is the case in developing countries, taken as representative of the entire population. Here, the importance of democratizing the process lies in what Professor Farmer sums up, in reference to the thrust of liberation theology, as eliciting "the experiences and views of poor people"[154] and integrating these views into health decision-making—views traditionally not given much weight in public policy deliberations, health-related or otherwise.

Contributing to health decision-making, whether on an individual basis or as a collectivity, is not confined to PHC. As the Committee on ESCR made explicit in 2000, an important element of the right to health is "the participation of the population in all health-related decision-making at the community, national and international levels."[155] This declaration envisages a broader involvement of civil society at all levels of health policy formulation, from the smallest unit of government through the central government to international institutions. The Brazilian Health system provides a remarkable instantiation of the utility and reward of engaging community input. As part of the 1996 health reform in that country, provision of comprehensive (and free) care was decentralized to municipalities, with funds provided by states and federal governments.[156] At the municipal level, communities take active part in budgetary decisions, allocation of funds, supervision of accounts and approval of the annual reports.[157] The result has been nothing short of phenomenal—more than 75 % coverage, in a country where half of the population lacked insurance in 1988.[158]

Community input in health decision-making is increasingly being channeled through civil society organizations (CSOs). The African Health Strategy defines CSOs as consisting of NGOs, Faith Based Organizations (FBOs), Community Based Organizations (CBOs), traditional leaders and healers as well as media

---

[153] Declaration of Alma-Ata, Article IV, VII, para 5.

[154] Farmer, p. 146. Decisions affecting the health of the population are typically made at the boardrooms of ministries of health, local government health departments or similar settings. Programs, plans or projects chosen at these fora, by and large, reflect the interests of the participants—the privileged few, not the experiences and views of the vast majority of the population whose spokesperson was conspicuously absent. The disservice occasioned by this lack of representation (of the poor) is potentially cured by the PHC principle.

[155] General Comment No. 14, para 11.

[156] Jurberg 2008, p. 248.

[157] Jurberg and Humphreys, p. 646.

[158] Ibid.

organizations, and urges countries to involve them in their national programs.[159] Thanks to globalization and internationalization of human rights, the number of CSOs in the region has risen sharply since the 1990s, with interests as diverse as the criteria for membership in individual organizations. Avenues through which CSOs could be useful in advancing regional and domestic goals are advocacy, community mobilization and, where appropriate, involvement in direct provision of services. And authorities are responding. Unrelenting pressure from CSOs was a catalyst in PHC reform in several countries including Mali.[160]

Aside from these strategies, CSOs have a role as watchdog of government activities. Even where the government reaches out to CSOs in its policy initiatives and agreement is struck on a set of goals and priorities, this does not, in any way, guarantee implementation according to the terms of the agreement. Neither accountability nor transparency of actions is innate to governance. Therefore, to hope for these virtues to mark and permeate government actions, in absence of a robust sanctioning regime, is a mistake. Incredibly, this hope—misplaced as it is— has characterized post-independence governance in Africa. The absence of a watchdog, a robust bulwark against abuse of public office, is a major reason for continuing paralysis of the social and economic fabrics of various nations in the region. Extant health quandary in the region is a visible reminder of years of neglect and abdication of responsibility on the part of public officials entrusted with stewardship of national resources.

Short of activism, the usefulness of the court system—the traditional watchdog of executive and legislative actions—is quite limited as courts can only adjudicate real cases (upon petition by aggrieved parties), and since lawsuits are rarely brought by private citizens to compel performance of a public duty, offending individuals have remained scot-free. This is a vacuum waiting for CSOs to fill. Unlike the judiciary, CSOs are unconstrained by technical rules and can choose from a wide array of options (particularly media campaign or legal action against policies or actions inimical to general welfare) to force fair governance. African CSOs have been particularly successful before the African Commission on Human and Peoples Rights (Commission), prevailing in several landmark cases. In *SERAC v. Nigeria,* for instance, the Commission held the government of Nigeria in violation of Article(s) 16 (right to health) and 24 (right to satisfactory environment) of the African Charter on Human and Peoples' Rights for not protecting the Ogoni people in South Eastern Nigeria from environmental degradation and health problems resulting from oil exploration and drilling by Shell Petroleum Development Corporation in that part of the country.[161]

---

[159] Africa Health Strategy, p. 24.

[160] WHO 2008, pp. 110–111.

[161] The Social and Economic Rights Action Center and the Center for Economic and Social Rights v. Nigeria, African Commission on Human and Peoples' Rights, Comm. No. 155/96 (2001).

But the usefulness of CSOs hinges greatly on whether governments regard them as threats or allies committed to the same cause. The former tainted and marred relationships between governments and CSOs prior to the triumph of democracy in most African countries toward the end of the 1990s. But democracy has not brought to an end the sometimes acrimonious relationship between CSOs and civilian administrations in many of these countries. Human rights scholar Makau Mutua's observation that governments in Africa "have historically adopted hostile—even coercive policies" against CSOs, sometimes viewing them "with suspicion, if not outright dread" and, in other cases, have "sought to either co-opt or muzzle them" remains true today, even as the current occupants of political positions in the region sanctimoniously and vociferously proclaim to have charted a different course from their predecessors.[162] A recent example is the enactment, in January 2009, of Ethiopia's Proclamation for the Registration and Regulation of Charities and Societies which prohibits CSOs in the country that receive 10 % or more of its funding from foreign sources from engaging in activities related to, inter alia, "[t]he advancement of human and democratic right ..."[163] Former U.N. High Commissioner for Human Rights, Mary Robinson, was exasperated: "I am very concerned about this legislation. ... It is regrettable to have legislation which might close the enabling space for civil society because it is actually part of the development of a country."[164] Despite mounting condemnations and criticisms from the United States, the European Union and CSOs, far and wide, the government in Addis Ababa refused to balk.

Conscious of the negative impact on development this sort of acrimonious relationship between CSOs and governments might engender, the African Health Strategy requires countries in the region to ensure not only the "participation of civil society" in the development and implementation of national health programs but also—and more important—to "create a conducive environment" for their meaningful and productive operation.[165] Health Ministries are specifically called upon to facilitate the emergence of CSOs and fund their activities.[166] By facilitating the emergence of CSOs and involving them in the design and implementation of health programs, governments tap into the expertise and insights of these organizations. These are important resources for developing and strengthening health systems in Africa.

---

[162] Mutua 2009, p. 1, 5.

[163] International Center for Not-for-Profit Law, 2009, http://www.icnl.org/knowledge/globaltrends/glotrends1-1.htm (accessed 6 January 2013). See Article(s) 2, 14, para 5.

[164] Irin News, Ethiopia: New Law on Charities Passed Despite Objections, 6 January 2009, http://www.irinnews.org/report.aspx?ReportId=82223 (accessed 4 April 2013).

[165] Africa Health Strategy, p. 24. See also NEPAD Health Strategy, p. 23.

[166] Africa Health Strategy, p. 16.

1.5 Conclusion

The arduousness and complexity of health sector constraints in Africa can, at times, be frustratingly overwhelming even to the most seasoned and astute public health scholar. Yet, how to detangle and deconstruct this seemingly inextricable maze is precisely the kind of intellectual resource students of human rights seek in public health scholarship. Steeped in this resource, in addition to reflections and insights from other fields, this chapter has labored not only to animate these challenges but more important, perhaps, also map out routes to extirpating them. The project of health MDGs, particularly in Africa, is facilitation of broader comprehensive health sector development, not just healthcare availability. For countries interested in this project, the first great lesson to imbibe is that improving access to health services, although a critical aspect of any reform initiative, is not per se a sufficient panacea. Diseases and illnesses do not just reveal a subpar performance of the physiological and biochemical functioning of the human system; they represent something more sinister. Morbidities (and human suffering that accompanies them) are manifestations of a much deeper socioeconomic and political pathology: the factors responsible for excess exposure or susceptibility to circumstances that combine to create the need for therapeutic intervention in the first place. More than anything else, including improving access to health services, challenging the status quo requires sustainable and unwavering action on multiple fronts, as meticulously elucidated in this chapter. This is the real antidote to the paralytic performance that has dogged health systems in Africa for decades.

The second lesson is that the tortured reliance on resource constraints as explanatory of the region's health sector woes serves no useful purpose. Even amidst scarcity, proper utilization of available resources would go a long way in improving general health and well-being. The illustration given with malaria (easy to prevent, diagnose, and treat) is a case in point. That malaria remains a prodigious killer disease in Africa in 2013 is an appalling indictment of health and political governance in the region. On this basis, therefore, to conclude as did Sam Nujoma, former President of Namibia and co-chair of the Millennium Summit, that " … despite all these challenges, … with more commitment and dedication, we will emerge victorious and meet most, if not all, of the MDGs come 2015" smacks of wishful thinking, ostensibly oblivious to the political reality and serious governance deficiencies in most countries in the region.[167] Neither Obasanjo's perverse ambition for a third term as president of Nigeria (despite unambiguous constitutional provisions to the contrary), nor continued recalcitrance of President Mugabe to relinquish power (notwithstanding overwhelming rejection and repudiation of his policies by Zimbabweans), was inspired by a burning desire to redirect the fortunes of either country toward health or general welfare. In short,

---

[167] Nujoma, From the Millennium Summit to 2015: The Challenges Ahead, U.N. Chronicle, http://www.un.org/wcm/content/site/chronicle/home/archive/issues2007/theMDGsareweontrack (accessed 4 April 2013).

1 Health and Millennium Development Goals in Africa

there is hardly any evidence that the kind of commitment and dedication envisaged by Nujoma has been or will be embraced any time soon by the political leadership in Africa.

The Abuja Declaration committing African countries to channel at least 15 % of their national budgets to health is undeniably a step in the right direction. Nonetheless, the fact that more than a decade after the agreement, very few countries have met the threshold speaks volumes. Health policies in Africa, both at national and international levels, are replete with dichotomies between goal and action, and this is where the existence of vibrant CSOs becomes crucial. The Committee on ESCR projects accountability and transparency as the principles upon which to anchor national health strategies and plans of action.[168] The accountability principle invites CSOs to demand that governments meet their domestic, regional, and international commitments. The mass media, academics, civic and religious leaders, market women, trade unions, and so forth are members of this partnership. The message to African CSOs is to cast health deterioration in the region as a human rights issue rooted in a subtle, yet insidious, class warfare. Proof (if there is need for one) is the regularity with which senior public officials, including presidents and prime ministers, from Africa are whisked abroad for medical treatment.

There is no more compelling evidence of classism and elitism than usurping public resources for private ends, in this case, to fund the best available treatment anywhere in the world—an exclusive preserve of the ruling class and its cohorts. Why is this important? This privilege, as contended in a pending lawsuit before a federal high court in Nigeria, has become a powerful disincentive to reforming the health system.[169] The lawsuit seeks a perpetual injunction restraining the government from "taking any public officer to foreign hospitals for medical checkup and/or treatment in any manner whatsoever and howsoever."[170] This is instructive for CSOs in Africa. Their operation should be anchored on the principle that populist (human rights) reform does not emanate from the top; instead, it starts with grassroot strident expression of dissatisfaction with, and rejection of, the state of affairs—a bottom-up approach.

To sum it all up, we return to a recurring theme in this discourse—and that is, how to conceptualize health. This is of critical importance for how we think of health powerfully shapes and influences what goes in and out of health policy baskets in Africa. Achieving "a state of complete physical, mental and social well-being" (WHO's definition of health)[171] or a modicum thereof involves tackling the

---

[168] General Comment No. 14, para 55.

[169] Suit No. FHC/IKJ/CS/M59/10(Unreported), Federal High Court Ikeja; Sahara Report, 'Falana Sues FG over Conditions of Public Hospitals', 29 July 2010, http://www.saharareporters.com/report/falana-sues-fg-over-conditions-public-hospitals (accessed 4 April 2013).

[170] Ibid.

[171] WHO Constitution, Preamble, adopted by the International Health Conference, New York, 19–22 June 1946, entered into force 7 April 1948.

root causes of diseases and health inequities which, in turn, depends on interventions by sectors other than health. Therefore, appropriate policy frameworks must incorporate, at the minimum, access to life's essentials (underlying health determinants) and basic health care, both of which are considered "core obligations" by the ICESCR and from which no derogation is allowed, even on grounds of resource difficulties.[172] Mechanisms should be put in place to ensure that lofty goals translate to real goods and services that can be readily accessed by anyone in need. This expansive conceptualization of health, especially its application and meaning to those on the lowest rung of social ladder (in terms of drawing attention to a broad spectrum of factors constraining their agency), should underline health policy decisions in every country in Africa. This is not, by any means, an imposition of a novel obligation but merely infuses life to commitments already undertaken in various regional and international human rights treaties to which a vast majority of these countries voluntarily subscribed. It is human rights pragmatism, a richly productive incarnation and reinforcement of a human rights approach to securing health for all.[173]

Health policy decisions should be anchored on the principle that social determinants of health such as food, housing, etc., are stricto sensu, not within the mandate of a Ministry of Health but, even so, their availability and equitable distribution are crucial to attaining the MDGs and advancing the right to health. This is the crux of multisectoral dimension of health and has two critical implications for Africa. First, health sector reform must be operationalized in tandem with strengthening other sectors (agriculture, industries, housing, and so forth) connected with providing or creating an enabling environment for availability of goods or conditions that promote good health. Second, multisectoral interventions must not only be harnessed, it must also be harmonized and streamlined to achieve a common goal: improving health. The leadership role of the Ministry of Health must involve active cooperation and collaboration with other sectors, including bilateral and multilateral partners, to find cost-effective and sustainable solutions to the numerous health challenges facing the region. As to whether attainment of the health MDGs is in the horizon for Africa, the reality is that in the end, it might be that despite massive international development assistance, all the summits and

---

[172] General Comment No. 14, para(s) 43, 47.

[173] "Human rights pragmatism" counterbalances state practice in Africa, especially in the realm of socioeconomic rights where, for the most part, the doctrine of *pacta sunt servanda* has had negligible impact in the practice of States. The idea goes beyond lofty goals to demand that the letter of human rights instruments mean something tangible, that the fruits of these words (goods and services) are concretized in the lives of designated beneficiaries. In other words, it advocates a new paradigm, separate and distinct from the current practice of subscribing to human rights instruments with little demonstrable consideration to practical implementation, and requires that governments must intend, and there must be a sense among the people, that the benefits of human rights treaties operative in their respective jurisdictions would be readily available to all, regardless of individual socioeconomic differentials.

1 Health and Millennium Development Goals in Africa

declarations, the best that can be hoped for is substantial improvement—indeed, a reversal—in the state of health in Africa. And this, in itself, is no mean feat, considering from whence the journey began.[174]

References

Abyad A, Homsi R (1993) A comparison of pregnancy care delivered by family physicians versus obstetricians in Lebanon. Fam Med 25(7):465–470

Agbakoba O, Mamah W (2002) Towards a peoples' constitution in Nigeria: a civic education manual for the legal community. Human Rights Law Service, Lagos

Alesina A, Weder B (2002) Do corrupt governments receive less foreign aid? Am Econ Rev 92(4):1126–1137

Anderson T (2010) Tide turns for drug manufacturing in Africa. Lancet 375(9726):1597–1598

Bateman C (2009) Cholera: getting the basics right. S Afr Med J 99(3):138, 140–142

Beck CA et al (2001) Discharge prescriptions following admission for acute myocardial infarction at tertiary care and community hospitals in Quebec. Can J Cardiol 17(1):33–40

Boff L (1989) Faith on the edge: religion and marginalized existence. Harper and Row, San Francisco

Cohen JT et al (2008) Does preventive care save money? Health economics and the presidential candidates. N Engl J Med 358(7):661–663

Commission on Social Determinants of Health (CSDH) (2008) Closing the gap in a generation: health equity through action on the social determinants of health. WHO Press, Geneva

Easterly W (2009) How the millennium development goals are unfair to Africa. World Dev 37(1):26

Farmer P (2003) Pathologies of power: health, human rights, and the new war on the poor. University of California Press, Berkeley

Franco Don A (2009) Poverty and the continuing global health crisis. Tate Publishing, Mustang

Gwartney J et al (1996) Economic freedom of the world: 1975–1995. Frasier Institute, Vancouver

Gwartney J et al (2010) Economic freedom of the world: 2010 annual report. Frasier Institute, Vancouver

Hagopian A et al (2004) The migration of physicians from sub-Saharan Africa to the United States of America: measures of the African brain drain, 2 Human Resources for Health (2004), http://www.human-resourceshealth.com/content/pdf/1478-4491-2-17.pdf

Heuston WJ et al (1995) Practice variations between family physicians and obstetricians in the management of low-risk pregnancies. J Fam Pract 40(4):345–351

---

[174] In so concluding, this author is in total agreement with Clemens & Moss who argued against a literal interpretation (which holds the MDGs as real practical targets) in favor of a "more nuanced view" which sees the "MDGs as a symbol of the kinds of outcomes toward which the world should strive." The reason, as they see it, is that "… there is a real risk that the MDGs, as currently conceived and promoted, could turn real development successes into imaginary failures." See Michael Clemens & Todd Moss, 'What's Wrong with the Millennium Development Goals?' Center for Global Development Brief, September 2005, 3, www.cgdev.org/files/3940_file_WWMGD.pdf (accessed 12 January 2013). In this view, therefore, simply because progress in Africa does not equal or surpass the numerical value designated as necessary to meet a certain benchmark should not be interpreted to mean failure as to do so would tantamount to trivializing lives saved and morbidities averted in the region as a result of MDG-generated initiatives.

Jurberg C (2008) Flawed but fair: Brazil's health system reaches out to the poor. Bull World Health Organ 86(4):248–249

Jurberg C, Humphreys G (2010) Brazil's march towards universal coverage. Bull World Health Organ 88(9):646–647

Kinfu Y et al (2009) The health worker shortage in Africa: are enough physicians and nurses being trained? Bull World Health Organ 82:225–230

Krikke EH, Bell NR (1989) Relation of family physician or specialist care to obstetric interventions and outcomes in patients at low risk: a Western Canadian cohort study. Can Med Assoc J 140(6):637–643

Kumar P (2007) Providing the providers—remedying Africa's shortage of health care workers. N Engl J Med 356:2564–2567

Mason PR (2009) Zimbabwe experiences the worst epidemic of cholera in Africa. J Infect Di Developing Countries 3(2):148–151

McCord C, Freeman HP (1990) Excess mortality in Harlem. N Engl J Med 322(3):173–177

Mohammed N (2009) The role of local manufacturers in improving access to essential medicines: creating opportunities for the scale-up of local pharmaceutical production. Medicine Transparency Alliance, November 2009

Mutua M (2009) Human Rights NGOs in East Africa: defining the challenges. In: Human Rights NGOs in East Africa: political and normative tensions. University of Pennsylvania Press, Philadelphia, p 5

Naicker S et al (2009) Shortage of healthcare workers in developing countries—Africa. Ethn Dis 19: S1-60–64

Narayan D et al (2000) Voices of the poor: can anyone hear us. Oxford University Press, New York

Nnamuchi O (2008) Kleptocracy and its many faces: the challenges of justiciability of the right to health care in Nigeria. J African Law 52(1):1–42

Nnamuchi O, Ortuanya S (2012) The human right to health in Africa and its challenges: a critical analysis of millennium development goal 8. Afr Hum Rights Law J 12(1):178–198

Obinna C, Duru R (2010) Fake drugs down to 5 %, says NAFDAC, Vanguard (online ed) 21 Sept 2010

Opara KO, Jiburum BC (2010) Skin cancers in Albinos in a teaching hospital in Eastern Nigeria—presentation and challenges of care. World J Surg Oncol 8(73). http://wjso.com/content/8/1/73

Raufu A (2002) Influx of fake drugs to Nigeria worries health experts. Lancet 324(7339):698

Ribadu N (2009) Capital loss and corruption: the example of Nigeria. Testimony before the House Financial Services Committee, 19 May 2009

Rose JH et al (2000) Generalists and oncologists show similar care practices and outcomes for hospitalized late-stage cancer patients. SUPPORT investigators. Study to understand prognoses and preferences for outcomes and risks for treatment. Med Care 38(11):1103–1118

Ryan S et al (2001) The effects of regular source of care and health need on medical care use among rural adolescents. Arch Pediatr Adolesc Med 155(2):184–190

UN (2007) Africa and the millennium development goals 2007 Update

UN (2010) The millennium development goals report

UN (2010) Treaty collection, chapter IV: human rights, No. 4: ICESCR status of ratification, as of Dec 20, 2010.

UN (2011) The millennium development goals report

UNDP (1997) Human development report 1997: human development to eradicate poverty. Oxford University Press, New York

UNDP (2009) Human development report 2009: overcoming barriers: human mobility and development. Palgrave MacMillan, New York

UNDP (2010) Human development report 2010: the real wealth of nations: pathways to human development. Palgrave MacMillan, New York

UNICEF (2009) The state of the world's children: special edition. Brodrock Press, Tarrytown, New York

WHO (1981) Global strategy for health for all by the year 2000. WHO Press, Geneva

WHO (1995) The World Health Report 1995: bridging the gaps. WHO Press, Geneva

WHO (2000) The World Health Report 2000: health systems: improving performance. WHO Press, Geneva

WHO (2001) Macroeconomics and health: Investing in health for economic development: report of the commission on macroeconomics and health. WHO Press, Geneva

WHO (2005) The World Health Report 2005: make every mother and child count. WHO Press, Geneva

WHO (2006) The World Health Report 2006: working together for health. WHO Press, Geneva

WHO (2008) The World Health Report 2008: primary health care now more than ever. WHO Press, Geneva

WHO (2009) World Malaria Report 2009. WHO Press, Geneva

WHO (2010) World Health Statistics 2010. WHO Press, Geneva

WHO (2011) World Health Statistics 2011. WHO Press, Geneva

Wilensky GR, Satcher D (2009) Don't forget about the social determinants of health. Health Aff Suppl. Web Exclusive 28(2):w194–w198

Wilkinson R, Marmot M (2003) Social determinants of health: the solid facts. WHO Regional Office for Europe, Copenhagen

World Bank (1993) World Development Report 1993: investing in health. Oxford University Press, New York

World Bank (2010) Doing business 2010: reforming through difficult times. IFC and Palgrave MacMillan, Washington DC

Chapter 2
Ensuring the Realization of the Right to Health Through the African Union (AU) System: A Review of Its Normative, Policy and Institutional Frameworks

Getahun A. Mosissa

Abstract The African continent has been and continues to be at the epicentre of a global public health crisis. Each year millions of lives in the continent continue to be wasted from diseases preventable with relative ease such as malaria, diarrhoea, tuberculosis (TB), pneumonia, measles, HIV/AIDS, malnutrition, etc. It is the continent where individuals have the lowest life expectancy in the world by any standard of measures. Maternal, under-five and adult mortality rate is the highest in the world. Evidence also show that the continent, sub-Saharan region in particular, is the most food insecure part of the world where over one in four persons are undernourished. In spite of these staggering facts, Africa's average total expenditure on health is one of the lowest in the world. The continent hosts poorly resourced health infrastructures and systems. Ordinary individuals, especially vulnerable persons, in the continent have the least possible access to health care and the underlying determinants of health as well as to other related social protection mechanisms such as social security and health insurance. These all raise very serious issues with the obligations of the States Parties to ensure the right to health for everyone within their jurisdictions. This contribution has accordingly the following two main objectives. The first is to identify the underlying obstacles

---

PhD Candidate, Dept. International and Constitutional Law, University of Groningen, The Netherlands and Lecturer, Jimma University, Ethiopia. I would like to thank Toebes and Nnamuchi for their insightful comments; and Koleva for her worthwhile contribution to the editorial works. Any errors or mistakes whatsoever, however, remain on my shoulder. For reactions and comments the author can be reached through the below e-mail addresses.

G. A. Mosissa (✉)
Department of International and Constitutional Law, University of Groningen, Groningen, The Netherlands
e-mail: getalex2000@yahoo.com; g.a.mosissa@rug.nl

B. Toebes et al. (eds.), *The Right to Health*, DOI: 10.1007/978-94-6265-014-5_2,   43
© T.M.C. ASSER PRESS and the authors 2014

to the realization of the right to health in the continent. In this respect, it particularly asks the extent to which the alleged lack of resources can be said to explain the inaccessability of health care and the underlying determinants of health. The second is to describe the relevant legal, policy and institutional frameworks available at the African Union (AU) level with the view to assessing their effectiveness in ensuring the right to health. In this regard, it is asked if and to what extent the two principal human rights organs of the AU with remedial powers, the Court and Commission, are able to practically hold the Member States accountable for their gross failures in realizing the right to health. Overall, it emerges from the discussion that the violation of the right to health in the continent is only a mirror of persistent socioeconomic injustices mainly resulting from lack of systemic accountability. This suggests that it is impossible to ensure the effective realization of the right to health without first addressing the structural accountability deficits not just in the health sector but also in the respective socioeconomic and political systems of the Member States as a whole.

Contents

2.1	Introduction	45
2.2	Human Dignity, the Right to Health and Social Justice	49
	2.2.1 The Normativity of the Right to Health	51
	2.2.2 The Principle of Social Justice	52
2.3	The Legal Basis of the Right to Health in the AU System	56
	2.3.1 Its Basic Features	56
	2.3.2 Its Key Pillars of Protections	59
	2.3.3 Impediment to the Realization of Basic Health Entitlements in Africa: Lack of Resources or Systemic Problem?	66
2.4	The Enforcement Mechanisms of the Right to Health in the AU System	71
	2.4.1 Introduction	71
	2.4.2 The Right to Health in the Practices of the Commission	73
2.5	Conclusion	88
References		89

There is still an enormous gap between the rhetoric of African governments, which claim to protect and respect human rights and the daily reality where human rights violations remain the norm.

[...]

So many people are living in utter destitution; so few of them have any chance to free themselves from poverty. Their dire situation is exacerbated by the failure of governments in the Africa region to provide basic social services, ensure respect for the rule of law, address corruption and be accountable to their people.[1]

2.1 Introduction

It would not take much effort to appreciate the extremely severe problem of poor health in Africa. Facts and figures abound and each source confirms that Africa has been and is still at the epicentre of a global public health crisis. The life expectancy in Africa is unacceptably the lowest in the world by any standards of measures.[2] According to one of the recent WHO reports, for instance, the average life expectancy in the continent was 53 years (against 68 years of global average) in 2008. Adult mortality rate (described as the probability of dying between 15 and 60 years per 1,000 population) was 392 (globally 180) in 2008. The distribution of disease burden estimated by percentage of total Disability Adjusted Life Years (DALYs) per 2004 data shows that over 70 per cent of deaths occurred from communicable diseases (compared to global average of 39.7 per cent) of which infectious and parasitic diseases such as HIV/AIDS, diarrhoea, malaria, TB accounted for the largest proportion.[3] Most Africans have the least possible access to basic goods and services: there are few health and other social services available to the population at large.[4] They are also the least protected against socioeconomic causes of vulnerability such as sickness, unemployment, low income, ageing, drought, famine, etc., because there are no or insufficient social protection

---

[1] Amnesty International Report 2009: The State of World's Human Rights (hereinafter Amnesty International Report 2009, available at www.amnesty.org last accessed 27 June 2013), p. 9.

[2] See the World Health Report 2000: Health Systems: Improving Performance, World Health Organization, Geneva (hereinafter World Health Report 2000, available at www.who.int/whr/2000/en/whr00_en.pdf last accessed 24 March 2013), Tables 2.2 and 2.3, pp. 29–30. In addition to those cited here and below, documents cited at footnote 48, 59, 88, 70 and 97 also provide interesting facts and figures confirming this assertion.

[3] See Health Situation Analysis in the African Region: Atlas of Health Statistics 2011, World Health Organization Regional Office for Africa (hereinafter Atlas of Health Statistics 2011, available through www.afro.who.int/en/clusters-a-programmes/ard/research-publications-and-library-services.html last accessed 24 March 2013), pp. x–xi.

[4] See the World Health Report 2010: Health Systems Financing: the Path to Universal Coverage, the World Health Organization, Geneva (hereinafter World Health Report 2010, available at www.who.int/whr/2010/10_summary_en.pdf last accessed 24 March 2013), Executive Summary, pp. x–xi.

mechanisms it was, for instance, estimated in the World Health Report 2010 that only between 5 and 10 per cent of the population were covered by some form of social protection systems.[5]

Ill-health and related impoverishments due to lack of access to basic health entitlements disproportionately affects those vulnerable parts of the population in Africa such as children, women, the poor and rural population (note that the majority of the African population live in rural areas mostly on subsistence farming). For instance, under-five and maternal mortality still remain to be grave concerns for most countries in the continent. This was shown in one of the most recent reports concerned with assessing Africa's progress towards MDGs.[6] According to this report, of 26 countries worldwide with under-five mortality rates above 100 deaths per 1,000 live births in 2010, 24 were in Africa.[7] Sub-Saharan Africa was the worst in this regard where 'one in around eight children die before the age of five (121 deaths per 1,000 live births)' and this was 'nearly twice the average in developing countries overall and more than 17 times the average in developed countries'.[8] The report also shows an unacceptably high rate of maternal mortality: the continent's average mortality ratio (MMR) was said to be 590 deaths per 100,000 live births in 2008. 'This means that, in 2008, a woman in Africa died as a result of pregnancy or childbirth every 2.5 min–24 h, 576 a day, and 210,223 a year.'[9]

The Africa Human Development Report, the first of its kind, can also help us to see the dire situation of health impoverishment through the prism of food insecurity in the continent which is, again, most severely affecting the vulnerable parts of the population. In particular, this is most severe in sub-Saharan Africa, the most food insecure part of the world, where it continues to impoverish the health of the population. As it states

> For too long the face of sub-Saharan Africa has been one of dehumanizing hunger. More than one in four Africans is undernourished, and food insecurity—the inability to consistently acquire enough calories and nutrients for a healthy and productive life—is pervasive. The spectre of famine, which has virtually disappeared elsewhere in the world,

---

[5] Ibid.

[6] See MDG Report 2012: Assessing Progress in Africa towards the Millennium Development Goals: Emerging Perspectives from Africa on the post-2015 Development Agenda, Economic Commission for Africa et al. (hereinafter MDG Report 2012: Assessing Africa's Progress, available at www.undp.org/dam/undp/library/MDG/english/MDGRegionalReports/Africa/MDG Report2012_ENG.pdf(final).pdf last accessed 25 August 2013), pp. 56–64.

[7] Ibid.

[8] Ibid., p. 59. 'The four main global killers of children under-five are pneumonia (18 per cent), diarrhoeal diseases (15 per cent), pre-term birth complications (12 per cent) and birth asphyxia (9 per cent). Malnutrition is an underlying cause in more than a third of under-five deaths. Malaria is still a major cause of child mortality in Africa (excluding North Africa), causing about 16 per cent of under-five deaths.' Ibid.

[9] Ibid., p. 65. In the report, Malaria, HIV/AIDS, TB were mentioned as among major driving factors behind MMR in the continent.

2 Ensuring the Realization of the Right to Health

continues to haunt parts of sub-Saharan Africa. Famines grab headlines, but chronic food insecurity and malnutrition are more insidious, often silent, daily calamities for millions of Africans.[10]

Paradoxically, the average proportion of expenditure on health is the lowest in the world, which does not reflect the state of ill-health in the continent.[11] It was in 2001 that the African leaders promised to increase the average national health expenditure on health to 15 % of the annual national budget by 2015[12] but only negligible number of countries has met or is on track to meet the target.[13]

These alarming figures raise very serious questions with respect to the international human rights obligations of the AU and its Member States. They particularly compel us to question the relevance and effectiveness of the international mechanisms for the protection of human rights mechanisms in Africa. Narrowing this question to the context of the right to health, the following discussion provides a review of the normative, policy and institutional frameworks in place at the AU level for the realization of the right to health in the continent. The following discussion shows that a great majority of countries in Africa are parties to numerous major international (that is, global and continental) human rights instruments providing for the right to health.[14] There have also been series of global and continental policy initiatives and commitments concerned with addressing the health situation in the continent including the most recent AU Social Policy Framework adopted in 2008. Nevertheless, only very little has been achieved on the ground.[15]

Several factors can be blamed for such gross infectiveness and failures. Resource constraint (scarcity), poor socioeconomic conditions, lack of

---

[10] See Africa Human Development Report 2012: Towards a Food Secure Future, UNDP (here inafter Africa Human Development Report 2012, available at www.undp.org/content/dam/undp/library/corporate/HDR/Africa HDR/UNDP-Africa HDR-2012-EN.pdf#page = 10&zoom = auto,0,243 last accessed 25 August 2013), p. 1.

[11] Africa's average total expenditure on health was only for 6.2 % of GDP in 2007 (global average by then was 9.7). See Atlas of Health Statistics 2011.

[12] See Abuja Declaration on HIV/AIDS, Tuberculosis and Other Infectious Diseases 2001, Abuja, Nigeria, Doc. OAU/SPS/ABUJA/3 (hereinafter Abuja Declaration, available at http://www.un.org/ga/aids/pdf/abuja_declaration.pdf last accessed 30 April 2013), para 26.

[13] See 'State of Health Financing in the African Region, Discussion Paper for the Interministerial Conference: Achieving Results and Value for Money in Health, 4–5 July 2012, Tunis, Tunisia', WHO Regional Office for Africa (hereinafter WHO 2012: State of Health Financing in Africa, available at http://www.hha-online.org/hso/system/files/health_financing_in_africa_edited_03_july_-_copy.pdf last accessed 30 April 2013), p. 7.

[14] These include the Universal Declaration of Human Rights (UDHR), International Covenant on Economic, Social and Cultural Rights (ICESCR), Convention on the Rights of the Child (CRC), Convention on Elimination of All Forms of Discrimination Against Women (CEDAW), International Convention on the Elimination of All Forms of Racial Discrimination (CERD), African Charter on Human and Peoples' Rights (African Charter or the Banjul Charter), African Charter on the Rights and Welfare of Child, the Protocol to the African Charter on the Rights of Women in Africa (Protocol on Rights of Women in Africa). See also footnote 52.

[15] See Sect. 2.3.3.

infrastructure development and poverty are among commonly cited factors impeding the realization of the right to health in the continent. This, however, sharply contradicts with overwhelming evidence indicating, for instance, the presence of abundant resources and endemic corruption. This author argues that the major underlying reason behind gross failures in ensuring the right to health has more to do with systemic, structural problems and less with scarcity. In making this argument, the author proposes to analyse the right to health in terms of three key pillars of protections that it guarantees under international law: the right to freedom of choice, basic health entitlements and access to justice. This approach provides us with very helpful framework in appreciating the extent to which the alleged lack of material resources could in fact be blamed for violation of the right to health in the continent. Accordingly, it will be seen that the obligation to ensure the first two key pillars falls within the elementary institutional responsibility of the State and by no means could be blamed on lack of resource constraints. Admittedly, ensuring the second element may involve substantial resource investment but this is not always the case. Not all the State Party failures in this respect can be attributed to the problem of scarcity as such.

The discussion, then, continues to ask if there exist strong and effective legal mechanisms, enforcement measures, so as to deal with the problem identified therein. In relation to this, the discussion proceeds from the basic normative principle regarding the responsibility of intergovernmental organizations like the AU which have joint responsibilities with its Member States for the protection of human rights in the continent. These responsibilities of the AU are clearly enshrined in its Constitutive Act and other relevant continental and global human rights treaties; that is, it is both a matter of constitutional and international legal responsibility for the AU to ensure the effective protection of human rights in the continent.[16] From this follows the obligation to ensure the existence and effective functioning of legal mechanisms to redress (potential) violations of human rights at the continental level. In this regard, the discussion assesses if and the extent to which the Court and Commission, the two principal human rights organs of the AU with remedial powers, have been playing meaningful role in addressing the problem of structural accountability in the continent. For reasons to be seen, the finding in this respect is quite disappointing.

Overall, by engaging in such a comprehensive review of legal, policy and institutional frameworks and practices of the protection of the right to health through the AU systems, this contribution intends to provide a useful insight into the underlying factors paralysing global and continental efforts to improve

---

[16] For the objectives and purposes of the AU, see Preamble *cum* Articles 3 and 4 of the Constitutive Act of the AU (AU Constitutive Act) adopted 11 July 2000 entered into force 26 May 2001 (available through www.au.int/en/treaties last accessed 10 May 2013). See also, *mutatis mutandis,* the responsibility of the AU enshrined in the Banjul Charter especially at Part II (concerning measures of safeguard) and in the ACRWC at Part II; Article 46 Statute ACtJHR and Articles 30 and 31 Protocol ACtHPR (both instruments cited at footnote 107). See generally Viljoen 2012, p. 156f, Yusuf and Ouguergouz 2012, Doumbé-Billé 2012.

2 Ensuring the Realization of the Right to Health   49

conditions resulting from systematic exclusion, marginalization and impoverishment. To this extent, it particularly aims to inform, from the perspective of the right to health, future academic and policy debates concerning the collective international responsibilities of the AU and its Member States in ensuring the realization of human rights and basic social justice in Africa.

2.2 Human Dignity, the Right to Health and Social Justice

But before proceeding to the review of the realization of the right to health through the AU system, the overarching theoretical arguments inspiring this discussion as regards the normative foundation and implications of the right to health in general are discussed. The objective here is to show how fundamental it is for individuals to have their right to health respected and, correspondingly, how compelling it is on the part of the State to ensure, in certain respects as a matter of priority, the right to health for everyone within its jurisdiction. The principal argument is that the right to health directly flows from the principle of respect for human dignity.[17] It is notable that international human rights law provides human dignity as the foundational normative principle[18] of all human rights. Thus, all persons have equal and inalienable rights derived from the inherent dignity of human being solely because they are all born free and equal in dignity and the rights thereof and that the recognition of this is the foundation of freedom, justice and peace in the world.[19]

---

[17] From the outset it should be stated that the theoretical idea and significance of human dignity has been debated generally and in relation to the right to health but here the sole focus is on its importance for the practical understanding of the normative essence and implications of the right to health as enshrined under international human rights law. For a general discussion on human dignity, see Klein and Kretzmer 2002, Rosen 2012, Dworkin 2011, Riley 2011, Kateb 2011, Spijkers 2011, Malpas 2010, Malpas and Lickiss 2010, Waldron 2007, Dworkin 2006, 1997, Weinrib 2005, Carozza 2003, Feldman 1999, 2000, Meyer and Parent 1992, Schacter 1983. In the context of the right to health, see generally Kaufmann et al. 2011, Malpas and Lickiss 2010, Aasen et al. 2009, Andorno 2009, Schroeder 2010, Eibach 2008, Chan and Pang 2007, Chochinov 2007, Häyry 2004, Harris and Sulston 2004, Brownsword 2003, Gentzler 2003.

[18] In this discussion the notion of 'norm' and 'principle' should be understood in the sense they are used in Alexy 2010a, b. According to Alexy, there are three essential aspects to deontic norms: command, prohibition and permission which he also analysed in the context of constitutional rights theory (see Alexy 2010b, pp. 114–138); on his theory of principle see ibid., at Chap. 3.

[19] This is the normative statements enshrined in the preambles of the United Nations Charter (UN Charter) and almost all of the international human rights treaties. For instance, the Preamble to UDHR provides, 'recognition of the inherent dignity and of equal and inalienable rights of all members of the human family is the foundation of freedom, peace and justice in the world... the disregard and contempt of the same has been the source of all forms of indignity and injustice...'. The Preambles to the twin Covenants, International Covenant on Civil and Political Rights (ICCPR) and ICESCR, repeat this saying, 'The States Parties to the present Covenant ...

But what does the principle of human dignity practically entail? There seems to be a general consensus that the concept of human dignity in human rights law refers to the inherent value that everyone possesses just by virtue of being a human person and hence worthy of unconditional respect;[20] an 'intrinsic', 'unconditional', 'incomparable', 'transcendental' value of humanity.[21] It is possible to construe the term 'by virtue of being a human person' as meaning by virtue of being a biological and moral person because a human being has, in essence, a biological and moral existence. This means the value of dignity pertains equally and inseparably to both the biological and moral aspects of humanness.[22] As having both the biological and moral existence, every person has equal and inherent needs required to live and function as such.[23] Based on this we can say that the core and primary essence of the principle of human dignity concerns the safeguarding of the physical and moral inviolability (respect-worthiness, respectfulness) of a person by asserting respect for the inherent being and needs of every person.[24] The ideal of

---

(Footnote 19 continued)

[recognize] that [the equal and inalienable rights of all members of human family declared in UDHR] drive from the inherent dignity of the human person'. The Preamble to the Banjul Charter also states, '[the States Parties recognize] on the one hand, that fundamental human rights stem from the attributes of human beings, which justifies their international protection and on the other hand, that the reality and respect of peoples' rights should necessarily guarantee human rights'....

[20] See footnote 17.

[21] See Rosen 2012, pp. 19–31 (discussing Kant's usage of the concept of dignity), Parfit 2011, Chap. 10 at Sections 34 and 35, (also discussing Kant's notion of value and dignity), Sulmasy 2010, pp. 13–17, Malpas 2010, pp. 19–20, Parent 1992, pp. 62–63. This does not mean that there is a universal conception on the idea and function of human dignity both generally and in human rights law. For more on this see the exchange between Carozza 2003, 2008, MCCrudden 2008, Riley 2010, at Sect. 1.2 (providing a very helpful intervention in the debates between the former two and several others); M'Honey 2012a, b and White 2012. See also Henry 2011, Rao 2011. There are also authors who reject the relevance of the notion of human dignity in the current human rights discourse altogether. See particularly Macklin 2003, Fyfe 2007, Hennette-Vauchez 2011.

[22] Usually the discussion on dignity concentrates on the moral aspects of being a human person and it rarely expresses the fact that the value of dignity equally pertains to the biological aspect of being human. For the purpose here we can say that by the natural fact of being born as free biological and moral beings, all human beings have equal dignity and, on this very basis, have the right to enjoy equally those basic biological and moral human needs inherent to their dignity.

[23] For more on the practical construction of the idea of human dignity see Nussbaum 2006, p. 69ff. (referring to the idea of life in dignity in its intuitive sense), Spijkers 2011 (discussing the sense in which the practical concept of human dignity has over the years been consistently employed in the legislative practices of the UN General Assembly); Henkin 1992, Parent 1992. The following authors have attempted to apply the principle of human dignity to the practical context of right to health and health care: Lickiss 2010, Malpas 2010, Sulmasy 2010 and in some of the essays in Aasenet et al. 2009, Kaufmann et al. 2011.

[24] In the Oxford Advanced Learner's Dictionary the word 'inviolable' is defined as 'that must be respected and not attacked or destroyed'. See also Articles 4 and 5 ACHPR, Article 1 Charter of Fundamental Rights of the European Union (EUCFR). Article 1 of EUCFR states, 'Human dignity is inviolable. It must be respected and protected'. For commentary on this provision, see Olivetti 2010. See Rosen 2012, pp. 57–58 (discussing the notion of respect-as-observance and

respect signified by human dignity itself has both negative and positive aspects. In the negative sense, it implies a prohibition of actions or behaviours infringing upon the inviolability of a human being. Whereas in the positive sense it prescribes a performance of positive actions required to ensure the inviolability of the same.[25] This shows that the principle of respect is the conceptual and normative essence of the notion of human dignity; in fact, it can be argued that without this ideal of respect there would not be any substantive meaning of human dignity as such.[26]

This brings us to the next important question: how does this principle of respect for human dignity inform our understanding of the nature of the right to health—that is, the nature of freedoms and entitlements that it guarantees and the State obligations thereof? My argument in this respect proceeds in two steps. The first pertains to the foundation of the normativity of the right to health and the second to general overarching aim of socioeconomic rights, where the right to health is provided as one among such rights. Ultimately, we arrive on the conclusion that, in the context of the right to health, respect for the dignity of human being means respect for those basic biological and moral health needs of everyone. In practical terms, this entails the realization of the right to health care and its underlying determinants in strict accordance with the principle of social justice.

2.2.1 The Normativity of the Right to Health

With regard to the first point, it is needless to say that many have discussed at great length the meaning and implications of the right to health under international law.[27] It is not my intention to repeat those discussions here but to state the nature of the normativity of the right to health in light of the principle human dignity. We have just said above that the principle of respect for human dignity implies respect for the inherent biological and moral needs of a person; health stands out as one among such fundamental needs. It is a matter of common sense that a person must have access to his or her daily biological and moral needs so as to live a healthy

---

(Footnote 24 continued)

respect-as-respectfulness, Parent 1992, p. 63 (discussing the idea of dignity as moral inviolability), Chaskalson 2002, pp. 134–135, Frowein 2002, pp. 121–124, Riley 2010, p. 133f, Klein 2002, p. 146ff, Kretzmer 2002, p. 167ff, Harris and Sulston 2004, p. 799ff, Dworkin 1997, pp. 198–199, 2006, pp. 9–21, Andorno 2009, Schacter 1983. See also Parfit 2011, Chap. 10, Sections 33 through 35.

[25] See Riley 2010, *especially* at Sect. 2.5; Parent 1992, p. 61ff.

[26] See footnote 17 & 24. This principle is referred to as the principle of respect for human dignity, the principle of human dignity or, in short, human dignity throughout this discussion.

[27] See generally Tobin 2012, Backman 2012, Toebes et al. 2012, and Toebes 1999. See also UN Doc. E/CN.4/2003/58, at Section I (Paul Hunt, discussing sources, contours and contents of right to health).

life.[28] In fact, at some basic level one would not be able to dispense with such conditions and still be able to live as a being with dignity: at such basic level they become matters of existential needs.[29]

Interestingly, this implies that a human life in which the essential conditions of life are not adequately available, is not a life of dignity and, hence, not a healthy human life.[30] This, in turn, establishes health as an integral component of the very notion of life of dignity. The essence of the right to health, its normativity, is clearly constituted by the nature of interest that it ultimately seeks to safeguard: a dignified human life. It does so by specifically requiring the realization of basic biological and moral health needs inherent in and indispensable for a life in dignity.[31] Based on this, it is logical to hold that the normativity of the right to health is one of the principal constitutive elements of the principle of respect for human dignity. In Sect. 2.4, we will be considering specific kinds of guarantees and corresponding State Party responsibilities flowing from the right to health. But for the purposes of this contribution it suffices to stress that because of such substantive relationships between human dignity and the right to health it is impossible for the State to satisfy the core normative demands of the former without properly attending to the requirements of the latter: the realization of basic material and moral health needs of a person.[32]

2.2.2 The Principle of Social Justice

The requirement of the right to health is part and parcel of the overarching State Party obligation under socioeconomic rights recognized in international law which, as I argue, concerns the realization of basic social justice for everyone in a society.[33]

---

[28] This is just one of the many vital imports of the capability approach developed by Nussbaum and Sen. See Nussbaum 2000, 2006, 2011, and Sen 1999, 2004, 2009.

[29] Nussbaum 2006, p. 71 (referring to the idea of 'threshold level' beneath which each central human capability need should not fall so as to ensure 'a truly human functioning').

[30] Ibid., pp. 76–78 (listing the ten central human capabilities need which, as she argues, is worked out from 'an intuitive idea of a life that is worthy of the dignity of the human being'; this is also discussed earlier in Nussbaum 2000 and more recently in Nussbaum 2011). See Shue 1996, at Chap. 1, Chaskalson 2002, p. 142 (stating that there can be little dignity in living under the conditions socioeconomic deprivations).

[31] See also Sect. 2.3.

[32] *Compare* this generally with the views of the Committee on Economic Social and Cultural Rights (CESCR) in, inter alia, General comment No. 3: The nature of States parties' obligations (Article 2, para 1) (Annex III), UN Doc. E/1991/23(SUPP) (hereinafter General Comment 3); General comment No. 14(2000): The right to the highest attainable standard of health (Article 12 of the International Covenant on economic, social and cultural rights), UN Doc. E/C.12/2000/4 (hereinafter General Comment 14).

[33] But we should not, however, see the argument from social justice as a new addition to this discussion. As it is to be seen in the subsequent paragraphs, the obligation of the State to ensure

That the realization of basic social justice constitutes the underlying aim of socio-economic rights can be substantiated with reference to the major human rights treaties providing for the same.[34] In essence, socioeconomic rights guarantee material and socioeconomic conditions of human dignity and, hence, wellbeing. There are several substantive principles of social justice that should guide the State Party's performance towards the realization of the socioeconomic rights but which cannot obviously be considered here. So, of the several principles of social justice, the following paragraphs pay attention to the principle of equality (and non-discrimination) and solidarity because of their vital importance in relation to the whole system of socioeconomic rights protection and the topic under discussion. In explaining these, I would like to focus on Articles 21 through 26 of UDHR which, taken together with other subsequent treaties such as ICESCR and ACHPR, provide a comprehensive account of basic social justice and impose commensurate obligations on States Parties towards their people.[35] In substance, these provisions establish that the State Party bears particularly compelling obligations in guaranteeing an adequate standard of living worthy of human dignity for all members of the society.[36]

Article 21 of UDHR is a crucial provision in that it, inter alia, recognizes the will of the people as the foundation of socioeconomic and political governance of a given society.[37] The provision also recognizes important rights flowing from or closely related to this: the right to equal participation in the government and the right to equal access to public services available in one's country.[38] Everyone has these rights of equality simply by virtue of being a member with equal dignity and worth.[39] These rights, in turn, have significant bearings on the ability of individuals to obtain those material conditions indispensable for their wellbeing and the

---

(Footnote 33 continued)

basic social justice flows directly from the fundamental principle of human dignity described above. In fact, to the extent social justice concerns the realization of those basic and indispensable material conditions of human life, it can be regarded as a sub-normative principle of human dignity. See generally Shue 1996, pp. 22–29 and 55–64 (discussing the notion of subsistence rights and the generic obligations flowing therefrom).

[34] Note that by socioeconomic rights regime I am referring to all those international legal norms (treaties) providing for the rights of individuals to have access to basic material goods and services available within their countries or systems.

[35] For commentaries on these provisions see several essays in Eide et al. 1992, Morsink 1999, *especially* at Chap. 6. See also Oraá 2009, pp. 197–203.

[36] See particularly Articles 22, 23, 25 and 26. See Morsink 1999 ibid, Eide et al. 1992 ibid.

[37] See Article 21 (3) which partly reads, 'The will of the people shall be the basis of the authority of the government; this shall be expressed in periodic and genuine elections which shall be by universal and equal suffrage ...'; for commentary on this provision see Rosas 1992.

[38] Article 21(1) and (2).

[39] See also Dworkin 1997, pp. 180–182 (critiquing the underlying assumption behind Rawls' contractual theory of justice. For Dworkin 'individuals have a right to equal concern and respect in the design and administration of the political institutions that govern them' and that this is 'a natural right of all men and women' in the sense that it is 'a right they possess not by virtue of birth or characteristic or merit or excellence but simply as human beings with the capacity to make plans and give justice') (emphasis added).

realization of their life-projects.[40] And, it is the State, a principal political institution which, as a matter of human rights law, bears a primary responsibility in ensuring the right to equal participation and access for all within its jurisdiction.[41]

Another equally important principle that should be mentioned here is the principle of solidarity. As enshrined in, inter alia, Articles 22 and 25 of UDHR, this principle essentially refers to the protection that must be afforded to vulnerable members of a society, those to whom basic material conditions of life are not available or who may be under an imminent risk of losing the same due to reasons beyond their control.[42] Both Articles recognize, among other things, the right of everyone to be secured against different causes of vulnerability. Article 22 states, 'Everyone, as a member of society, has the right to social security and is entitled to realization, …, of economic, social and cultural rights indispensable for his dignity and free development of his personality'.[43] And, Article 25(1) partly states, 'Everyone has … the right to security in the event of unemployment, sickness, disability, widowhood, old age or other lack of livelihood in circumstances beyond his [or her]'.

The principle of solidarity is not quite different from the principle of equality (and non-discrimination) just mentioned above; in fact, they are complementary normative principles. Hence, by directly speaking to the needs of vulnerable persons and the corresponding State obligations, the principle of solidarity clearly seeks to reaffirm the general right of everyone to equal respect and concern. This is so because as long as vulnerable persons do not, in fact, have equal access to basic material conditions of life, it is very difficult to say that the State is treating them as persons with equal worth and, hence, respect and concern. Accordingly, the principle of equality (and non-discrimination) and solidarity are both fundamental regulative principle(s) that States Parties to treaties providing for socioeconomic rights must comply with in the realization of basic social justice for everyone

---

[40] According to Gould, this right is justified on the basis of what she calls the principle of equal positive freedom, which she also considers as the foundation of (social) justice and democracy. See Gould 2004, pp. 37–39 and 71–74.

[41] See generally Fredman 2008, at Chaps. 1 and 2.

[42] Note that in referring to the principle of solidarity here I am specifically concerned with the legal obligation of the state to towards those vulnerable members of the society who are or might be, for reasons beyond their control, unable to cater for themselves and their dependents those basic material conditions of life. See General Comment 3, para 12; General Comment 14, *especially* at para 18 through 27 *cum* para 52); 'Principles and Guidelines on Implementation of Economic Social and Cultural Rights in the African Charter' adopted by the African Commission on its 50th Ordinary Session, 24 October 2011, (available at http://www.achpr.org/files/instruments/economic-social-cultural/achpr_instr_guide_draft_esc_rights_eng.pdf last accessed 20 March 2013) (hereinafter Principles and Guidelines), where the African Commission specifically underscores this obligation of the States with respect each of the socioeconomic rights guaranteed under the African Charter. See also Shue 1996, pp. 29–34. For some theoretical discussions on the idea of solidarity see generally Lotito 2010, p. 171, Hestermeyer 2012, pp. 46–51, Koroma 2012, Rangel 2012, Nussbaum 2006, pp. 36–39, 41–45 and 85–86 (discussing the Grotian, Aristotelian, Lockian and Marxian account of society and sociability), Fredman 2008, pp. 25–30.

[43] See also Articles 11(1) and 9 ICESCR; Article 18(3) ACHPR (compare this with Article 29(4) of the same on the duties of individuals towards their community).

2 Ensuring the Realization of the Right to Health

within their jurisdictions.[44] This is even more crucial with respect to the State Party's obligation to realize the right to health, for, as stated above, the interest that the right to health seeks to protect go to the very heart of human dignity and social justice.

Interestingly, it has clearly been shown that the most fundamental and pressing question pertaining to the right to health is the realization of the right to health care and the social determinants of health for everyone in a society in accordance with such principles as equality, fairness, justice and equity.[45] It is, thus, imperative that the right to health be ensured for everyone in society: 'not just the wealthy, but also those leaving in poverty; not just majority ethnic groups but minorities and indigenous peoples, too; not just those leaving in urban areas, but also remote villagers; not just men, but also women'.[46] So it is noteworthy that the question of social justice in the context of the right to health does not just refer to the distribution of goods and services to certain individuals as such but rather to the ensuring of background justice, fairness and equity in the distribution of those goods and services in a society.[47] Such a question of systemic justice is indeed 'a matter of life and death'.[48] The reason is that, as articulated by the Commission on the Social Determinants of Health (CSDH):

> [social justice] affects the way people live, their consequent chance of illness, and their risk of premature death. ... [The] inequities in health, avoidable health inequalities, arise because of the circumstances in which people grow, live, work and age, and the systems put in place to deal with illness. The conditions in which people live and die are, in turn, shaped by political, social and economic forces. Social and economic policies have a determining impact on whether a child can grow and develop to its full potential and live a

---

[44] See generally General Comment 16(2005): The equal rights of men and women to the enjoyment of all economic, social and cultural rights (Article 3 of the International Covenant on Economic, Social and Cultural Rights), UN Doc. E/C.12/2005/4; General Comment 20: Non-Discrimination in economic, social and cultural rights (Article 2, para 2, of the International Covenant on Economic, Social and Cultural Rights) UN Doc. E/C.12/GC/20. See also 'Report of the United Nations High Commissioner for Human Rights', UN Doc. E/2008/76 discussing the role of the twin principle of equality and non-discrimination in the protection of women's socioeconomic rights.

[45] On this see series of reports by Paul Hunt, the former UN Special Rapporteur on the Rights of everyone to the Highest Attainable Standard of Physical and Mental Health, between 2002 and 2008, available through UNOHCHR website http://www.ohchr.org/EN/Issues/Health/Pages/AnnualReports.aspx last accessed 15 April 2013). See also his Report to UN Human Rights Council (UN Doc. A/HRC/7/11, available at http://daccess-dds-ny.un.org/doc/UNDOC/GEN/G08/105/03/PDF/G0810503.pdf?OpenElement last accessed 15 April 2013) and to UN General Assembly (UN Doc. A/63/263).

[46] Clapham 2007, p. 128 (citing Paul Hunt).

[47] See generally Hunt and Backman 2008, Backman 2010.

[48] 'Closing the gap in a generation: health equity through action on the social determinants of health', Final Report of the Commission on Social Determinants of Health, Geneva, World Health Organization (hereinafter, Final Report CSDH 2008, available at http://whqlibdoc.who.int/publications/2008/9789241563703_eng.pdf last accessed 28 March 2013), p. 1.

flourishing life, or whether its life will be blighted. … The development of a society, rich
or poor, can be judged by the quality of its population's health, how fairly health is
distributed across the social spectrum, and the degree of protection provided from disadvantage as a result of ill-health.[49]

It may be very difficult to exaggerate how precarious and pervasive it is
especially for vulnerable persons not to have access to the material conditions of
life and, therefore, how aggravated the obligations of the State responsibilities
towards the same should be. It should, however, be clear enough that '[a] life that
achieves the full promise of human dignity requires, among other things, escape
from premature death, the resources to withstand debilitating disease, the ability to
read and write, and, in general, opportunities and freedoms unavailable in the
amidst of extreme poverty and deprivation'.[50] In my view, this is essentially what
comes out of the core normative demands of the principle of respect for human
dignity, the right to health and principle of social justice.

2.3 The Legal Basis of the Right to Health in the AU System

2.3.1 Its Basic Features

An apt starting point in considering the legal frameworks for the protection of the
right to health in Africa is an insight into the sources of the responsibilities of the
AU and, by extension, its Member States. The vast majority of African countries
are parties, to the major international (those adopted under the aegis of both the
UN and AU) human rights treaties providing for the right to health.[51] While it is
not necessary to discuss the contents of each of the treaties here, it is essential to
highlight the commonalities they share regarding the protection of the right to

---

[49] Final Report CSDH 2008, ibid. See Toebes 2012, p. 112ff. (referring to this same report in her
discussion of the social determinants of the right to health). See also Rio Political Declaration on
Social Determinants of Health, adopted at World Conference on Social Determinants of Health,
Rio De Jeneiro, Brazil, 19–21 October 2011 (hereinafter Rio Political Declaration, available at
http://www.who.int/social_determinants/en/ last accessed on 20th March 2013), paras 1–13;
Alma-Ata Declaration, para V. See generally Filho 2008 (discussing, especially drawing on the
experiences from Latin America, the role of human right-based approach to health policies and
programmes for the realization of social justice).

[50] Gauri and Brinks 2008, p. 1.

[51] For the recent update concerning the status of ratifications of African countries of international
human rights law, see Viljoen 2012, pp. 143–145 at Table 3.2 and pp. 285–287. Thus, at UN level
more than 90 % of African Countries (calculated at the exclusion of the new South Sudan) have
ratified ICESCR; ICCPR; CERD; CRC; CEDAW; at continental level it stands that out of 53
countries (excluding South Sudan) ACHPR is ratified by all countries; ACRWC by 46; Protocol
on the Rights of Women in Africa by 30 countries. As Nnamuchi and Ortuanya 2012 notes, all 53
member countries had ratified African Charter as of 15 March 1999 (at p. 179).

2 Ensuring the Realization of the Right to Health

health. Therefore, notwithstanding their formal sources (whether originating from global or regional frameworks) and the scope of protections afforded by each treaty,[52] there are several basic features that treaties providing for the right to health have in common. I would like to state three of such commonalities that I found pertinent for this discussion. One is that they all expressly recognize the right to health as a fundamental human right flowing from inherent human dignity aimed at ensuring basic material and moral health needs of a person. In fact, it is already argued above that the right to health is an integral component of the very notion of the right to human life in dignity.

The other is that they all define a particularly compelling obligation of the State Party.[53] The overarching compelling obligation of the State Party prescribed under international law ensuring the best (highest) attainable standard of physical and mental (moral) health for everyone within its jurisdiction.[54] From this of course follows several other specific obligations of both immediate and progressive nature.[55] But it is important to note that whether a given obligation of a State Party

---

[52] The following treaties recognize the rights of every person to the highest attainable standard of physical and mental health for every person. Article 25 UDHR, Article 12 ICESCR and Article 16 ACHPR. The protections enshrined in these treaties are further heightened by numerous thematic treaties aimed at safeguarding the interests of persons or group of persons who are or may be more vulnerable to discrimination, marginalization or exclusion in a society because of different background factors impairing, in one way or another, the equal and full enjoyment of their human rights. The following are major thematic treaties providing also for the protection of the right to health in Africa: CRC; CERD; CEDAW; Convention on the Rights of Persons with Disabilities (CRPWD); ACRWC; Protocol on Rights of Women in Africa. Hence, by subscribing to these binding legal instruments, States Parties have specifically undertaken to address those background factors as minority (childhood), gender, race, ageing, disability and other prohibited grounds of discriminations impairing the fullest enjoyment of the human right to health with utmost priority and urgency. In accordance with Articles 60 and 61 ACHPR, Article 31 Protocol AfCtJHR (footnote 107) and Article 7 Protocol AfCtHPR (footnote 107), all of these treaties are directly enforceable before the Commission and the Human Rights Court to the extent they are ratified by the State Party concerned. Further, the right to health is also enshrined in national constitutions as well. See Heyns and Kaguongo 2006, noting that the right health has been recognized 'in various formulations, in the constitutions of 39 African countries' (see at p. 706 and the accompanying footnote 246). See generally Marks and Clapham 2005, p. 199 (noting that right to health has been recognized in one way or another in more than a hundred national constitutions). For more on the right to health in the African Human Rights Systems, see for instance Yeshanew 2011, pp. 244–249; Viljoen 2012.

[53] This, in turn, is to contrast the characterization of the right to health as implying some sort of discretionary or programmatic policy measures. If the realization of the right to health is to be seen as constituting the discretionary policy choices of the State, then, it is up to the State concerned to take whatever steps it deems fit or not to take any actions at all—in either ways the State is under no obligation whatsoever (see generally Alexy 2010b, pp. 334–337). However, such a characterization is basically incompatible with the core demands of the principle of human dignity from which the normativity of the right to health directly flows.

[54] See for instance Article 16(1) ACHPR; Article 12(1) ICESCR.

[55] For the specific treatment of immediate and progressive State obligation, see Sepulveda 2003, at Chaps. 5 and 7, Fredman 2008, at Chap. 3. See also Arambulo 1999, Langford 2008.

(flowing from the right to health) is immediate or progressive requires a careful analysis of all the relevant factors including the nature of the interests in question; the specific circumstances of the individuals; the nature of measures (that should be) adopted; the level of available resources in a given country; and the expenses associated with operationalizing those measures.[56] In particular, the analysis of the immediate or progressive nature of those specific obligations treads differently on the different pillars of protections afforded by the right to health in international law. For instance, it will be demonstrated below that ensuring the right of individuals to freedom of choice in decisions affecting their health entails an immediate obligation. In addition, it can also be argued that the obligation to ensure access to basic health care for vulnerable persons in a society is also a matter of an immediate State obligation.

Finally, the way international treaties define the right to health and the obligations thereof essentially expresses its systemic character. So we can say that the right to health is also a systemic right in the sense that it requires the State Party to adopt, rationalize and operationalize multiple kinds legal, policy and institutional measures that must function together, as a system, in order to give effect to the protections afforded by the right.[57] This, of course, is not unique to the right to health because the same is more or less true for the protection of other human rights as well.[58] Nevertheless, the understanding of the right to health as a systemic right means that the responsibility of the state flowing from it essentially consists not just in providing specific material goods and services to certain individuals but also in (ensuring) the establishment of those underlying systems through which basic material conditions of health are continuously produced and made available to all members of a society.[59]

---

[56] Hence, it is accordingly suggested here that the Committee's distinction between the immediate and progressive realization of the State under ICESCR as expressed first, in General Comment 3, then, in other subsequent general comments should be understood in this sense. See also Sepulveda 2003, at Chap. 5 (Sect. 2.3) and 7, Fredman 2008, pp. 70–87.

[57] See generally General Comment 14.

[58] See Hunt and Beckman 2008, p. 82 (making a helpful analogy between the implications of the protection of the right to fair trail and right to health, in which they argued that as right to fair trial implies the establishment of court systems, the right to health also implies the establishment of health systems (the paper is available at http://www.hhrjournal.org/index.php/hhr/article/view/22/106 last accessed on 1 March 2013). See also Backman 2012, p. 113ff.

[59] In this sense it can be said that the following documents generally recognize the systemic nature of the right to health: General Comment 14; Declaration of Alma-Ata, International Conference on Primary Health Care, Alma-Ata, USSR, 6–12 September 1978 ((hereinafter Alma-Ata Declaration, available at http://www.who.int/publications/almaata_declaration_en.pdf last accessed in February 2013); Rio Political Declaration, Social Policy Framework for Africa adopted at the First Session of the AU Conference of Ministers in Charge of Social Development', Windhoek, Namibia, 27–31 October, CAMSD/EXP/4(I) (hereinafter AU Social Policy Framework 2008, available at http://sa.au.int/en/content/social-policy-framework-africa (last accessed on 24 March 2013).

2.3.2 *Its Key Pillars of Protections*

The other point worth discussing here is the kind of protections afforded by the right to health under international law. Here, I would like to show that the right to health as enshrined under international law incorporates three key pillars (or components) of protections. These are the right to freedom of choice, the right to basic health entitlements and the right to access to justice.[60] Analysing the right to health in terms of its key components is very useful especially to disentangle and shed light on some of the issues often raised in connection with the corresponding nature of the State Party obligations. This is particularly so in relation to the discussion in this contribution which, among other things, is concerned with assessing the extent to which the often claimed lack of resources (i.e. scarcity) is, in fact, a major impediment to the effective realization of the right to health in Africa. After considering each of these components, we are able to see that the right to basic health entitlements indeed requires an investment from the State Party but this is not the case with respect to the obligation to ensure freedom of choice and access to justice. In fact, it is to be seen that, in Africa, it is not lack of resources as such but critical structural (systemic) problems that can best explain the unacceptable low level of health care and its underlying determinants (see Sect. 3.3). This assertion is to some extent also supported by the relevant juris-prudence of the African Commission on Human and Peoples' Rights (the African Commission, the Commission) (Sect. 4.2.1): the discussion thereof shows that almost all of the violations of the right to health occurred in the context of detention and grave humanitarian crisis but so far there is no single communica-tion before the Commission claiming the violation of the right to health on account of lack of resources as such.

Here, I might be criticized for not following the tripartite (i.e. respect, protect and fulfil) or quadruple (respect, protect, promote, fulfil) approach that both the CESCR and the African Commission use for assessing the state party obligations. I am aware of both the merits and demerits associated with such approaches but I may also have to mention that not all human rights tribunals follow this dimen-sional analysis.[61] It should, however, be noted that my aim here is neither to depart from nor to confirm such categorization of State Party obligations, both generally and in relation to the right to health. In fact, it is my understanding that, one the one hand, the key components of the right to health I have just mentioned concern

---

[60] See generally General Comment 14, para 8 where the CESCR stated, 'The right to health is not to be understood as a right to be healthy. The right to health contains both *freedoms and entitlements. The freedoms* include the right to control one's health and body, including sexual and reproductive freedom, and the right to be free from interference, such as the right to be free from torture, non-consensual medical treatment and experimentation. By contrast, *the entitle-ments* include the right to a *system of health protection* which provides equality of opportunity for people to enjoy the highest attainable level of health' (*emphasis added*).

[61] For a recent critical review of the typologies of State obligations see *particularly* Koch 2009, especially at Chap. 2.

the general normative contents of the right to health (that is, what it guarantees for the right holder under international law). On the other hand, the tripartite (or quadruple) and other related standards such as availability, accessibility and quality[62] are clearly about the quantitative and qualitative analysis of the State Party obligations in relation to each of these key components of the right to health (but this is not, at least directly, the focus of my discussion in this contribution).[63]

2.3.2.1 Right to Freedom of Choice

The right to have and make free choices in respect of matters affecting one's health forms one of the core pillars of the right to health under international law. In this sense, the right to health guarantees the right to be free from any sorts of external interferences, obstructions or influences in making decisions pertaining to one's health as well as in the enjoyment of one's healthy living.[64] In addition, it includes the right of every woman to autonomously choose and decide on matters of, for instance, family planning and the use of contraceptives.[65] To this extent, it is possible to say that the right to freedom of choice in matters affecting one's health is the least disputed component of the right to health under international law. However, it is also worth noting that it may involve some complex and controversial ethical and policy issues as well. For instance, should public institutions interfere legitimately to prevent choices that may harm individual's health in such cases as smoking, unsafe sexual behaviours, alcohol, drug; should health benefits or allowances be based on private conducts and to what extent and so forth.[66]

In my opinion, the protection of this intimate and fundamental interest of a person is part and parcel of the elementary justification and, hence, responsibility

---

[62] See General Comment 14, para 12, where the CESCR stated that the right to health in all its forms and at all levels contains the following interrelated and essential elements, the precise application of which will depend on the conditions prevailing in a particular State Party: availability, accessibility, acceptability and quality of health facilities. goods and services. See also Tobin 2012, at Chap. 4.

[63] For the sake of clarity, it can therefore be stated that when we speak of the State Party obligations vis-à-vis the right to health under international law, we are essentially concerned with the obligation to respect, protect, promote, facilitate and fulfil the right to freedom of choice, the right to basic health entitlements and the right to effective justice for everyone within its jurisdiction.

[64] See General Comment 14, para 8; Principles and Guidelines, paras 5 and 65; Tobin 2012, at Chap. 4 (III); Jayawickrama 2002, p. 883.

[65] See Articles 3, 4, 5 and 14 Protocol on Rights of Women in Africa; Article 12 CEDAW. See also Yeshanew 2011, pp. 248–249; Tobin 2012 ibid.; Toebes 1999, pp. 52–55; Jayawickrama 2002, pp. 886–887.

[66] Tobin 2012 assesses some of the issues the right to freedom of health involves particularly in the context of reproductive health, adolescence sexuality and related risks thereof (such as HIV/AIDS and other sexually transmitted diseases), medical treatment and medical experimentation (see at pp. 132–158).

2 Ensuring the Realization of the Right to Health

of a State. This means that it is required to ensure the right to freedom of choice immediately and with utmost priority for everyone under its jurisdiction. In other words, this obligation is not the subject of progressive realization[67] because the right to freely choose and pursue decisions regarding one's health goes to the very essence of human dignity. As such it aims to safeguard interests so intimate and fundamental to the wellbeing of a person such as autonomy, integrity and security. Accordingly, a State Party can hardly justify, even on account of lack of resources, its failure to, for instance, protect individuals against physical and mental pain; safeguard a patient against a treatment which he or she has not given effective consent to; and guarantee for every woman her reproductive health rights.

2.3.2.2 The Right to Basic Health Entitlements

The second key pillar of the right to health is the right to have access to basic health entitlements.[68] This generally entails, depending on the specific circumstance of the individuals concerned, both the right to have access to health care and the underlying determinants of health (such as adequate and safe drinking water, nutritious food, housing and essential medicines) in kind and the right to have access to the means required to obtain those goods and services.[69] Interestingly, the major theoretical arguments behind the right to health entitlements have already been presented above when discussing the principle of social justice as enshrined in the major UN and AU human rights treaties providing for the protection of socioeconomic rights (Sect. 2.2).

It should however be mentioned that this component of the right to health explains the reason why its human 'right-ness' was contested in the past. For instance, the background document to the 1978 Alma-Ata Conference on Primary Health Care makes it clear that the provision of the underlying determinants of health was considered for so long as a discretionary power of the State, not as something to be claimed on the part of the State as a matter of right and justice.[70]

---

[67] See General Comment 14, paras 30–37.

[68] See General Comment 14, para 8; Jayawickrama 2002, pp. 883–884. See also generally the Final Report CSDH 2008, the Rio Political Declaration; Alma-Ata Declaration, paras VI–VII. For the treatment of the idea of entitlements in general see Alexy 2010b, at Chap. 9.

[69] *See for instance* Article 25 UDHR; Articles 11 and 12 ICESCR; Article 16 African Charter. See also General Comment 14, paras 11–13; Principles and Guidelines, para 61ff; Alma-Ata Declaration, paras V–VII; the Rio Political Declaration; the Ottawa Charter for Health Promotion, First International Conference on Health Promotion, Ottawa, 21 November 1986 (available at http://www.who.int/healthpromotion/conferences/previous/ottawa/en/ last accessed on 10 May 2013) (hereinafter the Ottawa Charter). See generally Toebes 2012, pp. 112–118; Toebes 1999, at Chap. V; Jayawickrama 2002, pp. 871–880 and 888–889, Tobin 2012, Alexy 2010b, Chap. 9, at Sect. IV.

[70] Report of the International Conference on Primary Health Care, Alma-Ata, USSR, 6–12 September 1978, World Health Organisation (hereinafter Background Report to Alma-Ata Conference 1978, available at http://whqlibdoc.who.int/publications/9241800011.pdf last

While it goes beyond the scope of this contribution to consider those arguments here, it can certainly be said that one of the major reasons behind such contestation was the fact that the obligations flowing from it entails, inter alia, the adoption of specific social and economic measures including those that concern direct provision of those basic goods and services to the vulnerable members of the society.[71] In any case, it now seems that only few would deny, at least in theory, that the protections afforded by the right to health under international law also and necessarily include the right to have access to those basic health entitlements.[72]

This should not, however, be taken as suggesting that the debate surrounding this component of the right to health has fully been resolved. In particular, the question whether a State Part bears an immediate or progressive obligation vis-à-vis the right to basic health entitlement is still ongoing. This, in turn, has to do with, admittedly, the complex nature of the measures that the State Party should adopt and the corresponding level of resources required to operationalize those measures. Indeed, given the substantial amount of resources that it requires, it may be difficult for the State Party to ensure an immediate access to basic health entitlements for everyone in a society and this is even more so for countries in Africa especially as a result of the fragility of their economies. But, under human rights law, the complexity of the measures and the level of expenses involved therein are not the sole determining factors in judging whether the State obligation to realize a given right is immediate or progressive. As suggested above, it is also equally significant to take into account other important factors such as the nature of the right and the interest it seeks to safeguard; the particular circumstances of

---

(Footnote 70 continued)

accessed 24 March 2013). See generally AU Social Policy Framework 2008; the 'Africa Health Strategy 2007–2015: *Strengthening of Health Systems for Equity and Development in Africa*', CAMH/MIN/5(III), adopted at the Third Session of the AU Conference of Ministers of Health, Johannesburg, South Africa, 9–13 (hereinafter Africa Health Strategy 2007–2015, available at http://www.nepad.org/system/files/AFRICA_HEALTH_STRATEGY%28health%29.pdf (last accessed 25 March 2013).

[71] This is generally part and parcel of general justiciability debate on ESCR. On this see generally essays in the following publications: Auweraert et al. 2002, Ghai and Cottrell 2004, Coomans 2006, Baderin and Mccorquodale 2007, Langford 2008. See also Fredman 2008, Yeshanew 2011, Viljoen 2012.

[72] This does not suggest that there is a universal consensus to that effect. See Tobin 2012, pp. 1–6 (providing a concise overview of the current state of debate on right to health). But seeing particularly in the light of the substantive contents of the international human rights law, it clearly seems to me a *contra legem* to say that the right to health does not provide for the right to have basic entitlements. Especially since the 1978 Alma-Ata Conference the underlying conditions of health have, at least theoretically, become the dominant part of the discussions on the right to health. In this regard, the works of the CESCR (especially in General Comment 14) and Paul Hunt, in his capacity as the former UN Special Rapporteur on the Rights of everyone to the Highest Attainable Standard of Physical and Mental Health from 2002 to 2008 (cited at n. 45 above) have been very pivotal in expounding the practical understanding of the contents of the right to health and State obligations thereof.

the individuals concerned; the level of available resources; and the overall performance of the State in realizing the right.

Seen in this light, it can be argued that the right to basic health entitlements entails both immediate and progressive State obligations. For instance, it seems to me that a complete eradication of some of the social causes of ill-health solely through the actions of a State may be an impossible goal. But I also believe that, as a matter of human rights law, a State Party cannot justify its failure to provide basic health entitlements for vulnerable and disadvantaged individuals or groups in a society because doing so would essentially amount to repudiating the very *raison d'etre* of recognizing the right in the first place.[73]

2.3.2.3 The Right to Access to Justice

The third core pillar of protection incorporated in the right to health is the right to access to justice. Possibly the right to access to justice has rarely been discussed not just in relation to the right to health but also with respect to socioeconomic rights in general because these categories of human rights were previously not seen as giving rise to a justiciable claim as such.[74] This contribution is of course not the right place to discuss the idea of the right to access to justice in socioeconomic rights[75] for my aim is simply to argue that it is one of the key components of the right to health. But it is important to note that the right to access to justice essentially consists of the right to individual justice and constitutional justice.[76] The right to individual justice is very familiar in human rights scholarship as it refers to the rights of a person (victim) to obtain a relief from those competent organs in relation to the personal damage(s) that he or she has suffered due to the acts (or omissions) directed against his or her person or property.[77] In this regard, both the suffering and relief sought are essentially personal to the victim. So, we

---

[73] For the view of the CESCR see General Comment 14, para 30ff; General Comment 3, para 9. See generally Sepulveda 2003, Fredman 2008.

[74] See *for instance* footnote 71.

[75] For an interesting report on the role of the right of access to justice for the realization of socioeconomic rights see Inter-American Commission on Human Rights (IACoHR), Access to Justice as a Guarantee of Economic, Social, and Cultural Rights. A Review of the Standards Adopted by the Inter-American System of Human Rights, OEA/SER.L/V/II.129, Doc. 4, 7 September 2007 (also available through www.oas.org/en/iachr/reports/thematic.asp last visited 25 May 2013). See also IACoHR, the Work, Education and Resources of Women: the Road to Equality in Guaranteeing Economic, Social and Cultural Rights, OEA/SER.L/V/II.143, Doc. 59, 3 November 2011; IACoHR, Access to Justice for Women Victims of Sexual Violence: Education and Health, OEA/SER.L/V/II. Doc 65, 28 December 2011 (both documents available through the link mentioned hereinbefore).

[76] In making this distinction I generally follow the approach of Wildhaber and Greer who discussed the merits of such an approach in the context of the European Court of Human Rights (ECtHR). See Wildhaber 2002, 2006, 2007, Greer 2006. See also Mowbray 2010.

[77] See Greer 2006, pp. 165–169. See generally Shelton 2005; Francioni 2007.

can say that the main focus of the individual justice proceeding is essentially to retroactively condemn and redress previous violation(s) to the rights of an individual.

In contrast, there is also a notion of constitutional justice which concerns the right to have remedies against wider structural or systemic problems generally affecting the enjoyment of human rights in a given country. This, in turn, is premised on the understanding that the existence of a structural or systemic problem in a given country means that a violation to individual rights is certainly inevitable. When this is the case in a given country or system, a particular violation of an individual right is simply a mirror of what is in fact affecting the rights of everyone concerned in that country or system in general.[78] Thus, in constitutional justice the principal concern is to proactively identify and address those underlying structural defects or systemic obstacles impeding the effective realization of human rights in general. For instance, the right to constitutional justice in the context of the right to health means the removal of underlying structural factors impeding the realization of right to health for the population at large rather than a mere remedying of previous individual violations per se.[79] Such is the case when an issue before a tribunal, as an example, concerns structural policies resulting in the systematic exclusion and marginalization of the poor and other vulnerable persons in a society from health care and other social services. It should, however, be said that this notion of constitutional justice is more of a recent phenomenon in human rights discourse although there have been practices here and there, especially within some national legal systems, reflecting certain of its core elements.[80]

Both of these elements of the right to access to justice are very crucial components of the international protection of the right to health but I would like to emphasis the particular relevance of the notion of constitutional justice especially in the context of this discussion. As we have said above, the right to health is characteristically a systemic right requiring the adoption of a complex set of measures aimed at materializing the underlying health needs of the society as a whole. The reason is that health is a public good par excellence. As a result, any corresponding measures taken by the State Party should target a wider population and be in strict accordance with the principles of social justice. As such it is crucial that health care and related social services be rendered for everyone in accordance

---

[78] See citations at footnote 76.

[79] In this regard individual justice proceeding may also have some element of proactive dimension, at least in theory. But in practice, this is in fact not the case: there is simply little evidence that ensuring individual justice would also and necessarily result in constitutional justice for all. See generally Brinks and Gauri 2008, Landau 2012.

[80] To my knowledge a more structured discussion on the notion of constitutional justice dimension of right to access to justice began by former judge of the ECtHR, Wildhaber followed by the extensive treatment of the subject by Greer and more recently by Mowbray, all cited at footnote 76. With respect to the practices at national level such notions as 'writ action', 'actio popularis', 'public interest litigation', 'class action', 'amparo action' can be seen as approximating the ideal of constitutional justice mentioned in this discussion.

2 Ensuring the Realization of the Right to Health

with such principles as of fairness, justice, equality and equity.[81] The failure of the State to ensure access to health care and its underlying determinants in such a manner affects not just one or two persons but almost all individuals in the society. And it is the addressing of such systemic failures that characteristically falls within the scope of the right to constitutional justice thus described.

As it is the case with the right to freedom of choice, the obligation to ensure the right to access to justice is part and parcel of the elementary obligations of the State Party both generally and in human rights law;[82] it is the right that the State Party is required to realize immediately for everyone within its jurisdictions. In this regard, it should be stressed that the right to access to justice is the core element of the accountability of the States Parties for the realization of human rights.[83] For instance, in the context of the right to health, the interconnection between the right to access to justice and accountability can vividly be seen from a recent exposition of accountability by Potts.[84] Potts sees accountability as 'the process which requires government to show, explain and justify how it has discharged its obligations regarding the right to the highest attainable standard of health'. As such, it also 'provides rights-holders with an opportunity to understand how government has discharged its right to health obligations' and to vindicate their rights 'to effective remedies' if it is established the government has failed in discharging its obligations thereof.[85] It is therefore clearly observable that in

---

[81] See Hunt and Backman 2008; Backman 2012 (both discussing health systems in the light of the values enshrined in the Alma-Ata Declaration); Nnamuchi and Ortuanya 2012, p. 187 (discussing certain elements of governance that should be in place to meet the promises of human right to health through Millennium Development Goals (MDGs). See also World Health Report 2000, 'Health Systems: Improving Performance', World Health Organization (hereinafter World Health Report 2000, available at http://www.who.int/whr/2000/en/whr00_en.pdf last accessed 24 March 2013); the Report of Special Rapporteur on Right to Health, Paul Hunt, UN Doc. A/HRC/7/11 (available at http://daccess-dds-ny.un.org/doc/UNDOC/GEN/G08/105/03/PDF/G0810503.pdf?OpenElement last accessed 15 April 2013).

[82] See generally Francioni 2007, IACoHR (footnote 75).

[83] Hunt and Backman 2008, Potts, Accountability (footnote 84), pp. 17–18; Amnesty International Report 2009, pp. 8–9. See particularly UN Docs. A/63/263 at Section III, and A/59/422, paras 36–45 (Paul Hunt articulating the special significance of accountability in ensuring the effective realization of the right to health and health-related MDGs).

[84] See Potts 2008, Accountability and the Right to the Highest Attainable Standard of Health, Human Rights Centre, University of Essex (hereinafter, Potts, Accountability, available at http://www.essex.ac.uk/hrc/research/projects/rth/docs/HRC_Accountability_Mar08.pdf last accessed 21 February 2013).

[85] Ibid., p. 13. Interestingly, it has 'both prospective and retrospective' dimensions. In the former sense, 'it draws attention to its potential to improve performance: to identify what works, so it can be repeated, and what does not, so it can be revised'; in the latter sense, 'it draws attention to the remedies that should be available when there has been failure on the part of government to fulfil its obligations'. Ibid. This shows that Potts notion of accountability incorporates both aspects of the right to access to justice—the right to individual justice and constitutional justice thus described in this discussion.

Potts's conception of accountability, the right of individuals to an effective remedy, that is, the right to access to justice, holds significant place.

Hence, without the fundamental right of access to justice, which, in turn, goes to the very essence of accountability, it is almost inevitable that any legislative or policy commitment by the State remains utterly rhetorical. Hunt is very clear on this. 'Without accountability', says Hunt, 'human rights can become no more than window-dressing. Whether human rights are applied to development, poverty reduction, trade, health systems, neglected diseases, maternal mortality, HIV/AIDS or anything else, they require that accessible, transparent and effective mechanisms of accountability be established.'[86]

To summarize, it emerges from the discussion in this part that the treaties providing for the right to health, to which almost all of the AU Member States are parties to, define the right to health as a fundamental and systemic right consisting of the right to freedom of choice, basic health entitlements and access to justice. It also emerges that the obligations flowing from the right to freedom of choice and access to justice correspond to the core of the State Party's obligations both generally and in human rights law in such a way that they ought to ensure the same for everyone within the State's jurisdiction immediately. The realization of the right to basic health entitlements, however, entails both immediate and progressive obligations because of the nature of measures and level of resources involved in the materialization of the same for everyone in a society. Nevertheless, when it comes to the right to basic health entitlements of the vulnerable persons in the society, the State Party concerned still shoulders particularly aggravated, heightened, responsibilities that it cannot easily dispense with even on such grounds as resource constraints. This being said in general, we now have to specifically assess if the alleged lack of material resources indeed explains the dire shortage of access to health care and the underlying determinants of health.

2.3.3 Impediment to the Realization of Basic Health Entitlements in Africa: Lack of Resources or Systemic Problem?

The facts and figures provided in the introductory part clearly and alarmingly show the dire shortage of health care and the underlying determinants of health in Africa, most seriously in sub-Saharan region.[87] So it remains to be seen if the gross failures to ensure the right to basic health entitlements could be attributed to the alleged lack of resources. As revealed in the Background Report to Alma-Ata Conference 1978 (and, since then, in many other reports including the ones already cited in this writing), the following factors were responsible for the then existing

---

[86] UN Doc. A/63/263, para 8 (referring also to the work of Potts cited at footnote 84).

[87] See footnote 2–13.

dysfunctional health services in many countries, particularly in the developing world, where African countries line from the bottom up. According to the report, the then existing health services and systems were characterized by gross injustices, inequalities and inequities resulting, in turn, in the loss of millions of lives from what could have been prevented with relative ease. For instance, national health systems were described therein as essentially inefficient, poorly resourced and structured; available resources were particularly skewed towards expensive and tertiary health services only accessible to the rich and to those in political power; public health issues were not seen as forming the integral component of the wider social and economic development agenda of the countries. All these were further compounded by the problems pertaining to bad governance systems both generally and in relation to health sectors.[88]

For the participants of the said Conference, responding to these major global public health crises was a matter of urgent concern. Nonetheless, access to health care and related services in the African continent are still as fragile as they were 30 years ago. Thirty years after the Alma-Ata Conference, the health systems of most African countries still remain 'too weak' and 'too under-resourced' 'to support targeted reduction in disease burden and achieve universal access' to health services as well as to provide 'interventions' that could 'match the scale of the [existing health] problems' mainly because of the reasons pertaining to the fragmentations of national policies and the inefficient utilization of available resources.[89] Still 30 years later, the health systems in the continent are infected with gross injustices, inequalities and inequities. For instance, the AU Social Policy Framework 2008 stresses that '[t]he benefits of health services do not equitably reach those with the greatest disease burden'; that there is no 'social protection' systems in place to safeguard the vulnerable and marginalized persons including those in a dire economic situations; that there is lack of community empowerment and participation at the national level; and that there is no effective administrative and accountability mechanisms in place to monitor and remedy those injustices in the sector, indicating, in turn, the 'vicious circle' between ill-health, poverty and bad governance in the continent.[90]

---

[88] See Background Report to Alma-Ata Conference 1978, pp. 37–38. See also the Final Report CSDH 2008; World Health Report 2007: Everybody business: strengthening health systems to improve health outcomes: WHO's framework for action, World Health Organization, Geneva (hereinafter World Health Report 2007, available at http://www.who.int/whr/2007/en/index.html last accessed 10 February 2013); World Health Report 2008: Primary Health Care (Now More Than Ever), World Health Organization, Geneva (hereinafter World Health Report 2008, available at http://www.who.int/whr/2008/en/index.html last accessed 15 April 2013).

[89] See AU Social Policy Framework 2008, at Sect. 1.1; Africa Health Strategy 2007–2015, at in this chapter See Abuja Declaration, para 26; WHO 2012: State of Health Financing in Africa.

[90] See AU Social Policy Framework 2008 at Executive Summary and Section 1; Africa Health Strategy 2007–2015 at in this chapter. See also citations at footnote 2–13 and 88. The AU Social Policy Framework 2008, Africa Health Strategy 2007–2015 and the Rio Political Declaration also mention problems relating to the global economic order affecting in one way or another the African national health systems but this will not be discussed here. On the role of international

These observations indicate that the fragility of the health services in Africa has less to do with the lack of resources than it has to do with the institutional decision-making system of the States Parties concerned.[91] In fact, many agree that it is not scarcity as such but, following Acemoglu and Robinson, the lack of 'inclusive' governance systems or, conversely, the prevalence of the 'extractive' nature of the continent's political and economic institutions that underlie the current state of structural and systematic exclusion of the population at large from practically every aspect of socioeconomic and political domain.[92] The AU Social Policy Framework 2008 emphatically confirms this fact by expressing the presence of endemic corruption in the continent. It clearly recognizes that corruption is 'the single greatest obstacle to development globally'; it has 'significantly contribute[d] to a skewed distribution of the benefits of development and growth'; '[m]ost profoundly, corruption and associated crimes [has destroyed] the trust relationship between the people and the state'.[93]

In fact, the longstanding and recurrent problem of Africa is a resource-curse much less than it is a resource-scarcity. The continent's abundant resources have for so long been a 'curse', a source of 'misery' to most peoples in the continent instead of being a means to ensuring their wellbeing and dignity.[94] As an example, the African Human Development Report 2012 clearly states that the most food insecure part of the world, the sub-Saharan Africa, has abundant agricultural resources.

> But shamefully, in all corners of the region, millions of people remain hungry and mal-nourished—the result of glaringly uneven local food production and distribution and chronically deficient diets, especially among the poorest. This is a daily violation of people's dignity, with many governments not fulfilling their basic responsibility of protecting their citizens from hunger. [...]
>
> Agricultural productivity remains low—much lower than in other regions. Many sub-Saharan African countries are net food importers and even depend on food aid during all-too-frequent humanitarian crises. Where food is available, millions cannot afford it or are

---

(Footnote 90 continued)

cooperation for the realization of right to health in Africa, see Nnamuchi and Ortuanya 2012. See generally A/59/422, paras 32–35 and 42–46; Maastricht Principles on Extraterritorial Obligations of States in the area of Economic, Social and Cultural Right, adopted on 28 September 2011, Maastricht, The Netherlands (available at http://www.rtfn-watch.org/uploads/media/Maastricht_ETO_Principles__EN.pdf last accessed 20 April 2013).

[91] See also (footnote 78) above.

[92] Acemoglu and Robinson 2012, p. 70ff. See the reports cited at footnote 2–13 and 88; Amnesty International Report 2009, footnote 1.

[93] See AU Social Policy Framework 2008, at Sect. 2.2.18. See also Africa Health Strategy 2007–2015, at Sect. 4.1.1, para 31ff.

[94] See particularly Viljoen 2012, p. 544. In its 2009 report, footnote 1, Amnesty International also indicated that 'Millions across the region continued to be deprived of their basic needs in spite of the sustained economic growth in many countries in Africa during past years. People faced enormous challenges in securing a daily livelihood, often aggravated by marginalization or political repression, attempts to muffle their voices and render them powerless' (at p. 1).

2 Ensuring the Realization of the Right to Health

prevented from buying or trading it by underdeveloped markets, poor roads, long distances to markets and high transport costs. [...]

Misguided policies, weak institutions and failing markets are the deeper causes of sub-Saharan Africa's food insecurity. This tainted inheritance is most evident in households and communities, where unequal power relations trap vulnerable groups—subsistence farmers, the landless poor, many women and children—in a vicious cycle of deprivation, food insecurity and low human development....[95]

Therefore, rather than resource constraints, the critical stumbling block obstructing the effective realization of basic health entitlements in the continent is essentially systemic in nature which mainly results from the extractive socioeconomic and political institutions in the continent. This, in turn, also speaks indirectly to the failure of the respective national legal systems in addressing the underlying systemic problem affecting not just the health sector but the entire socioeconomic spectrum of the Member States.[96] No doubt, in some respects financial constraint may indeed be a genuine problem of governments in Africa but it cannot justify decades of acute ill-health and impoverishment in the continent. On the contrary, there is overwhelming evidence here and there indicating decades of systematic and widespread social and political exclusion, marginalization, highly endemic and institutionalized corruption practices and absence of any meaningful accountability mechanisms in the continent.[97] In the presence of such evidence, the claim from resource-scarcity is nothing more than a smokescreen.

There have been series of initiatives, both globally and at the AU level, aimed at addressing the structural problems obstructing the realization of the right to health and other human rights. This is in fact one of the overarching aims of the AU Social Policy Framework 2008 mentioned above. The Policy Framework intends to deal with this persistent structural problem through continental policy-making and coordination. The approach taken therein is identifying the major continent-wide social problems and their underlying causes and, then, providing

---

[95] See footnote 10 at p. 2ff.

[96] Amnesty International Report 2009, footnote 1, pp. 8–9 (describing the problem of accountability and prevalence of impunity in the region).

[97] See particularly World Health Report 2010; Africa Human Development Report 2012; MDG Report 2012: Assessing Africa's Progress). See also Durojaye 2010, Alao 2010, Nnamuchi and Ortuanya 2012, p. 184ff, Viljoen 2012, p. 272ff. Since its first launch in 1995, African countries have been consistently in the category of low Corruption Perception Index of the Transparency International with the score of well below average (it is not more than one or two countries that approach the average 5/10 or 50/100 scale). For its recent report, see Corruption Perceptions Index 2012 (available at http://cpi.transparency.org/cpi2012/results/ last accessed 10 May 2013). Similarly, the Ibrahim Index of Africa Governance (IIAG) also provides us with the detailed account of governance crisis in the continent by breaking down into specific thematic issues as safety and rule of law (which covers rule of law, accountability, personal and national security) and participation and human rights (which covers participation, human rights and gender). Looking at its key findings of the 2012 index, it only shows a fragmented and unsustainable nature of any record of progress in each area since 2006. The 2012 IIAG can be found at http://www.moibrahimfoundation.org/iiag/ last accessed 10 May 2013).

policy recommendations that should be adopted by all stakeholders, especially national authorities. Accordingly, it has identified eighteen core thematic or priority areas[98] at the heart of which lies the problem of lack of access to basic health entitlements and structural accountability in the continent.[99]

To this extent, the Policy Framework could be hailed as both comprehensive and a landmark. However, the old question still remains: how effective would it be in bringing structural changes and thereby ensuring the right to health and basic social justice for those most in need? This question arises because the effectiveness of any legislative or policy commitment regarding the protection of human rights is essentially tied to the existence of a strong legal accountability mechanism through which the State Party can be held responsible both at the national and international level.[100] In addition to what has already been said in this section, an epigraphic note to this contribution also well-summarizes the fact that 'there is still an enormous gap between' the numerous legislative and policy rhetoric of the governments in the continent, on the one hand, and 'the daily reality where human rights violations remain the norm', on the other.[101] Interestingly, lack of effective legal accountability mechanisms is not limited to the national system. As the following discussion also shows, the legal accountability mechanisms available at the AU level are almost dysfunctional which undermines the practical value of not just the AU Social Policy Framework 2008 but the entire framework of human rights commitments and policy initiatives of the AU and its Member States.

---

[98] These are population and development, labour and employment, social protection, health (including HIV/AIDS, TB, malaria and other infectious diseases), migration, education, agriculture, food and nutrition, the family, children, adolescents and youth, ageing, disability, gender equality and women's empowerment, culture, urban development, environmental sustainability, the impact of globalization and trade liberalization in Africa and good governance, anti-corruption and rule of law. And there are also four additional areas of special concern: drug and substance abuse and crime prevention; sport; civil strife and conflict situations; and foreign debt (see at Executive Summary and Section 2).

[99] Ibid. at Sect. 1.1, paras 1–2.

[100] It should be mentioned that the AU Social Policy Framework 2008 envisages some kind of political accountability mechanisms. Among other things, the AU Commission is tasked with the monitoring of the actual implementation of the policy recommendation by receiving and reviewing of biennial progress reports from each Member State. It is also responsible to produce the overall status of social development in the continent every 2 years highlighting particularly the emerging issues and continuing challenges as well as to issue a comprehensive evaluation report on the implementation of the social policy framework every 5 years' (see at Sect. 3.2.3). Nonetheless, this mechanism is immaterial for the States can still refuse to cooperate with its specific recommendations and still face no legal consequence whatsoever; it may even be very doubtful if failure to implement those recommendations would be met with any sort of political consequences both from the Commission and other political institutions of the Union as such. This actually means that this mechanism has a limited role, if any, in addressing the kind of systemic injustices and failures I have been stressing in this discussion.

[101] See footnote 1 above citing Amnesty International Report 2009, p. 9.

2.4 The Enforcement Mechanisms of the Right to Health in the AU System

2.4.1 Introduction

There is no question that AU has the legal responsibility to ensure not just the availability but also the effective functioning of the human rights protective (enforcement) mechanisms especially at the continental level. Currently, the Court and Commission are the two principal AU human rights institutions with the mandate to remedy violations of human rights in the continent. Although the statutory mandates of the Court and the Commission differ (in scope and nature), the two regimes are complementary to one another.[102] While the Court's principal function is essentially adjudicatory (protective mandate in the strict sense of the term);[103] the Commission is tasked with broader protective[104] and promotional[105] mandates but, awkwardly, it cannot directly compel the States Parties concerned to comply with its decisions as such.[106] It should be noted that it is not the aim of this discussion to compare and contrast the functions of the two institutions but to see the extent to which they are practically contributing to addressing the structural accountability deficits impeding the effective realization of the right to health in the continent.

Seen in this light, there is nothing that could be said about the actual role of the Court because, though it formally became operational in 2004, it is yet to become the Court of the continent in the full sense of the term due to the low rate of

---

[102] See Article 2 Protocol ACtHPR; para 6 of Preamble to Protocol ACtJHR (see footnote 107).

[103] See Article 3 Protocol ACtHPR; Article 28 Statute of ACtJHR (see footnote 107).

[104] See Articles 30 *cum* 45 (2), 48, 55 and 62 African Charter. The protective function of the Commission, which is quite broader than the protective function of the Court, concerns the power to examine periodic State reporting and individual communications and to conduct on-site investigations.

[105] See Article 30 *cum* (1) (a–c), (3), (4) 45 African Charter. Hence, as part of its promotional mandate, the Commission is tasked with broad range of activities as studying, researching and documenting human rights problems in the continent and organizing seminars, symposiums and conferences as well as providing trainings for particularly national institutions, issuing guiding principles and rules for the national legislations and practices relating to fundamental human and peoples' rights.

[106] According to the Banjul Charter, after consideration of communications (interstate or individual), the Commission shall prepare reports indicating its findings and recommendations thereof. See at Articles 52, 53, 58 and 59. This means that it does not have a legal power to make a binding judgment. It seems from the wording and spirit of the Charter that the findings and recommendations of the Commission would become binding and hence compelling on the State concerned if and when adopted accordingly by the Assembly of OAU/AU.

ratifications to its statute and related complications.[107] It is also yet to pronounce any judgment in relation to the topic under consideration. This means that it is a very important institution but with untested remedial power. Obviously, one can speculate on the immense potential of the Court in enhancing the standard of human rights protection in the continent but this goes beyond the scope of this contribution. However, the future ability of the Court to address the structural obstacles to the realization of social justice in general and the underlying conditions of the right to health in particular are determined by the extent to which it would be able to integrate issues of individual justice with that of constitutional justice.[108]

In fact, it is possible to see the call upon the Court in the AU Social Policy Framework 2008 to '[a]ccord high priority' to the questions of basic social justice as particularly suggesting the careful examination of the background factors underlying those complaints over which it will assume jurisdiction in the light of the structural accountability deficits in the continent, not just in the light of the individual justice as such. In this way it may be possible that some of the structural problems could be exposed to rigorous continental judicial scrutiny which, if so decided, the State concerned is legally bound to remedy within the period that the Court indicates under the pain of possible legal sanctions from the Assembly of the AU.[109] The hope is that this might ultimately push Member States to strengthen their national accountability mechanisms as well—but, it might have to wait for a while before its full judicial authority will be put to test over cases concerning

---

[107] The establishment and full operationalization of the African continental judicial organ is complicated with various institutional hurdles and fragmentations. The first instrument, the Protocol to the African Charter on Human and Peoples' Rights, was adopted on 9 June 1998 and entered into force on 2 January 2004 (available at http://www.au.int/en/sites/default/files/PROTOCOL_AFRICAN_CHARTER_HUMAN_PEOPLES_RIGHTS_ESTABLISHMENT_AFRICAN_COURT_HUMAN_PEOPLES_RIGHTS_1.pdf, last accessed 10 May 2013) (hereinafter Protocol ACtHPR). As it stands now this Protocol has only 26 ratifications of which only five countries have accepted the individual complaint mechanisms (the status of ratification can be accessed through http://www.au.int/en/sites/default/files/achpr.pdf, last visited on 13th May 2013). In parallel, there was also an initiative to establish the Court of Justice of the Union and the protocol to that effect was adopted on 11th July 2003 and entered into force on 11th February 2009 (available at http://www.au.int/en/sites/default/files/PROTOCOL_COURT_OF_JUSTICE_OF_THE_AFRICAN_UNION.pdf, last accessed 10 May 2013) (hereinafter Protocol CJAU). This protocol has only 16 ratifications (see at http://www.au.int/en/sites/default/files/Court%20of%20Justice.pdf , last visited 13 May 2013). To further complicate the matter (or one would say, to solve the problem before it gets worse), it was decided to merge the two judicial organs into one judicial organ which will have dual jurisdictional functions and henceforth be known as the African Court of Justice and Human Rights. The 'merger' protocol was adopted on 1 July 2008 (available at http://www.au.int/en/sites/default/files/PROTOCOL_STATUTE_AFRICAN_COURT_JUSTICE_AND_HUMAN_RIGHTS.pdf, last accessed 10 May 2013) (hereinafter Protocol ACtJHR and its Statute as Statute ACtJHR). This Protocol has so far only five ratifications (it will need 10 more to enter into force) (see at http://www.au.int/en/sites/default/files/Protocol%20on%20Statute%20of%20the%20African%20Court%20of%20Justice%20and%20HR.pdflast visited 13 May 2013).

[108] See AU Social Policy Framework 2008, at Sect. 3.2.4.

[109] See Article 46 Protocol ACtJHR.

basic social justice in the continent. This makes the Commission the only functioning human rights organ so far as the practical assessment of the legal enforcement of the right to health through the AU system is concerned.[110]

2.4.2 The Right to Health in the Practices of the Commission

The Commission is the oldest, in fact, the only human rights organ established in the Banjul Charter with fairly broad promotional and protective mandates and it has now been in operation for about 30 years.[111] The question is, therefore, if it has been able to deal with those issues of structural injustices undermining the realization of the right to health in the continent in its nearly 30 years of operation. Answering this question obviously requires a review of some of its decisions raising relevant issues with the protection and promotion of the right to health.

2.4.2.1 Decisions of the Commission on the Right to Health

It seems that the Commission's decisions raising, in a more relevant sense, the violation of the right to health can generally be seen as concerning the following three major situations[112]: detention (including prisons and medical institutions), humanitarian crisis and poverty (lack of access to basic socioeconomic means needed to obtain health care and related goods and services). It should be noted that this categorization is merely based on the underlying situations leading to the alleged violations of the right to health (and nothing more) with the view to provide a clear picture as to the contexts engaging the responsibility of the State concerned. In this regard, it can be said that the major part of the Commission's decisions concerns detention situations and that only few of them deal with situations of humanitarian crisis. With respect to the third situation we cannot find any (relevant) substantive discussion by the Commission but only a very general and indirect reference to the right to health in some of its decisions; that is, in all the communications concerning the third situation, we could only find the Commission making a general normative statement in just a paragraph or so but without providing substantive arguments to that effect. For this reason it is not necessary to

---

[110] But one should note that because of what is just said above (footnote 106) the term 'legal enforcement' is employed here only in its loose sense to express its decisions would become enforceable if and when approved by the Assembly of the AU.

[111] The Commission was officially inaugurated on 2 November 1987 (note that the Banjul Charter entered into force on 21 October 1986).

[112] For the discussion on the practices of the Commission vis-à-vis the protection of socioeconomic rights, see *for instance* Yeshanew 2011, Viljoen 2012, Ssenyonjo 2011, 2012.

74   G. A. Mosissa

discuss them here and I will, therefore, make reference to such communications just for the sake of completeness.[113]

As will be discussed below, the nature of violations established by the Commission under these three scenarios (though we cannot say much on the third one) raise very serious issues with each of the core pillars of the protections afforded by the right to health already discussed above expressing as such the gross contempt for the fundamental principle of respect for human dignity. For instance, it is to be observed that the Commission's decisions pertaining to detention situations clearly show violations of the core elements of the right to have freedom of choice such as the right to have respect for one's integrity, autonomy and wellbeing; the right to basic health entitlements commensurate with the circumstances and needs of the detainees. Most importantly, the decisions also show absence of systemic accountability (pertaining to the third core pillar of the protections afforded by the right to health) as the nature of the violations addressed by the Commission were not isolated incidents as such but rather carried out by the direct participation of or aid from the State Party. The absence of systemic accountability is even more serious in relation to the decisions of the Commission pertaining to the second scenario (situations of humanitarian crisis) which express gross, systematic and widespread violations of not just the right to health but of virtually all human rights recognized in the Banjul Charter and other human rights treaties.

In the Context of Detention

The right to health of persons in detention clearly engages a special kind of State Party responsibility which directly emerges from the very fact of the detention itself. Without going into detail, the Commission emphasized that this responsibility has both a substantive and a procedural element. So, in its substantive sense, the State Party is required to ensure respect for the dignity of the detainees by making available to them all those basic material and moral conditions of human life and health and by securing them against all forms of violence, inhumane and degrading treatments; in its procedural sense, it is required to guarantee due process of law and access to prompt and effective remedies.[114]

---

[113] Communication 276/03 , *Centre for Minority Rights Development (Kenya) and Minority Rights Group International (on behalf of Endorois Welfare Council)/Kenya* (hereinafter *Endorois case*, decided on merits, 46th Ordinary Session (November 2009), Communication 157/96, *Association pour la sauvegarde de la paix au Burundi/Kenya et al. (hereinafter ASP-Burundi)*, decided on merits, 33rd Ordinary Session (May 2003), Communications 25/89-47/90-56/91-100/93, *Free Legal Assistance Group* et al./DRC (joined) (hereinafter *Free Legal Assistance*), decided on merits, 18th Ordinary Session (October 1995).

[114] This can be seen from the following decisions of the Commission: Communication 241/01, *Purhoit and Moore/The Gambia* (hereinafter *Purhoit*), decided on merits, 33rd Ordinary Session (May 2003); Communications 105/93-128/94-130/94-152/96, *Media Rights Agenda* et al./Nigeria (joined) (hereinafter *Media Rights Agenda* et al.), decided on merits, 24th Ordinary Session (31 October 1998); Communications 137/94-139/94-154/96-161/97, *International PEN et al./Nigeria*

2 Ensuring the Realization of the Right to Health

Thus, in *Purhoit and Moore/The Gambia* (*Purhoit*), for instance, subject of the complaint were the arbitrary and discriminatory nature of the legislation governing persons with mental disability and the substandard living condition in the detention centre.[115] As the Commission stated, the right to the health 'is vital to all aspects of a person's life, wellbeing, and is crucial to the realization of all the other fundamental human rights and freedoms. This right includes the right to health facilities, access to goods and services to be guaranteed to all without discrimination of any kind.'[116] It emphasized that this obligation, especially owing to their conditions and needs, is more compelling in relation to those persons with mental disability who ought to be accorded a special treatment that aims to ensure the attainment and sustenance of optimal level of independence and integration. In particular, persons with mental disability 'should never be denied their right to proper health care, which is crucial for their survival and their assimilation into and acceptance by the wider society'. Accordingly, the Commission found that the respondent State had failed to ensure the availability of clear therapeutic objectives and resources necessary to ensure a treatment required by and commensurate with the special conditions and needs of persons with disabilities[117] and for this reason they were denied the right to have a decent, dignified and normal human life.[118] The *Purhoit* case also revealed serious violations of the State responsibility to ensure equal and effective access to procedural guarantees for persons with mental disabilities including the right to have equal access to free and effective legal aid, the right to have the review of treatment or diagnosis resulting in their detention and the right to appeal against the decision of detention.[119]

The Commission has also addressed the particular significance of the right to health of persons particularly detained in the context of criminal law.[120] This entails the right to be provided with those basic conditions indispensable for their health and wellbeing,[121] the right to have prompt and effective access to medical services

---

(Footnote 114 continued)

(hereinafter *International PEN et al.*) (joined), decided on merits, 24th Ordinary Session (31 October 1998); Communications 54/91-61/91-96/93-98/93-164/97-196/97-210/98, *Malawi Africa Association* et al./*Mauritania* (joined) (hereinafter *Malawi Africa Association* et al.), decision on merits, 27th Ordinary Session (11 May 2000); Communication 334/06, *Egyptian Initiative for Personal Rights and INTERIGHTS/Arab Republic of Egypt* (hereinafter *EIPR/INTERIGHTS*), decided on merits, 9th Extraordinary Session (01 March 2011). For very helpful discussion on the normative function of human dignity in the detention situation see generally Riley 2011.

[115] *Purhoit*, paras 4–8.

[116] Ibid., para 80.

[117] Ibid., paras 81–85.

[118] Ibid., para 61.

[119] Ibid., paras 50–54 and 70–72.

[120] The relevant decisions of the Commission in this regard are the following: *Media Rights Agenda et al., International PEN* et al., *Malawi Africa Association et al.* and *EIPR/INTERIGHTS* (all cited at footnote 114).

[121] See *Media Rights Agenda* et al. at para 91; *International PEN* et al. at para 112, *Malawi Africa Association et al.* at paras 120 and 122. See also *Purhoit* at para 61.

such as access to qualified physicians and (adequate) medications and the right to have effective access to a legal counsel (lawyers).[122] As the Commission makes it clear in each of the communications just referred to, the State concerned bears a heightened, in fact, an absolute and exclusive responsibility to ensure the personal safety, integrity and wellbeing of persons under detention not just as a matter of law but because of the fact of detention itself which creates a complete situation of dependency of those persons on the State for their livelihood. Especially in the case of *EIPR/INTERIGHTS* mentioned above, the Commission underscored the two most important rationales behind the right to have prompt and effective access to medical services for persons under custody: that it is an indispensable element of the protection of detainees against torture, cruel, inhuman and degrading and other kinds of ill-treatments and that it is an integral element of the right to fair trial.[123] Hence, the right to have prompt access to medical services constitutes the most effective mechanism to ensure the protection of detainees against abusive treatments as well as to bring meaningful accountability to the detention systems.[124] It also plays a critical role in ensuring that illegally obtained confessions and evidence will not be adduced against those persons accused of criminal offenses, a matter which becomes an absolute necessity for those accused of serious offenses leading to grave punishments. Hence, the State is under a heightened legal obligation to prevent torturous confessions and other evidence obtained through such methods as well as to facilitate and avail individuals with effective opportunities to have access to medical expertise without any conditions whatsoever so that they will be able to challenge the evidence brought against them.[125]

In the Context of Humanitarian Crisis

The second instance in which the Commission has addressed the violations of the right to health pertains to the situations of humanitarian crisis, which in fact one can call *human crisis*,[126] which at their background have some basic systemic

---

[122] The Commission discussed this in detail in relation to *EIPR/INTERIGHTS*.

[123] See at paras 163–190 and 209–232.

[124] Ibid., at para 172 (stating that right to medical services should be provided promptly and regularly), paras 180–81 (stating that the link between effective prevention of torture and other inhuman treatments, and right to have access to prompt and regular access to lawyer has been established in the works of international human rights bodies).

[125] Ibid., at para 212ff.

[126] This in turn, may be due to either a 'constitutional' crisis or armed conflicts of both internal and international character. For the purpose here, constitutional crisis essentially refers to the gross violations of basic human rights through the direct actions or involvement of State machineries (usually police, military, security and secret service agents). This may be manifested through massive and arbitrary detentions, tortures, summary and extrajudicial killings. Internal armed conflicts on the other hand concern a fighting between a government and other groups (rebellions, insurgents, etc.) and hence does not, at least theoretically, involve civilian populations.

2 Ensuring the Realization of the Right to Health 77

failures in the countries concerned, affecting the entire population or certain specific groups of the population.[127] For instance, the case of *Malawi Africa Association* et al. shows the worst and egregious form of violations committed by the Respondent State against certain ethnic communities following the incident of military takeover of government. As the series of communications filed before the Commission show, there were widespread, massive, arbitrary and routine arrests, detentions (in extremely harsh, deplorable and inhumane conditions, also referred to as 'death camps'), torture (and other forms of inhumane treatments), massacres, persecutions, extrajudicial killings, summary executions, slavery, discriminations, expulsions, confiscations and destructions of livestock, harvests and villages by the State machineries particularly military forces just because those populations happen to be members of certain ethnic groups.[128] In declaring violations of, inter alia, the rights guaranteed under Articles 4[129] and 16[130] of the African Charter, the Commission stated that:

> 120. [...] Denying people food and medical attention, burning them in sand and subjecting them to torture to the point of death point to a shocking lack of respect for life, and constitutes a violation of Article 4 (see para 12). Other communications provide evidence of various arbitrary executions that took place in the villages of the River Senegal valley (see paras 18 and 19) and stress that people were arbitrarily detained between September and December 1990 (see para 22).
>
> 122. The State's responsibility in the event of detention is even more evident to the extent that detention centres are its exclusive preserve, hence the physical integrity and welfare of detainees is the responsibility of the competent public authorities. Some prisoners died as a result of the lack of medical attention. The general state of health of the prisoners deteriorated due to the lack of sufficient foo[d]; they had neither blankets nor adequate hygiene. The Mauritanian state is directly responsible for this state of affairs and

---

[127] This is particularly the case in *Malawi Africa Association et al.* (footnote 114); Communication 155/96, *Social and Economic Rights Action Center (SERAC) and Center for Economic and Social Rights (CESR)/Nigeria* (hereinafter *SERAC*), decided on merits, 30th Ordinary Session (27 October 2001); Communications 279/03-296/05, *Sudan Human Rights Organisation & Centre on Housing Rights and Evictions (COHRE)/Sudan* (joined) (hereinafter *Darfur case*), decided on merits, 45th Ordinary Session (27 May 2009); Communication 27/99, *Democratic Republic of Congo/Burundi, Rwanda, Uganda* (hereinafter *DRC case*), decided on merits, 33rd Ordinary Session (03 May 2003).

[128] See paras 115–122 (describing in part some of the situations that took place in detention places). See also its overall holdings in which it 'Declare[d] that, during the period 1989–1992, there were grave or massive violations of human rights as proclaimed in the African Charter; and in particular of Articles 2, 4, 5 (constituting cruel, inhuman and degrading treatments), 6, 7(1)(a), 7(1)(b), 7(1)(c) and 7(2)(d), 9(2), 10(1), 11, 12(1), 14, 16(1), 18(1) and 26', basically finding violations of, for all intents and purposes, the entire substantive provisions of the African Charter.

[129] Which reads, 'Human beings are inviolable. Every human being shall be entitled to respect for his life and integrity of his person. No one may be arbitrary deprived of this right'.

[130] This provision reads as follows, '1. Every individual shall have the right to enjoy the best attainable state of physical and mental health. 2. State parties … shall take the necessary measures to protect the health of their people and to ensure that they receive medical attention when they are sick'.

78 G. A. Mosissa

the government has not denied these facts. Consequently, the Commission considers that there was a violation of Article 16.

In the *DRC case* the Commission found, more or less, a similar kind of gross human rights violations by Respondent States contravening their international obligations under general humanitarian law and the African Charter. The relevant part of its decisions reads as follows:

> 79. The [African] Commission finds the killings, massacres, rapes, mutilations and other grave human rights abuses committed while the Respondent States' armed forces were still in effective occupation of the eastern provinces of the Complainant State reprehensible and also inconsistent with their obligations under Part III of the *Geneva Convention Relative to the Protection of Civilian Persons in Time of War* of 1949 and *Protocol 1 of the Geneva Convention*.[131]
>
> 88. The looting, killing, mass and indiscriminate transfers of civilian population, the besiege and damage of the hydro-dam, stopping of essential services in the hospital, leading to deaths of patients and the general disruption of life and state of war that took place while the forces of the Respondent States were occupying and in control of the eastern provinces of the Complainant State are in violation of Article 14 guaranteeing the right to property, Articles 16 and 17 (all of the African Charter), which provide for the rights to the best attainable state of physical and mental health and education, respectively.

The *SERAC* case, a complaint against the former military regime of Nigeria concerning the situation of Ogoni people, also expresses gross human rights violations ensuing from basic constitutional crisis in the sense employed in this writing. This was basically triggered by the military junta's decision to engage in oil exploration in the Niger Delta in complete disregard to the basic rights and interests of the population, especially as regards the project's impact on human health and the surrounding environment.[132] As the communication shows, the Ogoni people had become victims of double sufferings. On the one hand, the pollution that resulted from the toxic substances and hazardous wastes from the oil exploration destroyed their wellbeing and livelihoods particularly because the 'contamination of water, soil and air [had] had serious short and long-term health impacts, including skin infections, gastrointestinal and respiratory ailments, and increased risk of cancers, and neurological and reproductive problems' and 'the pollution and environmental degradation to the level humanly unacceptable has made it living in the Ogoni land a

---

[131] See this also with para 89 of the same stating, 'Part III of the *Geneva Convention Relative to the Protection of Civilian Persons in Time of War 1949*, particularly in Article 27 provides for the humane treatment of protected persons at all times and for protection against all acts of violence or threats and against insults and public curiosity. Further, it provides for the protection of women against any attack on their honour, in particular against rape, enforced prostitution, or any form of indecent assault. Article 4 of the Convention defines a protected person as those who, at a given moment and in any manner whatsoever, find themselves, in case of a conflict or occupation, in the hands of a Party to the conflict or Occupying Power of which they are not nationals'.

[132] See paras 1–9 (describing background reasons leading to the violations in the case). These allegations were admitted by the (new civilian) Government of Nigeria in its Note Verbale ref. 27/2000 addressed to the Commission saying that 'there is no denying the fact that a lot of atrocities were and are still being committed by the oil companies in Ogoni Land and indeed in the Niger Delta area' (ibid., at para 42).

2 Ensuring the Realization of the Right to Health   79

nightmare'.[133] On the other hand, their livelihoods were also shattered by the ruthless military operations and other agents destroying their homes, villages, source of foods (farms, water sources, crops and animals) and causing massive displacements, evictions, detentions, torturing, killings and other forms of ill-treatments and terrorizations.[134] As the Commission states, '[t]hese and similar brutalities not only persecuted individuals in Ogoniland but also the whole of the Ogoni community[…]. They affected the life of the Ogoni society as a whole'.[135]

The *Darfur case*, which alleged the atrocities committed against the people of Darfur, can be seen as a typical example of the gross violations of human rights (including the right to health) resulting from internal armed conflicts. Among other things, the *Darfur case* reveals the practice of large-scale killings (including extrajudicial executions), rape and torture, forced displacements, evictions, looting, destruction of foodstuffs, crops, livestock, poisoning of wells, denial of access to other water sources, and the destruction of public facilities and private properties and the disruption of the livelihoods of the Darfurian people, all through the direct participation of the state concerned and the agents it has sponsored.[136] For instance, the Commission concluded that 'the Respondent state and its agents, the Janjawid militia, actively participated in the forced eviction of the civilian population from their homes and villages' and that '[i]t failed to protect the victims against the said violations'; moreover, it, 'while fighting the armed groups, targeted the civilian population, as part of its counter insurgence strategy'. According to the Commission, all these acts and omissions clearly amount to cruel and inhuman treatment which threaten the very essence of the dignity of the said population.[137]

In finding the violation of the right to health, the Commission also held that 'the destruction of homes, livestock and farms as well as the poisoning of water sources, such as wells, exposed the victims to serious health risks and', therefore, 'amounts to a violation of Article 16 of the Charter'.[138] There are several more violations that the Commission has established in the *Darfur case*. For instance, in finding the violations under Article 22 of the African Charter,[139] the Commission stated the following.

---

[133] See Ibid., together with paras 51–54 and 67.

[134] Ibid., at paras 55 and 61–67.

[135] Accordingly, the Commission declared violation of, inter alia, right to inviolability of human life and wellbeing, health (which embraces right to food, shelter and water) and health environment all by the direct actions of the state and by sponsoring of or tolerating other non-state actors. In essence therefore, the Government has failed in terms of its elementary duty to respect and ensure respect (protect) for the basic rights and freedoms of the Nigerians living in Ogoniland (see ibid., at paras 54, 55, 58, 62–67).

[136] See for instance at paras 145–68. It concluded that by not acting diligently to protect the population concerned against violations perpetrated by its forces and other agents, the State Party violated Articles 4 and 5 of the African Charter (see at paras 205–216).

[137] Ibid., para 164.

[138] Ibid., para 112 (see also at paras 206–11 making reference to General Comment 14 as well).

[139] Article 22 states, '1. All peoples shall have the right to their economic, social and cultural development with due regard to their freedom and identity and in the equal enjoyment of the

The attacks and forced displacement of Darfurian people denied them the opportunity to engage in economic, social and cultural activities. The displacement interfered with the right to education for their children and pursuit of other activities. Instead of deploying its resources to address the marginalization in the Darfur, which was the main cause of the conflict, the Respondent State instead unleashed a punitive military campaign which constituted a massive violation of not only the economic social and cultural rights, but other individual rights of the Darfurian people. Based on the analysis hereinabove, concerning the nature and magnitude of the violations, the Commission finds that the Respondent State is in violation of 22 of the Africa Charter.[140]

At this point, it may be important to stress that the *Malawi Africa Association et al., Darfur case, SERAC* and *DRC case*—all pertaining to the situation of humanitarian crisis in the sense described above—have one basic feature in common: they all manifest very serious systemic failures. In other words, the facts and evidence recorded therein overwhelmingly establish gross, massive and widespread violations of human rights where the States Parties concerned directly participated, through highly orchestrated means, in the shattering of the dignified existence and livelihood of the entire populations in question. This means that there is hardly any right recognized in the African Charter that the actions and omissions of the States Parties did not violate. In addressing the violations therein, the Commission took, in four of the communications, the painstaking approach to disentangle the facts and restate them in the terms of the substantive provisions of the Charter. Although this kind of approach is not wrong per se, I would argue that it is both redundant and ineffective in situations like this. For instance, it was the very same facts that the Commission addressed under almost all of the substantive provisions of the African Charter including right to life, bodily integrity, security, prohibition of torture and degrading treatments, property, housing, food, health, peaceful existence, so and so forth. More fundamentally, such an approach gives the false impression that the violations are the result of isolated incidents while, in fact, they are highly systematic and widespread in nature. It is generally true that it is the claim of the parties to a dispute that sets a general framework as to how a tribunal should analyse a given case but it is also true that the tribunal has an inherent power not just to determine the issues involved in the case but also how to resolve the issues. In my opinion, it would have been more effective had the Commission declared in *Malawi Africa Association et al., Darfur case, SERAC* and *DRC case* that the States Parties concerned committed gross, massive, widespread and systematic violations of the African Charter and other related treaties of the AU.[141]

(Footnote 139 continued)

common heritage of mankind. 2. States shall have the duty, individually and collectively, to ensure the exercise of the right to development'.

[140] Ibid., at para 224. Similarly, it also found violation of the right to property under Article 14 (para 205), right of the family under Article 18 (para 216).

[141] This is supported by Article 58 of the Banjul Charter which refers to communications concerning a 'special case' expressing 'series of serious or massive violations of human and peoples' rights'.

In this regard, it should be clear that I am not in any way suggesting that the declaration of violations under the relevant substantive provisions of the Charter is superfluous. Indeed, it might be necessary to specify the individual rights violated by the States Parties concerned but this could have easily been indicated in the operating part of the Commission's decisions under consideration. The facts stated in four of the communications clearly indicate, for instance, that the right to health of the populations was violated in the worst ever possible manner one could imagine. We should, however, note the fact that this violation of the right to health was part and parcel of the widespread actions of the States Parties systematically carried out in order to silence those populations—the facts do not prove that the violations of the right to health was due to an isolated actions of the States Parties. That is why, in the situation where the very existence and livelihood of the population is actually under attack, analysing the facts and evidence therein as concerning the violation of a particular human right (as the right to health) is less effective and redundant.

All in all, the foregoing discussion on the jurisprudence of the Commission provides us with useful insights as to how it addressed the violations of the right to health in the context of detention and humanitarian crisis. Apart from this, we may not find any relevant authoritative normative guidance regarding the general positive obligations of the State Party to ensure equal access to health care and its underlying determinants for all within its jurisdiction. This is so because, on the one hand, in each of these communications the Commission found violations of the right to health on account of the direct actions or participation of the State Parties in the said violations. On the other hand, the positive obligation of the State to ensure the realization of the right to health care and its underlying determinants for the socioeconomically vulnerable parts of the society entails the adoption of deliberate, concrete and targeted legislative, policy and institutional measures. This clearly and minimally presupposes the existence of a thin functioning of the elementary principles of the rule of law for, this should be obvious, in the absence of this principle the normative basis upon which individuals can make a claim to have access to health care and basic social justice is simply non-existent. In any case, and as far as I am concerned, none of communications before the Commission so far has engaged, in a direct and relevant manner, the positive obligations of the State Party to realize the right to health and basic social justice.

2.4.2.2 The Right to Health in Other Activities of the Commission

The Commission has also dealt with some of the issues affecting the enjoyment of the right to health in its promotional and standard setting functions, especially in its Special Mechanisms. Ten out of sixteen Special Mechanisms[142] currently in

---

[142] The list of the special mechanisms is available through http://www.achpr.org/mechanisms/ (last visited 9 May 2013). For an interesting discussion the types, possible legal basis, function and effectiveness of the Commission's Special Mechanisms, see Viljoen 2012, pp. 369–378.

operation concern, directly or indirectly, the promotion of right to health.[143] Since the Commission started establishing these mechanisms in the late 1990s, the commission has issued a series of resolutions and declarations based on the works of or certainly with the participation from these special mechanisms. Beyond this, it is very difficult to explain their impact on the identification of specific systemic obstacles existing at the national level.

It should be mentioned that some have hailed the Commission's adoption of the Principles and Guidelines on the implementation of socioeconomic rights in the continent (already referred to in this discussion) and the Guidelines on State Reporting under the Banjul Charter (Reporting Guidelines) which, in turn, is a short-hand version of the Principles and Guidelines.[144] Both are notable works of the Working Group on ESCR. Nonetheless, neither the Principles and Guidelines nor the Reporting Guidelines add any new substantive legal principles or standards to the area of socioeconomic rights. They are mere consolidations of already existing principles of interpretations of socioeconomic rights and the corresponding State obligations being developed in its own decisions, in the works UN human rights institutions and its specialized agencies (such as WHO and IFAO) as well as in the jurisprudence of various national and supranational human rights tribunals. One might, however, be surprised to observe that neither the Principles and guidelines nor the Reporting Guidelines makes any reference to the 2008 AU's Social Policy Frameworks discussed in this contribution.[145] Thus, while it is not worth repeating here, it should be said that the protection of the rights of vulnerable persons is particularly emphasized in each of the documents. Both the Principles and Guidelines and Reporting Guidelines stress the need to pay due and appropriate regard to equality, non-discrimination, equity and accessibility in the provision of health care and other social services and to provide social protection measures for those without minimum income. Also, they both emphasize institutional principles such as accountability, transparency and participation as

---

[143] Thus, it can be said that the Committee on the Protection of the Rights of People Living With HIV (PLHIV) and Those at Risk, Vulnerable to and Affected by HIV or risking HIV/AIDS; the Working Group on Rights of Older Persons and People with Disabilities, the working Group on Extractive Industries, Environment and Human Rights Violations; the Working Group on Indigenous Populations/Communities, the Working Group Economic Social and Cultural Rights (ESCR); the Special Rapporteur on Refugees and Internally Displaced Persons; and the Special Rapporteur on the Rights of Women deal as part of their mandate with the socioeconomic dimensions of right to health whereas Special Rapporteur on Prisons and Conditions of Detention, Committee for the Prevention of Torture, Working Group on Death Penalty and Extrajudicial, Summary or Arbitrary Killings can address some of the issues pertaining to the promotion and protection of right to health as well.

[144] Also referred to as Tunis Reporting Guidelines, adopted on 24 November 2011 (available at http://www.achpr.org/instruments/economic-social-cultural-guidelines/ last accessed 22 December 2012).

[145] One apparent reason may be that which is mentioned by Viljoen 2012, p. 297 that 'to a large extent, the Commission has performed its activities in splendid isolation from the rest of the continent, including the AU organs'.

2 Ensuring the Realization of the Right to Health

fundamental norms that must be ensured and complied with not only in the delivery of health services but also in the designing and execution of other public policies aimed at the realization of human rights in general.[146]

2.4.2.3 Effectiveness of the Commission's Practices

Thus, the main question is whether the above discussions would give us a reason to believe that the Commission is playing a meaningful role in the effort to ensure the realization of right to health and its underlying conditions. That is, whether the practices of the Commission could be said to match the kind of underlying obstacles behind lack of systemic justice and therefore could be seen as a strong legal accountability mechanism of the AU System. This question may need further exploration in itself but remaining within the scope of this discussion it is possible to make the following observations.[147]

It could be said that there are some achievements that the Commission has been able to accomplish in its nearly 30 years of existence. Among these are the establishment of the Special Mechanisms and the examination of the individual communications (although it has decided very few cases compared to the number of years

---

[146] See Principles and Guidelines, at para 60 ff (concerning Right to Health under Article 16 of the African Charter).

[147] On the recent assessment of the effectiveness of the Commission's functions see Viljoen 2012, particularly pp. 295–299, Yeshanew 2011, particularly pp. 210–215; Chirwa 2008, pp. 334–336

See also Ssenyonjo 2011 (reviewing Commission's 30 years of jurisprudence, Ssenyonjo certainly sees its jurisprudence especially since 2001 as positive development. Okafor 2010 also sees the Commission as institution of collective human security struggle with important positive contribution to that vision but the Commission is yet to live up to that expectation and I am afraid the following assessments does not seem to be as positive as that of Okafor and Ssenyonjo. I should say that both authors discuss the Commission's work in terms of the ideal normative developments it has brought to the field but they are also quite aware of the ineffectiveness of those decisions as well. Okafor, whose argument is basically more of the constitutional and institutional design of the Commission than its current practical functioning (at p. 317), clearly notes that the Commission's engagement with socioeconomic rights is minimal (at p. 332). For Ssenyonjo, it is up to the States Parties and other relevant actors as CSOs/NGOs to support the Commission's decisions by practically implementing those norms developed by the Commission (at pp. 395–397). To this extent there may not be disagreements between their arguments and what is to be said in the following. However, the following assessment is basically about the effectiveness of the Commission's works in fact not just in theory vis-à-vis its (actual and potential) ability to bring strong legal accountability regime required to address those background injustices and inequities, i.e. systemic problems, impeding the effective realization of basic social justice in the continent (the collective human security that Okafor is also concerned with). In this regard, a normative development on the right to health, if any, is important but insufficient to give the Commission's office a positive assessment. Its methods, areas of concentrations, creativeness, practical outcomes and relevance (especially to the continent's urgent needs), authoritativeness, legitimacy, ability to influence grassroots level decision-making must also be part of that assessment as well.

it has been in operation). There are, however, several reasons to doubt the viability and effectiveness of these mechanisms in addressing the problem of structural accountability deficits—i.e. the lack of constitutional justice—in the continent. As far as the Special Mechanisms are concerned, the Commission may be criticized for being too late in establishing mechanisms aimed at addressing issues of socioeconomic rights and for being driven more by 'pressures from interest groups' than by its own 'careful and proactive' considerations and rationalization of its functions and the goals enshrined in the Banjul Charter.[148] What is even more disappointing is that, in the context of this discussion, there has been no practically meaningful outcome that could be hailed wholeheartedly (one should note that I have already stated my reservations as regards the Principles and Guidelines just mentioned above).[149]

In relation to the examination of the individual communications, there is an abundance of reasons to criticize the practices of the Commission. To begin with, its decisions mostly come far too late to constitute an effective remedy.[150] So, restating the old saying, 'justice delayed, justice denied', one may say here that judgment delayed is remedy denied. For instance, even though almost all of the communications discussed above concern very grave situations of human rights violations, the time taken by the Commission to render its final decisions do not, by any standard, reflect that sense of urgency and gravity.[151] This, in turn, has very serious negative implications for the capacity of the Commission in bringing accountability for violations of human rights. This is so because there would not be any meaningful point in rendering a decision on a particular communication after

---

[148] As Viljoen 2012 (at p. 297 and 299), 2009 (at pp. 512–513) and Murray 2010 (at p. 356ff.) observe, the Commission's activities (agenda) are essentially drawn by and in the interest of NGOs/CSOs and has nothing to do with its readiness to critically engage with the continent's major social issues.

[149] Viljoen is also critical about their effectiveness and efficiency as follows. 'While these mechanisms are important promotional tools, they confront States with allegations of specific violations only to a limited extent. Time, energy and resources devoted to these mechanisms have detracted from the Commission's core protective function. Again, delays and the failure to adopt reports by these mechanisms, their omission from the Commission's Activity Reports, and the lack of dissemination of these reports are major impediments to their effectiveness and impact'. See Viljoen 2012, at p. 297.

[150] Viljoen 2012, p. 296ff, Yeshanew 2011, p. 210ff; Ssenyonjo 2011, p. 395.

[151] For instance, the *Malawi Africa Association et al.* (cited at footnote 114) was decided nearly 10 years after the receipt of the first communication. The first communication against Mauritania (No. 54/91) was filed by Malawi Africa Association on 16 July 1991 and decided (joined communications) on 11 May 2000. The *SERAC case* (cited at footnote 127) was decided after five and half years after the receipt of the communication (on 14 March 1996 and decided at its 30th Ordinary Session held between 13 and 27 October 2001). The *Darfur case* (cited at footnote 127) was decided 6 years after the complaint by Sudan Human Rights Organization was received on 18 September 2003 and it was decided at the 45th Ordinary Session held between 13 and 27 May 2009. The case of *EIPR/INTERIGHTS* (cited at footnote 114) which concerned about situation of death penalty, was decided in nearly 5 years (to be precise, 4 years and nine months) after the communication was received at its 40th Ordinary Session held between 15 and 29 November 2006 and it was decided at its 9th Extraordinary Session held from 23 February to 3 March 2011.

2 Ensuring the Realization of the Right to Health 85

factors responsible for a particular human rights violation had disappeared. For instance, when the Commission delivered its findings in *Malawi Africa Association* and *SERAC* (which represent the worst forms of human rights violations) the regimes responsible for the said violations were no longer in place. As such the decisions of the Commission therein can hardly be regarded as constituting effective remedy for the complainants and, more generally, such is also not in line with the kind of accountability that international human rights law seeks to ensure. Of course it is possible that some of the reasons for the delays may be attributable to the conducts of the parties themselves but not all of them; in fact, the Commission is to blame for most of the postponements, which it can also not justify on the ground that its office functions on a part-time basis.

Besides this, the decisions of the Commission are usually muddled in incoherence, redundancy and inconsistency[152] such that the reasoning therein is generally unable to establish an authoritative normative standard in relation to the issues raised in the communication. As an example, the *SERAC* case was seen by some as a 'landmark' decision concerning socioeconomic rights but looking closely at its reasoning, this is hardly the case. I have argued above that *SERAC* concerns the violation of socioeconomic rights only on its surface while, deep inside, the facts therein indicate a major constitutional crisis resulting from the direct actions of the military junta in the Niger Delta: as the facts clearly show, the police, military and other State machineries (including secret agents sponsored by the regime) directly carried out widespread, systematic and gross violation of the livelihood of the Ogoni people as whole. Leaving this aside, while the standards the Commission employed in deciding *SERAC* was borrowed from the UN CESCR's General Comment 14[153], it did not provide us with any clear justification regarding the particular relevance of those standards especially given the background situations and nature of violations involved in the communication. There is nothing major that the decision added to the already existing jurisprudence of socioeconomic rights that could make *SERAC a* jurisprudentially landmark decision. Of course for those of us who were eager to see the Commission saying something about socioeconomic rights (because it openly refused to do so during the first season of its existence), the decision may be seen as landmark; even then it is only because it somehow shows a change to its own institutional perspective on socioeconomic rights rather than any jurisprudential advancement thereof.[154]

These are all issues that could be resolved by the Commission but there also remain other fundamental problems undermining the effectiveness of the Commission in addressing the accountability deficit in the continent. The decision of

---

[152] See Viljoen 2012, p. 296.

[153] See at paras 44–47 (in fact, it is almost a common practice of the Commission to rely on jurisprudences drawn from elsewhere without providing the due justification need in a given case).

[154] See Yeshanew 2011, p. 210 n 340 (citing, inter alia, Umozurike 1988); Viljoen 2012, p. 299; Ssenonjo 2011, pp. 366–385 (analysing its practices on ESCR by dissecting into two periods: pre-2001 of scanty decisions and activities and post-2001 of increased engagement).

the Commission is legally non-binding for it only has the power to make non-binding recommendations, which it cannot make public without the approval of the AU Executive Council.[155] In this regard, there are incidents where the latter refused to approve its findings, perhaps indirectly accusing the Commission of being biased. And, in practice, the Member States also did not show any sign of compliance with its decisions as such.[156] One may immediately say that these are not the problems for which the Commission should be responsible. However, the truth is that the Commission has a longstanding legitimacy crisis in the eyes of the AU Member States. In particular, it is seen as being used by NGOs/CSO as a tool to embarrass the States appearing before it and not as an objective human rights institution, a fact we should see in the light of the influence they have in the works of the Commission both practically and financially.[157] As Viljoen, pioneer in African human rights law, observes, its meetings (Sessions) are usually dominated by the activities and statements of CSO/NGOs.[158] It also appears from the discussion by Murray, who has also written a lot on the works of the Commission, that the programmes and activities of the Commission are basically organized around or even designed to serve the interests of CSO/NGOs.[159] It is therefore of little surprise that States are particularly sceptical about anything that comes out of its office.

Further, and even more fundamental, the methods through which the Commission conduct its business are hardly rationalized to the practical contexts and needs of the African continent. The Commission still remains unknown to the overwhelming number of populations who are most in need of the processes and outcomes of its functions. Even if it is theoretically known to some of the ordinary Africans, there are major practical reasons preventing them from approaching its office, among which are illiteracy, poverty, remoteness and the utter ineffectiveness of its decisions. It is also hardly the case that the Commission is even known to the ordinary public servants in the continent. This is mainly because of the fact that, for the last three decades or so, it has been focusing largely on the old-style methods of human rights promotion and protection—conducting litigation, issuing resolutions and organizing elite-driven seminars. So far, conducting litigations (and issuing of resolutions) seems to be the major outcome of the activities of the Commission but soon to be ignored by the Member States they are mainly addressed to. Other authors have already pointed at some of the limitations of litigation-based strategies for ensuring social justice for the poor.[160] For human rights institution like the Commission, which only has the power to make non-

---

[155] See Article 59 (1) Banjul Charter.

[156] See Viljoen 2012, p. 297, 2009, p. 512, Viljoen and Louw 2007, Chirwa 2008, p. 333, Yeshanew 2011, p. 211, Okafor 2010, p. 335.

[157] See Murray 2010, p. 344ff; Viljoen 2009, pp. 512–513; Viljoen 2012, p. 297.

[158] Viljoen 2009 ibid.

[159] See at footnote 157.

[160] See generally Landau 2012; Brinks and Gauri 2010.

2 Ensuring the Realization of the Right to Health

binding recommendations,[161] I do not think litigation can even be considered as an ideal strategy in the first place. This should be seen especially in the light of the fact that only a very negligible number of individuals may be able to practically access its office and that it receives a very low level of cooperation from the Member States. In addition to litigation, the Commission also organizes, as part of its promotional mandate, some elite-driven seminars. In fact, it is fair to say that, for most part of its existence, the Commission has been preoccupied with organizing seminars only to be attended by few professional elites and NGOs/CSO and that its commissioners are often busy with giving lectures and presentations, again, to few professional elite groups including those living overseas.

We have already seen that the jurisprudence of the Commission on poverty-related violations of the right to health is thin. This is because none of the communications discussed above alleged that the State has violated its positive obligation to ensure access to health care and its underlying determinants. So there is little that we could say as regards the Commission's view regarding the obligations of the Member States towards the socioeconomically vulnerable parts of the society. Of course the Commission has indicated that, drawing on the UN CESCR, it would analyse State Party's obligations in the light of the general obligation to respect, protect, promote and fulfil. But what these actually entail in the context of the continent where the great majority of the populations are rural residents and are living under chronic poverty still remains unexplained. Perhaps to one's surprise, even though the Commission operates in the continent where poverty is chronic; ill-health, maternal and child mortality is rampant (one of the highest in the world); corruption is endemic; and democratic accountability is in deficit for so long, it is, to my knowledge, yet to make any systematic or country-specific study; concrete policy recommendations; or establish a special mechanism on any one of these. One should recall that corruption and lack of structural accountability are underscored in this contribution as the major underlying impediments to the effective realization of the right to health care and basic social justice in continent.[162]

Therefore, by looking into its past approaches and practices, it is unfortunately very difficult to conclude that the Commission has been acting in such a way as to respond to the structural injustices and accountability deficits prevailing in the continent. There is simply no evidence that could warrant that conclusion. Instead, the Commission is described by some as 'the least effective human rights institution of the three regions'[163] or as a 'toothless bulldog'.[164] In my opinion, even such characterizations may not fully express the extent to which the Commission has failed, particularly in relation to the promotion and protection of socioeconomic rights in Africa. In this regard, we should note that the African Charter did

---

[161] Following Okafor, we can say that the Commission is the institution that can only persuade but not compel (Okafor 2010, p. 335).

[162] See also Viljoen 2012, p. 299.

[163] Chirwa 2008, p. 335.

[164] Ibid., at footnote 113 (citing Udombana 2000).

not conceive the office of the Commission as a 'toothless bulldog'. By vesting it with such robust promotional and fairly protective mandates, the Charter envisages the Commission as a continental institution that can engage actively and critically with local institutions and be a vehicle of change by constructively guiding the Member States through in-depth research, training and providing them with articulate, practical and alternative policy recommendations aimed at addressing concrete human rights problems.[165]

In the area of the right to health, for instance, the Commission could have contributed significantly by drawing key crosscutting issues from the wealth of reports of the Member States; launching its own thematic and county-specific investigations into national systems and practices; publishing its own robust reports and recommendations; and by using effectively its findings and experiences in its grassroots level promotional and training activities. This would, in turn, not only play a significant role in enhancing the protection of human rights but also in establishing its authority and legitimacy as an objective voice of human rights and basic social justice in the continent. But this would clearly require the Commission to make some critical programmatic and methodological choices. Thus, it should particularly focus on practical and robust promotional, training and research activities pertinent to the continent's dire needs. Such activities should not repeat its past failures or ineffectiveness. It should adopt methods well-rationalized into the contexts of individuals in need of its protective functions; it should actively and critically engage with local actors; I should aid governments through concrete and practical human rights protective guidelines. In this way, it is very possible that the Commission can contribute substantially to the quest for legal accountability in the area of the realization of basic social justice in Africa.

2.5 Conclusion

Health is an integral component of the very essence of human life in dignity and, hence, the right to health is all about ensuring respect for the inherent dignity of the human being. The right to health secures human dignity by guaranteeing to everyone the right to have those basic biological and moral health needs inherent in and indispensable for his or her dignified living and, to this extent, by imposing a compelling obligation on the State Party to realize the same in strict accordance with the basic principles of social justice such as equality (non-discrimination) and solidarity. It is, therefore, utterly impossible for the State to respect the inherent dignity of a human being without first ensuring the right to health of all persons within its jurisdiction. In particular, we have seen that the right to health as recognized in human rights law incorporates the right to have freedom of choice, the right to have access to basic health entitlements and the right to have access to

---

[165] See footnote 105–106.

2 Ensuring the Realization of the Right to Health

justice. However, the discussion has shown that neither of these is in fact ensured by governments in Africa. The empirical facts with which I have started this discussion shockingly indicate the dire and persistent shortage of access to health care and its underlying determinants; and the decisions of the African Commission also establish very serious violations of the right to health in the continent, particularly in the context of detention and humanitarian crisis. So, whether it is seen through the solid empirical facts or the decisions of the Commission, it is clear that the governments in Africa have failed miserably in ensuring the right to health and, hence, the dignity of most Africans.

Nevertheless, the chronic failure has hardly anything to do with a lack of resources (scarcity) as such. In fact, it emerges from the analysis in this contribution that States Parties cannot, under any circumstances, justify their failure to ensure the right to freedom of choice and access to justice on account of resource constraints. It is equally unacceptable that the State justifies its failure to ensure the right to health care and the underlying determinants of health for the vulnerable members of society on the ground of a lack of material resources. On the contrary, it is argued that the general problem of systemic, structural accountability persisting in the continent can best explain why the continent has been and continues to be at the heart of a global public health crisis for an unacceptably long period of time. Rather disappointingly also, the principal remedial institutions currently available at the AU level, the Court and the Commission, were unable to play meaningful roles in dealing with this underlying systemic problem. It might be encouraging to note that the AU has now integrated the question of the right to health into issues of basic social justice in the continent. But again there is no mechanism to ensure that such discretionary policy recommendations would result in some practical effects at the grassroots level. Ensuring the realization of the right to health through the AU system requires the existence of a strong legal accountability mechanism. Accordingly, it is imperative that the AU and its Member States work, as a matter of priority, towards revitalizing and rationalizing[166] these remedial institutions. Without this, the claim of the AU and its Members as being concerned with the protection and promotion of human dignity, human rights and social justice is simply nothing more than empty political rhetoric.

References

Aasen H et al (eds) (2009) Human rights, dignity and autonomy in health care and social services: Nordic perspectives. Intersentia, Antwerp

Acemoglu D, Robinson J (2012) Why nations fail: the origins of power, prosperity and poverty. Profile Books, London

Alao A (2010) Natural resource management and human security in Africa. In: Abass A (ed) Protecting human security in Africa. OUP, Oxford

---

[166] See generally Mbondenyi 2009.

Alexy R (2010a) A theory of legal argumentation: the theory of rational discourse as theory of legal justification (trans. Adler R, MacCromick N). OUP (paperback), Oxford

Alexy R (2010b) A theory of constitutional rights (trans. Rivers). OUP (paperback), Oxford

Andorno R (2009) Human dignity and human rights as a common ground for a global bioethics. J Med Philos 34:223

Arambulo K (1999) Strengthening the supervision of the international economic, social and cultural rights: theoretical and procedural aspects. Intersentia, Antwerpen

Auweraert P et al (eds) (2002) Social, economic and cultural rights: an appraisal of current european and international developments. Maklu, Antwerp

Backman G (2012) Health systems and the right to health. In: Backman G (ed) The right to health: theory and practice. Studentlitteratur, Lund

Backman G (ed) (2012) The right to health: theory and practice. Studentlitteratur, Lund

Baderin M, Mccorquodale R (eds) (2007) Economic, social and cultural rights in action. OUP, Oxford

Brinks V, Gauri D (2008) A new policy landscape: legalizing social and economic rights in the developing world. In: Gauri V, Brinks D (eds) Courting social Justice. Judicial enforcement of social and economic rights in the developing world. CUP, Cambridge

Brownsword R (2003) Bioethics today, bioethics tomorrow: stem cell research and the "Dignitarian alliance". Notre Dame J. L. Ethics Pub Pol'y 17:15

Carozza P (2003) "My friend is a stranger": the death penalty and the global ius commune of human rights. Tex L Rev 81:1031

Carozza P (2008) Human dignity and judicial interpretation of human rights: a reply. EJIL 19(5):931

Chan H, Pang S (2007) Long-term care: dignity, autonomy, family integrity, and social sustainability: the Hong Kong experience. J Med Philos 32:401

Chaskalson A (2002) Human dignity as a constitutional value. In: The concept of human dignity in human rights discourse. Kluwer Law International, The Hague

Chirwa D (2008) African regional human rights system: the promise of recent jurisprudence on social rights. In: Langford M (ed) Social rights Jurisprudence. Emerging trends in international and comparative law. CUP, Cambridge

Chochinov H (2007) Dignity and the essence of medicine: the A, B, C, and D of dignity conserving care. BMJ 335:184

Clapham A (2007) Human rights: a very short introduction. OUP, Oxford

Coomans F (ed) (2006) Justiciability of economic and social rights: experiences from domestic systems. Intersentia, Antwepen

Doumbé-Billé (2012) The AU: principles and purposes. In: Yusuf A, Ouguergouz F (eds) The AU: legal and institutional framework: a manual on the pan-African organization. Martinus Nijhoff Publication, Leiden

Durojaye E (2010) Corruption as a threat to human security in Africa. In: Abass A (ed) Protecting human security in Africa. OUP, Oxford

Dworkin R (1997) Taking rights seriously. Bloomsbury Academic, London

Dworkin R (2006) Is democracy possible here? Principles for a new political debate. Princeton University Press, Princeton

Dworkin R (2011) Justice for hedgehogs. Harvard University Press, Cambridge (paperback)

Eibach U (2008) Protection of life and human dignity: the German debate between Christian norms and secular expectations. Christ Bioeth 14(1):58

Eide A et al (eds) (1992) The universal declaration of human rights: a commentary. Scandinavian University Press, London

Feldman D (1999) Human dignity as a legal value: Part 1. Public Law: 682

Feldman D (2000) Human dignity as a legal value: Part 2. Public Law: 61

Filho A (2008) A human rights approach to quality of life and health: applications to public health programming. Health Hum Rights 10(1):93

Francioni F (2007) The rights of access to justice under customary international law. In: Francioni F (ed) Access to justice as a human right. OUP, Oxford

2 Ensuring the Realization of the Right to Health

Fredman S (2008) Human rights transformed: positive rights and positive duties. OUP, Oxford

Frowein J (2002) Human dignity in international law. In: Kretzmer D, Klein E (eds) The concept of human dignity in human rights discourse. Kluwer Law International, The Hague, pp 121

Fyfe R (2007) Dignity as theory: competing conceptions of human dignity at the Supreme Court of Canada. Sask L Rev 70:1

Gauri V, Brinks D (2008) Introduction: the elements of legalization and the triangular shape of social and economic rights. In: Gauri V, Brinks D (eds) Courting social justice. Judicial enforcement of social and economic rights in the developing world. CUP, Cambridge

Gentzler J (2003) What is a death with dignity? J Med Philos 28(4):461

Ghai Y, Cottrell J (eds) (2004) Economic, social & cultural rights in practice. The role of judges in implementing economic, social & cultural rights. Interights, London

Gould C (2004) Globalizing democracy and human rights. CUP, Cambridge

Greer S (2006) The European Convention on Human Rights: achievements, problems and prospects. CUP, Cambridge

Harris J, Sulston J (2004) Genetic equity. Nat Rev 5: 796

Häyry M (2004) Another look at dignity. Camb Q Healthc Ethics 13:7

Henkin L (1992) Human dignity and constitutional rights. In: Meyer M, Parent W (eds) The constitution of rights: human dignity and the American values. Cornell University Press, Ithaca

Hennette-Vauchez S (2011) A human dignitas? Remnants of the ancient legal concept in contemporary dignity jurisprudence. Int J Const L 9:32

Henry L (2011) The jurisprudence of dignity. U Pa L Rev 160:169

Hestermeyer H (2012) Reality or aspiration?–Solidarity in international environmental law and world trade law. In: Hestermeyer H et al (eds) Coexistence, cooperation and solidarity. Martinus Nijhoff Publication, Leiden

Heyns C, Kaguongo W (2006) Constitutional human rights law in Africa. S Afr J Hum Rts 22:673

Hunt P, Backman G (2008) Health systems and the right to the highest attainable standard of health. Health Hum Rights 10(1):81

Jayawickrama N (2002) The judicial application of human rights law: national, regional and international jurisprudence. CUP, Cambridge

Kateb G (2011) Human dignity. The Belknap Press, Cambridge

Kaufmann P et al (eds) (2011) Humiliation, degradation, dehumanization. Human dignity violated. Springer, Berlin

Klein E (2002) Human dignity in German law. In: The concept of human dignity in human rights discourse. Kluwer Law International, The Hague

Klein E, Kretzmer D (eds) (2002) The concept of human dignity in human rights discourse. Kluwer Law International, The Hague

Koch I (2009) Human rights as indivisible rights: the protection of socio-economic demands under the European Convention on Human Rights. Martinus Nijhoff Publication, Leiden

Koroma A (2012) Solidarity: evidence of an emerging international legal principle. In: Hestermeyer H et al (eds) Coexistence, cooperation and solidarity. Martinus Nijhoff Publication, Leiden

Kretzmer D (2002) Human dignity in Israeli jurisprudence. In: The concept of human dignity in human rights discourse. Kluwer Law International, The Hague

Landau D (2012) The reality of social rights enforcement. Harvard In L J 53(1):401

Langford M (2008) The justiciability of social rights: from practice to theory. In: Langford M (ed) Social rights jurisprudence. Emerging trends in international and comparative law. CUP, Cambridge

Langford M (ed) (2008) Social rights jurisprudence. Emerging trends in international and comparative law. CUP, Cambridge

Lickiss N (2010) On human dignity: fragments of exploration. In: Malpas J, Lickiss N (eds) Perspectives on human dignity: a conversation. Springer

Lotito P (2010) Article 27—workers' right to information and consultation within the undertaking. In: Mock W, Demuro G (eds) Human rights in Europe: commentary on the charter of fundamental rights of the European Union. Carolina Academic Press, Durham

M'Honey C (2012a) There is no such thing as a right to dignity. I.CON 10(2):551

M'Honey C (2012b) There is no such thing as a right to dignity: a rejoinder to Emily Kidd White. I.CON 10(2):585

Macklin R (2003) Dignity is a useless concept. It means no more than respect for persons or their autonomy. BMJ 327:1419

Malpas J (2010) Human dignity and human being. In: Malpas J, Lickiss N (eds) Perspectives on human dignity: a conversation. Springer, Dordrecht

Malpas J, Lickiss N (eds) (2010) Perspectives on human dignity: a conversation. Springer, Dordrecht

Marks S, Clapham A (2005) International human rights lexicon. OUP, Oxford

Mbondenyi M (2009) Invigorating the African system on human and peoples' rights through institutional mainstreaming and rationalization. NQHR 27(4):451

MCCrudden C (2008) Human dignity and judicial interpretation of human rights. EJIL 19(4):655

Meyer M, Parent W (eds) (1992) The constitution of rights. Human dignity and the American values. Cornell University Press, Ithaca

Morsink J (1999) The Universal Declaration of Human Rights: origins, drafting, and intent. University of Pennsylvania Press, Philadelphia

Mowbray A (2010) A study of the principle of fair balance in the jurisprudence of the European Court of Human Rights. Hum Rights L Rev 10(2):289

Murray R (2010) The role of NGOs and civil society in advancing human security in Africa. In: Abass A (ed) Protecting human security in Africa. OUP, Oxford

Nnamuchi O, Ortuanya S (2012) The human right to health in Africa and its challenges: a critical analysis of millennium development goal 8. AHRLJ 12(1):178

Nussbaum M (2000) Women and human development. The capabilities approach. CUP, Cambridge

Nussbaum M (2006) Frontiers of justice: disability, nationality, species membership. The Belknap Press, Cambridge

Nussbaum M (2011) Creating capabilities: the human development approach. The Belknap Press, Cambridge

Okafor O (2010) The African commission on human and peoples' rights as a collective human security resource: promises, performances, and prospects. In: Abass A (eds) Protecting human security in Africa. OUP, Oxford

Olivetti M (2010) Article 1—human dignity. In: Mock W, Demuro G (eds) Human rights in Europe: commentary on the charter of fundamental rights of the European Union. Carolina Academic Press, Durham

Oraá J (2009) The Universal Declaration of Human Rights. In: Isa F, de Feiter K (eds) International human rights law in a global context. Universidad de Deusto, Bilbao

Parent W (1992) Constitutional values and human dignity. In: Meyer M, Parent W (eds) The constitution of rights. Human dignity and the American values. Cornell University Press, Ithaca

Parfit D (2011) On what matters 1. OUP, Oxford

Rangel V (2012) The solidarity principle, Francisco de Vitoria and the protection of indigenous peoples. In: Hestermeyer H et al (eds) Coexistence, cooperation and solidarity. Martinus Nijhoff Pub, Leiden

Rao N (2011) Three concepts of dignity in constitutional law. Notre Dame L Rev 86:183

Riley S (2010) Human dignity: comparative and conceptual debates. Int. J L C 6(2):117

Rosen M (2012) Human dignity: its history and meaning. Harvard University Press, Cambridge

Schacter O (1983) Human dignity as a normative concept. Am J In L 77:848

Schroeder D (2010) Dignity: one, two, three, four, five, still counting. Camb Q Healthc Ethics 19:118

Sen A (1999) Development as freedom. OUP, Oxford

Sen A (2004) Elements of a theory of human rights. Philos Public Aff 32(4):315

Sen A (2009) The idea of justice. The Belknap Press, Cambridge

Sepúlveda M (2003) The nature of the obligations under international economic, social and cultural rights. Intersentia, Antwerpen

Shelton D (2005) Remedies in international human rights law, 2nd edn. OUP, Oxford

Shue H (1996) Basic rights: subsistence, affluence, and U.S. foreign policy, 2nd ed. Princeton University Press, Princeton

Spijkers O (2011) The United Nations, the evolution of global values and international law. Intersentia, Antwerpen

Ssenyonjo M (2011) Analysing the economic, social and cultural rights jurisprudence of the African Commission: 30 Years since the adoption of the African charter. NQHR 29(3):358

Ssenyonjo M (2012) Economic, social and cultural rights in the African Charter. In: Ssenyonjo M (ed) The African regional human rights system: 30 Years after the African Charter on Human and Peoples Rights. Martinus Nijhoff Pub, Leiden

Sulmasy D (2010) Human dignity and human worth. In Malpas J, Lickiss N (eds) Perspectives on human dignity: a conversation. Springer, Dordrecht

Tobin J (2012) The right to health in international law. OUP, Oxford

Toebes B (1999) The right to health as a human right in international law. Intersentia, Antwerpen

Toebes B (2012) The right to health and health-related rights. In: Toebes B et al (eds) Health and human rights in Europe. Intersentia, Antwerp

Toebes et al (eds) (2012) Health and human rights in Europe. Intersentia, Cambridge

Viljoen F (2009) The African regional human rights system. In: Krause C, Scheinin M (eds) International protection of human rights: a textbook. Åbo Akademi University, Institute for Human Rights, Åbo/ Turku

Viljoen F (2012) International human rights law in Africa, 2nd ed. OUP, Oxford

Viljoen F, Louw L (2007) State compliance with the recommendations of the African Commission on Human and Peoples' Rights, 1994–2004. AJIL 101:1

Waldron J (2007) Dignity and rank. Arch Europ Soc XLVIII(2):201

Weinrib L (2005) Human dignity as a rights-protecting principle. Nat J Const L 17:325

White E (2012) There is no such thing as a right to human dignity: a reply to Conor O'Mahony. I.CON 10(2):575

Wildhaber L (2002) A constitutional future for the European Court of Human Rights? Hum Rights L J 23:161

Wildhaber L (2006) The European Court of Human Rights 1998–2006: history, achievements, reform. N.P. Engel Pub, Strasbourg

Wildhaber L (2007) The European Court of Human Rights: the past, the present, the future. Nat J Const L 20:183

Yeshanew S (2011) The justiciability of economic, social and cultural rights in the African regional human rights system: theories, laws, practices and prospects. Åbo Akademi University press, Åbo

Yusuf A, Ouguergouz F (2012) The AU: legal and institutional framework. A manual on the pan-African organization. Martinus Nijhoff Pub, Leiden

Part II
Asia

Chapter 3
Equality and the Right to Health:
A Preliminary Assessment of China

Shengnan Qiu

Abstract In relation to the right to health, formal inequality and discrimination based on gender, race and certain other grounds are prohibited by law in China. Nevertheless, unequal access to health care between individuals and socio-economic groups are the result of discriminatory policies embedded in Chinese society and exacerbated by the transition from a centrally planned economy to a market economy. The current health system is not based on the principles of equality and equity, and therefore it is not designed to address the disadvantages experienced by some vulnerable groups. This contribution reviews Chinese concepts of equality; examines the legislative protection of healthcare equality in the country; explains the current health schemes, under the Hukou system; and explores uneven economic development strategies that have led to unequal access to health care during the economic transitional period.

Contents

3.1	Introduction	98
3.2	Equality and the Right to Health	100
	3.2.1 International Debates	100
	3.2.2 International Treaties Ratified by China	103
	3.2.3 Chinese Concepts of Equality	103
3.3	Formal Health Equality in China	105
3.4	Substantive Health Equality in China	108
	3.4.1 Unequal Access to Health Care Caused by Current Health Schemes	108
	3.4.2 Health Inequalities Caused by Hukou	113
	3.4.3 Health Inequalities Caused by Uneven Economic Development	115
3.5	Conclusion	117
References		119

S. Qiu (✉)
University of Essex, Colchester, UK
e-mail: shengnan.qiu@gmail.com

B. Toebes et al. (eds.), *The Right to Health*, DOI: 10.1007/978-94-6265-014-5_3,
© T.M.C. ASSER PRESS and the authors 2014

3.1 Introduction

Two types of equality are implicated in the context of the right to health: formal equality and substantive equality.[1] Formal equality requires the removal of legal barriers to equality and includes the prohibition of direct discrimination. Substantive equality demands examination and remediation of social conditions that generate economic, social or other disparities.[2] The two concepts are not mutually exclusive; substantive inequalities can be the result of formal inequality (or direct discrimination) or indirect discrimination. For example, distributive policies without explicit non-discrimination provisions may fail to address the needs of sub-populations living in the economic and social conditions.

In relation to the right to health, Chinese law prohibits formal inequalities and discrimination based on gender, race and certain other grounds.[3] Despite this prohibition, health inequalities between socio-economic groups, as well as between individuals remain embedded in Chinese society. According to the Committee on Economic, Social and Cultural Rights (CESCR) in its General Comment 14, services related to health care and the determinants of health must be:

> [B]ased on the principle of equity, ensuring that these services, whether privately or publicly provided, are affordable for all, including socially disadvantaged groups. Equity demands that poorer households should not be disproportionately burdened with health expenses as compared to richer households.[4]

The current Chinese health system is not based on the principles of equality or equity and therefore is not adequately designed to promote the achievement of substantive equality or redress disadvantages that contribute to ill health; rather, it serves to deepen the existing disadvantages experienced by some vulnerable groups that lead to health disparities.

The failure of the health system to address the needs of vulnerable members of society stems from economic reform policies that began in the late 1970s. After Deng Xiaoping's inaugural speech at the Third Plenary Session of the Communist Party in 1978, China began a program of economic reform in which public ownership and collectivism—crucial to the centrally planned economy—were abandoned in favour of a market-driven approach.[5] The government paid great attention to economic development during this process, whilst neglecting the

---

[1] Hunt 1996, p. 88.

[2] Fredman 2010, p. 291.

[3] See: The Constitution of the People's Republic of China 1982 (adopted at the 5th Session of the 5th National People's Congress and promulgated for implementation by the proclamation of the National People's Congress on 4 December 1982; amendments have been made on 12 April 1988, 29 March 1993, 15 March 1999, and 14 March 2004), Articles 21, 26, 36, 42, 44 and 45.

[4] General Comment 14, UN Doc E/C.12/2000/4, 11 August 2000, para 12.

[5] Zou 2008, pp. 1–10.

detrimental consequences that this particular model of development would have on the availability and accessibility of health care throughout the country.

The greatest impact of this change has been felt in rural areas. Along with the collapse of the collective agricultural system and the resulting migration of large numbers of people from rural areas to urban centres, has been the relocation of healthcare facilities and health professionals from rural areas to more densely populated cities. In addition to its deleterious effects on the availability of healthcare services in rural areas, the economic transition has impacted the economic accessibility of health care for rural populations: The move to a market-based economy has meant that most people in rural areas now have to pay their own total health expenditure unless they have private health insurance. As private health insurance plans were immature and lacking regulatory oversight when the transition began, most people chose not to pay for insurance.

The new household expense on health care made it inaccessible for many who live in poverty. For others living on the cusp of poverty, the cost of treating an unexpected illness contributed to their impoverishment. For example, it is estimated that 30 % of people living below the official poverty line become impoverished *because* of the costs associated with suffering from serious illness.[6] When a family's financial resources are directed toward medical costs, illness can impact the quality of life for the entire family, not only the person who is ill. For example, using resources earmarked for children's education to cover medical costs can result in depriving children of the opportunity to go to school.[7] Education, being a determinant of health,[8] is a means through which enabling conditions for achieving health and wellbeing are established. Thus the financial burden of illness contributes to the circle of poverty for families left without some form of health insurance.

The transition to a market economy involved the conversion of state-owned enterprises into private-owned enterprises. Because employers played an important role in the accessibility of health care, through the provision of insurance to employees, when ownership models changed, so too did responsibilities for healthcare insurance provision. Although there was no legal obligation for the new privately owned enterprises to provide healthcare insurance, there was an expectation on the part of the State that they would.[9] The perceived responsibility for providing insurance for health care, shifted from the State (as the employer) to the new owners of the enterprises. This meant that alongside the new challenges of competing in the free market, newly privatized enterprises had to also find a way to supply health insurance to employees. As a result, profitable enterprises could

---

[6] World Bank 1993.

[7] Although the government provides 12-year tuition-fee free education, students' parents have to pay for other expenses, such as, books and food, which can be a heavy burden on students' families.

[8] General Comment 14, UN Doc E/C.12/2000/4, 11 August 2000.

[9] There was a moral imperative for them to do so. See: Zuo 2008, pp. 285–299.

provide health insurance to employees, but those with little or no profits were either unable or unwilling to fulfil this responsibility.[10] A situation has therefore emerged where employees of enterprises that have remained state-owned have the benefit of healthcare insurance while only some people working in the private sector have the benefit of health insurance paid for by their employers. For example, a 1992 survey conducted in 22 cities, and which included 406 enterprises and 5,920 workers, showed that employees of state-owned enterprises were 23.6 times more likely than employees of private enterprises to have health insurance.[11] Thus, for many individuals, financial access to healthcare services was restricted as a result of their employment status.

This chapter aims to assess the extent to which the principle of equality has been embedded in the implementation of the right to health in China since the 1978 economic reforms. First, it briefly reviews international debates on equality and the right to health. Human rights treaties ratified by China and Chinese concepts of equality lay the foundation for this discussion. It then examines formal and substantive health equality. Formal equality is assessed by focusing on Chinese legislation related to the right to health, while substantive equality is discussed in terms of four dimensions of the enjoyment of the right to health in China: current health insurance provision; the effect of one's *Hukou* or residency status; the unequal distribution of healthcare services throughout the country; and uneven economic development strategies that have exacerbated health inequalities during the economic transitional period. A conclusion that there is little opportunity for correction of health inequalities in China follows at the end.

3.2 Equality and the Right to Health

3.2.1 International Debates

As a human rights principle, equality is often combined with non-discrimination to prohibit unjustifiable and differential treatment on grounds such as gender, race or other status.[12] Discrimination based on status may be corrected through the adoption of a rights-based approach.[13] Not only must legislation and policies comply with the principle of equality, administrative measures should also be

---

[10] Hsiao 1995.

[11] Hu et al. 1999.

[12] See: Articles 2, 3, 26 of the International Covenant on Civil and Political Rights, Articles 2, 12 of the International Covenant on Economic, Social and Cultural Rights, Articles 1 and 4 of the Convention to the Elimination of All Forms of Discrimination Against Women, Articles 2, 24 of the Convention on the Rights of the Child, General Comment No 14, etc.

[13] The term 'rights-based approach' is used widely by practitioners to refer to the application of human rights norms to practice. See: Fredman 2010.

adopted to guarantee the equal enjoyment of rights, including the right to health. Where economic, social and cultural rights are concerned, positive measures by the government are often required to achieve equal distribution of resources and enjoyment of rights. Thus, two types of equality are implicated in the context of the right to health: formal equality and substantive equality.[14] To be rights compliant, policies and strategies made by governments must adhere to the principle of equality from both perspectives. Considering this, substantive inequalities are often corrected through non-judicial mechanisms, such as political and administrative accountability mechanisms,[15] resource re-allocation, and addressing the social and economic determinants of health.

Through interpretation in UN documents and practice, the meaning of equality and non-discrimination is clarified, with some treaties sharing a common understanding of the concepts. For example, the definition of equality presented in Article 1 of the Convention on the Elimination of All Forms of Discrimination Against Women (CEDAW) was adopted by CESCR when discussing discrimination against women in its General Comment 16.[16] According to the normative understanding of equality, legislation and policies must not be discriminatory in nature, and they must also avoid resulting in discriminatory effects. Besides respecting formal equality, international human rights instruments embrace substantive equality by imposing duties on State parties to remove obstacles that lead to unequal enjoyment of the right to health, such as Article 12 of the CEDAW.

Although the ICESCR anticipates the progressive realization of the rights outlined therein, some obligations under the ICESCR are considered to have immediate effect, particularly non-discrimination and equal treatment.[17] Article 2(2) of the ICESCR proscribes discrimination of any kind based on race, color, gender, language, religion, political or other opinion, national or social origin, property, birth or other status. This is considered by the CESCR to apply in relation to access to health care and the underlying determinants of health.[18] The CESCR, in its General Comment 14 on the right to health, stresses that measures designed to eliminate health-related discrimination can be adopted even where there are severe resource constraints, such as through 'the adoption, modification or abrogation of legislation or the dissemination of information'.[19] States parties therefore have immediate obligations to guarantee that the right to health will be pursued without discrimination of any kind, either *de jure* or *de facto*.[20] In addition, states parties

---

[14] Hunt 1996, p. 88.

[15] Potts 2008.

[16] The Convention to the Elimination of All Forms of Discrimination Against Women (adopted in 1979 by the United Nations General Assembly); the General Comment 16, UN Document E/C.12/2005/4, CESCR, para 11.

[17] The International Covenant on Economic, Social and Cultural Rights (adopted in 1966 by the United Nations General Assembly), Article 2(1).

[18] General Comment No. 14, UN Doc E/C.12/2000/4, 11 August 2000.

[19] Ibid, para 18.

[20] Ibid; UN Doc A/61/338 (13 September 2006).

must ensure the equitable distribution of all health facilities, goods and services and that these resources are allocated in an appropriate way, whether privately or publicly funded.[21] This means that healthcare services, as well as services related to the underlying determinants of health, should be equally available and affordable for all regardless of how the healthcare system is organized. Participation, especially by vulnerable populations, is key to accessibility; when disadvantaged groups are able to participate in developing policies and programmes that affect them, inequalities can be reduced.

However, it needs to be pointed out that equality does not necessarily call for equal treatment; in fact, certain circumstances or conditions may require different treatment. Women, for example, may require additional care during maternity, while infants may require more care than a full-grown adult. What is more, discrimination against women is often intertwined with discrimination on other grounds, such as race, colour, language, religion, political or other opinion, national or social origin, property, birth or other status, which requires greater awareness on behalf of those who create policy and deliver health care that is accessible and acceptable. That is, different or special services and programmes may need to extend beyond immediately obvious circumstances or conditions to address the ways in which grounds for discrimination may intersect to amplify disadvantage. For example, according to the CESCR, as a vulnerable group, women might be prioritized in terms of the provision and distribution of aid and resources in times of internal or international armed conflicts.[22]

CEDAW specifically prohibits discrimination in Article 1. The proscription encompasses the notion of 'effect or purpose'. The word 'effect' includes indirect discrimination resulting from an action that may not be intentionally discriminatory and if the purpose of a distinction, exclusion or restriction is to impair or nullify women's rights, it is discriminatory.[23] Thus, the term 'equality' in CEDAW extends to substantive equality. This is further confirmed by CEDAW Article 4(1), which calls for 'temporary special measures aimed at accelerating *de facto* equality between men and women'.[24] CEDAW Article 2 also refers to 'the principle of equality of men and women',[25] while Article 12 emphasizes equal access to health facilities, and goods and services between men and women.[26] International health organs, such as the World Health Organization, also consider health equality as an important aim of health systems.[27]

---

[21] Ibid.

[22] General Comment 14, UN Doc E/C.12/2000/4, 11 August 2000, para 40.

[23] CEDAW, Article 1.

[24] Ibid, Article 4(1).

[25] Ibid, Article 2.

[26] Ibid, Article 12.

[27] See: WHO 2000.

3 Equality and the Right to Health: A Preliminary Assessment of China   103

3.2.2 *International Treaties Ratified by China*

China has ratified human rights treaties embracing equality and non-discrimination, including CEDAW, the International Covenant on Civil and Political Rights (IC-PR), ICESCR and the Convention on the Rights of the Child (CRC).[28] As China has adopted a monist system with regard to international law,[29] international treaties, if ratified or acceded to, will automatically have the same legal effect within China as national laws.[30] Further incorporation into national law is unnecessary, as a ratified international treaty can be directly applied in domestic courts. However, in practice, due to legal and political implications, courts are hesitant to refer to international treaties when making decisions. As a result, the right to health under international law is not yet effectively justiciable in Chinese courts.

Notwithstanding this hesitancy, the right to equality has been recognized as one of the basic legal rights held by Chinese citizens.[31] The government has stated its aim to achieve a 'harmonious society'; with equality being a key component of this goal,[32] it could provide political impetus toward the equal treatment of individuals across the country. Although Article 3 of the Constitution adopts the terminology 'equality before the law', conceptions of equality transcend equality before the courts. For example, equality before the law is now considered to include, *inter alia*, the equal enjoyment of every right stipulated by law; equality between men and women; and equality between socio-economic groups.[33] However, before examining formal equality and substantive equality in relation to the right to health in the Chinese context, Chinese concepts of equality will be briefly introduced.

3.2.3 *Chinese Concepts of Equality*

The concept of equality originally appeared in China as equality before the law.[34] In feudal societies there was an acknowledged informal agreement that individuals must be treated equally before the court, regardless of the class to which they

---

[28] The International Covenant on Civil and Political Rights (adopted in 1966 by the UN General Assembly resolution 2200A(XXI)); the Convention on the Rights of the Child (adopted in 1989 by UN General Assembly resolution 44/25).

[29] Mo 2002.

[30] Ibid.

[31] Many international human rights treaties share the endorsement of equality as a basic human rights principle. China ratified the ICESCR in 2001, the Convention on the Rights of the Child in 1992, and CEDAW in 1980.

[32] The idea of 'harmonious society' was raised at the Sixteenth General Meeting of the Chinese Communist Party. It contains: democracy and rule of law, equality and justice, trust and friendship, activity, stability and order. See: Hu 2005.

[33] Li 2005.

[34] Zhang 2007, p. 2.

belonged. This may have been more self-serving than altruistic, as equal access to justice was a desirable social norm and ensuring it served to garner respect for, and therefore strengthen, the ruling power. In reality, however, equality before the law in feudal societies had its limitations. A famous case during the Song Dynasty (AD 960–1279) exemplifies the limits of equality where high ranking members of society are involved: the emperor was found guilty of a crime and to show that he must be punished as others would be, while being mindful of his dignity as an emperor at the same time, Judge Bao's sentence was that the robe of emperor be beaten as symbolic punishment for his crime.[35] One can conclude from this that the law itself applied equally to all, even if the punishment was reduced for some. However, this would not satisfy the concept of equality in modern society.

The modern conception of equality was introduced in China in the nineteenth century when people were encouraged to critique feudal society.[36] It was not until 1912 that the equality principle was legally formalised through Article 5 of the *Provisional Constitution of the Republic of China,* which stipulated that 'Citizens of the Republic of China are equal, with no differences of race, class and religion'.[37] This article represented the first codification of equality in Chinese history. However, as the Republic government was unstable, the *Provisional Constitution* had little influence on practice.[38] Furthermore, when the PRC was founded in 1949, although it embraced the idea that individuals from all social classes and groups must equally enjoy social benefits without any distinction, initial studies on equality focused mainly on economic equality under socialist rule as political preference tends to influence the direction of academic research in China.[39] It is only recently that there has been a move towards Western conceptions of equality, such as those reflected in the writings of scholars such as Rawls, Dworkin, Sen and others that have emerged in China.[40] In addition, there was no significant development in Chinese conceptions of equality, and academic voices had, and still have, little influence on the government's decision-making process. Thus, the principle of equality has little reflection in health resource allocation and related policies.

---

[35] The Song Dynasty lasted from 960 to 1127; the case happened in 1025 and it has been written as a famous Chinese opera to praise 'being equal before the law'.

[36] Rousseau's *The Social Contract,* Montesquieu's *The Spirit of the Laws,* and Spencer's *Principles of Sociology,* were translated into Chinese around this time. Meanwhile, scholars who had studied abroad played important roles in introducing the modern concept of equality. They are: Kang Youwei, Liang Qichao, Lu Xun, Chen Duxiu, Tan Sitong, ShenJiaben, etc.

[37] The Provisional Constitution of the Republic of China, adopted on 11 March 1912. The ruling of the Republic of China was replaced by the People's Republic of China in 1949. The People's Republic of China had its own Constitution after it was founded.

[38] The Republic government was set up by the Nationalist Party in 1911.

[39] For example, Zhang 2007, Liu 2010.

[40] See: Yang 2001, Wang 2010a, b.

3.3 Formal Health Equality in China

As noted previously, an important role of legislation in realizing the right to health is to remove barriers to access through the prohibition of discrimination based on certain grounds. Existing inequalities can be addressed through an individual rights-based approach, and enforced through judicial procedures.[41]

The principle of equality was emphasized in the *Constitution 1982*. Article 4 stipulates that all nationalities are equal and Article 33 stipulates that all citizens are equal before the law. However, as a constitutional right, the right to be treated equally was not invoked in litigation until 2002. The reason for this may have been the reluctance of any court to be the first to accept such equality cases. However, in 2002, a Mr. Jiang sued the Chengdu Branch of the People's Bank of China[42] on grounds that the recruiting advertisement for a position at the bank contained discriminatory terms relating to a candidate's height.[43] When considering the case, Chengdu Wuhou of the Primary People's Court did not address the case as a constitutional one. Rather, the Court found that according to the *Banking Law of the People's Republic of China*, the recruiting activities of the Chengdu Branch were not part of its financial functions and therefore not specific administrative activities. As the Court found that the Chengdu Branch of the People's Bank of China had edited its advertisement, the case was thereby withdrawn. Mr. Jiang's case was the first to claim the right to be treated equally in China, in this case with regard to employment. Although it was not in reference to the right to health, the case illustrates the court's hesitation to decide on equality as a constitutional right. In some circumstances, the constitutional right itself might not be directly invoked in litigation, even where equality is an issue. Although unequal treatment is prohibited in the Constitution, there has been no case regarding health equality claimed in Chinese courts.

---

[41] See: Fredman 2010.

[42] The People's Bank of People's Republic of China is not a commercial bank, but a financial organ owned by the government which regulates primary financial activities in China's financial market.

[43] One of the basic requirements for male bank employee was that the candidate's height must be over 168 cm. Mr. Jiang claimed that the action of the Chengdu Branch of the People's Bank violated Article 33 of the *Constitution* relating to the equality of citizens before the law. In addition, since the People's Bank is not a commercial bank but a bank owned by the state which carries out financial functions, Mr. Jiang also claimed the height requirement in the recruiting advertisement violated his right to work in governmental organizations. After having been aware of the action by Mr. Jiang, the Chengdu Branch of the People's Bank deleted the height requirement in its recruiting advertisement. Before Mr. Jiang's case, discriminatory requirements related to height, gender, and age among other things were often set out in recruiting advertisements. However following that case, requirements on height gradually disappeared in recruiting advertisements, even though the first case challenging the issue was deemed inadmissible in legal practice. However, discrimination on gender and age still exists today, even with regard to governmental recruitment. Case details available at http://www.people.com.cn/GB/shehui/46/20020129/657782.html. Accessed 12 October 2012.

Due to lack of implementation of constitutional rights, in practice equality rights are more likely to be claimed under other legislation. Besides prohibiting direct discrimination against vulnerable groups, laws seek to prevent substantive inequalities that might result from varying differences in socio-economic conditions. This reflects the philosophy of equality that proposes that a just society should ensure that individuals have equal opportunities, including opportunities to attain their highest standard of health. The following statutes are not exhaustive but offer examples that endeavor to promote and protect equality for all. They outline the government's positive duties to eliminate pre-existing conditions that may cause substantive health inequalities as well as prohibit formal health inequalities.

Article 3 of the *Law on the Protection of Disabled Persons of the People's Republic of China* stipulates that people with disabilities shall enjoy equal rights with other citizens in political, economic, social, cultural and family life.[44] Article 4 further requires the state to give special assistance to eliminate the barriers people with disabilities face in enjoying other legal rights.[45] As economic independence is often a precondition for people to enjoy other social benefits, as well as the determinants of health, there are also policies to encourage employers to provide work opportunities to people with disabilities. In turn, people benefiting from these policies may have a more opportunities to achieve their highest attainable level of health.

Article 2 of *the Law on the Protection of Women of the People's Republic of China* emphasizes that women enjoy equal rights with men in political, economic, cultural, social and family life and other areas. Realizing equality between women and men is one of the basic national policies. The state is required to take necessary measures to progressively improve the protection of women's rights and interests in order to eliminate all forms of discrimination. Specifically, abuse, abandonment and mutilation of women are prohibited.[46] Article 25 stipulates that employers must provide female employees with a safe and suitable working environment and provide pre- and post-natal care when necessary.[47] Article 26 further emphasizes the need to guarantee the legal rights and interests of female employees during the prenatal period.[48] Article 27 requires that the state develop social insurance, social assistance, and health care to provide support to women

---

[44] The Law on the Protection of Disabled Persons of the People's Republic of China (adopted at the 17th meeting of the Standing Committee of the 7th National People's Congress on 28 December 1990, amended 24 April 2008, entered into force 1 July 2008).

[45] Ibid.

[46] The Law on the Protection of Women of the People's Republic of China (adopted at the 17th meeting of the Standing Committee of the 10th National People's Congress on 28 August 2005, entered into force 1 December 2005).

[47] Ibid. As mentioned earlier, economic reforms left many uncovered by health insurance and women were no exception. As economic reforms started in late 1970s, while the Law on the Protection of Women entered into force in 2005, women were not protected by this article during the economic transitional period.

[48] Ibid.

who are elderly, ill, or incapable of working.[49] The law thus seeks to remove barriers to women's enjoyment of social rights, including their health-related rights. However, in reality, women experience barriers to the determinants of health; for example, women have fewer work opportunities than men. Gender was once a legitimate ground for discrimination in employment recruitment, even for government positions and this was not removed until 2008 when the *Law on Labor Contracts* entered into force. Moreover, the *Law on Labor Contract* also stipulates that marriage and reproductive plans of employees should not create restrictions for women in labor contracts.

The right to health also contains an entitlement to participation for individuals and communities with regard to all health-related decision-making, including setting priorities, making decisions, planning, implementing and evaluating strategies, which may affect their development.[50] Through participation and accountability, those in charge of resource distribution or planning must justify their actions to the public or else adopt other strategies or policies that satisfy the public. The principle of participation and accountability can be practiced through democratic elections. In China, according to the *Election Law,* each citizen over 18 has the right to vote and to run for office. By allowing these political rights, individuals are able to participate in the decision-making process equally, which is of crucial importance to promoting good governance, and in turn, health policy development and health resource distribution. However, in practice, in the National People's Congress, each representative from rural areas represents a constituency with three times the population of constituencies in urban areas. Furthermore, the ratio of representatives from rural areas to urban areas is unbalanced in the National People's Congress; representatives from rural areas hold significantly fewer seats than representatives from urban areas.[51] Therefore, in reality, people from rural areas are not equally represented, which may lead to uneven resource distribution.

It is thus observed that Chinese legislation protects status-based formal equality and imposes duties on the government to take positive measures to promote substantive equality to some extent. Despite attention to vulnerable socio-economic groups, such as people with disabilities, the elderly, minority nationalities and women, the existing legislation neglects groups with diseases such as HIV/AIDS and Hepatitis B.[52] At times, diseases become barriers for individuals to receive education or gain employment—important determinants of health. This can in turn lead to economic barriers to health care, particularly when medicines are paid for out-of-pocket.

---

[49] Ibid.

[50] UN Doc, E/CN.4/2005/51 (2 February 2005) paras 59–61; Yamin 2009.

[51] This situation remained unchanged until 2012.

[52] Zhou 2007.

3.4 Substantive Health Equality in China

Although laws prohibit direct discrimination, significant health inequalities between sub-populations result from the uneven distribution of resources, including health resources, in China. Health inequalities are caused and perpetuated by the different health schemes under the *Hukou* system, inequitable development strategies, and social and environmental factors. The existence of different health schemes leads to unequal access to health-related services, goods and other resources. These health schemes are not created with the goal of redressing disadvantages; on the contrary, they perpetuate the existing disadvantages experienced by some individuals and groups.

The *Hukou* system is an obstacle to accessing health care and related goods and services for some segments of the population. Uneven development strategies lead to inequalities in terms of the availability and accessibility of health resources throughout the country. A controversial consequence of China's recent economic reforms is the uneven distribution of wealth. In 1982, Deng Xiaoping made this remark about China's development strategy: 'let some people and some areas get wealthy first, and let wealthier people and areas assist others to get wealthy in the future'.[53] Under such a strategy, often referred to as the "trickle down" approach to development, economic policies paid closer attention to efficiency than to equality. As a result, some became wealthy, but there were no policies obligating the wealthy to contribute to services that would also benefit low income or impoverished citizens. Nor were there policies in place to redistribute wealth. Thus, the development strategy articulated by Deng Xiaoping does not ensure that the public enjoys the benefits of development equally.

3.4.1 Unequal Access to Health Care Caused by Current Health Schemes

In July 2005, the Development Research Centre of the State Council (the DRCSC) of China published a series of reports, which assessed the performance of the health system. The reports reviewed the health reforms since 1978 that have been subject to the goals of economic reform, and reached the conclusion that having health reforms subject to economic reform has proven to be unsuccessful.[54] To further scrutinize the failure, the report recognized that the nature of the health service is such that it should be seen as a public good rather than a commercialized good.[55] Although it is possible that the commercialized service model can push health service suppliers to provide better services as a result of competition, the

---

[53] Deng 1993, p. 111.

[54] Ibid, p. 4.

[55] Ibid, p. 6.

3 Equality and the Right to Health: A Preliminary Assessment of China

problem is that equal access to health services may not be ensured in a free competitive market without strong policies in place to protect vulnerable populations. The government cannot discharge its obligations regarding health by simply sending health services out into a free market.

The report also recognized that China's social sector was lagging behind the country's rapid economic growth.[56] As a strategy to stimulate local government to expand production and increase income, the central government introduced a financial responsibility system, which divides revenue and expenditure between central and local government. Local government was allowed to keep increased revenue after handing in a fixed amount to the central government.[57] At the same time, however, the central government imposed no social obligations on local government. As a result, there was no imperative or incentive for local government to contribute financially to the health sector. Health financing was allocated primarily through local budgets, and therefore declined to varying degrees across the country, in some cases, dramatically.[58] Healthcare schemes should therefore not simply rely on the market but demand the government's intervention and subsidy.[59] Notably the report failed to point out the lack of overall governmental accountability, as well as the lack of internal monitoring within the health system. The rising inequality in access to health care undermines the government's professed commitment to a harmonious society, which was specifically identified as a national priority at the Sixth Plenary Sessions of the Communist Party's Central Committee in 2006 (immediately after the official publication by the government of its assessment of its performance on healthcare reform).[60] Furthermore, the government has committed itself to achieving universal health coverage by 2020.[61] At the practical level, various health schemes have been explored and implemented since 2006. However, the reformed health system shows little evidence that health resources are distributed with consideration to promoting equal access for vulnerable groups. The new health system contains the following four public health schemes apart from private health insurance.

(a) The Urban Labour Medical Insurance Scheme (ULMIS)

The ULMIS was evaluated long before an assessment report was issued in 2005; the government began a pilot programme in Jiujiang and Zhenjiang to look at the feasibility of a new medical scheme for urban labourers in 1994. A number of issues were considered at that time: how to balance the payment

---

[56] Development Research Centre of the State Council of the People's Republic of China 2005, p. 25.

[57] The State Council Document 1979 No. 176.

[58] Development Research Centre of the State Council of the People's Republic of China 2005, p. 26.

[59] Development Research Centre of the State Council of the People's Republic of China 2005, p. 27.

[60] See: http://www.gov.cn/ztzl/ygzt/. Accessed 12 October 2012.

[61] Ibid.

responsibilities of the premium between employers and employees; how to manage a social pooling account of health care and a personal healthcare account; which diseases to cover and to what extent medical expenses should be reimbursable; and what payment system should be adopted to supervise healthcare provider's delivery of quality health services.[62] Another 40 cities joined the pilot programme by 1996 and the ULMIS was formally adopted in 1998.[63] The scheme consists of a pooled fund for inpatient stays and individual medical savings accounts for outpatient visits. The basic health scheme is financed by employment taxes paid by employers and employees.[64] Government revenue does not contribute to this scheme. Under the ULMIS, individuals receive 50–80 % reimbursement for their medical costs.[65] By the end of 2009, the number of people who had joined the ULMIS had reached 219 million.[66] The ULMIS has gradually been extended to also cover immigrant labourers moving from rural areas to urban areas.[67]

(b) The Urban Resident Medical Insurance Scheme (the URMIS)

Urban residents here refers to individuals who live in urban areas but are unemployed or self-employed. These residents often include children, students, and the disabled population among others. Some individuals within this group once had their health care needs covered by identifying as dependents of family members who were employed. However, after the economic reform they were excluded from their previous healthcare schemes, even if they represent vulnerable groups with particular healthcare requirements. The *Guidance on the pilot medical scheme for urban residents by the State Council* (*the Guidance*) was issued in 2007.[68] In February 2008, the government announced a subsidy of at least 40 Yuan (approximately 4 British Pounds) to each uninsured urban resident as assistance towards insurance premiums. The pilot scheme started in 79 selected cities that had an above average development level and was extended to cover over half of urban residents by 2009. Population coverage increased from 42 million in 2007 to

---

[62] Hou and Ye 1998, pp. 65–84.

[63] Ibid.

[64] Hu 2008.

[65] The specific rate of reimbursement that individuals receive is subject to the level of medical institutions and hospitals they choose. The lower level of medical institutions they choose the higher reimbursement rate they receive. This is to encourage individuals to start from a lower level of medical institutions.

[66] Wang 2007.

[67] People who work in urban areas but are registered in rural areas with rural Hukou have been left out of any health scheme for a long period. A large amount of migration labours created a large 'floating population'. By 2004, the Chinese Ministry of Agriculture estimated that the number of such migrant labourers is over 100 million; see: http://www.agri.gov.cn/. Accessed 12 October 2012.

[68] The State Council Documents, GuoFa 2007 No. 20; See: Gordon et al. 2002, Ho 1995.

3 Equality and the Right to Health: A Preliminary Assessment of China

181 million by the end of 2009. However, the URMIS is only available to citizens who hold urban *Hukou*.[69]

(c) The New Rural Cooperative Medical Insurance Scheme (the NRCMIS)

The rural population accounts for 80 % of the whole population in China. The previous rural cooperation health scheme was built upon the organization of production teams. When production teams disappeared, the rural cooperation health scheme disappeared accordingly.[70] As a result, for over 25 years people living in rural areas had difficulty in accessing health services and medicines.[71]

In response, the NRCMIS was launched in 2002 on a pilot basis. It was originally funded by a government subsidy of approximately 20 yuan (approximately 2 pounds) per person per year, with a further required annual contribution of 10 yuan (approximately 1 pound) per member per year. However, the NRCMIS only covers inpatient care and the reimbursement rate is low.[72] By 2006, the pilot coverage had extended to 41 % of the population living in rural areas. Although some scholars criticized the system's voluntary nature and suggested that it was financially vulnerable due to under-funding,[73] it was approved by the State Council. The NRCMIS became operational nationally in 2007. In 2009, 200 billion RMB (approximately 20 billion pounds) was invested in health centres and facilities at the county level, which encompasses 5,689 centres across the nation. By the end of 2009, 833 million individuals living in rural areas had joined the NRCMIS.[74] However, as the NRCMIS is a voluntary scheme, many people choose not to participate. Furthermore, as with the URMIS, the NRCMIS is restricted to individuals who hold rural *Hukou* only. Its effectiveness in reducing out-of-pocket medical expenditure and impoverishment caused by long-term medical expenses is therefore doubted.

(d) The Government Medical Insurance Scheme (the GMIS)

Government employees are a special group in China.[75] They enjoy social benefits, such as health care and pension, above any other employment group. The GMIS, which covers government current and retired employees, schoolteachers and university students, has not undergone the same type of reforms that the other schemes have. It is financed by the government budget

---

[69] The Hukou system is a special population administrative system in China.

[70] Huang 1988, Feng et al. 1995.

[71] Li 2007, also see: Liu et al. 1995, Gu et al. 1993.

[72] The reimbursement of the NRCMS varies in different provinces. At the time of writing, the highest rate is 80 %, in Shandong Province.

[73] Ramesh and Wu 2009, see also, Wagstaff et al. 2007, Yip and Hsiao 2009, Liu 2004.

[74] China Health Statistics Yearbook 2010.

[75] As government employees enjoy so many priorities, being employed by the government is often called 'eating from the emperor's barn'.

and the beneficiaries do not need to contribute any premiums.[76] Government employees are able to get 90 % reimbursement of their health costs. This is the highest reimbursement rate available through any healthcare scheme. A report from the China Social Science Institute discovered that in 2006, 80 % of the government's health expenditure was spent on government employees.[77] The GMIS has posed a huge burden on the government's health budget, which is controversial considering the fact that the government contributes more to this scheme than others.[78] Recognizing this, in 2009, government began experimenting with its employees in Beijing by converting their health scheme from the GMIS into the ULMIS.[79] As this conversion is still at the experimental stage, it has not been officially confirmed whether or not the transition will be undertaken nationwide.

3.4.1.1 Concluding Remarks

In recent years, the government has made rapid progress on improving the coverage of health insurance schemes. The coverage rate for the whole population has dramatically increased from less than 20 % in the late 1990s to almost 95 % in 2011.[80] However, broad coverage is not the only goal of a health system; equal access to health resources is also imperative to the right to health. There are four parallel public health schemes currently in operation. The ULMIS, which relies on contributions from both employees and employers[81]; the URMIS, which receives contributions from the government and the insured[82]; the NRCMS, which also relies on contributions from the government and the insured[83]; and the GMIS, which relies on contributions from the government only. The government therefore makes different contributions to each scheme and the reimbursement rate of medical costs varies across different schemes, which leads to different levels of economic access to health benefits. This is particularly troubling because the health scheme to which one has access is determined by occupational and other status, and has little to do with the actual needs of the individual. In this light, consideration for equality and equity is lacking in the practical implementation of health schemes cross the country. As it can be seen that health schemes are distinguished by urban and rural residence status, the *Hukou* system deserves a close examination.

---

[76] Gail et al. 1995.

[77] Ibid.

[78] Dong 2010.

[79] Jinghua Times, An Experimental Reform on Government's Employees' Health Scheme 2009.

[80] China Daily 2011.

[81] Decisions on the Establishment of the Urban Labour Medical Insurance Scheme 2005.

[82] Guidelines on the Pilot Urban Resident Medical Insurance Scheme, the State Council 2007 No. 20.

[83] Guidelines on the Establishment of the New Rural Cooperative Medical Scheme 2008.

3.4.2 Health Inequalities Caused by Hukou

Since China was founded in 1949, every citizen of China has been required to register their place of official residence—where they were born (*Hukou*)—for the purpose of administration. The *Regulation on Citizen Registration of the People's Republic of China* of 1958 distinguished between residents living in urban areas and those living in rural areas. The *Hukou* registration record officially identifies an individual as a resident of a specific area and includes information such as name, date of birth, marriage status. The enjoyment of social benefits, including health benefits, depends on the type of *Hukou* one holds. Citizens have no freedom to choose their *Hukou*[84] and are divided into two categories: citizens registered in urban areas with urban *Hukou* and citizens registered in rural areas with rural *Hukou*. During the planned economy period in China, *Hukou* functioned as a form of identity necessary for individuals to work and also to enjoy health benefits.[85] Individuals with urban *Hukou* were generally covered by health schemes for the urban population while individuals with rural *Hukou* were covered by health schemes for the rural population.[86] Registered residency was the first entrance requirement for accessing health care. More specifically, if a person was registered to live in city A, he or she could only access primary health care in city A and not in any other city.[87] Nevertheless, as the whole country operated under a centrally planned system, although individuals were covered by different health schemes, the level of enjoyment of health benefits with both types of *Hukou* was roughly the same.[88] However, after the economic reform of 1978, health schemes based on the previous economic structure collapsed and the new health schemes that emerged provide differing levels of access to health benefits. The level of health benefits one enjoys depends on the health scheme under which one is covered.

Due to the high demand for laborers during the rapid economic development in urban areas, since the 1980s a great number of individuals from rural areas migrated to urban areas to live and work. As *Hukou* constitutes a certificate for social benefits, these individuals lose access to their social benefits once they leave their area of registration. There are policies in place, which permit individuals to temporarily live in urban areas without an official urban *Hukou*. However, a temporary residents permit is only proof of permission to stay, not a title for

---

[84] There are some circumstances in which one can change one's *Hukou* status. For example, rural *Hukou* can be transformed into urban *Hukou* if one passes the university entrance exam. This condition of transformation somehow implies that urban *Hukou* is a sort of award so that the urban *Hukou* has priority over the rural *Hokou*.

[85] See: Wang 2006.

[86] More specifically, as introduced previously, individuals with urban *Hukou* can join by the ULMIS, the URMIS or the GMIS; individuals with rural *Hukou* can only join the NRCMIS.

[87] This does not include emergency situations.

[88] Health care universally covered the whole population. Therefore, health care was available for everyone when needed.

qualifying as a beneficiary of the health scheme operating in that area. Most migrant workers are employed as 'temporary employees' and are neither covered by the ULMIS nor by the URMIS.[89] Meanwhile, as they do not live in rural areas and reimbursement is subject to the area in which one is registered, it is not convenient for them to join the NRCMIS from a long distance. As a result, migrant laborers have been left outside the health system. Furthermore, as they are mainly hired to work in physically demanding or precarious conditions, they represent vulnerable groups at high risk of being exposed to occupational dangers and disease threats.[90] By 2004, the Chinese Ministry of Agriculture estimated the number of migrant laborers to be over 100 million.[91] Their dependents face similar challenges when living with them in urban areas. They need to pay directly for health services—a huge burden when considering the paucity of their family incomes.[92] The situation therefore impairs the equal enjoyment of health benefits for this group based on their socio-economic position. As health is a crucial precondition for participating in other social activities, this further hinders the enjoyment of other rights and participation in society.

Although discrimination based on nationality, race, gender, and religion is prohibited by law, the law neglects discrimination based on *Hukou*. Yet *Hukou* greatly affects access to many opportunities and social benefits in China. Having an urban *Hukou* is sometimes required as a precondition for getting a permanent job in urban areas. Thus, unequal opportunities for gaining employment due to the restrictions imposed by one's *Hukou* may subsequently lead to inequality in the enjoyment of health benefits.

Economists argue that inequalities of this kind are inevitable during the process of economic development, as development 'does not start in every part of the economy at the same time'.[93] However, it is precisely because of this that the government has an obligation to remove pre-existing inequalities for individuals from various socio-economic backgrounds and address inequalities caused by uneven economic development. Although the *Hukou* system was originally designed for the purpose of administration, it has come to play more than just an administrative role, affecting the way that social resources are distributed and enjoyed. The fact that *Hukou* determines enjoyment of health entitlements is an infringement on the principle of equality, which is central to the right to health (Table 3.1 and Graph 3.1, Table 3.2 and Graph 3.2).

---

[89] The ULMIS has gradually extended to cover immigrant labours, but as it is on a voluntary basis, the coverage rate is low.

[90] Monda et al. 2007.

[91] Hu 2006.

[92] The high expenditure on health services may lead to less education opportunities for their children.

[93] See: Arthur 1954. This pattern is evidenced in the history of the U.S., with inequality rising during the rapid industrialization period from 1870 to 1920, and then declining thereafter.

3   Equality and the Right to Health: A Preliminary Assessment of China

Table 3.1 Number of beds by region in medical institutions in 2008[a]

	East	Middle	West	Total
Number of beds in medical institutions	1,704,780	1,250,431	1,081,272	4,036,483
Number of beds in hospitals and health centers	1,568,102	1,163,769	1,016,374	3,748,245
Beds per 1,000 population in medical institutions	3.47	2.79	2.83	3.05
Beds per 1,000 population in hospitals and health centers	3.2	2.59	2.66	2.84

[a] China Health Statistics Yearbook 2008

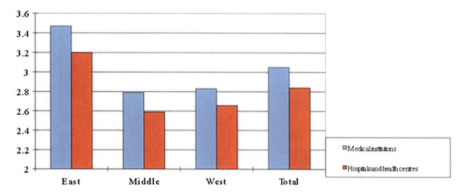

Graph 3.1 Beds per 1,000 population in China 2008

3.4.3 Health Inequalities Caused by Uneven Economic Development

Economic development is assumed to provide more possibilities for the advancement of social welfare benefits in the future. However, the principle of equality must not be neglected in this process. The economic development strategy for China since 1978 has been to allow some areas to be developed before others. It is precisely because of such discrepancies that the government has an obligation to protect vulnerable people and remove pre-existing inequalities.

Although China's economy has transformed from a planned to a market economy, some industries, such as those relating to natural resources, remain under the control of the central government. Provinces in the South and in the East have most rapidly developed because of preferential policies and the relative ease of securing convenient transportation.[94] As most hospitals have become self-funded since the economic reforms, health resources and advanced medical technologies became concentrated in wealthier areas.[95] This uneven distribution of

---

[94] Zhou 2007.
[95] Ramesh and Wu 2009.

Table 3.2 Number of health personnel by region in 2008[a]

	East	Middle	West	Total
Health personnel	22,39,598	15,52,799	12,37,641	50,30,038
Doctors	9,18,165	6,33,224	5,30,869	20,82,258
Nurses	7,64,436	5,00,017	3,88,844	16,53,297
Doctors per 1,000 population	1.87	1.41	1.39	1.58
Nurses per 1,000 population	1.56	1.11	1.02	1.25
Total personnel	27,54,381	19,15,224	14,99,445	61,69,050

[a] China Health Statistics Yearbook 2008

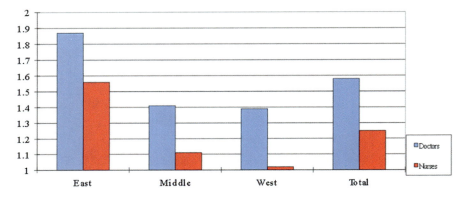

Graph 3.2 Health personnel per 1,000 population in China 2008

health resources has perpetuated inequalities in terms of availability and accessibility of quality health services between regions. This outcome is driven by profit chasing by the medical industry rather than as a consequence of national strategies. The strategy of prioritizing economic development indirectly leads to inequalities in terms of the enjoyment of health goods and services.

The tables above, published by the Ministry of Health of China, show imbalance in the regional distribution of health facilities and health personnel across the East, the middle, and the West of China.[96] This reflects the differences in accessibility of health services between regions.

In 2007, there were almost 30 % more beds per 1,000 people in medical institutions in the East than those in the middle of China and 30 % more than those in the West. As to health personnel, there were significantly more doctors in the East than

---

[96] The East includes provinces of Heilongjiang, Jilin, Liaoning, Beijing, Tianjin, Hebei, Shandong, Jiangsu, Shanghai, Zhejiang, Fujian, Guangdong, Hainan, Taiwan; the Middle includes Shanxi, Henan, Anhui, Hubei, Hunan, Jiangxi; the West includes Chongqing, Sichuan, Yunnan, Guizhou, Shaanxi, Qinghai, Gansu, Ningxia, Xizang, Guangxi, Neimeng.

3 Equality and the Right to Health: A Preliminary Assessment of China

in the middle and West of China. At the same time, however, the number of health personnel in the West was lower than that in the middle of the country. To some extent, this phenomenon demonstrates that although health facilities can be specifically allocated to some regions in accordance with national strategies and programmes, health personnel's mobility is driven by other factors, such as, working environment and potential opportunities for career development. Differences also exist in the quality of services available; hospitals in the East are equipped with more advanced medical technologies and facilities than those elsewhere in the country.

3.5 Conclusion

The right to health has been officially recognized by the government through its ratification of the ICESCR and other international human rights treaties, although these treaties have not yet been fully realized by society at large as a route to social justice. Nonetheless, the government considered the satisfaction of the population's health needs as one of its responsibilities even before it recognized the right to health as a human right. China once made great achievements in health care in spite of having less financial resources available than in the years immediately following the transition. However, along with the deconstruction of the planned economy in 1978, there was a corresponding deterioration of the health system. For a considerable period of time, 80 % of the population was left outside the entire healthcare system, despite rapid economic development during the same period. Acknowledging the situation, the government began pilot projects on health schemes for different groups, such as urban laborers, urban residents, and rural residents, and made substantial progress in healthcare provision. The government shows a willingness to achieve universal coverage of health care in the process of working toward a harmonious society. However, the fact that the government applies different health schemes to different groups based on pre-determined social conditions has impaired the equal enjoyment of health resources. According to a WHO report of 2000, the equality of access to health care in China was fourth from last, globally.[97]

In a special report published in 2005 examining the health and economic reforms since 1978, the Chinese government admitted the failure of its health reforms, including inequalities of accessing health care and medicines.[98] In October 2008, the government proposed a plan for building a new health

---

[97] World Health Organization 2000.

[98] Development Research Centre of the State Council of the People's Republic of China 2005, p. 26.

system, calling for comments from various sources.[99] The proposal emphasizes the willingness of the Chinese government to make efforts to ensure each citizen is covered by health schemes within the new health system. Nevertheless, it is based on goodwill initiatives and uses vague language to describe the targets of the new health system. As to how to achieve this goal and what measures to adopt, the proposal lacks significant detail. The proposal was therefore more of an expression of the government's attitude on health system reforms than a specific guideline that could be followed to achieve such reforms.[100] The government called for public participation through online comments regardless of the fact that less than half of the population has access to the Internet in China.[101] Thus, participation in the decision-making process was limited to a small segment of the population wealthy enough to have access to the Internet. Consequently, the majority of the population was effectively denied participation in this process.

In assessing the protection of the right to health in China, it has been shown that since 1978 rapid economic expansion has neglected the principles of equality and equity. Access to public health insurance is no longer guaranteed and differing levels of economic development across China have led to the unequal enjoyment of health care for many vulnerable individuals and groups. This is often closely linked to an individual's identity or profession. Thus, even though direct discrimination is expressly prohibited by legislation, many health inequalities can be attributed to national policies and strategies that have afforded a greater share of health resources to the fastest developing industrial regions. The right to health imposes obligations on the government to pay more attention to vulnerable individuals and groups in order to improve their conditions so as to enable them to enjoy their highest attainable standard of health. However, the on-going health reforms have not attempted to promote equity or eradicate the established discriminatory practice of *Hukou*, whereby a person's eligibility for social entitlements is linked to their registered residency status.

Different health schemes, *Hukou,* and uneven economic development all result in the breach of China's obligation make health care and health services accessible to all.[102] Regrettably, although General Comment 14 requires that judicial and other remedies should be available for such violations,[103] there is little opportunity for correction of inequalities caused by systematic and strategic reasons through existing accountability mechanisms in China.

---

[99] Opinions on China's healthcare system reforms 2008.

[100] It is an abstract policy to guide the direction rather than plan details on how to practice.

[101] China's Internet Development Report 2008.

[102] General Comment 14, paras 12, 18 and 19.

[103] General Comment 14, para 59.

References

Arthur LW (1954) Economic development with unlimited supplies of labour. Manchester Sch 22:139–191

China Daily (2011) The universal coverage of primary health care in China has reached 95 %. http://politics.people.com.cn/GB/1026/15092329.html. Accessed 25 Nov 2013

China Health Statistics Yearbook (2008) http://www.moh.gov.cn/publicfiles/business/htmlfiles/zwgkzt/ptjty/200805/35671.htm. Accessed 25 Nov 2013

China Health Statistics Yearbook (2010) www.moh.gov.cn/publicfiles/business/htmlfiles/zwgkzt/ptjnj/year2010/index2010.html. Accessed 19 Oct 2012

China's Internet Development Report (2008) http://download.xinhuanet.com/it/document/cnnic22.doc. Accessed 25 Nov 2013

Deng X (1993) Works of Deng Xiaoping, vol III. The Central Communist of China Editing Committee, Beijing

Development Research Centre of the State Council of the People's Republic of China (2005) Economic system reform and China's medical and health work: the economic, political and social context for changes in China's medical and health system. China Dev Rev 7(1):25–50

Dong D (2010) The Government health insurance scheme is a tumour of social equality and justice. Accessed 12–22 June 2012

Feng X et al (1995) Cooperative medical schemes in contemporary rural China. Sci Med 41(8):1111–1118

Fredman S (2010) Positive duties and socio-economic disadvantage: bringing disadvantage onto the equality agenda. Eur Hum Rights Law Rev 3:290–304

Gail H et al (1995) Distribution of medical insurance in China. Soc Sci Med 42(8):1119–1130

Gordon G et al (2002) Equity in health care access to: assessing the Urban health insurance reform in China. Soc Sci Med 55(10):1779–1794

Gu X et al (1993) Financing health care in rural China: preliminary report of a nationwide study. Soc Sci Med 36(4):385–391

Guidelines on the Pilot Urban Resident Medical Insurance Scheme, the State Council (2007) No. 20. www.gov.cn/zwgk/2007-07/24/content_695118.htm. Accessed 12 Sep 2012

Ho LS (1995) Market reforms and China's health care system. Soc Sci Med 41(8):1065–1072

Hou W, Ye Z (1998) The book of urban workers basic medical insurance system. China Yanshi Press, Beijing

Hsiao WC (1995) The Chinese health care system: lessons for other nations. Soc Sci Med 41(8):1047–1055

Hu J (2005) Building up a socialist harmonious society. News.xinhuanet.com/ziliao/2005-03/23/content_2732356.htm. Accessed 12 Sep 2012

Hu S (2006) Health care of the rural population in China. Sociology and anthropology China. www.sachina.edu.cn/Htmldata/article/2006/08/1173.html. Accessed 12 Sep 2012

Hu S (2008) Reform of how health care is paid for in China: challenges and opportunities. Lancet 372(9652):1846–1853

Hu T et al (1999) The effects of economic reform on health insurance and the financial burden for urban workers in China. Health Econ 8:309–321

Huang S (1988) Transforming China's collective health care system: a village study. Soc Sci Med 27(9):879–888

Hunt P (1996) Reclaiming social rights: international and comparative perspectives. Ashgate, Dartmouth

Li B (2005) Human rights law. High Education Press, Beijing

Li H (2007) A study on China's rural cooperative health system. Economy Science Press, Beijing

Liu Y (2004) Development of the rural health insurance system in China. Health Policy Plan 19(3):159–165

Liu Z (2010) Several theoretical questions of equal protection of rights. J Gansu Polit Sci Law Inst 108:1–8

Liu Y et al (1995) Transformation of China's rural health care financing. Soc Sci Med 41(8):1085–1093

Mo J (2002) Obligations under two covenants and China. World Econ Polit 8:15–28

Monda KL et al (2007) China's transition: the effect of rapid urbanization on adult occupational physical activity. Soc Sci Med 64(4):858–870

Opinions on China's Health Care System Reforms (2008). Accessed 25 Nov 2013

Potts H (2008) Accountability and the highest attainable standard of health. www.essex.ac.uk/hrc/research/projects/rth/docs/HRC_Accountability_Mar08.pdf. Accessed 15 Jan 2013

Ramesh M, Wu X (2009) Health policy reform in China: lessons from Asia. Soc Sci Med 68(12):2256–2262

The State Council Document (1979) No. 176. www.gov.cn/zwgk/index.htm. Accessed 12 Sep 2012

The State Council Documents GuoFa (2007) No. 20. www.gov.cn/zwgk/index.htm. Accessed 12 Sep 2012

Wang J (2010a) The principle of equality in Hobbes's concepts of natural rights. Legal Syst Soc 4:268–269

Wang L (2010b) True meaning of Rawls's democratic equality. Soc Sci Res 1:124–129

Wang W (2006) The Chinese Hukou system. Shanghai Culture Press, Shanghai

Wang Z (2007) Discussion on urban residents' basic medical insurance system. Chin Health Serv Manage 23(10):677–678

World Bank (1993) Country study: China: long term issues and options in the health transition 1992. World Bank, Washington, DC

World Health Organization (2000) The World Health Report 2000—health systems: improving performance. WHO, Geneva

Yamin A (2009) Suffering and powerlessness: the significance of promoting participation in rights-based approaches to health. Health Hum Rights 11(1):5–22

Yang W (2001) Utilitarianism: egalitarian or the purpose. Soc Sci Res 1:120–123

Yip W, Hsiao W (2009) Non-evidence based policy: how effective is China's new cooperative medical scheme in reducing medical impoverishment. Soc Sci Med 68(2):201–209

Zhang H (2007) On the thoughts and practice of revolution and Mao Zedong economic equality in newly-founded China. J Jiaying Univ 5:2–10

Zhou YR (2007) 'If you get AIDS…you have to endure it alone': understanding the social constructions of HIV/AIDS in China. Soc Sci Med 65(2):284–295

Zou D (2008) China: 30 Years of reform and opening-up (1978–2008): report on China's economic development and institutional reform. People Press, Beijing

Chapter 4
The Right to Health in Japan: Its Implications and Challenges

Tokuko Munesue

Abstract This contribution focuses on the meaning and challenges of realizing the right to health in Japan, based on the author's experience with monitoring the right to health in Japan. The first section summarizes the outcome of monitoring the right to health in Japan, which includes the country's legal commitments to the right to health, domestic laws, public health financing, and the state of people's health. The second section explores the significance of this right in Japan, the policy approach to human rights, and the right to health as a guiding principle of relevant policies. It is suggested that a number of guideposts commonly accepted with respect to the right to health, in particular the notions of "availability," "accessibility," "acceptability," and "quality" ("AAAQ") as well as the notions of "accountability" and "participation" are important in Japan. The last section will focus on the challenges for Japan to implement the right to health, by creating a system to monitor human rights and using and developing human rights indicators at a national level.

Contents

4.1	Introduction	122
4.2	Overview of the Extent to Which the Right to Health Is Observed in Japan	122
	4.2.1 Legal Commitments with the Right to Health	122
	4.2.2 State of Domestic Laws	123
	4.2.3 Status of Public Health Financing	124
	4.2.4 State of People's Health	125
4.3	Meaning of the Right to Health in Japan	126
	4.3.1 Significance of the Right to Health as a Guiding Principle for Policy	127
	4.3.2 Importance of the Element of "Accessibility"	127

T. Munesue (✉)
Faculty of Law, Institute of Human and Social Science, Kanazawa University,
Kakuma-machi, Kanazawa, Ishikawa 920-1192, Japan
e-mail: rindy@par.odn.ne.jp

B. Toebes et al. (eds.), *The Right to Health*, DOI: 10.1007/978-94-6265-014-5_4,
© T.M.C. ASSER PRESS and the authors 2014

121

4.3.3	Creating "Accountability" and "Participation" in Relation
to Environmental Health Issues	129
4.4 Conclusions: Challenges Toward Realization of the Right to Health in Japan	130
References..	131

4.1 Introduction

This author has monitored the right to health in Japan and published two reports on the outcome of this process in 2012.[1] It should be noted at the outset that Japan has not formally guaranteed the right to health. As such, the question arises: what is the significance of the right to health in Japan, a country with a high standard of health but without formal recognition of the right to health? This contribution will summarize the findings from the monitoring process and discuss the validity, implications and challenges with respect to the realization of the right to health in Japan.

4.2 Overview of the Extent to Which the Right to Health Is Observed in Japan

4.2.1 Legal Commitments with the Right to Health

Japan has ratified several major international human rights treaties stipulating a right to health, namely, the International Covenant on Economic, Social, and Cultural Rights (ICESCR) (ratified in 1979), the Convention on the Elimination of All Forms of Racial Discrimination (CERD) (ratified in 1995), the Convention on the Elimination of All Forms of Discrimination Against Women (CEDAW) (ratified in 1985), the Convention on the Rights of the Child (CRC) (ratified in 1994), and the Convention on the Rights of Persons with Disabilities (CRPD).[2] It has also ratified key international human rights treaties on civil and political rights that relate to health such as the International Covenant on Civil and Political Rights (ICCPR) and the Convention against Torture and Other Cruel, Inhuman, or Degrading Treatment or Punishment (CAT). In addition, Japan has ratified 49 International Labor Organization (ILO) conventions, some of which relate to health, and it is a signatory to the Geneva Conventions and Additional Protocols.

Article 98, Section 2 of the Constitution of Japan stipulates that "the treaties concluded by Japan and established laws of nations shall be faithfully observed."

---

[1] Munesue 2012a No. 298, pp. 1–33, Munesue 2012b No. 300, pp. 2–65.

[2] Japan has not ratified the Convention on the Protection of the Rights of All Migrant Workers and Members of Their Families.

The treaties Japan has ratified have the effect of domestic law once promulgated and are typically considered to take precedence over "black-letter" domestic law. This means that Japan has adopted the monistic school when it comes to the implementation of international treaties at the domestic level. However, this does not automatically mean that Japanese courts apply the rights. Generally, whether or not a court may immediately apply the rules of the ratified treaty is determined by the clarity of the treaty's language and provisions, and the nature of obligations it imposes, in the light of views in the country and the domestic legal system. In Japan, there is a firmly entrenched belief that the ICCPR, which imposes immediate obligations on the State Parties to "respect" individual's rights, is directly applicable, while the ICESCR, which imposes an obligation to progressively realize rights, is not directly applicable.[3] In this regard, the Tokyo District Court ruled on the right to health in a suit seeking to reverse a determination directing the establishment of standards on pesticide residues in foods. The Court held that "the right to health asserted by the plaintiffs... is ambiguous, and determining its specific meaning in a certain way is difficult. There are doubts as to whether this is an independent, definite right," and the plaintiff's action was dismissed.[4]

That said, Article 25 of the Constitution of Japan stipulates that "[a]ll people shall have the right to maintain the minimum standards of wholesome and cultured living" (Section 1) and "[i]n all spheres of life, the State shall use its endeavors for the promotion and extension of social welfare and security, and of public health" (Section 2). Inoue has argued that this provision forms a direct basis for the right to health in the Constitution of Japan.[5] However, Japanese court decisions have not yet recognized the right to health emanating from Article 25 of the Constitution.

4.2.2 State of Domestic Laws

While various laws cover aspects of population and individual health under Japanese domestic law, the right to health is not explicitly stipulated, and therefore the principles and aims of realizing this right have not been established. On the other hand, what is remarkable in realizing the right to health in Japan is the existence of the universal health insurance system. The entire population is mandatorily enrolled in the public medical insurance system, which allows people to receive necessary medical care at a fixed price. It was implemented through amendment of the National Health Insurance Act of 1958 and amid Japan's rapid economic growth. Public medical insurance benefits were subsequently enhanced in the

---

[3] Cf. the Shiomi case, Sup. Ct. Mar. 2, 1988 Hanrei Jihyo [Case Law Reports] No. 1363, p. 68.

[4] Tokyo District Ct. Apr. 23, 1997 Hanrei Jiho [Case Law Reports] No. 1651, p. 39. For a very similar approach before the Dutch courts see the Chapter on the Netherlands in this same volume.

[5] Inoue 2001 pp. 4–5.

1960s–1970s, and in 1973 medical expenses for people 70 years old and over became fully covered.

However, the period of Japan's rapid economic growth came to a close beginning with the first oil shock in 1972. Amid subsequent slow economic growth and aging of the population, restructuring of public finances became a serious policy issue, and the medical insurance system faced substantial reorganization. As a result, partial "out-of-pocket" costs for the older person were introduced and the benefit rate for individual employees was lowered. Structural reform of healthcare including the establishment of a medical system for older people (age 75 and over) is gradually being introduced and continues to the present.

4.2.3 Status of Public Health Financing

As of 2009, Japan's GDP totaled US$ 5,035.141 billion, giving it the second largest GDP behind the United States.[6] Japan's national healthcare expenditures totalled US$ 423.1 billion and represented 8.30 % of its GDP.[7] National healthcare expenditures per capita totalled US$ 3321.47.[8] In addition, Japan's public healthcare expenditures (public expenditures and premiums) totalled US$ 338.4 billion. Public healthcare expenditures account for 80 % of national healthcare expenditures.[9] Public healthcare expenditures account for 17.90 % of annual expenditures.[10] In addition, private healthcare expenditures account for 18.50 % of national healthcare expenditures, with 14.91 % borne by patients.[11]

Compared to public health financing in other OECD countries (40 countries), Japan has a lower national healthcare expenditure per capita, a lower national healthcare expenditure as a share of GDP, and a lower rate of increase in national healthcare expenditures when compared with OECD averages.[12]

---

[6] According to the latest data from 2012, Japan's GDP was US$ 5,963.969 billion, making it third behind the US and China. This report uses data from 2009, when all of the related data came out, to allow comparison of the GDP and medical expenditures.

[7] WHO Western Pacific Region 2011.

[8] Ibid.

[9] Ibid.

[10] Ibid.

[11] Ibid.

[12] OECD 2013. This chapter uses statistical data from the WHO with regard to Japan's health insurance financing, but the OECD and WHO have different statistical data for the year 2009, so specific numbers have been omitted. According to data from the OECD, the OECD average for national healthcare expenditures per capita was US$ 3,233 versus Japanese healthcare expenditures per capita of US$ 2,878. The OECD average for national healthcare expenditures as a share of GDP was 9.6 versus 8.5 % for Japan. The OECD average rate of increase in national healthcare expenditures was 4.0 versus 2.4 % for Japan.

4 The Right to Health in Japan: Its Implications and Challenges

Approximately 50 % of Japan's national healthcare expenditures are devoted to labor costs of health professionals. In this regard, Japan has 289,669 physicians, with 2.25 physicians per 1,000 population.[13] This number is lower than the OECD average of 3.1 physicians per 1,000 population and ranks Japan 30th among 40 OECD countries.[14] Japan has 99,426 dentists, with 0.78 dentists per 1,000 population.[15] Japan has 267,751 pharmacists, with 2.1 pharmacists per 1,000 population.[16] Japan has 1,295,670 nurses, with 10.15 nurses per 1,000 population[17]; this number is somewhat higher than the OECD average of 8.4 nurses per 1,000 population.[18] Japan has 27,789 midwives, with 0.22 midwives per 1,000 females.[19]

4.2.4 State of People's Health

The average life expectancy at birth in Japan is 79.59 years for males and 86.44 years for females. Life expectancy for both males and females is becoming higher.[20] In addition, Japan has an infant mortality rate of 2.40 per 1,000 population, with a mortality rate of 2.60 for males and 2.10 for females.[21] Japan has the highest average life expectancy among OECD countries (40 countries) and is second only to Iceland in terms of its low infant mortality rate.[22] On the other hand, 9.60 % of newborns in Japan have a low birth weight (2,500 g and under), and this figure appears to be rising (8.50 % for males and 10.80 % for females).[23] This figure is the fifth highest among OECD countries.[24]

In terms of mortality rates due to major illnesses, Japan's mortality rate due to ischemic heart disease is 38 per 100,000 population for men and 17 per 100,000 population for women. These low numbers place Japan second only to South Korea among the OECD countries.[25] Japan's mortality rate due to stroke is 53 per 100,000

---

[13] Op. cit. WHO.

[14] Op. cit. OECD.

[15] Op. cit. WHO.

[16] Ibid.

[17] Ibid.

[18] Op. cit. OECD. According to data from the OECD, there were 9.5 nurses (per 1,000 of population) in 2009.

[19] Op. cit. WHO. According to data from the OECD, there were 32.5 midwives per 100,000 females of population in 2009 compared to an OECD average of 69.8 midwives.

[20] Ibid.

[21] Ibid.

[22] Op. cit. OECD. The OECD average is 4.4.

[23] Op. cit. WHO.

[24] Op. cit. OECD. The OECD average is 6.7 %.

[25] Ibid. The OECD average is 117.

men and 30 per 100,000 women, compared to the OECD average of 54.[26] Japan's mortality rate due to all cancers (malignant neoplasms) is 189 per 100,000 men and 93 per 100,000 women. The mortality rate due to lung cancer is 44 per 100,000 men and 12 per 100,000 women. Breast cancer accounts for 10.8 deaths per 100,000 women while prostate cancer accounts for 8.4 deaths per 100,000 men. All of these numbers are lower than the OECD averages.[27] That said, cancer has been the leading cause of death among Japanese since 1981. The latest data show that Japan had 360,963 deaths per year due to cancer, its highest number in 2012.[28]

In terms of the morbidity rates for major illnesses, diabetes affects 5.0 % of the population from age 20 to age 79, and type 1 diabetes affects 2.4 % of the population from age 0 to age 14; both figures are lower than OECD averages.[29] Japan's morbidity rate for all cancers is 201.1 per 100,000 population while its morbidity rate for breast cancer is 42.7 per 100,000 population and its morbidity rate for prostate cancer is 22.7 per 100,000 population; all of these numbers are lower than the OECD averages.[30] Japan's morbidity rate for HIV is 0.01 % and the incidence of new AIDS cases is 3.4 per 1 million population, both of which are lower than the OECD averages.[31]

4.3 Meaning of the Right to Health in Japan

Japan has excelled in promoting and maintaining population health with lower health expenditure and fewer health professionals than other developed countries, and as such Japan's performance might be rated very high in terms of a cost-effective analysis. At the same time, although Japan has ratified several international human rights treaties that mention the right to health, it has not formally entrenched the right in the Constitution or laws. Furthermore, domestic court decisions have not recognized the right to health. This underscores the fact that countries like Japan that have not established the right to health as a concrete right, can also develop policies to preserve and promote people's health and can obtain good health care performance and achieve high scores on commonly used health metrics. As such, the question arises: what is the significance of the right to health as a human right in Japan? Does it still hold value?

---

[26] Ibid.

[27] Ibid. Respective OECD averages are 208, 124, 52, 20, 20.1, and 22.4.

[28] Ministry of Health, Labor and Welfare 2013.

[29] Op. cit. OECD. Respective OECD averages are 6.5 and 16.9 %.

[30] Ibid. Respective OECD averages are 260.9, 71.6, and 70.5.

[31] Ibid. The respective OECD average is 0.16 % and 14.0.

4.3.1 Significance of the Right to Health as a Guiding Principle for Policy

It is said that there are two ways of advancing human rights, including the right to health.[32] One way is via the courts, tribunals and similar processes (the "judicial" approach) and another approach is by using human rights principles to inform policy-making processes and decisions so that policies and programs are put in place that promote and protect human rights (the "policy" approach).

In this regard, there is a need for more legal research and practice that focuses on the latter approach in the context of Japan. However, the policy approach is significant in Japan because it is due to the development of the public medical insurance system and other health systems that Japanese people have achieved a high level of general health. Japan has been faced with the necessity of restructuring these systems due to a period of slow economic growth, aging of the population, and changes in patterns of disease. In fact, these systems have been revised in succession since the 1980s. In a country like Japan, applying the right to health as a guiding principle is important when the policy makers consider to revise these laws and systems. This author is of the opinion that the fundamental elements of the right to health, namely the so-called "AAAQ" (availability, accessibility, acceptability, and quality),[33] as well as the notions of "accountability" and "participation" have an effect, procedure-wise, on ensuring the right to health. The formal adoption of the right to health and the implementation of its implications into domestic law and policies would help ensuring that these principles are applied in a consistent and coherent fashion.

4.3.2 Importance of the Element of "Accessibility"

When the situation of Japan is reexamined according to the elements of the right to health, it is found that even though health-related systems obtain excellent health outcomes, these systems are not without problems. Of the "AAAQ," "accessibility" is of particular importance in Japan as exemplified in the following.

First, Japan has adopted a universal health insurance system that allows for necessary medical care at a fixed out-of-pocket cost, as mentioned above. However, in recent years, some people have not had access to needed healthcare since they were unable to pay premiums or the medical facility's fee. Under the National Health Insurance system, an individual is asked to return their Health Insurance

---

[32] Hunt 2009 p. 21.
[33] UN CESCR 2000, para 12.

Certificate when their premiums are in arrears for a year, excluding a natural disaster or other particular circumstances stipulated by the government, and the individual is issued a Certificate of Eligibility. When the individual with the Certificate of Eligibility visits a medical facility, the individual must pay the full amount of healthcare costs covered by insurance at the medical facility's accounting office. The individual will then receive a 70 % reimbursement at a later date from the insurer. According to statistics from the Japanese Medical and Dental Practitioners for the Improvement of Medical Care (2010), 4.36 million households were in arrears with their premiums, representing 20.6 % of the households (21.13 million households) covered by National Health Insurance. Japan had 1.28 million households (6.1 %) that were issued a Short-term Health Insurance Certificate[34] and 307,000 households (1.5 %) that were issued a Certificate of Eligibility.[35] People who have difficulty paying their premiums will presumably have difficulty paying 100 % of fees out-of-pocket to a medical facility. In actuality, a privately conducted survey found that one in 73 individuals with a Certificate of Eligibility, who would otherwise be regularly insured, received care (2009).[36]

Second, given the increase in chronic disease, such as cancer and diabetes, as well as the aging of the population, there is an increasing burden on health care. Patients with chronic diseases who need long-term care can incur exorbitant medical expenses which they cannot pay for and may forgo treatment as a result.

Third, results of a Survey of the Actual Number of Physicians Needed in Hospitals and Other Facilities put out by the Ministry of Health, Labor and Welfare in 2010[37] indicated that 18,288 physicians are needed to meet the growing health care demands of the population. The number of physicians that needed to be hired was 1.11 times the number of physicians at the time. The prefectures or cities with the greatest number of physicians needed (relative to the number of physicians at the time) were Shimane Prefecture (1.24 times the number of physicians at the time), Iwate Prefecture (1.23 times the number of physicians at the time), and Aomori Prefecture (1.22 times the number of physicians at the time). The departments with the greatest number of physicians that needed to be hired were Rehabilitation (1.23 times the number of physicians at the time), Emergency Medicine (1.21 times the number of physicians at the time), and Respiratory Medicine (1.16 times the number of physicians at the time). These figures indicate a dearth of physicians and uneven distribution of physicians in different regions and departments.

---

[34] A Health Insurance Certificate that is valid for several months as opposed to a normal Health Insurance Certificate, which is valid for 1 year (except in special circumstances).

[35] Ministry of Health, Labor and Welfare 2011.

[36] Japanese Medical and Dental Practitioners for the Improvement of Medical Care (Hodanren) 2010.

[37] Ministry of Health, Labor and Welfare 2010.

4.3.3 Creating "Accountability" and "Participation" in Relation to Environmental Health Issues

The most pressing problem in connection with the right to health in Japan is the nuclear accident which was caused by the Great East Japan Earthquake which occurred in March 2011. In this regard, it is worth observing that Japan has responded to the previous accident at JCO's uranium conversion facility in a village in Tokai. The UN Committee on Economic, Social, and Cultural Rights (CESCR or "the Committee") examined the relationship between the Government's response to the accident at the uranium conversion facility and Article 12 of the ICESCR (the right to health) in the second periodic reporting examination of Japan on ICESCR in 2001. The Committee recommended Japan to ensure that there is "increased transparency and disclosure to the population concerned of all necessary information, on issues relating to the safety of nuclear power installations."[38] The Committee also urged Japan to "step up its preparation of plans for the prevention of, and early reaction to, nuclear accidents."[39]

The Great East Japan Earthquake that occurred in March 2011 led to an accident at the Tokyo Electric Power Company's (TEPCO) Fukushima Daiichi Nuclear Power Plant. Approximately 900 peta-becquerels of radioactive material was released as a result of the accident. When this is converted to an equivalent iodine-131 dose, this amount is about one-sixth of that from the Chernobyl Nuclear Power Plant accident. The TEPCO nuclear power plant accident resulted in vast stretches of land, representing 1,800 km^2, of Fukushima Prefecture potentially having an air dose of radiation of 5 MSV^{40} a year or more. As of June 2012, there was no evidence of serious pollution-related health problems caused by radioactive material released from the power plant. However, the undeniable fact is that radioactive material escaped and residents were partially exposed to radiation.[41]

In the face of this situation, in the third periodic reporting examination of Japan on ICESCR in 2013, the Committee recommended "once again, that the State Party increase transparency on issues relating to the safety of nuclear power installations and step up its preparedness to nuclear accidents."[42] The Committee

---

[38] UN CESCR 2001, para 49.

[39] Ibid.

[40] "MSV" is an abbreviation of "millisievert". It is a unit of dose equivalence.

[41] Independent Commission to Investigate the TEPCO Fukushima Nuclear Accident (2012) Commission Report of the National Diet's ICIFNA. (English version): http://warp.da.ndl.go.jp/info:ndljp/pid/3856371/naiic.go.jp/en/. Accessed 17 January 2014. The Independent Commission to Investigate the TEPCO Fukushima Nuclear Accident was an independent investigative body under the auspices of the National Diet. Based on the Act for the Independent Commission to Investigate the TEPCO Fukushima Nuclear Accident (enacted Oct. 30, 2011), the commission sought to explore the causes of the accident at TEPCO's Fukushima Daiichi Nuclear Power Plant and offer suggestions.

[42] UN CESCR 2013, para 25.

also urged Japan to "provide the population with comprehensive, credible and accurate information on potential hazards, preventive measures and response plans, and to ensure prompt disclosure of all information when disasters occur."[43]

The Special Rapporteur on the right of everyone to the enjoyment of the highest attainable standard of physical and mental health visited Japan in November 2012 and inspected disaster-stricken areas and met relevant people. In his report on the mission to Japan publicized in 2013, the Special Rapporteur urged the Government to implement the following recommendations in the formulation and implementation of it nuclear emergency response system: health monitoring of the affected population; policies and information on radiation dose; decontamination; transparency and accountability within the regulatory framework; compensation and relief; and effective community participation in all aspects of the decision–making processes.[44] The Special Rapporteur repeatedly referred to the accountability of the Government and TEPCO and people's participation in his report.[45]

Such repeated nuclear accidents and the responses of the Government make clear that the notions of the Government's accountability for violations of the right to health and people's participation in the decision-making process over important decisions that affect health are lacking in Japan and that monitoring on this point is urgently needed.

4.4 Conclusions: Challenges Toward Realization of the Right to Health in Japan

When we reexamine Japan's situation in the light of the above-mentioned elements of the right to health, many problems are present that underscore the importance of the right to health for Japan. To ensure the effective implementation, it is first necessary to include the right to health as a concrete right under the Constitution and national laws. If circumstances require, amendment of appropriate legislation and regulations may be needed.

Second, Japan should seek to create a monitoring system to promote and protect human rights, including the right to health. In this regard, unlike some other countries Japan has not yet established a national human rights institution independent from Government. Japan was recommended to establish one in conformity with UN treaty body recommendations, such as the Committee on Economic, Social, and Cultural Rights.[46]

Third, in the light of the significance of the right to health as a guiding principle for policy, Japan should also examine the development and use of human rights

---

[43] Ibid.

[44] UN General Assembly 2013.

[45] Ibid.

[46] Ibid, para 8.

indicators appropriate for the Japanese context. Indicators can be developed with reference to the practices of the OHCHR[47] and the national human rights institutions of other countries, and they can be used by policy makers and relevant civil society organizations. Such indicators can be useful tools to enhance the Government's accountability for violations of the right to health and enhance the participation of the public in the process of the formulation, implementation and assessment of relevant policies.

References

Hunt P (2009) The right to the highest attainable standard of health: opportunities and challenges. In: Matsuda R, Munesue T (eds) Reexamination of the right to health: seeking Japan's challenges from recent international discussions. Research Center Ars Vivendi of Ritsumeikan University, vol 9, pp 20–33 (only in Japanese)

Inoue H (2001) General introduction: formulation and development of laws covering healthcare and long-term care. In: Japan Association of Social Security Law (ed) Social security law, vol 4, Houritsu Bunka Sha, pp 1–24 (only in Japanese)

Japanese Medical and Dental Practitioners for the Improvement of Medical Care (Hodanren) (2010) Results of surveys (2008 & 2009) on the ratio of insured individuals receiving care with a Certificate of Eligibility for National Health Insurance

Ministry of Health, Labor and Welfare (2010) Overview of the survey on the actual number of physicians needed in hospitals (in Japanese)

Ministry of Health, Labor and Welfare (2011) The status of (municipal) financing of national health insurance in 2009 (in Japanese)

Ministry of Health, Labor and Welfare (2013) Overview of vital statistics (final count) for 2012 (in Japanese)

Munesue T (2012a) The right to health in Japan (ver. 1). National Health Japan, No. 298, pp 1–33 (only in Japanese)

Munesue T (2012b) The right to health in Japan (ver. 2). National Health Japan, No. 300, pp 2–65 (only in Japanese)

OECD (2013) Health data. http://www.oecd.org/health/health-systems/oecdhealthdata.htm. Accessed 21 Jan 2014

OHCHR (2012) Human rights indicators—a guide to measurement and implementation. http://www.ohchr.org/Documents/Publications/Human_rights_indicators_en.pdf. Accessed 21 Jan 2014

UN CESCR (2000) General comment 14 on the right to the highest attainable standard of health, UN Doc. E/C.12/2000/4. http://www.unhchr.ch/tbs/doc.nsf/(symbol)/E.C.12.2000.4.En. Accessed 21 Jan 2014

UN CESCR (2001) Concluding observations on the second periodic report of Japan, UN Doc. E/C.12/1/Add.67. http://tbinternet.ohchr.org/_layouts/treatybodyexternal/Download.aspx?symbolno=E%2fC.12%2f1%2fAdd.67&Lang=en. Accessed 27 Jan 2014

UN CESCR (2013) Concluding observations on the third periodic report of Japan, UN Doc. E/C.12/JPN/CO/3. http://tbinternet.ohchr.org/_layouts/treatybodyexternal/Download.aspx?symbolno=E%2fC.12%2fJPN%2fCO%2f3&Lang=en. Accessed 27 Jan 2014

UN General Assembly (2013) Report of the special rapporteur on the right of everyone to the enjoyment of the highest attainable standard of physical and mental health, Anand Grover,

---

[47] OHCHR 2012.

Mission to Japan (15–26 November 2012), UN doc. A/AHR/23/41/Add.3. http://daccess-dds-ny.un.org/doc/UNDOC/GEN/G13/160/74/PDF/G1316074.pdf?OpenElement. Accessed 27 Jan 2014

WHO Western Pacific Region (2011) Country health information profile Japan, Western Pacific Regional health Databank. http://www.wpro.who.int/countries/jpn/11JPNtab2011_finaldraft.pdf. Accessed 17 Jan 2014

Part III
Middle East

Chapter 5
Codification and Implementation of the 'Right to Health' in the Arab World

Salman Rawaf and Sondus Hassounah

Abstract This chapter offers an analysis of the implementation of the 'Right to Health' in countries of the Arab World. We have mapped out the current status of individuals' health rights, from the State's perspective, through empirical analysis of the constitutional enactments of the 23 countries of the Arab world that address health and health care. We further examined other indices of national commitment to health and health care, such as the approach to identification of health as a right, the universality of each health system and the existing gaps (if any) between constitutions and service provision. As such, we merged the human rights framework for Availability, Accessibility, Acceptability and Quality ('AAAQ') with Public Health and Health system performance indicators.

Contents

5.1	Introduction	136
5.2	Overview of Health Systems in the 'Arab World'	137
5.3	Methodology	138
5.4	Findings and Discussion	140
	5.4.1 The Right to Health in the Constitutions and National Laws	141
	5.4.2 Access to Health care	143
5.5	Conclusion	146
Annexes		148
References		162

S. Rawaf (✉) · S. Hassounah
Department of Primary Care and Public Health, Imperial College London - Charing Cross Campus, The Reynolds Building, St Dunstan's Road, W6 8RP London, UK
e-mail: s.rawaf@imperial.ac.uk

S. Hassounah
e-mail: s.hassounah@imperial.ac.uk

B. Toebes et al. (eds.), *The Right to Health*, DOI: 10.1007/978-94-6265-014-5_5,
© T.M.C. ASSER PRESS and the authors 2014

5.1 Introduction

The most established definition of the right to health, also referred to as 'the right of everyone to the enjoyment of the highest attainable standard of physical and mental health', is provided by Article 12 of the International Covenant on Economic Social and Cultural Rights (ICESCR) of the United Nations.[1] An authoritative explanation of this treaty provision is provided by General Comment 14, an explanatory document to Article 12 of the ICESCR.[2] The right to health means that governments must create the conditions that enable its residents to lead healthy lives, for example: make adequate housing and nutritious food available, ensure the availability of health services, as well as warrant healthy and safe working conditions. This has been echoed by General Comment 14, which sets out that the right to health extends not only to timely and appropriate health care but also to the underlying determinants of health.[3] Furthermore, according to General Comment 14, the right to health contains both freedoms and entitlements.[4] Freedoms include the right to control one's health and to be free from non-consensual medical treatment or experimentation, while entitlements comprise of the right to a system of health protection which provides equality of opportunity,[5] the capacity and the basis for which people could be able to enjoy the highest attainable level of health.[6]

Building up on that, with particular focus on 'entitlement', it is fundamentally crucial to attest that Universal Health Coverage (UHC) is at the core of any, and every, platform of rights to health. As "the single most powerful concept that public health has to offer",[7] UHC is defined by the World Health Organization (WHO) as part and parcel of Governments' obligations to ensure that all people have access to needed preventive, curative, rehabilitative as well as promotive health services, of sufficient and effective quality, in an equitable manner, and while also safeguarding that people do not suffer financially for seeking such services.[8] Although General Comment 14 does not refer to UHC explicitly, it does refer to the State obligation 'To adopt and implement a national public health strategy and plan of action'.[9]

---

[1] Article 12, General Comment 14 of the International Covenant on Economic Social and Cultural Rights of the United Nations.

[2] General Comment No. 14 (2000).

[3] WHO/OHCHR Joint Factsheet 323 August 2007.

[4] General Comment No. 14 (2000).

[5] Health and Poverty Reduction Strategies. UNHCR Human Rights: Health and Human Rights Publications Series, Issue No 5, December 2008.

[6] Constitution of the World Health Organization. The Constitution was adopted by the International Health Conference and signed on 22 July 1946 by the representatives of 61 States, and entered into force on 7 April 1948.

[7] Margret Chan: Universal Health Coverage. Lancet Themed issue 7/09/2012.

[8] World Health Report 2010.

[9] Paragraph 43(f) of General Comment 14.

5 Codification and Implementation of the 'Right to Health' in the Arab World

In today's Arab world, irrespective to income level, we are observing a positive shift in the mindset for governance, highlighting the 'right to health' as a national goal.[10]

The fundamental notion: that it simply does not mean that massive amounts of financial resources need to be employed to create well-operating health systems, and that 'the right to health does not mean the right to be healthy, nor does it mean that poor governments must put in place expensive health services for which they have no resources'[11] regretfully eludes the multitude of sovereign states that make up the Arab world. Hardly any Government shows compulsory responsibility for universal and comprehensive health and health care in order to guarantee that equitable and encapsulating right for all citizens residing in their countries— whether native or migrant.

5.2 Overview of Health Systems in the 'Arab World'

The Arab region covers a vast territory, from the Gulf in the east to the Atlantic Ocean in the west, from the mountain ranges of Lebanon and the Syrian Arab Republic in the north to the equatorial plateau and the plains of Somalia in the south. Encapsulating the Middle East and North Africa (MENA), its indigenous population[12] comprises Arabic-speaking people native to the region.[13] Countries of the Arab world, particularly the Middle East, are immensely diverse and have many inequalities, for example, the GDP per capita ranges from USD 92,501 in Qatar to USD 1,361 in Yemen (2011 est.),[14] and shockingly, only 53 % of Yeminis[15] have access to safe-drinking.[16] Within the 22 countries comprising the Arab world, a total of approximately 350 million people live in 13,154,295 km^2, with over half under 25 years of age.

Populations' health and their health systems are contextually affected by a plethora of factors, and accordingly, need to be grappled using a multidisciplinary approach. Health achievements are strongly impacted by a country's GDP. However they are not exclusively moulded by it. The priority assigned to

---

[10] See in the Annex Table 5.3 > United Arab Emirate > State Policy: Government Strategy 2011–2013.

[11] Mary Robinson, former UN High Commissioner for Human Rights. As quoted in: Nygren-Krug H. 25 Questions and answers on health and human rights. World Health Organization health and human rights publication series No 1. Geneva: WHO 2002:11.

[12] UNDP: About Arab States.

[13] The World Bank: Arab World.

[14] World Bank Data—GDP per Capita in current USD.

[15] World Bank Data—Improved sanitation facilities (% of population with access).

[16] World Water Assessment Programme (WWAP) 2012. Chap. 7, p. 210.

investment in health, whether monetary or non-monetary, compared to other types of investments play a significant role, as do the effectiveness and fairness of delivery systems. This can be vividly seen as health expenditure in the region varies from country to country (between 8.4 % of GDP in Iraq to 1.8 % in Qatar), yet there is no straightforward effect on health indicators. This is quite a tricky area to explore because, although the increase in a country's GDP spent on health is quite crucial to alleviate the health state of its population, it is even more important 'how' these finances are spent.

The region is affected by many health issues, and several countries face a multitude of health-related concerns. The same countries are battling through dual disease burdens: a persistent, though much reduced, burden of communicable diseases, and a rapidly growing burden of non-communicable diseases (NCDs) including mental health-related illnesses.[4] Lifestyle factors and risk-taking behaviours such as smoking, lack of exercise, substance abuse, overconsumption of fatty and salty foods, disregard to the use of seat belts and traffic rules contribute to a significant proportion of the overall mortality and morbidity.[4,8]

Currently, most health services in the region are based on a curative model which seeks to 'cure' rather than 'prevent' illness. This is becoming increasingly expensive to maintain and ineffective in addressing the emerging challenges in health. Yet, many governments remain focused on expanding the infrastructure to meet the growing population without adequate attention to improving efficiency or evaluating the appropriateness of investments in the current stock of technology. Health-service delivery will need to be reconfigured to integrate the provision of preventive and promotion services.

5.3 Methodology

This work reports the findings for the empirical analysis of the constitutional enactments of the 23 countries of the Arab world that address health and health care. It also examines other indices of national commitment to health and health care such as the approach to identification of health as a right; the 'universality' of each health system; and the existing gaps (if any) between constitutions and service provision. The following search methodology was adopted:

(1) In regard to constitutional enactments, all constitutions examined were extracted from official governmental online platforms, ministerial publications, official translation documents, and UN agencies.[17] Keywords such as 'Health', 'Health care', 'Health Financing', 'Health services', Health Insurance' or all pertaining to the 'Medicinal' or overarching welfare of the health

---

[17] UNPAN—United Nations Public Administration Network, WIPO—World Intellectual Property Organization, UNOPS—UN Office for Project Services, and UNHCR—UN High Commissioner for Refugees.

Table 5.1 Availability and accessibility

Hospital beds/1,000 pop (source-year)	Access to medicine (essential medicines) (source-year)		Total expenditure on health as % of GDP (source-year)	General government expenditure on health as % of total government expenditure (source-year)	Private expenditure on health as % of total expenditure on health (source-year)	Private prepaid plans as a % of private expenditure on health (source-year)	OOP expenditure as % of total expenditure on health (source-year)
	Median availability of selected generic medicines (%)—Public	Median availability of selected generic medicines (%)—Private					

Table 5.2 Acceptability and quality

Physicians density/1,000 pop (per 1,000 population)	Environmental and public health workers density (per 1,000 population)	Health management & support workers density (per 1,000 population)	Total health workforce[a] (per 1,000 population)

[a] Total Health workforce encapsulates: Physicians, Dentistry personnel, Pharmaceutical personnel, Laboratory health workers, Environmental and public health workers, Community and Nursing and midwifery personnel, traditional health workers, other workers as well as Health management & support workers density per 1,000 population (unless otherwise indicated)

of the population were sought out and extracted from the text (see Annex Table 5.3). Only official English translations were used; which were cross-checked with their original Arabic versions.

(2) Concerning indices of national commitment to health and health care, we attempted to approach the identification of health as a right and the 'universality' of each health system between constitutions and service provision by using the criteria set out by General Comment 14 (AAAQ)[18] as a guiding principle, marrying it with routinely collected data and indicator based figures. We believe the chosen sets of indicators are the best available data to reflect the impact of the health care system of each country on its population and its responsiveness to their need (see Annex Table 5.4).

Tables 5.1 and 5.2 show the sets of indicators we used to reflect each criterion.

The constitutions, royal decrees and referendums in countries[19] used in this work span almost 60 years (1952–2012) in the time frame between which they have been promulgated and/or entered into force.

Due to the recent political instability in many of these countries and the contagious effect of revolutionary uprisings—as populations unanimously call for a more democratic and decent quality of life—there have been many and significant changes (not always for the better) in regard to their constitutions. We have attempted to collate the most recent and most up-to-date official documentation pertaining to constitution. The latest documents collected were as of 31 January 2013.

5.4 Findings and Discussion

People are ultimately responsible for their own health but they need to be supported to make better decisions about their own health and welfare. Nonetheless, there are widespread systematic failures that influence the decisions individuals

---

[18] See General Comment 14 on the Right to Health, in relation to the availability, accessibility, acceptability and quality of health care.

[19] The countries (Ranked according to population size in 2010) highlighted in this work are: Arab Republic of EGYPT; People's Republic of ALGERIA; Kingdom of MOROCCO; Republic of SUDAN & Republic of South SUDAN; Republic of IRAQ; Kingdom of SAUDI ARABIA; Republic of YEMEN; Arab Republic of SYRIA; Republic of TUNISIA; Federal Republic of SOMALIA; United Arab Emirates (UAE); National Transitional Council of LIBYA; Hashemite Kingdom of JORDAN; State of PALESTINE; State of KUWAIT; Islamic Republic of MAURITANIA; Sultanate OMAN, State of QATAR; Kingdom of BAHRAIN, Republic of LEBANON, Union of COMROS, and Republic of DJIBOUTI.

Note: At the time when this population-size ranking took place (2010) North and South Sudan were a single country and so have been placed together in the population overall ranking. Note that in areas other than constitutional analysis, 'Sudan' is accounted for as a single entity (encapsulating both Northern and Southern countries) as health metrics have not yet been calculated and recorded for them separately.

5   Codification and Implementation of the 'Right to Health' in the Arab World

currently make in regard to their health seeking behaviour.[20] Many of the countries we examined lack standard or all-encompassing legislation directly pertaining to the health of the population.[21] We observed that although, as expected, different countries exemplify their health laws differently, they exhibited some similarities. One of the commonalities is that the majority of the countries under scrutiny do not actually have explicit and clear-cut statutory or constitutional provisions safeguarding the health rights.

The 23 countries, constituting the Arab states and territories as part of the Arab League, share many aspects of culture, history and even patterns of disease. However they also show polarization in a large number of aspects; from GDP per capita, population size and state of political and social stability. Although the 'Arab World' is perceived as a single unit of analysis, it is crucial that we remain conscious of the political, monetary and geo-demographic differences between these countries.

5.4.1 The Right to Health in the Constitutions and National Laws

We have ranked countries according to their population sizes in 2010 and then carefully examined their constitutions for the availability of laws pertaining to health and health care. The plotted results include specific clarification on each country's enactments pertaining to health and/or health care as well as, whenever appropriate, the social determinants of health. Table 5.3 elaborates on each country's health-related laws, the specific phrasing of these laws, the time at which the constitution has been promulgated and any significant nuances related.

As shown in Table 5.3 (in the Annex to this chapter), five out of the 23 countries (20 %) still struggle with notions as simple as integrating health or health care into their constitutions. These five constitutions were found to show complete absence of either health or medical care as an obligation of the state and/or a right of its people. The remaining 80 % of the countries have some sort of statement within an agreement, or a law, addressing health or health care. In almost all of these constitutions, the laws are universal, rather than limited to particular groups.

---

[20] Securing our Future Health: Taking a Long-Term View Final Report Derek Wanless April 2002, pp. 119–122.

[21] Table 5.3 (in the Annex to this Chapter): 'The Right to Health in the Constitutions and National Laws of countries of the Arab world'. Note: *Grey shaded* denotes the absence of either health or medical care in the constitution as an obligation of the state and/or a right of its people.

Essentially, most constitutions only have statements of entitlements,[22] rather than more detailed and broken-down duty proclamations towards their residents.[23] These imprecise and broad definitions exemplify the lack of accountability by governments. It is worth noting that as countries have adopted their constitutions during different historical periods, which in itself poses as a critical determining factor in terms of whether or not (and how explicitly) constitutions address health or health care. To a large extent, constitutions mirror the period of their development. This is also true for the status of constitutional law development as well as international law at the time. An example of this would be the oldest constitution in our list (being that of (the) Jordan)—ratified and promulgated on the 1st of January 1952—where Health and medical care are not represented in the constitution as an obligation of the state and/or a right of its people, versus Egypt's newly adopted constitution, which was signed into law on 26 December 2012. The latter contains 3 explicit articles (Articles 10, 62 and 72)[24] addressing health, and an additional four (Articles 63, 66, 68 and 71)[25] discussing the social determinants

---

[22] See: Provisions for Health and Health Care in the Constitutions of the Countries of the World Eleanor D. Kinney & Brian Alexander Clark, p. 290.

[23] Meaning, the statement broadly states a right to health or health care or public health services. That is in comparison to a more scrutinised and specific definition, such as a *statement of duty*; which imposes a duty to provide health care or public health services or a *programmatic* statement, which in its turn is even more specific specifying approaches for the financing, delivery or regulation of health care and public health services (for example: The citizens' health care is financed from the state budget, by employers, by personal and collective insurance payments, and from other sources under conditions and according to a procedure determined by law).

For further clarification, the following is an example of an entitlement statement: "Every citizen has the right to health care. The State shall maintain public health and provide the means of prevention and treatment…" (Constitution of Iraq—Article 31), whereas a more broken down duty proclamation would be something along these lines: "The State guarantees assistance for the citizen and his family in cases of emergency, sickness, disability and old age according to the scheme of the social security and shall work for the solidarity of the society in bearing the burdens resulting from national disasters and catastrophies….") (Constitution of Oman—Article 12). Further reference can be found in http://indylaw.indiana.edu/instructors/Kinney/Articles/kinney_Constitutions.pdf.

[24] In regards to **Article 10:** "… The State shall ensure maternal and child health services free of charge, and enable the reconciliation between the duties of a woman toward her family and her work. The State shall provide special care and protection to female breadwinners, divorced women and widows". **Article 62:** "Health care is a right of every citizen, and the State shall allocate a sufficient percentage of the national revenue. The State shall provide health care services and health insurance in accordance with just and high standards, to be free of charge for those who are unable to pay. All health facilities shall provide various forms of medical treatment to every citizen in cases of emergency or life danger. The State shall supervise all health facilities, inspect them for quality of services, and monitor all materials, products and means of health-related publicity. Legislation to regulate such supervision shall be drafted." **Article 72:** "The State shall provide for people with disabilities health, economic and social care, and shall provide them with employment opportunities, raise social awareness toward them, and adapt public facilities to suit their needs."

[25] In regards to **Article 63:** "All individuals have the right to a healthy environment. The State shall safeguard the environment against pollution, and promote the use of natural resources in a manner that prevents damage to the environment and preserves the rights of future generations."

of health. However, it is worth mentioning that, how 'new' or 'old' a constitution is, has very little to do with how 'modern' or 'fair' health laws are. For example, the constitution of Somalia, although adopted fairly recently (August 2012), shows no traces of the State's responsibility towards its residents to guarantee their health rights, as would be expected of a constitution drafted in the 21st century.[26]

On the other hand, some countries go as far as setting regularly updated government strategies with populations' health at their core. For the period 2011–2013, the UAE created a national strategy that aims to "ensure access for all citizens and residents to primary health care, to improve the quality of health care services as well as ensure universal access to health care services by ensuring availability of health care services in all regions, and developing health insurance and implementing scheme". Similarly, in Qatar, a national development strategy[27] has been developed, building on situational analyses and identified priorities, to heavily invest in the health and development infrastructure. It is, however, uncommon to find this level of clear aims and direction in health policy and strategies, especially in a regularly updated manner, in countries of the Arab world. Thus the UAE example and another positive example from Sudan, addressing its Human Resources for Health (HRH) capacity building strategic plan,[28] are encouraging steps towards more explicit and transparent prescriptions for the duties of the state towards its people.

5.4.2 Access to Health care

'Access to Health care' is a broad term of multidimensional complexity due to the multiple factors determining its characterization. According to the WHO, a well-functioning health system responds to population's needs and expectations in a

---

(Footnote 25 continued)

Article 66: "The State shall provide social insurance services. All citizens unable to support themselves and their families in cases of incapacity, unemployment and old age have the right to social insurance guaranteeing a minimum sustenance." **Article 68:** "Adequate housing, clean water and healthy food are given rights. The state adopts a national housing plan, based on social justice, the promotion of independent initiatives and housing cooperatives, and the regulation of the use of national territory for the purposes of construction, in accordance with public interest and with maintaining the rights of future generations." **Article 71:** "The State shall provide care for children and youth; shall support their development spiritually, morally, culturally, educationally, physically, psychologically, socially and economically; and shall empower them for active political participation."

[26] In regard to the constitution of Somalia, which was adopted in August 2012, and is quite new in terms of when it was adopted, yet still health and medical care are not represented in the constitution as an obligation of the state and/or a right of its people.

[27] See Qatar Development Strategy 2011–2016.

[28] See Sudan's National Human Resources for Health Strategy 2012–2016.

balanced manner.[29] This can be achieved through improving the health status of individuals and communities; safeguarding the population against health threats and financial consequences of ill-health; providing equitable access to people-centred care; and by creating the possibility for people to participate in the decisions affecting their health and health system.[30]

Access encapsulates almost all aspects of the health system (HS), including service delivery, health financing, human resources for health (HRH) and essential medicines, to name a few. For that reason we chose to marry up the AAAQ framework with indicators representative of the later mentioned HS building blocks. Table 5.4 (in the Annex to this chapter) plots the various indicators chosen against the criterion for availability, accessibility (which includes both physical and financial), acceptability and quality.[31] We observe that availability and accessibility are very much intertwined, and could therefore not be strictly separated. Furthermore, due to its qualitative nature as a measure, it was quite challenging to quantify 'quality' and 'acceptability' in metric terms.

As seen in Table 5.4 (in the Annex to this chapter) there is massive variability in availability and accessibility to health care across the Arab region. This is substantiated by, even more, discrepancy in the countries' financial architecture (see Fig. 5.1). Libya, for example, houses the largest number of hospital beds/1000 population in the region,[32] yet a recent assessment of it shattered health system has shown that occupancy is at a 20 %.[33] In another example, Out of Pocket (OOP) expenditure as a percentage of total expenditure on health in Yemen is at a catastrophic level of 75 %, which is by all means unacceptable and constitutes a serious tension with the right to health. There is a direct correlation between how much governments spend on its health system (with reservations on how efficient the spending is, naturally) and how close its people are to devastating health financing consequences.

For further breakdown, Table 5.3 (in the Annex to this chapter) elaborates more on the intimate relationship between three health financing metrics (Total expenditure on health as a percentage of GDP,[34] General government expenditure

---

[29] See WHO's Key components of a well-functioning health system http://www.who.int/healthsystems/EN_HSSkeycomponents.pdf.

[30] Ibid.

[31] General Comment 14: Para 12 "The right to health in all its forms and at all levels contains the following interrelated and essential elements, the precise application of which will depend on the conditions prevailing in a particular State party: (a) Availability (b) Accessibility (c) Acceptability (d) Quality."

[32] See in the Annex Table 5.4 > Libya Hospital beds/1000 population.

[33] WHO CC-Imperial College London. Libya: Post-Conflict Health System Assessment (part 1). Rawat et al. 2013.

[34] Total health expenditure is the sum of public and private health expenditure. It covers the provision of health services (preventive and curative), family planning activities, nutrition activities, and emergency aid designated for health but does not include provision of water and sanitation (source: World Bank Data).

5 Codification and Implementation of the 'Right to Health' in the Arab World

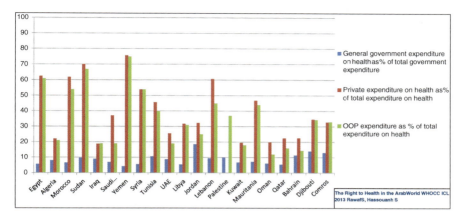

Fig. 5.1 Financing for Health care: public and private expenditure. The Right to Health in the Arab World WHOCC ICL 2013 Rawaf S, and Hassounah S

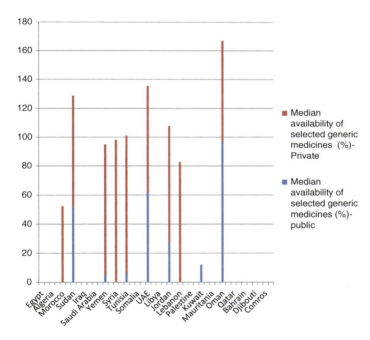

Fig. 5.2 Median availability of selected generic medicine (%) private and public. The Right to Health in the Arab World WHOCC ICL 2013, Rawaf S and Hassounah S

on health as a percentage of total government expenditure[35] and OOP expenditure as a percentage of total expenditure on health[36]) for countries of the Arab world. Additionally, Table 5.4 (in the Annex) and Fig. 5.2 show the discrepancy in the availability in essential medicines for the public; between Oman, having the highest number of essential medicines available in the public sector, and Yemen, having the lowest. This shows the lack of scrutiny in legislation as the state ensures the availability of drugs for the people.

In regard to acceptability and quality, as mentioned earlier, it is often quite challenging to quantify these criteria in a numeric form as they are more qualitative due to their seeming nature. Nonetheless, we approached this area attempting to correlate the availability of health professionals (in the multitude of specialities of health) to these criteria. There are many limitations to this approach, as the mere availability of health professional is not necessarily indicative to/of the level of quality of how acceptable services are to the public. We are well aware of such limitations and feel strongly regarding highlighting them.

5.5 Conclusion

The primary and core function of governments is to guarantee the rights of their population, including the right to health; to have strategic objectives focused on populations' interest; and to have people-centred policies. Overall, there has been noticeable progress in regards to better commitment to the health rights and universal health coverage in some countries in the Arab world. However, other countries still fall behind, embodying poor forms for governance that lack the capability of effectively safeguarding their residents health and well-being. Such countries, sadly, often lose more than the adequate health status of their residents (as an immediate effect). On the long run, they also suffer the brain drain and good medical expertise that they might have once had due to the dire conditions and frustrations caused to the health workforce operating within such inapt health systems.

---

[35] Public health expenditure consists of recurrent and capital spending from government (central and local) budgets, external borrowings and grants (including donations from international agencies and nongovernmental organizations), and social (or compulsory) health insurance funds. Total health expenditure is the sum of public and private health expenditure. It covers the provision of health services (preventive and curative), family planning activities, nutrition activities, and emergency aid designated for health but does not include provision of water and sanitation (source: World Bank Data).

[36] OOP expenditure as a percentage of total expenditure on health, also known as Private health expenditure includes direct household (out-of-pocket) spending, private insurance, charitable donations, and direct service payments by private corporations (source: World Bank Data).

Quantifying and measuring health care, and its progress, is quite a challenge, and is an ever-changing art form in its self. More developed countries, such as the United States and the United Kingdom, still continue to tweak and change their metrics to accommodate the ever changing health needs and population landscape. Thus it is not to be underestimated how complex and multidisciplinary it is to create indicators and metrics that are as closely reflective to the underlying status of health condition(s), or health system operation, as possible. The recurrent theme in health rights violations mainly pertains to poor comprehensive legal commitment at the national level, yet, this is compounded by poor efficiency mechanisms put in place for effective use of resources and challenges in accessibility, both physical and financial, or in terms of available skilled workforce. To enable structural and systematic improvement in terms of accessibility and availability of health and health care, we believe it is paramount to be able to quantify the performance of the existing models of care. And to reiterate, we realise that, given the complexity of health and health seeking behaviour, there is much difficulty to create, update and standardise such criteria. It is therefore incumbent upon governments in the region to adopt a more pragmatic model of measurable health outcomes and pre-set targets; marrying them up with updated strategic plans based on reliable and current information.

Across the board, both, the Public Health and Human Rights frameworks move to the same drumbeat of equity and dignity of human life. To reinforce this interlink in health rights, we find it acumen to strongly highlight UHC as the "single, most powerful concept public health has to offer",[37] which is, and can be further recognized as the core concept of the right to health.

---

[37] Dr. Margaret Chan-Director-General of the World Health Organization in her statement to the press at the launch of the World Health Report: Health Systems Financing: The Path to Universal Coverage.

Annexes

Table 5.3 The right to health in the constitutions and national laws of Arab states

Arab Republic of Egypt	
Enactment	**Signed into law by President on 26 December 2012** **Article 10** '........... The State shall ensure maternal and child health services free of charge, and enable the reconciliation between the duties of a woman toward her family and her work. The State shall provide special care and protection to female breadwinners, divorced women and widows **Article 62** Healthcare is a right of every citizen, and the State shall allocate a sufficient percentage of the national revenue The State shall provide healthcare services and health insurance in accordance with just and high standards, to be free of charge for those who are unable to pay All health facilities shall provide various forms of medical treatment to every citizen in cases of emergency or life danger The State shall supervise all health facilities, inspect them for quality of services, and monitor all materials, products and means of health-related publicity. Legislation to regulate such supervision shall be drafted **Article 72** The State shall provide for people with disabilities health, economic and social care, and shall provide them with employment opportunities, raise social awareness toward them, and adapt public facilities to suit their needs → **Social Determinants of Health:** **Article 63** All individuals have the right to a healthy environment. The State shall safeguard the environment against pollution, and promote the use of natural resources in a manner that prevents damage to the environment and preserves the rights of future generations **Article 66** The State shall provide social insurance services. All citizens unable to support themselves and their families in cases of incapacity, unemployment and old age have the right to social insurance guaranteeing a minimum sustenance **Article 68** Adequate housing, clean water and healthy food are given rights. The state adopts a national housing plan, based on social justice, the promotion of independent initiatives and housing cooperatives, and the regulation of the use of national territory for the purposes of construction, in accordance with public interest and with maintaining the rights of future generations **Article 71** The State shall provide care for children and youth; shall support their development spiritually, morally, culturally, educationally, physically, psychologically, socially and economically; and shall empower them for active political participation

(continued)

5 Codification and Implementation of the 'Right to Health' in the Arab World 149

Table 5.3 (continued)

	→ **Removed articles (regression)**
	Article 16
	The State shall guarantee cultural, social and health services, and work to ensure them particularly for villages in an easy and regular manner in order to raise their standard
	Article 17
	The State- shall guarantee social and health insurance services and all citizens have the right in accordance with the law to pension in cases of incapacity, unemployment and old age
People's Republic of Algeria	
Enactment	**Revised Constitution approved by the Referendum of November 28th, 1996.**
	Article 54
	All citizens have the right for the protection of their health. The State ensures the prevention and the fight of endemics and epidemics
	→ **Social Determinants of Health:**
	Article 55
	All citizens have right for work
	The law guarantees the right for protection, security and hygiene at work
	The right to rest is guaranteed; the law defines the relevant clauses
*Kingdom of Morocco**	**Adopted by referendum in 1996 and underwent reform for political/power related articles in 2011**
	Health and medical care are **NOT** represented in the constitution as an obligation of the state and/or a right of its people
Republic of Sudan	
Enactment	**Enforced by president in 1998**
	Article 13: Public Health, Sport and Environment
	The state shall promote public health, encourage sports and protect natural environment, its purity and its natural balance, to ensure safe, sustainable development for the benefit of all future generations
Republic of South Sudan	
Enactment	**Transitional constitution promulgated on 9 July 2011 (Date of South Sudan's Independence)**
	Part 2-Bill of Rights/Public Health Care
	31. All levels of government shall promote public health, establish, rehabilitate and develop basic medical and diagnostic institutions and provide free primary health care and emergency services for all citizens
	CHAPTER VIII- HIV/AIDS COMMISSION
	150. (1) There shall be established an independent commission to be known as the HIV/AIDS Commission

(continued)

Table 5.3 (continued)

Republic of Iraq	
Enactment	**Approved by referendum on 15 October 2005** (to replace the Law of Administration for the State of Iraq for the Transitional Period (TAL), previously adopted by a Governing Council appointed by the Coalition Provisional Authority after the Iraq War)
	Article 30:
	First: The State shall guarantee to the individual and the family—especially children and women—social and health security, the basic requirements for living a free and decent life, and shall secure for them suitable income and appropriate housing
	Second: The State shall guarantee social and health security to Iraqis in cases of old age, sickness, employment disability, homelessness, orphanhood, or unemployment, shall work to protect them from ignorance, fear and poverty, and shall provide them housing and special programs of care and rehabilitation, and this shall be regulated by law
	Article 31:
	First: Every citizen has the right to health care. The State shall maintain public health and provide the means of prevention and treatment by building different types of hospitals and health institutions
	Article 32:
	The State shall care for the handicapped and those with special needs, and shall ensure their rehabilitation in order to reintegrate them into society, and this shall be regulated by law
Kingdom of Saudi Arabia	**Royal Decree embodying the Basic Law of Governance dated 1992**
	Article 31:
	The state shall look after public health and provide health care for every citizen
Republic of Yemen	
Enactment	**Amended constitution dated 2001** (Note: a new draft for the constitution is currently being drafted and is henceforth expected impending the 2014 presidential elections)
	Article (55):
	Health care is a right for all citizens. The state shall guarantee this by building various hospitals and health establishments and expanding their care. The law shall organize the medical profession. The expansion of free health services and health education among the citizens

(continued)

5 Codification and Implementation of the 'Right to Health' in the Arab World 151

Table 5.3 (continued)

Arab Republic of Syria	
Enactment	**Amended constitution put forward in 2012**
	Article 22
	1. The state shall guarantee every citizen and his family in cases of emergency, sickness, disability, orphan-hood and old age
	2. The state shall protect the health of citizens and provide them with the means of prevention, treatment and medication
	Article 23
	The state shall provide women with all opportunities enabling them to effectively and fully contribute to the political, economic, social and cultural life, and the state shall work on removing the restrictions that prevent their development and participation in building society
	Article 25
	Education, health and social services shall be the basic pillars for building society, and the state shall work on achieving balanced development among all regions of the Syrian Arab Republic
Republic of Tunisia	
Enactment	**Adopted in 1959 and under gone amendments in 2002 and 2008** (Note: New/Post uprising constitution is expected to be due in April 2013)
	Article 34
	'… The law sets the basic principles for the following:
	• the system of property and real rights;
	• education; public health; labor law and social security'.
	Article 35
	Subjects other that those falling within the domain of the law come under the general regulatory power. Texts related to these subjects can be modified by decree upon recommendation by the Constitutional Council
*Federal Republic of Somalia[c]**	**Adopted August 2012**
	Health and medical care are **NOT** represented in the constitution as an obligation of the state and/or a right of its people
United Arab EMIRATES	
Enactment	**Came into effect 1971 and permanently adopted 1996**
	Article 19
	Medical care and means of prevention and treatment of diseases and epidemics shall be ensured by the community for all citizens
	The community shall promote the establishment of public and private hospitals, dispensaries and cure—houses

(continued)

Table 5.3 (continued)

State Policy (Government Strategy 2011–2013)	The UAE Government aims to ensure access of all citizens and residents to primary health care, and to improve the quality of healthcare services provided in the country to global standards. It also seeks to reduce lifestyle diseases and increase the readiness of the health system to deal with epidemics and health risks The UAE Government's strategic directions to build a world-class healthcare system include the following: 1. Ensure universal access to healthcare services by ensuring availability of healthcare services in all regions, and developing health insurance and implementing scheme 2. Provide world-class healthcare services by improving governance in the healthcare system, enhancing healthcare services, medical diagnosis and operations while leveraging partnerships, pursuing the accreditation of hospitals and other healthcare providers in the UAE, and upgrading the standards for healthcare professionals 3. Reduce epidemic and health risks by promoting a healthy way of life that reduces the prevalence of diseases, strengthening preventive medicine, and developing readiness to deal with health epidemics 11
Libya-National Transitional Council	
Enactment	**Post revolution/President over throw constitution-**Issued by National Transitional Council (NTC) in August 2011 and is to be used till dissolution council **Article (7)** Human rights and his basic freedoms shall be respected by the State. The state shall commit itself to join the international and regional declarations and charters which protect such rights and freedoms. The State shall endeavor to promulgate new charters which shall honor the human being as being God's successor on Earth
Hashemite Kingdom of Jordan*	**Ratified and promulgated 1 January 1952** Health and medical care are **NOT** represented in the constitution as an obligation of the state and/or a right of its people
Republic of c Lebanon	**Adopted 1926 with several amendments up to 1995** Health and medical care are **NOT** represented in the constitution as an obligation of the state and/or a right of its people
The State of Palestine*	
Enactment	**Amended and promulgated in 2003** **Article (45)** The law shall regulate the services of social security, disability and old age pensions, care for families of martyrs, prisoners, orphans, and care for those injured in the national struggle, and those requiring special care. The state shall guarantee them, within the bounds of its capabilities, the services of education, health and social security and shall give them priority in employment opportunities in accordance with the limitations laid down by law **Article (46)** The state shall organize health insurance as an individual right and a public interest. It shall guarantee, within the boundaries of its capabilities, basic health care for those financially unable

(continued)

5 Codification and Implementation of the 'Right to Health' in the Arab World 153

Table 5.3 (continued)

State of Kuwait	
Enactment	**Ratified and put into force 1963**
	Article 15 [*Health Care*]
	The State cares for public health and for means of prevention and treatment of diseases and epidemics.
Islamic Republic of [c] Mauritania*	**1991 Constitution with amendments in 2006**
	Health and medical care are **NOT** represented in the constitution as an obligation of the state and/or a right of its people
Oman, Sultanate	Promulgated in 1996—Followed by decree ratification in 2011 which mainly altered power-related articles in response of popular uprising.
	Article 12
	–The State guarantees assistance for the citizen and his family in cases of emergency, sickness, disability and old age according to the scheme of the social security and shall work for the solidarity of the society in bearing the burdens resulting from national disasters and catastrophes.
	–The State cares for public health and the means of prevention and treatment of diseases and epidemics. It endeavours to provide healthcare for every citizen and encourages establishing private hospitals, polyclinics and medical institutions under its supervision and according to regulations determined by the Law. It also works for the conservation of the environment, its protection and prevention of pollution.
State of Qatar	**Ratified 8th June 2004 by H.H. as the permanent constitution and has been used since**
	Article 23
	The State shall foster public health; provide means of prevention from diseases and epidemics and their cure in accordance with the law.
Kingdom of Bahrain	
Enactment	**Promulgated by the King in 2002** (was preceded by emergency law since 1975)
	Article 8:
	a. Every citizen is entitled to health care. The state cares for public health and the State ensures the means of prevention and treatment by establishing a variety of hospitals and healthcare institutions.
	b. Individuals and bodies may establish private hospital, clinics or treatment centres under the supervision of the state and in accordance with the law.

(continued)

Table 5.3 (continued)	
Republic of Djibouti	
Enactment	**Adopted 1992**
	'Health' not specifically elaborated on; the only related text is:
	TITLE II- ON THE RIGHTS AND DUTIES OF THE PERSON- ARTICLE 10
	'... Anyone who is deprived of his liberty shall have the right to be examined by a doctor of his own choosing'.
Union of Comoros	
Enactment	**Adopted December 2001**
	Belief: The right of health and education for all

* Constitution whereby health and medical care are **NOT** represented as an obligation of the state and/or a right of its people.

Table 5.4 Access to Health care: Analysis of AAAQ framework—Availability, Accessibility

Country (Ranked by population size -2010)	Availability and Accessibility							
	Hospital beds/1,000 pop (source-year)	Access to medicine (essential medicines) (source-year)		Total expenditure on health as % of GDP (source-year)	General government expenditure on health as % of total government expenditure (source-year)	Private expenditure on health as % of total expenditure on health (source-year)	Private prepaid plans as a % of private expenditure on health (source-year)	OOP expenditure as % of total expenditure on health (source-year)
		Median availability of selected generic medicines (%)—Public	Median availability of selected generic medicines (%)—Private					
1. Egypt	1.7 (WB/WDI-2010)	N/A	N/A	4.7 (WHO/GHO-2010)	5.7 (WHO/GHO-2010)	62.6 (WHO/GHO-2010)	1.7 (WHO/GHO-2010)	61 (WHO/NHAD-2010)
2. Algeria	1.7 (WB/WDI-2004)	N/A	N/A	4.2 (WHO/GHO-2010)	8.1 (WHO/GHO-2010)	22.1 (WHO/GHO-2010)	5.1 (WHO/GHO-2010)	21 (WHO/NHAD-2010)
3. Morocco	1.1 (WB/WDI-2009)	**0 (GHO-2004)**	52.5 (GHO-2004)	5.2 (WHO/GHO-2010)	6.6 (WHO/GHO-2010)	62 (WHO/GHO-2010)	13.7 (WHO/GHO-2010)	54 (WHO/NHAD-2010)
4. Sudan*	0.7 (WB/WDI-2009)	51.7 (GHO-2006)	77.1 (GHO-2006)	6.3 (WHO/GHO-2010)	9.8 (WHO/GHO-2010)	*70.2 (WHO/GHO-2010)*	1 (WHO/GHO-2010)	67 (WHO/NHAD-2010)
5. Iraq	1.3 (WB/WDI-2009)	N/A	N/A	*8.4 (WHO/GHO-2010)*	9 (WHO/GHO-2010)	**18.8 (WHO/GHO-2010)**	**0 (WHO/GHO-2010)**	19 (WHO/NHAD-2010)
6. Saudi Arabia	2.2 (WB/WDI-2009)	N/A	N/A	4.3 (WHO/GHO-2010)	7 (WHO/GHO-2010)	37.1 (WHO/GHO-2010)	*33.4 (WHO/GHO-2010)*	19 (WHO/NHAD-2010)
7. Yemen	0.7 (WB/WDI-2009)	5 (GHO-2006)	90 (GHO-2006)	5.2 (WHO/GHO-2010)	**4.3 (WHO/GHO-2010)**	75.8 (WHO/GHO-2010)	1.3 (WHO/GHO-2010)	*75 (WHO/NHAD-2010)*
8. Syria	1.5 (WB/WDI-2010)	N/A	98.2 *(GHO-2003)*	3.4 (WHO/GHO-2010)	5.6 (WHO/GHO-2010)	54 (WHO/GHO-2010)	**0 (WHO/GHO-2010)**	54 (WHO/NHAd-2010)

(continued)

Table 5.4 (continued)

Country (Ranked by population size -2010)	Availability and Accessibility							
	Hospital beds/1,000 pop (source-year)	Access to medicine (essential medicines) (source-year)		Total expenditure on health as % of GDP (source-year)	General government expenditure on health as % of total government expenditure (source-year)	Private expenditure on health as % of total expenditure on health (source-year)	Private prepaid plans as a % of private expenditure on health (source-year)	OOP expenditureas % of total expenditure on health (source-year)
		Median availability of selected generic medicines (%)—Public	Median availability of selected generic medicines (%)—Private					
9. Tunisia	2.1 (WB/WDI-2009)	6 (GHO-2004)	95.1 (GHO-2004)	6.2 (WHO/GHO-2010)	10.7 (WHO/GHO-2010)	45.7 (WHO/GHO-2010)	11.2 (WHO/GHO-2010)	40 (WHO/NHAD-2010)
10. Somalia	**0.4 (WB/WDI-1997)**	N/A	N/A	N/A	N/A	N/A	N/A	N/A
11. UAE	1.9 (WB/WDI-2008)	61.6 (GHO-2006)	73.9 (GHO-2006)	3.7 (WHO/GHO-2010)	8.8 (WHO/GHO-2010)	25.6 (WHO/GHO-2010)	15.7 (WHO/GHO-2010)	19 (WHO/NHAD-2010)
12. Libya	*3.7 (WB/WDI-2009)*	N/A	N/A	3.9 (WHO/GHO-2010)	5.5 (WHO/GHO-2010)	31.8 (WHO/GHO-2010)	0 (WHO/GHO-2010)	31 (WHO/NHAD-2010)
13. Jordan	1.8 (WB/WDI-2009)	27.8 (GHO-2004)	80 (GHO-2004)	2.6 (WHO/NHAD-2010)	*18.6 (WHO/NHAD-2010)*	32.3 (WHO/GHO-2010)	N/A	25 (WHO/NHAD-2010)
14. Lebanon	3.5 (WB/WDI-2009)	**0 (GHO-2004)**	83 (GHO-2004)	7 (WHO/GHO-2010)	9.5 (WHO/GHO-2010)	60.8 (WHO/GHO-2010)	22.1 (WHO/GHO-2010)	45 (WHO/NHAD-2010)
15. Palestinian Territories	1.2 (WB/WDI-1996)	N/A	N/A	16 (WHO/GHO-2011)	10 (WHO/GHO-2011)	N/A	N/A	37 (WHO/GHO-2011)
16. Kuwait	2 (WHS 1997)	12 (GHO-2004)	**0 (GHO-2004)**	2.6 (WHO/GHO-2010)	6.8 (WHO/NHAD-2010)	19.6 (WHO/GHO-2010)	9.4 (WHO/GHO-2010)	18 (WHO/NHAD-2010)

(continued)

Table 5.4 (continued)

Country (Ranked by population size -2010)	Availability and Accessibility							
	Hospital beds/1,000 pop (source-year)	Access to medicine (essential medicines) (source-year)		Total expenditure on health as % of GDP (source-year)	General government expenditure on health as % of total government expenditure (source-year)	Private expenditure on health as % of total expenditure on health (source-year)	Private prepaid plans as a % of private expenditure on health (source-year)	OOP expenditure as % of total expenditure on health (source-year)
		Median availability of selected generic medicines (%)—Public	Median availability of selected generic medicines (%)—Private					
17. Mauritania	**0.4 (WB/WDI-2006)**	N/A	N/A	4.4 (WHO/GHO-2010)	7.3 (WHO/GHO-2010)	46.9 (WHO/GHO-2010)	0.6 (WHO/GHO-2010)	44 (WHO/NHAD-2010)
18. Oman	1.8 (WB/WDI-2009)	*96.7 (GHO-2007)*	70.3 (GHO-2007)	2.8 (WHO/GHO-2010)	6.2 (WHO/GHO-2010)	19.9 (WHO/GHO-2010)	23.4 (WHO/GHO-2010)	**12 (WHO/NHAD-2010)**
19. Qatar	1.2 (WB/WDI-2009)	N/A	N/A	**1.8 (WHO/GHO-2010)**	5.5 (WHO/GHO-2010)	22.5 (WHO/GHO-2010)	27.9 (WHO/GHO-2010)	16 (WHO/NHAD-2010)
20. Bahrain	1.8 (WB/WDI-2009)	N/A	N/A	5 (WHO/GHO-2010)	11.4 (WHO/GHO-2010)	22.6 (WHO/GHO-2010)	29 (WHO/GHO-2010)	14.4 (WHO/NHAD-2010)
21. Djibouti	1.4 (WB/WDI-2010)	N/A	N/A	7.2 (WHO/GHO-2010)	14.1 (WHO/GHO-2010)	34.7 (WHO/GHO-2010)	0.9 (WHO/GHO-2010)	34.4 (WHO/NHAD-2010)
22. Comros	2.2 (WB/WDI-2006)	N/A	N/A	4.5 (WHO/GHO-2010)	13.1 (WHO/GHO-2010)	32.8 (WHO/GHO-2010)	0 (WHO/GHO-2010)	33 (WHO/NHAD-2010)

Table 5.5 Access to Health care: Analysis of AAAQ framework—Acceptability and Quality

Country (Ranked by population size-2010)	Acceptability and Quality			
	Physicians density/ 1,000 population	Environmental and public health workers density (per 1,000 population)	Health management & support workers density (per 1,000 population)	Total health workforce[**] (per 1,000 population)
1. Egypt	2.83 (WHO GAHW-2009)	0.13 (WHO GAHW-2004)	0.07 (WHO GAHW-2004)	8.96 (WHO GAHW-2009[a])
2. Algeria	1.21 (WHO GAHW-2007)	0.07 (WHO GAHW-2007)	0.03 (WHO GAHW-2007)	7.46 (WHO GAHW-2007)
3. Morocco	0.62 (WHO GAHW-2009)	0.02 (WHO GAHW-2004)	0.2 (WHO GAHW-2004)	2.17 (WHO GAHW-2009[b])
4. Sudan*	0.28 (WHO GAHW-2008)	0.07 (WHO GAHW-2006)	0.7 (WHO GAHW-2006)	2.9 (WHO GAHW-2006[c])
5. Iraq	0.69 (WHO GAHW-2009)	0.1 (WHO GAHW-2004)	1.33 (WHO GAHW-2004)	5.16 (WHO GAHW-2009[d])
6. Saudi Arabia	0.94 (WHO GAHW-2008)	N/A	2.42 (WHO GAHW-2008)	6.83 (WHO GAHW-2008[e])
7. Yemen	0.3 (WHO GAHW-2009)	0.04 (WHO GAHW-2004)	0.53 (WHO GAHW-2004)	1.84 (WHO GAHW-2004[f])
8. Syria	1.5 (WHO GAHW-2008)	N/A	0.56 (WHO GAHW-2006)	6.12 (WHO GAHW-2008[g])
9. Tunisia	1.2 (WHO GAHW-2009)	0.09 (WHO GAHW-2004)	1.61 (WHO GAHW-2004)	8.1 (WHO GAHW-2009[h])
10. Somalia	**0.035 (WHO GAHW-2006)**	**0.005 (WHO GAHW-2005)**	**0.009 (WHO GAHW-2005)**	**0.254 (WHO GAHW-2005[i])**
11. UAE	1.93 (WHO GAHW-2007)	N/A	N/A	7.04 (WHO GAHW-2007[j])
12. Libya	1.9 (WHO GAHW-2009)	N/A	N/A	9.66 (WHO GAHW-2009[k])

(continued)

Table 5.5 (continued)

Country (Ranked by population size-2010)	Acceptability and Quality			
	Physicians density/ 1,000 population	Environmental and public health workers density (per 1,000 population)	Health management & support workers density (per 1,000 population)	Total health workforce[**] (per 1,000 population)
13. Jordan	2.45 (WHO GAHW-2009)	*0.25 (WHO GAHW-2004)*	3.15 (WHO GAHW-2004)	*14.37 (WHO GAHW-2009[l])*
14. Lebanon	*3.54 (WHO GAHW-2009)*	N/A	N/A	8.95 (WHO GAHW-2009[m])
15. Palestinian Territories	2.08 (WHO GAHW-2011)	N/A	N/A	3.56 (GHO-2011[n])
16. Kuwait	1.79 (WHO GAHW-2006)	N/A	*4.13 (WHO GAHW-2009)*	13.66 (WHO GAHW-2009[o])
17. Mauritania	0.13 (WHO GAHW-2009)	0.057 (WHO GAHW-2009)	1.3 (WHO GAHW-2009)	2 (WHO GAHW-2009[p])
18. Oman	1.9 (WHO GAHW-2008)	0.076 (WHO GAHW-2008)	1.6 (WHO GAHW-2007)	12.82 (WHO GAHW-2008[q])
19. Qatar	2.76 (WHO GAHW-2006)	N/A	N/A	12.94 (WHO GAHW-2006[r])
20. Bahrain	1.4 (WHO GAHW-2008)	0.4 (WHO GAHW-2004)	2.4 (WHO GAHW-2004)	9.37 (WHO GAHW-2008[s])
21. Djibouti	0.2 (WHO GAHW-2006)	0.025 (WHO GAHW-2005)	0.29 (WHO GAHW-2005)	2.12 (WHO GAHW-2005[t])
22. Comros	0.15 (WHO GAHW-2004)	0.02 (WHO GAHW-2004)	0.34 (WHO GAHW-2004)	0.74 (WHO GAHW-2004[u])

Key to Tables 5.3, 5.4, 5.5

Bold = Lowest
Italics = Highest

*Including North and South
**Total Health workforce encapsulates: Physicians, Dentistry personnel, Pharmaceutical personnel, Laboratory health workers, Environmental and public health workers, Community and Nursing and midwifery personnel, traditional health workers, other workers as well as Health management & support workers density per 1,000 population (unless otherwise indicated)

WB: World Bank
GHO: Global Health Observatory
WDI: World Development Indicator
GHWA: Global Health Workforce Atlas
NHAD: National Health Accounts Directory

(a) Physicians, Dentistry, Pharmaceutical and Nursing personnel figures are for 2009 while Laboratory health workers, Environmental and public health, Health management & support workers, and other workers figures are for 2004 (There are no figures for Community traditional health workers)
(b) Physicians, Dentistry, Pharmaceutical and Nursing personnel figures are for 2009 while Laboratory health workers, Environmental and public health, Health management & support workers, and other workers figures are for 2004 (There are no figures for Community traditional health workers)
(c) Physicians, Dentistry, Pharmaceutical and Nursing, Environmental and public health, Health management & support workers, and other workers personnel figures are for 2006 while Laboratory and Community traditional health workers figures are for 2004
(d) Physicians, Dentistry, Pharmaceutical and Nursing, Environmental and public health, figures are for 2009 while Laboratory, Health management & support workers, other workers personnel and Community traditional health workers figures are for 2004
(e) Physicians, Pharmaceutical, and Nursing, Health management & support workers, other workers figures are for 2009 while Dentistry figures are for 2004 (There are no figures for Community, traditional health workers Environmental and public health or Laboratory)
(f) Pharmaceutical, Laboratory, Environmental and public health, Health management & support workers, other workers and Community traditional health workers figures are for 2004 while Physicians and Dentistry personnel figures are for 2009 (There are no figures for Nursing personnel)
(g) Physicians, Dentistry, Pharmaceutical and Nursing personnel figures are for 2008, while Health management & support, and other health workers figures

5 Codification and Implementation of the 'Right to Health' in the Arab World

are for 2006 (There are no figures for Community, traditional health workers Environmental and public health or Laboratory)

(h) Physicians, Dentistry, Pharmaceutical and Nursing personnel figures are for 2009, while Environmental and public health, Laboratory, Health management & support, and other health workers figures are for 2004 (There are no figures for Community, traditional health workers,)

(i) Physicians, Pharmaceutical and Nursing personnel figures are for 2009, while Health management & support, and other health workers figures are for 2004 (There are no figures for Dentistry, Community, traditional health workers, Environmental and public health or Laboratory)

(j) Figures displayed are only for Physicians, Dentistry, Pharmaceutical, Nursing and Midwifery personnel (2007). There is no available data for Environmental and public health, Laboratory, Health management & support, and other health workers.

(k) Figures displayed are only for Physicians, Dentistry, Pharmaceutical, Nursing and Midwifery personnel (2009). There is no available data for Environmental and public health, Laboratory, Health management & support, and other health workers.

(l) Physicians, Dentistry, Pharmaceutical, Nursing and Midwifery figures are for 2009 while Laboratory, Environmental and public health, Health management & support workers, other workers personnel and Community traditional health workers figures are for 2004

(m) Physicians, Dentistry, Pharmaceutical and Nursing personnel figures are for 2009, while Health management & support, and other health workers figures are for 2005 (There are no figures for Community, traditional health workers Environmental and public health or Laboratory)

(n) Figures displayed are only for Physicians, Dentistry and Pharmaceutical personnel (2011). There is no available data for Nursing and Midwifery Environmental and public health, Laboratory, Health management & support, and other health workers.

(o) Figures displayed are only for Physicians, Dentistry, Pharmaceutical, Nursing and Midwifery personnel (2009). There is no available data for Environmental and public health, Laboratory, Health management & support, and other health workers.

(p) Physicians, Dentistry, Pharmaceutical and Nursing, Environmental and public health, Health management & support workers, Community and other workers personnel figures are for 2009 while Laboratory workers figures are for 2004

(q) Physicians, Dentistry, Pharmaceutical and Nursing, Laboratory health workers, Environmental and public health, & support workers, and other workers figures are for 2008, while Health management figures are for 2007 (There are no figures for Community traditional health workers)

(r) Figures displayed are only for Physicians, Dentistry, Pharmaceutical, Laboratory, Nursing and Midwifery personnel (2006). There is no available data

for Environmental and public health, Health management & support, and
other health workers.

(s) Physicians, Dentistry, Pharmaceutical and Nursing, Laboratory health
workers, support workers, and other workers figures are for 2008 while figures for 'Environmental and public health workers and Health management &
support workers are for 2004 (There are no figures for Community traditional
health workers)

(t) Pharmaceutical, Laboratory, Environmental and public health, Nursing personnel, Health management & support workers, other workers and Community traditional health workers figures are for 2005 while Physicians and
Dentistry personnel figures are for 2009

(u) Pharmaceutical, Laboratory, Environmental and public health, Health management & support workers, other workers and Community traditional health
workers figures are for 2004 while Physicians and Dentistry personnel figures
are for 2009 (There are no figures for Nursing personnel)

References

Chan M (2010) World health report: health systems financing: the path to universal coverage. http://www.who.int/dg/speeches/2010/launch_WHR_20101122/en/index.html

Chan M (2012) Universal health coverage lancet themed issue (2012). http://www.thelancet.com/themed-universal-health-coverage

Constitution of the World Health Organization (1948). http://www.who.int/governance/eb/who_constitution_en.pdf

Health and Poverty Reduction Strategies. UNHCR Human Rights: Health and Human Rights Publications Series, Issue No 5. (2008). http://www.ohchr.org/Documents/Publications/HHR_PovertyReductionsStrategies_WHO_EN.pdf

International Covenant on Economic, Social and Cultural Rights. General Comment No. 14 (2000). Article 12: The right to the highest attainable standard of health. http://www.unhchr.ch/tbs/doc.nsf/(symbol)/E.C.12.2000.4.En

Kinney ED, Clark BA—Provisions for Health and Health Care in the Constitutions of the Countries of the World. p 290. http://indylaw.indiana.edu/instructors/Kinney/Articles/kinney_Constitutions.pdf

Qatar Development Strategy (2011–2016). http://www.gsdp.gov.qa/gsdp_vision/docs/NDS_EN.pdf

Rawaf S et al (2013) Libya: post-conflict health system assessment, part 1. World Health Organization collaborating Centre for Public Health Education and Training, Imperial College London

Robinson M (2002) 25 questions and answers on Health and Human rights. Health and Human Rights Publication Series, issue no. 1 July 2002, WHO, p 8, question 3. http://www.who.int/hhr/NEW37871OMSOK.pdf

Sudan's National Human Resources for Health Strategy (2012–2016). http://www.who.int/workforcealliance/countries/Sudan_HRHPlan_2012-16.pdf

United Nations Development Program: About Arab States. http://arabstates.undp.org/content/rbas/en/home/regioninfo/

Wanless D (2002) Securing our future health: taking a long-term view final report pp 119–122. http://si.easp.es/derechosciudadania/wp-content/uploads/2009/10/4.informe-wanless.pdf

WHO—World Health Report (2010). http://www.who.int/whr/2010/whr10_en.pdf

World Bank: Arab World. http://data.worldbank.org/region/ARB

World Bank Data—GDP per Capita in current USD. http://data.worldbank.org/indicator/NY.GDP.PCAP.CD/countries

World Bank Data—Improved sanitation facilities (% of population with access). http://data.worldbank.org/indicator/SH.STA.ACSN/countries

World Health Organization's Key components of a well-functioning health system. http://www.who.int/healthsystems/EN_HSSkeycomponents.pdf

World Health Organization / Office of the High Commissioner for Human Rights. Joint Factsheet WHO/OHCHR/323 (2007). http://www.who.int/mediacentre/factsheets/fs323_en.pdf

World Water Assessment Programme (2012) The United Nations World Water Development Report 4: Managing Water under Uncertainty and Risk. Paris, UNESCO. Chapter 7, p 210. http://unesdoc.unesco.org/images/0021/002156/215644e.pdf

Chapter 6
The Right to Health and Access to Health Care in Saudi Arabia with a Particular Focus on the Women and Migrants

Lara Walker

Abstract This chapter focuses on the right to health in the Kingdom of Saudi Arabia and looks specifically at the position of vulnerable groups when it comes to the realisation of the right to health. The groups considered are women and migrant workers. The chapter looks at the underlying determinants of the right to health in relation to these groups, specifically the determinants that arise from the concept or practice of gender inequality. In the context of the Kingdom, these inequalities arise from traditional, cultural, and social practices that may affect the health of women and migrant workers. The chapter begins by examining the overall human rights protection in the Kingdom and discusses a variety of disadvantages faced by these groups, which are generally caused by cultural and social practices. It then explains how these disadvantages can have a negative impact in a variety of aspects of these groups' lives and focuses specifically on the right to health. The chapter shows that it is impossible for the 'right to the highest attainable standard of health' to be achieved for these groups unless there are fundamental changes in social and cultural practices that are deeply embedded in the traditions and laws of the Kingdom.

Contents

6.1 Introduction 166
6.2 General Human Rights Protection in Saudi Arabia 167
6.3 The Right to Health in Saudi Arabia 170
6.4 General Health 173

Lara Walker is Lecturer in Law at the University of Sussex.

L. Walker (✉)
University of Sussex, Brighton BN1 9RH, UK
e-mail: lw264@sussex.ac.uk

B. Toebes et al. (eds.), *The Right to Health*, DOI: 10.1007/978-94-6265-014-5_6,
© T.M.C. ASSER PRESS and the authors 2014

6.5	Vulnerable Groups	174
	6.5.1 Women	174
	6.5.2 Migrant Workers	183
6.6	Conclusion	188
References		190

6.1 Introduction

The Kingdom of Saudi Arabia (also: 'the Kingdom') is located in the Middle East, and borders with both the Persian Gulf and the Red Sea. The capital city is Riyadh, and the Kingdom is split into thirteen different provinces. As of July 2012, the estimated population of the Kingdom was just over 26.5 million. This includes around 5.5 million non-nationals.[1] However, the latest Human Rights Watch World Report suggests that there are at least 9 million foreign workers.[2] Due to the fact that there are a high number of immigrants from Asia and the Middle East,[3] the larger number is probably more realistic and the true number of immigrants may never be known.[4] There are also migrants from the West, who work in the oil industry. The economy is oil based and the petroleum sector accounts for approximately 45 % of the GDP.[5]

This chapter considers the right to health in the Kingdom and focuses on groups that may be susceptible to infringements of their right to health, particularly women and migrant workers. The chapter begins by giving an overview of human rights protection in the Kingdom. It then looks specifically at the general protection given to the right to health in the Kingdom by examining international conventions to which Saudi Arabia is a party. Following this, the chapter moves on to the protection of the right to health in relation to vulnerable groups. The protection of the right to health in the Kingdom of these groups is influenced by general societal and cultural attitudes towards them. Therefore, it is important that the chapter begins by considering how these groups are treated generally before focussing more specifically on the right to health.

---

[1] CIA World Factbook, available at https://www.cia.gov/library/publications/the-world-factbook/geos/sa.html, accessed 25 January 2013.

[2] See Human Rights Watch World Report 2013, p. 603.

[3] CIA World Factbook. See also Human Rights Watch 2010.

[4] Human Rights Watch World Report 2011 states that '8.3 million migrant workers legally reside in Saudi Arabia; an unknown number of other migrant workers are undocumented' (p. 578).

[5] CIA World Factbook.

6.2 General Human Rights Protection in Saudi Arabia

The Kingdom of Saudi Arabia faces general problems in the context of human rights as they are inadequately protected by the legal system. This is a major issue that has frequently been pointed out by international bodies and organisations, including intergovernmental and non-governmental human rights organisations.[6] Saudi law does not protect many basic rights and even the few protected rights are subject to strict limitations. Instances include freedom of association, assembly and expression.[7] There are also serious concerns with the deficiency of official accountability,[8] arbitrary detention,[9] and the mistreatment and torture of detainees.[10] In many States around the world, 'traditional values are often deployed as an excuse to undermine human rights.'[11] General information available suggests that this is a particular problem in Saudi Arabia. Therefore, where human rights are generally undermined as a result of traditional values, groups that are particularly affected by these traditional values will have reduced human rights protection. This can include the right to health, particularly access to health care. A major cause for concern are the rights and the protection of women and children and the protection of migrant workers.[12]

Historically, women in Saudi Arabia have faced serious obstacles to their participation in society and this is a problem that continues to challenge them. This is due to the fact that the Saudi woman must obtain permission from the man who is their legal guardian before they can do certain things.[13] The legal guardian may be the husband, father or son of the woman and permission is required in order to work, travel, study, marry or access medical care.[14] Officials (both private and public actors working in an official capacity (such as doctors or lawyers)) regularly request permission from the legal guardian, even when this is not mandatory or stipulated under government guidelines. This is the case in hospitals, where some

---

[6] For example, see: Human Rights Watch World Report 2013, pp. 603–608, Amnesty International Annual Report 2012 and Blanchard 2012, pp. 1–5.

[7] Ibid. See also Freedom House 2012a.

[8] Ibid. See also Freedom House 2012b.

[9] This is common in terms of activists, who have tried to peacefully express their human rights, beliefs and been detained for this. 'In November, 16 men, including nine prominent reformists, who had tried to set up a human rights association, were given sentences ranging from 5 to 30 years in prison by the Specialised Criminal Court, which was set up to deal with terrorism-related cases, following a grossly unfair trial... Several of them had already been detained for three-and-a-half years without charge and interrogated without the presence of their lawyers.' (Amnesty International Report 2012).

[10] For example, see Human Rights Watch World Report 2013, pp. 606–607 and Amnesty International Report 2012.

[11] Human Rights Watch World Report 2013, p. 20.

[12] Idem, p. 603.

[13] Idem, p. 603.

[14] Idem, pp. 603–605.

require a guardian's permission before women are admitted or are allowed to consent to medical procedures for themselves or their children.[15] A guardian may also be consulted before the woman is discharged, despite the fact there are national regulations to the contrary.[16] This is serious and affects not only a woman's right to access health care, but also the rights of children and adolescents. Another detrimental factor is that Saudi women are not allowed to drive.[17] This could also affect the access of women and children to health care and makes them more reliant on their legal guardian. A further factor that could contribute to poor health in women is that women are traditionally not allowed to participate in sport.[18] They are denied access to sport lessons in schools and are not allowed to use public leisure centres. By failing to eliminate these discriminatory practices, the Saudi government is failing in its commitment to guarantee women and girls their right to education, employment, freedom of movement, health and equality in marriage.

This general practice conflicts with traditional human rights principles, particularly equal treatment. In this respect, the Convention on the Elimination of all forms of Discrimination Against Women (CEDAW), to which Saudi Arabia is party,[19] is of primary importance. This requires that States take all appropriate measures to:

> (...) modify the social and cultural patterns of conduct of men and women, with a view to achieving the elimination of prejudices and customary and all other practices which are based on the idea of the inferiority or the superiority of either of the sexes or on stereotyped roles for men and women.[20]

It is questionable whether the right to health can truly be protected in the Kingdom despite adequate 'access' to health care and healthcare facilities without these cultural practices being addressed. Discrimination or equality in access to health care is seen as an underlying determinant of the right to health.[21] Therefore, this chapter will consider what impact, if any, these traditional cultural practices have on women's right to health in Saudi Arabia.

---

[15] It has been reported that in July, a hospital delayed amputating a woman's hand because there was no legal guardian present, after she had been involved in a bad car accident that had killed her husband. (Human Rights Watch World Report 2013, p. 603).

[16] See Sect. 6.5.1 below.

[17] See, Amnesty International Report 2012.

[18] Human Rights Watch 2012.

[19] The Convention has applied in the Kingdom since September 2000. See, http://treaties.un.org/Pages/ViewDetails.aspx?src=TREATY&mtdsg_no=IV-8&chapter=4&lang=en, accessed 7 August 2013.

[20] Article 5(a) CEDAW. See also UN Human Rights Committee (2000), General Comment 28 on Equality between Men and Women (General Comment 28), particularly para 5.

[21] 'More determinants of health are being taken into consideration such as…gender differences.' (UN Human Rights Committee (2000), General Comment no 14, para 10. See also para 18 and P Hunt, 'Reducing Maternal Mortality', p. 6, available at http://www.unfpa.org/webdav/site/global/shared/documents/publications/reducing_mm.pdf, accessed 6 August 2013).

6 The Right to Health and Access to Health Care in Saudi Arabia

This chapter then goes on to discuss migrant workers' right to health and their ability to access health care. It is considered that migrant workers are treated very differently from citizens and treatment also differs greatly between different migrant groups. Migrant workers face different obstacles depending on nationality and nature of employment. Those that work for large private firms, normally in the oil sector and traditionally coming from Western States, tend to be treated very well and receive numerous benefits from their firms. However, migrant workers travelling from Asia, South East Asia and North Africa are much more vulnerable.[22] They generally come to work in the country as domestic workers and are essentially controlled by the family they work for.[23] They generally live with the family, meaning that hours of work, what and when they eat, and holidays are usually non-negotiable. The workers are expected to adapt to the host family's needs.

The practice of employing foreign domestic workers is deeply embedded in the culture of the Kingdom. The workers are completely at the mercy of the host family as they control their visa,[24] so if they become unemployed they are usually no longer allowed to reside in the Kingdom. There have been recent attempts to change the current sponsorship system, so that domestic workers will instead be sponsored by agencies, but the law is not in effect as yet.[25]

It is also common for the employers to keep the migrants' passports,[26] so they are unable to leave the Kingdom even if they wanted to. Domestic migrant workers are generally in a vulnerable position as they 'are excluded from labour laws'[27] and they are subject to a variety of situations that may adversely affect their health, such as long working hours, lack of rest, lack of food and poor living quarters.[28] They may also get little chance to contact their family back home or to establish friends and a social life in Saudi Arabia. This could have an adverse impact on both their physical and/or their mental health. Migrant workers may also have problems actually accessing health care when they do need it if their employers do not give them time off to visit the doctors. Therefore, overall human rights protection of domestic migrant workers is generally poor.

As there is a lack of commitment to human rights generally, particularly in the case of females and migrants, the right to health is not adequately protected in Saudi Arabia. Although there have been various improvements in relation to health care and facilities, further developments are still needed. These mainly relate to structural organisation and the cost of providing free services on an overburdened

---

[22] Examples are Ethiopia, Kenya and Indonesia. See Human Rights Watch World Report 2013, p. 120, 133 and 327.

[23] See, Minority Rights Group International 2012, and US Department of State 2012.

[24] Human Rights Watch World Report 2013, p. 605.

[25] Idem.

[26] US Department of State 2011, part d. Freedom of Movement, Internally Displaced Persons, Protection of Refugees, and Stateless Persons.

[27] Minority Rights Group International 2012.

[28] See US Department of State 2012, n 23.

system.[29] Throughout the Kingdom, there is a number of specialist hospitals, with excellent highly specialised equipment, but due to lack of accountability and poor reporting, there is paucity of reliable information. This makes it impossible to create a clear picture of how effective the Saudi healthcare system is as a whole, particularly how well the system responds to the requirements of the 'AAAQ'.[30] However, it is clear that there are problems with women's, children's and migrant worker's access to health care. These difficulties arise from the place and treatment of these groups in Saudi society.

6.3 The Right to Health in Saudi Arabia

The right to health is recognised in a number of international treaties and documents, but unsurprisingly Saudi Arabia is not party to many of these. The only international treaties that have been ratified by Saudi Arabia are CEDAW; the Convention on the Rights of the Child (CRC); the Convention against Torture (CAT); the International Convention on the Elimination of all forms of Racial Discrimination (CERD); and the International Convention on the Prevention and Punishment of the Crime of Genocide.[31] Both the CEDAW and the CRC contain provisions on the right to health. The CEDAW requires State parties to take 'all appropriate measures to eliminate discrimination against women in the field of health care',[32] and the CRC requires states to 'strive to ensure that no child is deprived of his or her right to access to ... health care services'.[33] However, in respect of CEDAW, where the text of the Convention conflicts with Islamic law, 'the Kingdom is not under obligation to observe the contradictory terms of the Convention.'[34] Therefore, although it is very helpful that Saudi Arabia has ratified CEDAW, it is questionable to what extent the provisions of the instrument are adhered to in the Kingdom.[35]

The main problem is that it is unclear what the Islamic Law actually is. The sharia is the prevailing law in Saudi Arabia. However, sharia is not codified in statutes or a written text, so it is subject to varying interpretations.[36] Sharia is a

---

[29] For a general overview of the structure and allocation of health services in the Kingdom see: Almalki et al. 2011 and Colliers 2012.

[30] See General Comment 14 on the right to health (General Comment 14), para 12: availability, accessibility, acceptability and quality.

[31] Information on ratifications available at http://treaties.un.org/Pages/Treaties.aspx?id=4&subid=A&lang=en, accessed 28 February 2013.

[32] Article 12(1) CEDAW.

[33] Article 24(1) CRC.

[34] A full list of reservations by State is available at http://www.un.org/womenwatch/daw/cedaw/reservations-country.htm accessed 2 August 2013.

[35] See the discussion above on Article 5 CEDAW.

[36] See, Van Eijk 2010, p. 157.

6 The Right to Health and Access to Health Care in Saudi Arabia

religious law that derives from the Koran and the Sunna.[37] In Saudi Arabia, these texts are seen as primary sources of law.[38] However, there has been disagreement as to whether reservations in this area, which have been made by a number of Islamic States, are actually necessary. This is because it is stated that the text of the Koran promotes equality between men and women.[39] However, it has not necessarily always been interpreted this way. Shah argues that certain provisions in the Koran allow for a different interpretation, which has led to the belief among some Muslims that women are inferior to men.[40] Of note is a provision, which suggests that men are the protectors and maintainers of women because they have more strength than women and they can support them.[41] It has been suggested that this provision constitutes the basis for male guardianship.[42] It is clear that because Sharia law is not codified, it is subject to a variety of interpretations,[43] meaning that it is ambiguous what a reservation based on Islamic Law actually entails. Any discriminatory practice or non-fulfilment of the rights in CEDAW based on this reservation arises from the interpretation given to the Koran by practitioners in the Kingdom and their interpretation of the Islamic sharia.[44]

Notably, Saudi Arabia has not ratified the International Convention on Civil and Political Rights (ICCPR).[45] Nor has the Kingdom ratified the International Covenant on Economic, Social and Cultural Rights (ICESCR).[46] This is unfortunate because even though CEDAW and CRC contain provisions on the right to health, the ICESCR is the main document for promoting social rights, such as health. Since the Kingdom is not a party to the ICESCR information is scarce on the protection of economic, social and cultural rights in the Kingdom at an international level. There is a weak international commitment to human rights, not only economic, social and cultural, but also civil and political. This is unsatisfactory and highlights that even when important Conventions have been ratified they afford little benefit to Saudis. In relation to vulnerable groups, women's rights may be better protected than the rights of migrant workers since Saudi Arabia has

---

[37] See, Van Eijk 2010, Sect. 4.5 and Ariany 2013, Sect. 3.2.

[38] Article 7 The Basic Law of Governance No: A/90, Dated 27th Sha'ban 1412 H (1 March 1992) (The Basic Law of Governance). See also Ariany 2013, p. 538.

[39] Ariany 2013, p. 542 and Shah 2006, p. 886.

[40] Shah 2006, p. 887.

[41] Sura 4:32 and see Shah 2006, pp. 887–890.

[42] Shah 2006, pp. 887–890.

[43] Shah 2006 and Ariany 2013, Sects. 2.4.2 and 3.2.4.

[44] Van Eijk 2010, p. 157.

[45] For a list of state parties see, http://treaties.un.org/Pages/ViewDetails.aspx?src=UNTSONLINE &tabid=2&mtdsg_no=IV-4&chapter=4&lang=en#Participants, accessed 17 September 2013.

[46] http://treaties.un.org/Pages/ViewDetails.aspx?src=TREATY&mtdsg_no=IV-3&chapter=4 &lang=en, accessed 27 February 2013. http://treaties.un.org/pages/ViewDetails.aspx?src= TREATY&mtdsg_no=IV-4&chapter=4&lang=en, accessed 28 February 2013.

ratified CEDAW, but not the Convention on the Protection of the Rights of Migrant Workers and Members of their Families.[47]

At the regional level, Saudi Arabia has agreed to the Cairo Declaration on Human Rights in Islam (a soft law document) and it has acceded to, but not ratified, the Arab Charter on Human Rights.[48] However, the Charter, which came into force on 30 January 2008 has been criticised by NGO's experts and academics.[49] The latest version of the Charter is an improvement, but it is still subject to criticism.[50] One particular concern is that there are no enforcement mechanisms[51] or guarantee of an effective remedy if an individual's rights are breached.[52] Fundamentally, as previously noted, the Kingdom has not ratified the Charter nor the two major human rights treaties.

Despite the lack of commitment to human rights at the international level, to international human rights standards, there appears to be some commitment at the national level. This can be seen in the Basic Law of Saudi Arabia, also known as the basic system of governance, which is a charter divided into nine chapters.[53] Chapter five refers to rights and duties. The main rights that are covered are economic, social and cultural rights, such as welfare rights, science and culture, education and environment and nature. The right to health care is referred to specifically in Article 31, which declares that: '[t]he state takes care of health issues and provides health care for each citizen'.[54] Given the referral to the word *citizen*, this could create additional problems for vulnerable groups, such as migrant workers, because non-citizens are implicitly denied protection under this provision. This can be compared with Article 36 of the same document, covering arrest and imprisonment, which provides security for all citizens and residents.[55] This would imply that Article 31 applies to citizens only and citizenship is governed by Regulations defined by statute.[56] This immediately demonstrates lack of compliance with the AAAQ, which among other things requires that health care must be accessible to all without discrimination.[57] Although these rights exist, they are protected in accordance with the Islamic Shari'ah, which is subject to interpretation,[58] and not by international

---

[47] See, http://treaties.un.org/Pages/ViewDetails.aspx?mtdsg_no=IV-13&chapter=4&lang=en, accessed 2 August 2013.

[48] http://www.arabhumanrights.org/en/countries/country.aspx?cid=16, accessed 28 February 2013. For information on the Charter see WHO, 'Arab Charter on Human Rights', available at www.who.int/hhr/Arab%20Charter.pdf, accessed 17 September 2013.

[49] Al-Midani and Cabanettes 2006, p. 148.

[50] Rishmawi 2005, pp. 361–376.

[51] Al-Midani and Cabanettes 2006, p. 149.

[52] Rishmawi 2005, p. 370.

[53] The Basic Law of Governance.

[54] Idem.

[55] Idem.

[56] Idem.

[57] General Comment 14, para 12(b).

[58] Ariany 2013, Shah 2006 and Van Eijk 2010.

human rights standards, which are codified in law. Considering the lack of commitment to the various international treaties and the issues considered in the introduction, particularly in relation to women and migrant workers, it is doubtful how effective and extensive the rights contained in chapter five of the basic law actually are.

6.4 General Health

Saudi Arabia is classified by the World Bank as a high-income country.[59] In terms of the information available, it would appear that the overall standard of living and general health of those living in Saudi Arabia is good. The healthcare system operates on a two-tiered system. The first tier relates to primary health care and the second tier covers advanced hospitals and specialised treatment facilities.[60] Ongoing changes and developments in the healthcare system are generally helpful, although some progress still has to be made.[61] Privatisation of public hospitals is a potential future problem.[62]

The average life expectancy of Saudi citizens is 72 years.[63] This is lower than the average life expectancy of countries in the high-income group, which is 80[64]; however, it is higher than the regional[65] average, which is 66.[66] The number of physicians working in the Kingdom is relatively low compared to the population. There are around 24,802, which works out as 9.4 qualified physicians per 10,000 people.[67] This is much lower than the rate for the high-income group, which is 27.7 and also lower than the regional average set at 10.9.[68] General observations are that although the overall health of the population is relatively good, and the general infrastructure of the health system is good, the system could be improved by increasing the number of personnel working in the Kingdom, particularly Saudi nationals.[69]

---

[59] World Bank 2011 available at http://data.worldbank.org/country/saudi-arabia, accessed 7 April 2013.

[60] See Almalki et al. 2011, and http://www.saudiembassy.net/about/country-information/health_ and_social_services/the_health_care_network.aspx, accessed 26 March 2013.

[61] Almalki et al. 2011.

[62] Idem, p. 792.

[63] World Health Organisation 2012, p. 58.

[64] Idem, p. 60.

[65] Under the WHO classifications, Saudi Arabia is in the Eastern Mediterranean Region. For a list of States in this region and further information see http://www.who.int/about/regions/emro/en/index.html, accessed 17 September 2013.

[66] World Health Organisation 2012, p. 60.

[67] Idem, p. 128.

[68] Idem, p. 130.

[69] Almalki et al. 2011, p. 789.

The purpose of this chapter is not to consider the overall health of the population, but to focus on specific vulnerable groups, to examine whether their right to health is impeded in any way and their access to health care is adversely affected. As mentioned in the introductory section, the groups selected are women and migrant workers, since they tend to be treated in a discriminatory way because of traditional, cultural and social practices. In light of the difficulties faced by these groups in their daily lives, their access to health care will be discussed in more detail, in order to identify whether the underlying cultural and social practices also affect their right to health.

6.5 Vulnerable Groups

6.5.1 Women

As explained above, women face discrimination across many areas of life in Saudi Arabia. This is evident in the way they are treated in society. Difficulties related to child birth and access to medical care have negative consequences on the rights of women and health of their children. These difficulties, examined through the lens of relevant human rights instruments will be discussed as well as how this may affect their children's right to access health care also.

6.5.1.1 The Right to Health as Prescribed in CEDAW

Although Saudi Arabia is not party to the ICESCR, women's right to health is protected by Article 12 of CEDAW to which Saudi Arabia is a party. Article 12 recognises women's right to access all healthcare services. This Article is divided into two sections. The first section covers non-discrimination or equal access for men and women and the second section covers health issues that apply specifically to women such as maternal health.

6.5.1.1.1 Non-discrimination

Article 12(1) requires that: 'States Parties shall take all appropriate measures to eliminate discrimination against women in the field of health care in order to ensure, on a basis of equality of men and women, access to healthcare services, including those related to family planning.' Sullivan argues that this provision does not create a clear duty to provide health care in itself, but rather ensures 'women access to health care on a basis of equality with men'.[70] It is true that no

---

[70] Sullivan 1995, p. 378.

6 The Right to Health and Access to Health Care in Saudi Arabia

clear duty is established by the text. Therefore, the protection of the right to health would be clearly problematic in States where overall access to health care is minimal and that State has only ratified CEDAW and not the ICESCR. However, given that the major problem in Saudi Arabia is equality rather than access to health care generally, the provision as formulated in Article 12(1) should present no problems for Saudi women, even though the right to health in general is not protected in the Kingdom.

In terms of non-discrimination norms, Sullivan considers that the 'prohibition of gender discrimination on the nature and scope of obligations regarding women's right to health should be considered in light of the standard applicable to discrimination in general international law'.[71] This could be problematic as Saudi Arabia has not ratified the main UN human rights documents, which establish this norm, the ICCPR and the ICESCR. However, given the strong emphasis on non-discrimination and equality throughout CEDAW (e.g. Articles 5(1), 10(h), 11(1)(f), 12(1) and 16(1)(d)), this should not pose any problems. In fact, the concept of gender equality that is embodied in the Women's Convention is seen as broader than the non-discrimination norm (contained in other international Conventions such as the ICCPR and ICESCR) because, 'it encompasses the restructuring of gender relations of power.'[72] Despite this, given the proviso that the Convention will not apply if it conflicts with Islamic law; it is unclear to what extent the rights in CEDAW are actually protected in Saudi Arabia, particularly those that refer to equality and non-discrimination.[73]

It is extremely important that access to health care for women is non-discriminatory in Saudi Arabia if the highest attainable standard of health is to be met. The CEDAW Committee,[74] emphasises that 'States should not restrict women's access to health services or to clinics that provide those services on the ground that women do not have the authorization of husbands, partners, parents or health authorities'.[75] State Parties shall take all appropriate measures to eliminate discrimination in the field of health care in order to ensure equal access to healthcare services, which should then improve health, including those related to family planning. It is recommended that State parties should identify the test they apply to assess whether women and men have equal access to health care in their country.[76] In this respect, access to health care will only be considered 'acceptable' where the services are 'delivered in a way that ensures that a woman gives her fully informed consent, respects her dignity, guarantees her confidentiality and

---

[71] Idem, p. 386.

[72] Idem, p. 386.

[73] See, Van Eijk 2010, p. 157.

[74] This is the body responsible for monitoring the Convention. For more information see http://www.un.org/womenwatch/daw/cedaw/committee.htm, accessed 30 September 2013.

[75] UN Committee on the Elimination of Discrimination against Women (1999) General Recommendation 24 on Women and Health, para 14 (General Recommendation 24).

[76] Idem.

is sensitive to her *needs and perspectives*.'[77] The societal culture to treat women unequally in Saudi Arabia fails to comply with any of these factors that are required in order to ensure that health care is acceptable and accessible as required by the AAAQ.[78] Therefore, women's access to health care in the Kingdom cannot be considered as acceptable,[79] because women will often be unable to make final decisions on their care, and they will not always be able to choose the option that best meets their particular needs. Therefore, the services cannot be confidential as required by the AAAQ. Overall, the CEDAW Committee suggests that Article 12 requires:

> The duty of States parties to ensure, on the basis of equality between men and women, access to healthcare services, information and education implies an obligation to respect, protect and fulfil women's rights to health care. States parties have the responsibility to ensure that legislation and executive action and policy comply with these three obligations. They must also put in place a system, which ensures effective judicial action. Failure to do so will constitute a violation of Article 12.[80]

In relation to adequate protection of the right to health for women in Saudi Arabia, the Committee has noted that there is a lack of data and information on health and have stated their concern about the practice of male guardianship:

> The Committee expresses concern about the lack of information and data on health problems… as well as access by women and girls from rural areas and non-Saudi nationals to adequate healthcare services. The Committee expresses concern that women may require permission of their male guardian to access health facilities.[81]

Therefore, because Saudi women require permission before they participate in most things including daily activities, the utility of CEDAW as a weapon against gender oppression is severely limited as women in the country continue to face discrimination in all aspects of their lives. In particular, it is unlikely that the right to 'access all' medical services is met since women often require permission from their male guardian before they can seek medical care or advice or even receive emergency treatment. This would suggest that Article 12(1) CEDAW is not sufficiently protected in Saudi Arabia. Even though the Article does not create a concrete right this does not matter because men can generally access healthcare facilities and receive appropriate treatment immediately because no permission is

---

[77] Idem.

[78] See, n 30 above.

[79] This refers to acceptable as required by the AAAQ. In this context, access to health care will only be acceptable where, all health facilities, goods and services are respectful of medical ethics and culturally appropriate, i.e. respectful of the culture of individuals, minorities, peoples and communities, sensitive to gender and life-cycle requirements, as well as being designed to respect confidentiality and improve the health status of those concerned (General Comment 14, para 12).

[80] General Recommendation 24, para 13.

[81] UN Committee on the Elimination of Discrimination Against Women, Fortieth Session 2008 CEDAW/C/SAU/CO/2 Concluding Comments of the Committee on Saudi Arabia.

6 The Right to Health and Access to Health Care in Saudi Arabia

required. Therefore women would need to be treated in the same way as men if Article 12(1) is to be complied with.

6.5.1.1.2 Article 12(2)

In contrast to Article 12(1), 12(2) creates a concrete right to access certain types of health care. This goes beyond a prohibition of discrimination,[82] or a reference to equality, and requires that appropriate services are required in relation to maternal and reproductive health. States are required to 'ensure women receive appropriate services in connection with pregnancy, confinement and the post-natal period, granting free services where necessary, as well as adequate nutrition during lactation.'[83] In this regard, General Recommendation no 24 emphasises that State reports should show how these services are provided (including antenatal services) and how the free services are supplied and allocated where necessary.[84]

6.5.1.2 Maternal Health and Family Planning in Saudi Arabia

When evaluating the compliance by a State of the right to health and specifically women's access to health care, maternal health is a paramount concern. This is highlighted in various documents such as General Comment 14, which urges States to reduce maternal mortality.[85] This is advanced further in goal 5 of the Millennium Development Goals, which aims to improve overall maternal health.[86] Moreover, General Comment No. 14 (para 44(a)) elevates maternal health to a status comparable to a core obligation in relation to which derogation is impermissible even on grounds of resource constraints.

In general, maternal health in Saudi Arabia seems to be improving. In 1999, only 87 % of women were receiving maternal health care, but by 2003, this had increased to 96 %.[87] The latest figures suggest that in terms of antenatal care, 97 % of mothers receive at least one visit from skilled personnel.[88] However, in this respect, it is noted that the 'definition of skilled personnel differs from the standard definition.'[89] It is unclear whether these persons are higher or lower

---

[82] Sullivan 1995, p. 378.

[83] Article 12(2).

[84] General Recommendation 24, paras 26–27.

[85] General Comment 14, para 21.

[86] See http://www.undp.org/content/undp/en/home/mdgoverview/mdg_goals/mdg5/, accessed 2 August 2013.

[87] Millennium Development Goals Report Saudi Arabia 2005, p. 45, available at http://www.un.org/summit2005/MDGBook.pdf, accessed 26 February 2013.

[88] World Health Organisation 2012, p. 104.

[89] Idem, p. 107. It is unclear how the definition differs. The report simply states that it differs. A skilled health personnel is somebody such as a doctor nurse or midwife, who has specific training

qualified than the standard definition. There is no information on the percentage of mothers, who had at least four visits from a skilled personnel.[90] According to the data, 100 % of births were attended by skilled health personnel, but again the definition varies from the standard definition.[91] There is also no information available on post-natal visits.

It is unfortunate that there is a lack of information available in this area and there is no clear definition of the term 'skilled health personnel' in this case. However, in comparison to the data provided for the rest of the region, the statistics for Saudi Arabia are relatively good. This is because only 72 % of women in the region get at least one antenatal visit and only 59 % of births are attended by a skilled personnel.[92] Since the data suggests that all births in Saudi Arabia are attended by some form of skilled personnel, it is unsurprising that maternal mortality rates are relatively low. In 2010, the maternal mortality rate was 24 per 100,000 live births.[93] This is higher than the neighbouring State of the United Arab Emirates where the rate is 12[94]; however, it is much lower than the regional average, which is 250.[95] Despite this, the Kingdom is rated as a high-income country and in this case, the maternal mortality rate is quite high in comparison to the other countries within this classification, as the average rate for this group is 14.[96] Hunt emphasises that '[p]reventable maternal mortality occurs when there is a failure to give effect to the rights of women to health, equality and non-discrimination.'[97] Therefore, it might be unsurprising that the figures are higher compared to other States in the income group because discrimination, arising from the culture of guardianship, poses the risk of delaying access to necessary medical care and procedures. The rate might also be higher because migrant workers may not always have access to the necessary health care. However, if this group does not receive adequate health care, then it is unlikely that this group will be included in the statistics, which suggest 100 % of births are attended by a professional.

On the basis of the information provided, it would appear that the maternal health in the Kingdom is good, especially in the case of Saudi nationals. However,

---

(Footnote 89 continued)

in pregnancy and childbirth. It would not include traditional birth attendants. (WHO, Health Statistics and health information systems at, http://www.who.int/healthinfo/statistics/indantenatal/en/index.html, accessed 18 September 2013.

[90] World Health Organisation, Statistics 2012, p. 104. WHO recommends that pregnant women get at least four visits from a skilled health personnel. (WHO, Health statistics and health information systems, n 89 above).

[91] World Health Organisation 2012, p. 104.

[92] Idem, p. 106.

[93] Idem, p. 78.

[94] Idem, p. 78.

[95] Idem, p. 82.

[96] Idem, p. 82.

[97] P Hunt, 'Reducing Maternal Mortality', p. 3, available at http://www.unfpa.org/webdav/site/global/shared/documents/publications/reducing_mm.pdf, accessed 7 August 2013.

6 The Right to Health and Access to Health Care in Saudi Arabia   179

it is questionable whether these statistics are accurate as they may not include information on migrant workers who might not have sufficient access to health care.[98] A further consideration is whether the maternal mortality rate is higher than other countries in the high-income group because of women's place in society and the concept of guardianship. Pregnant women may be denied access to health care in emergency situations if their guardian is not present and this could be why the maternal mortality rate is slightly higher than in comparable countries.

In 2009, the still birth rate was 8 per 1000 live births.[99] This is very low as the rate for the region is four and the rate for high-income countries is 10.[100] Therefore, in relation to births that are recorded, the live birth rate is very high and the medical care good. There is no information available on the number of newborns with low birth weights, however, only 5.3 % of children under 5 years of age are underweight.[101] Interestingly, 6.1 % are overweight.[102] The infant mortality rate within the Kingdom has dropped drastically in the past 30 years. In 1970, it was as high as 118 per 1000 live births, but dropped to 21 per 1000 live births in 2005.[103] The latest figures suggest that the infant mortality rate in 2010 was only 15.[104] Although the regional rate is 68, the rate in the Kingdom is higher than other high-income States where the average rate is 5.[105] Again, this could be related to a delay in accessing medical care if a guardian is not present. It should also be noted that the rates for Saudi Arabia may not be accurate and could in fact be higher than stated due to a lack of information on adolescent health, and the fact there is often a lack of appropriate health care available for non-Saudi children.[106] It is unknown whether infant mortality rates are higher within this portion of the population or indeed whether there are significant differences between the rural and urban population in this area. There is also lack of data on the frequency of post-natal visits in the Kingdom.[107] This is unfortunate as follow-up care is important for mothers and their babies.

Although access to maternal health care is of relatively good quality, it is unlikely that women have adequate access to reproductive health services and suitable information on the choices available to them in this area. Paragraph 34 of the General Comment on the right to health urges States to refrain from limiting access to contraceptives and other means of maintaining sexual and reproductive information, including sexual education and information. In this respect, Article

---

[98] See Sect. 6.2.

[99] World Health Organisation 2012, p. 59.

[100] World Health Organisation 2012, p. 61.

[101] World Health Organisation 2012, p. 116.

[102] World Health Organisation 2012, p. 116.

[103] Human Development Report (2007/08) Table 10.

[104] World Health Organisation 2012, p. 59.

[105] World Health Organisation 2012, p 61.

[106] This will be discussed below at 6.5.2.3.

[107] World Health Organisation 2012, p. 104.

12(1) of CEDAW, which applies in Saudi Arabia, requires that both men and women have equal access to family planning, but does not specify whether these facilities should be available for women to access alone in private or if it is acceptable for couples to always access these services together and therefore "equally". It is most likely that the former is correct or more precisely it should be up to the individual to decide whether they want to access the services alone or with a partner. Access undertaken together does not necessarily guarantee equality if one party is weaker than the other.

The latest figures on the contraceptive prevalence rate in the Kingdom suggest that between 2005 and 2010, the rate was very low at just 24 %.[108] There is no data on the unmet demand for contraception.[109] The lack of data and the low contraceptive prevalence rate are most likely related to the general lack of protection of women's rights in the Kingdom. If women are required to get permission from their husband's or male guardian before gaining information about or being given contraceptives, then, they cannot exercise their right to free and informed choice. This is also inconsistent with the concept of 'acceptability', which requires that all health facilities are designed to respect confidentiality.[110] Unfortunately, because Saudi Arabia is not party to the ICESCR, it is questionable to what extent the AAAQ can be enforced and followed in Saudi Arabia. Helpfully, this point is emphasised in General Recommendation no 24 (which refers specifically to Article 12 CEDAW) where further problems are recognised if confidentiality is not protected in respect of women:

> While lack of respect for the confidentiality of patients will affect both men and women, it may deter women from seeking advice and treatment and thereby adversely affect their health and well-being. Women will be less willing, for that reason, to seek medical care for diseases of the genital tract, for contraception or for incomplete abortion and in cases where they have suffered sexual or physical violence.[111]

The low rate of contraceptive usage could be a combined result of male guardians refusing permission for women to have access to contraceptives and women not wanting to approach their guardians to ask for permission about matters which are personal to them. It is considered that the latter would be particularly true where the guardian is the woman's father or son. In this context, the link between Article 12 and other provisions of CEDAW has been recognised. These are Article 10, which requires States to ensure equal access to education, particularly 10(h) which requires that women and girls have access to specific educational information and advice on family planning, and Article 16(1)(e) which requires that women have the same rights as men to decide freely and responsibly on the number and spacing of their children and to have access to the information and means necessary to

---

[108] Idem.

[109] Idem.

[110] General Comment 14, para 12(c).

[111] General Recommendation 24, para 12(d).

6 The Right to Health and Access to Health Care in Saudi Arabia 181

enable them to access those rights.[112] Fundamentally, in relation to Saudi Arabia, all these rights are underpinned by the requirement on States to take all appropriate measures to 'modify the social and cultural patterns of conduct of men and women, with a view to achieving the elimination of prejudices and customary and all other practices, which are based on the idea of the inferiority or the superiority of either of the sexes or on stereotyped roles for men and women'.[113] Therefore, ultimately if contraceptive use is to increase, societal and cultural attitudes towards women will have to change. The best way to do this is to abolish the practice of male guardianship in order to ensure that women's rights are truly respected and CEDAW is complied with. This will be a hard task to fulfil as this practice is deeply embedded in the culture of the Kingdom.

Abortion is generally illegal in Saudi Arabia with a very narrow exception.[114] The law states that an abortion may only be performed to save a woman's life, if the pregnancy is less than 4 months old and it is proven beyond doubt that the continued pregnancy greatly endangers the mother's health.[115] The pregnancy is believed to greatly endanger the mothers health, if it could cause death, or damage to her physical or mental health.[116] Abortion is not permitted for any other reason such as foetal impairment, rape or incest.[117] In excess of 4 months, abortion is only permitted if a panel of approved specialists state that the continuation of the pregnancy will result in the mother's death and all other means to eliminate the danger have been exhausted.[118] Additional requirements for abortion at any stage in the pregnancy are that: it must be performed in a government hospital; a panel of three medical specialists must sign a recommendation before the abortion can be performed; and written consent must be obtained from the patient as well as her husband or guardian.[119] This again shows the hierarchal structure in society where women can effectively be controlled by men, showing the impact of cultural practices in relation to access to maternal health care.

There is little statistical data available on abortions in the Kingdom. However, a study implies that there are very few legal abortions carried out in Saudi Arabia.[120] It was reported that in 2010, only ten Saudi residents obtained a legal abortion and that all ten abortions were carried out in another country.[121] Due to the lack of

---

[112] General Comment 24, para 28.

[113] CEDAW, Article 5(a).

[114] Ministerial Resolution No. 218/17/L of 26 June 1989 of the Ministry of Health Article 24, available at http://www.hsph.harvard.edu/population/abortion/SAUDIARABIA.abo.htm, accessed 17 September 2013.

[115] Idem, Article 24.

[116] Idem, Article 24.

[117] See, http://www.alranz.org/findoutmore/internationalperspective/abortioninthe.html, accessed 17 September 2013 and Ministerial Resolution No. 218/17/L, Article 24(1).

[118] Ministerial Resolution No. 218/17/L, Article 24(4).

[119] Idem, Article 24(4).

[120] Johnston 2013.

[121] Johnston 2013.

reliable statistical data on this subject, it is difficult to develop clear conclusions on abortion in Saudi Arabia. However, in light of the strict law and lack of accurate data, there may be a high number of illegal abortions being carried out because '[n]o data often means no recognition of the problem.'[122] This will create risks to the mother's health and can increase maternal mortality rates. This suggests that the relatively low maternal mortality rates reported may be inaccurate.

6.5.1.3 Other Health Issues

In addition to the general problems women face in accessing health care, they also face other difficulties which impact on their health—and which, again, arise from inequality and underlying social determinant to health. An example of this is the fact that women are generally not allowed to participate in sport and they face considerable problems in accessing gyms and suitable facilities.[123] Human Rights Watch has concluded that in 'Saudi Arabia, authorities cite cultural norms and religious teachings in denying women and girls the right to participate in sporting activities'.[124] If women are not participating in physical activity, then, this can have a negative impact on their overall health. The percentage of women, who are classified as obese in the Kingdom significantly outweighs the number of obese males. In 2008, 43.5 % of females were classified as obese compared to 29.5 % of males.[125] It is a dire medical problem that almost half the female population in the Kingdom is classified as obese, and this could be directly related to the fact that women are not encouraged to exercise. Obesity has many negative impacts on the general health of a person and this adversely impacts the cost of health care and other health-related government expenditure in a country.[126] Some health effects of obesity are: high blood pressure, diabetes, heart disease, joint problems, sleep apnea, cancer, metabolic syndrome and it can also affect the psychological health of individuals.[127] In fact it has been reported that in Saudi Arabia, overall, there 'has been an alarming increase in the prevalence of chronic diseases, such as diabetes, hypertension and heart diseases'.[128]

The efficiency of a healthcare system and its compatibility with the AAAQ is on its own not enough to ensure that the right to health is protected in a particular country. This is particularly true where selected groups of individuals have

---

[122] CSDH 2008, p. 30.

[123] Human Rights Watch 2012.

[124] Human Rights Watch World Report 2013, p. 21.

[125] Human Rights Watch 2012, p. 117.

[126] According to a Stanford Hospital, obesity-related illnesses cost the US over $150 billion a year. http://stanfordhospital.org/clinicsmedServices/COE/surgicalServices/generalSurgery/bariatricsurgery/obesity/effects.html, accessed 22 March 2013.

[127] Ibid and see also Jia and Lubetkin 2005.

[128] Almalki et al. 2011, p. 791.

6 The Right to Health and Access to Health Care in Saudi Arabia 183

significant health problems due to underlying determinants to health such as gender inequity. According to the Commission on the Social Determinants to Health (CSDH), gender 'biases in power, resources, entitlements, norms and values, and the way in which organisations are structured and programmes are run damage the health of millions of girls and women.'[129] These gender-based inequities can influence health through a number of routes from basic access to healthcare services and relevant information to unfair divisions of 'leisure and possibilities of improving one's life'.[130]

Non-availability of leisure facilities and physical education lessons for women and girls appears to have an impact on the overall health of Saudi females.[131] An example of this impact is high prevalence of obesity in females, which carries the risk of triggering a variety of other health issues, each with its own problems and costs.

6.5.2 Migrant Workers

The position of migrant workers in the Kingdom is unclear. Some of the information available suggest that all migrant workers must have private medical insurance since they are not eligible for state funded health care.[132] However, other information suggests that compulsory private health insurance is being introduced through a different scheme.[133] This scheme requires all those who work in the private sector to have health insurance regardless of their nationality or citizenship.[134] In this respect, it is noted that most Saudi's work in the public sector,[135] not the private sector; so, in general they have less need for private insurance. What is unclear is whether all migrant workers need private health insurance regardless of their employment type or if only those who work in the private sector need health insurance as in the case of Saudi citizens. Thus, the current position is somewhat unclear. A conclusion that fits with all these

---

[129] CSDH 2008, p. 22.

[130] CSDH 2008, p. 22.

[131] In this respect, it is noted that those who work for some private companies can access leisure facilities. Companies which have their own compounds often have private leisure facilities that employees and their families are free to use (Human Rights Watch 2012, p. 13).

[132] See http://www.telegraph.co.uk/health/expathealth/8701829/Expat-guide-to-Saudi-Arabia-health-care.html, accessed 26 March 2013, and International Labour Organisation (1999) available at http://www.ilo.org/public/english/standards/relm/ilc/ilc87/r3-1b6.htm, accessed 26 March 2013.

[133] Almalki et al. 2011, p. 787.

[134] Idem.

[135] In 2011, statistics showed that only 1 in 10 Saudis worked for the public sector. See http://www.voanews.com/content/saudi-arabia-youth-bulge-private-sector-economy/1709481.html, accessed 5 August 2013.

hypothesis is that all immigrants, who work in the private sector must have private health insurance. It is submitted that the majority of migrant workers fit into this category as they work for private companies or for families as domestic workers. Therefore, a reasonable starting point is that nearly all immigrants must have private medical insurance in order to access health care in the Kingdom.

The position of migrant workers in the Kingdom is very different depending on a variety of factors. Almost all non-nationals are required to have compulsory private health insurance. However, those coming from the West, who primarily work in the oil sector are usually provided with suitable health insurance by their employers and generally enjoy a high standard of living in the Kingdom. However, for those from Asia and Africa, who may enter the country illegally or through the *kafala* sponsorship system,[136] the position is likely to be very different, despite the fact they are also employed in the private sector. Migrant workers in the Kingdom can be split into three categories and the position of the workers is different depending on what category they fit into. These are those who work for oil companies or other large private sector firms who are protected by labour laws and provided with benefits by their employer and other forms of migrant workers such as labourers or domestic workers.[137] The latter can be split into two categories, namely, male and female.[138] It is noted that because of the human rights commitments of Saudi Arabia, technically only women migrant workers are protected by the international framework on the right to health. This is because Saudi Arabia is only party to CEDAW and not the ICESR; so, technically the commitment to protect the right to health at the international level only applies to women.[139]

The overall information on the number of migrant workers varies as highlighted in the introduction Therefore, since the true number of migrant workers residing in the Kingdom is unclear, it is likely the information on the health of this group is also likely to be inaccurate.

---

[136] The kafala sponsorship system 'ties migrant workers' residency permits to "sponsoring" employers, whose written consent is required for workers to change employers or leave the country. Employers often abuse this power in violation of Saudi law to confiscate passports, withhold wages and force migrants to work against their will or on exploitative terms' (Human Rights Watch 2013).

[137] See Human Rights Watch 2009.

[138] 'Although both men and women migrate, migration is not a gender-neutral phenomenon. The position of female migrants is different from that of male migrants in terms of legal migration channels, the sectors into which they migrate, the forms of abuse they suffer and the consequences thereof. (CEDAW, General Recommendation 26 on women migrant workers (General Recommendation 26).

[139] See Sects. 6.3 and 6.5.1.1 above.

6.5.2.1 Workers with Good Access to Health Care and Resources

Those working for large private firms have access to good-quality health care and health-related information. This is because the Kingdom has a sufficient number of primary healthcare facilities and good hospitals.[140] Further, the underlying factors which prevent equal access to health care and affect health do not apply to this group because they are not subject to traditional cultural practices and social beliefs. This is evidenced by the fact that women from this group have access to private leisure facilities on company compounds. They are treated differently overall when in private places and therefore access to suitable health care should be good.

6.5.2.2 Domestic Workers and Other Labourers

Saudi Arabia hosts around 1.5 million domestic workers, the highest number in the Middle East.[141] This group of workers could be susceptible to inequities in relation to health care. However, there is generally no data on the health of migrant workers. This is because the statistics available cover the overall health of the entire (legal) population and are not segregated into information on migrant workers and citizens. However, as noted in Sect. 6.2, these type of workers do face poorer working conditions and therefore could be subject to poorer health due to problems arising from underlying determinants to health. CEDAW explains that domestic workers or labourers may:

> suffer from a lack of arrangements for their safety at work, or provisions for safe travel between the worksite and their place of accommodation. Where accommodation is provided, especially in female-dominated occupations such as factory, farm or domestic work, living conditions may be poor and overcrowded, without running water or adequate sanitary facilities, or they may lack privacy and hygiene.[142]

Therefore, this group is particularly vulnerable and their health is at risk for a number of reasons. Firstly, they are generally subject to poor working conditions including long hours and little rest, both of which could impact on their health generally and therefore the right to the highest attainable standard of health.[143] Secondly, there are no extensive labour laws in place for this group, hence the long working hours. This means that their employer controls everything in terms of their work and their right to remain in the Kingdom, including their sponsorship.[144] The fact that sponsorship is controlled by the employer would suggest that the employer should also make arrangements to ensure that medical insurance is in

---

[140] See, Almalki et al. 2011.

[141] Human Rights Watch 2009, p. 5.

[142] General Recommendation 26, para 17.

[143] See above at Sect. 6.2.

[144] See n 136.

place since migrant workers are required to have this. It is unclear whether or not the employer actually has to provide this insurance or if many large firms just choose to do this. However, since migrant domestic workers are generally on a low income, it is unclear how they would be able to afford the cost of private health insurance if they had to pay for this themselves. Further, because it appears as though domestic workers are not treated particularly well in the Kingdom, it is questionable whether these employers will actually arrange adequate health insurance when organising the sponsorship. There does not seem to be any information available on this or comments on the likelihood of employers providing insurance. Without insurance coverage, the workers will have very limited access to health care since access to basic services is reserved for citizens. Any other access to basic services is through the UNHRC. The UNHCR has an office in Riyadh, which has provided subsistence to a small number of families on a needs-based assessment.[145] However, as this assistance is only available for families with refugee status, who are unable to work, it is unclear what help would be provided for migrant workers who possess neither refugee status nor compulsory health insurance.

Human Rights Watch has recommended that the government 'adopt comprehensive labour and immigration reforms for domestic workers that protect their freedom of movement, guarantee limits on working hours in parity with other sectors, and abolish the current sponsorship system.'[146] This is all particularly important if domestic migrant workers' rights are to be protected adequately, specifically the right to the highest attainable standard of health. As with women, migrant workers face difficulties due to traditional practices (such as the practice of Saudi families to employ domestic workers as a live-in cook and cleaner) in the State. It is unclear to what extent these practices adversely affect this group's right to health care, but the sponsorship system needs updating and has to be regulated if it is to be ensured that domestic migrant workers have appropriate health insurance. More research is needed in this area and proper statistics on numbers of migrant workers and the percentage of these, who actually have the compulsory medical insurance is essential.

6.5.2.3 Particular Problems Relating to Women and the Children of Migrant Workers

Many women travel to Saudi Arabia in order to become domestic workers. These women, as explained previously, are usually at the mercy of their employers and their employees may withhold their passports and could require them to work for long hours without regular holidays Therefore, these women are at risk of suffering from underlying determinants to health such as discrimination based on gender and

---

[145] US Department of State 2011, section D.

[146] Human Rights Watch 2009, p. 5.

status.[147] These problems are accentuated by their living and working conditions,[148] which are 'shaped by political, social and economic forces.'[149] There is also a question of whether domestic workers would get time off to visit a doctor if they did need to access healthcare facilities and also how they would travel to those facilities.

As with women generally who face inequities in relation to their access to health care and other services, women migrant workers also suffer from inequities which can threaten, among other issues, their health. This is because they may not be able to access health services, including reproductive health services, particularly where insurance or national health schemes are not available to them, or are unaffordable.[150] Since women have different health requirements compared to men, this is an area which requires special attention.[151]

There are potential risks if a worker becomes pregnant because she may face coercive abortion or lack of access to safe reproductive health and abortion services, which put the health of the mother at risk.[152] Since some of these risks are also apparent in respect of Saudi women, who may not be able to access appropriate information in this area for a variety of reasons, it is likely that migrant workers will also face problems with access to suitable maternal health care and appropriate advice. Within the Kingdom, there appears to be a system of superiority, which places men above women and domestic migrant workers below Saudi citizens. Therefore, women domestic workers are at a high risk of facing abusive practices. However, it is difficult to find information on this or the health and access to health care of migrant workers. Therefore, it is very unclear what the position is in this area and whether this is a real risk faced by women migrant workers in the Kingdom. Absence of data on overall health in the Kingdom and particularly in this area is not only unhelpful, but a major cause for concern.

Where the domestic worker continues with her pregnancy by trying to conceal it from her employer, because pregnancy could also lead to dismissal affecting immigration status and possibly leading to deportation, this could put her health at risk. Similarly, if the employers continue to let her work and remain in the country, this could also place her health at risk. This is essentially because she will have to work long hours often in poor conditions in the absence of adequate maternity leave and without the benefits of affordable obstetric care, which could result in serious health risks.[153] It is clear that migrant domestic workers face poor working

---

[147] See n 21.

[148] CSDH 2008, Foreword.

[149] CSDH 2008, Foreword. In this context, the social impact comes from the way Saudi citizens are accustomed to living, economic forces in the migrants country of origin are encouraging immigration for better wages and the political circumstances are shaped by the fact that the Saudi government is not changing the law in order to better regulate the current system.

[150] General Recommendation 26, para 17.

[151] Idem, para 17.

[152] Idem, para 18.

[153] Idem, para 18.

conditions and there is generally a lack of legal protection in this area. This could suggest that their health is at risk and women face greater risks for the reasons explained. However, no clear conclusions can be drawn in this area as data on the health of migrant workers specifically and their ability to access quality health care is unavailable.

In relation to children of migrant workers, Saudi Arabia is party to the United Nations Convention on the Rights of the Child (CRC). Article 24 lays down a wide range of standards, which should be attained to ensure that a child's right to health is wholly fulfilled. Under the Article, Saudi Arabia is obliged to make quality health care accessible to all children. This immediately creates a problem as non-Saudi workers' children, without legal residence, do not have access to health services.[154] The Committee on the Rights of the Child recommended that the Kingdom 'develop and implement policies and practices to better protect and serve children of migrant workers.'[155]

As compulsory health insurance is seemingly a requirement of lawful residency in the Kingdom, migrants, without health insurance, may now be classified as residing illegally in the country. However, because employers control sponsorship and should arrange health insurance, it is unclear to what extent this insurance will actually be compulsory. This is especially true in terms of domestic workers where there are no clear labour laws and no checks and balances are in place. This could result in employers exploiting illegal immigrants, thereby exacerbating poverty on the part of the workers. This may also affect their health as they will not be able to access health care unless they have insurance. This could create problems with the health of the population as the workers may carry diseases that could then spread into the general population, such as measles. This is a cause for concern and it is unfortunate that there is no clear data available in relation to the health of migrant workers.

6.6 Conclusion

In general, Saudi Arabia has a good-quality health system. However, it is not protecting those most vulnerable such as women and migrant domestic workers. These groups are sometimes denied access to adequate health care. The health care that Saudi women receive does not fully comply with the recommendations made by human rights Committees on the right to health. The starting point is that women are not always treated equally in Saudi society and therefore immediately it is apparent that they are unlikely to gain equal or immediate access to health care. Fundamentally, health care for these groups is not always accessible, it is not

---

[154] Committee on the Rights of the Child, Forty-First session, CRC/C/SAU/CO/2 17th March 2006, p. 14.

[155] Idem.

fully acceptable and therefore it lacks quality. The primary cause for this is because women do not always get the final say in their health care and therefore cannot always choose treatment or make decisions in relation to their general health that best suit their needs. This is an inherent problem in Saudi culture, which is encapsulated by the practice of male guardianship.

This practice conflicts with human rights norms generally and, in particular, the principle of non-discrimination or equality. Even though Saudi Arabia is not party to the ICCPR or the ICESCR, it is party to CEDAW, which in effect takes the non-discrimination provisions further. Therefore, by continuing to allow the practice of male guardianship, the Kingdom is not complying with its obligations under CEDAW, particularly the general equality clause in Article 5(1), which prevents discrimination on social, cultural or customary grounds and Article 12(1), which prevents discrimination on access to health care. Therefore, any discrimination on access to health care or delay in accessing care, where a male would be able to access treatment immediately, renders the State noncompliant with Article 12(1) or 5(1) of CEDAW. Denial of access to health care in emergency situations could be contributing to the higher rate of maternal mortality in the country compared to other countries in the same income group. Further, despite the fact that abortion is only allowed for health reasons, even where the risk to the mother is considered to be sufficient by male personnel, the law still requires that the abortion can only be performed with the consent of the male guardian. Therefore, even though Article 12(2) CEDAW establishes a clear right to appropriate maternal health care, this cannot be realised unless women are treated equally in society.

The societal culture in general has other underlying factors that are detrimental to health. A prime example is the fact that Saudi women are traditionally not allowed to participate in sport and are prohibited from entering public gyms. Saudi girls are denied physical education in schools. This means that Saudi women in general are unable to exercise and, as a result, a high percentage of the female population is obese. This means also that women are more likely to suffer from illnesses related to obesity, placing additional preventable burdens on the healthcare system. The problems with health care and the right to health in Saudi Arabia, in the case of women, are inextricably linked to the culture of male guardianship. Had it been that this practice did not exist, it is likely that the health services provided for women would be very good and of a high standard.

In the case of migrant workers, their position in society is different depending on what field they work in. General observations are that migrant domestic workers tend to be treated badly and poor working conditions could have an adverse effect on their health. In terms of access to health care for this group, no clear conclusions can be drawn. This is because there is a lack of credible data on numbers of migrant workers and there is no separate data on the health of this group. This is unfortunate because the standard attained should be equal across the State and as the standard of health is relatively high (compared with other countries in the region) the health of migrant workers should be too. Further, it is unclear whether this group does actually have access to health-related services as it is questionable whether they have suitable private health insurance, which should be compulsory for these workers.

Access to health care and the right to health for both these vulnerable groups is hampered by traditional, cultural and social practices, which adversely affect the day-to-day life of these groups in a variety of aspects. In order for improvements to be made in the area of health, practices, customs and traditional views will need to be changed in the Kingdom. The law and practice in relation to health cannot be changed in isolation from these views and major changes will need to be made if access to health care for these vulnerable groups is to be improved and the system in Saudi Arabia is to comply with General Comment 14 on the right to health.

As explained in the latest Human Rights Watch World Report, the human rights community is not against customary and traditional laws in general, but the 'aspects of them that violate rights.'[156] Traditional and cultural practices need to be transformed, so that laws and customs can 'develop in order to remove discriminatory elements'.[157] Modification of these laws is imperative and some would say imminent because in light of continuous developments in society culture cannot or should not remain locked in, it must alter with time, even if developments are minor.[158] There have been changes in Saudi culture in recent times; for example, the London 2012 Olympic games saw the first women participant from Saudi Arabia. However, big changes still need to be made in relation to traditional practices relating to Saudi women and migrant domestic workers if all those living in the Kingdom are to be treated equally and have equal access to quality health care and health-related information.

References

Almalki M, Fitzgerald G, Clark M (2011) Health care system in Saudi Arabia: an overview. Eastern Mediterr Health J 17:784
Al-Midani M, Cabanettes M (2006) Arab Charter of Human Rights 2004. Boston Univ Int Law J 24:147
Amnesty International (2012) Amnesty International Annual Report 2012—Saudi Arabia, 24 May 2012. http://www.amnesty.org/en/region/saudi-arabia/report-2012. Accessed Feb 2013
Ariany B (2013) The conflict between women's rights and cultural practices in Iraq. Int J Hum Rights 17:530
Blanchard CM (2012) Saudi Arabia: Background and US Relations. www.fas.org/sgp/crs/mideast/RL33533.pdf. Accessed July 2013
CIA World Factbook. https://www.cia.gov/library/publications/the-world-factbook/geos/sa.html. Accessed Jan 2013
Colliers International (2012) Kingdom of Saudi Arabia Healthcare Overview. www.colliers.com/.../ksahealthcareoverviewcihq12012.ashx. Accessed July 2013

---

[156] Human Rights Watch World Report 2013, p. 28.

[157] Idem.

[158] Idem.

6 The Right to Health and Access to Health Care in Saudi Arabia

Commission on the Social Determinants of Health (CSDH) (2008) Closing the gap on a generation. http://whqlibdoc.who.int/hq/2008/WHO_IER_CSDH_08.1_eng.pdf. Accessed Feb 2013

Freedom House (2012a) Freedom in the world 2012—Saudi Arabia, 4 June 2012. http://www.unhcr.org/refworld/docid/4fcc9536c.html. Accessed Feb 2013

Freedom House (2012b) Countries at the crossroads 2012—Saudi Arabia, 20 September 2012. http://www.unhcr.org/refworld/docid/505c172a2d.html. Accessed Feb 2013

Human Rights Watch (2009) Slow movement protection of migrants rights in 2009. http://www.hrw.org/news/2009/12/16/slow-movement. Accessed Mar 2013

Human Rights Watch (2010) Slow reform protection of migrant domestic workers in Asia and the Middle East. http://www.hrw.org/reports/2010/04/28/slow-reform. Accessed Mar 2013

Human Rights Watch (2012) "Steps of the Devil" Denial of women and girls' right to sport in Saudi Arabia. www.hrw.org/sites/default/files/reports/saudi0212webwcover.pdf. Accessed Mar 2013

Human Rights Watch (2013) Saudi Arabia: Protect migrant workers' rights. http://www.hrw.org/news/2013/07/01/saudi-arabia-protect-migrant-workers-rights. Accessed Aug 2013

Human Rights Watch World Report (2011). http://www.hrw.org/sites/default/files/reports/wr2011.pdf. Accessed Jan 2013

Human Rights Watch World Report (2013). https://www.hrw.org/sites/default/files/wr2013_web.pdf. Accessed Feb 2013

Hunt P, 'Reducing maternal mortality'. http://www.unfpa.org/webdav/site/global/shared/documents/publications/reducing_mm.pdf. Accessed Aug 2013

International Labour Organisation (1999). http://www.ilo.org/public/english/standards/relm/ilc/ilc87/r3-1b6.htm. Accessed 26 Mar 2013

Jia H, Lubetkin EI (2005) The impact of obesity on health-related quality-of-life in the general adult US population. J Public Health 27:156. http://jpubhealth.oxfordjournals.org/content/27/2/156.full.pdf+html. Accessed Mar 2013

Johnston WR (2013) Historical abortion statistics, Saudi Arabia. http://www.johnstonsarchive.net/policy/abortion/ab-saudiarabia.html. Accessed April 2013

Ministerial Resolution No. 218/17/L of 26 June 1989 of the Ministry of Health Article 24. http://www.hsph.harvard.edu/population/abortion/SAUDIARABIA.abo.htm. Accessed Mar 2013

Minority Rights Group International (2012) State of the World's Minorities and Indigenous Peoples 2012—Saudi Arabia, 28 June 2012. http://www.unhcr.org/refworld/docid/4fedb3f055.html. Accessed Feb 2013

Pallot P (2011) Expat guide to Saudi Arabia: health care. http://www.telegraph.co.uk/health/expathealth/8701829/Expat-guide-to-Saudi-Arabia-health-care.html. Accessed Mar 2013

Rishmawi M (2005) The revised Arab Charter on Human Rights: a step forward? Hum Rights Law Rev 5:361

Royal Embassy of Saudi Arabia. http://www.saudiembassy.net/about/country-information/health_and_social_services/the_health_care_network.aspx. Accessed Mar 2013

Shah N (2006) Women's human rights in the Koran: an interpretative approach. Hum Rights Q 28:868

Stanford Medicine, BMI Clinic. http://stanfordhospital.org/clinicsmedServices/COE/surgicalServices/generalSurgery/bariatricsurgery/obesity/effects.html. Accessed Mar 2013

Sullivan D (1995) The nature and scope of human rights obligations concerning women's right to health. Health Hum Rights 1:369

The Basic Law of Governance No: A/90, Dated 27th Sha'ban 1412 H (1 March 1992). http://www.saudiembassy.net/about/country-information/laws/The_Basic_Law_Of_Governance.aspx. Accessed Jan 2013

UN (2008) Human Development Report 2007/08. http://hdr.undp.org/en/reports/global/hdr2007-2008/. Accessed April 2013

UN (2005) Millennium Development Goals Report Saudi Arabia. http://www.un.org/summit2005/MDGBook.pdf. Accessed Feb 2013

UN, Arab Human Rights Index. http://www.arabhumanrights.org/en/countries/country.aspx?cid=16. Accessed Feb 2013

UN, Treaty Collection. http://treaties.un.org/pages/ViewDetails.aspx?src=TREATY&mtdsg_no=IV-4&chapter=4&lang=en. Accessed July 2013

UN Committee on the Rights of the Child, Forty-First session, CRC/C/SAU/CO/2 17th March (2006). http://www.unhchr.ch/tbs/doc.nsf/898586b1dc7b4043c1256a450044f331/6145a0cf3438dc54c1257168004c5998/$FILE/G0641006.pdf. Accessed Mar 2013

UN Human Rights Committee (2000) General Comment No. 28 on Equality of rights between men and women (Article 3), Doc CCPR/C/21/Rev.1/Add.10, March 2000. http://www.unhchr.ch/tbs/doc.nsf/0/13b02776122d4838802568b900360e80. Accessed Aug 2013

UN Committee on the Elimination of Discrimination against Women (2008) General Recommendation no 26 on women migrant workers, CEDAW/C/2009/WP.1/R, December 2008. www2.ohchr.org/english/bodies/cedaw/comments.htm. Accessed Aug 2013

UN Committee on the Elimination of Discrimination against Women (1999) General Recommendation No. 24 on Women and Health, U.N. Doc. A/54/38 at 5, 20th Session 1999. http://www.un.org/womenwatch/daw/cedaw/recommendations/recomm.htm. Accessed Aug 2013

UN Committee on the Elimination of Discrimination Against Women, Fortieth Session (2008) CEDAW/C/SAU/CO/2 Concluding Comments of the Committee on Saudi Arabia. http://www2.ohchr.org/english/bodies/cedaw/docs/CEDAW.C.SAU.CO.2_en.pdf. Accessed Feb 2013

US Department of State, 2011 Country Reports on Human Rights Practices—Saudi Arabia, 24 May 2012. http://www.unhcr.org/refworld/docid/4fc75a672.html. Accessed Feb 2013

US Department of State, 2012 Trafficking in Persons Report—Saudi Arabia, 19 June 2012. http://www.unhcr.org/refworld/docid/4fe30c9cc.html. Accessed Feb 2013

Van Eijk E (2010) Sharia and national law in Saudi Arabia' In: Otto J (ed) Sharia Incorporated (LUP 2010) 193–180

World Health Organisation (2012) World Health Statistics 2012. http://www.who.int/gho/publications/world_health_statistics/2012/en/index.html. Accessed Jan 2013

World Bank (2011). http://data.worldbank.org/country/saudi-arabia. Accessed April 2013

Chapter 7
The Realization of the Right to Health for Refugees in Jordan

Katharine Heus and Thamer Sartawi

Abstract This chapter presents an assessment of the realization of the right to health for refugees in Jordan. A host to Palestinian, Iraqi, and Syrian refugees, Jordan has one of the highest densities of refugees per capita of any country in the world. The central aim of this contribution is to assess where primary responsibility for the realization of the right to health for these acutely vulnerable subgroups lies, both in theory and in practice. This is done through an analysis of the health status, core obligations, and the accessibility, availability, acceptability, and quality of care framework. It is found that while in theory primary responsibility lies with the Government of Jordan, in practice the international community has assumed a greater role in realizing the right to health across each of the main refugee communities. In particular, the United Nations Relief and Work Agency and the United Nations High Commission for Refugees have assumed a central role in realizing the right to health for refugees in Jordan. We posit that this Government of Jordan to United Nations responsibility-shift has resulted in the entrenchment of parallel social protection structures that has led to the creation of multiple UN "surrogate states." While providing access to key services, these parallel structures exacerbate fragmentation in the Jordanian health system, compromising the realization of the right to health for both refugees and non-refugees alike. Integration of these parallel service structures into the Jordanian health system is proposed as a potential avenue for advancing the realization of the right to health for all residents in Jordan, including refugees.

Katharine Heus is a Graduate at the Global Public Health Unit, School of Social and Political Sciences, University of Edinburgh. Thamer Sartawi is a Medical doctor, Holder of MSC Global Public Health Unit, School of Social and Political Sciences, University of Edinburgh.

K. Heus (✉) · T. Sartawi
School of Social and Political Sciences, University of Edinburgh, Edinburgh EH8 9AD, UK
e-mail: katharineheus@gmail.com

T. Sartawi
e-mail: Thamer.sartawi@gmail.com

B. Toebes et al. (eds.), *The Right to Health*, DOI: 10.1007/978-94-6265-014-5_7,
© T.M.C. ASSER PRESS and the authors 2014

Contents

7.1	Introduction	194
7.2	The Jordanian Health System	196
7.3	Jordan and International Norms	197
	7.3.1 Human Rights Law	197
	7.3.2 Refugee Law	198
	7.3.3 Right to Health and Core Obligations	199
7.4	Right to Health for Palestinian Refugees in Jordan	203
	7.4.1 GOJ, UNRWA and Citizenship	203
	7.4.2 UNRWA and Palestinian Refugees	206
	7.4.3 Health Status	207
	7.4.4 AAAQ Analysis	207
	7.4.5 Core Obligations	209
	7.4.6 Parallel Structures and the Rise of the "Blue State"	210
7.5	The Right to Health for Iraqi Refugees	211
	7.5.1 UNHCR and GOJ Dichotomy	212
	7.5.2 Health Status	214
	7.5.3 AAAQ Analysis	215
	7.5.4 Core Obligations	217
	7.5.5 Parallel Structures	217
7.6	Right to Health for Syrian Refugees in Jordan	218
7.7	The Right to Health and UN Surrogacy	219
7.8	Sustainability and Looking Forward	222
7.9	Conclusion	224
References		225

7.1 Introduction

The Hashemite Kingdom of Jordan is a small, upper-middle income country located in the heart of the Middle East. A constitutional monarchy, the head of state is King Abdullah II bin Hussein who succeeded his father King Hussein bin Talal in 1999 who had ruled Jordan for more than four decades. Since gaining independence from British rule in 1946, Jordan has faced significant internal and external challenges to its stability and development as an independent nation.[1] The most prominent among these include the 1948 and 1967 Arab-Israeli wars, the 2003 US-led invasion of Iraq, and the ongoing Syrian revolution turned civil war, which have cumulatively resulted in mass influx of refugees into the Kingdom.

Jordan's geographic proximity to each of these conflict zones, relative political stability, and tolerant attitude toward displaced peoples has resulted in this country becoming the principal host for Palestinian, Iraqi, and, most recently, Syrian

---

[1] World Bank (n.d.): Jordan Country Profile http://www.worldbank.org/en/country/jordan [last accessed: 2 October 2013]. Patterson 2007 offers an overview of the Kingdom of Jordan in his comprehensive assessment of the right to health in Jordan.

7 The Realization of the Right to Health for Refugees in Jordan

refugees.[2] With a total population of 6.249 million people[3]—37 % of whom are 15 years old or younger[4]—Jordan hosts over 3 million refugees, with the number increasing daily.[5] Even before the onset of the Syrian crisis, Jordan had the greatest density of refugees per capita of any country in the world.[6] And while refugees in Jordan face serious affronts to the realization of a wide number of human rights, our analysis will focus on a major component of refugee protection—the "right to the highest attainable standard of health" as outlined in Article 12 of the International Convention on Economic, Social, and Cultural Rights (ICESCR)[7] and further clarified through General Comment 14.[8]

This chapter will evaluate the realization of the right to health for Palestinian, Iraqi, and Syrian refugees in Jordan as case studies of long-term, medium-term, and acute refugee crises. We will assess the realization of this right through an analysis of the health status and assessment of progress across the core obligations.[9] Additionally, the AAAQ framework, which considers the availability,[10] accessibility,[11] acceptability,[12] and quality of care[13] will be used to guide an in-depth examination of the realization of this right. Unfortunately, due to the contemporary nature of the Syrian refugee crisis, it is not possible to conduct the same kind of analysis for this group and so, instead, a general discussion of this emerging crisis will be undertaken. In turn, these three case studies will be used as a platform from which the distribution of responsibility for the realization of the right to health can be examined.

Throughout this chapter, we attempt to determine who bears primary responsibility for the realization of the right to health for refugees in Jordan both in theory and in practice. By examining the distribution of responsibility across the main refugee populations, we show that the dynamic interaction between UN agencies and the Government of Jordan (GOJ) has resulted in the creation of

---

[2] Jordan is often portrayed as a safe haven for refugees in the Middle East and North Africa region; see Chatelard 2010 and Patterson 2007.

[3] World Bank (n.d.) Jordan Country Profile http://www.worldbank.org/en/country/jordan [last accessed: 2 October 2013].

[4] ESCWA Demographic Profile of Jordan (n.d) http://www.escwa.un.org/popin/members/Jordan.pdf [last accessed: 2 October 2013].

[5] Ibid. Furthermore, UNHCR estimates that Jordan currently hosts 600,000 Syrian refugees, constituting 10 % of the Jordanian population, see Koren 2013.

[6] UNHCR Global Report 2012b, p. 84.

[7] United Nations International Committee on Economic, Social and Cultural Rights (ICESCR) 1976 Article 12.

[8] United Nations CESCR 2000 General Comment No. 14: The Right to the Highest Attainable Standard of Health (herein: General Comment 14).

[9] Ibid.

[10] General Comment 14, para 12(a).

[11] General Comment 14, para 12(b).

[12] General Comment 14, para 12(c).

[13] General Comment 14, para 12(d).

parallel social welfare structures that have evolved into multiple "UN surrogate states."[14] We posit that these surrogate state structures have assumed the primary responsibility for the realization of refugees' varied economic, social and cultural rights—including the right to health.

7.2 The Jordanian Health System

> At the heart of the right to the highest attainable standard of health lies an effective and integrated health system, encompassing medical care and the underlying determinants of health, which is responsive to national and local priorities and accessible to all.[15]
>
> Hunt and Backman (2008)

As Hunt and Backman elucidate, the health system is of central importance to the realization of the right to health; and before proceeding to our analysis it will be useful to have a basic understanding of the Jordanian health system (JHS). The JHS is well known regionally for its commitment to improving the health of its population[16]; this is apparent in a number of significant health indicators including decreasing infant and maternal mortality rates, and increasing average life expectancy, which is now 74 years.[17] Jordan's total health expenditure is consistently among the highest in the region, reaching 9.5 % of GDP in 2009 and dropping slightly to 8.3 % of GDP in 2010[18]; in terms of finance and provision however the JHS is highly fragmented.[19]

The JHS consists of three major health service providers including the public and private sectors, as well as national and international nongovernmental organizations (NGOs/iNGOs). The public sector is composed of the Royal Medical Services (RMS), the Ministry of Health (MOH), and to a lesser extent, university hospitals, which provide services to university and hospital staff and their dependents.[20] The RMS offers primary, secondary, and tertiary healthcare to members of the Jordanian army, the public security police force, civil defense, intelligence agency, Royal Jordanian Airline employees, as well as retired military personnel and their dependents among others.[21] Through the Civil Insurance Program (CIP), the MOH provides services and insurance coverage to government

---

[14] Kagan 2012 offers an interesting assessment of the proliferation of UN surrogate states in the MENA region. He recognizes that UN surrogacy has arisen in Jordan, and proposes that this has been particularly acute in response to the Palestinian and Iraqi refugee crises.

[15] Hunt and Backman 2008, p. 82.

[16] World Bank 2012: Country Cooperation Strategy 2012–2015, p. 2.

[17] Jordanian Department Of Statistics 2011.

[18] WHO 2013 Global Health Expenditure—Jordan National Expenditure on Health 1996–2011.

[19] Ekman 2007.

[20] Jordanian Ministry of Health 2011—Jordan National Health Strategy 2008–2012.

[21] Ibid.

employees and their dependents, the certified poor (income < JD 600), handicapped persons, blood donors, cancer, and end-stage kidney disease patients, and on a voluntary basis, to the elderly and pregnant women.[22]

The private sector has a good reputation for its highly qualified personnel, advanced diagnostic modalities, and for generally providing a high standard of care; however, the majority of Jordanian citizens are unable to access private sector services as they are either not covered by health insurance, are unemployed, or are unable to afford private insurance premiums.[23] The final component of the JHS consists of UN agencies and NGOs that operate on a nonprofit basis, and which have particular significance in the case of refugees.[24]

The 2008 Jordanian National Health accounts—an analysis of the JHS's sources of finance—revealed that public health expenditure constituted 57 % of funding, while private health expenditure constituted 37.49 %, with donor funds constituting the remaining 5.51 %.[25] Further analysis of health expenditure showed a high proportion of out of pocket payments (OPP)—with OPPs from households comprising 42.3 % of total health expenditure. Additionally it was found that only approximately 20 % of the population had health insurance coverage. Thus, the high levels of OPPs and low insurance coverage constitute major barriers to accessing affordable, high-quality healthcare services as Jordanian households must shoulder a substantial portion of healthcare costs themselves.[26] The complexity and fragmentation of the health system presents significant challenges to the realization of the right to health for both refugee and non-refugee populations in Jordan.

7.3 Jordan and International Norms

7.3.1 Human Rights Law

Jordan is a party to a number of international human rights agreements, including the International Convent on Economic, Social, and Cultural Rights (ICESCR), the International Convention on Civil and Political Rights (ICCPR), the Convention of the Rights of the Child (CRC), the Convention on Elimination of Discrimination Against Women (CEDAW), the Convention on the Elimination of all Forms of Racial Discrimination (CERD), the Convention Against Torture (CAT) and the Convention on the Rights of Persons with Disabilities (CRPD).[27] Jordan has also

---

[22] Ibid.

[23] Ibid.

[24] World Health Organization 2009—Country Cooperation Strategy for WHO and Jordan 2008–2013 http://www.who.int/countryfocus/cooperation_strategy/ccs_jor_en.pdf [Last accessed: 2 October 2013].

[25] Ibid.

[26] Ibid.

[27] NCHR 2010, UNDP 2013, p. 78.

affirmed its commitment to Human Rights through the Universal Islamic Declaration of Human Rights.[28]

Despite this apparent acknowledgment of human rights at the international level, Jordan has taken a minimalistic approach to incorporating both the rights of refugees and the right to health into domestic legislation.[29] While Jordan is a signatory to the aforementioned Conventions, Jordan has not ratified optional protocols of these conventions, which would allow individuals to submit human rights abuse complaints to the UN thereby effectively preventing refugees from accessing a means of redress.[30]

In his comprehensive review of the right to health in Jordan, Patterson finds that, "it does not appear that Jordan has incorporated any of the international instruments that it has ratified into domestic law, thus denying citizens' the right to access to effective judicial remedy at a national level."[31] The Jordanian Constitution only mentions health once, in Article 23, in reference to safe working conditions and offers little further guidance in regard to the rights of refugees.[32] In order to unpack the realization of the right to health for refugees in Jordan, it is necessary to examine not only human rights law, but also refugee law and international humanitarian law.

7.3.2 Refugee Law

Jordan has not ratified the United Nations High Commission for Refugees (UN-HCR) 1951 Refugee Convention, or the 1967 Protocol Relating to the Status of Refugees, and there is effectively no Jordanian refugee legislation to speak of.[33] This is particularly significant in light of Article 23 of UNHCR's 1951 Convention, which mandates that refugees are to have guaranteed access to public relief services—including health—on par with host country citizens.[34] Over the past six decades, the GOJ has largely[35] treated those seeking asylum as "foreigners" or "guests" and therefore, the domestic law applicable to all out of state individuals has generally also been applied to those seeking refuge.[36]

---

[28] UNHCR 2010.

[29] Backman et al. 2008, p. 2064, NCHR 2010, Patterson 2007, pp. 2–3, UNDAF 2007, p. 11.

[30] UNDP 2013.

[31] Patterson 2007.

[32] Patterson 2007.

[33] Davis 2012.

[34] UN 1951, Protocol Relating to the Status of Refugees.

[35] efugees of the 1948 war were granted Jordanian citizenship and are the exception here as the categorization of refugees as foreigners largely applies to those who sought refuge to Jordan after 1954.

[36] See Zaiotti 2006 for a broader discussion of refugee policy in the Middle East.

The Jordanian Constitution offers little guidance in regard to the rights of refugees, as the only reference to this group is in regard to prohibiting the "extradition of political refugees ... on account of their political beliefs or for their defense of liberty"[37]—a stipulation that has proven important in regard to international claims around the violation of the principle of non-refoulement on the part of the GOJ, but which again has not been substantially integrated into national Jordanian policy.[38]

7.3.3 Right to Health and Core Obligations

The duty to "respect, protect, and fulfill"[39] the right to "the highest attainable standard of physical and mental health"[40] as outlined in Article 12 of the ICESCR necessitates certain actions on the part of both State and non-state actors. Signatories to the ICESCR are legally obligated to "respect the right to health by, inter alia, refraining from denying or limiting equal access for all persons."[41] The State has an obligation to "respect and guarantee the safe delivery of services"[42] and to protect and ensure "equal access to health care and health-related services," including those provided by third parties.[43] The obligation to fulfill the right to health necessitates that States not only "give sufficient recognition to the right to health in the national political and legal systems," but that this recognition extends to the provision of equal access to health care encompassing primary care and the wider determinants of health "such as nutritiously safe food and potable drinking water, basic sanitation and adequate housing and living conditions."[44] In this regard, the capacity of the Jordanian state and the national health system are critical determinants of the right to health.

This is complicated by the fact that refugees are non-nationals residing in a country facing mass population influxes, presenting a significant challenge to the capacity of the State's health and social service systems. Article 2.3 of the ICESCR states that, "developing countries, with due regard to human rights and their national economy may determine to what extent they would guarantee the economic rights recognized by the present Covenant to non-nationals."[45] As a

---

[37] U.S. Committee for Refugees and Immigrants 2009.

[38] Backman et al. 2008, Human Rights Watch (HRW) 2006.

[39] General Comment 14, para 33; WHO (n.d.) Human Rights-Based Approaches Note further outlines the duty to "respect, protect, fulfill" the right to health, while Meier and Fox 2010 offer an interesting discussion of this duty in regards to international obligations.

[40] ICESCR 1976, Article 12, para 1.

[41] General Comment 14, para 34.

[42] Toebes 2013, p. 133.

[43] General Comment 14, para 35.

[44] General Comment 14, para 36. Much of this discussion emerged from the commentary offered by B. Toebes—for a full discussion see: Toebes 2013.

[45] ICESCR Article 2, para 3.

developing country that, unlike many of its neighbors, is not oil-rich, the Jordanian government has come under considerable economic strain due partially to the emergence of very large refugee subpopulations. It is widely understood that the realization of the varied and complex rights such as the right to health outlined in the ICESCR cannot be reached comprehensively immediately, instead a mechanism has been created to encourage a step-wise approach to fulfilling these rights.[46] Article 2.1 of the Covenant asserts that the States' duty to "protect, respect and fulfill"[47] the right to health is subject to resource availability and progressive realization.[48]

This is highly significant in the Jordanian context as this country has experienced repeated waves of refugee influxes, each of which have brought hundreds of thousands of refugees to this relatively small, arid, and resource poor country. It is in part because of the limited resources and the scale of the repeated refugee crises that the international community has become entrenched in the realization of the right to health for refugees in Jordan. Additionally, Article 2.1 of the ICESCR obligates all States party to the Covenant to "… take steps, individually and through international assistance and cooperation, especially economic and technical, to the maximum of its available resources, with a view to achieving progressively the full realization of the rights recognized in the present Covenant by all appropriate means…"[49] As the right to health is also outlined in this Covenant, Article 2.1 denotes a duty on the part of the international community to work toward the attainment of the right to health in countries and for communities requiring international assistance.[50]

In the Jordanian context, a significant array of international actors have become engaged with the provision of health services and with the attainment of broader economic, social, and cultural rights for refugees. The international community has often taken the lead in realizing second-generation rights for refugees in Jordan, which "… grant individuals rights to basic socio-economic services (food, clothing, water, housing, and healthcare)."[51] The length of the refugee crises—over 60 years for the Palestinian community, and nearly a decade for the Iraqi community—poses a challenge to the concept of acute humanitarian crisis demanding international action.[52] And while Geneva Law "only applies fully during international armed conflicts,"[53] it has been suggested that, "human rights

---

[46] Hunt and Backman 2008.

[47] General Comment 14, para 33.

[48] Hunt 2006, p. 1. A special thanks to B. Toebes for her comments, guidance and insights on this matter.

[49] ICESCR Article 2, para 1.

[50] Toebes 2013, p. 133.

[51] Toebes 2013, p. 134.

[52] United States Department of State: Human Rights Report Jordan 2010.

[53] Toebes 2013, p. 136.

law forms an important additional framework, in particular during non-international armed conflicts, emergencies, and disasters."[54]

General Comment 14 recognizes the exceptional circumstances presented by humanitarian crises and suggests that, "the role of WHO, the Office of the UNHCR, the International Committee of the Red Cross/Red Crescent and UNICEF, as well as non governmental organizations and national medical associations, is of particular importance in relation to disaster relief and humanitarian assistance in times of emergencies," and this extends to both refugees and internally displaced persons.[55] Interestingly, all these actors have been or are currently engaged with the realization of the right to health for refugees in Jordan—albeit, as will become clear in the case studies below, some are more heavily engaged than others.

General Comment 20 offers further insight here as it states that the realization of the rights outlined in the ICESCR should not be subject to discrimination on the basis of identity or result in differential treatment on the grounds of status[56]; specifically, General Comment 20 describes how "both direct and indirect forms of differential treatment can amount to discrimination," and the example of "...requiring a birth registration certificate for school enrolment may discrimination be against ethnic minorities or non-nationals who do not possess, or have been denied, such certificates."[57] This same principle extends to the right to health and thereby, both State and non-State actors must respect, protect, and fulfill not only the right to health, but also the right to nondiscrimination on the grounds of nationality.[58]

Accordingly, in line with General Comment 20, the core obligations outlined in General Comment 14 must be progressively realized in accordance with the resources available to both the Jordanian State and the international community, for all those residing in Jordan regardless of their "... civil, political, social or other status."[59] General Comment 14 further suggests that, "equality of access to health care and health services has to be emphasized."[60] It is interesting to note, however, that due to the finitude of resources available, the focus of the debate around the right to health for refugees in Jordan is limited to the realization of the core obligations, rather than the general obligations.[61] The significant challenge faced in meeting even these central tenets of the right to health for refugees—the "minimum" requirements—is in and of itself quite revealing.[62]

---

[54] Ibid, p. 134.

[55] General Comment 14, para 18.

[56] UN CESCR 2009 General Comment 20: Non-discrimination in economic, social and cultural rights (Herein: General Comment 20).

[57] General Comment 20, para 10(b).

[58] General Comment 20, para 10(b).

[59] General Comment 14, para 18.

[60] General Comment 14, para 19.

[61] General Comment 14, para 30.

[62] Hunt and Backman 2008, p. 84.

The six core obligations outlined in General Comment 14 can be considered duties "... of immediate effect"[63] and necessitate certain actions on the part of the State to ensure that "at the very least minimum essential levels"[64] of health services are reached. Drawing on the principles outlined in the Alma Ata Declaration,[65] these core obligations take on a particular significance in this context as they offer guiding principles of minimum actions that the GOJ has primary responsibility for realizing. These six core obligations include the obligation to:

(a) ... ensure the right of access to health facilities, goods and services on a non-discriminatory basis, especially for vulnerable or marginalized groups;

(b) ... ensure access to the minimum essential food which is nutritionally adequate and safe, to ensure freedom from hunger to everyone;

(c) ... ensure access to basic shelter, housing and sanitation, and an adequate supply of safe and potable water;

(d) ... provide essential drugs, as from time to time defined under the WHO Action Programme on Essential Drugs;

(e) ... ensure equitable distribution of all health facilities, goods and services;

(f) ... adopt and implement a national public health strategy and plan of action, on the basis of epidemiological evidence, addressing the health concerns of the whole population ... the process by which the strategy and plan of action are devised, as well as their content, shall give particular attention to all vulnerable or marginalized groups.[66]

Hunt and Backman synthesize these obligations into four central tenants, encompassing: (1) the preparation of a "comprehensive national health plan for the development of the health system;" (2) ensuring "access to health-related services and facilities on a non discriminatory basis..."; (3) ensuring "the equitable distribution of health related services;" and (4) the establishment of "effective, transparency, accessible and independent mechanisms of accountability...".[67] Hunt and Backman also discuss the provision of a basic package of health services as an additional core obligation.[68]

While primary responsibility lies with the Jordanian state, in the context of limited resources and a very large refugee population, establishing an acceptable pace of realization and assessing the appropriate allocation of resources is challenging.[69] This finitude of resources legitimizes international engagement with the

---

[63] General Comment 14, para 12.

[64] Hunt and Backman 2008, p. 84.

[65] General Comment 14, para 43.

[66] General Comment 14, para 43 a–f.

[67] Hunt and Backman 2008, p. 85.

[68] Ibid.

[69] Patterson 2007.

realization of the right to health for refugees in Jordan.[70] When examining progress across these core obligations in practice for the three main refugee communities in Jordan, it becomes critical to question the distribution of de facto responsibility for progress in these regards, as the international community has come to play a significant role.

The remainder of this chapter consists of a case-by-case examination of the realization of the right to health for refugees in Jordan, commencing with the longest standing group—Palestinian refugees—progressing through the largest group—Iraqi refugees—and concluding with the most recent group—Syrian refugees.

7.4 Right to Health for Palestinian Refugees in Jordan

The 65 year long Palestinian refugee situation is the longest running crisis of statelessness in modern history.[71] The 1948 Arab-Israeli wars resulted in the occupation of Palestine and the forceful displacement of more than 700,000 Palestinians from their homeland.[72] Palestinians have suffered decades of disadvantage due to prolonged statelessness. It is a difficult task to comprehensively assess the realization of human rights, including the right to health, for Palestinian refugees in Jordan over the past six decades. In our opinion, an overview of the main actors engaged with refugee health is a useful starting point for determining where primary responsibility for realizing the core obligation lies both in theory and in practice. In this case study, the roles of both the United Nations Relief and Works Agency (UNRWA) and Jordanian state are considered.

7.4.1 GOJ, UNRWA and Citizenship

The GOJ's categorization of the legal status of Palestinians has been undertaken in response to various crises that have occurred over the past 6 decades, which have cumulatively resulted in the assignment of Palestinians residing in Jordan into 6 categories.[73] Political events such as the 1970 civil war in Jordan, the 1981 severance of legal and administrative ties with the West Bank, and the 1991 Gulf War

---

[70] Sincere thanks to Stefanie Jensen for her comments and insights regarding non-nationals, and to Obi Nnamuchi for his editorial support and assistance with the discussion around the finitude of resources.

[71] Rempel 2006.

[72] Ibid.

[73] Al Abed 2004: This categorization of the 6 groups of Palestinians is done in addition to east banker Jordanians who lived on the east bank of the Jordan River before 1948. They are referred to as being Jordanians of Jordanian origin, in contrast to the 1948 Palestinian refugees who are more widely referred to as Jordanians of Palestinian origin.

have all shaped the Palestinian population's experience in Jordan. But, the 1948 war (*nakbah*) and the 1967 war (*nakseh*) were the major incidents that created the Palestinian refugee crisis in Jordan and in the region.

Of these six groups, the first two groups we identify are classified as Jordanian "citizens of Palestinian origin" including: (1) those originating from Palestinian land occupied in 1948, and (2) those originating from the conflict in 1967.[74] Refugees displaced in the 1948 war in Palestine were granted citizenship in accordance with Jordanian Law No. 6 of 1954 on Nationality, Article 3(b), which states that a Jordanian national is "[a]ny person who, not being Jewish, possessed Palestinian nationality before 15 May 1948 and was a regular resident in the Hashemite Kingdom of Jordan between 20 December 1949 and 16 February 1954."[75] Both subgroups are given a national identification (ID) number and 5-year Jordanian passports, however, the latter subgroup is given additional identification cards, called "yellow cards" to indicate their 1967 origins.[76]

Three additional subgroups include: (3) Jordanian-Palestinians of 1967 who reside in the West Bank, (4) Jordanian-Palestinian from Jerusalem, and (5) Palestinian refugees from Gaza. These subgroups do not have a national ID number, but are given Jordanian passports and identification cards—"green cards" for the first two groups and "blue cards" for the 1967 Gaza refugees[77]—which serve to indicate both their descent and their legal status in Jordan. The sixth category includes Palestinian citizens who have been issued Palestinian passports by the Palestinian Authority who reside neither in Jordan nor in the occupied Palestinian territories. The importance of the national ID number arises from the fact that holding it is essential for refugees' eligibility to enjoy basic human rights on par with Jordanian citizens.

The GOJ's rigid categorization has a myriad of political, social, and economic ramifications that have influenced the attainment the right to health for Palestinian refugees in Jordan. The case of Palestinian refugees from Gaza is rather unique as, in contrast to the 1948 refugees, the 130,000 refugees displaced during the 1967 war were given the status of "foreign nationals"[78] and issued temporary Jordanian passports.[79] The "foreign national" status presumes that these refugees are able to

---

[74] Ibid.

[75] Law No. 6 of 1954 on Nationality (last amended 1987) http://www.refworld.org/docid/3ae6b4ea13.html [Last accessed: 3 October 2013].

[76] Al Abed 2004.

[77] Al Abed 2004.

[78] Pérez 2011, p. 1034.

[79] Ibid. Gaza was under Egyptian administration during the 1948 and 1967 wars in Palestine, and Gaza inhabitants held Egyptian legal documents. During the 1948 war Gazan's who fled to the West Bank as well as refugees of the 1967 war originally from Gaza were not given Jordanian citizenship status as they already possessed Egyptian legal documents. Accordingly, Jordan classified these refugees as foreigners—a status that has persisted for 46 years even though these refugees are eligible for citizenship under Jordanian Law due to their prolonged residence in Jordan.

return to their home countries; however, that option is not viable due to the ongoing Israeli occupation of Palestinian land.[80]

Although Article 4 of the Jordanian Nationality Law allows Arab individuals residing in the country for more than 15 years to be eligible for Jordanian citizenship, the GOJ has disallowed 1967 refugees from claiming citizenship in accordance with their right as outlined in this law.[81] The GOJ claims that granting citizenship to these refugees from Gaza would be inconsistent with their right of return to Palestine—thus claiming that this exception to the citizenship is undertaken for the protection of this refugee population.[82] Regardless of government claims, state denial of citizenship for these refugees has significant ramifications for the realization of a number of different human rights including the right to health, education, employment, property ownership, forming unions, voting, and political representation in parliament.[83] Michael Perez attributes the unequal status of Palestinian refugees from Gaza to be as a result of "... their international exclusion from the contemporary order of citizens and states."[84]

The experience of Palestinian refugees in Jordan provides an exemplary case of long-term statelessness and the challenges this status poses for the realization of the right to health. The differential citizenship status of Palestinian refugees in Jordan is integral to understanding the challenges facing both UNRWA and the Jordanian government in regard to upholding the right to health for these populations. While the 1954 Nationality Law granted citizenship to Palestinians who sought refuge after the 1948 war, refugees of the 1967 war—mainly from Gaza—have not been granted citizenship status and thus live in a state of legal limbo. The Government's decision to classify refugees from Gaza as foreign nationals has resulted in the continued denial of human rights on the basis of legal status. This has pressured the Gaza refugee community to refrain from demands around the realization of the full scope of the universal human rights to which they are entitled, to a rather narrow focus on the demand for a national ID number, which has effectively become a gateway for the right to have rights in Jordan.[85]

---

[80] Ibid, p. 1036.

[81] Ibid, p. 1045.

[82] Ibid, p. 1036—the notion of a substitute homeland "Watan Badil" claim is only put forward with regards to the 1967 Gaza refugees, however, it is interesting to note that such claims have not been put forward with regards to the 1948 refugees.

[83] Ibid, p. 1037.

[84] Ibid, p. 1036.

[85] Pérez 2011, p. 1036.

7.4.2 UNRWA and Palestinian Refugees

UNRWA was established in 1949 under UN General Assembly Resolution 302 (IV) with a mandate to provide relief and work services for Palestinian refugees according to their needs.[86] UNRWA's mission is to "help Palestine refugees achieve their full potential in human development under the difficult circumstances in which they live."[87] UNRWA defines Palestinian refugees as: "any person whose normal place of residence was Palestine during the period 1 June 1946 to 15 May 1948 and who lost both home and means of livelihood as a result of the 1948 conflict, and descendants of such persons, including legally adopted children, through the male line."[88]

UNRWA's definition of a Palestinian refugee "does not define refugee status"[89] and instead attempts to establish eligibility criteria for accessing UNRWA services.[90] It is worth noting, however, that the 1951 Refugee Convention does not apply to Palestinian refugees and therefore the rights of these refugees are not guaranteed under international refugee law and instead fall under UNRWA's mandate.[91] Accordingly, in the aftermath of the 1967 war, UNRWA broadened its eligibility criteria to include refugees displaced by the conflict. The UN General Assembly's Resolution 2252 states that UNRWA is "to continue to provide humanitarian assistance, as far as practicable, on an emergency basis, and as a temporary measure, to persons in the area who are currently displaced and in serious need of continued assistance as a result of the June 1967 and subsequent hostilities,"[92] which further substantiates UNRWA's commitment to refugees as long as the conflict remains unresolved.

By 2012, UNRWA provided services to approximately 4.67 million registered Palestinian refugees, dispersed across 58 camps in Jordan, Syria, Lebanon, Gaza, and West-Bank; a third of these refugees reside in UNRWA serviced refugee camps.[93] Nearly 2 million Palestinian refugees live in Jordan, of which 17 % are

---

[86] UNRWA Medium Term Strategy 2010–2015, p. 9.

[87] Ibid.

[88] UNRWA's consolidated Eligibility and Registration instructions (CERI) (n.d.) http://www.unrwa.org/userfiles/2010011995652.pdf [Last accessed: 2 May 2013].

[89] Ibid.

[90] Ibid.

[91] Article 1D of the 1951 Refugee Convention states that the "convention shall not apply to persons who are at present receiving from organs or agencies of the United Nations other than the United Nations High Commissioner for refugees protection or assistance." Since Palestinians receive assistance from a UN body (UNRWA), they are excluded from UNHCR mandate. See: http://www.unhcr.org/4ca34be29.pdf [Last accessed 3 October 2013] and Bocco 2009.

[92] Bocco 2009—the resolution was updated in 2004 in the General Assembly, further strengthening UNRWA's mandate to attend to the needs of Palestinian refugees.

[93] UNRWA: http://www.unrwa.org/etemplate.php?id=86 [Last accessed: 2 October 2013].

located in 13 refugee camps throughout the country.[94] Jordan is well known as the largest host of Palestinian refugees in the world, with 40 % of the total displaced Palestinian refugee population residing in the Kingdom.[95]

7.4.3 Health Status

The health of Palestinian refugees in Jordan has been steadily improving due in part to UNRWA's successful provision of a wide range of services.[96] This improvement is evident in low infant and maternal mortality rates,[97] high immunization rates, and a fair control over communicable diseases.[98] Mirroring a near global trend, there has been an epidemiological transition within this community with noncommunicable diseases (NCDs) surpassing communicable diseases as the leading cause of morbidity and mortality.[99] UNRWA's services now include the provision of drugs and therapies for diabetics, the supply of antihypertensive medication, lipid lowering drugs, and other expensive drugs for free.[100] This significantly reduces the financial burden facing Palestinian refugees, which the general Jordanian population continues to face from high OOPs.

7.4.4 AAAQ Analysis

The realization of the right to health can be seen as a result of the complex interaction of accessibility, availability, acceptability and the quality (AAAQ) of care.[101] While in theory, the GOJ is primarily responsible for the realization of AAAQ for vulnerable groups residing in the country, in practice, this does not appear to be the case for refugee populations. In particular, perhaps in part because of the size of the Palestinian refugee population, these groups face multiple barriers to accessing public health services and CIP or RMS health insurance. Studies have revealed that RMS health insurance distribution among the displaced Palestinians population in Jordan was significantly lower for both camp and non-camp refugees with coverage levels at 3 and 8 %, respectively. The prevalence of RMS

---

[94] Ibid.

[95] UNRWA 2010b.

[96] Riccardo et al. 2012.

[97] Ibid, p. 5. For example, with regards to infant mortality for Palestinian refugees in Jordan is 22.3/1000 compared to 18.4/1000 for the Jordanian population.

[98] Ibid, p. 11.

[99] Leaning et al. 2011, p. 9, Yach et al. 2004, Adeyi et al. 2007.

[100] Leaning et al. 2011.

[101] Toebes 1999, p. 665.

insurance in rural Jordanian villages, cities, and nomadic regions reached up to 51 % and it can be assumed that the situation remains largely the same today.[102]

As refugees of the 1967 war do not hold Jordanian citizenship, they are not eligible for employment in the public sector, and are therefore systematically excluded from the CIP and RMS insurance schemes. For 1967 refugees, co-payments reach up to 40 % of the total cost of accessing public sector services, posing significant financial barriers for public healthcare access, which makes them the most vulnerable Palestinian refugee population in Jordan.[103] By 2007, 71 % of Palestinian refugees registered with UNRWA had no insurance, whereas 3 % held private insurance and 26 % held public insurance.[104] Uninsured refugees are entitled to access public health services on par with uninsured Jordanian citizens, which entails incurring a 20 % copayment fee for services.[105] As access to public healthcare services and health insurance is significantly constrained by financial barriers, the majority of 1948 refugees holding Jordanian citizenship and all 1967 refugees regard UNRWA as their main health service provider.[106]

UNRWA's health system is quite comprehensive and operates through a network of 23 primary care centers located in all Palestinian refugee camps in Jordan, providing primary healthcare to registered refugees free of charge.[107] UNRWA subsidizes the cost of secondary and tertiary care for the refugees through public sector and other service providers.[108] The clinics provide preventive and curative services for acute and chronic conditions, as well as outpatient care, laboratory, oral and radiology services, medical supplies, and physical rehabilitation therapies.[109] Additionally, UNRWA focuses on the provision of family planning services, prenatal and neonatal care, child immunization, dental care, and chronic disease management. The wide variety of services and the vast distribution of UNRWA clinics significantly improve accessibility, availability, and affordability of healthcare for Palestinian refugees.

As the refugees have come to rely primarily on UNRWA health services, the quality of these services emerges as a major determinant of the standard of care. Although UNRWA clinics are readily available and free at the point of use, most refugees report dissatisfaction with the quality of services provided in the clinics—with particular dissatisfaction arising in regards to the performance of UNRWA clinics in managing chronic illnesses and disabilities, family planning services, and

---

[102] Jordanian Ministry of Health 2011—Jordan National Health Strategy 2008–2012.

[103] UNRWA 2013, Health in Jordan. Available at: http://www.unrwa.org/activity/health-jordan [Last accessed: 12 October 2013].

[104] Lapeyre et al. 2011, pp. 105.

[105] Ibid.

[106] Ibid.

[107] World Health Organization 2009—Country Cooperation Strategy for WHO and Jordan 2008–2013 http://www.who.int/countryfocus/cooperation_strategy/ccs_jor_en.pdf [Last accessed: 2 October 2013].

[108] Ibid.

[109] Ibid.

7 The Realization of the Right to Health for Refugees in Jordan

hospital services.[110] As the demand for more inclusive, high-quality primary healthcare and advanced secondary or hospital care services continues to grow, the ability of UNRWA's health system to match the health needs of the population is central to upholding the right to health for Palestinian refugees in Jordan. When UNRWA is unable to satisfy refugee health demands, refugees must resort to the public and private sectors as alternative health service providers. The costs of accessing care in the private sector and the high copayments for accessing care in the public sector, compounded with high rates of poverty, lack of insurance and unemployment, present significant barriers for most Palestinian refugees in Jordan, especially for camp residents, the abject poor, and refugees from Gaza.

7.4.5 Core Obligations

From the above assessment, it appears that UNRWA is satisfying many of the core obligations. In regards to designing a "comprehensive, national health plan for the development of a health system"[111] for Palestinian refugees, UNRWA is undoubtedly taking the lead; UNRWA's most recent strategy paper—the "2010–2015 Medium Term Strategy" (MTS)—reaffirms the agency's longstanding commitment to the livelihood of Palestinian refugees.[112] This report outlines four human development goals, including: "long and healthy life; knowledge and skills; a decent standard of living; and, human rights enjoyed to the fullest."[113] The explicit incorporation of health and human rights positions UNRWA at the forefront for the realization of the right to health for Palestinian refugees.

Of the 15 strategies adopted in the MTS, the 3 main health strategies of relevance to the core obligations include "ensur[ing] universal access to quality comprehensive primary health care," "protect[ing] and promot[ing] family health" and "prevent[ing] and control[ling] diseases."[114] The MTS signifies UNRWA's commitment to progressing across the core obligation of planning for the construction of a comprehensive health system. Furthermore, the agency's centrality is recognized by the GOJ, evident in that the Jordanian Ministry of Health's plan to reach universal coverage by 2012 included UNRWA as the primary insurer for 11.4 % of the population. This encompasses 600,000 Palestinian refugees that are acutely vulnerable and excluded from other insurance schemes.[115]

---

[110] Lapeyre et al. 2011, pp. 100–105.

[111] Hunt and Backman 2008, p. 85.

[112] UNRWA Medium Term Strategy 2010–2015.

[113] World Health Organization 2009—Country Cooperation Strategy for WHO and Jordan 2008–2013 http://www.who.int/countryfocus/cooperation_strategy/ccs_jor_en.pdf [Last accessed: 2 October 2013].

[114] Ibid.

[115] Ibid.

It is clear that the GOJ on its own is not realizing the second core obligation mentioned by Hunt and Backman—ensuring "access to health-related services on a non-discriminatory basis."[116] UNRWA has stepped in to ensure that progress is made for these highly vulnerable groups, and has taken on significant responsibility in regards to ensuring the "equitable distribution of health-related services and facilities."[117] Thus, based on the above AAAQ assessment, UNRWA is taking concrete steps to advance towards greater health equity within the Palestinian refugee community. This is perhaps most clearly apparent in the vast network of camp and non-camp-based facilities the agency has established encompassing 24 clinics and facilities.[118]

In regard to Hunt and Backman's fourth core obligation, which centers on the transparency and accountability of actors,[119] there is clear monitoring and evaluation by UNRWA, which is obligated to do so in line with wider UN mandates.[120] Despite providing a wide range of support to the Palestinian refugee community, UNRWA faces a variety of structural and operational challenges, with resource scarcity and reduced donor funding being the most significant.[121] Nonetheless, the organization strives to improve both the efficiency and quality of services it provides to maximize its capacity for social protection of refugees across a basic basket of services—especially in regard to highly vulnerable subpopulations such as the abject poor.[122]

7.4.6 Parallel Structures and the Rise of the "Blue State"[123]

Throughout its years of operation UNRWA has assumed central responsibility for ensuring the livelihood of Palestinian refugee communities in Jordan. The agency continuously provides services such as education, health care, and other social services, as well as micro-financing opportunities and it has also invested in refugee camp infrastructure, all of which are ultimately directed to "a single beneficiary population—that of Palestinian refugees and their descendants."[124]

---

[116] Hunt and Backman 2008, p. 85.

[117] Ibid.

[118] UNRWA 'Health in Jordan' Summary: http://www.unrwa.org/activity/health-jordan [last accessed: 6 October 2013].

[119] Hunt and Backman 2008, p. 85.

[120] See: UN (n.d.) http://www.un.org/en/strengtheningtheun/accountability.shtml [last accessed: 6 October 2013].

[121] As UNRWA's funding has decreased over the past years from 100 USD per refugee to 60.6 USD per refugee, the organization is under substantial financial pressure to perform and deliver services for refugees with only limited means. UNRWA Medium Term Strategy 2010–2015, p. 3.

[122] Lapeyre et al. 2011, pp. 100–105, UNRWA Medium Term Strategy 2010–2015, p. 41.

[123] Bocco 2009, p. 234.

[124] Rosenfeld 2009.

However, UNRWA does not assume responsibility for enforcing law and governance in the refugee camps where it operates.[125] Consequently, the GOJ's role was confined to law enforcement in the camp.[126] This decades' long interaction between UNRWA and Palestinian refugees has led to a redefinition of the organization's mandate from being a relief and work organization responding to an acute humanitarian crisis to becoming the primary protection and development agency for Palestinian refugees in Jordan and other countries of operation.[127]

In this context, an international refugee organization whose original mandate was to provide basic healthcare and relief services has now been portrayed as a strategic stakeholder in the implementation of long-term health policies in the GOJ's universal healthcare plan, most evident in Jordan's research MTS.[128] The preeminent role of UNRWA is evident in its continued commitment as the major provider of relief and work services for three generations of Palestinian refugees. UNRWA—an agency initially established as a temporary measure—has progressively taken on a "quasi state function" that provides parallel public services with "non-territorial administration."[129] Widely referred to as "the Blue State,"[130] UNRWA's quasi-state establishment is strongly present in the Jordanian context.

The vulnerability produced by the prolonged statelessness of the Palestinian refugee population is a systemic barrier that hinders the realization of the right to the highest attainable standard of health. As UNRWA serves to ameliorate the effects of disadvantages and vulnerabilities for Palestinian refugees in Jordan, realizing the right to health for this refugee community is ultimately determined by UNRWA's ability to increase its capacity to meet refugee's evolving health demands and tackle the wider determinants of health. In our opinion, the current GOJ-UNRWA quasi-state arrangement is unlikely to be challenged, given the absence of a long-lasting just solution that guarantees the right of return for Palestinian refugees to their homeland.

7.5 The Right to Health for Iraqi Refugees

While the case of Palestinian refugees discussed above is widely considered to be the longest-standing refugee crisis that the Middle East has ever experienced, the refugee crisis that resulted from the US-led invasion of Iraq is often considered the most acute.[131] A culmination of factors including the reign of Saddam Hussein,

---

[125] Bocco 2009.

[126] Kagan 2012.

[127] Takkenberg 2009.

[128] Jordan Ministry of Health 2011.

[129] Bocco 2009, p. 234.

[130] Ibid.

[131] Devi 2007, p. 1815, Bettis 2010, p. 262, Doocy et al. 2011, p. 273.

the US-led invasion in 2003, and prolonged sectarian violence led to the displacement of three to four million Iraqis since 2003.[132] The scale of the refugee crisis should not be underestimated: over 1.13 million individuals were internally displaced and an additional 2.2 were externally displaced.[133] Of those forced to seek refuge outside Iraq, most traveled to Syria and Jordan, with relatively smaller numbers arriving in Lebanon and Egypt.[134]

In 2007, it was estimated that there were 400,000–750,000 Iraqis refugees in Jordan, though estimates of up to 1 million have been deemed conceivable.[135] In recent years, many Iraqis have returned home and a much smaller number have sought permanent relocation both regionally and internationally.[136] While the GOJ has consistently upheld that this number remains around 450,000,[137] in early 2013 it was estimated that 150,000–450,000 Iraqi refugees remained in Jordan.[138] The GOJ has largely resisted using the term "refugees" to describe displaced Iraqis, but there is a consensus within the international community that the Iraqis who sought asylum in Jordan during the period leading to, and following the US-led invasion of Iraq, are refugees as per the definition outlined in the 1951 Refugee Convention.[139]

7.5.1 UNHCR and GOJ Dichotomy

In contrast to the Palestinian case where a distinct UN agency was created to manage the crisis, UNHCR took the lead in coordinating the response to the Iraqi refugee crisis in Jordan.[140] UNHCR opened its first office in Amman in 1991 in response to the emerging refugee crisis resulting from the first Gulf War.[141] In 1998, UNHCR and the GOJ negotiated a Memorandum of Understanding (MOU),

---

[132] Bettis 2010, p. 262, Chatelard 2010, Kenyon Lischer 2008.

[133] UNHCR 2013 http://www.unhcr.org/pages/49e486426.html.

[134] Crisp et al. 2009: 1, Bettis 2010: 262, International Organization for Migration 2009, as cited in Kenyon Lischer 2008, p. 95.

[135] Fafo 2007, p. 3. Figures listed here are based on synthesis of UNHCR, NGO and Government data. Furthermore, Chatelard 2010 suggests that the actual number is probably closer to 1 million, whereas Davis 2012 suggests that, at the peak of the crisis, the number was between 400,000 and 750,000. Finally, data presented by the U.S. Committee for Refugees and Immigrants 2009 World Refugee Survey estimates the figure is closer to 450,000 refugees from Iraq. Conflicting estimates of the total number of Iraqi refugees in Jordan make it quite difficult to ascertain an example number, and so instead the wide range proposed here will be accepted.

[136] International Crisis Group 2008 Middle East Report No. 77, p. 14.

[137] Crisp et al. 2009, p. 9.

[138] Ibid.

[139] UNICEF, WHO and Johns Hopkins 2009, HRW 2006.

[140] Ibid.

[141] UNHCR 2010 Global Report Jordan, Crisp et al. 2009, Chatelard 2010.

which was undertaken to "safeguard the asylum institution in Jordan, to enable UNHCR ... to provide international protection to people falling within its mandate" and reaffirmed both parties' commitment to the principle of non-refoulement.[142] The 1998 MOU also stipulated that asylum seekers and refugees in Jordan should "receive treatment as per the internationally accepted standards," "should receive legal status," and furthermore that the UNHCR would "... endeavor to find recognized refugees a durable solution be it voluntary repatriation to the country of origin or resettlement in a third country."[143]

The 1998 MOU is significant because the GOJ maintains that this defines both parties' terms of engagement with asylum seekers and refugees.[144] Under the 1998 MOU, the UNHCR bears primary responsibility for "adjudicating refugees claims" and "for the designation of refugee status."[145] In anticipation of a mass exodus from Iraq as a result of the US-led invasion, the GOJ and UNHCR negotiated a Temporary Protection Regime (TPR), which UNHCR sees as outlining the distribution of responsibility in regard to social protection for Iraqi refugees in Jordan.[146] The GOJ however, maintains that this TPR applies only to camp-based Iraqi refugees, of which there were very few as the majority settled in urban areas.[147] Wider readings of the 2003 TPR support the GOJ's interpretation, and therefore, the GOJ's position that the 1998 MOU still holds can be assumed valid.[148] The substantial divergence between the GOJ and the UNHCR's positions has resulted in confusion regarding who bears primary responsibility for the welfare of these refugees.[149] This debate is significant because the resultant confusion has allowed each party to exonerate itself from bearing primary responsibility.

One manifestation of this debate can be seen in the numbers of Iraqi refugees registered by UNHCR. While wider estimates posit that the number of Iraqi refugees in Jordan is upward of 450 000, by 2010 UNHCR had only registered 50 000.[150] UNHCR has maintained that registration ground to a halt out of concern that the agency's inability to relocate individuals within the designated six-month period would result in their forced expatriation.[151] In comparison to estimates that place the actual number of Iraqi refugees at 450,000, there is a staggering discrepancy between the number of registered and unregistered Iraqi refugees.[152]

---

[142] UNHCR and GOJ MOU 1998. For a more detailed discussion see: HRW 2006.

[143] HRW 2006.

[144] UNHCR and GOJ MOU 1998.

[145] HRW 2006, p. 10.

[146] Kenyon Lischer 2008, p. 65.

[147] Davis 2012.

[148] See HRW 2006, p. 5 for a discussion of camps in the Iraqi refugee crisis.

[149] Ibid, p. 6.

[150] UNHCR Global Report Jordan 2010.

[151] Ibid.

[152] Martin and Taylor 2012.

In the context of a tepid international reaction to the Iraqi crisis, UNHCR faced significant budgetary challenges and struggled to balance the costs of registering thousands of claimants with the cost of providing adequate social services, while simultaneously attempting to permanently resettle the refugees already registered.[153] These financial constraints, in combination with uncertainty between the GOJ and UNHCR, resulted in most Iraqi refugees being classified as "foreigners" or "guests."[154] Much like the Palestinian population, the Iraqi population is also distinct from other foreigners who come to Jordan due to their heightened state of vulnerability as individuals fleeing conflict, and their constrained ability to return to their respective homelands.

With the GOJ and UNHCR pointing fingers at each other, many Iraqis have fallen through the cracks and have had to make due without substantial support from either actor. The shifting of responsibility between the GOJ and the UNHCR[155] has forced Iraqi refugees to live in a precarious state of legal limbo that has had significant ramifications for the realization of a number of their human rights, not least of which is their right to the highest attainable standard of health.[156]

7.5.2 Health Status

While the typical image of refugee camps brings up images of rows of UN tents stacked along border areas, the case of Iraqi refugees in Jordan is unique from this common—and perhaps largely inaccurate—perception for two main reasons.[157] Firstly, Iraqi refugees mostly "originated from urban areas in their country of origin and have taken up residence in urban areas of their country of asylum."[158] With the exception of the Ruweished camp, most Iraqi refugees settled in urban centers, with the large majority—an estimated 70 %—taking up residence in Amman.[159] The urban location and spatial integration is one unique feature of the Iraqi refugee population in Jordan.[160]

---

[153] Leaning et al. 2011 p. 7, United States Committee for Refugee and Immigrations 2009, p. 2.

[154] Mowafi and Spiegel 2008, p. 1713.

[155] Crisp et al. 2009.

[156] HRW Silent Treatment 2006 offers an extensive discussion of the difference between the number that have been registered with UNHCR, and the number of Iraqis present in Jordan (pp. 6–9). Significantly, as stated in this report, the GOJ does not recognize the UNHCR asylum-seeker cards that the Refugee Commission has issue to some Iraqis in lieu of refugee status.

[157] Guterras and Spiegel 2012, p. 673.

[158] Crisp et al. 2009, p. 4.

[159] Mateen et al. 2012, Fafo 2007, Davis 2012, p. 4, Doocy et al. 2011.

[160] Davis 2012 has undertaken a comprehensive assessment of urban refugees in Amman and the complexities around mainstreaming healthcare. Furthermore, the Iraqi refugee population in Jordan is not the only urban refugee population to speak of and Guterras and Speigal 2012 offer an interesting overview of adapting health responses to urban environments.

7 The Realization of the Right to Health for Refugees in Jordan

The second distinctive feature is that the majority are from the middle and upper classes of Iraqi society; many are well-educated professionals who have middle-class health needs and expectations for state provision of comprehensive social services.[161] The Iraqi population left a middle-income country with a history of a reasonably well-developed welfare system—albeit one that began to decay during the reign of Saddam Hussein—and arrived in a lower-middle income country from which it expects a similar level of social support and engagement.[162]

The Iraqi refugee population has a high burden of noncommunicable diseases and chronic conditions, notably cardiovascular disease, diabetes, and cancer.[163] In their 2011 assessment of the health status of around 7,000 of the roughly 50,000 UNHCR registered refugees, the WHO reported that nearly 4 out of every 5 individuals seeking care "require chronic disease management."[164] This burden of disease, and expectation of a certain quality and accessibility of care has fundamentally determined the care seeking patterns of the Iraqi population in Jordan.[165]

7.5.3 AAAQ Analysis

The urban location and spatial integration of Iraqi refugees mounted pressure on UNHCR to change its approach with regards to ensuring both availability and accessibility of health services.[166] Early on in the Iraqi refugee crisis, both the international community and the GOJ professed a desire to reframe their approach from that undertaken in response to the Palestinian crisis.[167] Accordingly, in 2007, after a ministerial meeting convened by the WHO, Iraqi nationals were permitted to access public health centers by assuming the same status as uninsured Jordanian nationals.[168]

Thus Iraqi refugees became susceptible to the systemic limitations of the Jordanian health system mentioned above such as high reliance on OPPs for accessing drugs and private sector health care where the quality is widely regarded as superior, but were granted access to the public health system.[169] This posed a significant challenge to the host country, as the Iraqi refugee community was

---

[161] Crisp et al. 2009. Furthermore, the Jordanian refugee population was found by Crisp et al. to be on average of higher socioeconomic status than those who sought refuge in Syria and Lebanon. Davis 2012, p. 9; International Crisis Group 2008: Middle East Report No. 77, p. 13.

[162] Davis 2012, p. 9.

[163] Devi 2007, p. 1816, UNICEF, WHO, Johns Hopkins Joint Assessment 2009.

[164] Mateen et al. 2012, p. 446.

[165] UNICEF, WHO, Johns Hopkins Joint Assessment 2009, p. 21, Mateen et al. 2012.

[166] Crisp et al. 2009.

[167] Davis 2012, p. 4.

[168] UNICEF, WHO and Johns Hopkins 2009, Devi 2007.

[169] Crisp et al. 2009.

found to have "disproportionate level of intensive healthcare needs and high levels of psychological traumas," both of which "require a great deal of resources and follow-up" care.[170] In comparison to the wider Jordanian population, Iraqi refugees have a tendency to seek healthcare more frequently, which may in part be due to their "high level of health and education awareness, and the legacy of free health services they received in Iraq."[171]

Though information about access to health facilities for refugees is limited, available reporting suggests that the Iraqi population is "wary of trusting Jordanian public health systems," as they are used to a relatively high quality and heavily subsidized centralized healthcare system in Iraq.[172] For this reason, despite the high costs, many Iraqis choose to seek care at private facilities.[173]

In 2009, the WHO reported that the cost of accessing care was the greatest barrier to care for Iraqi refugees, "with 59 % of respondents indicating medical care is not affordable."[174] Human Rights Watch suggests that costs associated with accessing health care are one of the greatest expenses that refugee families in Jordan face.[175] The prevalence of chronic diseases and medications required to treat these conditions further increases the cost of care.[176] Access to care for this population is reasonable with the majority of individuals reporting that they do seek care when a member of the household needs medical attention[177]; however, the cost of accessing this care is substantial.

In respect to the quality of care available to Iraqi refugees, those registered with UNHCR have access care at NGO clinics such as those run by the UNHCR, Caritas, or CARE, whereas those not registered with UNHCR largely choose to visit private clinics rather than attend government run institutions.[178] In some regards, the Iraqi refugee population actually has access to a higher quality of care than do uninsured Jordanian nationals, as they have the opportunity to seek care at NGO-run clinics and institutions.[179] However, the cost of accessing this care is a serious barrier especially since a large proportion of the Iraqi population is struggling to find employment.

---

[170] Devi 2007, Davis 2012.
[171] UNICEF, WHO and Johns Hopkins 2009.
[172] Davis 2012, p. 9.
[173] UNICEF, WHO and Johns Hopkins 2009.
[174] Ibid, p. 15.
[175] HRW 2006, p. 64.
[176] UNICEF, WHO and Johns Hopkins 2009.
[177] Ibid.
[178] Ibid.
[179] HRW 2006.

7.5.4 Core Obligations

UNHCR has taken the lead in assuring that those registered with the agency have access to primary heath care, and when necessary, secondary and tertiary care.[180] However, most Iraqi refugees access health services on an ad hoc basis in line with their personal needs, rather than through a health plan framework and must incur the costs of accessing such care.[181] Unlike Palestine refugees for whom UNRWA has become the primary health service provider, UNHCR acts primarily as a coordinator of health services.[182] With diminishing numbers of Iraqi refugees in Jordan, there is not a comprehensive health plan as necessitated by Hunt and Backman as a key core obligation beyond the aforementioned integration into the JHS.[183] However, this does not account for Iraqi refugees not registered with the UNHCR and consequently, the second core obligation proposed by Hunt and Backman is not currently being realized as the equity, nondiscrimination and the distribution of services have not systematically been accounted for.

In this context, it is challenging not only to decipher if there is an "equitable distribution of health related services," but it is also challenging to establish what the health needs of this community are.[184] And while the middle class demographics of the Iraqi refugee population might lead one to believe that there is an opportunity for increased participation, substantial political and operational barriers remain limiting the realization of Hunt and Backman's fourth core obligation— effective "mechanisms of accountability."[185] The legal limbo in which Iraqi refugees find themselves, as well as exclusion from employment in the formal sector and the lack of political representation hinder meaningful participation and hamper progress across each of the core obligations outlined in General Comment 14.[186]

7.5.5 Parallel Structures

The legacy of the six decades long Palestinian refugee experience has fundamentally informed both the GOJ and the international community's reactions to subsequent refugee crises in Jordan.[187] With the Iraqi refugee crisis, UNHCR and the GOJ were aligned in their desire not to duplicate the parallel structures that

---

[180] UNHCR Jordan Country Profile 2013.

[181] HRW 2006.

[182] Mowafi and Spiegel 2008.

[183] Bocco 2009.

[184] Davis 2012.

[185] Hunt and Backman 2008, p. 85.

[186] General Comment 14, para 3.

[187] Crisp et al. 2009, p. 10.

formed in Jordan in response to the mass displacement of Palestinians.[188] Unlike in the Palestinian case, a new UN agency was not established and the provision of services for Iraqi refugees fell under the mandate of the UNHCR. The GOJ largely focused on third-party country resettlement and where possible, limited integration into the public system most significantly in regards to education and healthcare.[189]

In many other aspects, however, the GOJ and the UNHCR have come head to head, with one critical point of contention being the responsibility for the designation of refugee status.[190] The asylum claims of most Iraqi refugees were not registered by UNHCR and the Iraqi refugee community effectively assumed the status of "foreign nationals" in Jordan.[191] Therefore, as with the Palestinian case, many Iraqi refugees in Jordan also live in a precarious state of legal limbo.[192] Over the course of the past decade, the many challenges Iraqi refugees face in attaining adequate legal status in Jordan has proven to be the most significant barrier for the realization of their human rights.[193]

7.6 Right to Health for Syrian Refugees in Jordan

In 2011, the spark of social and political change spread throughout the Arab world with revolutions in Tunisia, Egypt, Libya, and Yemen resulting in the toppling of their respective regimes in what became known as the Arab Spring. In Syria, small nonviolent demonstrations calling for regime change rapidly spread across the country and by July 2012 the Red Cross declared that Syria was in the midst of a full-blown civil war between military and rebel forces. This rapid escalation of violence resulted in a sevenfold increase in registered refugees from May 2012 to December 2012—from 70,000 to 500,000. As of September 2013, the GOJ estimates that approximately 1.3 million Syrians reside in the country.[194]

Any assessment of the right to health for refugees in Jordan must include the Syrian refugee community; however, this analysis is limited in that it is not possible to conduct a comprehensive assessment of the realization of this right for a number of reasons. First of all, information available is too limited to conduct a comprehensive assessment. Secondly, the Syrian refugee crisis is changing by the minute making it challenging to assess the lasting impacts on health and the

---

[188] Davis 2012.

[189] Davis 2012.

[190] Davis 2012, p. 10.

[191] Ibid.

[192] Ibid.

[193] Crisp et al. 2009.

[194] The Jordan Times (15 September 2013) Jordan Hosts 2130 Syrian Army Defectors. Available at: http://jordantimes.com/jordan-hosts-2130-syrian-army-defectors——majali.

7 The Realization of the Right to Health for Refugees in Jordan

various actors' reactions. And thirdly, with the numbers of refugees rapidly escalating, so too are the health needs of this community. Together, these factors make the Syrian refugee crisis a discussion of the right to health in a conflict setting rather than in a protracted refugee setting. It is, however, possible to map out the response of the international community and the Government of Jordan's thus forth, and begin to evaluate the impact of their response on the realization of the right to health for Syrian refugees in Jordan.

Thus forth, a substantial deal of coordination appears to be taking place between the various stakeholders; UNHCR appears to have assumed central responsibility for coordinating the public health response in close coordination with the GOJ.[195] UNHCR has assumed primary responsibility for the registration of Syrian refugees and so far, has done so in a comprehensive manner.[196] At the time of writing, UNHCR had registered 525,000 Syrian refugees in Jordan, with an additional 700,000 unregistered refugees residing in Jordan. This is vastly different in regard to UNHCR's response to the Iraqi refugee crisis where around 50,000 refugees were ever registered.[197]

However, in the absence of sufficient international financial support—clearly evident in UNICEF's recent announcement of their inability to conduct comprehensive immunizations due to lack of adequate funding—the Jordanian health system is coming under an intensive strain which greatly jeopardizes the immediate realization of the right to health for these refugees. The debates presented above with regard to the realization of the right to health for Iraqi and Palestinian refugees extend to the Syrian refugee context as well. As the Syrian refugee crisis escalates and threatens to become protracted, this refugee population is at risk of increased social and economic vulnerability. This demands long-term planning and highlights the necessity of directing humanitarian assistance toward addressing long-term vulnerabilities and realization of refugee rights.

7.7 The Right to Health and UN Surrogacy

Over the course of our analysis we examined the various elements that influence the realization of the right to health for Palestinian, Iraqi, and Syrian refugees in Jordan. Particular attention was paid to the interaction between the international community and the GOJ in upholding the cultural, economic and social rights of these refugees. This interaction has taken the form of the GOJ's minimal engagement, which has necessitated considerable action on the part of the international community.

---

[195] UNHCR 2013.
[196] Ibid.
[197] UNHCR Global Report Jordan 2010.

In line with their obligation to assist in times of humanitarian crisis, the international community—and most significantly UNRWA for Palestinian and UNHCR for Iraqi and Syrian refugees—has established a complex network of social service structures that run parallel to the State. We feel that these parallel state structures have effectively evolved into what Kagan has termed "UN surrogacy."[198] In this section, we will reflect on the various refugee experiences in Jordan in an attempt to unpack the implications of the UN surrogacy on the realization of the right to health for refugees.

The lack of integration of international human rights and refugee laws at the national level has significantly hindered government accountability in regards to its internationally recognized obligation to "protect, respect and fulfill"[199] the right to health across a number of the core obligations of all individuals residing within its borders—regardless of their legal status.[200] Across all three scenarios, the GOJ's willingness to accept refugees and basic adherence to the customary law principle of non-refoulement has been paramount, as Jordan has provided millions of individuals with a "safe-haven" in the face of war and conflict.[201] However, commendable this may be, the GOJ's scope of engagement with refugees has not significantly broadened beyond these two factors.

The lack of alignment between domestic policy and international standards has significant implications for the debate around the division of responsibility for the right to health for refugees between the Jordanian state and the international community. Jordan's ratification of the ICESCR without reservations means that the country has a duty to progressively realize the right to the highest attainable standard of care to the greatest extent of its capacity; however, the Jordanian state's capacity is recognizably limited when the scope of the crisis is taken into consideration—looking only at the numbers, with a refugee population of over 3 million, the Jordanian state faces a challenge it cannot overcome alone.[202]

We contend that the international community has not only become the primary provider of social welfare services for refugees ranging from registration, to cash-transfers, to vocational trainings, and to the provision of education and health services, but has actually assumed primary responsibility for meeting the needs of refugees in Jordan. This has resulted in what Kagan has termed a de facto "state-to-UN responsibility shift"[203] from the Jordanian state to UN-agencies and other international actors.

Kagan suggests the UN surrogacy results in a particular division of responsibility between the state and the international community, where the UN agencies assume responsibility for upholding positive liberties such as education, health and

---

[198] Kagan 2012.

[199] General Comment 14, para 33.

[200] For a discussion of accountability and the realization of the right to health—see Yamin 2008.

[201] Kagan 2012, p. 311, Slaughter and Crisp 2008.

[202] Kenneth 2004.

[203] Kagan 2012, p. 316.

7 The Realization of the Right to Health for Refugees in Jordan

social welfare, and the State maintains responsibility for the protection of liberties such as non-refoulement, and the overall security of refugees in host communities.[204] In line with this argument, the UNRWA "blue state"[205] has emerged in Jordan as a surrogate state for Palestinian refugees and UNHCR for Iraqi and Syrian refugees.[206]

There are both benefits and drawbacks of the impact of the UN surrogate state on refugees' wellbeing and livelihoods. In this arrangement, UN agencies assume "unnatural roles"[207] that are usually performed by states for their citizens.[208] One beneficial element of UN surrogacy is that it effectively slows "the downward spiral of refugee protection"[209] that would ensue if host countries were left to deal with the refugee crises singlehandedly. Although UN agencies' assumption of these roles can initially be beneficial in providing access to the most basic basket of services, over time, refugees come to rely on UN agencies as the primary protector of their wellbeing—this disproportionate reliance ultimately renders the state irrelevant for realizing the basic rights of these communities, including the right to health. With time, as refugees grow accustomed to relying upon international agencies and NGOs as primarily responsible for their well being, this may create inflated expectations in regards to continued care.

However, UN agencies' relatively limited capacity and shrinking resource base prohibits them from being able to "fully substitute for a host government,"[210] thereby creating a gap that leaves many refugees underprovided for. This gap is widened by the effective retrenchment of the host government's responsibility for refugee protection. This retrenchment is an expression of the GOJ's "tendency to see refugees as a problem to be managed rather than as people with rights."[211] As the UN surrogate states have assumed de facto responsibility for achieving the highest attainable standard of health, the realization of this right is contingent upon the UN surrogate states' capacity to solve the "problem"[212] posed by refugees in their host countries.

UN surrogate state structures pose significant challenges to the Jordanian health system. As the core obligations center on establishing an "effective health system available to all,"[213] these parallel health structures obscure progress in this regard. The fragmented nature of refugee healthcare delivery system exacerbates existing fragmentation within the JHS and poses significant challenges for moving beyond

---

[204] Ibid.

[205] Bocco 2009, p. 234.

[206] Kagan 2012, p. 308.

[207] Ibid, p. 309.

[208] Ibid.

[209] Ibid.

[210] Ibid.

[211] Kagan 2012, p. 311, Hathaway 2007.

[212] Ibid.

[213] Hunt and Backman 2008, p. 89.

the status quo, compromising its effectiveness in serving both the refugee and Jordanian population. Although some coordination does exist between the UN surrogate states and the GOJ in regard to secondary and tertiary health services, primary health services are the major responsibility of UN agencies and iNGOs. And since it has been widely argued that the realization of the right to health is largely contingent upon primary health care,[214] the realization of this right falls heavily upon the UN surrogate states rather than the Jordanian state.

7.8 Sustainability and Looking Forward

The division of responsibility between the UN surrogate states and the GOJ fundamentally calls into question whether the right to health is being realized for refugees in Jordan to the fullest extent possible. It is interesting to question if the principle of nondiscrimination is being violated in this case, as the above assessment clearly revealed that each refugee group is progressing toward the realization of the right to health at a different pace, and at the hands of different coordinators and providers. This does not necessarily counter the universality of human rights, which necessitates that there are certain actions that all individuals are entitled to, but it does bring into question the division of responsibility between the various actors engaged with refugee health as differential realization of the right to health is evident across each group.

In reflecting on the global health literature, we see similarities between the widely discussed issues around vertical, disease-specific programs and the effects of UN surrogacy. We believe that key criticisms around vertical programs— mainly in that they both contribute to health system fragmentation and a lack of equity[215]—can be applied to questions around the sustainability of UN surrogacy in regards to the provision of health care services for refugees in Jordan.

Our analysis recognizes the basic divergence of mandate between UN structures and global public-private health partnerships (GPPHP): the UN has a mandate to uphold more inclusive rights in its operations, while GPPHP are more exclusively focused on the realization of one specific right, for example, access to essential medicines.[216] The basic premise of this comparison is that both kinds of parallel structures serve identified subpopulations rather than the population at large: vertical programs serve disease-specific populations and the UN surrogate states serve specific refugee populations.[217] Additionally, both types of structures rely on

---

[214] WHO 1978 Declaration of Alma-Ata, WHO 2008: Primary Health Care (Now More than Ever), Rifkin and Walt 1986.

[215] Buse and Harmer 2007, England 2007, Ranson et al. 2007, p. 30.

[216] Clear examples of GPPHP include the GAVI Alliance, which provides immunizations (www.gavialliance.org) and also The Global Fund to Fight AIDS, TB and Malaria, which attempts to provide access to necessary medication (www.theglobalfund.org).

[217] Balbanova et al. 2010, Buse and Harmer 2007, Kagan 2012.

7 The Realization of the Right to Health for Refugees in Jordan

funding from the international community, raising similar concerns around aid effectiveness and the use of international funds.[218]

Similarities between the negative effects of the entrenchment of both types of parallel structures can be identified as they both lead to: (1) increased health system fragmentation;[219] (2) "the insufficient use of resources;"[220] (3) "poor harmonization,"[221] and ultimately; (4) "depriving specific stakeholders a voice in decision-making."[222] We believe that similar solutions such as those proposed to counter the adverse effects of vertical programs on national health systems such as alignment with the principles of aid effectiveness[223] and increased donor coordination,[224] can be applied to the realization of the right to health for refugees in Jordan.

An oft-proposed remedy to the over-reliance on vertical interventions is to shift the focus toward horizontal, system-wide, approaches.[225] Our main proposed solution includes minimizing duplication through the integration of parallel structures into national health systems. Integration of these structures and expansion of the national public health systems would work toward enhancing the sustainability of the provision of healthcare, which is necessary for advancement toward realizing the right to health for these vulnerable populations. The UNHCR recognizes the importance of incorporating health systems strengthening into their refugee health policies; in countries such as Somalia in the 1970s,[226] Malawi in the 1980s[227] and in Guinea in the 1990s,[228] the UNHCR directed its funding and technical assistance to support national health systems with the goal of meeting refugee health needs.[229]

However, the task of adopting a strategy of UN surrogate health service integration into the JHS is challenging. In regard to the ongoing Syrian refugee crisis, the combination of inconsistent international funding and the substantial strain on the Jordanian health system has limited the different stakeholders' abilities to fulfill their various commitments to the preexisting refugee groups. This less than optimal engagement has resulted in a potentially avoidable public health crisis looming low in the horizon.[230] With no end to the Syrian civil war in sight, we

---

[218] Balbanova et al. 2010, Buse and Harmer 2007.

[219] Balbanova et al. 2010.

[220] Buse and Harmer 2007.

[221] Ibid.

[222] Ibid.

[223] OECD Paris Declaration on Aid Effectiveness 2005, OECD Accra Agenda for Action 2008, Sridhar 2009, WHO Aid Effectiveness and Health 2007.

[224] UNHCR 2009—Facilitating the Transition http://www.unhcr.org/4a8030d69.pdf [last accessed: 14 October 2013], Martin and Taylor 2012.

[225] Vergeer et al. 2009, World Health Report 2008, Freedman 2005.

[226] Godfrey and Mursal 1990 as cited in Rowley et al. 2006.

[227] Kunz 1990 as cited in Rowley et al. 2006.

[228] Van Damme 1998, as cited in Rowley et al. 2006.

[229] Rowley et al. 2006, p.162.

[230] UNFPA 2013, UN News Center 2013.

have a good reason to believe that the Syrian refugee crisis will most likely evolve into a prolonged state of refuge as was seen a mere decade ago with Iraqi refugees. So, while not currently imminent, it is necessary to plan for this long-term displacement.

We propose that the integration of UN health services could provide a platform for addressing the long-term health needs of refugees. One way this could be done would be through shifting a proportion of aid toward investment in health system strengthening strategies that are sustainable in the long run. Although admittedly applying this may be difficult when faced with acute health crises, the precedence for long-term investment does exist in Jordan in regards to other services, as was implemented in the case of education for Syrian refugees.[231]

In order to proceed with a plan of increased integration to progress toward a greater realization of the core obligations of the right to health, it will be necessary to harness political will and commitment on the part of both the GOJ and the international community to increase the capacity of the Jordanian health system. While harnessing this political will may prove challenging, adopting health system strengthening strategies in this setting would greatly benefit not only the refugee population, but also the general Jordanian population. A possible arrangement would entail a redefinition of the roles of the international community and the GOJ, with the former potentially financing health service expansion programs through the health system of the latter entity. This arrangement could be seen as a practical step toward building a more comprehensive health system that is available, accessible, and acceptable to all. If these measures were to be adopted, they might result in a reduction of inequity and discrimination and lead to a more inclusive healthcare system, which could provide a platform for a sustainable advancement toward the realization of the right to health for refugees in Jordan.

7.9 Conclusion

The right to health framework has much to offer for understanding the challenges facing refugee communities today. Nonetheless, this approach has yet to be adequately incorporated into the refugee health discourse. The realization of the right to health for refugees in Jordan is a highly complex issue and we recognize that at this point in time, there may be more questions than answers. Outstanding questions include: how can the right be enforced in a refugee setting? Who is responsible for monitoring and evaluating this enforcement? And ultimately, do refugees have adequate access to redress? The UN Committee on Social, Economic and Cultural Rights itself has "raised concerns regarding the awareness of the Jordanian population to the concept of the right to health,"[232] and so an

---

[231] UNHCR 2012a Participatory Assessment; CARE Jordan Baseline Assessment 2012.

[232] ICESCR 1976.

7 The Realization of the Right to Health for Refugees in Jordan

additional outstanding question surrounds how to elevate the right to health framework within the Jordanian health policy agenda.

Nonetheless, the central element when examining the rights of refugees remains to be the root causes of displacement—in this case war and conflict. We believe that structural elements beyond the control of the Jordanian state, such as the absence of a long-lasting and just solution for the Palestinian refugees and their inability to return, as well as insecurity in Iraq, and the ongoing civil war in Syria, are the most prominent barriers that hinder the realization of a wide spectrum of human rights for refugees in Jordan—not least of which is the right to health. While conflict resolution should be the ultimate goal, it is necessary to move toward the continued realization of the right to health of refugees in Jordan at a pace that upholds and respects both their dignity and well-being.

References

Adeyi O, Smith O, Robles S (2007) Public policy and the challenge of chronic non-communicable diseases. World Bank, Washington

Al Abed O (2004) Palestinian refugees in Jordan. FMO Research Guide, Oxford. http://www.forcedmigration.org/research-resources/expert-guides/palestinian-refugees-in-jordan/fmo025.pdf. Accessed 14 Oct 2013

Backman G, Hunt P, Khosla R, Jaramillo-Strouss C, Mekuria FikreB, Rumble C, Pevain D, Acuiro Paez D, Armijos Pineda M, Frisancho A, Tarco D, Motlagh M, Darcasanu D, Vladescu C (2008) Health systems and the right to health: an assessment of 194 countries. Lancet 372:2047–2085

Balbanova D, McKee M, Mills A, Walt G, Haines A (2010) What can global health institutions do to help strengthen health systems in low income countries? Health Res Policy Syst 8:22

Bocco R (2009) UNRWA and the Palestinian refugees: a history within history. Refugee Surv Q 28(2–3):229–252

Bettis R (2010) The Iraqi refugee crisis: whose problem is it? Transnatl Law Contemp Probl 261:262–290

Buse K, Harmer A (2007) Seven habits of highly effective global public-private health partnerships: practice and potential. Soc Sci Med 67:259–271

CARE Jordan (2012) Baseline assessment of community identified vulnerabilities among Syrian refugees living in Amman. data.unhcr.org/syrianrefugees/download.php?id=1177. Accessed 14 Oct 2013

Chatelard G (2010) Jordan: a refugee haven. Migration information source (August). http://www.migrationinformation.org/feature/display.cfm?ID=794. Accessed 14 Oct 2013

Crisp J, Janez J, Riera J, Samy S (2009) Surviving in the city: a review of UNHCR's operation for Iraqi refugees in urban areas of Jordan, Lebanon and Syria. United Nations High Commissioner for Refugees Policy Development and Evaluation Services. http://www.unhcr.org/4a69ad639.pdf. Accessed 14 Oct 2013

Davis R (2012) Urban refugees in Amman, Jordan. Institute for the study of international migration, center for contemporary Arab studies (November). http://ccas.georgetown.edu/document/1242773779568/Amman_27NOV_pages.pdf. Accessed 10 Oct 2013

Devi S (2007) Meeting the health needs of Iraqi refugees in Jordan. Lancet 370:1815–1816

Doocy S, Sirois A, Anderson J, Tileva M, Biermann E, Storey JD, Burnham G (2011) Food security and humanitarian assistance among displaced Iraqi populations in Jordan and Syria. Soc Sci Med 77:273–282

Ekman B (2007) The impact of health insurance on outpatient utilization and expenditure: evidence from one middle-income country using national household survey data. Health Res Policy Syst 5(6)

England R (2007) The dangers of disease specific programmes for developing countries. BMJ 334:565

ESCWA—United Nations Economics and Social Commission for Western Asia (n.d.) Demographic Profile of Jordan. http://www.escwa.un.org/popin/members/Jordan.pdf. Accessed 14 Oct 2013

Fafo (2007) Iraqis in Jordan: characteristics and numbers. http://www.fafo.no/ais/projectoverview.htm. Accessed 14 Oct 2013

Freedman L (2005) Achieving the MDGs: health systems as core social institutions. Development 48(1):19–24

Godfrey N, Mursal H (1990) International aid and national health policies for refugees: lessons from Somalia. J Refugee Stud 3(2):110–134

Guterras A, Spiegel P (2012) The state of the world's refugees. JAMA 308(7):673–674

Hathaway JC (2007) Forced migration studies: could we agree to just 'date'? J Refugee Stud 20(3):349–369

Human Rights Watch (2006) The silent treatment—fleeing Iraq, surviving in Jordan 18 (10 E). http://www.hrw.org/reports/2006/11/27/silent-treatment. Accessed 14 Oct 2013

Hunt P (2006) The right to the highest attainable standard of health: opportunities and challenges. Castan Centre for Human Rights Law, Monash University, Melbourne, Australia, 1 May

Hunt P, Backman G (2008) Health systems and the right to the highest attainable standard of health. Health Hum Rights 10(1):81–92

International Crisis Group (2008) Middle east report: failed responsibility, Iraqi refugees in Syria, Jordan and Lebanon. http://www.crisisgroup.org/en/regions/middle-east-north-africa/iraq-iran-gulf/iraq/077-failed-responsibility-iraqi-refugees-in-syria-jordan-and-lebanon.aspx. Accessed 14 Oct 2013

International Organization for Migration (2009) Emergency needs assessments, four years of Post-Samarra displacement in Iraq. http://www.internal-displacement.org/8025708F004CE90B/(httpDocuments)/EA591F6527B7A796C125773B004E71E9/$file/IOM_Displacement_Reports_Four_Years_of_Post-Samarra_Displacement.pdf. Accessed 13 Oct 2013

Jordanian Department of Statistics (2011) Population of Jordan by governance and sex. http://www.dos.gov.jo/dos_home_e/main/ehsaat/alsokan/2011/2-2.pdf. Accessed 22 Sept 2013

Jordanian Ministry of Health (2011) Jordan national health strategy 2008–2012. http://www.moh.gov.jo/MOH/Files/National_Health/Health%20Strategic_1%20_1.pdf. Accessed 14 Oct 2013

Kagan M (2012) The UN 'surrogate state' and the foundation of refugee policy in the Middle East. Scholarly works paper 781. http://scholars.law.unlv.edu/facpub/781/. Accessed 14 Oct 2013

Kenneth R (2004) Defending economic, social and cultural rights: practical issues faced by an international human rights organization. Hum Rights Q 26(1):63–73

Kenyon Lischer S (2008) Security and displacement in Iraq: responding to the forced migration crisis. Int Secur 33(2):95–119

Koren M (2013) Jordan: Syrian refugees are 10 % of population. National Journal 24 September 2013. http://www.nationaljournal.com/domesticpolicy/jordan-syrian-refugees-are-10-percent-of-our-population-20130924. Accessed 29 Sept 2013

Kunz D (1990) Serving the health needs of refugees in Malawi: an integrated approach. Refugee policy group working paper II (January), Washington DC

Law No. 6 of 1954 on Nationality (last amended 1987) Kingdom of Jordan. http://www.refworld.org/docid/3aeb4ea13.html. Accessed 14 Oct 2013

Lapeyre F, Al Husseini J, Bocco R, Brunner M, Zureik E (2011) The living conditions of the Palestine refugees registered with UNRWA in Jordan, Lebanon, The Syrian Arab Republic, the Gaza Strip and the West Bank. Lebanon, The Syrian Arab Republic, the Gaza Strip and the West Bank. http://graduateinstitute.ch/files/live/sites/iheid/files/sites/admininst/shared/iheid/800/bocco/UNRWA-FinalSynthesisReport2007.pdf. Accessed 14 Oct 2013

Leaning J, Spiegel P, Crisp J (2011) Public health equity in refugee situations. Confl Health 5:6

Martin A, Taylor A (2012) Urban refugees in Amman: mainstreaming of healthcare. institute for the study of international migration and center for contemporary Arab studies. http://ccas.georgetown.edu/document/1242773779488/Urban+Refugees+in+Amman+-+Mainstreaming+of+Healthcare.pdf. Accessed 14 Oct 2013

Mateen F, Carone M, Al-Saedy NyceS, Ghosn J, Mutuerandu T, Black R (2012) Medical conditions among Iraqi refugees in Jordan: data from United refugees information system. Bull World Health Organ 90(6):444–451

Meier BM, Fox AM (2010) International obligations through collective rights: moving from foreign health assistance to global health governance. Health Hum Rights 12(1):61–72

Mowafi H, Spiegel P (2008) The Iraqi refugee crisis: familiar problems and new challenges. JAMA 299(14):1713–1715

National Center for Human Rights (NCHR) (2010) Human rights situation in the Hashemite Kingdom of Jordan for 2010. Seventh annual report of the national centre for human rights. http://www.nchr.org.jo/english/Publications.aspx. Accessed 14 Oct 2013

OECD Paris Declaration on Aid Effectiveness (2005). http://www.oecd.org/dataoecd/11/41/34428351.pdf. Accessed 14 Oct 2013

OECD Accra Agenda for Action (2008). http://www.oecd.org/dac/effectiveness/paris declarationandaccraagendaforaction.htm, http://www.nchr.org.jo/english/Publications.aspx. Accessed 14 Oct 2013

Patterson D (2007) The right to health in Jordan. Right to Health in the Middle East Project, Law School, University of Aberdeen. http://www.abdn.ac.uk/law/hhr.shtml, http://www.nchr.org.jo/english/Publications.aspx. Accessed 14 Oct 2013

Pérez P (2011) Human rights and the rightless: the case of Gaza refugees in Jordan. Int J Hum Rights 15(7):1031–1054

Ranson K, Poletti T, Bornemisza O, Sonorp E (2007) Promoting health equity in conflict-affected fragile states. The Conflict and Health Programme, London School of Tropical Medicine and Hygiene

Rempel T (2006) Who are Palestinian refugees? In Palestinian displacement: a case apart? Refugee studies center in association with the Norwegian Refugee Council. http://www.fmreview.org/FMRpdfs/FMR26/FMR26full.pdf. Accessed 14 Oct 2013

Rifkin SB, Walt G (1986) Why health improves: defining the issues concerning 'comprehensive primary health care' and 'selective primary health care'. Soc Sci Med 23:559

Riccardo F, Khader A, Sabatinelli G (2012) Low infant mortality among Palestine refugees despite the odds. WHO Bull 89:304–311. www.who.int/bulletin/volumes/89/4/10-082743/en/index.html. Accessed 14 Oct 2013

Rosenfeld (2009) From emergency relief assistance to human development and back: UNRWA and the Palestinian refugees, 1950–2009. Refugee Surv Q 28(2–3):286–317

Rowley EA, Burnham GM, Drabe RM (2006) Protracted refugee situations: parallel health systems and planning for the integration of services. J Refugee Stud 19(2):158–186

Slaughter A, Crisp J (2008) A surrogate sate? The role of UNHCR in protracted refugee situations. UNHCR new issues in refugee research—research paper no. 168. http://www.unhcr.org/4981cb432.html. Accessed 14 Oct 2013

Sridhar D (2009) Post-Accra: is there space for country ownership in global health? Third World Q 30(7):1363–1377

Takkenberg L (2009) UNRWA and the Palestinian refugees after sixty years: some reflections. Refugee Surv Q 28(2–3):253–259

The Jordan Times (2013) Jordan Hosts 2130 Syrian army defectors. http://jordantimes.com/jordan-hosts-2130-syrian-army-defectors—majali. Accessed 15 Oct 2013

Toebes B (1999) Towards an improved understanding of the international human right to health. Hum Rights Q 21(3):661–679

Toebes B (2013) Health and humanitarian assistance: towards an integrated norm under international law. Tilburg Law Rev 18:133–151

United Nations Populations Fund (UNFPA) (2013) UNFPA Executive Director visits Syrian refugee camps in Turkey and Jordan to highlight urgent needs. http://www.unfpa.org/public/cache/offonce/home/news/pid/13830;jsessionid=5B2A8B2015EA32D4D294BE9514C40AE6.jahia02. Accessed 15 Oct 2013

United Nations (n.d) Strengthening the UN—Accountability. http://www.un.org/en/strengtheningtheun/accountability.shtml. Accessed 14 Oct 2013

United Nations (1951) Convention and protocol relating to the status of refugees. http://www.unhcr.org/4ca34be29.pdf. Accessed 2 Oct 2013

United Nations (1967) Protocol relating to the status of refugees. Treaty series: 606. http://www.refworld.org/docid/3ae6b3ae4.html. Accessed 14 Oct 2013

United Nations Committee on Economic, Social and Cultural Rights (ICESCR) (1976) International covenant on economic, social and cultural rights. http://www.ohchr.org/EN/ProfessionalInterest/Pages/CESCR.aspx. Accessed 10 Aug 2013

United Nations Committee on Economic, Social and Cultural Rights (CESCR) (2000) General Comment No. 14: The right to the highest attainable standard of health (Article 12 of the Covenant) 11 August. http://www.unhchr.ch/tbs/doc.nsf/(symbol)/E.C.12.2000.4.En. Accessed 14 Oct 2013

United Nations Committee on Economic, Social and Cultural Rights (CESCR) (2009) General Comment No. 20: Non-discrimination in economic, social and cultural rights (Article 2, para 2 of the international covenant on economic, social and cultural rights). http://www.refworld.org/docid/4a60961f2.html. Accessed 14 Oct 2013

United Nations Development Assistance Framework (UNDAF) (2007) Jordan 2008–2012. http://www.undg.org/docs/13036/Jordan-UNDAF-2013-2017-sgn-EN.pdf. Accessed 14 Oct 2013

United Nations Development Program (UNDP) (2013) Jordan Poverty Reduction Strategy: final report

UNHCR and Government of Jordan (1998) Memorandum of Understanding (5 April). http://mawgeng.unblog.fr/files/2009/02/moujordan.doc. Accessed 14 Oct 2013

UNHCR (2009) Facilitating the transition from asylum to return and reintegration in Iraq. http://www.unhcr.org/4a8030d69.pdf. Accessed 14 Oct 2013

UNHCR (2010) Global Report—Jordan. http://www.unhcr.org/4dfdbf4f13.html. Accessed 14 Oct 2013

UNHCR (2012a) Participatory Assessment. http://data.unhcr.org/syrianrefugees/settlement.php?id=57&country=107&region=36. Accessed 14 Oct 2013

UNHCR (2012b) Global Report. http://www.unhcr.org/cgi-bin/texis/vtx/home/opendoc PDFViewer.html?docid=51b1d61f5&query=refugee%20per%20capita. Accessed 29 Sept 2013

UNHCR (2013) Country operations profile—Jordan. http://www.unhcr.org/pages/49e486566.html. Accessed 14 Oct 2013

UNICEF, WHO and Johns Hopkins Joint Assessment (2009) The health status of the Iraqi population in Jordan

United Nations New Center (2013) Syrian refugee crisis worsens with aid efforts grossly underfunded, UN warns. 9 April. http://www.un.org/apps/news/story.asp?NewsID=44602#.U11RneA8egx. Accessed 15 Oct 2013

UNRWA (n.d.). http://www.unrwa.org/etemplate.php?id=86. Accessed 2 Oct 2013

UNRWA (n.d.) Health in Jordan—Summary. http://www.unrwa.org/activity/health-jordan. Accessed 6 Oct 2013

UNRWA (n.d.) Consolidated Eligibility and Registration instructions (CERI) http://www.unrwa.org/userfiles/2010011995652.pdf. Accessed 2 May 2013

UNRWA (2010a) Medium Term Strategy 2010–2015. http://www.unrwa.org/userfiles/201003317746.pdf. Accessed 30 April 2013

UNRWA (2010b) UNRWA in Numbers. http://www.unrwa.org/userfiles/20120317152850.pdf. Accessed 2 May 2013

United States Committee for Refugee and Immigrations (2009) World refugee survey–Jordan. http://www.refworld.org/docid/4a40d2aac.html. Accessed 15 Oct 2013

United States Department of State (2010) Human Rights Report Jordan. http://www.state.gov/j/drl/rls/hrrpt/2010/nea/154464.htm. Accessed 15 Oct 2013

Van Damme W (1998) Medical assistance to self-settled refugees: Guinea, 1990–1996. Studies in Health Services Organisation and Policy 11. ITG Press, Antwerp, Belgium

Vergeer P, Canavan A, Rothmann I (2009) A rethink on the use of aid mechanisms in health sector early recovery. Development Policy and Practice, Amsterdam. Accessed 14 Oct 2013

World Bank (n.d.) Jordan Country Profile. http://www.worldbank.org/en/country/jordan. Accessed 2 Oct 2013

World Bank (2012) Country Cooperation Strategy 2012–2015. http://documents.worldbank.org/curated/en/2012/02/15780007/jordan-country-partnership-strategy-period-fy11-fy15. Accessed 4 May 2013

WHO (n.d.) A human rights-based approaches note. http://www.ohchr.org/Documents/Issues/ESCR/Health/HRBA_HealthInformationSheet.pdf. Accessed 15 Oct 2013

World Health Organisation (1978) Declaration of Alma-Ata: International Conference on Primary Health Care, Alma-Ata, USSR. http://who.int//hpr/NPH/doc/declaration_almaata.pdf. Accessed 14 Oct 2013

World Health Report (2008) Primary health care (now more than ever). World Health Organisation. http://www.who.int/whr/2008/en/. Accessed 15 Oct 2013

World Health Organisation (2009) Country cooperation strategy for WHO and Jordan 2008–2013. http://www.who.int/countryfocus/cooperation_strategy/ccs_jor_en.pdf. Accessed 2 Oct 2013

World Health Organisation (2007) Aid effectiveness and health. WHO/HSS/healthsystems/2007.2 working paper no. 9. http://www.who.int/hdp/publications/aid.pdf. Accessed 15 Oct 2013

World Health Organisation (2013) Global health expenditure—Jordan National Expenditure on Health 1996–2011. http://apps.who.int/nha/database/StandardReport.aspx?ID=REP_WEB_MINI_TEMPLATE_WEB_VERSION&COUNTRYKEY=84645. Accessed 2 Oct 2013

Yach D, Hawkes C, Gould CL, Hofman KJ (2004) The global burden of chronic diseases: overcoming impediments to prevention and control. JAMA 291:2616–2622

Yamin AE (2008) Beyond compassion: the central role of accountability in applying a human rights framework to health. Health Hum Rights 10(20):1–20

Zaotti R (2006) Dealing with Non-Palestinians refugees in the middle east: policies and practices in an uncertain environment. Oxford University Press

Part IV
The Americas

Chapter 8
The Right to Health: The Next American Dream

Dabney P. Evans

Abstract The American Dream is a strongly held notion that permeates the American psyche. The subtext of the dream is the assumption of equal opportunity for education and the subsequent career opportunities that presumably follow. Assuming equality of opportunity (a large assumption indeed), potential success is based on individual talent and effort resulting in part in the development of the individualistic societal norms of the 'self-made man,' 'every man for himself,' and 'rugged individualism' ideologies that are predominant in the US today. The archetype of the American Dream is the "self-made man" who, through will and determination gains an education, career success, and material wealth exemplified by home ownership. Human rights language would refer to these as the right to education, work, property, and housing. US constitutional law strongly protects civil and political rights. US federal law has even come to protect some economic, social, and cultural rights such as education as part and parcel of the American Dream. Until the 2010 passage of the Patient Protection and Affordable Care Act (ACA), the right to health has for the most part been excluded from both the notion of the American Dream as well as protection under US federal law. This chapter provides an overview of the historical development of the American Dream, an examination of global health models, and the U.S. model more specifically. It also explores the ACA and the 2012 US Supreme Court ruling as it relates to the international conceptualization of the human right to health, specifically focusing on the human rights principles of accessibility and nondiscrimination and how the ACA may contribute to an expanded notion of the American Dream including the right to health.

D. P. Evans (✉)
Institute of Human Right, Emory University, Atlanta, GA, USA
e-mail: Dabney.Evans@emory.edu

B. Toebes et al. (eds.), *The Right to Health*, DOI: 10.1007/978-94-6265-014-5_8,
© T.M.C. ASSER PRESS and the authors 2014

Contents

8.1	Introduction and Framework	234
8.2	The American Dream	236
8.3	Models of Health Care	241
	8.3.1 The US Healthcare System	242
	8.3.2 Universal Health Care (UHC)	243
8.4	Starting Point for the Next American Dream: The Patient Protection and Affordable Care Act	245
	8.4.1 ACA Intent and Implementation	246
	8.4.2 ACA Ruling by the Supreme Court of the United States	248
8.5	ACA and the Right to Health	251
8.6	Conclusions and Recommendations	253
References		256

8.1 Introduction and Framework

The framework used in this analysis will include the major documents outlining the right of everyone to the highest attainable standard of physical and mental health (hereinafter referred to as the right to health) as defined in Article 12 of the International Covenant on Economic, Social and Cultural Rights (ICESCR), and further clarified by General Comment 14.[1,2] These documents are further supported by the work of the United Nations (UN) Special Rapporteur on the right of everyone to the highest attainable standard of physical and mental health (hereinafter referred to as the UN Special Rapporteur on the right to health).[3] Two themes from these sources are most relevant to this chapter: accessibility and nondiscrimination, both of which have been identified as major barriers to care in the US.[4]

Accessibility is defined most explicitly in the AAAQ (Availability, Accessibility, Acceptability and Quality) framework of General Comment 14, which provides a comprehensive and authoritative source for understanding the major elements of the right to health.[5] Accessibility encompasses geographical/physical

---

[1] United Nations. International covenant on economic, social and cultural rights (ICESCR). New York, United Nations, 1966. United Nations General Assembly resolution 2200 (XXI), UN GAOR, 21st Session, Supp. No. 16, at 49, UN Doc. A/6316, entered into force 3 January 1976. New York: United Nations, 1976 (hereinafter referred to as ICESCR).

[2] Committee on Economic, Social and Cultural Rights. The right to the highest attainable standard of health: 11/08/2000. E/C.12/2000/4, CESCR General Comment 14. Twenty-second session Geneva, 25 April–12 May 2000 Agenda item 3 (hereinafter referred to as GC14).

[3] Office of the United Nations High Commission on Human Rights. "Special Rapporteur on the right of everyone to the enjoyment of the highest attainable standard of physical and mental health" Available: http://www.ohchr.org/EN/Issues/Health/Pages/SRRightHealthIndex.aspx (accessed 25 November 2013).

[4] Lovett-Scott and Prather 2014.

[5] GC14, at para 12.

8 The Right to Health: The Next American Dream

accessibility, economic/financial accessibility, and information accessibility as well as nondiscrimination particularly for the most vulnerable populations.[6]

Nondiscrimination itself is the second theme germane to the discussion of the US context as explored in this chapter. The principle of nondiscrimination is central to the normative character of the right to health as noted in the ICESCR.[7] With regard to health, discrimination in access to health care is prohibited including on the basis of health status.[8] General Comment 14 outlines the State obligation to provide health insurance to those without sufficient resources.[9] Further, the former UN Special Rapporteur on the right to health, Paul Hunt examined the issue of nondiscrimination in the enjoyment of the right to health as a major focus during his tenure.[10] The current UN Special Rapporteur on the right to health has emphasized that "the full realization of the right to health is contingent upon the availability of adequate, equitable and sustainable financing for health" including the sources of adequate funds, the ways in which funds are pooled, and their allocation within health systems.[11] With this foundation as a basis, this chapter examines the US context as it relates to the right to health bearing in mind that the US has not *yet* ratified the ICESCR.[12,13] At the international level, it is worth noting the Cold War divide that undermined initial US support for the right to health and which is perpetuated today despite the fact that all human rights are interdependent.[14]

This chapter provides an overview of the historical development of the American Dream, an examination of global health models, and the US model more specifically. It also explores the Patient Protection and Affordable Care Act ACA and the 2012 US Supreme Court ruling as it relates to the international conceptualization of human right to health specifically focusing on the human rights principles of accessibility and nondiscrimination and how the ACA may contribute to improved accessibility and decreased discrimination vis-à-vis an expanded notion of the American Dream including the right to health.

---

[6] Idemat, para 12(b).

[7] ICESCR, supra n 1 at Articles 2.2 and 3.

[8] GC14, at para 18.

[9] Idemat, para 19.

[10] Hunt 2003, para 61. Similar views are found in Hunt 2005, para 51.

[11] Grover 2012, para 1.

[12] Supra n 1. United National Treaty Collection "International Covenant on Economic, Social and Cultural Rights" Available: http://treaties.un.org/Pages/ViewDetails.aspx?src=TREATY&mtdsg_no=IV-3&chapter=4&lang=en (accessed 25 November 2013).

[13] The US has only ratified one human rights treaty that includes the right to health, namely the International Convention on the Elimination of all forms of Racial Discrimination emphasizing the importance of the principle of nondiscrimination to this discussion. The US has ratified other treaties, which include health-related rights such as the International Covenant on Civil and Political Rights among others.

[14] Meier 2010.

8.2 The American Dream[15]

"It is called the American Dream because you have to be asleep to believe it."

American comedian George Carlin[16]

In discussing the application and interpretation of international human rights law in any specific country, it is important to understand the context. In the case of the US, an important cultural paradigm is that of the so-called 'American Dream.' The 'American Dream' is principally based on the second sentence of the US Declaration of Independence and its oft-quoted reference to the rights to life, liberty, and the pursuit of happiness.[17] The phrase 'American Dream was coined by historian James Truslow Adams in his optimistic Depression era book.[18]

> The American Dream is that dream of a land in which life should be better and richer and fuller for everyone, with opportunity for each according to ability or achievement ... a dream of social order in which each man and each woman shall be able to attain to the fullest stature of which they are innately capable, and be recognized by others for what they are, regardless of the fortuitous circumstances of birth or position.[19]

It is on the very premise of equality of opportunity that the 'American Dream' is based. Coupled with an enduring belief that that those who work hard and play by the rules will be rewarded, the subtext of the dream is the assumption of an equal opportunity for education and the subsequent career opportunities that presumably follow.[20] Assuming equality of opportunity, (which as it turns out is a large assumption indeed), potential success is based on individual talent and effort resulting in part in the development of the individualistic societal norms of the 'self-made man,' 'every man for himself,' and 'rugged individualism" ideologies that have perpetuated from the country's founding until today.[21,22]

While equality of opportunity is the very foundation of the 'American Dream' it is important to acknowledge that vast segments of the US population were initially excluded from the dream exalted in the US Declaration of Independence. After all, at the time of its proclamation, slavery was legal and the 'men' referenced in the

---

[15] The concept of the American Dream as it relates to the right to health in the US was first explored by this author in Evans 2012.

[16] Carlin HBO Films 2006.

[17] The United States of America, Declaration of Independence 1776.

[18] Cullen 2004.

[19] Ibid at pp. 214–215.

[20] Time Magazine 2012 (hereinafter referred to as Time Magazine).

[21] John Locke is widely credited as being the father of rugged individualism. See for example Moulds 1965, pp. 97–109. Locke's philosophy greatly influenced a number of American Revolutionaries as reflected in the American Declaration of Independence *vis-à-vis* the concepts of republicanism and liberal theory. See for example Becker and Harcourt 1922, p. 27.

[22] Obama's Remarks to Congress on Health Care (NPR radio broadcast Sept 9, 2009). Available at: http://www.npr.org/templates/story/story.php?storyId=112695048&sc=emaf (accessed 25 November 2013) (hereinafter referred to as Obama's remarks to Congress).

8 The Right to Health: The Next American Dream

Declaration were literally men (only) and also limited to White, Christian property owners. It is not by chance then that the symbolic high water mark of the US civil rights movement was framed by Dr. Martin Luther King in terms of the American Dream.[23] His dream included, "[…]decent wages, fair working conditions, livable housing, old-age security, health and welfare measures, conditions in which families can grow, have education for their children and respect in the community."[24]

Over time, the archetype of the American Dream has evolved and is embodied by the "self-made man" who through will and determination gains an education, career success, and material wealth best exemplified by home ownership.[25] Human rights language would refer to these as the rights to education, work, property, and housing. Thus, the right to own property and the ideal of home ownership, referred to in contemporary human rights parlance as the right to housing, have always been strong components of the 'American Dream.' Property has traditionally been treated as a civil right and concurrently as a good to be sold in the market.[26] However, it also maintains a social function.[27]

Similarly, the right to education has also been subsumed under the umbrella of the 'American Dream' presumably because of the positive lifelong opportunities that may come as a result of education. Despite its exclusion from the US constitution, today the federal prohibition of discrimination on the basis of race may be found in numerous acts of legislation related to education.[28,29] Further, there is an underlying social expectation for a publicly funded school system demonstrating the evolving possibilities for an expanded notion of State protected rights.

The inclusion of property and education is based on the American Dream ethos, however, the same expectation does not hold in the area of health. Like property, health has also been treated as a market good rather than as a public good.[30] However, health (facilities, services, goods) have been viewed as at best an entitlement rather than a right.[31] National protections against racial discrimination

---

[23] Time Magazine, supra n 20.

[24] King Jr. 1961, p. 7.

[25] Henry Clay is credited with coining the phrase self-made man in his 1832 Senate Speech, "The American System." See Clay 1994.

[26] C. Golay and I. Cismas, The Right to Property from a Human Rights Perspective (International Centre for Human Rights and Democratic Development). http://dd-rd.ca/site/_PDF/publications/humanright-en.pdf. Accessed 13 August 2013.

[27] Ibid.

[28] Reports Submitted by States Parties under Article 9 of the Convention; Third Periodic Reports of States Parties Due in 1999; Addendum United States of America, (10 October 2000).

[29] See for example Emergency Insured Student Loan Act of 1969, Sect. 1078(c) (2) (F), Higher Education Act of 1965s. 1011 et seq., The Equal Education Opportunities Act of 1974, Sect. 1703, Elementary and Secondary Education Act of 1965, Sect. 6301 et seq,. General Education Provisions Act, Sect. 1228 (a) and Federal Family Education Loan Program, sect. 1087–1 (e)(3).

[30] Rudiger (2008).

[31] Ibid.

related to property demonstrate the regulatory role that the US government could also play in regard to the protection of health, if it so desired. The narratives relating to the rights to property and education demonstrate how, despite reluctance on the part of the American public to acknowledge the role of the State in the development of the public sector in support of the "self-made man" and State reluctance to explicitly obligate itself to such responsibilities, it is impossible to ignore the role the State has played in the development and perpetuation of the American Dream mentality. Limitations of space prevent a further exploration of the similarities and differences between the rights to property and education to the right to health viewed through the lens of the American Dream; however, it should be pointed out that the U.S. federal, if not Constitutional law, has come to protect *some* economic, social, and cultural rights, such as education as part and parcel of the American Dream above and beyond the traditionally valued civil and political rights found in the U.S. Constitution, while largely still excluding the right to health. As will be discussed in the conclusions such action would require both political will for policy change and a cultural attitude adjustment.

The implications of the American Dream ethos on the issue of the right to health in the US cannot be understated. Given that the US Constitution is the oldest existing constitution in the world and that the presence of economic, social and cultural rights (ESCR) in constitutional documents was not common at the time of its drafting, it is not surprising that a right to health was not guaranteed in its original text.[32] Such inequalities in health were not a deliberate concern within the original US constitutional framework.[33] However, health inequalities across race and social class have developed and become exacerbated by inequalities in other aspects of legal protection over time. Despite the fact that opinion polls dating back to the 1930s have shown support for health insurance and access to health care by the American public, health as a right has still remained excluded from the 'American Dream' and US constitutional and federal law.[34] Inequalities in health care are exacerbated by individualistic notions stemming from the 'American Dream' and are often articulated in the idea that individuals should 'pull themselves up by their bootstraps.' This colloquialism assumes, however, that one has boots and bootstraps to begin with. Most modern societies are premised on a similar notion of opportunity that at least in theory anyone can aspire to economic advancement. But in reality not everyone has the same opportunities or likelihood for such advancement. Equality of opportunity and equality of outcome are separate and distinct measures with one measuring a starting point and the other measuring the result. Advances in opportunity depend in large part on "cultural capital" or nonfinancial social assets, something that many social groups are

---

[32] Sunstein 2005, p. 4.

[33] The role of the State and its impact on health was not introduced until the nineteenth century. See for example, Virchow 2006, pp. 2102–2105.

[34] Hoffman 2009.

8 The Right to Health: The Next American Dream 239

lacking.[35] This, coupled with a lack of political will, has contributed to the exclusion of the right to health from the 'American Dream.' Still, nearly every US President in the past century has attempted some level of reform related to health (See Table 8.1).

The ACA is the largest comprehensive health reform law since the 1960s.[36] It makes preventive care more accessible and affordable to Americans.[37] Prior to signing the ACA, US President Barack Obama harkened to a part of the American character, which he described as,

> that large-heartedness, that concern and regard for the plight of others...too, is part of the American character... a recognition that we are all in this together, and when fortune turns against one of us, others are there to lend a helping hand; a belief that in this country, hard work and responsibility should be rewarded by some measure of security and fair play; and an acknowledgment that sometimes government has to step into help deliver on that promise.[38]

This statement acknowledges the sentiments of the 'American Dream' as well as notions of individual responsibility while simultaneously recognizing the potential role and responsibility of government as a safety net. More recently, Obama referred to the courage to stand together for "the right to healthcare in the richest nation on Earth for every person."[39]

The concept of the 'American Dream' has served as a cause for hope as generations of Americans have envisaged steady personal and national progress.[40] While civil and political rights have traditionally been the most strongly supported rights in the American context, the partial acceptance of some economic, social, and cultural rights and the passage of the ACA signal, a hope for the possibility of ways in which concepts of a right to health could also be incorporated into the 'American Dream.'

Yet, the global economic recession and the widening gap between the rich and the poor suggest that as the costs of key goods and services, including health care, have risen rapidly, it is more difficult than ever for Americans to fulfill the Dream.[41] Moreover, at this time, the right to health as understood in international

---

[35] Muller 2008, available at http://www.foreignaffairs.com/articles/63217/jerry-z-muller/us-and-them. Accessed 25 November 2013.

[36] Ibid.

[37] Patient Protection and Affordable Care Act pp. 111–148 (hereinafter referred to as ACA).

[38] Obama's Remarks to Congress on Health Care, supra n 22.

[39] Remarks by the President at the "Let Freedom Ring" Ceremony Commemorating the 50th Anniversary of the March on Washington. Available at: http://www.whitehouse.gov/the-press-office/2013/08/28/remarks-president-let-freedom-ring-ceremony-commemorating-50th-anniversa (accessed 18 September 2013).

[40] Time Magazine, supra n 20.

[41] J Biden, Why Middle Class Americans Need Health Care Reform. Available at http://www.whitehouse.gov/assets/documents/071009_FINAL_Middle_Class_Task_Force_report2.pdf (accessed 25 November 2013).

240   D. P. Evans

Table 8.1 US executive action towards a right to health

1912	Teddy Roosevelt champions national health insurance[a]
1942	Franklin Delano Roosevelt signs the Social Security Act which included public health services (Title VI) and considered universal health insurance[b]. He also establishes wage and price controls during WWII creating competition among businesses for employees. Health insurance becomes a workplace benefits
1945	Harry Truman proposes that national insurance be paid with voluntary fees, a policy which is denounced by the American Medical Association as socialized medicine[d]
1965	Lyndon Johnson authorizes the creation of Medicare and Medicaid[e]
1974	President Richard Nixon proposed a "Comprehensive Health Insurance Plan" (CHIP) with universal coverage and special coverage for the working poor and unemployed[f]
1976	President Jimmy Carter proposes unsuccessfully a national health insurance plan[g]
1986	Ronald Reagan signs legislation (referred to as COBRA) that ensures insurance coverage for laid off workers for up to 18 months.
1993	Bill Clinton unsuccessfully proposes health care reform including universal coverage and stronger government regulation[h]
1997	Bill Clinton introduces the Children's Health Insurance Program (CHIP) which provides insurance for children who do not otherwise qualify for Medicaid
2003	George W. Bush introduces the Medicaid Part D prescription drug plan
2010	Barak Obama signs the Patient Protection and Affordable Care Act (ACA)[i]

[a] Kiplinger, "The Evolution of US Health Care Plans" Available: http://www.kiplinger.com/infographics/evolution_of_healthcare/map.html?si=1 (hereinafter referred to as Kiplinger)
[b] Achenbaum 1986, pp. 25–26
[c] Kiplinger, supra n 36
[d] Hoffman 2009
[e] Both Medicare and Medicaid are national insurance programs serving specific segments of the US population. Medicare is aimed at Americans aged 65 and older or those younger than 65 with disabilities. Medicaid serves low income adults and children
[f] Hoffman 2009
[g] Kinney 2008
[h] Kiplinger, see a above
[i] Vicini and Stempel 2012

human rights law is not guaranteed fully or even recognized as a right by the US. The human rights paradigm represents health as a fundamental right that should be available to all based on need, a view widely accepted globally. In diametric opposition to this moral and ideological vision is the view that health is a commodity in a market-based economy to which those who can afford to pay are welcome to purchase.[42] Inequalities are not viewed as the concern of markets; rather they are collateral damage. In contrast the egalitarian human rights approach views rights violations as problems for which the government bears responsibility.[43] Free markets have brought the US to its current crossroads where as Medical Anthropologist Paul Farmer states, "health care can be considered a commodity to

---

[42] O'Connell 2005.

[43] Yamin 2005, p. 1159.

8 The Right to Health: The Next American Dream

be sold, or it can be considered a basic social right. It cannot comfortably be considered both of these at the same time."[44] Others believe that health can be viewed as both a human right and a public—rather than a market—good, concurrently.[45]

8.3 Models of Health Care

Thus far, the American context as it relates to the conceptualization of the American Dream has been explored. In order to further understand the potential role that the right to health might play in a new formulation of the American Dream, a brief examination of global models of healthcare systems as well as the existing US healthcare system is necessary. Worldwide, four models of healthcare systems exist:

- The **Bismarck Model** includes nonprofit employer-based private insurance financed by employers and employees through payroll deductions. Coverage is universal and services and fees are tightly regulated. Examples include Germany, Japan, France, and the Netherlands (See Chap. 13);
- In the **Beveridge Model,** medical treatment is a public service provided by a mix of public and private providers where care is provided and financed by government through taxation and with payment directly from States to providers. Examples include the UK, most Scandinavian countries, Italy, and Cuba;
- The **National Health Insurance Model** is characterized by a single payer (the State) while providers are private. Coverage is universal with every citizen paying a monthly premium. Examples include Canada, Taiwan, and South Korea; and
- The **Out-of-Pocket Model** requires that care is paid for by the patient without assistance from private insurance or government. The world's poorest countries have the highest percentage of out-of-pocket health care along with the US where out-of-pocket payment account for 17 % of healthcare costs.[46] Out-of-pocket payments also disproportionally impact the poor within countries.[47,48]

---

[44] Farmer 2005, p. 175.

[45] Rudiger 2008.

[46] Reid 2009.

[47] Grover 2012, at para 2.

[48] Koivusalo and Mackintosh 2004.

8.3.1 The US Healthcare System

The section title above is a bit of a misnomer. After all, a 'healthcare system' seems to refer to an organized structure that provides healthcare facilities, goods, and services. In fact, the US does not have a healthcare system as such; rather we have what one public health expert has referred to as, an "illness care industry."[49] In reference to the healthcare models outlined above, the US is distinct in that all of these models exist simultaneously. Which model an individual participates in is largely a function of demographics where working people under age 65 enjoy a Bismarck model, military personnel, veterans, and Native American populations participate in the Beveridge model, those over 65 participate in a Single Payer system via Medicare and the 50 million uninsured fall into the Out-of-Pocket category.[50] The fact that these models exist simultaneously has led to the belief that, "we don't have a 'health care system.' Rather we have an illness and injury care industry within which multiple providers, provider systems and payment systems operate."[51] While the human rights paradigm does not dictate which model States ought to subscribe to, the UN Special Rapporteur on the right to health has called for an appropriate balance between the public and private sectors in both the financing and administration of health systems.[52,53]

While all other developed countries have settled on one of these models for the provision of health care, American exceptionalism at its worst is characterized by for profit insurance companies and businesses offering fragmented and decentralized "systems" of health care for separate classes of people that lack coverage.[54,55] The notable absence of government regulation in the US system coupled with an emphasis on the private actors as primary agents has resulted in a system that has profits, but also high premiums and administrative costs.[56] Three major problems facing the US are the growing uninsured population, the rising costs of health care, and poor health outcomes.[57] Each of these challenges has implications for the theme of nondiscrimination among vulnerable populations—a theme with which the human rights paradigm is preoccupied. In 1997, 37 million Americans were without healthcare access and by 2010 that number had grown to approximately 40 million.[58] Moreover, health outcomes have been declining with the US slipping in global rankings from 18th in 1980 to 25th in 2002 in infant mortality

---

[49] Keck 2012.

[50] Reid 2009.

[51] Keck 2012.

[52] Grover 2012, at para 3.

[53] GC 14, at para 17.

[54] Reid 2009.

[55] Lovett-Scott and Prather 2014 in Chap. 4.

[56] Editorial 2002, p. 1871 (hereinafter referred to as Where health care is not a right).

[57] Wilensky 2012, pp. 1479–1481.

[58] Lovett-Scott and Prather 2014, at Chap. 4.

rates and from 14th to 23rd in life expectancy, with healthcare spending accounting for nearly 20 % of the US federal budget.[59,60] More recently, the US ranked 39th in infant mortality rates and 37th for the effectiveness of its health care "system" despite spending an average of twice as much per capita on health care as other developed nations, all of whom have some form of universal healthcare coverage.[61,62] The current "American illness industry" has resulted in a tiered system, which separates categories of individuals (most often by socioeconomic status) resulting in unequal health services and poor health outcomes.[63,64] Worse still, the current US system emphasizes treatment instead of prevention. Seven in ten deaths in the US are related to preventable diseases and three-quarters of US healthcare dollars are spent treating such diseases. However, only three cents of each dollar spent on health care in the US goes towards prevention.[65] Support for prevention may also move the US further in the direction of a system of universal coverage since no country has achieved Universal Health Care (UHC) as long as it has relied on out-of-pocket payments for basic preventive care or medical treatments.[66]

8.3.2 Universal Health Care (UHC)

The World Health Organization (WHO) defines Universal Health Care (UHC) as "securing access to adequate healthcare for all at an affordable price" and WHO Director General Margaret Chan has called UHC "the single most powerful concept that public health has to offer, because you can realize the dream and

---

[59] Lovett-Scott and Prather 2014, at Chap. 4.

[60] Rodin 2012, p. 861.

[61] Lovett-Scott and Prather, at Chap. 4.

[62] Rodin and De Ferranti 2012.

[63] Tiered health systems are defined as those where a State or government health system provides basic health services while a parallel private system provides an additional level of coverage for those who can afford to pay. Such a system exists in a number of European States. In the US Medicare, Medicaid, the State Children's Health Insurance Program and Veteran's Health would be considered in the first tier while all employer and private insurance would fall into the latter category. Many of the American uninsured fall between the cracks of the two existing tiers.

[64] MacNaughton 2009, p. 47.

[65] American Public Health Association 2012. "Why do we need the Affordable Care Act? Critical Health Systems Problems facing the United States." Available at: http://www.apha.org/NR/rdonlyres/19BEA341-A7C3-4920-B2BC-65BDC846B803/0/WhyWeNeedtheACA_Aug2012.pdf (hereinafter referred to as American Public Health Association) (accessed 25 November 2013).

[66] Savedoff et al. 2012, p. 924, 932.

aspiration of health for every person."[67,68] A recent resolution on UHC passed by the UN General Assembly and endorsed by the US, aims to avoid significant direct payments at the point of delivery of care and suggests mechanisms for pooling risks to avoid catastrophic healthcare spending and impoverishment.[69,70] This historic resolution opened the door for what has been called the "3rd global health transition," namely how health care is financed and how health systems are organized.[71] This type of historical overhaul of poorly functioning systems is not without precedent with an overwhelming majority wanting health to be seen as a collective or public good where everyone in a country can enjoy generalized access to the healthcare services they need without incurring financial hardship.[72,73] UHC can be measured in terms of guaranteed rights, contractual financial protections (via pooled funds such as taxation or mandated contributions to healthcare schemes), and the utilization of healthcare services.[74] Each of these measures includes roles for both the State and the individual both in terms of duties and obligations, notions shared with the human rights paradigm, and softly echoed in the ACA.

With the exception of the US, the 25 wealthiest nations all have some form of UHC.[75] Savedoff et al. identified three common characteristics in the development of UHC across States. First, persistent and widespread domestic pressures demand the creation of public programs or regulations that expand access to care, improve equity, and pool financial risks.[76] Second, policies and programs must buy more health services for greater numbers of people.[77] Finally, greater shares of health spending are pooled (a necessary part of requirement of UHC) rather than paid for out-of-pocket.[78] As a result of widespread and persistent domestic pressure UHC emerges in most States over time as a matter of incremental negotiation rather than design and including a large role for the State, although specificities vary across the regulation and provision of services, financing models, and service provision.[79]

---

[67] Mark Tran "UN set to vote in favour of universal health coverage." 12 December 2012. Available at: http://www.guardian.co.uk/global-development/2012/dec/12/un-vote-universal-health-coverage. (Accessed 25 November 2013).

[68] Rodin and De Ferranti 2012.

[69] UN General Assembly 6 December 2012. Available at: http://www.un.org/ga/search/view_doc.asp?symbol=A/67/L.36 (Accessed 25 November 2013).

[70] Pooling in the field of health care refers to the redistribution of health care risks, costs, and benefits. See for example Savedoff et al. 2012.

[71] Rodin and De Ferranti 2012.

[72] Rodin and De Ferranti 2012.

[73] Savedoff et al. 2012.

[74] Ibid.

[75] Rodin and De Ferranti 2012.

[76] Savedoff et al. 2012.

[77] Ibid.

[78] Ibid.

[79] Ibid.

Thus, as the US engages in healthcare system reform, we must consider the lessons learned from the experience of others, who have already established UHC as a guide in the development of their health systems. In the US, the movement towards UHC has begun with slow, but relatively persistent progress, beginning with the inception of the Medicare and Medicaid programs.[80] As previously mentioned, a number of executive actions towards healthcare system reform have been initiated and plans for UHC were put forward by Presidents Nixon, Carter, and Clinton as well as the implementation of partial programs such as CHIP (See Table 8.1).[81] The stage has been set for UHC in the US as half of all US health spending is publicly financed and the majority of private insurance premiums are publicly subsidized at present.[82] At the signing of the ACA, President Obama alluded to the principle of UHC in his remarks:

> [W]e are a nation that faces its challenges and accepts its responsibilities. We are a nation that does what is hard. What is necessary. What is right ... and we have now just enshrined, as soon as I sign this bill, the core principle that everybody should have some basic security when it comes to their health care.[83]

The basic security called for by President Obama signals the need for a minimum safety net for all Americans. It is highly distinctive from the progressive realization of the right to health called for in the ICESCR. However, as a first step, the principle of UHC in the US has been established by the mandatory insurance requirement present in the ACA, which has been upheld by the US Supreme Court and which will be discussed in greater detail in the following section.[84]

8.4 Starting Point for the Next American Dream: The Patient Protection and Affordable Care Act

The existing US healthcare system faces unsustainable spending increases, poor health outcomes, and a lack of universal coverage including health disparities among various populations exacerbated by discriminatory industry practices.[85] The ACA establishes UHC as a national goal and outlines the responsibilities of individuals, employers, and the State with regard to that goal.[86] Each of these

---

[80] Ibid.

[81] Ibid.

[82] Ibid.

[83] The White House Blog. "On behalf of my mother" Available at: http://www.whitehouse.gov/blog/2010/03/23//behalf-my-mother (accessed 25 November 2013).

[84] Savedoff et al. 2012.

[85] ACA, supra n 37. See also US Department of Health and Human Services. The Health Care Law and You. Available at: http://www.hhs.gov/iea/acaresources/brochures/health-care-law-and-you.pdf (accessed 25 November 2013).

[86] Shaffer 2013, e-1-4.

challenges will be examined in turn before considering the ways in which the ACA addresses these points.

Healthcare spending in the US is unsustainable and is expected to reach 20 % of gross domestic product (GDP) by 2020.[87] In 2011, the Medicare program alone accounted for 15 % of the US federal budget and is expected to rise as the US population ages.[88] Rising healthcare costs negatively contribute to both the federal deficit as well as limiting the ability to spend towards and realize other social services, such as education, housing, and economic development.[89] It is worth noting that the ACA does not add to the US federal deficit.[90]

Despite such high spending, US health outcomes are poor. The US spends far more on medical care than any other industrialized nation, but ranks 36th in terms of life expectancy.[91,92] The Institute of Medicine reported in 2012 that "the current generation of children and young adults in the United States could become the first generation to experience shorter life spans and fewer healthy years of life than those of their parents".[93]

Lastly, the Congressional Budget Office estimated that 55 million Americans under the age of 65 are currently uninsured representing one out of five Americans in that population.[94] Most uninsured go without health coverage because they cannot afford it. The uninsured are less likely to receive preventive care, and less likely to seek care as quickly when they are sick or injured. This results in higher costs when they do seek treatment.[95] A major accomplishment of the ACA is that 30 million previously uninsured Americans will be covered by its implementation, although that coverage is not defined or viewed explicitly as a guaranteed right to health or health insurance.[96]

8.4.1 ACA Intent and Implementation

As stated earlier, the ACA establishes UHC as a national goal and outlines the responsibilities of individuals, employers, and the State with regard to that goal.[97]

---

[87] Universal health coverage, supra n 67.

[88] American Public Health Association, supra n 65.

[89] Ibid.

[90] ACA, supra n 37. See also US Department of Health and Human Services. The Health Care Law and You. Available at: http://www.hhs.gov/iea/acaresources/brochures/health-care-law-and-you.pdf (accessed 25 November 2013).

[91] Lovett-Scott and Prather 2014.

[92] Universal health coverage, supra n 67.

[93] American Public Health Association, supra n 65.

[94] Ibid.

[95] Ibid.

[96] Wilensky 2012.

[97] Shaffer 2013.

8 The Right to Health: The Next American Dream   247

The intent of the ACA is to expand insurance coverage and provide stronger regulation of the private insurance industry towards the improved efficiency and effectiveness in healthcare delivery with an eye towards prevention and improved health outcomes.[98] It does so by rolling out in stages, granting further reaching guarantees as time goes on. Since President Obama signed the ACA into law in early 2010, several major benchmarks have been achieved (See Fig. 8.1).[99] In July 2010, the first tangible protections for a vulnerable population were offered in the form of temporary coverage for those who had previously been denied coverage due to a preexisting condition, roughly 129 million Americans.[100] Later in 2010, the first set of ACA protections entered into force including requirements that insurance companies:

- offer free preventive services without charging a deductible or co-pay;
- not deny coverage to a customer because of paperwork or other unintentional errors;
- no longer set lifetime spending limits on key benefits;
- are limited in their ability to set annual dollar limits on coverage; and
- no longer deny coverage for children with pre-existing conditions.[101]

In 2011, additional protections entered force including increased coverage for seniors and a requirement that health insurers seeking to increase their rates by 10 % or more be reviewed by a State or federal agent. Figure 8.1 details the implementation of the ACA in stages. By 2012, additional preventive care services for women, including "well woman visits" and contraception were covered.[102] In 2013, States will have access to new funding for preventive services for people with Medicaid at low or no cost. By 2014, the full protections of the ACA will enter into effect including insurance company bans on discriminating against pre-existing conditions, charging higher rates due to gender or health status and annual and lifetime dollar limits. Middle class families will receive tax credits to help pay for private insurance coverage and Medicaid coverage will be expanded to families of four with incomes of up to $29,000. Those without coverage can use Affordable Insurance Exchanges, marketplaces where consumers can choose a

---

[98] ACA, supra n 37. See also US Department of Health and Human Services. The Health Care Law and You. Available at: http://www.hhs.gov/iea/acaresources/brochures/health-care-law-and-you.pdf (accessed 25 November 2013).

[99] The White House. "Explore the Timeline of Health Reform in Action." Available at: http://www.whitehouse.gov/healthreform (accessed 25 November 2013) (hereinafter referred to as Timeline).

[100] DeParle 2012.

[101] Timeline, supra n 99.

[102] Well-woman visits are annual preventive care visits that include preconception and other services prior to prenatal care. See Women's Preventive Services Guidelines, "Health Resources and Services Administration" (date, year). Available at: http://www.hrsa.gov/womensguidelines/ (accessed 25 November 2013).

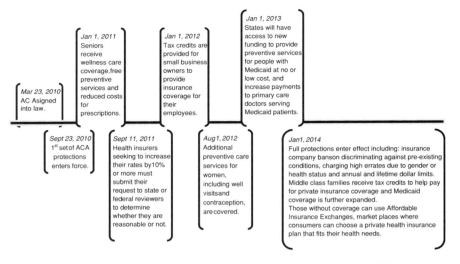

Fig. 8.1 Implementation timeline for the ACA, adapted from timeline, supra n 99

private health insurance plan that fits their health needs.[103] The exchanges offer a menu of standardized private health insurance plans from which individuals can select a plan. The goal to increase efficiency in healthcare delivery can already be seen with a cumulative savings of $10.7 billion as a result of Medicaid fraud protection measures alone. Moreover, towards the goal of increased insurance coverage, 2.5 million Americans under the age of 26 have received coverage by registering under their parents' health insurance plans and an additional 2 million workers have received coverage as a result of tax credits to small business owners for the provision of insurance coverage.[104,105] Each of these major benchmarks addresses the twin human rights themes of access and nondiscrimination among vulnerable populations.

8.4.2 ACA Ruling by the Supreme Court of the United States

Shortly after being signed into law, the ACA was almost immediately challenged in a series of legal cases. Ultimately, these consolidated cases came to the Supreme Court of the United States (SCOTUS). In July 2012, SCOTUS ruled on four aspects of the ACA in *National Federation of Independent Businesses v. Sebelius, Secretary of Health and Human Services*:

---

[103] See www.healthcare.gov for the federal exchange website.

[104] Timeline, supra n 99.

[105] For select State-specific data regarding implementation see, Corlette et al. 2013.

8 The Right to Health: The Next American Dream

- The question of the power of the US Congress to enact the individual mandate;
- The severability of the individual mandate from other portions of the ACA;
- Whether the Anti-Injunction Act bars consideration of the individual mandate's constitutionality prior to its penalties entering force in 2015,[106] and
- Whether the ACA Medicaid expansion constituted an unconstitutional coercion of states.[107]

The ACA was upheld in its entirety in a 5–4 ruling (with the exception of the final bullet).[108] In the interest of brevity, this chapter will discuss only the first and last bullet points which are of direct relevance to an expanded notion of the American Dream and the right to health. On the first point, the individual mandate refers to the term used in the ACA, which requires individuals to purchase health insurance. At question was whether Americans could be required to purchase health insurance as a matter of Congressional powers to regulate commerce and tax and spend. Surprisingly, the SCOTUS did not directly address the individual mandate as a matter of interstate commerce under the Commerce clause of the US Constitution as many expected. Rather, in delivering the majority opinion of the court, Chief Justice John Roberts, held that the individual mandate was a tax as defined in Article 1, para 8 of the US Constitution as opposed to a penalty.[109] Based on the fact that the tax by statute can never exceed the cost of insurance and that individuals have a choice to purchase insurance or otherwise pay the tax, SCOTUS found that the tax was not so punitive as to exceed the constitutional powers afforded to the US Congress to lay and collect taxes.[110,111]

Taxation has historically been a powerful tool for public health regulation and protections, as for example in the case of tobacco taxation. In viewing the individual mandate to purchase health insurance as a tax SCOTUS had adopted a potentially powerful methodology for the guaranteeing the right to health among the American population. However, rather than viewing it as a right to health, the individual is in fact obligated to purchase health insurance under the ACA. Under the SCOTUS ruling health insurance coverage, care is viewed as a choice where those who cannot afford coverage will get tax credits and those who can afford coverage and choose not to purchase it will no longer be subsidized.[112] This view differs significantly

---

[106] The Tax Anti-Injunction Act is a US federal law (26 U.S.C. para 7421((a)), which limits law suits on the grounds of taxation regardless of payment of the tax in question.

[107] Parento and Gostin 2012, (hereinafter referred to as Parento).

[108] *National Federation of Independent Businesses* v. *Sebelius*, Secretary of Health and Human Services 2012.

[109] *National Federation of Independent Businesses* v. *Sebelius*, at 567, Slip opinion C.J. Roberts, at 39.

[110] Congressional Budget Office. Estimates for the Insurance Coverage Provisions of the Affordable Care Act Updated for the Recent Supreme Court Decision. July 2012. Available at: http://www.cbo.gov/sites/default/files/cbofiles/attachments/ 43472-07-24-2012-CoverageEstimates.pdf (accessed 25 November 2013).

[111] U.S. Const. Article I, § 8.

[112] DeParle 2012.

from viewing health as a universal right. Most people who do not buy insurance fail to do so because they cannot afford it, not because they are exercising a "right to be uninsured."[113] The economic viability and effectiveness of the mandate is also questionable given that the tax is small relative to both the cost of insurance and income.[114] Therefore, the individual mandate is an invitation to purchase health insurance rather than an obligation.[115] Nor is it a right to health per se.

With regard to the coercion of states, SCOTUS found that Congress may not revoke existing State Medicaid funding as a penalty for those who decline to participate in Medicaid expansion under the ACA.[116] Medicaid, the US health program for people of low income is highly valued by the American public with 67 % supporting its expansion.[117] Viewed by SCOTUS as distinct from the existing Medicaid program, which was designed for disabled, blind, elderly, and needy families, the ACA proposed expansion to the entire nonelderly population with income below 133 % of the federal poverty guidelines (roughly $31,000 for a family of four).[118,119] While Justice Ginsberg argued that "adults earning less than $14,586 *surely* rank among the Nation's poor," Chief Justice Roberts viewed the Medicaid expansion as an element of a comprehensive national plan to provide universal health insurance coverage.[120,121] Based on the SCOTUS ruling that Congress may not revoke existing State Medicaid funding as a penalty for those who decline to participate in Medicaid expansion, states have the choice to opt out of the ACA Medicaid expansion. States can continue to receive current Medicaid funding, but will lose new money if they choose not to insure everyone via the expansion.[122]

---

[113] Ibid.

[114] The penalty in 2014 is $95 per adult and $47.50 per child or 1 % of family income, whichever is greater. By 2016, these numbers will increase up to $695 per adult and $347.50 per child or 2.5 % of family income, whichever is greater. See The Henry J Kaiser Family Foundation. "The Requirement to Buy Coverage Under the Affordable Care Act." Available at: http://healthreform.kff.org/the-basics/requirement-to-buy-coverage-flowchart.aspx (last accessed 25 November 2013).

[115] Parento and Gostin 2012.

[116] Ibid.

[117] Kaiser Family Foundation. "Key Findings of the July Kaiser Family Foundation Health Tracking Poll." 31 July 2012. Available at http://kaiserfamilyfoundation.files.wordpress.com/2013/01/8339-f.pdf (accessed 25 November 2013).

[118] *National Federation of Independent Businesses* v. *Sebelius*, supra n 108.

[119] The US Poverty Guidelines (also referred to as the federal poverty level) are a federal poverty measure issued annually by the US Department of Health and Human Service used to determine eligibility for federal programs. For 2013, the poverty guideline for a family of four is $23,550. See Annual Update of the HHS Poverty Guidelines, Federal Register. (date, year) Available at: https://www.federalregister.gov/articles/2013/01/24/2013-01422/annual-update-of-the-hhs-poverty-guidelines (accessed 25 November 2013).

[120] *National Federation of Independent Businesses* v. *Sebelius*, Slip opinion, J. Ginsburg.

[121] Ibid. Slip opinion C.J. Roberts.

[122] Cruze 2012.

8 The Right to Health: The Next American Dream

Much like the individual mandate, the SCOTUS decision has the effect of converting the Medicaid expansion from a requirement for universal coverage of the ACA to an option for States.[123] While no state was projected to lose money by participating in the expansion, state's decisions about how to respond will have significant impacts as Medicaid expansion amounts for half of the increased insurance coverage provided by the ACA accounting for 16 of 32 million additional insured persons.[124] By lifting the state requirement to participate in the Medicaid expansion, SCOTUS has removed a primary enforcement mechanism of the ACA.[125] The challenge to incentivize states to participate in the Medicaid expansion depends on numerous factors including current Medicaid thresholds, amount paid for uninsured populations, number likely to enroll after expansion, federal contributions towards care, and other budget considerations and timing preferences.[126]

8.5 ACA and the Right to Health

As previously mentioned, two principal themes from human rights are most relevant to the ACA. These include access to healthcare goods, facilities, and services as well as nondiscrimination, particularly among vulnerable populations such as the poor. From a human rights perspective, States' obligations include what this author refers to as the "mantra of human rights"—the tripartite typology of obligations to "respect, protect, fulfill."[127] The obligation to respect requires States to refrain from directly or indirectly violating the right to health.[128] The obligation to protect requires States to take measures that prevent other actors from violating the right to health.[129] The obligation to fulfill requires States to take positive actions in facilitating, promoting, and providing the right to health.[130] The ACA does much to move the US in the direction of the respect, protect, fulfill framework of human rights, specifically as it relates to the themes of access and nondiscrimination, as clarified further in Table 8.2.

Most health professionals have a limited definition of access equating it to merely transportation and insurance coverage.[131] True access includes being able to get to

---

[123] Ibid.

[124] Congressional Budget Office, supra n 110.

[125] Ibid.

[126] Ibid.

[127] GC 14, at para 33.

[128] Ibid.

[129] Ibid.

[130] Committee on Economic, Social and Cultural Rights. 'The right to adequate food' 1999, agenda item 7.

[131] Lovett-Scott and Prather, Chap. 1.

252 D. P. Evans

Table 8.2 Benefits of ACA and their relationship to Right to Health Themes[a]

ACA benefit	Right to health theme	Tripartite typology
Strengthens protections against fraud	Information accessibility	Protect
Requires transparency in insurance rate increases	Information and financial accessibility	Protect
Provides rebates from insurers who spend too much	Financial accessibility	Protect
Offers tax credits for small business owners and individuals	Financial accessibility	Fulfill
Offers affordable insurance for those with pre-existing conditions; After 2014 prohibits denial of coverage for pre-existing conditions	Nondiscrimination and financial accessibility	Respect; Protect
Creates gender parity in insurance	Nondiscrimination and financial accessibility	Respect
Funds National Health Service Corps for scholarships & loan repayments for health care professionals working in underserved areas	Nondiscrimination and financial accessibility	Fulfill
Reduces medication costs and lowers insurance costs for seniors	Nondiscrimination and financial accessibility	Fulfill
Creates state based exchanges	Nondiscrimination	Fulfill
Improves consumer protections such as lifetime limits on coverage and coverage of preventive services	Nondiscrimination	Protect
Offers insurance coverage until age 26	Nondiscrimination	Fulfill
Creates community health centers	Non-discrimination	Fulfill

[a] Adapted from DeParle 2012. The addition of human rights themes and the tripartite typology are the work of this author

and from health services, having the ability to pay for the services needed, and getting needs met once one enters the health system.[132] The previously mentioned AAAQ framework of the human rights paradigm outlines four overlapping dimensions to access: physical, economic, and information accessibility as well as accessibility to healthcare goods, services, and facilities in a nondiscriminatory manner.[133] Information accessibility is addressed most directly by the ACA provisions related to transparency including increased Medicaid fraud protections, the right to an independent review of insurance plan decisions and the requirement that insurance premiums cannot be raised by more than 10 % without public justification.[134] Financial accessibility is attended to in numerous provisions such the creation of the affordable exchanges providing competitive marketplaces for insurance, tax credit to individuals and small businesses, discounts on brand name medications for Medicare recipients, and the 80/20 rule where 80 % of every healthcare dollar collected by insurance companies must be spent on health care itself.[135]

---

[132] Idem, Chap. 3.

[133] GC 14, at para 12b.

[134] ACA supra n 37.

[135] Ibid.

8 The Right to Health: The Next American Dream 253

Nondiscrimination, particularly among vulnerable groups is a concern of human rights and one that is addressed within the context of the ACA. Groups whose vulnerability receives attention under the ACA include the uninsured, the poor (Medicaid recipients), the elderly (Medicare recipients), and those with preexisting conditions.[136] Examples of specific provisions attending to these populations include increased access to long-term care for the disabled, increased access to an expanded network of community health centers for low-income populations, and access to critical supports for pregnant and parenting teens.[137] An immediate provision has allowed those under age 26 to stay on their parent's insurance plans while future provisions will guarantee gender parity in insurance rates and prohibit discrimination based on pre-existing conditions.[138] The ACA also offers an increased focus on public health via preventive care.[139] Preventive services offered for free include cancer screenings, vaccination, contraception, birth control, mental health screening, and tobacco cessation as well as wellness visits for seniors.[140] Table 8.2 below displays some benefits of the ACA as they relate to the human rights themes of access and nondiscrimination and where they fit into the tripartite typology of respect, protect, and fulfill.

8.6 Conclusions and Recommendations

The notion of the American Dream is one that permeates American culture and policy. Long-standing tensions exist between the American fascination with the individual's capability to make his way in the world and the role and responsibilities of government in ensuring that he has equal opportunity to achieve his potential.[141] These tensions are exacerbated by the assumptions and stereotypes that pervade American culture in regard to vulnerable populations, such as minorities or those living in poverty. These views are particularly problematic with regard to economic, social, and cultural rights such as the right to health as these rights have not traditionally been viewed as a part of the American Dream.

Values and policy modifications are necessary in order to build and sustain the political will to support notions of the right to health as a part of the 'American Dream' in the future. As suggested by the brief examination of global models of health care, a close examination of others and a replication of their successful practices, particularly those facing resource constraints, may prove useful.[142]

---

[136] Ibid.

[137] Ibid.

[138] Ibid.

[139] Ibid.

[140] Ibid.

[141] Time Magazine, supra n 20.

[142] Lovett-Scott and Prather 2014, Chap. 17.

The major challenges facing the US healthcare system are a growing uninsured population, the rising costs of health care, and poor health outcomes.[143] Starting points to address each of these barriers include an emphasis on prevention and examination of models and trajectories towards UHC.

UHC has been identified as a powerful public health tool and one which addresses the existing fragmented US system. Policies that reduce reliance on out-of-pocket spending and improve institutions that manage pooled funding have been shown to address healthcare system concerns of equity, efficiency, and sustainability.[144] UHC may be achieved through many financing structures, but pooled expenses predominate in successful models. Moreover, the political process must be ubiquitous and persistent as political action is the major force behind pooled financing of health expenditures.[145] While the introduction of the individual mandate of the ACA may be perceived as coercive to some, the societal and legal consensus that everyone is entitled to affordable health insurance coverage supports the obligation of individuals to pay the ACA tax.[146]

The groundwork for an evolution in the American Dream paradigm towards inclusion of the right to health has been laid by the ACA. This is evidenced by its attention to issues of access and nondiscrimination among vulnerable populations. As illustrated in Table 8.2, the ACA formally and positively contributes to the prevention of the discrimination and improved information and financial accessibility to healthcare goods, services, and facilities. The ACA provides a level of health protection via regulation of the US insurance industry that has been unseen previously. Interestingly, many of the requirements of the ACA may be categorized as fulfilling the human right to health either by facilitating or directly providing benefits to the American public. These entitlements are guaranteed despite the failure of the US government to ratify the ICESCR. Further, the SCOTUS ruling validates taxation as a methodology for ensuring the protection of the right to health in the US. This decision elevates the right to health to the same level as education, property, and other civil rights that have similarly been accepted in the US as taxable rights.[147]

Despite this leap forward in US treatment of the right to health, the ACA still leaves room for improvement. If the ACA is fully implemented, 30 million Americans will remain uninsured.[148] Depending on the decision of States with regard to participation in Medicaid expansion, these numbers could and likely will be higher.[149] Former UN Special Rapporteur on the right to health, Paul Hunt has

---

[143] Wilensky 2012.

[144] Savedoff et al. 2012.

[145] Ibid.

[146] Editorial 2002.

[147] See for example, Hunt in "Reclaiming Social Rights: International and Comparative Perspectives" (1996) discussing the relationship between civil and political rights to social rights.

[148] Freeman 2012.

[149] Ibid.

stated that, "rigorous policy-making demands an analysis of the distributional impact of reforms on the well-being of different groups in society, especially the poor and vulnerable."[150] While the ACA does explicitly address the vulnerabilities of a number of groups, such as the poor and elderly, others are left out entirely. Among those excluded from the ACA are undocumented immigrants who have been barred from purchasing even unsubsidized insurance through the exchanges.[151] Such exclusion emphasizes the need to preserve and improve upon the universal access framework created by the ACA. Else, the ACA itself risks de facto and de jure discrimination in access to healthcare services, which may contravene the nondiscrimination clause of the right to health under Article 12 of the ICESCR.

While the human rights regime is neutral on the type of healthcare system in a given State, the State must regulate and supervise the activities of non-State actors including *vis a vis* the right to health.[152] The challenge for the US now is to build upon the foundation of the ACA by continuously inquiring the best ways in which to improve access to care, reduce discrimination, and incorporate the right to health into both the US healthcare system and cultural mindset.[153] Values and policy modifications will be necessary in order to build and sustain the political will to support notions of the right to health as a part of the 'American Dream' in the future. As Truslow Adams suggested, "that American dream of a better, richer, and happier life for all our citizens of every rank, which is the greatest contribution we have as yet made to the thought and welfare of the world."[154] Adams' dream and that of Dr. Martin Luther King Jr. after him are both expansive with an optimistic view towards universality. The contributions of many US presidents and policymakers have gradually led the US to its current position. However, the ACA is only the first step in the evolution of the right to health as a part of the American Dream. The next iteration of the American Dream demands more, including full engagement of the US in the international human rights regime and its processes as well as ratification of the ICSCR. The US is at the cusp of a new era and there is still much work to be done.

References

Achenbaum A (1986) Social security visions and revisions. Cambridge University Press, New York

American Public Health Association (2012) Why do we need the Affordable Care Act? Critical Health Systems problems facing the United States. www.apha.org/NR/rdonlyres/19BEA341-A7C3-4920-B2BC-65BDC846B803/0/WhyWeNeedtheACA_Aug2012.pdf. Accessed 25 Nov 2013

---

[150] Hunt 2003, para 82.

[151] Parento and Gostin 2012.

[152] GC 14, at para 35.

[153] Lovett-Scott and Prather 2014.

[154] Time Magazine, supra n 20.

Becker CL (1922) The declaration of independence: a study of the history of political ideas. Harcourt, Brace and Company, New York

Brown v. Board of Education (1954) 347 US 483

Clay H (1994) The American System. In: Byrd RC, The Senate, 1789-1989: Classic Speeches, 1830–1993. Government Printing Office, Washington, D.C, 1994. http://www.senate.gov/artandhistory/history/resources/pdf/AmericanSystem.pdf

Cullen J (2004) The American dream: a short history of an idea that shaped a nation. Oxford University Press

Committee on Economic, Social and Cultural Rights. The right to the highest attainable standard of health: 11/08/2000. E/C.12/2000/4, CESCR General Comment 14. Twenty-second session Geneva, 25 April–12 May 2000 Agenda item 3

Committee on Economic, Social and Cultural Rights. The right to adequate food: 05/12/1999. E/C.12/1999/5, CESCR General Comment 12. Twentieth session Geneva, 26 April–14 May 1999 Agenda item 7

Corlette S, Monahan C, Lucia K (2013) Moving to high quality, Adequate coverage: state implementation of new essential health benefit requirements. Georgetown University's Health Policy Institute. http://www.rwjf.org/content/dam/farm/reports/reports/2013/rwjf407484

Cruze D (2012) Justice in health care reform. Emory Health Magazine. Woodruff Health Sciences Center. http://emoryhealthmagazine.emory.edu/issues/2012/fall/features/justice-in-health-care-reform/index.html

DeParle N (2012) A Supreme Court upholds President Obama's health care. The White House Blog 11 July 2012

Editorial (2002) Editorial: where health care is not a right. Lancet 359:1871

Evans DP (2012) The synergistic approach: racial discrimination and the right to health. LAP Lambert Academic Publishing

Farmer P (2005) Pathologies of power: health, human rights and the new war on the poor. University of California Press, California

Freeman J (2012) Health reform, ACA and primary care: Is there still a conundrum? Medicine and Social Justice. http://medicinesocialjustice.blogspot.com/2012_11_01_archive.html. Accessed 19 June 2014

Grover A (2012) Interim report of the special rapporteur on the right of everyone to the highest attainable standard of physical and mental health UN doc.A/67/302

(The) Henry J Kaiser Family Foundation. The requirement to buy coverage under the Affordable Care Act. http://healthreform.kff.org/the-basics/requirement-to-buy-coverage-flowchart.aspx. Accessed 25 Nov 2013

Hoffman C (2009) National Health Insurance, A brief history of reform efforts in the U.S. http://www.kff.org/healthreform/upload/7871.pdf. Accessed 13 Aug 2013

Hunt P (2003) Report of the Special Rapporteur on the Right to the Highest Attainable Standard of Physical and Mental Health" UN doc.E/CN.4/2003/58, 13 Feb 2003

Hunt P (2005) Report of the Special Rapporteur on the Right to the Highest Attainable Standard of Physical and Mental Health UN doc.E/CN.4/2005/51, 11 Feb 2005

International Convention on the Elimination of all forms of Racial Discrimination, G.A. Res. 2106 (XX), U.N. Doc. A/RES/2106 (XX) 21 Dec 1965

Keck C (2012) Personal communication. San Francisco, California, 2 Oct 1012

King ML Jr (1961) Speech to the AFL-CIO, 11 Dec 1961. http://www.thekingcenter.org/archive/document/mlk-speech-4th-constitutional-convention-afl-cio

Kinney ED (2008) Recognition of the International Human Right to Health and Health Care in the United States. Rutgers Law Review 60:337. http://www.pegasus.rutgers.edu/~review/vol60n2/Kinney_Macro_web.pdf

Koivusalo M, Mackintosh M (2004) Health systems and commercialisation: in search of good sense. Social Policy and Development Programme. http://www.unrisd.org/80256B3C005BCCF9/(httpPublications)/32A160C292F57BBEC1256ED10049F965?OpenDocument. Accessed 25 Nov 2013

Lovett-Scott M, Prather F (2014) Global health systems comparing strategies for delivering health systems. Jones & Bartlett Learning, Burlingham

MacNaughton G (2009) Untangling equality and non-discrimination to promote the right to health care for all. Health Hum Rights 11(47):47–63

Meier BM (2010) Global health governance and the contentious politics of human rights: mainstreaming the right to health for public health advancement (December 1, 2010). Stanford J Int Law 46(1) 2010. Available at SSRN: http://ssrn.com/abstract=1816625

Moulds H (1965) John Locke and rugged individualism. American J Econ Sociol 24(1):97–109

Muller JZ (2008) Us and them: the enduring power of ethnic nationalism, March/April FOREIGN AFFAIRS. http://www.foreignaffairs.com/articles/63217/jerry-z-muller/us-and-them. Accessed 25 Nov 2013

Naderi PS, Meier BD (2010) Privatization within in the Dutch context: a comparison of the health insurance systems of the Netherlands and the United States, Sage Publications, pp 603–618. http://hea.sagepub.com/content/14/6/603.refs.html. Accessed 25 Nov 2013

National Federation of Independent Businesses v. Sebelius, Secretary of Health and Human Services, 567 US 05 (2012)

O'Connell P (2005) The right to health and the privatisation of Irish Health Care. Medico–Legal Journal of Ireland 11(2):76 et seq

Parento EW, Gostin LO (2012) The Supreme Court's Landmark Decision on the Affordable Care Act, Healthcare Reform's Ultimate Fate Remains Uncertain. O'Neill Institute for National and Global Health Law. Briefing Paper No. 7. July 9, 2012

Patient Protection and Affordable Care Act (ACA) [P.L. 111-148]

Reid TR (2009) The healing of America. Penguin Press, New York

Report by the Independent Expert on Human Rights and Extreme Poverty (2006) U.N. Doc. E/CN.4/2006/43/Add.1 (Mar. 27, 2006)

Reports Submitted by States Parties under Article 9 of the Convention (10 October 2000) Third Periodic Reports of States Parties Due in 1999; Addendum United States of America, U.N. Doc CERD/C/351Add.1

Rodin J, De Ferranti D (2012) Universal health coverage: the third global health transition. Lancet 380:861–862

Rudiger A (2008) From market competition to solidarity? Assessing the prospects of U.S. health care reform plans from a human rights perspective. Health Hum Rights Int J 10(1). http://ssrn.com/abstract=1984251. Accessed 25 Nov 2013

Savedoff WD, de Ferranti D, Smith AL, Fan V (2012) Political and economic aspects of the transition to universal health coverage. Lancet 380:924–932

Shaffer ER (2013) The affordable care act: the value of systemic disruption. Am J Public Health 103(6):969–972

Sunstein CR (2005) Why does the American constitution lack social and economic guarantees? 56 Syracuse L Rev 56:1

Rodin J (2012) Universal health coverage: the third global health transition. Lancet 380:861–862

Vicini J, Stempel J (2012). US top court upholds healthcare law in Obama triumph". http://www.reuters.com/article/2012/06/28/us-usa-healthcare-court-idUSBRE85R06420120628, 28 June 2012. Accessed 25 Nov 2013

Virchow RC (2006) Report on the typhus epidemic in Upper Silesia. Am J Public Health 96(12):2102–2105

Wilensky GR (2012) The Shortfalls of 'Obamacare'. N Engl J Med 367:1479–1481

Yamin A (2005) The Right to Health Under International Law and its Relevance to the United States. Am J Public Health 95:1156 et seq

Chapter 9
The Brazilian Human Rights Indicators System: The Case of the Right to Health

Aline Albuquerque

Abstract This chapter focuses on the Brazilian government's project to build a National Human Rights Indicators system (NHRI) for the right to health as outlined in Article 12 of the International Covenant on Economic, Social and Cultural Rights (ICESCR). First, the notion of human rights indicators is developed based on reflections from three key documents: the Report on Indicators for Monitoring Compliance with International Human Rights Instruments (HRI/MC/2006/7), the Report on Indicators for Promoting and Monitoring the Implementation of Human Rights (HRI/MC/2008/3), and the Guidelines for Preparation of Progress Indicators in the area of economic, social, and cultural rights. Subsequently, the major initiatives undertaken by the Secretariat of Human Rights to create the NHRI are assessed, such as the development of the Monitoring Technical Committee (CTA). This chapter draws upon the right to health according to the Brazilian Constitution and the law, the current health indicators used by the Brazilian Ministry of Health, and indicators proposed by the Brazilian government, taking into account the unique attributes of the Public Health System and the context of social and economic inequalities in Brazil. This contribution examines which health-related indicators proposed by the United Nations Office of the High Commissioner for Human Rights (OHCHR) and the Inter-American Commission on Human Rights are appropriate for Brazil; it considers which indicators might be useful to other countries; it explores which health indicators used by the Brazilian Ministry of Health are applicable to the NHRI; and it contributes to the discussion on the use of human rights indicators to evaluate government progress toward accomplishing their health-related human rights obligations.

A. Albuquerque (✉)
UNESCO Chair of Bioethics, University of Brasilia, Human Rights Secretariat, Brasilia, Brazil
e-mail: alineaoliveira@hotmail.com

B. Toebes et al. (eds.), *The Right to Health*, DOI: 10.1007/978-94-6265-014-5_9, 259
© T.M.C. ASSER PRESS and the authors 2014

Contents

9.1   Introduction 260
9.2   Guidelines Set Forth by the UN High Commissioner for Human Rights
      and the Inter-American Commission on Human Rights for the Construction
      of Human Rights Indicators 262
9.3   Indicators of the Right to Health 267
9.4   The Brazilian Human Rights Indicators System: The Case of the Human Right
      to Health 270
      9.4.1   The Brazilian Human Rights Indicators System: Historical Process
              of Elaboration and Theoretical Bases 270
      9.4.2   The Current Stage of Development of the Brazilian Human Rights
              System Related to the Human Right to Health 273
9.5   Final Considerations 276
References 277

9.1 Introduction

As noted in General Comment 14 on the right to the highest attainable standard of
health, the use of indicators for monitoring the fulfillment of States' human rights
obligations is useful to improve governmental transparency, to encourage the role
of civil society in monitoring progress, and to inform the country's National Public
Health Strategy.[1] The OHCHR affirms that quantitative and qualitative indicators
are useful tools for promoting and monitoring the implementation of human rights
in a given State.[2] In addition, it points out that "human rights indicators are tools
for States to assess their own progress in implementing human rights and compliance with the international treaties."[3] Similarly, the 1993 Vienna Declaration
and Programme of Action specifically echoes this idea in relation to economic,
social, and cultural rights. The 2000 Human Development Report also affirms that
statistical indicators are powerful tools for the achievement of human rights
because they strengthen accountability procedures.[4] In the Inter-American Human
Rights System, Article 19 of the Protocol of San Salvador[5] directs "the States
Parties to [...] undertake to submit periodic reports on the progressive measures

---

[1] U.N. Committee on ESCR (CECSR), General Comment No. 14: The right to the Highest
Attainable Standard of Health, para 43, U.N. Doc. E/C.12/2000/4 (11 August 2000) (Hereafter:
General Comment 14), para 43 (f).

[2] OHCHR 2013.

[3] OHCHR 2013.

[4] UNDP 2000.

[5] The Additional Protocol to the American Convention on Human Rights in the area of Economic,
Social, and Cultural Rights, more commonly known as the "Protocol of San Salvador," was
opened for signature in the city of San Salvador, El Salvador, on 17 November 1988. The Protocol
prescribes social, economic, and cultural rights, as well as the right to health, to work, and to
education, which were treated generically in the American Convention on Human Rights.

9 The Brazilian Human Rights Indicators System: The Case of the Right to Health 261

they have taken to ensure due respect for the rights set forth in this Protocol."[6] In order to accomplish this, the Inter-American Commission on Human Rights produced the Guidelines for Preparation of Progress Indicators in the Area of Economic, Social, and Cultural Rights.[7]

Although the international community recognizes the relevance of human rights indicators, there remain challenges to establishing national indicator systems. The complexity of distinguishing between human rights indicators and social indicators[8] requires defining them in a unique way that captures the essential aspects of a particular right as well as the overarching principles of nondiscrimination and equality. Involving civil society at all stages of the process ensures that the process itself—and not only the outcome—promotes participation and empowerment. Furthermore, ensuring civil society participation in its development requires a true political commitment from the government of the country in question. Another challenge is the lack of disaggregated data by prohibited grounds of discrimination such as sex, disability, and ethnicity and how to analyze the indicators in the light of a human rights perspective. Data scarcity can be linked to resource and capacity constraints, or a lack of political will.

Recognizing the importance of human rights indicators for monitoring state performance and informing public policies, the Brazilian State included them in the National Human Rights Program (NHRP-3), which was edited in 2009 by the President of the Republic at the time. Thus, NHRP-3 reaffirms the obligation to "[establish] a Human Rights indicators system."[9] Brazil, during its participation in the 2008 Universal Periodic Review, voluntarily committed itself to elaborate new instruments for the internal monitoring of human rights, which led to the establishment of a national indicators system and annual reports on the situation of human rights in the country, including the right to health.[10] To this end, Brazil has been making efforts to establish a national indicators system for human rights since 2008.

The Brazilian government's sustained commitment to building a human rights indicators system presents an opportunity to advance the monitoring of economic, social, and cultural rights, including the right to health. The goal of this chapter is to analyze the development process, identify its theoretical basis including conceptual and methodological aspects, and consider the extent to which proposals from the UN High Commissioner and the Inter-American Commission on Human Rights have been incorporated. The development process is understood as laying the theoretical basis for the project as well as for the set of human rights indicators

---

[6] Organization of American States 1999, Article 19.

[7] Inter-American Commission on Human Rights, "Guidelines for Preparation of Progress Indicators in the Area of Economic, Social and Cultural Rights" (2008). Available from http://cidh.org/countryrep/IndicadoresDESC08eng/Indicadoresindice.eng.htm.

[8] It is important to highlight Paul Hunt's Report "A human rights-based approach to health indicators," elaborated in 2006, as Special Rapporteur on the right of everyone to the enjoyment of the highest attainable standard of physical and mental health.

[9] Brazil 2009.

[10] United Nations 2012.

to be used. There is a particular emphasis on "result" indicators, given that these indicators emphasize the experience of the right-holders, rather than on governmental actions. As such, the Brazilian government has decided to build its system primarily around a set of result indicators. Due to the complexity of establishing a full set of indicators for each right, the government has chosen to examine, specifically, the right to the highest attainable standard of physical and mental health, prescribed in Article 12 of the UN International Covenant on Economic, Social and Cultural Rights (ICESCR), and in Article 10 of the Protocol of San Salvador, adopted within the scope of the Organizations of the American States.[11]

The set of indicators employed by the Brazilian State is assessed in the light of the underlying theoretical basis of the project and the indicators proposed by the said agencies. As such, this article is organized as follows: (a) an explanation of the proposals formulated by the UN High Commissioner and by the Inter-American Commission on Human Rights, consolidated in the 2008 Report on Indicators for Promoting and Monitoring the Implementation of Human Rights, and in the Process Indicators in Respect of Rights contemplated in the 2011 Protocol of San Salvador; (b) a study of the indicators formulated by the UN Special Rapporteur on the Right to the Highest Attainable Standard of Physical and Mental Health, as well as specific literature on the subject, pointing out the scarcity of the latter; (c) research on guidelines that document the process of the elaboration of indicators used in the Brazilian Human Rights Indicators System; (d) an analysis of the theoretical framework that includes conceptual and methodological aspects, and of the set of indicators for the right to health defined by the Brazilian State, based on the proposals from the UN High Commissioner and from the Inter-American Commission on Human Rights.

First, the content advocated by the UN High Commissioner and by the Inter-American Commission on Human Rights for a national human rights indicators system will be described.

9.2 Guidelines Set Forth by the UN High Commissioner for Human Rights and the Inter-American Commission on Human Rights for the Construction of Human Rights Indicators

The Report on Indicators for Promoting and Monitoring the Implementation of Human Rights includes contributions from the OHCHR Report on the use of indicators to determine the attainment of economic, social, and cultural rights[12] and the

---

[11] The objective of the National System of Human Rights Indicators, in the first stage of the project, is to deal with the following rights: the right to education; the right to health; the right to work, the right to life, and the right to environment.

[12] OHCHR 2011.

document entitled, "Progress Indicators in Respect of Rights Contemplated in the Protocol of San Salvador." The OHCHR's report was prepared at the request of the human rights treaty bodies.[13] The OHCHR has conducted extensive research and investigated the practical usage of indicators by national and international organizations. The conceptual and methodological framework presented in the document stresses the need for strictly defined human rights indicators based on a suitable methodology and available information from trusted sources.[14]

In relation to conceptual aspects, human rights indicators must be derived from the normative content of each right, according to what is established in international human rights treaties and in the General Comments by the respective Committees. The primary goal of human rights assessments is to evaluate the efforts of the duty-bearer aiming to fulfill its obligations to respect, protect, and fulfill human rights. It is crucial to measure the consolidated efforts through "result" indicators as well as the "intention or commitment" of the State through "structure" and "process" indicators. In the specific case of the economic, social, and cultural rights, the process and result indicators are perhaps more relevant, as "progressive realization" requires States and monitoring agencies to monitor progress over an indefinite period of time.[15]

In addition, there are universal principles of rights, such as nondiscrimination, equality, indivisibility, accountability, participation, and empowerment, which must be taken into account in indicator selection. Similarly, monitoring the "accessibility" of health care, especially for vulnerable populations, might prevail over other key aspects of the right outlined in General Comment 14, including availability, acceptability, and quality.[16] This is because monitoring access provides a better indication of the extent to which a state is promoting the equal realization of the right

---

[13] OHCHR 2008a.

[14] OHCHR 2008a.

[15] OHCHR 2011.

[16] The four elements of the human right to health are: availability, accessibility, acceptability and quality of healthcare systems. (A) Availability: each State must have a sufficient number of public healthcare facilities, goods and services, as well as healthcare policies and programs. The mentioned services also encompass those related to basic health, such as clean and potable water, and appropriate sanitation. Also important is the number of hospitals, clinics and other healthcare facilities; healthcare personnel; essential medication defined in the Action Programme on Essential Medication of the World Health Organization, made available by the State. (B) Accessibility: it is defined as the commitment made by the States so that healthcare facilities, goods and services are available to all, with no discrimination of any kind. It is subdivided into: (I) non-discrimination: healthcare facilities, goods and services must be accessible, in fact and in law, to the marginalized and vulnerable parts of the population; (II) physical accessibility: healthcare facilities, goods and services must be physically reachable by the entire population, especially those marginalized and vulnerable groups, minorities, indigenous people, women, children and adolescents. People living in rural areas are included in this category; (III) economic accessibility: healthcare facilities, goods and services must be available to all, and the payment for the services must observe the principle of equity; (IV) access to information: it is the right to ask for, receive and divulge information and ideas. (C) Acceptability: it is defined as the respect for ethics and cultural standards by the healthcare services providers. (D) Quality: it is the

to health, in accordance with the principle of nondiscrimination. Ensuring physical and economic access for all residents is essential to the realization of the right to health.[17] These principles are captured by indicators that overlap with the various human rights outlined in international and regional instruments, highlighting the indivisible nature of rights. For example, statistics indicating the proportion of underweight children are connected to the right to food, the right to health, and to the underlying principles of equality and nondiscrimination.

The first step in the process of selecting human rights indicators is to define attributes.[18] The text of normative human rights documents must be translated into a list of characteristics for each right, making it easier to identify the metrics that are most appropriate for monitoring the realization of such rights. The most important function of the attributes is to correlate the indicator and the normative provision on which it is based. Regarding the right to health, the attributes are extracted from Article 25 of the Universal Declaration of Human Rights, Article 12 of the ICESCR, and General Comment no. 14. Additionally, General Comment no. 3 and no. 4 by the Committee on the rights of the Child, and General Recommendation no. 24 by the Committee on the Elimination of Discrimination against Women[19] are considered.

The OHCHR opted for the configuration of structure-process-result indicators aiming to capture the commitments, efforts, and results from the "debtors." This configuration does not correspond to the tripartite obligations to "respect, protect and fulfil" human rights as stressed by the OHCHR. The structure indicators reflect the ratification and adoption of legal instruments, as well as the existence of institutional mechanisms that support the attainment of human rights. The process indicators capture the policies and programs that will gradually realize human rights, expressing causality between the structure and result indicators. The result indicators reflect the extent of the realization of rights, for individuals or collectively.[20]

Regarding the methodological aspects, the OHCHR affirms that the indicators must be based on two types of information: administrative socioeconomic data and data on human rights violations. Socioeconomic statistics refer to the quantitative information gathered by the State, by means of administrative records and statistical research, usually conducted by national statistics agencies. Hence, basing

---

(Footnote 16 continued)
conformity of healthcare facilities, goods and services to the scientific, medical and quality-related standards (CESCR 2000).

[17] OHCHR 2008b.

[18] There is a difference between human rights indicators and health indicators. According to Hunt (2006), health indicators may be used to monitor aspects of the progressive realization of the right to health provided: (a) they correspond, with some precision, to a right to health norm, such as article 12 of ICESCR; (b) they are disaggregated by at least sex, race, ethnicity, rural/urban and socio-economic status [...]; (c) they are supplemented by additional indicators that monitor [...] essential and interrelated features of the right to health.

[19] OHCHR 2008a.

[20] OHCHR 2008a.

the indicators on information coming from governmental agencies that use a standardized methodology confers a higher degree of transparency, credibility, and accountability to them in their monitoring process. The criteria for the selection of quantitative indicators, which are expressed in numbers, percentages, and indices[21] must be: relevant, valid, reliable, simple, fitting, and based on objective information. They must also be able to be compared over time and be disaggregated by sex, age, or other prohibited grounds of discrimination.[22] Disaggregation is vital as it allows for the detection of inequalities that could be otherwise overlooked using averages, hindering the achievement of the objectives established by public policies and programs.[23] Hence, disaggregation based on vulnerable and marginalized groups is useful.

Data analysis on information extracted from human rights indicators must be undertaken in light of the normative understanding of human rights. In general, indicators do not present a complete view of the extent to which a right has been realized or violated; however, as stated by the OHCHR, they are useful to: (a) determine the effectiveness of laws and normative acts; (b) set clear goals for public policies and programs and allow for more direct policies and programs geared toward vulnerable groups and to monitor their results; (c) establish objective criteria for the verification of the gradual realization of the right; (d) serve as a basis for complaint mechanisms regarding human rights violations by governments and international organizations; (e) inform debates on the allocation of scarce resources and strengthening the social consensus about relevant options.[24] Regarding right to health indicators specifically, the OHCHR advocates five attributes that relate to Article 12.2 ICESCR: sexual and reproductive health; healthcare and infant mortality; occupational and labor health; control, disease prevention and treatment; and access to essential healthcare service and medication. For each attribute, there are lists of structure, process, and result indicators.[25]

The proposal formulated by the Inter-American Commission on Human Rights focused on progress indicators related to economic, social, and cultural rights identified in the Protocol of San Salvador. The divergent aspects of the two proposals are emphasized in this study, while the conceptual and methodological elements shared by the approaches of the OHCHR and the Commission are not discussed in full. The Commission has chosen process indicators to verify the degree of accomplishment and effectiveness of human rights. It also observes that the indicators must be trustworthy, pertinent, empirically verifiable, sensible, relevant, independent, precise, valid, accessible, and available. In addition, it mentions the three types of indicators—structure, process, and result—that must be situated within three related conceptual categories: inclusion of the right; State

---

[21] OHCHR 2011.

[22] OHCHR 2008a, b.

[23] OHCHR 2008a.

[24] OHCHR 2011.

[25] OHCHR 2008a.

capacity; and financial context and budgetary commitment, as well as of three transversal principles: equality, access to justice, and access to information and participation.[26]

The first difference between the two concerns the conceptual categories, as they are not included in the OHCHR proposal. The first conceptual category regards the inclusion of the right into the legal system, into the institutional apparatus, and its insertion into public policies. For example, process indicators in the context of this category might include the verification of existing jurisprudence regarding the right, or the verification of the scope and coverage of the public policies established as a means to implement the right. The second category refers to the financial context, which encompasses State resource availability and allocation. This identifies whether there are available resources in the budget and whether they are being allocated in a way that promotes the realization of the right to health; it is not enough to guarantee use in public health programs and policies, as occurs in Brazil. Finally, the third category refers to institutional or State capacities—administrative, political, technical, and institutional; it aims to identify the problems and obstacles faced by decision-makers and to foster the adoption of administrative measures, so as to make economic, social, and cultural rights effective.[27]

According to the Commission, the obligation to ensure that economic, social, and cultural rights are carried out according to the principles of equality and nondiscrimination is to take immediate effect.

The Commission focuses on the right to health. It considers health a public good and recognizes that States must take measures aimed toward its realization. Such measures are: (a) the provision of basic healthcare; (b) the extension of healthcare services and products to all the individuals under the jurisdiction of a State; (c) universal immunization against the main infectious diseases; (d) the prevention and treatment of endemic, occupational, and other diseases; (e) health education aimed at prevention; (f) health care to meet the demands of high-risk populations and vulnerable groups.[28]

The OHCHR and the IACHR adopt similar methodologies regarding the development of human rights indicators. Both draw from normative tools to inform indicator selection: the OHCHR uses the International Covenant on Economic, Social and Cultural Rights and the IACHR uses Article 10 of the Protocol of San Salvador. However, the OHCHR uses attributes as a way to confer a concrete basis for indicators, while the IACHR uses Article 10 of the Protocol of San Salvador. Both prefer the use of structure, process, and result indicators as opposed to the Brazilian proposal, as will be discussed below. Another similarity between the OHCHR and the IACHR is that neither approach focuses on the living standards of individuals or whether individuals are effectively enjoying their rights; instead, both approaches are tied to the fulfillment of the obligations on the

---

[26] IACHR 2008.

[27] IACHR 2008.

[28] IACHR 2008.

9 The Brazilian Human Rights Indicators System: The Case of the Right to Health

part of the State. In other words, there is an important difference between the adoption of laws, policies, and programs on the part of the State, and their impact on the individual's health and enjoyment of the right to health. While the two approaches can be complementary, understanding their distinction is useful to the process of elaborating a human rights indicators system[29] as it allows for a more critical analysis of the two approaches when seeking to adapt them to the needs and reality of each country.

Neither document analyzes the usefulness of categorizing information according to the sources from which it was collected, such as human rights indicators, information on human rights violations, or information originating from administrative statistics, opinion polls, and expert inquiries.[30] The IACHR suggests dividing information into three categories in order to improve the possibility of analysis and better organize the information collected: incorporation of the right; state capabilities; and the financial context and budgetary commitment.[31] These categories are unique to the IACHR and they are not mentioned by the OHCHR. Both proposals understand the importance of disaggregating data according to prohibited grounds of discrimination in order to understand the experience of vulnerable and marginalized groups. Both also incorporate universal principles, although the IACHR places emphasis on the principles of access to justice and access to information, which are not mentioned by the OHCHR. Specifically in relation to the right to health, the OHCHR proposes attributes from which indicators are developed, while the IACHR proposes only indicators. The framework adopted by the Brazilian government uses attributes to develop indicators.

The model adopted by the Brazilian government, similar to the proposals by OHCHR and IACHR, is based on structure, process, and result indicators. The State obligations to respect, protect, and fulfill are used as a reference. Contrary to the IACHR proposals, the focus of the Brazilian government is not on financial expenditure, but on individual access to health, which cannot be inferred from the amount of money spent on health care. Also, in Brazil, emphasis is placed on result indicators, as they are better suited to express the enjoyment of the right to health, while the structure and process indicators are more suitable to demonstrate the progressive realization of the right.

9.3 Indicators of the Right to Health

In the field of public health, human rights represents one way of establishing the relationship between States—the main supplier of healthcare products and services—and individuals—the legal owners of such rights. The use of human rights

---

[29] Raworth 2005.

[30] Malhotra and Fasel 2005.

[31] IACHR 2008.

indicators by public healthcare agents is gradually improving. In addition, the use of indicators promotes a better understanding of the health status of the population and the performance of the healthcare systems. The World Health Organization's (WHO) Indicator Registry is a source of indicators not only for the WHO, but for other organizations as well. There is also the Global Health Observatory, which is a repository of data that contains an extensive list of health-related indicators.[32] Monitoring government adherence to human rights obligations is possible through health-related indicators. For example, the infant mortality rate can be used to verify the degree of fulfillment of the duty to provide healthcare services to children.[33] From a human rights perspective, new indicators must be established to introduce the human rights approach to public health; these indicators may be different from health-related indicators, which often fail to encompass any consideration of vulnerable groups. However, "many existing health indicators may be used, provided they are disaggregated on various grounds, such as sex, race and ethnicity."[34]

The UN Special Rapporteur on the Right to the Highest Attainable Standard of Physical and Mental Health uses the health-related indicators based on human rights principles. According to the Special Rapporteur, careful attention must be given to vulnerable and marginalized groups; to the active participation of the individuals affected; and to efficient, transparent, and accessible mechanisms for monitoring and giving account of their actions.[35] Hence, health-related indicators and indicators for the human right to health may impose similar standards. Human rights indicators may make use of traditional health-related indicators, proposed by the WHO, for example, by using disaggregation and the incorporation of new indicators, such as the ones relating to participation and accountability.[36]

Hunt affirms "that there is no alternative but to use indicators to measure and monitor the progressive realization of the right to the highest attainable standard of health."[37] Indeed, government progress toward meeting the healthcare demands of the population can be best understood using a combination of measures that establish points of reference in relation to each disaggregated indicator.[38] In this way, public policymakers or monitoring agencies can establish goals, and they can monitor the indicators so that adjustments can be made when undesirable outcomes appear or desirable outcomes are not met. It is important to point out that the outcome may have failed due to reasons beyond a State's control, and may not demonstrate that a State has failed to fulfill its obligations. Hence, indicators of the human right to health can be useful to assist policymakers in the field of health to

---

[32] WHO 2012.

[33] Gruskin and Ferguson 2009.

[34] Hunt 2006.

[35] Hunt 2006.

[36] Hunt 2006.

[37] Hunt 2006.

[38] Hunt 2006.

9 The Brazilian Human Rights Indicators System: The Case of the Right to Health 269

design programs and policies, and to monitor their outcomes. The indicators can also be used to help agencies and entities monitor the government's work in providing healthcare products and services to the population.

The mere appropriation of health-related indicators by a national human rights indicator system does not immediately turn them into "human rights indicators" or "indicators of the right to health." Hunt points out three criteria according to which health-related indicators might be understood as indicators of the right to health.[39] The first criterion presupposes a correspondence, with a certain degree of precision, between the health-related indicator and a norm of the human right to health deriving necessarily from Article 12 of the International Covenant on Economic, Social and Cultural Rights and from Article 10 of the Protocol of San Salvador. The second criterion imposes the disaggregation of data concerning a health-related indicator by gender, age group, race, ethnicity, rural or urban population, and socio-economic status. This criterion mirrors the importance of vulnerable and marginalized groups, as underscored by the OHCHR and the WHO.[40] Hunt states that some health problems imply special disaggregation, such as sexual and reproductive health, in which age disaggregation is crucial due to the health of adolescents. The third criterion regards the necessity of complementing health-related indicators with additional indicators that follow the five special characteristics of the human right to health: (a) the requirement that the State has a strategy and a national plan of action that include the right to health; (b) the participation of individuals and groups in the design of health policies and pro-grams, particularly from marginalized and vulnerable groups; (c) access to information about health, which implies the existence of indicators to measure the population's access to health information; (d) international assistance of donor States in relation to the human right to health; (e) effective and efficient mecha-nisms of accountability.[41]

Hunt formulates an approach that seeks to reconcile existing health-related indicators, such as infant and maternal death rates, and new indicators that enhance the understanding of specific aspects of the right to health, such as, the partici-pation of people affected by certain healthcare policies or programs and the ren-dering of accounts on the part of the State to show its responsible conduct. He stresses that health-related data should be disaggregated to capture inequalities and discrimination in order for it to be useful as a right to health indicator. Therefore, there is a specific category of indicators that encompass the nexus between the fields of health and of human rights, which are the indicators of the human right to health.[42]

In fact, among States' obligations listed in General Comment no. 14 is the duty to have indicators and points of reference related to the human right to health,

---

[39] Hunt 2006.

[40] OHCHR 2008a, b.

[41] Hunt 2006.

[42] Hunt 2006.

which allow the monitoring of any progress made. In a specific item about indicators and points of reference, the Committee establishes that national healthcare strategies must identify indicators with the intention to monitor, in the national and international scopes, the fulfillment of the obligations prescribed in Article 12 of the ICESCR. The indicators for the human right to health must encompass all the aspects of this right, "from the ongoing work of WHO and the United Nations Children's Fund (UNICEF) in this field."[43] Hence, once the indicators of the human right to health are identified, the States must establish national points of reference for the Committee to monitor their fulfillment.[44]

9.4 The Brazilian Human Rights Indicators System: The Case of the Human Right to Health

9.4.1 The Brazilian Human Rights Indicators System: Historical Process of Elaboration and Theoretical Bases

With the intention to carry out the task of developing a national human rights indicators system, in 2007 the Brazilian Government, by means of the Secretariat for Human Rights of the Presidency of the Republic, began a series of studies in Brazil by approaching civil society organizations working in this field. It also approached the Applied Economic Research Institute (IPEA), the Brazilian Institute of Geography and Statistics (IBGE), and Ministries whose competence relates to certain human rights. At the heart of such a task, the Brazilian Government made efforts to consolidate governmental and nongovernmental experiences on the use of human rights indicators. One example of this was a seminar in 2007, in which civil society organizations, the government, and research and statistics institutions[45] participated.

In 2008, within the scope of the Universal Periodic Review, Brazil restated its commitment to elaborating a national indicators system for human rights, affirming that such measures aim to strengthen human rights protection in the country.[46] Indicators deliver specific information regarding the state or the status of an event, activity or result, and can be quantitative or qualitative in nature. Quantitative human rights indicators alone may not be used to evaluate the State's commitment to its obligations; however, they provide a guideline for making such an assessment.[47]

---

[43] CESCR 2000.

[44] CESCR 2000.

[45] Telles et al. 2011.

[46] United Nations 2012.

[47] Malhotra and Fasel 2005.

In 2011, recognizing the three-year gap between the aforementioned measures and the release of information concerning the establishment of a Brazilian Human Rights Indicators System, the Secretariat of Human Rights of the Presidency of the Republic developed the "Information on Human Rights Project: Identifying Potentialities and Elaborating Indicators," in partnership with the Brazilian Agency of Cooperation, the UN Populations Fund and the UN Development Programme. The intention of this was to encourage support for the establishment of the national human rights indicators system. On that occasion, the Secretariat for Human Rights of the Presidency of the Republic, by means of General Coordinator of Information and Human Rights Indicators, reaffirmed the need for the development of a tool to assist "the formulation of policies and action, using data that express the Brazilian social reality in the perspective of the human rights, and not only in the sociological, geographic or economic perspective."[48] In addition, the Secretariat noted that the data available on vulnerable and marginalized groups in Brazil were not disaggregated, rendering it unhelpful in the development of public policies and programs that might be useful for those subpopulations.[49]

In February 2012, the Secretariat for Human Rights of the Presidency of the Republic conducted workshops for members of civil society, the academic community, governmental institutions, and international agencies. First, the workshops provided a platform for discussions with specific groups, such as civil society, the academic community, and governmental bodies, about the attributes of the human rights selected by the Secretariat, which are: the right to health, the right to education, the right to life, the right to social security, and the right to work.[50] In the following phase, the specific groups gathered in plenary sessions to share the outcomes of the initial discussions. The discussions held in the workshops afforded civil society an opportunity to participate in the development of the theoretical basis of the System alongside the government. The Secretariat for Human Rights of the Presidency of the Republic created the Technical Monitoring Committee (CTA) with the purpose of soliciting participation from civil society. Consequently, organizations from civil society presented a document to the Secretariat for Human Rights of the Presidency of the Republic, listing "the problems that they observed in the structure of the System."[51]

Also in 2012, the Secretariat for Human Rights of the Presidency of the Republic edited Administrative Rule no. 619, issued on May 22, 2012, which establishes the CTA, with the purpose being to define the methodological framework for the SNIDH, as well as to monitor the System's process of elaboration. The Technical Committee consists of representatives from the Secretariat for Human Rights of the Presidency of the Republic, the Applied Economic

---

[48] Telles et al. 2011.

[49] UNFPA 2011.

[50] Telles et al. 2011.

[51] INESCa 2012.

Research Institute (IPEA), the Brazilian Institute of Geography and Statistics (IBGE), organizations from civil society assigned by the Platform on Economic, Social, Cultural and Environmental Rights (the Dhesca Platform), and from the UN Agencies, assigned by the UN Development Programme. The Brazilian Human Rights Indicators System will encompass the following topics: access to justice, culture, education, freedom of speech, the environment and sustainable development, housing, social security and assistance, health care, public security, work and income, and life and participation in public issues.[52]

The first meeting of the Committee was held in August and comprised representatives from agencies and organizations. In the meeting, attendees discussed conceptual and methodological landmarks of the Brazilian Human Rights Indicators System with the intention to reach an agreement on the System's theoretical underpinnings.[53] It was decided that the System would not make a distinction between human rights indicators based on human rights violations on the one hand, and indicators based on data provided by administrative statistics, opinion polls, and experts' inquiries on the other. The CTA chose the structure-process-result indicators triad, with an emphasis on result indicators due to the fact that the enjoyment of rights by individuals is the core objective of the indicators system. Therefore, the System does not to focus on public policies and programs. The CTA considers attributes to be central to the identification of human rights indicators because "by identifying the major attributes of a right, the process of selecting suitable indicators or clusters of indicators is facilitated."[54] It also rejects the typology proposed by the IACHR: incorporation of the right, state capacities, and financial context and budgetary commitment. Regarding universal principles, the CTA emphasized the principles of equality, indivisibility, universality, and non-discrimination. It suggested the disaggregation of data related to vulnerable and marginalized groups, including gender, race, and geography, as well as the disclosure of Brazil's economic and social inequalities.[55]

Regarding the methodology, data must be collected in accordance with the international standards in order for it to be useful at the international level:

> [Q]uantitative indicators have to be explicitly and precisely defined, based on an acceptable methodology of data collection, processing and dissemination, and have to be available on a regular basis. The main methodological issue relates to data sources and generating mechanisms, criteria for selection of indicators and the amenability of the framework to support contextually relevant indicators.[56]

---

[52] SDHa 2012.

[53] INESCb 2012.

[54] OHCHR 2008a.

[55] SDHb, INESCb.

[56] OHCHR 2008a.

9 The Brazilian Human Rights Indicators System: The Case of the Right to Health   273

Making data regularly available allows for historical comparisons[57] to enable governments to track their progress over time in accordance with the "progressive realization" of the right to health.

In addition, the CTA formed Technical-Executive Groups regarding the rights to life, health, work, and education, with the aim to continue the development of a larger system. In other words, these Groups, formed by members from statistics institutions, civil society, the academic community, and governmental agencies and entities, have the task of defining the attributes of each right, as well as a corresponding set of indicators. The Technical-Executive Group related proposed attributes and indicators as detailed below to the human right to health.

9.4.2 The Current Stage of Development of the Brazilian Human Rights Indicators System Related to the Human Right to Health

The Technical-Executive Group responsible for the human right to health (hereinafter called "GTE Health") consists of two representatives from the Ministry of Health, one representative from the Applied Economic Research Institute, one representative from civil society, and two representatives from the Secretariat for Human Rights of the Presidency of the Republic. GTE Health conducted four meetings to define the attributes of the human right to health and the corresponding indicators. The meetings consisted of: (a) an evaluation and confirmation of the attributes proposed by the Ministry of Health and the Secretariat for Human Rights of the Presidency of the Republic and (b) indicators identification, subdivided into the following stages: evaluation of the indicators proposed by the Ministry of Health and by the Secretariat for Human Rights of the Presidency of the Republic; analysis of the indicators proposed by the OHCHR and the IACHR; proposal of new indicators; and, finally, identification of gaps[58] in indicators.

Following the work of GTE Health, the OHCHR identified five attributes for the human right to health: sexual and reproductive health, health care and infant mortality, occupational and labor environment, disease control, prevention and treatment, and access to essential healthcare services and medication.[59] When reviewing the attributes proposed by the OHCHR, the Ministry of Health suggested that sexual and reproductive health be kept, that the indicator referring to infant healthcare be modified to remove the isolated emphasis on infant mortality,[60] and that an attribute for healthy and protected childhood be inserted. The

---

[57] Telles et al. 2011.

[58] SDHc 2012.

[59] OHCHR 2008a.

[60] The infant mortality rate is one aspect of child health that encompasses policies and programs that have a much wider scope, like the policies/programs related to violence against children.

Ministry of Health stressed the use of the word "protected," as it is connected to the duty of the State to adopt measures to ensure children's security and address violence against children. Regarding the occupational and labor environment, the Ministry of Health proposed that it be separated into two: workers' health, and environmental health, in order to adapt the attributes to a more current context. It was proposed that accessibility of services and disease control, prevention and treatment should be treated as one, since the term "attention to health" includes disease prevention and treatment. Access to medication would have to be part of another attribute, according to the Ministry of Health, since the Brazilian Public Health System provides not only essential medication, but also high-cost drugs, prostheses, and other healthcare-related goods. Based on the proposals from the Ministry of Health, GTE Health adopted the following attributes for the human right to health: (a) sexual and reproductive health, (b) healthy and protected childhood, (c) equitable access to quality healthcare services, (d) workers' health, (e) environmental health, and (f) access to pharmaceutical assistance, prostheses, and other health products.[61]

Among the indicators proposed by the OHCHR and the IACHR, GTE Health contemplated the inclusion of attributes related to sexual and reproductive health, maternal mortality rate, and maternal mortality rate due to its cause (for example, due to unsafe or illegal abortion). Regarding healthy and protected childhood, GTE Health included the infant mortality rate, and mortality rate for those less than five-years old, including children from indigenous groups, the latter being an ongoing problem in Brazil. Regarding the attribute related to equal access to quality healthcare services, basic healthcare coverage and family expenditure on health care in relation to the family income is included. Regarding environmental health, the percentage of the population with access to potable water and the percentage of the population with access to basic sanitary services is included. Workers' health and access to pharmaceutical assistance, prostheses, and other health-related products are not indicators proposed by the OHCHR and the IACHR but were incorporated by GTE Health. GTE Health opted for a series of indicators related to issues that are specifically related to Brazil, such as "mortality rate due to work-related accidents among people insured under the Social Security," "work-related accidents and diseases among people insured under the Social Security," and "acute exogenous intoxication rate by agrochemicals" and "mortality rate by exogenous substances." Hence, Brazil gives greater emphasis to these attributes and to the issue of agrochemical use and their impact on the population's health.

GTE Health then began to identify indicators, focusing on only the result indicators, as explained above. Therefore, at this stage of the work, most indicators of the human right to health proposed by the OHCHR and the IACHR were not incorporated into their analyses because they were argued to be too specific or not applicable. For example, "prevalence of deaths, injuries, diseases and incapacities caused by an unhealthy environment"; "prevalence of deaths, injuries, diseases

---

[61] SDHc.

and incapacities caused by an unhealthy and unsafe work environment"; "mortality rate and the prevalence of communicable and noncommunicable diseases (such as HIV/AIDS, malaria, and tuberculosis)"; "number of hospital discharges by gender" and "service utilization rate" are not indicators used by Brazil. For example, the first and the second indicators are so overarching that they cannot be calculated and the last ones are imprecise and not valid and reliable. Others are not useful for capturing the Brazilian reality, such as "number of people covered by health insurance plans"; "number of women in reproductive age with anemia", and "number of children with abnormalities due to foetal malformation caused by the use of alcohol and other drugs." There are other indicators that, although relevant to the right to health, cannot be used in Brazil due to a lack of administrative data and research capacity. For example: "number of illegal abortions, by age, location (urban or rural) and socio-economic circumstances"; "healthcare coverage for the elderly"; "percentage of disabled people that have access to public and private healthcare"; and "treatment of disabled people in community healthcare facilities." Other indicators are not appropriate for the human rights approach including: "suicide rate"; "ratio of people who make use of harmful substances"; and "number of healthcare professionals who perform child birth delivery." The first two indicators are arguably related to individual lifestyle choices. The last one has already been addressed in Brazil; it is not only child delivery performed by healthcare professionals that can be safe to the mother. Thus, an indicator that does not capture the use of traditional birth attendants and focuses only on the professionals available would present an inaccurate illustration of access to birth attendants. Finally, some indicators are more suitable for the human right to life, including "mortality rate by age and sex"; "life expectancy at birth and up to year of age, and life expectancy adjusted to health"; and "domestic violence assistance rate."[62]

There is some overlap between the Brazilian Human Rights Indicators System and the proposals put forward by the OHCHR, mainly with regard to attributes. Despite some similarities, it was necessary to diverge from the proposals to select attributes to fit the Brazilian context. For example, the notion of 'attention to healthcare' and healthy and 'protected' childhood has particular significance in the Brazilian context. GTE Health proposed a smaller group of indicators than that advocated by the OHCHR and the IACHR. The reasons for this are related to relevancy, resource constraints, practical considerations, and disagreement among decision-makers. The need to adapt indicators to the realities in the country in which they are applied is recognized and, as such, indicators must reflect the healthcare challenges that still hinder the implementation of the right to health in Brazil. Some indicators could not be incorporated due to a lack of data on certain issues or populations. Others were deemed methodologically inappropriate due to their vague nature. Furthermore, there is some disagreement between GTE Health, the OHCHR, and the IACHR regarding the pertinence of certain indicators as

---

[62] SDHb, SDHc, SDHd and SDHe.

human rights indicators, since it is necessary to have a correlation between the health indicator and the normative understanding of the human right to health. GTE Health has attempted to adhere to the proposals by the UN Special Rapporteur for the Right to the Highest Attainable Standard of Physical and Mental Health, in order to select indicators that are in accordance with the international treaties on human rights. Similarly, GTE Health recognizes that the disaggregation of data with emphasis on vulnerable and marginalized groups is the key guiding principle for indicators of the human right to health.

9.5 Final Considerations

The human rights indicators system adopted by the Brazilian government reflects the choices made concerning concepts, attributes, and indicators referring to each right. This process included the participation of civil society organizations in all phases of its development. The attributes and indicators reflect the incorporation of the models devised by the UN and the WHO. While process indicators are used to highlight policies and programs that are in place, the particular emphasis on result indicators allows the system to focus on the experience of the right-holders, rather than on governmental actions. It also focuses on vulnerable populations, which is reflected in the emphasis on the disaggregation of data. Underlying this project is the assumption that a gap exists between health-related laws, policies, or programs, on the one hand, and the actual enjoyment of the right to health by the individual, on the other. The differences between the health indicators selected by the Brazilian government and those proposed by the OHCHR and the WHO can be classified as follows:

(1) the Brazilian system prescribes specific attributes for environmental health, workers' health, and access to medication as being the responsibilities of the State. The system also included indicators related to these topical issues, showing the government's concern with environmental health, and the importance of monitoring work-related illnesses;
(2) some indicators were excluded in Brazil because they cover issues that are not considered topical in the current context of Brazil, for example, the indicator related to younger women who have anemia, or the perinatal mortality rate;
(3) some indicators, despite being suitable from a human rights perspective, cannot be used in Brazil due to a lack of available data, for example, the ones referring to access to public healthcare services by the elderly or unsafe abortion;
(4) indicators that are vague or inadequate from a human rights perspective are not used in Brazil.

The Brazilian system deviates from the framework adopted by the UN and the WHO, making it a useful illustration of how international guidelines must not be incorporated without a thorough analysis of their compatibility with the context in which they are being inserted. Such an analysis must consider the significance of international guidelines to the specific health concerns of the population. It must also consider what data are available, and if these parameters can be adapted to serve the purpose at hand, which is monitoring the State's fulfillment of human rights.

It is known that each country has its own social, economic, and cultural realities. However, the Brazilian experience can be useful to demonstrate that the process of building a national system of indicators for human rights presupposes a genuine commitment from the government, as well as participation from civil society throughout the entire process, including in the selection of indicators. Similarly, having a conceptual idea of human rights indicators at the beginning of the process is recommended, as this eases the process of selecting attributes and indicators. It is important to point out that the governmental agencies that deal with statistics are fundamental to the entire process, as well as other specialized agencies. Most of the Brazilian data are not disaggregated, which challenges the usefulness of the indicators system for monitoring accessibility for vulnerable populations. The delay in the construction of the Brazilian system highlights the need for the commitment of all actors—civil society, agencies, and the government. In other words, it involves collaboration between society and the State, and as such the advances brought about by human rights that derive from social and governmental engagement.

References

Literature

Gruskin S, Ferguson L (2009) Using indicators to determine the contribution of human rights to public health efforts. Bull World Health Organ 87:714–719

Hunt P (2006) Informe del Relator Especial sobre el Derecho de toda Persona al Disfrute del más alto nivel posible de salud física y mental. Comision de Derechos Humanos: www.ohchr.org/EN/Issues/Health/Pages/AnnualReports.aspx. Accessed 20 Oct 2012

Malhotra R, Fasel N (2005) Report of Turku expert meeting on human rights indicators: www.humanrightsimpact.org/resource-database/publications/resources/view/102/user_hria_publications/. Accessed 20 Oct 2012

Raworth K (2005) Measuring human rights. In: Gruskin S et al (eds) Perspectives on health and human rights. Routledge, New York, pp 393–411

Telles J et al (2011) Por um Sistema Nacional de Indicadores de Direitos Humanos. Revista Brasileira de Monitoramento e Avaliação. n. 2, Julho–Dezembro, 2011

Documentation

Brasil (2009) Brasil. Decreto n° 7.037, de 21 de dezembro de 2009. www.planalto.gov.br/ccivil_03/_Ato2007-2010/2009/Decreto/D7037.htm. Accessed 20 Oct 2012

CESCR (2000) Committee on Economic, Social and Cultural Rights - CESCR. Observación general 14, El derecho al disfrute del más alto nivel posible de salud (artículo 12 del Pacto Internacional de Derechos Económicos, Sociales y Culturales). 2000. www.umn.edu/humanrts/gencomm/epcomm14s.htm. Accessed 20 Oct 2012

INESCa. www.inesc.org.br/noticias/noticias-do-inesc/2012/fevereiro/sociedade-civil-aponta-problemas-na-construcao-do-sistemas-de-indicadores-dos-direitos-humanos. Accessed 20 Oct 2012

INESCb. www.inesc.org.br/biblioteca/inesc-noticia/edicao-no34-30-08-2010/sistema-de-indicadores-dos-direitos-humanos. Accessed 20 Oct 2012

IACHR (2008) Inter-American Commission of Human Rights—IACHR. Guidelines for preparation of progress indicators in the area of economic, social and cultural rights. http://cidh.org/pdf%20files/Guidelines%20final.pdf. Accessed 20 Oct 2012

OHCHR (2008a) Office of the High Commission for Human Rights—OHCHR. Report on Indicators for Promoting and Monitoring the Implementation of Human Rights (HRI/MC/2008/3). http://www2.ohchr.org/english/issues/indicators/docs/HRI.MC.2008.3_en.pdf. Accessed July 2014

OHCHR (2008b) Office of the High Commission for Human Rights—OHCHR; World Health Organization—WHO. The right to health—Fact Sheet no. 31. www.ohchr.org/Documents/Publications/Factsheet31.pdf. Accessed 20 Oct 2012

OHCHR (2011) Office of the High Commission for Human Rights—OHCHR. Report of the United Nations High Commissioner for Human Rights to the Economic and Social Council, Geneva 4–29 July 2011 (E/2011/90). http://www.ohchr.org/Documents/Issues/ESCR/E_2011_90_en.pdf. Accessed 20 Oct 2012

OHCHR (2013) Office of the High Commission for Human Rights—OHCHR. www.ohchr.org/EN/Issues/Indicators/Pages/HRIndicatorsIndex.aspx. Accessed 20 Oct 2013

SDHa (2012) Secretaria de Direitos Humanos da Presidência da República—SDHa. Portaria n° 619, de 12 de maio de 2012. Disponível em: ftp://ftp.saude.sp.gov.br/ftpsessp/bibliote/informe_eletronico/2012/iels.mai.12/Iels97/U_PT-PR-SDH-619_220512.pdf. Accessed 20 Oct 2012

SDHb (2012) Ata da 1ª Reunião do Comitê Técnico de Acompanhamento do Sistema Nacional de Indicadores de Direitos Humanos realizada em agosto de 2012. www.dropbox.com/sh/gzc7uuppg07sc81/DuVlDUJf0t/Saude. Accessed 20 Oct 2012

SDHc (2012) Ata da 1ª Reunião do Grupo Técnico-Executivo do Direito à Saúde do Sistema Nacional de Indicadores de Direitos Humanos realizada em outubro de 2012. www.dropbox.com/sh/gzc7uuppg07sc81/DuVlDUJf0t/Saude. Accessed 20 Oct 2012

SDHd (2012) Ata da 2ª Reunião do Grupo Técnico-Executivo do Direito à Saúde do Sistema Nacional de Indicadores de Direitos Humanos realizada em outubro de 2012. www.dropbox.com/sh/gzc7uuppg07sc81/DuVlDUJf0t/Saude. Accessed 20 Oct 2012

SDHe (2012) Ata da 3ª Reunião do Grupo Técnico-Executivo do Direito à Saúde do Sistema Nacional de Indicadores de Direitos Humanos realizada em outubro de 2012. www.dropbox.com/sh/gzc7uuppg07sc81/DuVlDUJf0t/Saude. Accessed 20 Oct 2012

SDHf (2012) Ata da 4ª Reunião do Grupo Técnico-Executivo do Direito à Saúde do Sistema Nacional de Indicadores de Direitos Humanos realizada em outubro de 2012. 2012. www.dropbox.com/sh/gzc7uuppg07sc81/DuVlDUJf0t/Saude. Accessed 20 Oct 2012

United Nations (2012). Informe nacional presentado con arreglo al párrafo 5 del anexo de la resolución 16/21del Consejo de Derechos Humanos. http://daccess-dds-ny.un.org/doc/UNDOC/GEN/G12/116/21/PDF/G1211621.pdf?OpenElement Accessed 24 Oct 2012

UNDP (2000). United Nations Development Program—UNDP. Human Development Report 2000. http://hdr.undp.org/sites/default/files/reports/261/hdr_2000_en.pdf. Accessed 20 Oct 2012

UNFPA (2011) United Nations Population Fund—UNFPA. www.onu.org.br/brasil-comeca-a-desenvolver-sistema-de-indicadores-sobre-direitos-humanos-em-parceria-com-pnud-e-unfpa/. Accessed 20 Oct 2012

WHO (2012) World Health Organization—WHO. https://www.who.int/gho/indicator_registry/en/. Accessed 23 Oct 2012

Chapter 10
Aboriginal-Specific Health Initiatives and Accessible Health Care in Canada; Are Goodwill Initiatives Enough

Rhonda Ferguson

Abstract This chapter examines aspects of two initiatives with the potential to improve access to culturally appropriate health care in Canada: the *Traditional Healer Travel Fund* as part of the *Non-Insured Health Benefits* program and the *Aboriginal Healing and Wellness Strategy* in Ontario. Representing only two of a number of current Aboriginal-specific initiatives across the country, they have been chosen because they exemplify the obstacles to and achievements of improved access to acceptable health care in the Canadian political, legal, and cultural context. The essential elements of the right to health as listed by the Committee on Economic, Social, and Cultural Rights in General Comment 14 are employed as the criteria for assessing congruencies between the above-mentioned initiatives and the human right to health. Underpinning this research is the question of whether goodwill initiatives are sufficient to ensure the availability and accessibility of culturally appropriate health care for Aboriginal Peoples. Ultimately, respect for the ongoing calls by First Nations, Métis, and Inuit communities to define and address local needs through Aboriginal-led and Aboriginal-driven initiatives is argued to be fundamental to the realization of the right to health. While "culturally appropriate" health care is best defined by the community using it, governments have an important role in facilitating availability and access through partnership, commitment, and reliable long-term support for Aboriginal-led and Aboriginal-driven initiatives. Tying government's role to human rights obligations will help to ensure greater accountability, respect for the principles of nondiscrimination and equality, and an enabling environment in which Aboriginal Peoples' self-determination can be exercised.

R. Ferguson (✉)
Irish Centre for Human Rights, National University of Ireland Galway, University Road, Galway, Ireland
e-mail: r.ferguson1@nuigalway.ie

B. Toebes et al. (eds.), *The Right to Health*, DOI: 10.1007/978-94-6265-014-5_10,   281
© T.M.C. ASSER PRESS and the authors 2014

Contents

10.1	Introduction	282
	10.1.1 Cultural Responsibility and Contextualization	284
	10.1.2 Background	286
10.2	Aboriginal Peoples and Health Care Entitlements in Canada, an Overview	287
	10.2.1 Who are the Aboriginal Peoples of Canada?	287
	10.2.2 Basic Overview of Aboriginal Health	288
	10.2.3 Barriers to Health Care	291
	10.2.4 Conceptions of Health	293
10.3	The Right to Health for Aboriginal Peoples	294
	10.3.1 Sources in International Law	295
	10.3.2 Sources in Canadian Law	295
	10.3.3 The Canada Health Act	296
	10.3.4 Treaty 6	296
	10.3.5 Judgments and Recognition	297
	10.3.6 Entitlements According to Status	298
	10.3.7 Indian Act	298
10.4	Aboriginal-Specific Initiatives	300
	10.4.1 NIHB	301
	10.4.2 Aboriginal Healing and Wellness Strategy	303
10.5	Conclusions	307
References		308

10.1 Introduction

The founding document of Canada's universal healthcare system, the Canada Health Act, promotes the availability and accessibility of quality health care for all citizens without discrimination. Notwithstanding the absence of an enshrined right to the highest attainable standard of mental and physical health in Canada, the Canada Health Act embodies many of its tenets. Consequently, Canadians, on average, enjoy good access to health care and a relatively high standard of health.[1] However, disaggregated data highlights persistent gaps in health status between Aboriginal[2] and non-Aboriginal populations—indications that the progressive realization of the right to health is not occurring for everyone equally. Specifically, the availability and accessibility of culturally appropriate care varies according to one's location (urban, off-reserve, or on-reserve), identity, and status with the country's Indian Registry. Additionally, what is 'culturally appropriate' varies

---

[1] World Health Organization 2013.

[2] According to the Royal Commission on Aboriginal Peoples (1996), the term "'Aboriginal peoples' refers to organic political and cultural entities that stem historically from the original peoples of North America, rather than collections of individuals united by so-called 'racial' characteristics". See Royal Commission on Aboriginal Peoples 1996, Vol. 1, A note about sources.

according to each community. While General Comment 14 states that culturally appropriate care is "respectful of the culture of individuals, minorities, peoples and communities",[3] this definition remains quite general. Communities themselves must define what is acceptable, though generally speaking, health care should be community-based, holistic and integrate traditional knowledge. While much of discourse surrounding Aboriginal health has shifted to focus on the determinants of health, access to culturally appropriate health care remains crucial for the improvement of well-being of individuals and communities.

This chapter examines aspects of federal and provincial-Aboriginal initiatives with the potential to improve access to culturally appropriate health care: the *Traditional Healer Travel Fund* as part of the *Non-Insured Health Benefits* (NIHB) program and the *Aboriginal Healing and Wellness Strategy* (AHWS) in Ontario. The essential elements of the right to health as listed by the Committee on Economic, Social, and Cultural Rights in General Comment 14—the availability, acceptability, accessibility, and quality of health care (AAAQ)—will be employed as the criteria for assessing congruencies between the above-mentioned initiatives and the human right to health. As such, this chapter: highlights the disproportionate disease burden borne by Aboriginal Peoples; provides an overview of two Aboriginal-specific healthcare initiatives; and assesses the extent to which the initiatives adhere to aspects of the normative content of right to health as outlined in General Comment 14. Underpinning these objectives is the question of whether goodwill initiatives involving federal, provincial, and territorial governments are sufficient to ensure the availability and accessibility of culturally appropriate health care for Aboriginal Peoples.

A host of initiatives could be employed here to exemplify opportunities to improve access to culturally appropriate care—the Kelowna Accord (2005)[4] and the Indian Health Transfer Policy (1988)[5] immediately come to mind. However, many of these initiatives have since expired or else their history exceeds the economy of this chapter. Indeed, because of changing political tides—one of the problems preventing long-term solutions—the Kelowna Accord never came to fruition.[6] The Indian Health Transfer Policy on the other hand has had some success in terms of transferring control to Aboriginal Peoples, though it has also

---

[3] UN Committee on Economic, Social and Cultural Rights 2010 at 12(c).

[4] The Kelowna Accord embodied a ten-year plan to reduce the health and welfare gap between Aboriginal and non-Aboriginal Canadians and emphasized Aboriginal control over health services. Negotiations involved five Aboriginal groups, as well as representatives from provincial and federal governments. In 2006 the new federal government reneged on its commitment to the agreements in the Kelowna Accord made by its predecessor. See Webster 2006, p. 275.

[5] The Indian Health Transfer Policy (1988) "provided a framework for the assumption of control of health services by First Nations people, and set forth a developmental approach to transfer centered on the concept of self-determination in health". Health Canada 2005. Interestingly, "self-determination" was removed from government discourse around the Indian Health Transfer Policy in 1999. Moreover, despite some success, the policy's usefulness for inter alia improving access to traditional healing is debatable. See Jacklin and Warry 2004, pp. 220–230.

[6] Webster 2006, p. 275.

been criticized as a government-led attempt to reduce spending on Aboriginal Health and an opportunity for the government to abandon its responsibilities toward Aboriginal Peoples, while doing little to improve access to culturally appropriate care.[7] In fact, numerous initiatives to improve Aboriginal health and health care through greater self-determination have been undertaken, with varying degrees of success, since the Indian Health Policy (1979) was presented.[8] Most recently, in British Columbia, the transfer of total control and resources for First Nations health from the federal government to the First Nations Health Authority in October 2013 might be hailed a success for Aboriginal self-government and self-determination.[9] However, it will take some time before the outcomes of the transfer will be understood.

The chapter is divided into five sections: the remainder of Sect. 10.1 introduces the topic and provides background information; Sect. 10.2 provides a brief socio-demographic overview of Aboriginal Peoples in Canada and highlights key metrics to describe the health status of Aboriginal Peoples; Sect. 10.3 introduces what the right to health and related entitlements mean in the context of Canada; Sect. 10.4 presents two Aboriginal-specific healthcare initiatives, challenges to their implementation, and discussion of how they relate the AAAQ elements of the right to health; and Sect. 10.5—the conclusion—projects a greater self-determination, balanced with long-term commitment, support, and recognition of responsibilities by all levels of government, as central to the realization of the right to health by Aboriginal populations.

10.1.1 Cultural Responsibility and Contextualization

This chapter has been undertaken with the notion of cultural responsibility in mind. In this context, cultural responsibility is understood as undertaking research in a way that is respectful to those affected, mindful of how the information presented might be used, and accessible to those to whom it relates.[10] As such, careful consideration has been given to ensure that the subject matter is the health care initiatives presented and how they adhere to dimensions of the right to health; it is not meant to illustrate the diverse experiences, or attempt to speak on behalf of, individuals. When possible, data gathered through research that adheres to the

---

[7] Speck 1989, 187, Jacklin and Warry 2004, pp. 220–230.

[8] The Indian Health Policy is a federal policy "to achieve an increasing level of health in Indian communities, generated and maintained by the Indian communities themselves". It is premised upon three pillars encompassing the issues of community development, the relationship between Indians and the government (with the government as an advocate for Indians), and the health care system. Health Canada 2005.

[9] First Nations Health Authority 2013.

[10] Personal Communication. Dr. Michael Hankard (Hankard 2013) University of Sudbury, Department of Indigenous Studies.

principles of Ownership, Control, Access, and Possession (OCAP) is used, as advocated by the Steering Committee of the First Nations Regional Longitudinal Health Survey and National Aboriginal Health Organization (NAHO) among other organizations.[11]

In Sect. 10.2 statistics on the health status of Aboriginal populations are presented. Some authors have cautioned about the "use of epidemiological statistics to draw attention to inequities in health status" arguing that doing so "run[s] the risk of perpetuating a view of Aboriginal communities as sick, disorganized, and dependent—a view that reinforces unequal power relations and that may be used to justify paternalism and dependence."[12] To avoid this, some suggest describing ill health as "connected to experiences of colonialism, racism, poverty, and despair".[13] A thorough discussion of root causes of ill health are beyond the scope of this research, yet attempts have been made to reinforce the fact that the full realization of the right to health for Aboriginal Peoples depends on addressing past abuses and rebuilding the relationship between Aboriginal Peoples and the government. Although access to health care is only one of many determinants of health, it nonetheless remains a vital component of health.

While international instruments provide the framework used, mapping this framework onto a local context in a way that is culturally responsible involves employing language that is meaningful, locally. Originating in New Zealand, the term, 'cultural safety' is widely considered a key element of health care that is accessible and appropriate for Aboriginal communities in Canada.[14] Cultural safety shares similarities with the notion of cultural appropriateness in General Comment 14, although the term "culturally appropriate" is not uniformly accepted by Aboriginal Peoples in Canada.[15] It is an approach to health care that views health challenges faced by Aboriginal populations in the context of post-contact history.[16] According to the Health Council of Canada report, cultural safety in health care is:

> [A]n outcome, defined and experienced by those who receive a service—they feel safe; based on respectful engagement that can help patients find paths to well-being; is based on understanding the power differentials inherent in health service delivery, the institutional discrimination, and the need to fix these inequities through education and system change; and requires acknowledgement that we are all bearers of culture—there is self-reflection about one's own attitudes, beliefs, assumptions, and values.[17]

---

[11] Schnarch 2004, p. 80.

[12] Browne et al. 2005, 31.

[13] Ibid.

[14] Brascoupe and Waters 2009, p. 6, 7; Health Council of Canada 2012, p. 4.

[15] Jacklin and Warry note that the term "culturally appropriate" is not universally accepted in the Wikwemikong community; some felt that the term does not reflect the diverse cultures within the community. Jacklin and Warry 2004, p. 232.

[16] Brascoupe and Waters 2009, pp. 6–7.

[17] Health Council of Canada 2012, at p. 5.

In regard to healthcare services, culturally safe practices involve trust-building, respect for the patient's beliefs and values, and decision-making opportunities for the patient.[18] In the context of Canada, the concepts of cultural safety and culturally appropriate care, as discussed in General Comment 14, can be considered complementary.

10.1.2 Background

Today in Canada, Aboriginal Peoples bear a disproportionate disease burden and report lower levels of physical and mental health and well-being than the non-Aboriginal population. Aboriginal Peoples not only face greater obstacles to the social determinants of health, but additional determinants particular to the history of colonization in Canada have had lasting, intergenerational impacts on individual and community health. The effects of the residential school system,[19] forced relocation from traditional lands,[20] and the outlawing of traditional practices[21] are still felt by communities. Aboriginal Peoples' interaction with Western medicine throughout the nineteenth and twentieth centuries have been marred by abuses such as those that occurred through racially segregated "Indian hospitals,"[22] medical experimentation,[23] and attempts to abolish healing practices.[24] Not surprisingly, these experiences have fostered a sense of distrust among many Aboriginal Peoples toward Western-based medicine[25] and have left lingering effects on the health and well-being of communities.

In addition to distrust, Aboriginal Peoples have cited racism and a lack of culturally appropriate options as barriers to health care, and effectively, to health.[26] To compound the issue, at the policy level, discriminatory rules, lack of coordination among levels of government, and pervasive paternalistic attitudes toward Aboriginal peoples hinder concerted efforts by Aboriginal leaders, communities, and governments to address the abuses of the past and the health concerns of the

---

[18] Ibid.

[19] The residential school system, which occurred between 1884 and 1948, forcibly removed children from their communities for the purpose of assimilation. The systemic physical, sexual and emotional abuse that occurred in the schools has been widely documented. See the Royal Commission on Aboriginal Peoples 1996, Vol 1, Part 2, Chap. 10.

[20] Royal Commission on Aboriginal Peoples 1996 Vol 1, Part 2, Chap. 11 (for the effects of the relocation on health, see Chap. 11, Sect. 4.3).

[21] Royal Commission on Aboriginal Peoples 1996 Vol 3, Chap. 3, Sect. 1.1.

[22] See generally, Lux 2010.

[23] Aboriginal Peoples were used as subjects in experiments relating to vaccine trials and nutrition. See generally Mosby 2013, Lux 1998.

[24] Royal Commission on Aboriginal Peoples Vol 3, Chap. 3, Sect. 1.1.

[25] Health Council of Canada 2012 at p. 15.

[26] Ibid, p. 4.

present. Notwithstanding these challenges, health initiatives aimed at improving health equity have been undertaken as a response to the fiduciary responsibilities owed by governments to Aboriginal peoples in some cases, and in others, as a result of the demands of Aboriginal Peoples for opportunities to exercise greater control over services.

The right to health encompasses more than simply the availability of health care services and products; it includes consideration of the determinants of health and is interdependent on the realization of other human rights listed in the International Bill of Human Rights.[27] This chapter is anchored firmly in the understanding of the right to health as it appears in Article 12 of the ICESR and elaborated by General Comment 14, however, the primary focus here is on the AAAQ of *health care* available to Aboriginal Peoples as exemplified by two initiatives. The principles of nondiscrimination and equality are important considerations; as essential overlapping dimensions of the right to health they must be ensured at all stages of service development and delivery.

10.2 Aboriginal Peoples and Health Care Entitlements in Canada, an Overview

10.2.1 Who are the Aboriginal Peoples of Canada?

The term Aboriginal describes indigenous Peoples in what is now known as Canada. According to the 2011 Census of Canada, 1,400,685 people self-identify as Aboriginal. Within this population, the census identified approximately 851,560 First Nations (North American Indians), 451,795 Métis, and 59,445 Inuit.[28] However, the actual number of Aboriginal persons in each category is believed to be higher than that reported by the Census findings; incomplete or nonparticipation by some First Nations communities[29] and reluctance to self-identify to government employees[30] contribute to inaccuracies in data collection. The terms First Nations, Inuit, and Métis refer to the three groups of Peoples recognized by the Constitution, yet each refer to a heterogeneous group of people that are culturally, linguistically, and geographically unique.[31] For the purpose of this chapter, however, the three broad categories of Peoples are frequently used due to the fact that much of the quantitative research available has employed such categories.

---

[27] UN Committee on Economic, Social and Cultural Rights 2000 at p. 3.

[28] Statistics Canada 2011, p. 6 http://www12.statcan.gc.ca/nhs-enm/2011/as-sa/99-011-x/99-011-x2011001-eng.pdf (Accessed 5 October 2013).

[29] Ibid at p. 6.

[30] Smylie 2009, p. 281.

[31] Ibid.

'First Nations' came into use during the 1970's to replace the term 'Indian,' which was the erroneous term given by early colonizers and offensive to many people (though it remains in key federal legislation regulating the relationship between Aboriginal Peoples and the government, such as the Indian Act).[32] There are 630 First Nations communities in Canada, which encompass over 60 distinct nations and languages.[33] Interestingly, there is no legal definition of First Nations. It can refer collectively to groups of Aboriginal Peoples or it may appear in singular form to replace the word "band" in a community name (e.g., Lac la Ronge First Nation).[34] Inuit (which translates to "the people" in Inuktituk) originate from the Arctic regions and belong to the larger circumpolar Inuit population.[35] Métis are a group of people "of mixed blood",[36] that is, of both Aboriginal and European ancestry, however, there is no agreement on what per se constitutes a Métis person or people.[37] In fact, among the various Métis organizations in the country there are divergent views on what criteria determine membership in this group. However, the following definition was accepted by the Métis National Council, British Columbia, Alberta, Saskatchewan, and Manitoba:

Métis means an Aboriginal person who self-identifies as Métis, who is distinct from Indian and Inuit and is a descendant of those Métis who received or were entitled to receive land grants and/or Scrip under the provisions of the Manitoba Act 1870 or Dominion Lands Act as enacted from time to time.[38]

Though these three categories are used to identify Aboriginal Peoples, and have a role in determining the rights and entitlements of individuals, they have "little or no correlation with culturally meaningful groupings."[39] Individuals may identify more closely with their band or nation, rather than broad classifications imposed by the state (i.e., one may primarily identify as Mi'kmaq, Ojibwe, or Anishinabek). There are other forms of imposed classification, such as the dichotomous status/nonstatus classification, which will be dealt with below.

10.2.2 Basic Overview of Aboriginal Health

Although health disparities between Aboriginal and non-Aboriginal populations are reducing, Aboriginal Peoples continue to rank lower on nearly all commonly

---

[32] Aboriginal Affairs and Northern Development Canada 2012.

[33] Assembly of First Nations (n.d.) http://www.afn.ca/index/php/en/about-afn/description-of-the-afn (Accessed 5 October 2013).

[34] National Aboriginal Health Organization 2013.

[35] Ibid.

[36] Ibid.

[37] Stevenson 2002, p. 241.

[38] Ibid, p. 242.

[39] MacIntosh 2008, p. 397.

used indicators for health—including life expectancy, prevalence of disease, infant mortality, and injuries. When data is disaggregated according to Métis, Inuit, and First Nations, health disparities become greater. A 2004 study by the Canadian Population Health Initiative showed that the life expectancy of Status First Nations women is five years lower than that of Canadian women, and the life expectancy of Status First Nations men is 7 years lower than that of Canadian men.[40] This gap is even greater when looking specifically at the Inuit population: the life expectancy of Inuit women and men is 12 and 8 years lower than that of non-Aboriginal women and men, respectively.[41]

The overall disease burden of both communicable and noncommunicable disease is greater for Aboriginal Peoples and statistics show that the disparities between some groups are even more pronounced. For example, according to the Inuit Tapiriit Kanatami organization, the rate of tuberculosis among first nations and Inuit populations is 31 and 185 times higher than that of Canadian-born, non-Aboriginals, respectively.[42] In 2010, it was noted by the organization that the rate of tuberculosis among Inuit has doubled over the past four years. According to the Chair of Inuit Tapiriit Kanatami's National Inuit Committee on Health, "[i]t is unconscionable that these conditions exist in a country that boasts of having one of the lowest TB rates in the world."[43] Chief Angus Toulouse cited "overcrowded housing, poor nutrition and lack of access to health care"[44] as important factors contributing to disease among Aboriginal Peoples.

The prevalence of chronic, non-communicable diseases is also on the rise among Aboriginal Peoples, with the increase in diabetes perhaps most alarming. Studies show 17.2 % of First Nations populations (living on-reserve) and 7.3 % of Métis have diabetes, compared to 5.0 % of non-Aboriginal population.[45] To complicate matters, treatment for diabetes is particularly difficult to administer: the required lifestyle changes, lack of local treatment options, and the high cost of healthy foods in remote communities sometimes prevent compliance with treatment plans.[46]

Overall, the rate of infant mortality among Aboriginal Peoples (and the total Canadian population) has decreased over the past 30 years, yet disparities between First Nations, Inuit, Metis, and the total Canadian Population remain significant. Researchers argue that despite gaps in data availability across provinces and territories, it is estimated that First Nations and Inuit have infant mortality rates are approximately two and four times higher than the total Canadian population.[47]

---

[40] Canadian Institute for Health Information 2004, p. 81.

[41] Ibid.

[42] Inuit Tapiriit Kanatami 2010.

[43] Ibid.

[44] Ibid.

[45] Public Health Agency of Canada 2011.

[46] Waldron et al. 2006, p. 100.

[47] Smylie et al. 2010, p. 146.

No comparable information is available for Métis, though the authors of the study assert that the "census socio-demographic profile of this population strongly suggests a population at risk for high infant mortality and morbidity."[48]

Suicide rates for Status First Nations and Inuit Peoples are also significantly higher than that of the non-Aboriginal population. Status First Nations Peoples have a suicide rate twice as high as the Canadian population (24 per 100,000 people) and Inuit Peoples have a rate ten times higher than that of the Canadian population (135 per 100,000).[49] Though there is a lack of data on suicide rates for all Aboriginal Peoples across the country.[50]

Aboriginal women are nearly three and a half times more likely to experience violence than non-Aboriginal women and three times more likely to experience spousal violence.[51] Moreover, Aboriginal women experience more severe forms of family violence, including life-threatening assault (54 % of Aboriginal women versus 37 % of non-Aboriginal women).[52] Registered Indian women (ages 25–44) are also five times more likely than other women of the same age to die from the violence they experience.[53] Despite the disproportionate rates of violence experienced by Aboriginal women in Canada, the Canadian government recently rejected calls at the United Nations' Universal Period Review to conduct a review of violence against Aboriginal women.[54]

10.2.2.1 Lack of Available Data

Despite an impressive amount of data collected on the health of the general population, the health status of subpopulations is less well known because disaggregated data for some measures is unavailable. Data on the health status, healthcare access, and socio-economic conditions of Métis and nonstatus Aboriginal Peoples is perhaps most scarce. Indeed, for some health metrics there is no disaggregated information available for Métis, despite the fact that many face health challenges similar to other Aboriginal Peoples. According to a statement by the Health Council of Canada in 2005:

> [T]he life expectancy of the Métis is unknown as are rates for infant mortality, low birth weight, and types of cancer that most commonly cause death in the Métis population. Other major mortality causes are unknown ... the rate and type of communicable diseases affecting the Métis are also unknown, with the exception of some data on HIV/AIDS.[55]

---

[48] Idem 2010, p. 146, 147.

[49] Kirmayer et al. 2007, p. 14.

[50] Idem, p. 15.

[51] Native Women's Association of Canada (n.d.), p. 2.

[52] Ibid.

[53] Indian and Northern Affairs Canada 1996, n.p. in Amnesty International 2004, p. 14.

[54] Canadian Broadcast Corporation 2013.

[55] Allard 2007, p. 16.

10 Aboriginal-Specific Health Initiatives and Accessible Health Care in Canada 291

Further surveillance and analysis of the health status of underrepresented populations such as Métis could serve to better inform policies and programs delivered to them. The absence of data in itself may be regarded as an indication of vulnerability to ill health; without empirical data demonstrating the issues particular to specific subpopulations, there is little evidence upon which improvements to health policies or programs can be initiated. Seen another way, the failure to collect useful data on subpopulations accentuates their vulnerability. Individuals and communities can become invisible while decision-makers avoid accountability.

Collecting and interpreting data in ways that identify health vulnerabilities is complicated by the fragmented nature of healthcare responsibilities in Canada. Agencies and organizations operating at local, provincial and federal levels may employ different research methodologies or protocols, rendering information from different sources incomparable. Funding cuts by the federal government to the country-wide Aboriginal health research organization, the NAHO, has forced this facility—which conducted nation-wide research on all Aboriginal Peoples, made information accessible online, and housed important historical information—to cease operations. Moreover, recent changes to the national census will make the relationships between socio-demographic and health data more difficult to determine in the future. In 2010 the federal government announced that completing the "long form"[56] version of the survey is no longer mandatory. This means that some questions related to socio-economic status are now optional, as opposed to obligatory. As a result, the usefulness of future census data to demonstrate connections between socio-economic conditions, group membership, and health status is limited. The absence of empirical data easily lends itself to the abdication of responsibility by government.

From available data, it is clear that despite universal health care, Aboriginal Peoples continue to experience a greater disease burden. The disparities in health status have multiple contributing factors rooted in post-contact history and present-day barriers to the determinants of health. This gap will not be reduced by health-specific research or initiatives alone, ensuring the AAAQ of health care remains essential to improving well-being.

10.2.3 Barriers to Health Care

Economic and physical access to health care is listed as essential to the right to health in General Comment 14.[57] While research conducted by the National Collaborating Centre for Aboriginal Health (NCCAH) does not use the same language, it lists a variety of socio-economic and geographic barriers among those

---

[56] The "long form" census is a version of the Census of Canada that covered a wide variety of questions, including questions relevant to socio-economic status and health.

[57] UN Committee on Economic, Social and Cultural Rights 2000, at 12 (b).

experienced by Aboriginal Peoples, particularly those who live in remote Northern communities. Barriers such as a lack of education and employment opportunities, low income, and poor housing conditions create situations where individuals are unable to pay for goods and services that are not covered under healthcare schemes and are billed by physicians.[58] Inability to pay for treatment means that individuals may delay or avoid visiting a doctor. Additionally, the conditions on reservations have led to people to migrate to urban areas, where some people end up homeless,[59] which poses additional challenges to accessing care such as difficulty proving that one has insurance coverage.[60] Geographic barriers include "lack of transportation infrastructure, [...] long wait times, inadequate human resources, and northern climate conditions"[61] (which impact road access and travel). Authors also cite communication and language barriers as challenges to accessing health care.[62]

In a 2012 report by the Health Council of Canada, interviewees across the country cited deep distrust and fear of racism in healthcare settings as reasons for not accessing available care.[63] Healthcare professionals and patients recounted hearing racial slurs and experiencing discrimination, for example, refusal by some doctors to prescribe painkillers based on the assumption Aboriginal Peoples are likely to abuse prescription drugs.[64] Interviewees reported incidents wherein Aboriginal people in emergency departments "were assumed to be under the influence of drugs or alcohol and not given proper assessments as a result."[65] These presumptions have been uncovered in other studies as well; Browne et al. discovered that healthcare professionals can adopt negative images of Aboriginal people presented by the media and in public discourse—"as irresponsible, dependent wards of the state, as 'getting everything for free,' and as passive recipients of government benefits"—and that these assumptions can shape the nature of relationship between Aboriginal patients and professionals.[66] The reluctance to seek health care when needed results in delayed treatment and poorer prognosis for Aboriginal Peoples.[67]

The fragmented nature of a healthcare system in which the responsibilities are divided between the federal and provincial governments create additional structural barriers to care. The Constitution Act (1867) mandates the federal government with jurisdiction over "Indians and lands reserved for Indians",[68] while the

---

[58] National Collaborating Centre for Aboriginal Health 2011, p. 2.

[59] Ibid.

[60] Ibid.

[61] Ibid.

[62] Ibid.

[63] Health Council of Canada 2012, p. 4.

[64] Ibid., p. 8.

[65] Ibid., p. 9.

[66] Browne et al. 2005, p. 30.

[67] National Collaborating Centre for Aboriginal Health 2011, at p. 2.

[68] The Constitution Act 1867, 30 & 31 Vict, c 3, http://laws-lois.justice.gc.ca/eng/const/page-1. html (Accessed 5 October 2013).

provinces are responsible for most health care matters.[69] Therefore, much of the responsibilities for health care rest with the provinces, giving them expertise and more experience in the provision of health services than the federal government, which is responsible for First Nations and Inuit health. The divisions of powers and responsibilities between governments lead to 'siloed' care.[70] Jurisdictional disputes and lack of cooparation are exemplified in the case of Jordan River Anderson, a First Nations child in Manitoba who suffered from a disorder which could not be treated in his community.[71] The child was sent to live in medical foster care while obtaining treatment away from his community. However, the provincial and federal governments could not agree on which government was responsible for funding his care in the foster home. The child died in hospital in 2005, 2 years after the ordeal began, without ever reaching the foster home. This case led to the development of the child first policy called "Jordan's Principle"[72] to resolve jurisdictional disputes involving First Nations children, though it has yet to be fully implemented. Generally, services geared toward Aboriginal Peoples can be characterized as "a complex myriad of mechanisms and jurisdictionally separated agencies, provincial departments and federal Ministries" with little coordination between these actors.[73]

10.2.4 Conceptions of Health

When undertaking an assessment of Aboriginal-specific health initiatives, the various conceptions of 'health' and 'well-being' held by Aboriginal communities must be appreciated. While there is no singular definition of health among Aboriginal Peoples as a heterogeneous group, Aboriginal conceptions generally involve a more holistic notion of well-being that includes recognition of the underlying and broad determinants of health, not unlike that promoted by General Comment 14 or the Constitution of the World Health Organization. Despite the impossibility of a general definition acceptable to Aboriginal Peoples, the Royal Commission on Aboriginal Peoples made this attempt:

> For a person to be healthy, [he or she] must be adequately fed, be educated, have access to medical facilities, have access to spiritual comfort, live in a warm and comfortable house with clean water and safe sewage disposal, be secure in cultural identity, have an opportunity to excel in meaningful endeavor, and so on. These are not separate needs; they are all aspects of the whole.[74]

---

[69] Ibid.

[70] MacIntosh 2008 at p. 404. See also MacIntosh 2006.

[71] Aboriginal Affairs and Northern Development Canada 2013.

[72] Ibid.

[73] MacIntosh 2008 at 403.

[74] Royal Commission on Aboriginal Peoples 1996, at p. 206.

The interconnectedness of all aspects of life—physical, mental, emotional, social, and spiritual—is a salient feature of many definitions. There are clear similarities between these holistic conceptions of health and the subject of ICESCR Article 12.

Similarly, the word 'healing' carries special meaning for Aboriginal Peoples, which is not compatible with Western approaches to healing.[75] Research conducted by the RCAP indicates the western approach to services "*perpetuates* ill health and social distress" for Aboriginal Peoples.[76] According to the Royal Commission on Aboriginal Peoples:

> Healing refers to personal and societal recovery from the lasting effects of oppression and systemic racism experienced over generations. Many Aboriginal people are suffering not simply from specific diseases and social problems, but also from a depression of spirit resulting from 200 or more years of damage to their cultures, languages, identities and self-respect.[77]

In this light, conventional determinants of health may not adequately capture the requirements for well-being or health; additional determinants that reflect the post-contact histories of Aboriginal Peoples, including the lasting effects of policies of assimilation and abuse through the country's residential school system, for example, must be considered influential to health and must inform healthcare. As recognized by the World Health Organization's Commission on Social Determinants of Health, these events cannot be seen only as "historical processes that devastated the traditional livelihood of Aboriginal Peoples... [rather] the process of colonization must be recognized as a contemporary reality".[78] Notwithstanding the fact that the current Aboriginal health crises cannot be fully understood without consideration of the history of colonization, access to healthcare—both traditional and western—remains a fundamental determinant of personal and community health.

10.3 The Right to Health for Aboriginal Peoples

The following provides a brief overview of the sources of the right to health for Aboriginal Peoples including international law sources, Canada's human rights machinery, treaties, and decisions.

---

[75] Royal Commission on Aboriginal Peoples 1996, at Chap. 3, Sect. 2.4.

[76] Ibid.

[77] Royal Commission on Aboriginal Peoples 1996, at p. 109.

[78] World Health Organization 2007, p. 24.

10.3.1 Sources in International Law

Canada has ratified a number of key international agreements that include reference to the right to health for everyone. In 1977 Canada ratified what is perhaps the most central UN treaty in regard to the right to health, the ICESCR, which explicitly lists health as a fundamental human right in Article 12. It has ratified the Convention on the Elimination of All Forms of Discrimination against Women and endorsed the Declaration on the Rights of Indigenous Peoples in 2010, after initially voting against the latter. The government originally stated that, while the country is committed to indigenous rights, it found "parts of the text [...] vague and ambiguous, leaving it open to different, and possibly competing, interpretations".[79] Canada has not yet signed the Optional Protocol to the International Covenant on Economic, Social, and Cultural Rights, nor has it ratified the International Labor Organization's Indigenous and Tribal Peoples Convention (No. 169), which outlines the right to health for indigenous peoples.

10.3.2 Sources in Canadian Law

Aboriginal Peoples, like other Canadians, do not have a constitutional right to health.

Moreover, the extent to which human rights can be used as tools to address the asymmetrical power structure that has come to define Aboriginal-state relations in Canada is debatable. Rights frameworks depend on the State as the duty bearer and, effectively, the distributor of entitlements. The idea that the law is the source of entitlements, contingent upon the State, is incongruent with traditional conceptions of entitlement, which may be based on custom, ancestry, or founded in nature. Ideally, national laws and policies would reflect these customs, but that has not always been the case. Canada's human rights machinery at the federal, provincial, and territorial levels have evolved from a legal system steeped in colonial history, with lasting colonial-based power structures: "[T]he courts are exclusively rooted in a Constitutional heritage that, in the case of Canada, for instance, draws all its legitimacy from the authority of the sovereign crown that established the framework for the colonization of the country".[80] The discrepancies between a rights framework rooted in a legal system with a colonial past and Aboriginal models of entitlement call into question the usefulness of 'rights' in the context of Canada. In addition to this, nevertheless, a human rights framework is an avenue through which entitlements can be claimed when enshrined in law, however, the original sources of those entitlements may be perceived.

---

[79] Aboriginal Affairs and Northern Development Canada 2010.

[80] Hall 2003, p. 42.

10.3.3 The Canada Health Act

The Canada Health Act (CHA) was adopted in 1984 and represents the highest form of health law in Canada. Without referencing a right to health specifically, the CHA includes many shared principals; indeed, the stated aim of the CHA is to "protect, promote and restore the physical and mental well-being of residents of Canada and to facilitate reasonable access to health services without financial or other barriers."[81] As Virginia Leary points out, at first glance, "the Canadian health care system appears to be grounded in core elements of the right to health including the availability, accessibility, and acceptability of quality health goods, services and facilities."[82] However, as she notes, a right to health is not enshrined in any of the documents establishing the Canadian health care system, nor in the country's Charter of Rights and Freedoms.

The CHA outlines the principles and conditions that must be met by each province and territory in order to receive funding from the federal government. Among the criteria listed are: Comprehensiveness (health insurance must cover all insured services); Universality (the insurance plan must cover everyone in the province equally), and; Accessibility (among other things, this principle asserts that a province's health care insurance plan must provide insurance for services "on uniform terms and conditions and on a basis that does not impede or preclude [...] reasonable access to those services by insured persons [...]".[83]

It is clear that there are some similarities between the CHA and the AAAQ requirements. Yet what the act does not do is *require* the government to make financial contributions to the provinces for health care. Moreover, the act enables the federal government to provide funding through monetary or tax transfer for care that is necessary for health, but "health" is not defined in the document. The implication of this is a narrow understanding of the term as determined largely by governments, rather than healthcare professionals or service-users. The value of listing health (and at the very least, health care) as a human right is that it translates needs into entitlements and provides avenues for recourse if needs are unmet.

10.3.4 Treaty 6

A right to health particular to Aboriginal Peoples is sometimes argued to stem from provisions of Treaty 6 (1876) between the Crown and the Plain and Wood Cree Indians. Historical interpretations reveal that the future health of the

---

[81] Canada Health Act 1984, c. 6, s. 3.

[82] Leary 2009, p. 473

[83] Canada Health Act 1984, c. 6, s. 12.

Aboriginal population was among the primary concerns of the first signatories.[84] Interpretations of this treaty as the source of a right to health are based on what is known as the "medicine chest" clause, which is the only provision in the Aboriginal treaty series to explicitly reference medicine.[85] It states that, "a medicine chest shall be kept at the house of each Indian Agent for the use and benefit of the Indians at the direction of such agent."[86] In 1966 the Saskatchewan Court of appeal ruled that the government does not have obligations to provide comprehensive health care to Aboriginal Peoples, and that only a 'first aid kit' must be provided.[87] However, Boyer argues that the previous judicial interpretations would not likely be upheld today if taken to the Supreme Court of Canada.[88] While the medicine chest may provide a source for limited health entitlements for those covered by the treaty, namely, a number of First Nations, it does not offer entitlements to all Aboriginal Peoples.

10.3.5 *Judgments and Recognition*

Section 35 of the Constitution Act (1982) 'recognizes and affirms' *pre-existing* Aboriginal rights.[89] As such, Section 35 does not *bestow* rights to Aboriginal Peoples; it affirms those that already exist. This provides some flexibility so that rights may 'evolve' over time,[90] but it also leaves much of the power to define rights to the Courts.

In *R. v. Van der Peet* the Supreme Court developed a test to identify what constitutes an existing right within the meaning of Section 35: it must be "an element of a practice, custom, or tradition integral to the distinctive culture of the Aboriginal group asserting that right."[91] Building on this, author Boyer argues that:

> Evidence concerning therapeutic ceremonies and healing practices of Aboriginal Peoples demonstrates that such ceremonies and practices were integral to the existence of Aboriginal society. The integral nature of these ceremonies and practices supports the existence of an Aboriginal right to health.[92]

---

[84] Boyer 2003, p. 19, a copy of Treaty No. 6 between Her Majesty the Queen and the Plain and Wood Cree Indians and other Tribes of Indians at Fort Carlton, Fort Pitt and Battle River with Adhesions available at https://www.aadnc-aandc.gc.ca/eng/1100100028710/1100100028783 #chp2 (Accessed 5 October 2013).

[85] Aboriginal Affairs and Northern Development Canada 1964.

[86] Boyer 2003, at p. 20.

[87] Idem, at p. 22.

[88] Ibid.

[89] Constitution Act 1982, para 35.1.

[90] *R v. Sparrow* 1990.

[91] *R. v. Van der Peet* 1996.

[92] Boyer 2003, p. 16.

Despite some arguments that a right to health can be gleaned from previous decisions, it would be difficult to derive obligations on the part of the State to provide comprehensive health care, including medicines, to all Aboriginal Peoples.

The Canadian Human Rights Commission also recognizes Aboriginal Peoples' collective rights to cultural and traditional practices and knowledge.[93] Considering the diverse understandings of health, traditional ceremonies and practices can be understood as health supporting. Equally important to the health of Aboriginal Peoples, the Commission notes that collective rights include the right to self-government.[94] Health-related rights, whatever their source, clearly encompass the notion of culturally appropriate care, including traditional medicines and healing practices.

10.3.6 Entitlements According to Status

Under the Ontario Health Insurance Plan (OHIP), everyone in Ontario has access to insured healthcare services and products without user-fees; this includes many primary care services and medically necessary secondary and tertiary care. What this does not include is, inter alia, prescription medicine, birth control, therapy and counseling, dental care, physiotherapy, vision care, alternative therapies, except under specific circumstances (i.e., emergency dental surgery). It also limits one's care options to that which is insured under OHIP, even when other (uninsured) options or treatments may be less invasive or preferred by the individual patient. Some Aboriginal Peoples have access to additional health benefits not covered by OHIP through the NIHB program discussed below. Understanding who does and does not receive NIHB requires a look into the Canadian legislation that has divided and classified Aboriginal Peoples, specifically, the Indian Act of 1876.

10.3.7 Indian Act

Of the 11 treaties regulating the relationship between Aboriginal Peoples and the Crown, the most cited, and perhaps most contentious treaty, is the Indian Act. Established in 1876 and amended multiple times, most recently in 2011, it encompasses matters pertaining to registered Indians, the band system, and land reservations. It establishes the authority of the Department of Indian Affairs to control the Indian Registry, affords unique rights to those who are registered, and imposes responsibilities on the government. The Indian Registry controls who is recognized as "Indian" by the government.

---

[93] The Canadian Human Rights Commission 2005, p. 13.

[94] Ibid.

10 Aboriginal-Specific Health Initiatives and Accessible Health Care in Canada   299

On the surface the Act may appear as a benign, perhaps even empowering, instrument to further Aboriginal rights including the right to health, however, in reality it is widely criticized on grounds relating to its discriminatory provisions, paternalistic nature, and divisive effects.[95] According to the provisions of the act, Aboriginal Peoples are classified as either 'registered Indians' or 'unregistered Indians'; registered, or "status" individuals, have entitlements related to health care and supportive of the determinants to health that are not afforded to those who are unregistered or without status. Status is a legal category constructed largely for legislative and policy purposes; it does not describe one's band membership or identity as an Aboriginal Person.[96]

Historically, the Indian Act promoted the assimilation of Aboriginal Peoples through enfranchisement (the loss of one's status). The Act imposed discriminatory criteria for gaining and losing one's status and was particularly detrimental to women and their children. For example, if a registered woman (or a woman who was eligible for registry) married a non-Aboriginal person, she would lose her status and her children became ineligible.[97] The privileging of paternalistic lineage while disregarding maternal lineage reflects the values of the European colonizers of the time.[98] Other methods of enfranchisement involved the removal of one's status in exchange for full citizenship, or voting rights in federal elections. In 1985, an Act to Amend the Indian Act remedied the discriminatory provisions against women.[99]

Section 6 of the Indian Act sets out the criteria which must be met in order for an individual to obtain Indian Status under the Registry, most of which refers to predetermined definitions of who may be considered Indian for the purposes of the Act. Essentially, a person may be registered if he or she is of "descent from persons whom the Canadian government recognized as members of an Indian band in Canada".[100] While bands now have authority to determine who can have membership in their band, they do not have control over the registry. There is no legal definition of who an unregistered Indian might be, nor any recognized formula for identifying a non-status Aboriginal, as status is a constructed and imposed identity without definition.

Until 2008, the relationship between the Indian Act and the enjoyment of human rights was also complicated by Section 67 of the Canadian Human Rights Act (CHRA), which stated "[n]othing in this Act affects any provision of the Indian Act or any provision made under or pursuant to that Act."[101] In other words, Section 67 exempted the Indian Act from the CHRA and therefore complaints pertaining to

---

[95] Among innumerable critiques of the Indian Act, see for example The Royal Commission on Aboriginal Peoples 1996 Vol 1, Part 2, Chap. 9.

[96] MacIntosh 2008 at p. 397.

[97] Indian Act 1985, para 12(1).

[98] Smylie 2009, at p. 284.

[99] Also referred to as Bill C-31.

[100] Aboriginal Affairs and Northern Development Canada 2011.

[101] Canadian Human Rights Act 1985, para 67 (repealed).

discrimination related to the Indian Act, including violations by First Nations governments or bands, were not permissible under Section 76.[102] This allowed for gaps in human rights coverage for individuals categorized as Indians under the Indian Act, and prevented challenges to the discriminatory nature of the Act itself. The repeal of Section 67 is a move toward the equal enjoyment of the CHRA and does not affect treaty or other rights of Aboriginal Peoples.

Metis and Inuit have historically been excluded from treaty negotiations, including the Indian Act,[103] though Inuit are entitled to some of its provisions. Similar to First Nations, matters that pertain to Inuit populations have fallen under the federal jurisdiction. Métis, as a People, fell within the legislative jurisdiction of the provinces[104] and were not recognized as Indian under the Indian Act until 2013 when a landmark decision by a federal court, the "Daniels decision," ruled that Métis and non-status Aboriginal Peoples are Indians under the Constitution.[105] This means that while federal government claimed jurisdiction for First Nations and Inuit there was "a de facto jurisdictional vacuum in respect to the Métis"[106] for nearly a century and a half. The 13-year legal battle culminated in recognition of Métis rights, though the federal government's responsibilities toward Métis are not yet clarified. The ruling does not enable Métis to register with the Indian registry, which means that the extent to which benefits afforded to registered Indians will be made accessible to Métis is unclear.

10.4 Aboriginal-Specific Initiatives

This section presents and an overview of two Aboriginal-specific healthcare initiatives and focuses on elements that aim to improve access to health care, particularly care that is culturally appropriate: the *Traditional Healer Services Travel Policy* (THSTP) as part of the NIHB program, which is the most inclusive countrywide health program available to Aboriginal Peoples in Canada, and Ontario's *Aboriginal Healing and Wellness Strategy*, which is the most comprehensive Aboriginal-specific provincial health policy in the country.[107] Both initiatives aim to promote health and access to health care, including culturally appropriate care, of Aboriginal Peoples Aboriginal Peoples.[108] Without specifically referencing a

---

[102] Canadian Human Rights Commission 2005 at p. 1.

[103] Smylie 2009, at p. 281.

[104] Constitution Act 1867, Section 91 (24)5.

[105] *Daniels v. Canada* 2013.

[106] Stevenson 2002 at p. 237.

[107] Lavoie and Gervais 2010, p. 133

[108] Health Canada 2012, http://www.hc-sc.gc.ca/fniah-spnia/pubs/nihb-ssna/_medtransp/2005_med-transp-frame-cadre/index-eng.php. Accessed 5 October 2013; Ministry of Community and Social Services 2012a, http://www.mcss.gov.on.ca/en/mcss/programs/community/programsfor aboriginalpeople.aspx (Accessed 5 October 2013).

right to health, these initiatives exemplify formal attempts to ensure access to and availability of culturally appropriate care, among other elements of the right to health.

10.4.1 NIHB

The NIHB program is a country-wide program that provides coverage for medically necessary services and goods, including drugs, dental care, vision care, medical supplies, counseling, and medical transportation for those eligible.[109] The program is offered in addition to provincial health care schemes to improve access to health care goods and services that might otherwise be physically or economically inaccessible for some eligible recipients.

According to Health Canada—the federal health department which oversees the NIHB program—a person is eligible for the NIHB program if he or she is a Canadian resident and meets one of the following criteria: "a registered Indian according to the Indian Act; an Inuk recognized by one of the Inuit Land Claim organizations; or an infant less than one year of age, whose parent is an eligible recipient".[110] Ontario has 189,903 eligible recipients—the highest number of eligible recipients of any province or territory.[111]

The NIHB program's THSTP improves the availability and accessibility of culturally acceptable health care by providing travel funding for eligible recipients to access traditional healers outside of one's community. Travel funding can be obtained for other reasons as well, including: doctor appointments outside one's home community, diagnostic tests and hospital care, and substance-abuse treatment.[112]

Recalling that General Comment 14 stresses the preservation of traditional knowledge, medicines, and healing traditions as important for the realization of the right to health for indigenous peoples, the THSTP, as part of the NIHB program, can be viewed as an attempt to address some of the historical abuses that stifled the preservation of knowledge, traditional healing practices, and the use of medicines. The historical discouragement and outlawing of practices, the removal of people from their lands, and the forced enrollment in residential schools separated people from the traditions and medicines that promoted well-being. Knowledge that is preserved through oral traditions is particularly vulnerable to disappearance and while assimilation efforts were not successful at destroying knowledge of traditional healing practices, they have had negative impact on the availability of healers today:

---

[109] Health Canada 2012.

[110] Ibid.

[111] Ibid.

[112] Ibid, para 1.3.

> [E]arly within the traumatic period known as "contact" (roughly 400–500 years ago), each community had their own healers and medicine people. Because of disease, war, colonialism and the resulting destruction of most of the First Nations population, access also decreased significantly [...] First Nations went from having local access to a medicine person on a community level in the 1660s, to accessing one on a regional level (such as within a particular territory), to a point where today healers are in such short supply that communities often bring them in from as far away as reserves in the U.S. Midwest.[113]

For groups that were historically hunter-gatherers, the reservation system, which designates areas of land for Aboriginal Peoples to reside, put an end to the movement that once allowed people to participate in knowledge and medicines exchanges.[114] The THSTP, as part of the NIHB, provides the opportunity to access healers and medicines when they are unavailable in the community and the cost of travel may otherwise prevent the trip.

While the THSTP attempts to promote access to traditional medicines and healing, the benefits offered under the policy are limited in terms of availability and accessibility. The primary obstacle to obtaining funding that would facilitate access to traditional healers is the criterion stipulating recognized identity; one must be recognized by the government as an Inuk or registered Indian to qualify for travel funding, or the NIHB program in general. This clearly limits access for a great number of Aboriginal Peoples in Canada who are not registered as Indian or not recognized as Inuk and who do not have the financial resources to pay for travel themselves.

Obtaining travel funding is not a simple process and there are practical challenges that often hinder one's access to funding: The complexity of the forms, the lengthy process, and the requirement that individuals pay out-of-pocket and receive reimbursements for travel render the benefits out of reach for many.[115] In regard to coverage for drugs and medicines generally, the application process can be especially lengthy when one attempt to obtain benefits for medicines that are not typically covered by the program, as the list of covered drugs contains the most cost-effective options.[116]

In order for travel costs to be covered by the program a physician or health professional[117] must refer the patient. Obtaining a referral has its own complications that are largely out of the control of the person seeking treatment. Dr. Hankard's study indicates that there may be reluctance on behalf of health care professionals to refer patients to traditional healers due to liability concerns and fear of drawing criticism from the Canadian Medical Association.[118] This is in spite of the fact that the Canadian Medical Association has formally embraced traditional practices such

---

[113] Hankard 2011, p. 82.

[114] Ibid.

[115] Ibid, pp. 85–87; National Collaborating Centre for Aboriginal Health 2011, p. 2.

[116] National Collaborating Centre for Aboriginal Health 2011, p. 2.

[117] Or First Nations and Inuit Health Branch representative (Non-Insured Health Benefits Medical Transportation Policy Framework, Sect. 8.4).

[118] Hankard 2013, p. 3

as sweat lodges, healing circles and traditional medicine.[119] The lack of quantitative data on the efficacy of traditional healing practices may be a concern for those working in a field in which decisions are based on empirical research. While participating in traditional ceremonies such as healing ceremonies can be important for well-being—and recognized as the right of Aboriginal Peoples in Canada—when it comes to the practical enjoyment of these rights, well-intentioned healthcare professionals can create obstacles for individuals.

The effort by Health Canada to make traditional healing options available to some Aboriginal Peoples without out-of-pocket cost adheres to some of the elements set out in General Comment 14, specifically the idea that health services should take "into account traditional preventive care, healing practices and medicines."[120] However, access to funding for travel for traditional healing practices is largely controlled by those operating from the lens of Western medicine. The possibility for tension between the concepts of quality care (as defined by the Western-based healthcare community) and culturally appropriate care (as defined by the community accessing it) calls into question how quality is measured, and by whom, in light of healing practices that exist outside of the rubric of Western-based medicine.

Furthermore, the program responds to the rights and responsibilities of Aboriginal Peoples and the federal government listed in the Indian Act. In this way, rather than being based on efforts to address the barriers to health care, or the historically rooted factors for disproportionate rates of disease, the program was born out of the fiduciary responsibility that the federal government has to First Nations and Inuit; it is not based on human rights obligations, which emphasize dignity, equality, and nondiscrimination.

10.4.2 Aboriginal Healing and Wellness Strategy

As the result of the combined efforts of the provincial government of Ontario, First Nations groups, and Aboriginal groups,[121] the Aboriginal Healing and Wellness Strategy (AHWS) was created in 1994 to address the unique health challenges faced by Aboriginal Peoples living on-reserve as well as in rural and urban areas. It was the first Aboriginal-specific provincial strategy of its kind in the country.

---

[119] Ibid.

[120] UN Committee on Economic, Social and Cultural Rights 2000, at 27.

[121] The original fifteen participating groups consisted of: seven independent First Nations groups (Chippewa of Nawash Unceded First Nation, Chippewas of Saugeen Frist Nation, Mohawk Council of Akwesasne, Shawanaga First Nation, Six Nations of the Grand River, Walpole First Nation, Temagami First Nation); four Province-wide and political organizations (Association of Iroquois and Allied Indians, Grand Council of Treaty 3, Nishnawbe Aski Nation, Ontario Federation of Indian Friendship Centres); and three associations which are no longer participants (Ontario Natives Women's Association, Ontario Métis Aboriginal Association, and the Union of Ontario Indians). The Métis Nations of Ontario has since joined the strategy.

Importantly, the strategy is "status-blind," which means that the programs and policies developed under it are available to Aboriginal Peoples regardless of identity, band, or place of residence. Programs and services supported by the strategy are not only open to all Aboriginal Peoples, but in some cases non-Aboriginals as well. This inclusive approach helps to bridge some of the gaps left by the jurisdictional divide between provincial and federal government responsibilities.

In 2010, the AHWS was renewed with greater emphasis on Aboriginal control over programs and services and improving services in Aboriginal communities.[122] The increased role of Aboriginal Peoples in the design, delivery and control over services, promotes empowerment and the enjoyment of the right to health, among other rights. This section explores some of the successes of the AHWS in improving the availability and accessibility of culturally appropriate services in Ontario as well as some of the challenges to its practical implementation.

Two main policy documents help guide the development of programs under the strategy: *For Generations to Come: The Time is Now* and the *Aboriginal Health Policy for Ontario*. The former focuses on family healing and the issue of family violence. The latter report directs the Ministry of Health and Long-Term Care in its planning and programming to address a number of key issues affecting the accessibility of health care for Aboriginal Peoples, including:

> [The] lack of Aboriginal influence in health planning; lack of Aboriginal involvement in legislation affecting the Aboriginal community; a need to identify strategic priorities in Aboriginal health; a need for ongoing provincial support for Aboriginal health; and, a need to clarify provincial versus federal responsibility for Ontario's Aboriginal population.[123]

As such, the Aboriginal Health Policy for Ontario informs programs under the AHWS as well as those delivered to the entire population with an aim to more effectively meet the needs of Aboriginal clients. Crucially, the policy underscores the need for support from both the provincial and federal government, and that the roles and responsibilities of each must be more clearly defined.[124] Clear roles and responsibilities will: help to uncover who is being overlooked by the provincial health care scheme or community-based programs and services; ensure that Aboriginal and health organizations understand where to turn to address various shortcomings in the practical implementation of programs and services; and, promote accountability at the provincial and federal level.

Through the AHWS and subsequent policy a combination of traditional and mainstream community-based programs have been developed. These include: community wellness programs, maternal and infant health programs, counseling, crisis intervention services, healing lodges, health education, women's shelters, and substance-abuse treatment.[125] Among the successes of the strategy advertised

---

[122] Ministry of Community and Social Services 2012b.

[123] Ontario Aboriginal Health Advocacy Initiative 1999.

[124] Ibid., p. 3.

[125] Ministry of Community and Social Services 2012a.

by provincial government, is the creation of Aboriginal Health Access Centres.[126] The ten Aboriginal Health Access Centres that have opened across Ontario are examples of community-led organizations that adhere to the principles outlined in the AHWS and the Aboriginal Health Policy for Ontario, providing inter alia traditional healing, primary care, cultural programs, and community development initiatives.[127]

For example, the De dwa da dehs nyes[128] Aboriginal Health Centre in Hamilton, Ontario provides primary and traditional care through health care teams that work together to offer a holistic approach.[129] Practitioner–patient relationships are cultivated by establishing trust—the absence of which is listed as a reason why some Aboriginal Peoples avoid accessing care through Western facilities.[130] To enhance communication and understanding between patients and practitioners, a "Patient Advocate" works at the Centre and local hospitals to promote access and empowerment in health care settings. A unique service available at De dwa da dehs nyes Health Centre is the creation of a traditional medicine dispensary, which will allow patients access to alternative medicines instead of, or in addition to, Western medicine. Drawing on the knowledge of the community, clients, and elders, the Centre seeks to train staff and inform programs in ways that are culturally appropriate, which in turn improves the accessibility of health care.

Similarly, the Southwest Ontario Aboriginal Health Access Centre offers a variety of traditional and Western treatment options. Clients are able to meet with a traditional healer, participate in ceremonies, and learn about traditional medicines. Additionally, the Centre has a Cultural Safety Trainer to educate health care practitioners working in local hospitals about traditional medicine and ceremonies, to improve cultural safety in programs and services operating outside of the Centre. These programs and services represent efforts to respond to the needs of the communities served by improving the accessibility of mainstream health care as well as the availability of culturally appropriate options.

The challenge to making these programs available to a larger number of people and in the future lies in funding, increasing human resources, and the long-term commitment of both the provincial and federal governments. While these successes adopt the concept of cultural safety and also appear to be in line with the progressive realization of the right to health, which includes making culturally appropriate care available and accessible, they operate with considerable financial and resource challenges that will likely only grow with time. Indeed the Southwest Ontario Aboriginal Health Access Centre already has wait lists for sessions with the traditional healer based at the Centre, whom is only available two days per

---

[126] Ibid.

[127] Ontario AHAC Network and Association of Ontario Health Centres 2010, p. 7.

[128] De dwa da dehs nyes describes the notion of "taking care of each other amongst ourselves". See http://aboriginalhealthcentre.com/.

[129] Health Council of Canada 2012, at 49.

[130] Idem at 58.

week. In fact it was clear soon after the Centres opened around Ontario that the demand for services was greater than the capacity of the Centres could deliver[131]: With insufficient resources to address the needs of the communities, most Centres experienced wait lists, financial difficulties recruiting staff, and the Centres were often excluded from government initiatives made available to other primary health care organizations.[132]

Although the Centres, along with the policy and strategy objectives, are improving health care options, funding challenges in 2005 led some to describe the Centres as "second class" and "in crisis."[133] Since 2007, with the support of the Ontario Association of Ontario Health Centres and the government of Ontario, which has provided increased funding for some services, the Centres are still in operation. Significant funding and human resource challenges persist, and consideration of the population growth trajectory for Aboriginal Peoples and the rise of chronic and noncommunicable disease indicate that the future will bring even greater demands on these and other facilities. Overarching strategies such as the AHWS and related policies must have long-term support and durability in order to build trust and meet the needs of the communities served. At the same time, there must be room for change and new developments, according to the priorities of communities.

The sustainability of existing programs and the growth of new projects to accommodate demand is dependent upon provincial and federal government commitment. The priorities of governments tend to change frequently, and according to the political party in power at national, provincial or territorial levels. The cessation of funding to organizations such as NAHO and changes to the country's census are examples of shifting priorities at the federal level. Moreover, short-term funding, or funding tied to specific outcomes, create a lack of stability for hollistic and locally focused programming that may be at odds with the priorities of the government agency responsible for allcoating funds through the AHWS or other initiatives. As one researcher points out, "[f]unding agencies' working definition of culturally appropriate services often does not match First Nations' vision."[134] Moreover, it has been found that "funders' expectations can be rigid in their reporting requirements or desired program outcomes. They can vary tremendously between funding streams and may even change mid-stream."[135] While government commitment to support Aboriginal-led and Aboriginal-driven health care is necessary, transitioning control from governments to communities requires that communities have the ability to make decisions based on local needs and what they deem to be culturally appropriate.

---

[131] Ontario AHAC Network and Association of Ontario Health Centres 2010, at p. 13.

[132] Ibid.

[133] Ibid.

[134] Maar 2004, p. 58

[135] Ibid.

10 Aboriginal-Specific Health Initiatives and Accessible Health Care in Canada

Meeting the human resource demands of Aboriginal Health Access Centres—and increasing the number of Aboriginal health care practitioners, generally—requires greater opportunities for Aboriginal Peoples to become health professionals. Stipulations within Canadian law are partially responsible for excluding Aboriginal Peoples from medicine. Until 1985 a condition of entering medical school (or law school) was enfranchisement[136]; essentially that means if a First Nations or Inuit person wished to become a doctor, he or she was required to denounce their Indian status and adjoining entitlements.[137] Although enfranchisement is no longer a requirement to study medicine or law, persistent economic and physical barriers to higher education must be addressed if the representation of Aboriginal Peoples in health care across the country is to improve. Remote and Northern Centres also have difficulties retaining staff, not only because of financial concerns, but because professionals tend to prefer residing in urban areas. High turnover rates and lack of specialist availability limit what kind of care is available at facilities based outside of urban centres. In short, when such services are dependent upon the goodwill of governments at both levels, their sustainability is in question. Continuing to incorporate concepts such as cultural safety into staff training and to mainstream this concept is crucial to improving access to health care, as well as other services used by Aboriginal Peoples.

10.5 Conclusions

Generally speaking, people residing in Canada—Aboriginal Peoples and Non-Aboriginal people—have good economic access to primary health care through provincial and territorial health insurance schemes. In Ontario (where nearly 40 % of Canada's population resides) and other regions of the country, progress is being made towards the availability and accessibility of health care that is culturally appropriate through the adoption and mainstreaming of culturally safe practices. Today, Aboriginal Peoples exercise greater participation in and control over policies and services than ever, many of which are status-blind and tailored toward the needs of the specific communities served. Importantly, the power to shape and deliver health services is gradually being turned over to communities. The programs developed under the AHWS are examples of how organizations and governments are collaborating to incorporate holistic conceptions of care and deliver services that are acceptable to the communities served.

However, despite these initiatives the health status of Aboriginal Peoples continues to lag behind that of non-Aboriginals and obstacles to accessing health care persist, as evidenced in the Health Council of Canada report from 2012.

---

[136] Voluntary and involuntary enfranchisment promoted by the Indian Act were deemed in violation of the ICCPR and also struck down by the Supreme Court of Canada in 1981. See Moss and Gardner-O'Toole 1991.

[137] MacIntosh 2008 at p. 398.

In part due to the geographic expanse of the country, challenges remain in regard to the physical accessibility of some health-related goods and services according to one's location (remote, rural, or urban) and residence (on-reserve or off-reserve). Other barriers to health care include policies that entitle some groups to goods and services, while excluding others; the unavailability of culturally safe services at some facilities; and a lack of traditional healers and practices.

Without referencing the right to health, many of the principles and formal objectives of the current initiatives outlined in this chapter capture aspects of the right to health espoused in General Comment 14, but do not include human rights-specific obligations to provide such care. These and other initiatives often come with an expiry date, and commitments to the goals contained therein are dependent upon the political climate in the country at a given time. Moreover, the jurisdictional divide and the continued lack of clarity surrounding which level of government is responsible for what and whom, complicate the possibility for enhanced accountability. Efforts by governments and communities could be strengthened if the commitments and objectives outlined above were tied to legal rights and obligations (in addition to the pre-existing rights of Aboriginal Peoples and affirmed Section 35.1 of the Constitution Act).[138] Legally entrenched entitlements ensure that when needs are not met, claims can be made in a way that respects the dignity of the rights-holders.

Crucially, improving well-being depends on rebuilding the relationship between Aboriginal Peoples and governments into one based on based on respect, agency and rights. Respecting the demands by Aboriginal Peoples for greater self-determination would help to create an enabling environment for Aboriginal-led policies and control over relevant services; improved access to resources—natural and monetary; and accessing the determinants of health. Using human rights as a framework for transforming this relationship would encourage the continued support of governments and ensure that increased ownership by First Nations, Métis and Inuit does not operate as an avenue for governments to escape responsibilities. Despite the formal end of colonization, its effects and processes are still with us. Decolonization and self-determination de facto and de jure will undoubtedly encourage ownership over services, programs, and resources to ensure the needs of the communities are met.

References

Aboriginal Affairs and Northern Development Canada (1964) Copy of Treaty No. 6 between Her Majesty the Queen and the Plain and Wood Cree Indians and other Tribes of Indians at Fort Carlton, Fort Pitt and Battle River with Adhesions. https://www.aadnc-aandc.gc.ca/eng/1100100028710/1100100028783#chp2. Accessed 5 Oct 2013

Aboriginal Affairs and Northern Development Canada (2010) Canada's Position: United Nations Draft Declaration on the Rights of Indigenous Peoples. http://www.aadnc-aandc.gc.ca/eng/1100100014078/1100100014079. Accessed 5 Oct 2013

---

[138] Constitution Act of Canada 1982, Section 35.1.

10 Aboriginal-Specific Health Initiatives and Accessible Health Care in Canada

Aboriginal Affairs and Northern Development Canada (2011) The Indian Register. http://www.aadnc-aandc.gc.ca/eng/1100100032475/1100100032476. Accessed 5 Oct 2013

Aboriginal Affairs and Northern Development Canada (2012) First Nations. http://www.aadnc-aandc.gc.ca/eng/1100100013791/1100100013795. Accessed 5 Oct 2013

Aboriginal Affairs and Northern Development Canada (2013) Jordan's Principle. http://www.aadnc-aandc.gc.ca/eng/1334329827982/1334329861879. Accessed 5 Oct 2013

Allard YE (2007) Métis concepts of health: Placing health within a social-cultural context. Social, economic and environmental (ecological) determinants of Métis health. National Collaborating Centre for Aboriginal Health, Ottawa, pp 1–5

Amnesty International (2004) Stolen sisters: a human rights response to discrimination and violence against indigenous women in Canada. AI Index: AMR 20/003/2004. http://www.amnesty.ca/sites/default/files/amr200032004enstolensisters.pdf. Accessed 5 Oct 2013

Assembly of First Nations (n.d.) Description of the AFN. http://www.afn.ca/index/php/en/about-afn/description-of-the-afn. Accessed 5 Oct 2013

Boyer Y (2003) Aboriginal health a constitutional rights analysis. Discussion Paper Series in Aborigial Health: Legal Issues No. 1, National Aboriginal Health Organization, Native Law Centre, Ottawa and Saskatoon

Brascoupe S, Waters C (2009) Cultural safety; exploring the applicability of the concept of cultural safety to aboriginal health and community wellness. J Aboriginal Health 5(2):6–41

Browne A, Smye V, Varcoe C (2005) The relevance of postcolonial theoretical perspectives to research in aboriginal health. CJNR 37(4):16–37

Canada Health Act (1984) Canada Health Act, RSC 1985, c C-6. http://canlii.ca/t/51w33. Accessed 19 June 2014

Canadian Broadcast Corporation (2013) Canada nixes UN review of violence on aboriginal women. http://www.cbc.ca/news/canada/manitoba/canada-nixes-un-review-of-violence-on-aboriginal-women-1.1860828. Accessed 5 Oct 2013

Canadian Human Rights Act (1985) Canadian Human Rights Act, RSC 1985, c H-6. http://canlii.ca/t/527nx. Accessed 19 June 2014

Canadian Human Rights Commission (2005) A matter of rights a special report of the Canadian Human Rights Commission on the Repeal of Section 67 of the Canadian Human Rights Act. http://www.chrc-ccdp.gc.ca/sites/default/files/report_a_matter_of_rights_en.pdf. Accessed 5 Oct 2013

Canadian Institute for Health Information (2004) Improving the health of Canadians. https://secure.cihi.ca/free_products/IHC2004rev_e.pdf. Accessed 5 Oct 2013

Constitution Act (1982) The Constitution Act, 1982. Schedule B to the Canada Act 1982 (UK), 1982, c 11. http://canlii.ca/t/ldsx. Accessed 19 June 2014

First Nations Health Authority (2013) BC First Nations Health Authority marks historic transfer of services from health Canada. http://www.fnha.ca/about/news-and-events/news/bc-first-nations-health-authority-marks-historic-transfer-of-services-from-health-canada. Accessed 5 Oct 2013

Hall AJ (2003) The American empire and the fourth world. McGill-Queen's University Press, Kingston

Hankard M (2011) Transforming relationships and accessing non-insured health benefits travel funding to see traditional healers from off-reserve. University of Sudbury aboriginal policy studies, vol 1(3):81–95

Hankard M (2013) Barriers to accessing traditional healer travel funding from off-reserve. Indigenous Policy J XXIV(1):1–24

Health Canada (2005) Ten years of health transfer first nation and inuit control. http://www.hc-sc.gc.ca/fniah-spnia/pubs/finance/_agree-accord/10_years_ans_trans/index-eng.php. Accessed 5 Oct 2013

Health Canada (2007) Indian health policy 1979. http://www.hc-sc.gc.ca/ahc-asc/branch-dirgen/fnihb-dgspni/poli_1979-eng.php. Accessed 5 Oct 2013

Health Canada (2012) Non-insured health benefits medical transportation policy framework. http://www.hc-sc.gc.ca/fniah-spnia/pubs/nihb-ssna/_medtransp/2005_med-transp-frame-cadre/index-eng.php. Accessed 5 Oct 2013

Health Council of Canada (2012) Empathy, dignity, and respect: creating cultural safety for aboriginal people in urban health care 2012. http://www.healthcouncilcanada.ca/rpt_det.php?id=437. Accessed 5 Oct 2013

Indian Act (1985) Indian Act RSC 1985, c. I-5. http://canlii.ca/t/52123. Accessed 19 June 2014

Inuit Tapiriit Kanatami (2010) Inuit TB rate doubles to 185 times the rate of Canadian-born non-aboriginals; First Nations rate 31 times higher. http://www.itk.ca/media-centre/media-releases/inuit-tb-rate-doubles-185-times-rate-canadian-born-non-aboriginals-first. Accessed 5 Oct 2013

Jacklin KM, Warry W (2004) The Indian health transfer policy in Canada: toward self-determination or cost containment? In: Singer A, Castro A (eds) Unhealthy health policy: a critical anthropological examination. AltaMira Press, Lanham, pp 215–234

Kirmayer LJ, Brass GM, Holton T, Paul K, Simpson C, Tait C (2007) Suicide among aboriginal people in Canada (Aboriginal Healing Foundation). http://www.ahf.ca/downloads/suicide.pdf. Accessed 5 Oct 2013

Lavoie J, Gervais L (2010) Towards the adoption of a national aboriginal health policy. In: White JP, Peters J, Dinsdale P, Beavon D (eds) Aboriginal policy research, vol IX., Health and well-beingThompson Educational Publishing, Toronto, pp 121–139

Leary V (2009) Health care in Canada: does a health care system based on shared values ensure respect for the right to health?. In Clapham A, Robinson M (eds) Swiss human rights book, vol 3. Ruffer & Rub, Berne, pp 472–480

Lux M (1998) Perfect subjects: race, tuberculosis, and the Qu'Appelle BCG Vaccine Trial. Can Bull Med Hist 15(2):277–295

Lux MK (2010) Care for the 'Racially Careless': Indian hospitals in the Canadian West, 1920–1950s. Can Hist Rev 93(3):407–434

Maar M (2004) Clearing the path for community health empowerment: integrating health care services at an aboriginal health access centre in Rural North Central Ontario. J Aboriginal Health 1(1):54–65

MacIntosh C (2006) Jurisdictional roulette: constitutional and structural barriers to aboriginal access to health. In: Flood C (ed) The frontiers of fairness. University of Toronto Press, Toronto

MacIntosh C (2008) The intersection of aboriginal public health with Canadian law and policy. In: Bailey TM, Caulfield T, Ries NM (eds) Public health law and policy in Canada, 2nd edn. LexisNexis, Canada, pp 395–439

Ministry of Community and Social Services (2012a) Aboriginal healing and wellness strategy. http://www.mcss.gov.on.ca/en/mcss/programs/community/programsfor aboriginalpeople.aspx. Accessed 5 Oct 2013

Ministry of Community and Social Services (2012b) Ontario's renewed aboriginal healing and wellness strategy. http://www.mcss.gov.on.ca/en/mcss/programs/community/ahws/AHWS_renewal_letter.aspx. Accessed 5 Oct 2013

Mosby I (2013) Administering colonial science: nutrition research and human biomedical experimentation in aboriginal communities and residential schools, 1942–1952. Histoire Sociale Soc Hist 46(91):145–172

Moss W, Gardner-O'Toole E (1991) Aborignal people: history of discriminatory laws. Law and Government Division. http://publications.gc.ca/Collection-R/LoPBdP/BP/bp175-e.htm. Accessed 5 Oct 2013

National Aboriginal Health Organization (2013) Terminology guidelines. http://www.naho.ca/publications/topics/terminology/. Accessed 5 Oct 201

National Collaborating Centre for Aboriginal Health (2011) Access to health services as a social determinant of first nations, Inuit and Métis Health. http://www.nccah-ccnsa.ca/Publications/Lists/Publications/Attachments/22/Access%20to%20Health%20Services%20(English).pdf. Accessed 5 Oct 2013

10 Aboriginal-Specific Health Initiatives and Accessible Health Care in Canada

Native Women's Association of Canada (n.d.) Fact sheet: violence against aboriginal women. http://www.nwac.ca/files/download/NWAC_3E_Toolkit_e.pdf. Accessed 5 Oct 2013

Ontario Aboriginal Health Advocacy Initiative (OAHAI Manual) (1999) Aboriginal health policy for Ontario. http://74.213.160.105/oahai/Acrobatfiles/Ahp.pdf. Accessed 5 Oct 2013

Ontario AHAC Network and Association of Ontario Health Centre (2010) Aboriginal health access centres: our health our future. http://www.cachc.ca/?page_id=95&did=9. Accessed 5 Oct 2013

Public Health Agency of Canada (2011) Diabetes in Canada facts and figures from a public health perspective. http://www.phac-aspc.gc.ca/cd-mc/publications/diabetes-diabete/facts-figures-faits-chiffres-2011/pdf/facts-figures-faits-chiffres-eng.pdf. Accessed 5 Oct 2013

Royal Commission on Aboriginal Peoples (1996) Royal commission report on aboriginal peoples. http://www.aadnc-aandc.gc.ca/eng/1307458586498/1307458751962. Accessed 5 Oct 2013

Schnarch B (2004) Ownership, control, access, and possession (OCAP) or self determination applied to research. J Aboriginal Health 1(1):80–95

Smylie J (2009) The health of aboriginal peoples. In: Raphael Dennis (ed) Social determinants of health, 2nd edn. Canadian Scholar's Press Inc., Toronto, pp 280–301

Smylie J, Fell D, Ohlsson A, Joint Working Group on First Nations, Indian, Inuit, and Métis infant mortality of the Canadian Perinatal Surveillance System (2010) A review of aboriginal infant mortality rates in Canada: Striking and persistent aboriginal/non-aboriginal inequities. Can J Public Health 101(2):143–148

Speck DC (1989) The indian health transfer policy: a step in the right direction of revenge of the hidden agenda? Native Stud Rev 5(1):187–213

Statistics Canada (2011) Aboriginal peoples in Canada: First Nations People, Métis and Inuit (National Household Survey 2011). http://www12.statcan.gc.ca/nhs-enm/2011/as-sa/99-011-x/99-011-x2011001-eng.pdf. Accessed 5 Oct 2013

Stevenson M (2002) Section 91(24) and Canada's legislative jurisdiction with respect to the Métis. Indigenous Law J 1:237–262

The Constitution Act (1867) 30 & 31 Vict, c 3. http://laws-lois.justice.gc.ca/eng/const/page-1.html. Accessed 5 Oct 2013

UN Committee on Economic, Social and Cultural Rights (2000) General Comment No. 14: The Right to the Highest Attainable Standard of Health (Art. 12 of the Covenant), E/C.12/2000/4. http://www.refworld.org/docid/4538838d0.html. Accessed 5 Oct 2013

Waldron J, Herring A, Young TK (2006) Aboriginal health in Canada: historical, cultural, and epidemiological perspectives, 2nd edn. University of Toronto Press, Toronto

Webster P (2006) Canadian Aboriginal people's health and the Kelowna deal. Lancet 368:275–276

World Health Organization (2007) Social determinants of health and indigenous peoples. http://www.who.int/social_determinants/resources/indigenous_health_adelaide_report_07.pdf. Accessed 5 Oct 2013

World Health Organization (2013) Canada: health profile. http://www.who.int/countries/can/en

Cases

Daniels v. Canada (2013) FC 6 (CanLII). http://canlii.ca/t/fvhv7. Accessed 29 November 2013

R. v. Sparrow (1990) CanLII 104 (SCC), [1990] 1 SCR 1075. http://canlii.ca/t/1fsvj. Accessed 29 Nov 2013

R. v. Van der Peet (1996) CanLII 216 (SCC), [1996] 2 SCR 507. http://canlii.ca/t/1fr8r. Accessed 29 Nov 2013

Chapter 11
The Right to Health in Peru: Persistent Vulnerabilities in the Context of HIV/AIDS

Ruth Iguiñiz, Nancy Palomino and Marco Barboza

Abstract Throughout the history of public health in Peru, health policy strategies aimed at communicable diseases have not been guided by human rights considerations. Instead, they have followed compulsory strategies aimed at controlling epidemics and preserving the well-being of the unaffected population. Initial policies and methods to face the emergence of HIV/AIDS were rooted in this tradition of public health, insensitive to the needs, sufferings, and rights of the sick until a new perspective began to surface: the human right to health. This chapter addresses the challenges of implementing human rights-oriented health policies in the context of HIV/AIDS in Peru. Looking at concepts of privacy and nondiscrimination as key components of the human right to health, we explore the ways in which health policies and legislation have succeeded and failed in incorporating the "human rights-based approach." This study is based on research conducted in Peru during 2008 as part of a study coordinated by Gayet of the Facultad Latinoamericana de Ciencias Sociales (FLACSO) across eight countries. The research concerned the incorporation of a human rights approach and the evolution of public policy from the first nationally registered case of HIV/AIDS. Policies aimed at prevention and treatment for those living with HIV/AIDS, and the incorporation of the right to health, nondiscrimination, and the right to privacy and confidentiality into policies and programs are examined in light of four populations that meet conditions of vulnerability: sex workers, people with nonheterosexual orientations, pregnant women, and people living with HIV. It surveys existing regulations in the country and secondary sources such as reports from civil society organizations, the

---

R. Iguiñiz (✉) · N. Palomino
School of Public Health and Administration, Universidad Peruana Cayetano Heredia,
Lima, Peru
e-mail: ruth.iguiniz.r@upch.pe

N. Palomino
e-mail: nancy.palomino@upch.pe

M. Barboza
Human Rights to Health Specialist, Lima, Peru
e-mail: barbozamarco@gmail.com

B. Toebes et al. (eds.), *The Right to Health*, DOI: 10.1007/978-94-6265-014-5_11,
© T.M.C. ASSER PRESS and the authors 2014

313

Office of the Ombudsman and UN Human Rights Reports to explore law implementation and its implications. Interviews were carried out with representatives of civil society organizations and the Ministry of Health, as well as researchers from academia and other key informants related to sexual health public policies.

Contents

11.1 Introduction 314
11.2 From the Control of Venereal Diseases to the Control of HIV/AIDS 316
    11.2.1 Health Policies Against Syphilis in Peru 317
    11.2.2 The Emergence of AIDS in Peru and the State Response 319
    11.2.3 The Incorporation of Social Participation and Human Rights Approaches 321
11.3 Populations and Civil Society Actors in the Context of the HIV Epidemic 323
    11.3.1 Communities of Lesbians, Gays, Transvestites, Transsexuals and Transgender people 323
    11.3.2 People Living with HIV–AIDS 325
    11.3.3 Sex Workers 325
    11.3.4 Non-Governmental Organizations 326
11.4 Human Rights in the Context of HIV 327
    11.4.1 Right to Life and Quality of Survival 327
    11.4.2 Right to Nondiscrimination 328
    11.4.3 Right to Privacy and Confidentiality 330
11.5 Major Contradictions and Gaps in the Recognition of Rights in the Context of HIV 333
    11.5.1 Tensions and Contradictions Surrounding the Rights of Women 333
    11.5.2 Tensions Between Criminalizing Contagion and the Rights of the General Population 334
11.6 Conclusions: Unresolved Tensions Between Public Health Policy and the Right to Health, Non-discrimination and Privacy 335
References 336

11.1 Introduction

Throughout the history of public health in Peru, health policy strategies against communicable diseases have involved compulsory measures aimed at controlling epidemics and preserving the well-being of the unaffected population. Initial policies and methods to face the emergence of HIV/AIDS were rooted in the tradition of public health, insensitive to the needs, sufferings and rights of the sick individuals until a new perspective began to surface: the human right to health.

The Peruvian state recognizes and has signed all major international declarations and conventions on human rights, including the International Convention on Economic, Social and Cultural Rights; the convention on the elimination of all forms of discrimination against women (CEDAW); the American Convention on Human Rights, the "Pact of San Jose, Costa Rica," the Inter-American Convention on the

11 The Right to Health in Peru: Persistent Vulnerabilities in the Context of HIV/AIDS   315

Prevention, Punishment and Eradication of Violence against Women ("Convention of Belem do Para"); the Declaration of the Rights of the Child; and the Convention on the Rights of Persons with Disabilities. It has also constitutionally entrenched the right to health in its chapter on social and economic rights, article 7: "all individuals are entitled to the protection of his/her individual, their family environment and community health; and the duty to contribute to its promotion and defense".

This chapter is based on research conducted in Peru during 2008 concerning the evolution of public health policy from the first nationally registered case of HIV/AIDS. This study focuses on the development of policies to prevent and treat HIV/AIDS, and the incorporation of the right to health, the right to nondiscrimination, and the right to privacy among four populations that meet conditions of vulnerability: sex workers, people with different sexual orientations, pregnant women, and people living with HIV. Conducted as part of a broader study which was coordinated by Cecilia Gayet of FLACSO in eight countries, our research team, including the authors of this chapter and Maria Teresa Arana, collected data on the existing regulations in the country and analyzed secondary sources such as reports from civil society organizations, the Office of the Ombudsman and UN Human Rights Reports to explore law implementation and its implications. Interviews were also carried out with representatives of civil society organizations and the Ministry of Health, as well as researchers from academia and other key informants knowledgeable on sexual health public policies and human rights.

For the purposes of this study, the right to health refers to "the enjoyment of the highest attainable standard of health conducive to living a life in dignity" as expressed by the Committee on Economic, Social, and Cultural Rights in General Comment 14. Within this framework, the right to health, "extend[s] not only to timely and appropriate health care, but also to the underlying determinants of health, such as access to safe and potable water and adequate sanitation, healthy occupational and environmental conditions, and access to health-related education and information, including on sexual and reproductive health."[1]

It is particularly relevant to HIV/AIDS to recognize that the right to health depends on, and contributes to, the realization of many other human rights such as the right to life, the right to freedom from discrimination, and the right to privacy. In this case our analysis looks for ways in which these rights interrelate in the context of HIV/AIDS-related health policy regulation and implementation in Peru.

In this context, discrimination means any distinction, exclusion, or restriction made on the basis of various grounds which has the effect or purpose of impairing or nullifying the recognition, enjoyment, or exercise of human rights and fundamental freedoms. "Accordingly, international human rights law proscribes any discrimination in access to health care, and the underlying determinants of health,

---

[1] United Nations 2003, p. 8. See also: CESCR General Comment No. 14, (E/C.12/2000/4), para 8.

[2] United Nations 2003, p. 8. See also: CESCR General Comment No. 14, paras 18–21 and A/54/38/Rev.1, CEDAW General Recommendation 24, 1999.

on the internationally prohibited grounds, including health status, which has the intention or effect of impairing the equal enjoyment of the right to health."[2]

The International Covenant on Economic, Social, and Cultural Rights (Article 2 (2)) and the Convention on the Rights of the Child (Article 2 (1)) identify the following non-exhaustive grounds of discrimination: race, color, sex, language, religion, political or other opinion, national or social origin, property, disability, birth or other status. According to the Committee on Economic, Social, and Cultural Rights, "other status" may include health status (e.g., HIV/AIDS) or sexual orientation.[3] It is linked to the marginalization of specific population groups and is generally at the root of fundamental structural inequalities in society which may make these groups more vulnerable to poverty and ill-health.

For the purposes of our study, the right to privacy refers to everyone's right to have his honor respected and his dignity recognized.[4] The International Covenant on Civil and Political Rights (Article 17) provides that "no one shall be subjected to arbitrary or unlawful interference with his privacy, family, home or correspondence, nor to unlawful attacks on his honor and reputation. Everyone has the right to the protection of the law against such interference or attacks." Thus, the right to privacy encompasses obligations to respect physical privacy, including the obligation to seek informed consent to HIV testing and the privacy of information, including the need to respect the confidentiality of all information relating to a person's HIV status, sexual identity and other intimate practices not against the law.

11.2 From the Control of Venereal Diseases to the Control of HIV/AIDS

Throughout the history of public health in Peru, strategies against communicable diseases have shared a compulsory character common to European approaches described as medical police since the second half of the eighteenth century. The policing role in the realization of public health (particularly with respect to the differential targeting of particular groups or classes) was configured in practices of inspection and surveillance, information and intelligence gathering, and direct intervention in private, familial and commercial matters.[5] Cueto, in his historical study of epidemics in Peru,[6] mentions the influence of the medical police approach to controlling epidemics (quarantine, the isolation or abandonment of the sick, burning the homes of those affected, migratory control of people) such as the Bubonic plague and Yellow fever at the beginning of the twentieth

---

[3] CESCR General Comment No. 14, para 18.

[4] American Convention on Human Rights, Article 11.

[5] Carrol 2002.

[6] Cueto 1997.

century. These procedures sought to preserve the well-being of the healthy population but were insensitive to the needs and suffering of the sick.

One of the key aspects of the medical police approach was the division of diseases into two groups according to the causes: natural, including contagious diseases and epidemics, and those produced by humans, mostly attributed to the physical consequences of loose morals and transgressions of the moral order.[7] As a result of this division public health initiatives have focused on two interventions: moral control (police) and prophylactic (for health), which has influenced public health responses to disease, for over two centuries.[8]

Initial policies and methods to face the emergence of HIV/AIDS were rooted in this tradition of public health, until a new perspective began to surface: health rights. On the other hand, the burden faced by stigmatized groups and individuals affected by HIV as well as the challenge of overcoming stigmatization in health services would also have an influence not only in the policies but also in their execution.

11.2.1 Health Policies Against Syphilis in Peru

Toward the end of the nineteenth century, the serious implications of sexually transmitted diseases such as syphilis and gonorrhea were becoming a concern for Peruvian society and the government began to develop state policies directed toward women sex workers. In June 1910, within the purview of the Department of Public Health, the Prostitution Health Services Office was created for the inspection and surveillance of "public" women and to provide free medical checks and treatment in state clinics. The police remained in charge of the "conservation of morality and public order."[9] The creation of this service noted that universal experience had proven the ineffectiveness of police regulation concerning prostitution and the prophylaxis of venereal diseases.

In 1911 the Public Assistance of Lima was established as a government body, which had as one of its sections the clinic for prophylaxis of venereal diseases. In the same vein, the Internal Regulations of the Public Assistance of Lima (1923) noted that it was a woman's obligation, if she had reached the age of 21 and had given herself to prostitution (sic), to register with the "Prostitute's Registry" that was overseen by the health inspection branch of the Public Assistance. It was compulsory for each registered sex worker to carry her "health card" and to show it as often as it was required, to notify any change of address to the Public Assistance, and to be hospitalized in that establishment until all danger of

---

[7] Rosen 1985.

[8] Barboza 2008.

[9] Rosen 1985.

contagion had passed. In addition to ongoing mandatory health checks for women, prostitution houses required a special licence granted by the police.

From 1996 onwards, many health providers and policymakers developing HIV prevention policies criticized the ineffectiveness of "sex worker health cards" and the regulations governing special licences which regulated brothels beginning in 1910. A double standard of moral control (police) and prophylactic (health) has vigilantly accompanied prostitution in Peru during the twentieth century. When it comes to epidemics of venereal diseases and, now with much more intensity, HIV, this control calls for the need to guarantee the "innocent" population—(whose behavior met the standards of morality such as wives and children)–safety, while portraying sex workers as the main threat.

For decades, there has been an unresolved controversy between the regulatory and abolitionist positions against prostitution in Peru. The regulationist position can be traced back to 1985.[10] From this perspective, the prostitute represented a necessary evil against the unbridled sexuality of men and the need to preserve the honor of "virtuous" women and their families. Thus, the justification for regulation was provided by the need for health surveillance to prevent the spread of syphilis and other venereal diseases. Other measures that were discussed and implemented for several decades in the twentieth century included confining brothels to certain areas of the city, restricting sex workers' mobility, and demanding that women sex workers permanently carry health cards to certify that they had undergone a gynecological examination. The establishments or brothels had to be licensed and pay fines if provisions were violated.

Abolitionist proposals intended to prevent and eliminate prostitution, incorporate sex education, prophylaxis of venereal diseases and eugenic measures via the municipal prenuptial sanitary control process which required blood and medical tests before marriage. Attempts to abolish the regulation of prostitution failed to position themselves against the regulatory positions, the latter being the current trend, even though several of these rules are changing. In 1983, the granting of licences and the control of activities relating to sexual commerce were transferred to the Provincial Municipalities. Peru's current legislation can be described as regulatory.

Currently the abolitionist position, represented by the NGO "Movimiento El Pozo," identifies customers as the main cause of prostitution because they benefit from the mechanisms of economic power, gender, and social complicity necessary to create and maintain a demand. Under this perspective, prostitution is seen as a violation of women's human rights and as a consequence of unequal power relations between the sexes, which ought to be removed.[11] In recent years, this position has been confronted by women's sex workers' associations seeking recognition of prostitution as sex work and of women sex workers as holders of all labor and human rights.

---

[10] Nencel 2000, p. 31.

[11] Interview 16.

The use of the health cards ceased to be compulsory between the 1980s and 1990s, nevertheless police officers continue to request health cards even without a legal basis. Most critics of the initiative denounced the fact that while the health card was mandatory, pelvic examinations were carried out in very poor biosecurity conditions and were not able to detect venereal diseases, and neither was HIV testing included. Furthermore, it generated a system of abuse, including sexual abuse, by the police and health professionals who were responsible for stamping and validating health cards.[12]

11.2.2 The Emergence of AIDS in Peru and the State Response

Although the first case of AIDS in Peru was diagnosed in 1983, the state did not actively address the issue until July 1990 with the enactment of Law 25275. The legislation made the prevention of and the fight against HIV a national health priority and made reporting diagnosed cases of AIDS compulsory and required full disclosure of infected individuals' identity. Furthermore, it established mandatory testing for AIDS for all persons applying for residence in Peru, pregnant women, gays, and sex workers. This law sought to control the epidemic by controlling women, sex workers, homosexuals or foreigners. All these populations have been subjected to differential treatment within the legal system because of either their gender, sexual identity, or nationality.

In 1993, a decade after the first confirmed case of AIDS, it was estimated that the number of people living with AIDS had reached 5,000. Given this rapid growth, the regulatory approach by the health sector was totally inadequate to address the magnitude and severity of the problem.

Fundamental changes in HIV/AIDS policy took place in 1996. A new law (Law 26626) established a set of provisions for the protection of the human rights of those affected. A specific health program—PROCETSS—was created to control STD and HIV/AIDS in Peru, which included, among others, the following objectives and strategies:

- To reduce the transmission of STDs, including HIV: by improving the rate of diagnosis, promoting behavioral changes such as condom use, ensuring the availability and accessibility of prophylactics, and reducing blood transmission and vertical transmission by introducing HIV-positive women and their partners to family planning programs.
- To reduce the individual, social, and economic impact of STDs, especially HIV and AIDS: by promoting quality care, recognition, and respect for the exercise

---

[12] Interviews 14, 16 and 21.

[13] Ministry of Health (hereafter MINSA), 1996.

of civil and labor rights by people living with HIV, by providing support for socially responsible behavior which prevents HIV transmission, and by ensuring nondiscrimination in health services.[13]

Despite these improvements in the law, the following year's national budget did not allocate the additional funds required to provide drugs to treat the most common curable STDs or to promote recognition and respect for the rights of people living with HIV/AIDS (PLWHA). Regulations did not expressly mention the state's obligation to provide HIV/AIDS drugs needed to improve PLWHA's quality of life and dignity. This is even more problematic in a fragmented health system[14] with very limited health coverage plans like the Peruvian health system.

Policies continued to focus on pregnant women, sex workers, and men who have sex with men as key vulnerable populations. Initiatives were directed at these populations with the overall goal being the protection of the general unaffected population, rather than the enjoyment of human rights by those living with the illness. For example, the new law established that universal screening of pregnant women required pretest counselling and informed consent, but did not change its compulsory character. However, the compulsory character of the legislation in Peru is mentioned and used as a very strong dissuasive element in the health sector. If the law was applied, and a woman did not give her consent for a required test or intervention, following services such as prenatal care would not be provided and she would be out of the system records.

This law also implemented an education programme on the prevention of STD-HIV for sex workers and men who have sex with men, in an effort to familiarize them with the health services and to control AIDS. It relied on people regularly attending health services for their checkups, as in the case of sex workers from authorized brothels, to outreach for people at risk.

An evaluation of the Ministry of Health's early plans for the prevention and control of HIV/AIDS in Peru indicated that there was no adequate political will dedicated to expanding the prevention and care of HIV/AIDS during the first years of the plan's implementation. It also suggested that affected groups and activists had weak negotiation capacity and were just beginning to organize their demands.[15]

---

[14] Peru's health sector is divided into health services provided by the state (public health services) and by private providers. The public health sector is also subdivided, according to the public institution providing the service, into the MINSA's health services; Essalud-public health insurance; and the police and armed forces' health services.

[15] ONUSIDA-policy, 2005.

11.2.3 The Incorporation of Social Participation and Human Rights Approaches

Citizens' participation in policy formulation or monitoring implementation, despite progress in recent years, is still very weak. Nevertheless, without the intense PLWHA and LGBT groups' demand for rights recognition, changes in the way in which policies incorporate the human rights approach would not have been possible.

Peruvian health policies against communicable diseases have tended to focus their policies and strategies in two main axes: (1) prevention—to prevent people from getting and/or spreading the disease and (2) health care—to attempt recovery or minimize the damage. A third axis, delineated in recent years and inspired by human rights, is to promote a favorable environment for the right to health.[16] A human rights approach to health has criticized the focus on so-called 'risk groups' because it strengthened the stigmatization of these populations. Instead it proposes to use the concept of vulnerability—as the result of concurrent factors including social and living conditions and other social determinants of health—which has been increasingly incorporated into policies.

The new plan called CONTRASIDA 2004–2006 restated as strategic objectives: the reduction of sexual transmission of STDs including HIV among the general and vulnerable populations, a decrease in blood and vertical transmission, and a reduction of the impact of individual, social and economic PLWHA. But more importantly, for the first time it included the strengthening of health and social institutions and creating a multisectoral coordination mechanism to ensure social organizations' involvement in policy implementation. This mechanism called the National Multisectoral HIV-related Coordination Mechanism (CONAMUSA), promoted by the Global Fund to Fight AIDS, Tuberculosis and Malaria (GFATM), incorporated representatives from vulnerable populations in the formulation and implementation of plans. As one of its first tasks, CONAMUSA led the process of formulating the HIV/AIDS Multisectoral Strategic Plan 2007–2011 (PEM, Plan Estratégico Multisectoral) to set the objectives, strategies, and goals in the fight against HIV. Later, this plan became part of the Ministry of Health's National Concerted Plan.[17]

Nevertheless, the emphasis on disease transmission common to a public health approach continues to focus on sanitary issues and controlling vulnerable populations, rather than empowering them, which disregards the entitlements of rights-holders. According to the latest publication from the Epidemiology Office, the backlog from 1983 to 2009: 97 % of cases were sexually transmitted, 2 %

---

[16] MINSA 2005.

[17] Ministry of Health 2007, Iguiñiz-Romero et al. 2011, p. 5.

[18] MINSA 2010, p. 39.

[19] MINSA 2012.

[20] Guezmes et al. 2002.

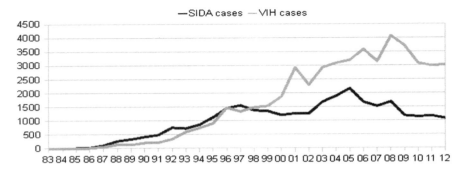

Fig. 11.1 Cases of AIDS and HIV reported in Peru, 1983–2012

were transmitted from mothers to newborns and 1 % for parenteral transmission (Fig. 11.1).[18] In 2010 there were 4,346 new cases of VIH in Peru.[19]

Although anyone can become infected, vulnerability increases for people with low socio-economic status in society. It is not known how many cases of transmission occur as a result of sexual violence. A study sponsored by the WHO found that 1 in 5 women had been sexually abused before the age of 15.[20] Other studies have documented sexual violence towards men, yet it is reported less frequently than sexual violence against women due to its implications to socially constructed notions of masculinity.[21]

In summary, we observed three phases in the response of the Ministry of Health, as the primary actor, in the fight against HIV/AIDS. The first (1996–2002) focuses on primary strategies to prevent HIV transmission, such as the prevention of vertical transmission, early diagnosis, and treatment of STDs and interventions to change behavior. These activities are mainly aimed at the promotion and protection of the right to health of the general population, because in that period the state did not provide free anti-retroviral treatment for PLWHA. It was only available without cost to pregnant women and newborns. During a second phase (2002–2007), the state incorporated treatment for children and adolescents through the Integral Health Insurance (2002), and with the provision of highly active anti-retroviral therapy (HAART) for adults PLWHA (2004). It also acknowledged the importance of working with social organizations and within human rights frameworks to obtain better results. A third phase (commencing in 2007) corresponds to the adaptation and standardization of technical regulations to the objectives, goals and outcomes outlined in the Multisectoral Strategic Plan (PEM) 2007–2011 which incorporated the specific goal (Obj. 7) to "Promote an enabling political, social and legal environment for the comprehensive approach to HIV/AIDS and sexual diversity from a human rights perspective, with the participation

---

[21] Quintana and Vásquez 1999.
[22] MINSA 2007, p. 42.
[23] Cáceres 2009, p. 35.

of the communities with the highest prevalence(MSM, SW and People in Prison) and PLWHA."[22] PEM was the result of a participatory process to guide and improve the state's response to the epidemic; however, it has not been incorporated into other national plans such as the National Human Rights Plan, the National Poverty Reduction Plan, and the National Gender Equality Plan, among other plans at the national and regional level.[23]

These phases should be seen as cumulative efforts, which together provide substance to the expansion of the right to health in relation to HIV.

11.3 Populations and Civil Society Actors in the Context of the HIV Epidemic

The presence of HIV/AIDS as an epidemic in Peru and the rest of the world has contributed to the emergence of social movements and demands focused on new identities, and the recognition of the rights of people with non-hegemonic sexualities. Research on sexual behavior and on the social construction of sexuality and power relations associated with gender, racism and sexual-orientation discrimination have unveiled mechanisms by which a part of society refused to acknowledge the citizenship and rights of women and people with non-hegemonic sexualities. Despite this, legal frameworks have not changed accordingly and homophobia, xenophobia, racism, sexism, violence towards vulnerable groups and intolerance of PLWHA continue to increase.

The fact that the epidemic was associated with immoral sexual behavior forced many organizations of PLWHA, activists from homosexual movements and groups of transvestites and transsexuals as well as sex workers' organizations to enter the public sphere and to demand their right to health and not to be discriminated against regardless of their HIV/AIDS status. Other efforts were deployed by NGOs and researchers specializing in HIV, with the support of international cooperation, which produced studies allowing a better understanding of the epidemic and its impact.

11.3.1 Communities of Lesbians, Gays, Transvestites, Transsexuals and Transgender people

Homosexuals, transvestites and transsexuals suffer from stigma and discrimination because of their sexual orientation and gender identity. Although consensual homosexual acts among adults in private have not been prohibited in Peru since 1923, a strong homophobic culture keeps many people who identify as LGBT or who engage in nonheterosexual practices fearful of social or moral sanctions. Hate

---

[24] Montalvo 2005.

crimes directed at members of this community were collected by the Truth Commission, in which the Shining Path and the MRTA killed people in several parts of the country accusing them of being homosexuals, drug addicts and prostitutes. These organizations justified the killings with the idea that they were eliminating undesirable citizens and carrying out prophylaxis at society's level, without much reaction from the general population.[24]

In addition to an intolerance toward various sexual practices and gender identity, the association between the AIDS epidemic and homosexuality in our continent stigmatized the disease and perpetuated discrimination and abuse.

A year before the onset of the first case of AIDS in Peru, in 1982, one of the most significant movements of rights activists and gay people formed the Homosexual Movement of Lima (MHOL), to subvert the culture and fight homophobia. It was composed mainly of intellectuals and artists, who would surprise Lima's traditional society by publicly announcing their sexual orientation and claiming their rights.

Years later some of its founders and members died from AIDS creating awareness and the commitment to fight the epidemic. In 1990, the MHOL supported the formation of PROSA, the first organization of people with HIV in Peru, which demanded rights beyond the context of HIV/AIDS. As the movement grew, new groups appeared (and disappeared) over time in Lima and other main cities, and it continues to play a key political role.

A group even more vulnerable within this context is the transgender population. Violence against this population during the internal war exacerbated and triggered a large migration of transgender people from areas of conflict to Lima. Since the 1980s, with the support of a religious congregation, the first Transgender self-support group called "Virgen de la Puerta" was formed in a marginal urban district of Lima. This group looked primarily to offer vocational training that would allow these people to enter into the labor market. Later in the 1990s new groups emerged; some of them linked to gender studies programs: *GPUC, Parentesis, Apertura, Colectivo Contranaturas, Colectivo Transforma, Diverse Women Group, Encuentros por el Arte, Asociación Angel Azul.*

In the early years of the twenty-first century, the Lesbian Gay Bisexual Trans Peruvian Network was formed involving many of these groups. Its main challenge was to articulate the different positions of their multiple members. Some of the groups prioritized working on HIV, while others focused on combating the "homosexualization" of AIDS, identity rights for transgender people, among other issues.

One of their main initiatives—in the context of the constitutional reform in 2002—was the creation of the Front for the Right to be Different which sought to include in the Peruvian Constitution a non-discrimination clause based on sexual orientation. An important indicator of progress in becoming political actors was the participation of two LGBT representatives in the Congressional election of 2006, and the presentation of several law proposals against discrimination based on sexual orientation. Although they did not win a seat in Congress, they appeared

11 The Right to Health in Peru: Persistent Vulnerabilities in the Context of HIV/AIDS

publicly for the first time as political actors and have continued to fight for their rights in many ways.

11.3.2 People Living with HIV–AIDS

At the beginning of the epidemic, when no treatment was available, the state did not respond to the suffering of PLWHA in a timely manner and the first response was prevention-focused. So PLWHA suffered discrimination and rejection not only in society, but from those closest to them due to a lack of knowledge about the disease, i.e. family rejection, isolation and even expulsion. As one interviewee reflects:

> In the beginning, because there was no treatment, just basically the promotion of self-help, people could use mental and spiritual resources, group support to address HIV and to overcome the stigma of discrimination, that is a persistent theme. Between the discovery of the first case of HIV there have passed so far, easily 25 years and there have not been substantial changes in the stigma against people with HIV. In the media people keep talking about HIV/AIDS as a deadly disease, PLWHA as having a terrible evil.[25]

The first mutual aid (self-help) groups (GAM) were formed linked to health services as spaces where the PLWHA gather. One of the first groups known, El Hongo, formed in the Hospital Nacional Cayetano Heredia in Lima even when there was no access to anti-retroviral treatment in Peru in order to support each other. Since then many other GAM have been created and played a key role in gaining access to treatment.

11.3.3 Sex Workers

Sex workers have always been heavily stigmatized in Peru. Social stigmatization and discrimination have condemned them to anonymity and isolation which increases their vulnerability to sexually transmitted diseases, to violations of their human rights by police violence, sexual violence and abuse in general.

Only in the last few decades, and with support from feminist organizations and NGOs, has a concern for the human and sexual rights of women sex workers become visible. The first NGO to address the issues faced by women involved in prostitution and to work directly with sex workers was the Movimiento el Pozo. Formed in 1978, it seeks to empower women providing opportunities for support and friendship to strengthen their self-esteem, training in alternative occupations and alternative income generation, and promoting their human and sexual and reproductive rights.

---

[25] Interview 2.

The involvement of sex workers, predominantly women, in teaching the use of condoms to fellow workers has contributed to the recognition of these women as rights-holders and key social actors for active health provision.

> It has contributed, here in Peru and elsewhere, to provide some kind of recognition for women who engage in prostitution, their importance in addressing the health problem, and recognizing them as persons. They have assumed a new identity, similar to what happened to gay men in the 1990s when homosexuality became spoken of and identified with concrete faces and individuals.[26]

The first association of sex workers in Peru, "Miluska Vida y Dignidad", appeared in 2002 and sought to disclose the abuse of sex workers at the hands of the police and the authorities. The organization demanded civil, labor, and health rights for sex workers. Currently, there are six organizations in Lima and some other regions of the country. While the context of HIV has been a major driving force for the development of organizations of vulnerable populations such as sex workers, they see their work and impact beyond that linked to HIV prevention.[27] While some stereotypes have begun to change, the stigma associated with sex work is still very strong and has prevented organizations from expanding.

11.3.4 Non-Governmental Organizations

NGOs working on HIV/AIDS developed with the first cases of HIV and they have formed networks over the years to better position themselves to advocate on behalf of diverse social actors, to create dialog with the state, and to promote international cooperation.

In 1997 eight civil society organizations and groups of PLWHA formed the *Collective for Life*[28] that has continued to grow and now comprises twenty groups. One of its priorities, achieved by the amendment of Law 26626, was to ensure free access to comprehensive treatment and timely and quality services for all PLWHA in Peru.

> On the Collective for Life, we dealt with access to treatment; the law 28243 which was what we wanted as PLWHA, a law that says you have free access to treatment and quality.[29]

In the same year, the Peru AIDS Network (Red Sida Peru) was formed by eleven NGOs nationally and internationally, with the objective to *contribute to the reduction of the impact of the epidemic, stigma and discrimination associated with*

---

[26] Interview 14.

[27] Interview 16 and 20.

[28] Cueto 2001, p 124.

[29] Interview 12.

[30] www.redsidaperu.org.pe

11 The Right to Health in Peru: Persistent Vulnerabilities in the Context of HIV/AIDS 327

HIV and AIDS on the affected and vulnerable people in particular, as well as the general population.[30]

11.4 Human Rights in the Context of HIV

11.4.1 Right to Life and Quality of Survival

LGBT populations' rights to life and health are continuously being violated by the use of violence against them. In Peru, hate crimes perpetrated by the state or citizens take place every week on average. Violence occurring at the hands of municipal and national police forces, whose responsibility is to protect the population, against the person or group that identifies as transvestite, transgender, gay, lesbian, or against sex workers are continuously reported. The following quote represents an example of the lack of respect for human rights among police officers: "I think there is an act of cruelty, I saw what happened in a police station in Piura, last year, there was a police officer who took three transvestites, sex workers, and he tossed a teargas bomb into the cell, I think it is ignominious."[31]

In the early years of the epidemic the struggle of PLWHA focused on the demand for the right to health care and access to medicine, because life and quality of survival were at risk. In fact, in the early years of the epidemic many people died due to a slow response from the State and the lack of effective treatment.

> Times were very hard, actually. In the GAM we did joint activities in order to collect some funds to support a member, (…), I remember it was to pay for basic medication required to alleviate some of the discomfort from opportunistic infections … was a bit rough this time, we knew we could do nothing to increase the opportunity to continue to live for those people, because we knew we could just reduce their suffering and, day after day we saw many friends die, very very hard times in our country on that issue.[32]

The neglect of the State to prioritize access to treatment motivated that in 2002 a group of 121 people requested precautionary measures before the Inter-American Court of Human Rights. Despite achieving a favorable ruling for six people, but the MOH did not abide by the ruling and one of the women in the group died without receiving treatment.[33]

With the discovery and availability of new treatments such as HAART, the HIV/AIDS mortality rate has decreased, which means it is now considered a chronic disease, rather than one that is imminently fatal. From a health system

---

[31] Interview 18.

[32] Interview 6.

[33] Chávez 2004, p. 26.

perspective, it opens a series of issues ranging from consumer needs and demands, administrative deficiencies, and public health policy regarding coverage, distortions between programming and effective administration of treatment regimens, quality of care and programme sustainability over time. For example, Peruvian policy guarantees free access to anti-retrovirals, which is a large demand on drug supply and other resources. This problem is not unique to the health care of PLWH, but rather an issue that has accompanied successive evolutions of the health system, which now also extends to HIV.

Chronic disease implies longer treatment durations and the need for care throughout one's life. From an individual perspective this means taking medication for life, as well as learning to live with a chronic disease and its social, economic, and political implications. It raises issues of rights entitlements, of adherence to treatment, of well-being, of full participation in society as individuals with rights.

11.4.2 *Right to Nondiscrimination*

With free access to HAART, PLWHA have replaced the fear of death with the fear of discrimination and rejection experienced at the health services. The administration and implementation of the HAART treatment program was not sensitive to the privacy and autonomy of PLWHA. The gradual incorporation of the right to nondiscrimination into health policies and plans taking place in the last decade have been partly promoted by civil society and PLWHA organizations and motivated by the limitations of the predominantly epidemiological approach of the health sector to address the epidemic.

The National Strategy for the Prevention of HIV/AIDS, Tuberculosis and Malaria of the Ministry of Health includes a strong area of prevention, which follows a human rights approach, in its work with vulnerable populations.

> Even though a rights approach is prioritized at the policy level, at the health service level PLWHA still face discrimination and stigmatization. Health records containing information about HIV status are openly shared among different health providers and non-medical personnel running the center. There are innumerable cases of people who did not get attention immediately even though their health was in great risk. Of pregnant women who were denied attention through emergency once identified as PLWHA. Although acts of discrimination take place in different settings, in health centers they put the lives of PLWHA at even greater risk.[34]

The strong association of the HIV epidemic with non-heterosexual practices has further increased discrimination towards LGBT populations and towards PLWHA. While there has been progress in terms of health coverage, the LGBT population, sex workers and PLWHA are still discriminated against when denied the same rights and services as the general population.

---

[34] Interview 6.

11 The Right to Health in Peru: Persistent Vulnerabilities in the Context of HIV/AIDS

Discrimination against sex workers is not recent, and the identification of sex workers as potential transmitters of HIV has increased their stigma. Models to control STD and provide health care in 'special' secluded facilities for sex workers were applied to deal with the HIV/AIDS epidemic. Prevention, control, and treatment for STDs and HIV continue to be provided only at special Units for Regular Medical Attention, HAART services and centers. Confinement to specific healthcare centers has contributed to the discrimination of users in several ways. First, specialization in these facilities prevents users from accessing comprehensive healthcare services that may be unrelated to sexual health. Second, as reported by Hunt, segregated health services makes people affected more reluctant to go to health services afraid of being identified and associated with or stigmatized as PLWHA, LGBT, or sex workers, which contributes to their and others' vulnerability to HIV infection.[35,36]

In addition to the stigma and discrimination associated with sexual and gender identity, age is also a variable of discrimination within the health services. Young people involved in consensual sexual practices do not have access to health care without the presence of a parent or tutor. This violation of young people's right to access health care has a strong impact on the increased rates of adolescent pregnancy and suicide experiences in recent years.[37]

Despite several campaigns to eliminate discrimination against people with HIV, both in health facilities and among the general population, it is still very much present. There is evidence that members of communities of Transsexual/Transgender, sexual workers and men who have sex with men (MSM) (in that order) are less accepted than heterosexual men and women living with HIV. In the first case people prefer to keep a distance from the 'trans' population and to avoid sharing a space or having any physical contact with them. In the second case, people would not have problems sharing a space or having physical contact with heterosexual PLWHA nor with children, for whom there is more sympathy.[38]

An additional problem identified in implementing human rights legislation against discrimination is that health providers are not familiar with legislation changes and human rights frameworks. One key issue aggravating discrimination is the tendency to identify with one category, MSM, gay men, bisexuals, transvestites and 'trans'. This has been identified as a violation of their different identities and also of their particular healthcare needs and therefore of the acceptability component of the right to health as stated in General Comment 14.

The National Human Rights Plan 2006–2010 states that campaigns should be established to protect and promote human rights and respect for the dignity of PLWHA, thereby trying to reduce the stigma and discrimination associated with HIV/AIDS. It even adds measures to eradicate all forms of stigma and

---

[35] United Nations 2007.

[36] UNGASS 2010, p. 124.

[37] Mesa de Lucha contra la Pobreza 2013.

[38] CARE 2006.

discrimination in public and private services, the media, the workplace, and also in recreation and sports (Presidencia de la República 2005).

There is a general perception among PLWHA that the country has adopted some anti-discrimination laws but their contents are not known by the majority of the population. Moreover, the existence of several protection mechanisms is not sufficient to enable vulnerable populations to claim their rights, to counteract their mistrust of the police and the authorities, nor to overcome the stigma associated with the disease and vulnerable populations. As one interviewee explained: "We may denounce this discrimination, because Law 26626 already established that this test (ELISA) was not mandatory, but the fear of becoming visible as a person with HIV, the fear and stigma were too big, I was afraid to say it publicly and confront the fact."[39]

11.4.3 Right to Privacy and Confidentiality

The Peruvian Constitution states in its Chap. 1, article 7 that every individual "has the right to honor and a good reputation, to individual and family privacy, and to own their own image and voice". In its article 10 it acknowledges individuals' rights to the "secrecy and inviolability of private communications and documents" and states that information systems, public or private, are forbidden from providing information that affects individual or familiar intimacy.[40]

The National Health Law in its article 15 recognizes the right of every user of the health system to respect for his/her personality, dignity and privacy. Thus, to provide information contained in medical records requires the written consent of the patient. Furthermore, article 25 states that any user of health services is entitled to request the reservation of information related to his or her medical and health history, with exceptions established by law (i.e., compulsory notification of HIV/AIDS cases, and maternal deaths).

Based on the legislation analyzed for this study, we identified that the right to privacy is also interpreted as the right to confidentiality. While most objectives and strategies to fight HIV/AIDS have been developed under the scope of national laws and human rights principles, this distinction has particular consequences in everyday practice within the health sector.

On the one hand, the right to confidentiality is mentioned when dealing with the processing and handling of health information collected through the health services. On the other hand, the right to privacy is understood as the individual and interpersonal relationships established at the health service facilities.

---

[39] Interview 6.
[40] Peruvian Constitution 1993, Article 2.6.

In the first case, emphasis is placed on securing the information provided by the user to the service provider as a result of clinical trials, and to the handling of such information with respect, without exposing the privacy of users. The Multisectoral Strategic Plan 2007–2011 (PEM) recognizes this right and states that its goal of strengthening the information system should ensure that the reporting of HIV and AIDS cases also guarantees the confidentiality of the identity of the people involved according to the law.[41] To ensure compliance with the mandatory reporting of STDs, and HIV and AIDS without violating the privacy of PLWHA, the PEM establishes that notification must be *confidential to protect the honor, dignity and privacy of individuals.*

Since the start of the mandatory reporting of HIV and AIDS cases in Peru in 1995, based on the experience of other epidemiological surveillance activities that were in place, the notification forms are coded and only report the initials of the person and the date of birth to ensure the confidentiality of the information handled at the different levels of the MOH and health sector.[42]

At the health center level, with regard to medical records and confidentiality within the health services, there have not been many problems keeping diagnosis in reserve and using codes in the medical history charts for this purpose. Representatives from different health and civil society institutions, however, recognize that respect for privacy /confidentiality requires constant vigilance as it depends on the commitment of the team of health professionals. "Currently they are strongly committed and know that this is a basic right. We have not had problems ... I think if the people working there are committed to keep the issue of confidentiality."[43] Nevertheless, cases of violations of the right to privacy /confidentiality can still be found and a few of them have been reported to regional health authorities or the Ombudsman.

In the second case, the right to privacy is understood as the interpersonal relationships established at the health centers where services are provided. This interaction should foster a sense of trust, comfort and respect for the privacy of users while in the service and is a key component of the quality of care and services. An initial concern for privacy during healthcare delivery can be traced to the late 1980s as a result of health providers' initiatives serving sex workers. Some health centers began to build partitions to divide large areas where women sex workers were lined up in beds for the regular gynecological examinations (almost in series) into smaller spaces for individual and personal attention.

Gradually the concept of the right to privacy in health has been included in legislation and protocols, and has gained strength. The 2006 National Guide to Treat Sexually Transmitted Infections[44] recognized the respect for privacy as a key element in the provider-user relationship. It established the need to ensure privacy at the

---

[41] MINSA 2006, Objective 9.

[42] Interview 22.

[43] Interviews 9 and 10.

[44] MINSA 2006.

physical spaces where care is provided; in the way to ask questions about sexual practices and symptoms; as well as regarding information obtained in medical records.

An important concern about the exercise of the right to privacy is that care services for PLWHA, LGBT people and sex workers are provided only at the Reference Center for Sexually Transmitted Infections (CERITS), and Units for Regular Medical Care (UAMP) making clear the medical condition or vulnerability of the people who are going to and are served at these establishments. Zambrano highlights PLWHA's awareness that merely attending the service identifies them as a potential gay, 'trans', sex worker or living with HIV/AIDS: "There are few gays and transvestites who are not afraid to disclose their sexual orientation or do not worry about being seen near those services. But most users, especially heterosexual men, prefer to travel long distances to receive treatment in a far area for fear of being identified and discriminated".[45]

It is also very interesting to note that among health professionals one of the first interpretations when asked about the right to privacy and confidentiality is directly related to secrecy. While the majority still prefer to keep their identity and diagnoses secret from their family, social groups, and health services; some professionals say that some PLWHA are less likely to keep family members uninformed of their HIV-seropositive diagnosis.

This change has been strongly promoted by regulation regarding access to HAART. It establishes as a mandatory requirement for treatment that the user has a Personal Support Agent who knows his/her diagnosis and supports him/her to maintain the long-term treatment.[46] Although the benefits of this type of support seem to be valuable, as evidenced by the quote below, its mandatory character, emphasis on treatment adherence and monitoring logic behind the initiative can be identified as a violation of the right to privacy and confidentiality of PLWHA.

> When we elaborate the HAART programme, we asked ourselves, how do we achieve adherence, we need someone who is there, vigilant ... one of the conditions set for receiving HAART is that at the evaluation he/she has to be accompanied by what is called your Personal Support. The personal support agent is really a relative, brother, sister, father, mother, uncle, godfather, couple. Then you say to him/her: you have to bring me someone to share the diagnosis with, so that someone begins to educate the family.[47]

Many health practice procedures invade the privacy of the individual from a personal perspective as well as from a system perspective through two main practices. On the one hand, physical examinations take place in crowded spaces with other individuals (medical professionals or patients) around, exposing individuals' histories to public scrutiny. On the other hand, medical examinations and laboratory tests and all personal information are all recorded, shared and archived in the medical history which are manipulated and shared by different providers within the healthcare system. With the expansion of public-private partnerships in the health

---

[45] Zambrano 2008.

[46] MINSA 2004.

[47] Interview 21.

sector, issues of private information might become problematic. While the State may claim a need to control information in the name of the public interest, private companies would maximize their benefits without much concern for individual rights. Pharmaceutical campaigns are in full range collecting individuals' information of drugs consumption, common illnesses and medical plans through their clients/customers' discount plans with no clear legislation or control by the state.

11.5 Major Contradictions and Gaps in the Recognition of Rights in the Context of HIV

Human rights, and specifically the rights of people in vulnerable conditions, have been included in regulations and policies. As mentioned in Sect. 11.2, the state's response to STDs and the HIV and AIDS epidemic has evolved from an epidemiological and controlist perspective focused on preserving the health and morale of the "healthy" population, to a perspective that incorporates human rights principles into health discourse, while maintaining the "control" aspect in plans and programs.

11.5.1 Tensions and Contradictions Surrounding the Rights of Women

A contradiction that emerges from the analysis of policies and regulations on HIV is the notion of "female subjects" and their rights. Whilst, on the one hand, they recognize the right to privacy of the general population and establish regulations to protect it from compulsory diagnostic tests (Law 26626), a subsequent amendment of the law in 2004 (Law 28243) excluded pregnant women from this protection.

Although different voices have been raised against mandatory testing for pregnant women, they are still subject to legal discrimination based on sex, and being pregnant. Identified as potential PLWHA and transmitters of HIV to infants, they are the only ones who systematically undergo mandatory testing as a mechanism to prevent vertical transmission. The screening of pregnant women, included as routine services, could become a systematic violation of women's rights to autonomy and privacy. Being a regular maternal healthcare procedure within public health facilities, there is the risk of delivering the service without the minimum requirements and considerations needed such as informed consent, and counselling before and after testing.

The failure to consider women as subjects of rights with ethical decision-making capacity has been a persistent issue in Peruvian legislation. Legally, the Peruvian Constitution in its second article recognizes the unborn as a subject with the right to life and to welfare. Not surprisingly, the first state response towards access to treatment favors children affiliated with the Comprehensive Health Insurance Plan 2002.

Additional examples of the failure to recognize the reproductive rights of women include the failure to comply with the recommendations from the United Nations Committee on Human Rights and CEDAW regarding the need to review the national legislation on abortion. This means that a woman cannot decide to legally interrupt her pregnancy if she is an HIV carrier or if her life is threatened; not even to decide autonomously on the best interest of her children's health and welfare.

11.5.2 Tensions Between Criminalizing Contagion and the Rights of the General Population

The controlist approach to dealing with the spread of communicable diseases is also present in the Penal Code. It states that the person who deliberately spreads the disease will be punished by the law. The criminalization of deliberate contagion as a criminal offence opens up space for the criminalization of sex workers, PLWHA or pregnant women living with HIV/AIDS.

This argument has been used for the persecution or violation of sex workers' rights by the national or municipal police and individuals. So far there have not been cases recorded or publicly known of prosecutions for transmitting a STD against LGBT or sex worker populations. To start a judicial process against an individual will require the disclosure of private information and the behavior of the litigants, and to expose them to public scrutiny and moral judgments.

At the system level, responsibility for contagion also reaches the health system, which is responsible for ensuring a "safe blood policy" and biosafety and laboratory biosecurity mechanisms to prevent the spread of the epidemic. Indeed regulation preceding the first responses to HIV/AIDS has evolved with the State's response to HIV. Nevertheless, cases of people (nine children infected and five resulting deaths in 2004, and one heterosexual woman infected in 2007) infected by blood or blood–derived products transfused at healthcare facilities has led to a public outcry, charges against the state and timely reactions by key state actors as the Ombudsman. It is significant to note that in both cases the children and the woman who do not belong to vulnerable or at-risk groups were socially identified as "innocent". As mentioned above, there are no cases raised by individuals that due to their sexual orientation, or social stereotypes might be morally judged as responsible for contracting the disease or even deserving it because of their immoral behavior.

11.6 Conclusions: Unresolved Tensions Between Public Health Policy and the Right to Health, Non-discrimination and Privacy

The history of policies to control sexually transmitted diseases such as syphilis in its time and now HIV/AIDS are in tension with the principles underlying human rights, including the right to privacy and non-discrimination, therefore limiting people's autonomy when interventions are mandatory or without due regard to the consent of the person.

Despite the fact that the construction of health policy frameworks has not been necessarily inspired by human rights principles, as evidenced by the development of the policies presented, there is a growing recognition of the inadequacy of compulsory approaches, which in turn has allowed a progressive incorporation of a rights-based approach to health.

It was only after the achievements and limitations of the health sector became visible, and knowledge of the HIV virus increased, that the need to incorporate other public institutions and civil society in the fight against HIV and AIDS was recognized. The characteristics of the HIV epidemic have obliged public health officials to call upon various institutions and social actors. The participation of these actors has raised awareness and generated a response to the issues of the discrimination and stigmatization of vulnerable populations—either by their health status (carriers of HIV infection), their non-conventional sexual orientation/preference, gender identities, involvement in sex work (male, female or 'trans') or other reasons—into policies.

Compared to the development of other health goals, those related to HIV show interesting developments regarding the recognition of the rights of vulnerable populations, which may be due to the extensive involvement of multiple social actors, to the influence of the international context, the possibility of international cooperation, resource availability and the existence of opportunities for dialog and sectoral coordination such as the National Coordinating Mechanism—CONAMUSA encouraged by the Global Fund.

After two decades since the beginning of the epidemic, the human right to health has expanded from the right to have access to healthcare services to the right to the enjoyment of the highest attainable standard of health conducive to living a life in dignity. It set the groundwork to expand the State's obligations, both regulatory and programmatic regarding health as an inseparable part of a broader system of entitlements and freedoms associated with the notion of human dignity.

While in the theoretical and normative fields there has been a significant evolution towards acknowledging and incorporating elements of the right to health, this has not been the case in the jurisprudence and legal doctrine, nor in the

---

[48] UNAIDS/Joint United Nations Programme on HIV/AIDS 2006.

healthcare delivery practices. Rather, they have retained the old formulations focused on health care, sanitation, and isolation, which has had a significant impact on regulations and the formulation of legislative initiatives on HIV/AIDS by state officials and civil society groups. For instance, HIV-related policies incorporate the rights approach either in a selective or a general way. In our analysis of the right to privacy and confidentiality, these are rights that have been circumscribed almost exclusively to the health sector and relationships established at the health center. However, since discrimination on multiple grounds persists in the country, the right to no-discrimination continues to be defined in general terms that fails to adequately address specific cases and situations, such as those experienced by PLWHA, sex workers and other vulnerable populations.

Even with valuable policy instruments such as the 2007–2011 Multisectoral Strategic Plan and other guidelines,[48] there are still weaknesses in the implementation and enforcement of rights. Many health providers and personnel tend to hold old prejudices and/or compulsory practices which run counter to a human right to health-based approach. Patterns of discrimination and stigma are widespread and shared, hence abuse and discriminatory actions against people who have less power or whose rights are not recognized. Rigid state institutions and procedures, and the lack of knowledge and understanding of human rights among health providers and the general population makes the scenario for the exercise of the rights to health one which is riddled with accidents, contradictions, advances and setbacks.

More importantly, the focus of HIV health policies on vulnerable populations limits their impact and prevents them from developing massive educational campaigns to inform the general population and reduce the risks of infection. While compulsory and regulatory approaches supported by conservative religious groups continue to exert pressure and influence sexual and reproductive health policies, the state not only neglects people's sexual and reproductive rights but also all citizens' right to access information and to be informed.

References

American Convention on Human Rights (1992) O.A.S.Treaty Series No. 36, 1144 U.N.T.S. 123, entered into force July 18, 1978, reprinted in Basic Documents Pertaining to Human Rights in the Inter-American System, OEA/Ser.L.V/II.82 doc.6 rev.1 at 25 1992

Barboza M (2008) Tecnología médica e innovaciones de salud en el Perú, desde una perspectiva de género (o de la rehabilitación liberadora a la vitalización). In: UNAM, Anales del Primer Encuentro Latinoamericano y del Caribe 'La sexualidad frente a la sociedad'. México D.F.: UNAM/ Fundación Arco Iris. pp. 143–144

Cáceres C (2009) Lecciones aprendidas de la colaboración con el Fondo Mundial en VIH y SIDA en el VIH / SINDROME DE INMUNODEFICIENCIA ADQUIRIDA / PROGRAMAS NACIONALES DE SALUD. IESSDEH-UPCH, Lima

CARE (2006) Cerrando Brechas. Care, Lima http://www.care.org.pe/Websites/FondoMundial/CERRANDOBRECHAS/Informe6/5R-VIH%20Q06-Informe.pdf Accessed June 2008

Carrol P (2002) Medical police and the history of public health. Med Hist 46:461–494

11 The Right to Health in Peru: Persistent Vulnerabilities in the Context of HIV/AIDS

Chávez S (2004) Cuando el fundamentalismo se apodera de las políticas públicas: políticas de salud sexual y reproductiva en el Perú en el periodo 2001-Junio 2003. Flora Tristán, Lima

Cueto M (1997) El regreso de las epidemias. Salud y sociedad en el Perú del siglo XX. Instituto de Estudios Peruanos, Lima

Cueto M (2001) Culpa y coraje: Historia de las políticas sobre el VIH/Sida en el Perú. CIES–FASPA, Lima

Guézmes A, Palomino N, Ramos M (2002) Violencia sexual y física contra las mujeres en el Perú. Estudio multicéntrico de la OMS sobre la violencia de pareja y la salud de las mujeres, UPCH-OMS, Lima

Iguiñiz-Romero R, Lopez R, Sandoval C, Chirinos A, Pajuelo J, Caceres C (2011) Regional HIV-related policy processes in Peru in the context of the Peruvian national decentralization plan and global fund support: Peru GHIN study. Glob Health Gov, Spring 4(2):1–14

Mesa de Lucha contra la Pobreza (2013) Prevención del Embarazo Adolescente. Seguimiento Concertado "Estado y Sociedad Civil". Reporte No.1-2013-SC/PSMN

Ministry of Health (1996) Doctrina, normas y procedimientos para el control de las enfermedades de transmisión sexual y el Sida en el Perú, PROCETSS. MINSA, Lima

Ministry of Health (2004) Norma Técnica para el Tratamiento Antirretroviral de Gran Actividad – TARGA en adultos infectados por el VIH. MINSA, Lima

Ministry of Health (2006) Norma técnica de salud para el manejo de las ITS. MINSA, Lima

Ministry of Health (2007) Plan estratégico multisectorial para la prevención y control de las ITS y el VIH / Sida en el Perú 2007-2011. MINSA, Lima

Ministry of Health (2012) Informe nacional sobre los progresos realizados en el País – Perú. MINSA, Lima

Ministry of Health - DGE (2010) Análisis de la situación de salud del Perú 2010. MINSA, Lima

Montalvo J (2005) Crímenes de homofobia en el contexto de la violencia política en el Perú: 1980–2000. http://es.geocities.com/raizdiversidad/articulos.html

http://www.oocities.org/es/crimenes_odio_nunca_mas/PERU.htm. Accessed 10 Apr 2013

Nencel L (2000) Mujeres que se prostituyen. Género, identidad y pobreza en el Perú. Flora Tristán, Lima

Presidencia de la República (2005) Plan Nacional de Derechos Humanos. 2006–2010. Decreto Supremo N° 017-2005-JUS. (Publicado en El Peruano, 11.12.05), Lima

Quintana A, Vásquez E (1999) Construcción social de la sexualidad adolescente. IES, Lima

Rosen G (1985) De la policía médica a la medicina social. Siglo XXI, México DF

UNAIDS /Joint United Nations Programme on HIV/AIDS (2006) International guidelines on HIV/AIDS and human rights. Consolidated Version. HR/PUB/06/9

UNAIDS/ONUSIDA, Proyecto POLICY Interagency Team (2005) Evaluación del Plan Estratégico del MINSA, 2001–2004 para la Prevención y Control del VIH / SIDA en el Perú. MINSA, ONUSIDA, Proyecto Policy, Lima

United Nations (2003) Reports of the UN special rapporteur on the right to health, Paul Hunt. E/CN.4/2003/58. 13 Feb 2003

United Nations (2007) Reports of the UN special rapporteur on the right to health, Paul Hunt. A/HRC/4/28. 17 Jan 2007

UNGASS (2010) Informe Nacional sobre los procesos realizados en la aplicación del UNGASS 2008–2009, Lima

Zambrano D (2008) La Implementación de la política de adherencia al tratamiento antirretroviral para personas viviendo con VIH/Sida en un Hospital de Lima, 2005. Dissertation, Universidad Peruana Cayetano Heredia, Lima

Part V
Europe

Chapter 12
The Right to Health for Vulnerable and Marginalised Groups: Russia as a Case Study

Natalya Pestova

Abstract The international human right to health seeks to deliver equal opportunity to enjoy the highest attainable standard of health for everyone and is specifically concerned with the health status of vulnerable and marginalised groups. To this aim it unequivocally prohibits discrimination and guarantees the equal access to health care for all. This contribution analyses the potential of the human rights framework to ensure equal health opportunities for women, children, indigenous peoples, prisoners, drug users and people with HIV by means of the Russian case study. This chapter will first establish the normative protection the right to health offers for disadvantaged groups via the principles of non-discrimination and equality, which are translated into the content of the right to health and the consequent states' obligations. Second, it undertakes a case study of the Russian public health system and assesses the health status of disadvantaged groups in the context of central government law and public health policy measures. From this empirical evidence, the systematic noncompliance of the State with its obligations in relation to the right to health of the vulnerable and marginalised groups is established: equal access to health care is particularly impeded for prisoners, drug users, indigenous people, women and adolescents; de facto discrimination is experienced by HIV-positive drug users despite the equality legislation available in Russia; and preventative measures, such as health information and education are not adequately provided to women, adolescents and indigenous groups. Based on the findings of the case study this carries out an analysis of the perspectives, challenges and dimensions of equal opportunity for disadvantaged communities to enjoy the highest attainable standard of health. It reaffirms that equal access to health care and non-discrimination are crucial conditions to combat health inequalities, and elaborates whether political willingness and purposeful rights-based action focusing on the specific health needs of vulnerable and disadvantaged people are capable of ensuring the much needed equal health opportunities for all.

N. Pestova (✉)
Irish Centre for Human Rights, National University of Ireland, Galway, Ireland
e-mail: pestovang@gmail.com

B. Toebes et al. (eds.), *The Right to Health*, DOI: 10.1007/978-94-6265-014-5_12,
© T.M.C. ASSER PRESS and the authors 2014

Contents

12.1	Introduction		342
12.2	Marginalised and Vulnerable Groups in the Light of the Normative Scope		
	of the Right to Health		343
	12.2.1	The Principles of Equality and Non-discrimination	345
	12.2.2	The Normative Content of the Right to Health	346
	12.2.3	Obligations of States	348
12.3	Russia as a Case Study		349
	12.3.1	Historical Context	349
	12.3.2	Legal Settings for the Right to Health in Russia	350
	12.3.3	Health Sector Financing	352
	12.3.4	Health Status of Disadvantaged Groups	353
	12.3.5	Analysis	366
12.4	Conclusion		369
References			370

12.1 Introduction

Disparities in health status across population groups based on physical characteristics, gender or the age of individuals exist in every society. At the same time, the systematic differences in health status among different socio-economic groups emerge as socially produced health inequalities[1] which are unfair, and as such, avoidable and amenable to change.[2] According to the WHO 'most health services are consistently inequitable' in terms of availability, access, quality and burden of payment.[3] Health inequalities emerging from vulnerability and social processes combined with inequities within the healthcare system result in asymmetrical health outcomes across the various sections of the population.[4] Respectively, addressing health inequalities requires purposeful action in the health sector along with the consideration of broader implications of poverty, social disadvantage, exclusion and marginalisation.[5]

In this context, international human rights law presents an important normative framework and tool for action in the effort to address health inequalities. From its beginnings, the human rights movement acted to assert the collective dignity and well-being of vulnerable and marginalised groups. The international human right to health exists as the appropriate mechanism to advance health equity and is set

---

[1] Whitehead and Dahlgren 2006, p. 23.

[2] Ibid., p. 4, 23.

[3] WHO 2008, p. 24.

[4] Ibid.

[5] Braveman and Gruskin 2003, p. 540.

forth in a range of international human rights treaties, including those adopted in the interests of disadvantaged sections of the population.[6]

Vulnerable groups and their health status are a matter of particular attention to the UN Committee on Economic, Social and Cultural Rights (UNCESCR)[7] and other treaty bodies established to monitor implementation of the international human rights treaties. In 2000, the UNCESCR adopted General Comment 14[8] clarifying the meaning and scope of the right to health as stipulated in Article 12 of the International Covenant of Economic, Social and Cultural Rights (ICESCR). It is a soft law instrument that is non-binding on states, but yet is the official source of the authoritative interpretation of the right to health. At its outset, General Comment 14 establishes that the right to health comprises the right to a system of health protection which as its outcome provides equality of opportunity for everyone to enjoy the highest attainable level of health.[9] The document refers to the particular aspects of the right to health for vulnerable groups embedded in the principles of equality and non-discrimination, the normative content of the right and the respective obligations of states. This chapter utilises General Comment 14 as a principal matrix for its analysis.

An attempt will be made below to revisit the potential of the human rights framework to address the inequalities in the health status of vulnerable and marginalised groups. Based on a case study of Russia, this article examines how these features unfold in norm and practice, what are the strengths or shortfalls of human rights in this regard and where the challenges lie in achieving equal health opportunities for all in diverse societies.

12.2 Marginalised and Vulnerable Groups in the Light of the Normative Scope of the Right to Health

This chapter refers to a group as marginalised if its members reside outside or do not equally participate in, the life of the mainstream society. These groups experience evident social disadvantages and include, for instance, indigenous peoples, minorities, Roma communities, prisoners, drug users and others. The origins of their marginalisation are different: they can be social exclusion in the

---

[6] International Convention for the Elimination of All Forms of Racial Discrimination 660 UNTS 195 (CERD), Convention on the Elimination of All Forms of Discrimination against Women 19 ILM 33 (CEDAW), Convention on the Rights of the Child 28 ILM 1448 (CRC), Migrant Workers Convention 30 ILM 1517 (MWC), Convention on the Rights of Persons with Disabilities 993 UNTS 3 (CRPD).

[7] Toebes 1999a, pp. 669–671.

[8] UNCESCR 2000, General Comment on the Right to the Highest Attainable Standard of Health 14. (hereinafter General Comment 14).

[9] Ibid., p. 8.

case of Roma communities or minorities, geographical isolation of indigenous peoples, institutionalisation of asylum seekers, social status and gender inequities in the case of women, criminalisation of drug use or freedom restriction for prisoners. Marginalisation is often accompanied with issues such as inadequate access to basic services, poverty, limited opportunities, poor education and an unhealthy lifestyle affecting the health status of these groups.[10]

By contrast, population groups that require special attention and protection due to their biological characteristics such as age, health status, physical or emotional needs will be referred to in this chapter as vulnerable. These groups include children, women,[11] elderly people, people with HIV/AIDS or persons with disabilities. Both vulnerable and marginalised individuals experience disadvantages when it comes to their health status. Disadvantages for marginalised groups flow from their position in society, and for vulnerable people from their physical circumstances. Marginalisation and vulnerability often overlap and invoke multiple health-related challenges. For instance, women as a group belong to both categories due to their social status and their specific health needs.[12] For the purpose of this study, reference made to 'disadvantaged' implies both vulnerable and marginalised groups.

General Comment 14 does not provide a definition of vulnerable or disadvantaged individuals, yet on eleven occasions it refers to vulnerable' and ten times it mentions 'marginalised' groups. It draws particular attention to vulnerable groups and elaborates on the measures to be taken by governments to maintain the health status of women, children, indigenous peoples, older persons, and people with disabilities.[13] However, it does not fully address the specific health-related needs in its interpretation of the governments' obligations towards these groups. This is not a major shortfall, considering that the health-related interests and needs of women, children and people with disabilities are specifically dealt with in General Comments and Recommendations of the bodies monitoring implementation of the international human rights treaties stipulating the right to health.[14]

Nor does General Comment 14 sufficiently attend to the marginalised groups with the exception of indigenous peoples.[15] It refers to prisoners, illegal immigrants and asylum seekers on one occasion,[16] three times it mentions minorities[17] and persons with HIV,[18] and there are no references to drug users and Roma

---

[10] WHO 'Women and health: today's evidence tomorrow's agenda' 2009, pp. 9–10.

[11] See for example WHO '10 facts on women's health', 2009. www.who.int/gender/documents/10facts_womens_health_en.pdf. Accessed 31 March 2013.

[12] The other examples of the overlapping statuses that create manifold disadvantages are, among others, a drug user with HIV in detention, a migrant woman or a Roma child.

[13] General Comment 14, paras 20–26.

[14] See for example UNCRC 2003a, b, UNCRC 2005a.

[15] The states' obligations in relation to their right to health have been specifically addressed in para 27.

[16] General Comment 14, para 34.

[17] Ibid., paras 12 (b), (c), 34.

[18] Ibid., paras 12(b), 18, 28.

communities. The fact that States' obligations in relation to the right to health for these groups have not been adequately clarified can be considered a shortcoming of General Comment 14. Despite that, the absence of systematic reference to particular groups by the UNCESCR should not be seen as deliberately excluding these communities from the scope of its application, nor should the list of disadvantaged groups that General Comment 14 refers to be interpreted as exhaustive. In fact, General Comment 14 systematically attends to both 'vulnerable and marginalised' groups in general, through several normative perspectives, as discussed further in this section.

12.2.1 *The Principles of Equality and Non-discrimination*

The principle of non-discrimination is the cross-cutting theme in international human rights treaties that guarantee the human right to health of disadvantaged groups. The Convention on the Elimination of All Forms of Discrimination against Women (CEDAW) explicitly requests States parties to take measures 'to eliminate discrimination against women in the field of healthcare'.[19] The Convention on the Rights of Persons with Disabilities (CRPD) elaborates fairly detailed the right to health without discrimination on the basis of disability.[20] The Convention on the Rights of the Child (CRC) provides for the right to the highest attainable standard of health for the child[21] and in its non-discrimination clause stipulates that 'States Parties shall respect and ensure the rights set forth in the present Convention to each child within their jurisdiction without discrimination of any kind'.[22]

Discrimination directly undercuts the opportunity to enjoy the right to health on an equal basis. The ICESCR prohibits any discrimination in access to health care and underlying determinants of health.[23] The UNCESCR defines discrimination as follows:

> any distinction, exclusion, restriction or preference or other differential treatment that is directly or indirectly based on the prohibited grounds of discrimination and which has the intention or effect of nullifying or impairing the recognition, enjoyment or exercise, on an equal footing, of Covenant rights.[24]

The principle of equality is a core concept of human rights, closely related to non-discrimination. Often used as interchangeable or complementary notions, the principles of equality and non-discrimination differ in their meaning.[25]

---

[19] CEDAW, Article 12.1.

[20] CRPD, Article 25.

[21] CRC, Article 24.

[22] Ibid, Article 2.

[23] ICESCR, Article 2.2, 3; General Comment 14, para 18.

[24] UNCESCR 2009, p. 7.

[25] San Giorgi 2012, pp. 66–67.

Discrimination can be described as 'the best-known dimension of the principle of equality. [...] It is a species of inequality'.[26] In the framework of the right to health, the concept of equality underpins the objective of the right to guarantee the system of health protection which provides equality of opportunity for people to enjoy the highest attainable level of health.[27] On the normative level, it translates into the requirement of equal access to health care[28] throughout the life cycle for all, including women, children, refugees, indigenous peoples, prisoners and other disadvantaged groups.[29]

For vulnerable and marginalised communities that systematically experience challenges with their health status, principles of equality and non-discrimination are the ones of most critical importance, direct relevance and immediate application. Both principles target health inequalities and unjustified differential treatment and aim to ensure equal health opportunities for all. The normative framework of the right to health set out in General Comment 14 entrenches these principles. It explicitly prohibits discrimination[30] and guarantees equal access to healthcare services, facilities and goods, as well as underlying determinants of health for disadvantaged groups.[31] The principles are translated across the dimensions of the normative content of the right to health[32] and through a number of specific States' duties in this respect[33] as will be outlined below.

12.2.2 The Normative Content of the Right to Health

The normative content of the right to health comprises the interrelated essential elements of availability, accessibility, acceptability and quality (AAAQ) that are set forth in General Comment 14.[34] The availability dimension requires states to have health care facilities, goods and services in sufficient quantity. The accessibility element is complex and comprises the four overlapping dimensions of non-discriminatory access, physical accessibility, affordability of health services, goods and facilities as well as accessibility of information concerning health issues. The acceptability dimension requires that 'all health facilities, goods and services must

---

[26] Ibid.

[27] General Comment 14, para 8.

[28] San Giorgi 2012, pp. 68–75.

[29] Ibid., pp. 54–55.

[30] General Comment 14, para 12 (b).

[31] General Comment 14, paras 17, 19.

[32] General Comment 14, para 12.

[33] Obligations concerned with equality are contained in the General Comment 14, paras 18, 19, 20, 22, 34, 35, 36; obligations translating the principle of non-discrimination are found in paras 18, 19, 21, 22, 26, 30, 34, 43(a), 54, 57.

[34] General Comment 14, para 12.

12 The Right to Health for Vulnerable and Marginalised Groups

be respectful of medical ethics and culturally appropriate'.[35] Finally, the fourth element requires the health facilities, goods and services to be of good quality and scientifically and medically appropriate.

The normative content of the right to health expressed in the AAAQ framework considers the vulnerable and marginalised groups across its essential elements. The notions of accessibility and acceptability could be highlighted as having particular relevance when it comes to these groups. Access without discrimination is an integral part of the accessibility element. It explicitly requires that 'health facilities, goods and services must be accessible to all, especially the most vulnerable or marginalised sections of the population, in law and fact, without discrimination on any prohibited grounds'.[36]

The physical accessibility requirement highlights the importance of safe physical access to health facilities, goods and services for all sections of the population and 'especially vulnerable or marginalized groups, such as ethnic minorities and indigenous populations, women, children, adolescents, older persons, persons with disabilities and persons with HIV/AIDS'.[37] This requirement is essentially important for pregnant women, who require immediate access to medical assistance due to their particular health status, or for persons with disabilities who need healthcare buildings to be wheelchair accessible.

The economic accessibility element requires that health facilities, goods and services be affordable for all, including socially disadvantaged communities and poorer households.[38] Although the General Comment failed to explicitly address vulnerable groups in the context of this element, it may be understood that vulnerable groups are not excluded, but are implied in the normative requirement of the health care to be 'affordable for all'.[39]

Finally, the acceptability element requires that health facilities, goods and services be culturally appropriate, sensitive to gender and age requirements, and respectful of the culture of individuals and groups.[40] The acceptability dimension is important for vulnerable groups such as children, women and elderly people on the grounds of their age and gender. It is also of particular relevance to minorities, indigenous peoples, migrants, asylum seekers and refugees, whose experience and perception of health care is based on their culture and nationality.

---

[35] Ibid., para 12(d).
[36] Ibid., para 12(b).
[37] Ibid.
[38] Ibid.
[39] Ibid.
[40] Ibid., para 12(c).

12.2.3 Obligations of States

The framework of the right to health addresses the status of vulnerable and marginalised groups through the spectrum of legal obligations of governments in relation to the right to health. These responsibilities, when considering disadvantaged groups, translate the principles of equality and non-discrimination, as well as the features of the normative content of the right highlighted in the preceding section, into detailed operational provisions. The tripartite classification of states duties to respect, protect and fulfil human rights has been developed by several human rights scholars[41] and is now commonly applied within the UN charter-based and treaty-based human rights mechanisms.[42] Within this framework the obligation to respect requires governments to refrain from certain forms of behaviour that interfere with the enjoyment of human rights. The duties to protect and to fulfil involve performance of specific tasks and taking action by governments to guarantee and ensure rights. The normative framework of the right to health represented in General Comment 14 incorporates this classification and elaborates on the specific obligations of states to respect, protect and fulfil the right. It simultaneously considers disadvantaged groups in relation to these obligations.

Under the duty to respect, states are required to refrain from denying or limiting equal access to health services for all persons, including prisoners or detainees, minorities, asylum seekers or illegal immigrants. States must abstain from enforcing discriminatory practices as a policy, and particularly from imposing discriminatory practices relating to women's health status and needs.[43] The obligation to protect entails, among other actions, adopting legislation or taking other measures ensuring equal access to health care and health-related services provided by third parties, and protecting all vulnerable or marginalised groups of society, in particular women, children, adolescents and older persons, in the light of gender-based expressions of violence.[44] The obligation to fulfil in general terms implies taking steps towards realisation of the right to health, through legal and policy measures, including allocation of sufficient expenditure to the health sector. The inadequate allocation of public resources which prevents vulnerable and marginalised groups from enjoying their right to health constitutes a violation of the obligation to fulfil the right to health.[45] General Comment 14 outlines a list of actions comprising the obligation to fulfil, which do not explicitly consider marginalised and vulnerable groups, with exception of the obligation to promote the right to health and ensure 'that health services are culturally appropriate and that

---

[41] Toebes 1999b, pp. 306–310.

[42] UNCESCR, 'Report on the Right to Food as a Human Right' (1987) UN Doc. E/CN.4/Sub.2/1987/23 was one of the first applications of the tripartite obligations of states in the UN system.

[43] General Comment 14, para 34.

[44] Ibid., para 35.

[45] Ibid., para 52.

12   The Right to Health for Vulnerable and Marginalised Groups   349

healthcare staff are trained to recognise and respond to the specific needs of such groups.[46]

In addition, General Comment 14 defines a set of core obligations of states in relation to the right to health, to ensure the satisfaction of, at the very least, minimum levels of the right to be guaranteed by the state.[47] Two core obligations explicitly refer to disadvantaged groups. First, the States parties must ensure the right of access to health facilities, goods and services on a non-discriminatory basis, especially for vulnerable or marginalized groups.[48] Second, states must adopt and implement a national health strategy and a plan of action, and the process by which these documents are devised, as well as their content, shall give particular attention to all vulnerable or marginalized groups.[49]

12.3 Russia as a Case Study

As established above, the human right to health is explicitly concerned with disadvantaged groups and incorporates the principles of non-discrimination and equality into its normative content and respective obligations of the states. As such it provides an authoritative normative framework and a tool for action to ensure equal opportunity to enjoy the highest attainable standard of health for all. Below, an assessment will be made of the health status of the vulnerable and marginalised groups in Russia in order to evaluate the state's compliance with the right to health for these groups and to seek the potential of the right to health as a suitable conceptual and operational framework to address the health inequalities in the diverse Russian society.

12.3.1 Historical Context

The assessment of the right to health of vulnerable populations in Russia has to be set within the historical context of the Soviet (1917–1991) and post-Soviet governance of the public health system. The communist government during the first two decades of its leadership (1917–1937) gradually took upon itself the entire responsibility for public health. The Soviet healthcare system was based on the principles developed by Nikolay Semashko (Semashko model) which included government responsibility for health, universal access to free services, a preventive

---

[46] Ibid., para 37.

[47] Ibid., para 43.

[48] General Comment 14, para 43(a).

[49] Ibid., para 43(f).

approach to 'social diseases', quality professional care, interlink between science and medical practice, and continuity of care.[50]

The Soviet healthcare policy was oriented towards substantive increase in medical personnel, hospital beds, outpatient hospitals, including parallel health-care facilities specialising in occupational diseases and health problems linked with industries. As a result, the system achieved impressive results as regards the health status of the Russian population.[51] The drastic measures concerning control and prevention of infectious diseases, involving mandatory immunisation and health checks resulted in the elimination of major epidemics.[52]

Despite the substantial expansion of the public health sector, the quality of services remained poor due to factors such as limited funding, corruption caused by the low financial status of the medical occupation and isolation of medical science from western developments, which also impeded progress in the Russian pharmaceutical industry.[53] The public health system was mainly preoccupied with prevention of infectious diseases, while healthy lifestyle choices were not promoted within society. As a result, non-communicable diseases gradually became a real threat to the nation's health[54] and by the end of the Soviet era in the late 1980s Russia 'was already confronting a health crisis which had been developing gradually over the previous two to three decades'.[55] The collapse of the Soviet Union led to disintegration of the health system mainly because the budget expenditure for health was significantly reduced. According to the World Bank, government spending for health care in the 1990s declined by one-third, and 'many secondary and rural facilities were closed and services discontinued'.[56] Consequently, the health status of the Russian nation during the transition times had significantly deteriorated.

12.3.2 Legal Settings for the Right to Health in Russia

The USSR ratified several international human rights treaties stipulating the right to health since the inception of the modern system of human rights. In 1991, Russia became an independent state and took over the international legal commitments of the former USSR. Currently, Russia is a party to the following international human rights treaties stipulating the right to health: the International Covenant on Economic, Social and Cultural Rights (ICESCR), the International Convention on Elimination of All Forms of Racial Discrimination (CERD), and

---

[50] Tragakes and Lessof 2003, p. 23; Mehanik 2011.

[51] Tragakes and Lessof 2003, pp. 22–25.

[52] Ibid., p. 8. Mortality rates from infectious diseases fell from 87 per 100,000 in 1960 to 21 in 1980 and 12 in 1991 (overall fall of 86 % in 30 years).

[53] Schecter 1992, p. 206.

[54] Tragakes and Lessof 2003, p. 9.

[55] Ibid.

[56] World Bank 2008, p. 13.

12 The Right to Health for Vulnerable and Marginalised Groups 351

the Convention on the Rights of the Child (CRC). It is a signatory only to the Convention on the Elimination of All Forms of Discrimination against Women (CEDAW) and to the UN Disability Convention. Russia is a party to the International Covenant on Civil and Political Rights (ICCPR) and the Convention Against Torture (CAT), both containing provisions relevant to the right to health. The state is also a party to several health-related conventions of the International Labour Organisation, including the Occupational Safety and Health Convention (ILO No. 155). Since its existence as an independent state, the Russian Federation has entered into several European regional human rights treaties, which also contain provisions on the right to health. As a member of the Council of Europe, Russia ratified the European Convention for the Protection of Human Rights and Fundamental Freedoms, the European Social Charter, as well as the European Convention for the Prevention of Torture with its two protocols. It has not ratified the Council of Europe Convention on Human Rights and Biomedicine.

Article 41 of the Russian Constitution stipulates the right of its citizens to health protection and free medical aid. It states that

> federal programmes for protecting and strengthening the health of the population shall be financed by the State; measures shall be adopted to develop state, municipal and private health services; activities shall be promoted which facilitate the strengthening of health, the development of physical culture and sport, ecological and sanitary-epidemiological well-being.

According to Article 18 of the Constitution this right shall be directly operative and determine the meaning of laws and the activities of the authorities, such as policy-making, implementation, and judicial action. The constitutional right to health has been furthered through Federal Law 'On the basis of health protection in the Russian Federation',[57] which reaffirmed the right of everyone to protection of health and to free medical care.[58] A comprehensive range of free healthcare services and treatment is defined by central government,[59] and only a few items including dental care, cosmetic surgery or homeopathy are excluded from the scope of free health care.

Overall, the domestic legislative framework in the field of public health consists of a vast number of legal instruments and by-laws, and regulates various aspects of the health sector. It was characterised as vast, open-ended, declarative, inconsistent and lacking effective enforcement mechanisms.[60] Furthermore, the sub-national authorities of the Russian Federation share the responsibility for public health and can enact legislation in this respect to regulate the healthcare sector within their territories.[61] More than 300 laws in this respect had been adopted within the sub-national territories of the Russian Federation by 2003.[62]

---

[57] Federal Law N 323-FZ "On the basis of health protection in the Russian Federation" 2011.

[58] Ibid., Article 18, 19.

[59] Ibid., Article 19.

[60] Tragakes and Lessof 2003, p. 189.

[61] Constitution of the Russian Federation 2003, Article 72.

[62] Tragakes and Lessof 2003, p. 188.

Russian legislation guarantees equal enjoyment of the right to health for vulnerable and marginalised groups through a number of legal instruments. The international human rights treaties, ratified by the State, are part of the domestic legal system. Respectively, the non-discrimination clauses of these treaties are directly applicable across the entire territory of the State. Article 19 of the Russian Constitution 'guarantees the equality of rights and liberties regardless of sex, race, nationality, language, origin, property or employment status, residence, religion, convictions, membership of public associations or any other circumstance'.[63] The Federal Law 'On the basis of health protection in the Russian Federation'[64] fails to explicitly and comprehensively mainstream these principles and norms into the operation of the health sector. As domestic legislation on public health in Russia is very extensive, it is beyond the scope of this chapter to assess whether the international and constitutional guarantees of equality and non-discrimination have been adequately entrenched in law.

12.3.3 Health Sector Financing

The health sector in Russia during the post-Soviet transition has experienced a chronically low level of funding. Throughout the 1990s public spending for health declined by one-third and it notably increased in 2006 with the launch of the National Project 'Health'.[65] Public expenditure on health care since 2001 has fluctuated between 2.7 and 3.6 % of GDP, the average level for middle-income countries.[66] Total health expenditure in Russia in 2009 according to the WHO estimate was 5.6 % of the GDP, which reflects the significant increase in financing of the health sector.[67] The same source informs us that government spending on health constitutes 63.4 % of total health expenditure, and the private share is 36.6 % respectively.[68] According to the World Bank, 'the large proportion of private expenditure in Russia reflects out-of-pocket payments for informal charges in health facilities and the purchase of pharmaceuticals'.[69] Often, patients choose to pay for the 'free' public health services to secure better or immediate provision. These payments comprise 82.1 % of private spending,[70] and involve formal and informal payments to medical personnel. According to one study, 600 million US dollars are spent annually on under-the-counter informal payments for medical

---

[63] Constitution of the Russian Federation 2003, Article 19.

[64] Supra note 57.

[65] National Project 'Health'.

[66] World Bank 2008, p. 12.

[67] WHO 2012, p. 138.

[68] Ibid.

[69] World Bank 2008, p. 12.

[70] Ibid., p. 139.

services in Russia.[71] Sukshin correctly summarised the situation as follows: '[t]he great mismatch between the practically all-inclusive entitlements on the one hand, and the limited official resources on the other, do not allow the system any chance of survival in the absence of widespread unofficial payments'.[72] And it is for this reason that the under-the-table payments appear to be a significant funding source for the Russian health system.

12.3.4 Health Status of Disadvantaged Groups

The evaluation of the health status of vulnerable and disadvantaged groups should be placed in the context of the overall key health outcomes in the country. The systematic increase in mortality in Russia over the last decades across all population groups is alarming. The UNDP located Russia 119th in the world in life expectancy, behind many developing countries.[73] Life expectancy is 66 years on average, with 60 years for men and 73 for women.[74] The mortality statistics per socioeconomic group are not known to the author, but according to the WHO 'the mortality crises of the last decades affected mainly the socially weaker groups'.[75] The major threats to life in Russia are cardiovascular diseases, which are responsible for 56 per cent of all deaths, external causes resulting from injury and violence, which account for 14 per cent of deaths, and cancer, accounting for 12 per cent of total mortality.[76] The burden of disease partly reflects the patterns of mortality: cardiovascular diseases, injuries, and mental health conditions are the dominating causes of illness. The leading factors contributing to the burden of disease and mortality are alcohol and tobacco use, stress, high blood pressure and high cholesterol, poor diet, physical inactivity, occupational risk factors, violence and conflict, poverty, unhealthy lifestyle, and risk-taking behaviour.[77]

The main current national healthcare policy measure in action is the National Project 'Health', started in 2006.[78] Its key objectives are the development of preventive out-patient primary care, an increase in accessibility and quality of specialised and high-technological health care, advancement of medical care for mothers and children, and promotion of a healthy lifestyle. This project does not focus on vulnerable and disadvantaged groups, except for women and children.

---

[71] Shukshin 2004, p. 105.

[72] Ibid.

[73] UNDP 2009, pp. 261–264.

[74] WHO 2009, p. 40.

[75] WHO regional office for Europe 2006, p. 9.

[76] WHO 2006, p. 144, these numbers are estimates only.

[77] WHO regional office for Europe 2006, pp. 10–11.

[78] National Project 'Health'.

Central government has also implemented various programmes to address specific health issues or disadvantaged groups, and some of these measures will be referred to in the following paragraphs.

12.3.4.1 Women

The right to health framework recognises women as a vulnerable group with specific gender-related health needs. Women's reproductive health rights, including the access to health care during pregnancy and childbirth,[79] access to sex and reproductive education and protection from maternal mortality[80] are among the specific objectives of the women's right to health stipulated in the ICESCR and CEDAW.[81] At the same time, their social status secondary to men is a major disadvantage for women in many cultures. In this regard, the issues of gender based domestic violence[82] and harmful traditional practices[83] emerge as human rights matters and are addressed by the right to health framework. As a party to the ICESCR, Russia has undertaken human rights responsibilities in relation to women's health. However, it is only a signatory to the CEDAW and is therefore not legally obliged to comply with the latter's provisions.

The health status of Russian women should be seen in its historical context. During the Soviet era the issues of family planning, contraception and sexuality were taboo in public policy, media and popular literature. Russia lagged behind in the production, promotion and distribution of contraception. In the 1980s, only 10 per cent of married women used hormonal or intrauterine contraception.[84] Due to poor sex education and lack of effective contraceptive means, abortion became the most widespread means of birth control.[85] Since the collapse of the Soviet Union, and along with media liberalisation and demonopolisation of the drugs market, access to contraceptives, sex education and related information have been enhanced dramatically. Rapid improvement in pregnancy control increased the share of women using modern contraception up to 40 per cent.[86] However, two decades into the post-Soviet period women's health status remains far from satisfactory. The lack of sexual and reproductive health education was pointed out by the UNCESCR in its Concluding Observations on the fifth periodic report of Russia. It recommended to update the school curricula with the respective modules

---

[79] ICESCR, Article 12, para 2(a), General Comment 14, para 44(a).

[80] General Comment 14, paras 21, 52.

[81] ICESCR, Article 12; General Comment 14, paras 12(b), 20, 21, 34, 35, 36, 37 51; CEDAW, Article 12; UNCEDAW 1999, General Recommendation 24.

[82] General Comment 14, paras 21, 35, 36, 51.

[83] Ibid., paras 21, 35, 36, 37, 51.

[84] UNDP 2009, p. 48.

[85] RAND 2001.

[86] UNDP 2009, p. 48.

12 The Right to Health for Vulnerable and Marginalised Groups

to enhance prevention of early pregnancy and sexually transmitted infections. The Committee also noted the limited access to sexual and reproductive health services, particularly in rural areas, and called on the government to 'increase knowledge of and access to affordable contraceptive methods in the State and to ensure that family planning information and services are available to everyone'.[87]

The USSR was the first state in the world to legalise termination of pregnancy, and nowadays the abortion rate in Russia is the highest in the world.[88] The conservative approach towards contraception and family planning in Soviet times explains the high figure of 120 abortions per 1,000 women of childbearing age in the 1980s.[89] The attitude to abortion has been challenged along with the post-Soviet transformations and improvement of reproductive literacy of the population. While in the 1990s an average woman would have 3.4 abortions during her lifetime, this figure had dropped to 1.3 by 2006.[90] Poor quality of the procedure of termination resulting in a high incidence of health complications and secondary sterility is another serious concern. Unsafe abortion as a main cause of maternal mortality in Russia has been criticised by the UNCESCR in 2002.[91] According to the World Bank women are more at risk to die from abortion in Russia than elsewhere in Europe and Central Asia and in 2003 abortions accounted for 16 per cent of maternal mortality.[92]

The majority of childbirths in Russia are being attended by skilled medical personnel at health facilities.[93] Despite this coverage, a high level of maternal mortality was noted by the UNCESCR in 2002.[94] In its fourth periodic report on the implementation of the ICESCR, the Russian government indicated a rate of 39.7 maternal deaths per 100.000 births in 2000.[95] The most recent statistics from the WHO disclose that the indicator dropped to 34 deaths in 2010.[96] Reducing maternal mortality by at least 50 % in the period 1990–2015 is one of the Millennium Development Goals (MDGs) adopted for Russia.[97] While the MDGs do not represent a formal basis for the national development planning, their objectives have been imbedded in strategic policy documents. The National Project 'Health'

---

[87] UNCESCR Concluding Observations Russian Federation 2011, p. 30.

[88] UN Department of Economic and Social Affairs, Population Division 2007, World Abortion Policies. www.un.org/esa/population/publications/2007_Abortion_Policies_Chart/2007Abortion Policies_wallchart.htm. Accessed 8 April 2013.

[89] UNDP 2009, p. 48.

[90] Ibid.

[91] UNCESCR 2003, p. 35.

[92] Marquez 2005, p. 7.

[93] WHO 2012, p. 22, 102.

[94] UNCESCR 2003, para 35.

[95] Russian Federation 2011, para 342.

[96] WHO 2012, p. 21.

[97] The MDG+indicators were developed in 2005 by a group of independent experts as part of an initiative of the UNDP within the framework of the preparation of the Human Development Report for the Russian Federation. See Institute for Complex Strategic Studies Moscow 2006.

aimed to reduce the rate of maternal mortality to 19.5 per 100,000 births by 2012.[98] Furthermore, the growth in the number of gynaecological complications during pregnancy, birth and postnatal period was an alarming feature of the women's health status over the last decades. The fourth periodic report of Russia to the UNCESCR provided statistics painting a bleak picture of women's reproductive health and particularly the level of gynaecological diseases, such as endometriosis, inflammatory ailments and complications arising during pregnancy, birth and postnatal period.[99] By 2004, the proportion of women suffering from various birth-related pathologies reached 78 per cent,[100] indicating an apparent deterioration of women's reproductive health.

In response to these challenges the 'Concept for Demographic Policy of the Russian Federation up to 2025'[101] proposes several measures for the improvement of accessibility and quality of free medical care for women. These include the development of family oriented prenatal technologies, equipment improvements at obstetric facilities and the development of high-technology medical care for women.[102] One of the primary focuses of the National Project 'Health' for 2009–2012 was increasing the accessibility and quality of health care for women during pregnancy and childbirth.

Empirical evidence leads to several observations as regards the compliance of the State with its obligations in relation to women's right to health. The reproductive and maternal health rights seem inadequately fulfilled in Russia.[103] In violation of the right to access to health-related information,[104] government failed to ensure adequate dissemination of sex, reproductive and family planning information and adequate education.[105] Challenges of maternal mortality, unsafe abortions and gynaecological complications indicate the violation of women's right to health in the form of the failure to ensure access to quality maternity, sexual and reproductive health services,[106] particularly in rural areas, as noted by the UNCESCR. At the same time, Russia is taking visible steps to enhance the access of women to high quality medical care during pregnancy and childbirth as follows from the content of the national policies and programmes.[107] These developments appear potentially capable of enhancing women's reproductive health status and according equal opportunity to enjoy the highest attainable

---

[98] National Project 'Health'.

[99] Russian Federation 2001, paras 337, 338.

[100] UNDP 2009, p. 164.

[101] Concept for Demographic Policy of the Russian Federation up to 2025, approved by Russian Presidential Decree No. 1351, 2007.

[102] UNDP 2009, p. 171.

[103] ICESCR, Article 12, para 2(a); General Comment 14, para 14.

[104] General Comment 14, paras 11, 12(b), 14.

[105] Ibid., paras 36, 37.

[106] Ibid., paras 12(d), 14, 21, 36.

[107] ICESCR, Article 12, para 2(a); General Comment 14, para 44(a).

12 The Right to Health for Vulnerable and Marginalised Groups

standard of health. Yet, the content and implementation of the policy measures require a separate rights-based assessment to draw more tangible conclusions in this regard.

12.3.4.2 Children

Article 12 of the ICESCR elaborates on the states' obligations to take steps to ensure the healthy development of children and a reduction in infant mortality. Article 24 of the CRC stipulates the right of a child to the enjoyment of the highest attainable standard of health, and the UN Committee on the Rights of the Child (UNCRC) in its General Comments provides for a range of measures to be taken to implement that right.[108] Russia has ratified the ICESCR and the CRC, taking upon it the obligation to respect children's right to health.

Infant mortality is one of the key aspects of a child's right to health and to life. As a party to the ICESCR, Russia is under the obligation to take steps to reduce infant mortality,[109] and failure to do so constitutes violation of the obligation to fulfil the right to health.[110] Infant mortality rates in Russia have declined noticeably over the last two decades, from 22 per thousand live births in 1990 to 9 in 2010.[111] In contrast with this positive trend, infant mortality among the indigenous populations ranges from 30 to 60 per thousand live births across the various north and north-east regions.[112] In its recent periodic report the State has disclosed that in some regions of the north the infant mortality is up to 16 per cent.[113] The UNCRC clarifies that governments have a positive duty to combat infant mortality among the indigenous populations.[114] However, the striking differences in the mortality rates between mainstream and indigenous populations is a clear indication of the failure of the state to comply with its human rights obligations as regards disadvantaged children of remote indigenous settlements. In its fourth periodic report to the UNCESCR, the government disclosed that 'the main causes of infant deaths are problems arising in the prenatal phase (44.2 %) and congenital defects (23.1 %)'.[115] It highlighted a notably high percentage of premature and immature births and stated that every third child born in Russia suffers from a complicated health condition.[116] This situation underlines the concern of the

---

[108] UNCRC 2003a, b, 2005a.

[109] ICESCR, Article 12, para 2(a); General Comment 14, paras 14, 22.

[110] General Comment 14, para 52.

[111] WHO 2012, p. 57.

[112] Global Environment Facility et al. 2004, p. 165.

[113] UNCRC 2012, para 294.

[114] UNCRC 2005b, para 50.

[115] Russian Federation 2001, p. 343.

[116] Ibid., p. 339.

preceding section in relation to the failure of the state to provide for access to reproductive and maternal healthcare services of appropriate quality.

Child immunization is carried out in accordance with a national inoculation scheme and is characterised by a high level of coverage. The Russian public health system provides a sound experience of dealing with communicable diseases inherited from the Soviet times.[117] Despite that, Russia is currently facing unprecedented difficulties in addressing the HIV/AIDS pandemic.[118] The UNCRC in its concluding observations to the fourth periodic report indicated the increase of mother to child transmission of HIV and recommended stronger measures to prevent transmission and 'guarantee anti-retroviral treatment to newborns whose mothers are infected with HIV'.[119] The fifth periodic report to the UNCRC indicates that the State took measures to address its failure to comply with human rights obligations to prevent mother to child HIV transmission and the duty to provide mothers with the anti-retroviral treatment.[120] It states that in 2009 between 80 and 89 per cent of women received antiretroviral treatment during pregnancy and childbirth, and the number of children diagnosed with HIV decreased to 54 per cent in the period from 2003 to 2009.[121]

The UNCRC also highlighted several challenges concerning adolescent health, such as a high suicide rate among young people and the neglect of this problem, poor state of reproductive health and sex education in schools, high incidence of teenage pregnancies and abortions, and insufficient promotion of good health practices in Russian schools.[122] This evidence highlights the disregard by the state of its obligation to provide adolescents with access to reproductive and sexual information, as well as to create awareness on safe and respectful social and sexual behaviours, diet and physical activity to facilitate their health and development.[123] In violation of its human rights obligations clarified by the UNCRC General Comment 4,[124] Russia fails to ensure access to mental health services for adolescents, which results in an increase in suicide and other self-destructive behaviour. The deterioration of the state of physical health of adolescents has been recently highlighted by the State in its fifth periodic report to the UNCRC in 2012.[125]

Over the last two decades the Russian government has been developing its social policy on children's protection. National measures adopted in this respect include the 'Plan of action for improving children's situation in the Russian

---

[117] See Sect. 12.3.1.

[118] See Sect. 12.3.4.4.

[119] UNCRC 2005c, paras 54–58.

[120] UNCRC 2003a, para 26.

[121] UNCRC 2012, para 168.

[122] UNCRC 2005c, paras 59–61.

[123] UNCRC 2003b, paras 26, 28.

[124] Ibid., para 22.

[125] UNCRC 2012, paras 162, 167.

12 The Right to Health for Vulnerable and Marginalised Groups 359

Federation for the period 1998–2000', the Presidential Programme 'Children of Russia', and the special federal programme 'Children of the north' among others. All these initiatives include measures on the protection of child health. The federal programme 'Healthy child' was in operation from 2002 to 2006. The National Project 'Health' introduced measures such as health check-ups for adolescents in 2011–2012, improvement of health care for children with hearing difficulties, neonatal screening and audio screening for newborns. It is debatable though whether these policy measures have been tailored to enhance the child's right to health. Certain progress should be noted with respect to the realisation of the right to health for the children of HIV-positive parents. Yet, the evidence demonstrated in this section suggests that the right to health of indigenous children and adolescents in Russia has not been adequately implemented.

12.3.4.3 Prisoners and Detainees

Russia has one of the highest rates of imprisonment with more than 600 people in detention per 100,000. Living conditions in many Russian prisons are reported to be substandard, aggravated by overcrowding, poor ventilation, humidity, poor lighting, lack of toilets and interruptions in water supply.[126] These factors inevitably have an adverse health impact and accelerate the spread of contagious diseases within detention centres. According to a WHO estimate in 2003, up to 10 per cent of approximately 870,000 prisoners in Russia had an active form of tuberculosis (TB) and around 7,000 HIV positive Russians were prisoners.[127] In 2002, the UNCESCR expressed concern with regards to the high infection rate of TB in Russian prisons, which was reportedly sixty times higher than among the general population. It recommended intensifying the State's efforts to combat TB, to guarantee medical treatment and to ensure adequate sanitary conditions in prisons.[128]

Access to health care is of crucial importance for people in detention, since being in prison according to the WHO is a health hazard in itself.[129] Physical access to medical services, facilities and goods for prisoners can be effectively limited due to restricted freedom. General Comment 14 failed to comprehensively clarify the States' duties as regards the right to health of this marginalised group. On one occasion it articulates that 'States are under the obligation to respect the right to health by refraining from denying or limiting equal access for…prisoners or detainees…to preventive, curative and palliative health services'.[130] However, it has failed to explicitly clarify the specific positive obligation to provide for the

---

[126] Bobrik et al. 2005, p. 36.

[127] WHO Regional Office for Europe 2003.

[128] UNCESCR 2003, paras 33, 61.

[129] WHO Regional Office for Europe 2003.

[130] General Comment 14, para 34.

health care for prisoners, which would be of better use to this group. Evidence provided below suggests that Russian prisoners are systematically denied access to adequate medical care. Where the denial results from the lack of appropriate services, the right to health of the prisoners is effectively violated by the failure of the state to provide essential health care for the group.[131] And if such services exist within or in the vicinity of detention, but access to those services is refused through negligence, or as punishment or a way of extorting information, the administration of the prison in this case acts in violation of the obligation to respect the right to health of the prisoners.[132] As illustrated further, the violation of the right to health in detention can lead to the infringement of the right to life, which points at the scale of the health challenges in the Russian punitive system.

The Human Rights Committee in 1997 considered the case of Vladimir Lantsov who died of pneumonia from the deplorable conditions during pre-trial detention and being refused health care. It concluded that Russia had failed to protect the life of the detainee, and had thus violated Article 6, para 1 of the ICCPR.[133] The former Special Rapporteur on the Right to Health, Paul Hunt, received several communications regarding the failure to ensure access to appropriate and prompt medical treatment for people in pre-trial detention, as well as the denial of food and water for several days.[134] The Russian advocate Mikhail Trepashkin imprisoned in 2006 attempted to defend his rights to life and access to medical care by different means. In a communication to the Special Rapporteur he claimed his life was under threat because the prison authorities denied him access to adequate treatment for life-threatening asthma.[135]

The evidence of the denial of medical care in the Russian punitive system comes to light in judicial proceedings. In 2008–2009 the European Court of Human Rights (ECtHR) considered the case of Vasiliy Alexanyan, who was kept in pre-trial detention without access to adequate health care and treatment for AIDS. The Court issued a number of directives on immediate hospitalisation and independent medical examination of Alexanyan, yet, Russian authorities failed to comply with those interim measures.[136] In 2010 the Court considered a case of a Russian convict, who was denied adequate treatment for diabetes which resulted in

---

[131] Maastricht Guidelines on Violations of Economic, Social and Cultural Rights 1997, Guideline 6.

[132] General Comment 14, para 34; Toebes 1999b, p. 318, 325.

[133] Communication No. 763/1997, Yekaterina Pavlovna Lantsova on behalf of her son Vladimir Albertvich Lantsov v. the Russian Federation.

[134] Report of the Special Rapporteur on the right of everyone to the enjoyment of the highest attainable standard of physical and mental health 2005, E/CN.4/2005/51/Add.1, para 19; Report of the Special Rapporteur on the right of everyone to the enjoyment of the highest attainable standard of physical and mental health, 2005 E/CN.4/2006/48/Add. 1, 2005, para 17.

[135] Report of the Special Rapporteur on the right of everyone to the enjoyment of the highest attainable standard of physical and mental health, A/HRC/7/11/Add.1, 2008, para 50.

[136] ECtHR, Alexanyan v. Russia, Final judgement on application No. 46468/06, 5 June 2009.

12 The Right to Health for Vulnerable and Marginalised Groups

his loss of vision.[137] In 2008, a district court in Syktyvkar established that women in the regional female correctional centre were not provided adequate medical care and hygienic conditions.[138]

The opaque Russian penitentiary system remains almost inaccessible to independent and unbiased evidence-based research of its internal conditions. A few public campaigns and legal actions give only a partial impression of the real situation and do not allow for drawing a complete account of the status of prisoners' right to health. The emerging statistics, cases, and evidence, however, give an apparent indication that Russian prisoners and detainees are deprived of equal opportunity to enjoy their human right to health. The conditions of detention in the first instance affect the detainees' health status, while access to adequate medical care and the underlying preconditions of health is often denied. Effective transparent accountability mechanisms, where the prisoners can safely articulate their health concerns, be heard, and challenge the denial of health care, do not exist. In this light the prisoners can be considered as one of the population groups that are most deprived of the equal opportunity to enjoy their right to health.

The Federal Law 'On the basis of health protection in the Russian Federation'[139] stipulates a number of guarantees for persons in detention as regards their right to health. Detainees have the right to receive medical care at their place of custody, including the right to have arranged consultations with specialist doctors. If medical care cannot be provided at the place of detention, the person has the right to receive assistance in medical institutions of public and community health. Pregnant women in detention, women during childbirth and postpartum period have the right to appropriate health care. These provisions entered into force in 2012 and their effectiveness within the Russian penal system remains to be seen.

12.3.4.4 Persons with HIV/AIDS

The HIV/AIDS epidemic in Russia is one of the fastest growing in the world. It started in the middle of the 1990s, and by 2000, close to 390,000 people had been diagnosed with HIV.[140] As estimated in 2011, the number of people living with HIV reached 1,300,000, with HIV prevalence among adults of 1.4 per cent.[141] Intravenous drug users, prisoners, young people and sex workers represent the highest HIV-risk groups. The Russian government was criticised for failure to protect these groups from disease and for subjecting them to mandatory and even

---

[137] ECtHR, Vasilyev v. Russia Decision as to the admissibility of application No.28370/05, 1 July 2010.

[138] Moscow Helsinki Group 2008, p. 130.

[139] Federal Law N 323-FZ "On the basis of health protection in the Russian Federation" 2011 Article 26.

[140] WHO, UNAIDS, UNISEF 2008, p. 4.

[141] From UNAIDS official website www.unaids.org/en/regionscountries/countries/russian federation/. Accessed 31 March 2013.

forceful testing in violation of the freedom to control one's health and body.[142] The epidemic is entering mainstream society due to the lack of awareness of HIV, poor understanding of the ways of its transmission and inadequate sex education.

Statutory legislation introduced in 1995 guarantees for the Russian citizens with HIV status equal enjoyment of the rights and freedoms stipulated in the national Constitution and domestic legislation,[143] as well as equal access to medical care.[144] It was an important development at the time, as people with HIV had been seriously stigmatised in the early years of the epidemic and often faced the denial of access to medical care.[145] Statutory law, however, treats stateless and migrant persons with HIV less favourably; they are not entitled to the similar scope of rights and are subjected to deportation on the basis of their HIV status.[146] In this context, the Constitutional Court of Russia challenged the legitimacy of the deportation on the basis of HIV status in favour of the migrants, who have established families in Russia and integrated into society.[147] The recent case of the European Court of Human Rights considered the refusal of Russian authorities to issue a residence permit to a non-national with HIV status and found a breach of Article 14 of the Convention taken in conjunction with Article 8 of the European Convention. The refusal of residence for the vulnerable individual, who has established family life in Russia, has been found discriminatory on the basis of the health status.[148]

While equality measures for persons with HIV are guaranteed in legislation, the access to treatment and the discrimination of certain groups remains a disturbing issue in Russia. According to UNAIDS/WHO statistics estimated anti-retroviral treatment coverage rates in 2011 were 22–34 %, which is below the average 56 % in sub-Saharan Africa.[149] Disadvantaged individuals such as migrants or drug users are not in touch with the public healthcare system and face difficulties as regards access to treatment. As recorded by the Human Rights Watch, in some parts of Russia drug users have been denied the necessary treatment for AIDS.[150] Access to treatment is a key dimension of the right to health; however, as the next section illustrates, the Russian government fails to ensure equal access to anti-retroviral treatment for drug users with HIV/AIDS.

---

[142] Stachowiak 1996.

[143] Federal Law N 38-FZ 'On prevention of the spread of HIV infection in the Russian Federation' 1995, Article. 5.

[144] Ibid., Article 14.

[145] Stachowiak 1996.

[146] Federal Law N 38-FZ 'On prevention of the spread of HIV infection in the Russian Federation' 1995, Article 11, para 2.

[147] Constitutional Court of Russian Federation Decision N 155-O, 12 May 2006.

[148] Kiyutin *v.* Russia, Application no. 2700/10.

[149] UNADIS 2013, p. 13.

[150] Human Rights Watch 2004.

12 The Right to Health for Vulnerable and Marginalised Groups 363

In 2003 the UNCESCR requested the government to take urgent measures to stop the spread of the disease,[151] and in this context highlighted the inadequacy of sex education within the state.[152] General Comment 14 clarifies the governments' duty to carry out prevention and education programmes on HIV/AIDS,[153] and, as a part of the obligation to fulfil the right to health, to organise information campaigns on HIV/AIDS.[154] Several policy measures have been taken in Russia to address the outbreak. In the early years of the epidemic the campaign 'Rational people, rational choices' was carried out to raise awareness among young people on HIV/AIDS and sexually transmitted diseases.[155] Within the last decade, the government took further steps to combat HIV within the frameworks of the Federal Target Program 'Anti-HIV and AIDS' and the National Project 'Health'. Funding for improved diagnosis, treatment, and prevention measures has significantly increased since 2006.[156] Yet the situation remains alarming in Russia, where according to UNAIDS 'a comprehensive national prevention strategy is still lacking'.[157] Almost 78,000 people had died of AIDS in Russia by 2011[158] and many lives could have been saved if prevention had been effective and access to treatment guaranteed to all. Inadequate sexual health education and poor understanding of HIV within the population perpetuate the spread of the epidemic and indicate the breach by the State of its obligations to promote and fulfil the right to health.[159]

12.3.4.5 Drug Users

Russia has one of the largest numbers of injecting drug users in the world, estimated as close to 1.8 million.[160] The Russian government has taken a 'zero-tolerance' approach towards substance misuse, and in this context systematically fails to respect, protect and fulfil the human right to health of people addicted to illicit drugs. Opioid substitution therapy is commonly recognised as the best practice for treating opioid drug dependence, yet drug users are denied access to this therapy, which is prohibited in Russian healthcare.[161] The Russian government restricts the

---

[151] UNCESCR 2003, para 62.

[152] UNCESCR 2011, para 30.

[153] General Comment 14, para 16.

[154] Ibid., para 36.

[155] Russian Federation 2001, paras 400–405.

[156] Institute for Complex Strategic Studies Moscow 2006, p. 17.

[157] UNAIDS Russian Federation Country Situation 2009 National Response, www.unaids.org/ctrysa/EURRUS_en.pdf. Accessed 31 March 2013.

[158] From UNAIDS official website www.unaids.org/en/regionscountries/countries/russian federation/. Accessed 31 March 2013.

[159] General Comment 14, paras 6, 37.

[160] UNAIDS 2010.

[161] Human Rights Watch 2007.

implementation of needle and syringe exchange harm reduction programmes for drug users. Harm reduction practices are internationally proven the best methods of addressing substance misuse and preventing HIV among drug users in the world.[162] In Russia, where more than one-third of injecting drug users lives with HIV,[163] these programmes are vital. In the absence of harm reduction programmes the spread of HIV among injecting drug users, who represent near to 80 per cent of all HIV cases, unfolds at a dramatic scale.[164]

Only 20 per cent of HIV-positive drug users in need receive anti-retroviral treatment.[165] Access to treatment is impeded as a result of the state policy on substance misuse. Statutory law qualifies drug use as an administrative offence, for which a person can be incarcerated for up to fifteen days.[166] The drug user willingly registered at the local health centre and undertaking treatment is exempted from responsibility. The treatment offered at state drug clinics, however, has been referred to by the Human Rights Watch as amounting to a violation of the right to health.[167] It drives drug users to avoiding specialised public health services. Yet, only 'registered'[168] drug users can have access to anti-retroviral treatment under the public health system. As a result of these clashing state policies penalising substance misuse while denying adequate treatment for drug dependency, drug users with HIV status are *de facto* denied access to anti-retroviral treatment.[169]

Physically safe access to healthcare services and goods for all on a non-discriminatory basis is the key element of the AAAQ normative framework of the right to health.[170] The UNCESCR in its Concluding Observations in the fifth periodic report urged the Russian government to apply the human rights-based approach to drug use and encouraged the State to consider opioid substitution therapy with use of methadone and buprenorphine, as well as needle and syringe exchange harm reduction and overdose prevention programmes.[171] Yet, the national government's approach to drugs and the resulting policies that impede both access to adequate treatment for substance misuse, as well as equal access to anti-retroviral treatment, effectively violate the State's international human rights obligations and disregard the constitutional and statutory rights of Russian citizens.

---

[162] Kimber et al. 2010.

[163] UNAIDS 2010.

[164] WHO Europe website www.euro.who.int/en/what-we-do/health-topics/communicable-diseases/hivaids/policy/injecting-drug-users-idu. Accessed 31 March 2013.

[165] According to the WHO Europe website www.euro.who.int/en/what-we-do/health-topics/communicable-diseases/hivaids/policy/injecting-drug-users-idu. Accessed 1 April 2013.

[166] Administrative Code of Russian Federation, Article 6(9).

[167] Human Rights Watch 2007.

[168] According to Barret et al. 2008, p. 8: 'Russian narcological clinics require all drug users who seek free treatment at state drug dependence treatment clinics to be placed on a state drug user registry.'

[169] Ibid.

[170] General Comment 14, para 12(b).

[171] UNCESCR 2011, Concluding Observations Russian Federation, para 29.

12.3.4.6 Indigenous Peoples

Indigenous peoples living along the northern coastline of Russian territory and in the Far East experience serious challenges in terms of their health status. In 2003, the UNCESCR flagged the low life expectancy of indigenous populations which was 15–20 years lower than the national average.[172] In 2004, the life expectancy of indigenous populations was estimated as not exceeding 50 years and according to the more recent statement from the Russian Association of the Indigenous Peoples of the North it has fallen to 40–45 years.[173] Excessive alcohol consumption is common among indigenous populations and alcohol intoxication is one of the main underlying factors leading to death from 'external causes', along with traumas, accidents and suicide.[174] Tuberculosis is another alarming health issue for indigenous communities. In 2001, the government stated that 'among the indigenous population of the Kola Peninsula the incidence of tuberculosis is seven times the Russian average'.[175]

General Comment 14 clarifies that indigenous peoples have the right to specific measures to improve their access to health services and care.[176] Two special federal programmes 'Children of the north' and 'Economic and social development of the small indigenous peoples of the north for the period until 2000' have been carried out by the Russian government as part of the international decade of indigenous peoples (1995–2004). In 2001 Russia reported to the UNCESCR that the type of trachoma[177] most common among the indigenous peoples of the north had been eradicated.[178] However, the situation in the North has significantly deteriorated since the fall of the Soviet Union, due to the environmental degradation caused by unsustainable natural resources development and lack of financing at subnational government level for even basic healthcare.[179] The UNCESCR in its Concluding Observations to the fifth Russian periodic report highlighted the gaps in the ambulatory system coverage in the regions North, Siberia and Far East, resulting from a territorial reorganisation.[180] The normative content of the right to health elaborates on the availability of and physical access to healthcare services and facilities as its key dimension,[181] and it is the obligation of states to ensure the access to health care.[182] Obviously, the human right to health

---

[172] UNCESCR 2003, Concluding Observations Russian Federation, para 31.

[173] George 2010.

[174] Global Environment Facility et al. 2004, p. 165.

[175] Russian Federation 2001, pp. 337–339.

[176] General Comment 14, para 27.

[177] The infectious disease affecting eyes that can cause irreversible blindness.

[178] Russian Federation 2001, para 391.

[179] George 2010.

[180] UNCESCR 2011, para 28.

[181] General Comment 14, paras 12 (a)(b).

[182] Ibid., paras 21, 22, 36.

of indigenous populations who are denied access to healthcare services and facilities will be compromised.[183]

12.3.5 Analysis

The effective measures of implementation of the right to health include domestic legislative change, national strategy or plans of action based on the human rights principles, and standards, budgetary measures and accountability mechanisms to ensure that all stakeholders in the health sector are held to account for their actions.[184] Likewise, the equality of opportunity for marginalised and vulnerable people to enjoy the highest attainable standard of health is to be achieved through the utilisation of these measures, which should disallow discrimination and embrace an integrated rights-based approach to their particular health-related needs. Based on the evidence provided in the case study this section evaluates whether the government's legal and policy measures in the field of public health advance the right to health for disadvantaged groups and consider their particular health needs.

12.3.5.1 Health Needs as the Right to Health Claims

Disadvantaged groups have particular health-related needs due to their physical vulnerability or marginalised social status. The significance of the human rights framework is that it transforms these needs into legal rights. The health status of the Russian disadvantaged groups, as the case study reveals, reflects the failure of the State to attend to these needs, which constitutes a violation of the right to health.

Women have distinct health-related needs connected with gender and their reproductive function. These include information regarding and access to contraception, opportunity to have a safe abortion, access to sexual and reproductive health education, family planning services, and adequate medical care during pregnancy and childbirth. In order to address the demographic concerns of population decline, current State policy places great emphasis on the development of maternal health services.[185] Yet, the right to health analysis reveals that government fails to adequately address the essential health needs of women in sex education, in understanding of and access to affordable contraceptive methods, family-planning information and services. Unsafe abortions, maternal mortality and gynaecological complications are yet to be fully eradicated. The failure of the

---

[183] Ibid., para 12.

[184] Ibid., paras 53–56, 59.

[185] National Project 'Health'.

12 The Right to Health for Vulnerable and Marginalised Groups

State to address these issues undermines the equal opportunity for women to enjoy the highest attainable standard of health.

Children's health has been a specific concern of Russian public health policies and initiatives over the last two decades. The Government successfully addressed important dimensions of child health care such as immunisation. Decline in infant mortality is also a positive development, with the exception of the areas of Far East and North, where the level of child mortality remains high, which can perhaps be linked to the poor access to health services in those regions. Specific health-related issues such as vulnerability of mental health in adolescent age and the importance of sexual and reproductive awareness, appear to be addressed less satisfactory in Russia. Social vulnerability of adolescents resulting in isolation, bullying, early pregnancy, suicide and self-harm remains poorly addressed, it affects their health status and undermines their equal enjoyment of the right to health.

Isolation of prisoners in segregated centres with harsh living conditions has a negative impact on detainees' physical and mental health. As established, prisoners face serious difficulties in terms of access to healthcare services in detention, indicating a violation of their right to health. Section 12.3.4.3 highlighted the high level of tuberculosis and HIV among Russian prisoners. These challenges point at the critical importance of improved conditions in detention and of the immediate access to health care for detainees as a matter of their equal enjoyment of the right to health.

Persons with HIV/AIDS require access to anti-retroviral therapy and have increased needs for medical assistance. While the laws guarantee equal access to medical care for Russian citizens with HIV, evidence suggests that drug users with HIV experience de facto discrimination in access to the anti-retroviral treatment in violation of their human right to health. Drug users in Russia are also denied opioid substitute therapy which is considered the most effective type of treatment for their condition. Specific needs of these groups in terms of access to appropriate treatment and medical assistance remain unmet. Penalising substance misuse and resisting to implement harm reduction programmes have a devastating impact on drug users' health status, putting them at increased risk of HIV contamination. This policy discourages drug users in seeking medical help, leads to the deterioration of their health status and contributes to health inequalities experienced by this group.

The lifestyle, harsh climate conditions and geographic isolation of the indigenous peoples of the North and Far East of Russia pose serious challenges to their health. Evidence of low life expectancy, high levels of infant mortality, suicide, traumas, alcohol consumption and tuberculosis all indicate the urgent need for targeted measures to address the situation, such as provision of healthcare services and facilities in disadvantaged regions, and promotion of a healthy lifestyle among the indigenous populations. Insufficient government action in this regard undermines the right to health of the indigenous peoples and fails to effectively address systematic health inequalities experienced by this group.

12.3.5.2 Legal and Policy Measures

In theory, the law is a powerful tool to guarantee equality in society, to address discrimination and modify societal attitudes. In practice, the efficiency of statutory legislation depends on various factors. The Russian case represents the situation where the legal rights stipulating equality are generously enshrined in the domestic legal system, but remain ineffective in practice. The international treaties stipulating the right to health, which have been ratified by Russia, are incorporated into the domestic law and are directly applicable. Russian statutory law positively incorporates certain dimensions of the international right to health, including the requirements on equality and non-discrimination. The Federal Law 'On the basis of health protection in the Russian Federation' guarantees equal access to medical care, to information on health status, and to family planning and other services for everyone.[186] It contains specific regulations as regards the access to health care for disadvantaged groups within the population such as women, children, persons in detention, and people with HIV. For instance, the Federal Law N 38-FZ stipulates equality and particular rights for persons with HIV. Yet, being in effect since 1995, this law proves to be ineffective for HIV positive drug users who experience systematic challenges in access to anti-retroviral treatment.[187]

National policies and action plans are operational vehicles for development in the public health sector. Over the last two decades, the national government has implemented a number of national programmes targeted at enhancing the health status of the population, including vulnerable groups. The national project 'Health' specifically aims to increase accessibility and quality of health care for women, and reduce the rate of maternal mortality. A range of programmes to address the particular health needs of children and adolescents have been implemented across the territories of the Russian Federation, though the adolescents' health status indicates the need for further policy action. Several measures have been implemented to tackle the spread of HIV; still, a comprehensive national strategy to address the epidemic systematically is lacking. Similarly, the central government's action to address the health challenges of the populations in the North, Siberia and the Far East is sporadic and lacks a focused strategic approach.

Overall, the statutory law and central government policy action addressing the health status and needs of vulnerable groups as well as increasing public health spending as illustrated in this chapter, indicate the State is taking steps towards realisation of the right to health for these groups. Nevertheless, there remain apparent inequalities in the health status of disadvantaged groups as compared to the rest of the population. The human rights principles of equality and non-discrimination in the formulation and implementation of public health policies and measures need to be mainstreamed. The State's policy towards substance misuse,

---

[186] Federal Law N 323-FZ "On the basis of health protection in the Russian Federation" 2011, Article 19, 22, 51.

[187] See Sect. 12.3.4.4.

for instance, fails to adhere to these principles. What is more, it undermines the legal guarantees of equal access to health care, depriving drug users of their right to health. The absence of a comprehensive national strategy to tackle the health needs of all vulnerable and marginalised groups constitutes a violation of the core obligation of the State with regard to the human right to health.[188] Random national policies fail to deal with the health-related needs of these groups in an integrated manner or, as in the case of drug users, reflect the unwillingness of the government to pursue the human rights-based approach to their needs.

12.4 Conclusion

The international human right to health outlaws discrimination and imposes on States the duty to ensure equal access to healthcare services, goods and facilities. It requires mainstreaming the principles of equality and non-discrimination into the operation of the health sector to guarantee equal opportunity to enjoy the highest attainable standard of health for all, including vulnerable and marginalised populations. To achieve this goal, public health legal and policy measures must consider the particular health-related needs of these groups, and respectively ensure access to appropriate healthcare services, facilities or goods.

The Russian case highlights the significance of these measures. It shows that unfavourable disparities in the health status of disadvantaged populations often result from a government's failure to embed the legal requirements of non-discrimination and equality into public healthcare policy and strategy. It results in the health sector operating without consideration and even in violation of these principles. As the case of HIV-positive drug users exemplifies, national policies can effectively trump the legal guarantee of equal access to medical treatment and cause de facto discrimination. This divergence of law and policy indicates that Russia is failing to comply with the principles of equality and non-discrimination, which are inherent to the right to health, in the operation of its health sector.

In violation of the principle of equality, access to health care in Russia is impeded for prisoners, drug users, indigenous peoples, women, children and adolescents. As this study reveals, the government systematically fails to consider the specific health needs of vulnerable and marginalised groups in the health sector organisation, which results in the weakening of their health status. In violation of the obligations to promote the right to health and to carry out preventive measures, the health-related information and education are not adequately provided to the population in general, and to women, adolescents and indigenous groups specifically.

Russia falls short of complying with two core obligations in relation to the right to health of disadvantaged groups. First, it fails to ensure the access of drug users

---

[188] General Comment 14, para 43(f).

with HIV status to healthcare services and treatment on a non-discriminatory basis.[189] Second, Russia is lacking a continuous comprehensive national health strategy and a plan of action, which would attend to the vulnerable and marginalised groups.[190] While sporadic programmes have been carried out for certain groups, these measures fail to attend to their health needs effectively, as study reveals. In the context of increased public health spending over the last few years, this is an unfortunate indication of the State's negligence towards the right to health of those groups of the population that are most in need of attention and affirmative action. A rights-based analysis of the allocation of public health expenditure to the needs of vulnerable groups would assist in the understanding of health inequalities in Russia.

The human rights framework allows disclosure of these trends and emerges as a useful matrix for analysis. But more than that, it converts the challenge of health inequalities into a matter of human rights concern to be addressed at law and policy making level. Primarily, it requires governments to comply with the obligations they undertake upon ratification of the human rights treaties stipulating the right to health. Specifically, the human rights principles of equality and non-discrimination, as well as the particular needs of vulnerable and marginalised people, have to be given adequate consideration by health sector laws, policies and need to be embedded in the organisation of the health sector. A public health budgeting closely linked to a rights-based analysis of health outcomes and inequalities would target the groups that are short of attention and require specific action.

Overall, the international human right to health through its normative and operational perspectives endeavours to deliver equality of opportunity to enjoy the highest attainable standard of health. To this aim, human rights research needs to link with an understanding of the health disparities faced by disadvantaged groups, the dynamics of their occurrence and to test the potential of the human rights framework to overcome the various forms of health inequalities. The gist of learning that emerged from this study, although not novel, is useful in this connection: political willingness and focused rights-based action attending to the specific health needs of vulnerable and marginalised people are crucial, obligatory and urgent to ensure the much needed equal health opportunities for all.

References

Barret D, Lines R, Schleifer R, Elliott R, Bewley-Taylor D (2008) Recalibrating the regime. The Beckley Foundation Drug Policy Programme, Report thirteen

Bobrik A, Danishevski K, Eroshina K, Mc Kee M (2005) Prison health in Russia: the larger picture. J Public Health Policy 26(1):30–59

---

[189] General Comment 14, para 43(a).

[190] Ibid., para 43(f).

12 The Right to Health for Vulnerable and Marginalised Groups

Braveman P, Gruskin S (2003) Poverty, equity, human rights and health. Bulletin WHO 2003, 81(7):539–545

Constitution of the Russian Federation (2003), adopted 12 Dec 2003 with the amendments and additions of 30 Dec 2008, English version of the Constitution. http://constitution.garant.ru/english/. Accessed 5 Jun 2014

George J (2010) Indigenous people of Russia battered by hardships. www.nunatsiaqonline.ca/stories/article/98789_indigenous_people_of_russia_battered_by_hardships. Accessed 31 Mar 2013

Global Environment Facility, United Nations Environment Programme, Arctic Monitoring and Assessment Programme, Russian Association of the Indigenous Peoples of the North, Siberia and Far East (2004) Persistent toxic substances, food security and indigenous peoples of the Russian North. www.amap.no/resources/pts_project.htm. Accessed 13 Mar 2013

Human Rights Watch (2004) Lessons not learned: Human rights abuses and HIV/AIDS in the Russian Federation. www.hrw.org/reports/2004/russia0404/russia0404.pdf. Accessed 1 Apr 2013

Human Rights Watch (2007) Rehabilitation required: Russia's human rights obligation to provide evidence-based drug dependence treatment. www.hrw.org/en/reports/2007/11/07/rehabilitation-required-0. Accessed 31 Mar 2013

Institute for Complex Strategic Studies Moscow (2006) The millennium development goals and Russia's National Projects: strategic choices. www.undp.ru/download.phtml?$481. Accessed 3 April 2013

Kimber J, Palmateer N, Hutchinson S, Hickman M, Goldberg D and Rhodes T (2010) Harm reduction among injecting drug users—evidence of effectiveness. In: EMCDDA Monographs, Harm reduction: evidence, impacts and challenges

Maastricht Guidelines on Violations of Economic, Social and Cultural Rights 1997

Marquez PV (2005) Dying too young: addressing premature mortality and Ill health due to non-communicable diseases and injuries in the Russian Federation. The World Bank, Europe and Central Asia Human Development Department. http://web.worldbank.org/WBSITE/EXTERNAL/COUNTRIES/ECAEXT/0,,contentMDK:20661159~pagePK:146736~piPK:146830~theSitePK:258599,00.html. Accessed July 2014

Mehanik A (2011) Semashko pyramid in expert №° 30-31(764). http://expert.ru/expert/2011/30/piramida-semashko/. Accessed 31 Mar 2013

Moscow Helsinki Group (2008) Human rights in regions of Russian Federation

National Project 'Health'. www.roszdravnadzor.ru/gos_programs/health. Accessed 1 Sept 2013

RAND (2001) Improvements in contraception are reducing historically high abortion rates in Russia, in 'Population Matters' Policy Brief. www.rand.org/pubs/research_briefs/RB5055/index1.html. Accessed 31 Mar 2013

Russian Federation (2001) Implementation of the International Covenant on Economic, social and cultural rights, fourth periodic report submitted by States parties in accordance with articles 16 and 17 of the Covenant, E/C.12/4/Add.10

San Giorgi MS (2012) The human right to equal access to health care. Intersentia, Amsterdam

Schecter K (1992) Soviet socialised medicine and the right to health care in a changing Soviet Union. Hum Rights Q 14:206–215

Shukshin A (2004) Ailing Russian health-care system in urgent need of reform. Bull WHO 82(5):391

Stachowiak J (1996) Systematic-forced-testing in Russia. www.thebody.com/wa/summer96/russian.html. Accessed 6 Apr 2013

Toebes B (1999a) Towards an improved understanding of the international human right to health. Hum Rights Q 21:661–679

Toebes B (1999b) Right to health as a human right in international law. Intersentia, Amsterdam

Tragakes E, Lessof S (2003) Health care systems in transition, European observatory on health systems and policies

UNAIDS (2010) Global report, fact sheet. Eastern Europe and Central Asia. www.unaids.org/documents/20101123_FS_eeca_em_en.pdf. Accessed 31 Mar 2013

UNADIS (2013) Right to health, right to life: why we need to act now on HIV and human rights, discussion paper, high level meeting on HIV and human rights in the European Union and Neighbouring Countries. http://ec.europa.eu/health/sti_prevention/docs/ev_20130527_discussion_paper_en.pdf. Accessed 1 Sept 2013

UNCEDAW (1999) General recommendation No. 24: Article 12 of the Convention (women and health) A/54/38/Rev.1

UNCESCR (2000) General comment on the right to the highest attainable standard of health 14, UN Doc. E/CN.12/2000/4

UNCESCR (2003) Concluding observations Russian Federation E/C.12/1/Add.94

UNCESCR (2009) General comment 20: Non-discrimination in economic, social and cultural rights (article 2, para 2, of the International Covenant on Economic, Social and Cultural Rights) UN Doc E/C.12/GC/20

UNCESCR (2011) Concluding observations Russian Federation E/C.12/RUS/CO/5

UNCRC (2003a) General comment No. 3 HIV/AIDS and the rights of the child CRC/GC/2003/3

UNCRC (2003b) General Comment No. 4 Adolescent health and development in the context of the Convention on the Rights of the Child CRC/GC/2003/4

UNCRC (2005a) General comment No. 7 implementing child rights in early childhood CRC/C/GC/7/Rev.1

UNCRC (2005b) General comment No. 11 Indigenous children and their rights under the convention. CRC/C/GC/11

UNCRC (2005c) Concluding observations: Russian Federation CRC/C/RUS/CO/3

UNCRC (2012) Fourth and fifth periodic reports of States parties due in 2011, Russian Federation, CRC/C/RUS/4-5

UNDP (2009) National human development report: Russian Federation 2008: Russia facing demographic challenges. http://hdr.undp.org/en/reports/nationalreports/europethecis/russia/NHDR_Russia_2008_Eng.pdf. Accessed 31 Mar 2013

Whitehead M, Dahlgren G (2006) Concepts and principles for tackling social inequities in health: levelling up Part 1. WHO Regional Office for Europe. www.euro.who.int/document/e89383.pdf. Accessed 31 Mar 2013

World Bank (2008) Public spending in Russia for health care: issues and options http://siteresources.worldbank.org/INTRUSSIANFEDERATION/Resources/PublicSpendingInRussiaforHealthCare.pdf. Accessed 31 Mar 2013

WHO (2006) About the new EU neighbours. Russian Federation. Health. 10 health questions. www.euro.who.int/data/assets/pdf_file/0006/99960/E88202.pdf. Accessed 31 Mar 2013

WHO (2008) The World Health Report 'Primary Health Care–Now More Than Ever'

WHO (2009) World Health Statistics 2009. www.who.int/whosis/whostat/2009/en/. Accessed 31 Mar 2013

WHO (2012) World Health Statistics 2012. www.who.int/gho/publications/world_health_statistics/2012/en/. Accessed 31 March 2013

WHO Regional Office for Europe (2003) Health in prisons update. Newsletter No 1. http://www.hipp-europe.org/. Accessed 25 Aug 2010

WHO regional office for Europe (2006) Highlights on health in the Russian Federation 2005. www.euro.who.int/data/assets/pdf_file/0003/103593/E88405.pdf. Accessed 31 Mar 2013

WHO, UNAIDS, UNISEF (2008) Epidemiological fact sheet on HIV and AIDS: core data on epidemiology and response. Russian Federation, http://apps.who.int/globalatlas/predefined Reports/EFS2008/full/EFS2008_RU.pdf. Accessed 8 Apr 2013

Chapter 13
The Challenges to Realising the Right to Health in Ireland

Adam McAuley

Abstract Political will is vital to realising the right to the highest attainable standard of health found in Article 12 of the International Covenant on Economic, Social and Cultural Rights and its related General Comment No 14 (General Comment No 14, para 12 (www.unhchr.ch/tbs/doc.nsf/(symbol)/E.C.12.2000.4.En)). Domestic stakeholders influence the political will to the realisation of this right. This chapter analyses the challenges in realising the right to health in Ireland where stakeholders wielded significant power. It reveals that there is no enforceable legal right to health in Ireland and that there is significant political discretion in realising the availability, accessibility, acceptability and quality objectives of General Comment No 14. The Catholic Church and medical profession have exercised a dominant influence over Irish health policy for decades. A consequence of this influence was that the Irish health system developed a unique mix of public and private health care which continues to hamper the realisation of the availability and accessibility objectives of General Comment No 14. The chapter discovers that there is a significant challenge in achieving the acceptability objective in Ireland with religious homogeneity. It discusses the role of the Catholic Church in access to health care with a focus on family planning. Finally, the chapter discusses Ireland's progress in achieving the quality objective of General Comment No 14 because all stakeholders desired improvements in the quality of healthcare delivery.

Contents

13.1	Introduction	374
13.2	The Role of Politics in the Right to Health	374
	13.2.1 The Constitution of Ireland 1937	375
	13.2.2 Statutory and International Right to Health in Ireland	378

A. McAuley (✉)
School of Law and Government, Dublin City University, Glasnevin, Dublin 9, Ireland
e-mail: adam.mcauley@dcu.ie

B. Toebes et al. (eds.), *The Right to Health*, DOI: 10.1007/978-94-6265-014-5_13,
© T.M.C. ASSER PRESS and the authors 2014

13.2.3	Conclusions on the Right to Health	380
13.3	Availability and Accessibility of Health Care in Ireland	381
13.3.1	Fostering Two-Tier Healthcare System	382
13.3.2	Impact of Economic Boom on Two-Tier Healthcare System	384
13.3.3	Impact of Financial Crisis on Ireland's Healthcare System	387
13.3.4	Conclusions on Availability and Accessibility Objectives	388
13.4	Acceptability of Healthcare Delivery in Ireland	389
13.4.1	Dominant Influence of Catholic Church on Family Planning Regulation	390
13.4.2	Preserving Prohibition on Abortion	391
13.4.3	Lingering Impact of Church Ethos on Access to Lawful Treatment	393
13.4.4	Conclusions on Acceptability Objective	394
13.5	Quality of Health Care in the Irish System	394
13.5.1	Improving Quality Assurance After Healthcare Scandals	395
13.5.2	Conclusions on Quality Objective	397
13.6	Conclusions	397
References		398

13.1 Introduction

Article 12 of the Covenant on Economic, Social and Cultural Rights 1966 (Covenant) recognises the right of everyone to the enjoyment of the highest attainable standard of physical and mental health. Article 12 provides scant guidance to states as what steps are necessary to realise the right to health. In 2000, the UN Committee on Economic, Social and Cultural Rights (CESCR) issued General Comment No 14 which lays down the availability, accessibility, acceptability and quality (AAAQ) objectives necessary to realise the right to health.[1] Political will is vital to realising the right to the highest attainable standard of health. This chapter assesses the existence and strength of the right to health under Irish law before considering the challenges in realising the AAAQ objectives with stakeholders who have exercised significant influence over health policy since the foundation of the Irish state in 1922.

13.2 The Role of Politics in the Right to Health

The absence, presence and strength of any legal right to health determines the scope of politics in health policy. A strong and enforceable right to health severely restricts the role of politics and the influence of stakeholders. The absence of a right to health confers significant political discretion in health policy. Stakeholders

---

[1] International Covenant on Civil and Political Rights 1966, Article 12.

13 The Challenges to Realising the Right to Health in Ireland

seek to wield influence on the exercise of this political discretion. This section determines the scope of politics by examining the strength of the right to health under the Constitution of Ireland 1937, statute and international human rights law.[2]

13.2.1 The Constitution of Ireland 1937

The presence of a constitutional right to health reflects a state's commitment to health care.[3] The Irish constitution contains a section entitled 'fundamental rights' and these rights reflect a patent rejection of the Westminster parliamentary model where parliament can confer, limit or extinguish rights. A referendum of the people is required to amend an existing right or add a new right to this section. The express constitutional rights are civil and political in nature reflecting similar rights adopted by European states during the period between the two world wars. The Irish constitution, however, contains no express constitutional socio-economic rights, such as a right to health. There is one express socio-economic duty to provide for children's 'free primary education'.[4] Two studies on comparative constitutional law arrived at different conclusions as to whether the Irish constitution is an outlier in possessing no express constitutional right to health. In 2003, a study found 67.5 per cent of the world's constitutions contained a health provision.[5] The second study found that 67.2 per cent of states do not recognise the right to health in their constitutions or legislation.[6] The disparity in these studies may be explained by the different types of provisions on health found in these states' laws. The Irish constitution could be amended to add an express right to health, which would restrict the scope of the political sphere to determine health policy. The CESCR has recommended such an amendment.[7] However, there is no political will to amend the constitution to confer express socio-economic rights.

---

[2] Ireland has ratified the European Convention for the Protection of Human Rights and Fundamental Freedoms 1950, European Social Charter 1961, International Convention on the Elimination of All Forms of Racial Discrimination 1966, International Covenant on Civil and Political Rights 1966, International Covenant on Economic, Social and Cultural Rights 1966, United Nations Convention on the Elimination of All Forms of Discrimination against Women 1979, United Nations Convention against Torture and Other Cruel, Inhuman or Degrading Treatment or Punishment 1984, European Convention for the Prevention of Torture and Inhuman or Degrading Treatment or Punishment 1987 and United Nations Convention on the Rights of the Child 1989. Ireland has signed but not yet ratified the United Nations Convention on the Rights of Persons with Disabilities 2006.

[3] Kinney and Clark 2004, pp. 285–286 and 298.

[4] Constitution of Ireland 1937, Article 42.4.

[5] Kinney and Clark 2004, p. 287.

[6] Backman et al. 2008, p. 2078.

[7] CESCR 1999, para 22 and CESCR 2002, para 23.

A majority of the members of the Constitution Review Group decided that socio-economic rights are essentially political, which should be the responsibility of the elected representatives and not be the concern of unelected judges.[8]

Judicial recognition of implied constitutional rights is a hallmark of judicial activism. Irish judges avoided judicial activism, which pleased the executive branch until the election of Seán Lemass as Prime Minister in 1959. Lemass was an economic and social reformer who wanted to drag Ireland into the twentieth century. Lemass recognised the prohibitive political cost in effecting social change through parliament. Thus, Lemass appointed Ó'Dálaigh as Chief Justice and Walsh to the Supreme Court on the same day in 1961 with an imprimatur: the Irish Supreme Court should be judicially active in a similar vein to the Warren Supreme Court in the United States (US). During the next twenty years, High and Supreme Court judges encouraged barristers to invoke constitutional rights. These courts struck down legislation for breaching express rights and identified 'unenumerated' or implied constitutional rights sourced by the judges from the 'Christian and democratic nature of the State'.[9] However, these implied rights are exclusively civil and political in nature such as bodily integrity,[10] privacy[11] and dignity.[12] Judges may have been reluctant to imply socio-economic rights because the Irish constitution expressly prohibits judges from constitutional interpretation by reference to the constitution's directive principles of social policy, which include a duty to safeguard the economic interests of weaker members of society and to contribute, where necessary, to support the sick.[13] The Irish directive principles of social policy were the source for similar principles in the Indian constitution. The Indian courts have demonstrated greater willingness than the Irish courts to invoke these directive principles in developing socio-economic rights.[14]

Irish judges have decided that their role in interpreting the Irish constitution does not extend to implying any universal socio-economic right. In *TD v. Minister for Education* Chief Justice Keane expressed the 'gravest doubts as to whether the courts at any stage' should assume the function of declaring socio-economic rights.[15] This judicial hostility caused a fierce debate surrounding the role of judicial activism amongst academics and even a Supreme Court judge.[16] Despite this judicial hostility, one cancer patient litigated a claim that her right to life and implied right to medical treatment was breached when a public hospital refused to

---

[8] Constitution Review Group 1996, pp. 235–236.

[9] *Ryan v. Attorney General* 1965 IR 294, pp. 312–313 *per* J. Kenny.

[10] *Ryan v. Attorney General* 1965 IR 294, p. 313 *per* J. Kenny.

[11] *Kennedy v. Ireland* 1987 IR 587, p. 592 *per* P. Hamilton.

[12] *In Re A Ward of Court (withholding medical treatment) (No 2)* 1996 2 IR 79, p. 163 *per* J. *Denham*

[13] Constitution of Ireland 1937, Article 45.4.1°.

[14] See: Bhagwati 1985 and Cassels 1989.

[15] 2001 4 IR 259 at p. 282. Similar sentiments were expressed by J. Hardiman at p. 361.

[16] See: Quinn 2000, Hogan 2001, Gwynn Morgan 2002, Whyte 2002 and Hardiman 2004.

13 The Challenges to Realising the Right to Health in Ireland

admit her for inpatient chemotherapy because of a bed shortage.[17] The patient settled her legal claim by accepting the state's offer to pay for a private bed in the very same public hospital.[18]

The Irish Supreme Court has imposed severe restrictions on the judicial enforceability of socio-economic rights. During the late 1990s, the High Court found that the state was failing to honour its constitutional duty of education to hundreds of children suffering with dyslexia, intellectual disabilities, hyperkinetic conduct and attention deficit disorders. The High Court adjourned proceedings so the government could adopt and implement a policy addressing these children's needs. The High Court's patience was sorely tested when government delayed implementing its adopted policy. The High Court's response was to issue an injunction against government requiring it to implement the policy. The government's appeal claimed that the constitutional separation of powers prohibited such an injunction. The Supreme Court rejected the government's claim but held that a mandatory order could only be issued when the government clearly disregarded its constitutional duty in a conscious and deliberate manner.[19] A majority of the Supreme Court found that the government's delay in implementing this policy was not conscious and deliberate.

The Irish judicial definition of justice explains their hostility to socio-economic rights. Judges recognise distributive and commutative justice.[20] Distributive justice is the distribution of common goods and tax revenue amongst members of a political community. Irish judges have decided that the government is responsible for distributive justice which must be administered fairly by allocating what is due to each individual by reference to the common good. Judges have decided that courts should not be involved in distributive justice to vindicate socio-economic rights. Commutative justice involves providing redress arising from an interaction or relationship between two or more individuals; for example, a court orders monetary compensation to a patient who is injured because of a doctor's negligence. Judges believe that courts are responsible for commutative justice. In *Re Health (Amendment) (No 2) Bill* 2004 the Supreme Court indicated that a court could engage in distributive justice by constraining distribution of tax revenue in order to satisfy a constitutional duty to provide shelter and maintenance for those with 'exceptional needs'.[21] The government and legislature's denial of distributive justice must be so pronounced that the court considers it to be commutatively unjust.[22] This situation would only arise if the government decided to abolish social welfare and public health care, which would never occur because such action would be so politically unpalatable. Irish judges do not want to dictate how

---

[17] Irish Times 2001a.

[18] Irish Times 2001b.

[19] *TD v. Minister for Education* 2001 4 IR 259.

[20] *O'Reilly and Others v. Limerick Corporation* 1989 ILRM 181, pp. 194–195 *per. J. Costello* approved by the Supreme Court in *TD v. Minister for Education* 2001 4 IR 259.

[21] *In Re Health (Amendment) (No 2) Bill 2004* 2005 1 IR 105, p. 166 *per CJ. Murray.*

[22] Rossa Phelan 1994, pp. 145–146.

a government spends tax revenue when there are fixed budgetary resources.[23] Irish judges believe that a court's adjudicatory function is inappropriate to consider and weigh the panoply of issues in determining policy, including health policy.

Although Irish judges refuse to imply a universal right to health, Irish judges have recognised a limited implied right to health for prisoners and children arising from their special relationship of dependency on the state. The judges found that imprisonment deprives a prisoner of the ability to access private and public health care. Therefore, the state must provide medical treatment for an ill prisoner.[24] The judges have stressed that an ill prisoner's constitutional right to bodily integrity and the prohibition on cruel and unusual punishment are breached where the state provides inadequate treatment.[25] However, the courts have decided that a prisoner is not entitled to medical treatment of their choice[26] and the state does not have to provide the best available medical treatment.[27] Despite the limited right to health, a 2010 study found that the medical needs of prisoners were not being met consistently by Irish prisons.[28] Furthermore, judges recognised that children have unique implied constitutional rights, including rights to be fed, live, reared and educated, and to have the opportunity of working and realising that child's full personality and dignity.[29] One Supreme Court judge added a right to medical treatment.[30] The High Court held that the state has a constitutional duty to provide for these rights where parents cannot meet the child's needs, however, the state does not have to meet a child's exceptional health needs.[31]

13.2.2 Statutory and International Right to Health in Ireland

The Irish courts have decided that the conferring of a statutory right to health is a political decision that lies with the government and legislature. There is no political will to confer such a right. Instead, the legislature imposes statutory discretions and duties in relation to health on statutory bodies rather than rights, for example the Health Acts 1953 to 2013 impose duties and discretions on the Health Services Executive (HSE) to provide health for those who cannot afford private

---

[23] Kinney and Clark 2004, p. 300.

[24] *The State (C) v. Frawley* 1976 IR 365, p. 372 *per P. Finlay* and *The State (Richardson) v. Governor of Mountjoy Prison* 1980 ILRM 82.

[25] See: *O'Reilly v. Governor of Wheatfield Prison*, unreported, High Court, *J. Hanna*, 22nd June 2007 and *McMenamin v. Governor of Wheatfield Prison*, unreported, High Court, *J. Hanna*, 29th June 2012.

[26] See: *McDonagh v. Frawley* 1978 IR 131.

[27] See: *The State (C) v. Frawley* 1976 IR 365.

[28] Barry et al. 2010.

[29] *G v An Bord Uchtála* 1980 IR 32, p. 56 *per C.J. Higgins*.

[30] *Eastern Health Board v. An Bord Uchtála* 1994 3 IR 207, p. 230 *per J. O'Flaherty*.

[31] *FN v. Minister for Education* 1995 1 IR 409, p. 416 *per J. Geoghegan*.

13 The Challenges to Realising the Right to Health in Ireland 379

health care. Where there is a statutory discretion, the HSE may provide health care but is not obliged to do so and the HSE determines the extent of any health care.[32] The HSE must provide health when there is a statutory duty to do so. A statutory right to health can be implied from a statutory duty but does not guarantee a level or quality of service unless this is specified in the duty which is also very rare.

Ireland has signed and ratified a significant number of human rights treaties concerned with health.[33] Indeed, international recognition of the right to health is more widespread than national recognition, which may be explained by the weakness of state accountability under international law.[34] A study of one hundred and seventy states found that ratification of human rights treaties containing provisions on health was not associated with any change in health status.[35] The Irish constitution contains a dualist approach to international law so an Irish court or state body can only give effect to a treaty where the legislature has transposed that treaty into domestic law.[36] Successive Irish governments have demonstrated little or no political interest in transposing human rights treaties into domestic law. The CESCR has expressed disappointment at Ireland's failure to transpose the Covenant into domestic law.[37] Ireland has transposed only one human rights treaty, the European Convention on Human Rights, which was required as part of the Northern Ireland peace process in order to establish common human rights standards in the Republic of Ireland and Northern Ireland. The European Convention does not contain an express right to health and the European Court of Human Rights (ECtHR) has rejected claims to a right to health as manifestly ill-founded.[38] The ECtHR has recognised that the right to life and the prohibition of degrading treatment imply a very limited duty on states for health care. The right

---

[32] *CK v. Northern Area Health Authority* 2002 2 IR 545, p. 557 *per P. Finnegan.*

[33] European Convention for the Protection of Human Rights and Fundamental Freedoms 1950, European Social Charter 1961, International Convention on the Elimination of All Forms of Racial Discrimination 1966, International Covenant on Civil and Political Rights 1966, International Covenant on Economic, Social and Cultural Rights 1966, United Nations Convention on the Elimination of All Forms of Discrimination against Women 1979, United Nations Convention against Torture and Other Cruel, Inhuman or Degrading Treatment or Punishment 1984, European Convention for the Prevention of Torture and Inhuman or Degrading Treatment or Punishment 1987 and United Nations Convention on the Rights of the Child 1989. Ireland has signed but not yet ratified the United Nations Convention on the Rights of Persons with Disabilities 2006.

[34] Backman et al. 2008, p. 2059.

[35] Palmer et al. 2009, p. 1987 and 1989.

[36] Constitution of Ireland 1937, Art. 29.6; *In Re Ó Laighléis* 1960 IR 93 concerning the European Convention on Human Rights, *Application of Woods* 1970 IR 154 concerning the Universal Declaration of Human Rights, *E v. E* 1982 ILRM 497 concerning a judgment of the European Court of Human Rights and *Kavanagh v. Ireland* 1996 1 IR 321 concerning a decision of the UN Human Rights Committee under the optional protocol of the Covenant on Civil and Political Rights.

[37] CESCR 1999, para 9.

[38] *Jazvinský v. Slovakia (Application nos 33088/96, 52236/99, 52451/99, 52453/99, 52455/99, 52457/99 and 52459/99)*, 7th September 2000.

to life may require a state to take appropriate steps to safeguard a person's life.[39] A positive duty to provide health care arises when state agents jeopardise a person's life by denying that person access to health services available to the general population. The ECtHR has suggested that state responsibility under the right to life may be engaged by state conduct in health policy. A state may have to provide health care to prisoners in order to avoid breaching the prohibition of degrading treatment.[40] Furthermore, a prisoner's health must be adequately secured by providing necessary medical treatment in light of the practical demands of imprisonment.[41] The prohibition of degrading treatment does not require the release of a prisoner on health grounds or admission to a public hospital for particular medical treatment.[42] Ireland is vindicating the ECtHR's limited implied right of access to health care, which is reflected in the Irish courts' approach in *Re Health (Amendment) (No 2) Bill* 2004 and the prisoner cases.

13.2.3 Conclusions on the Right to Health

There may be too much weight attached to the absence or presence of a legal right to health in relation to health provision. Some states fail to vindicate their constitutional rights to health while other states devote extensive resources to health in the absence of a constitutional right.[43] Thirteen of the twenty states with the highest per capita expenditure on health had no constitutional health provision in 2003. Per capita expenditure is a very crude indicator as there is no assessment of value for money, the quality of health care and whether expenditure is sufficient to address health care needs.[44] Legal rights to health can be used in strategic litigation to improve the right to health for particular groups, such as access to antiretroviral drugs and promote care of people who are elderly and mentally ill.[45]

Irish law is deficient since it contains neither a legal right to health enforceable in court nor one that imposes policy imperatives. The absence of a legal right to health confers discretion in political decision-making about health policy and organisation of the health system. Stakeholders wield their influence to determine health policy which can affect the realisation of AAAQ of General Comment No 14. The Catholic Church and the medical profession formed a strong alliance hampering the realisation of the objectives of the AAAQ in Ireland for decades, which is discussed in the following sections.

---

[39] *Nitecki v. Poland (Application no 65653/01)*, 21st March 2002.

[40] *Kudła v. Poland (Application no 30210/96)*, 26th October 2000.

[41] Ibid, para 94.

[42] Ibid, para 93.

[43] Kinney and Clark 2004, p. 294.

[44] Ibid, pp. 294–295.

[45] Palmer et al. 2009, pp. 1989–1990.

13.3 Availability and Accessibility of Health Care in Ireland

The availability and accessibility objectives of General Comment No 14 require a state to ensure that there is a healthcare system providing health care to all. There are three models upon which a state can organise and fund a healthcare system: voluntary health insurance, social health insurance and national health service (NHS).[46] The choice of one of these models or a combination of models is a political decision involving interactions between government and stakeholders.[47] In 1922, there was no political desire to choose any of these models when Ireland attained independence. The Irish health system in 1922 comprised hospital and general practitioner (GP) care with a very small number of people having social health insurance. GPs acted as gatekeepers to consultant and hospital care. The Catholic Church provided hospital care through their "voluntary" hospitals. Hospitals and hospital consultants received limited state funding to treat public patients whilst charging private patients for treatment. GP care was regulated by the Poor Relief (Ireland) Act 1851, where there was a dispensary doctor for each of the state's 723 dispensary districts. The system was financed by a levy on property owners.[48] This system was flawed because of regional variations in eligibility criteria for treatment and patients had no choice of doctor. Dispensary doctors were also entitled to treat and charge private patients. Thus, there was a two-tier health system for public and private patients where patients were accorded a different status on the basis of ability to pay for health care rather than their medical need.

In 1947, the Irish government recommended replacing the existing two-tier system with an NHS model providing free access to health care based on medical need, similar to the NHS model adopted by the United Kingdom in 1946.[49] In 1951, the Irish government initiated the first phase of this NHS model with free maternity care and services for children. The church and medical profession joined forces to oppose this proposal because it would eliminate income from their private patients. As a result of this opposition, the government abandoned the NHS model and retained the existing two-tier system. The government decided that access to health was to be determined by the patient's ability to pay which is reflected in the three categories of patients and their access to health care.[50] The first category comprises those on the lowest incomes who were entitled to health free of charge. The second category comprises middle income earners who were entitled to free hospital care or at a nominal charge but not free GP care. The third category comprises the highest income earners who had no entitlement to any free

---

[46] Toth 2013, p. 160.

[47] Ibid, p. 159.

[48] Adshead and Millar 2003, p. 10.

[49] Department of Health 1947.

[50] Considine and Dukelow 2009, p. 254.

health care. A government is entitled to decide that a nation's health needs should be met by private and public healthcare systems. A government must ensure that either system does not negatively impact on the other. Successive Irish governments have incubated a parasitic relationship between the private and public systems. The public system subsidises the cost of private health care. The consequence of this parasitic relationship is a significant detrimental impact on availability and accessibility to health care for public patients.

13.3.1 Fostering Two-Tier Healthcare System

The introduction of private health insurance in 1957 copper fastened the two-tier healthcare system. The medical profession proposed health insurance to protect their private income from 15 to 20 per cent of patients ineligible for free hospital care under the public health system.[51] Free market principles did not regulate this market because the Voluntary Health Insurance (VHI) had a statutory monopoly to provide insurance on the basis of open enrolment, community rating and lifetime cover. Open enrolment requires an insurer to enroll every patient regardless of risk status. Community rating provides that insurance premiums are the same irrespective of age, gender and state of health. Community rating operates on the basis of inter-generational solidarity where younger subscribers subsidise older subscribers in the expectation that they will be subsidised in later years by a new generation of younger subscribers. Lifetime cover confers on a patient the right to renew their policies, irrespective of age, risk status or claims history. The principles allow anyone to subscribe to insurance regardless of age or health status and pay the same premium.

Irish patients opted to obtain private health insurance in the past even though they were eligible to subsidised public health care. Irish patients obtained health insurance because the public system was inefficient and there was tax relief on insurance premium.[52] Private health insurance guaranteed to a private patient shorter waiting time for a hospital bed than a public patient in the very same hospital.[53] Private insured patients were more likely to be treated in a private bed in a public hospital even though 50 per cent of private beds were in private hospitals.[54] Governments failed to adopt a common waiting list on the basis of medical need rather than ability to pay.[55] Three factors cemented the two-tier hospital system. First, governments allowed public and voluntary hospitals to designate public beds as private beds to make up for shortfalls following cuts in

---

[51] Adshead and Millar 2003, p. 12.

[52] Considine and Dukelow 2009, p. 266.

[53] Ibid, p. 267.

[54] Ibid, p. 277.

[55] Ibid, p. 276.

13 The Challenges to Realising the Right to Health in Ireland   383

public expenditure during recessions.[56] The number of private beds grew from 10 per cent in 1972 to 20 per cent by 1987. A bed designation system with a maximum 80–20 per cent split between public and private beds was not established until 1991.[57] However, patients who designate themselves as private patients have tended to exceed this 20 per cent limit which may indicate that public hospitals are failing to adhere to this bed designation system. Second, the public hospital system subsidised private health care because no government required insurers to pay the full economic cost of a private patient staying in a private bed in a public hospital.[58] In addition, there was no provision made for recovering the cost of a private patient occupying a public bed. Wren argues that this subsidisation aided expansion of the private health system.[59] Third, hospital consultants breached their contracts with the state by treating too many private patients and insufficient number of public patients. Governments failed to take steps to ensure that hospitals and consultants adhered to the public/private mix. The failure to address this two-tier system significantly undermines availability of and access to health care for public patients.

In 1994, the health insurance market was opened to competition with the removal of the VHI's statutory monopoly, like other health insurance markets such as that found in the Netherlands. The Health Insurance Authority (HIA) was established to regulate the market.[60] The principles of community rating, lifetime cover and open enrolment were modified with maximum age limits and prescribed waiting periods. New insurers could limit these principles by devising insurance products to attract younger people who are generally healthier and do not utilise as much health services. The VHI is being left with older subscribers who tend to be greater users of health because they tend to be ill more frequently. The 1994 Act recognised that this could be a problem and establishes a risk equalisation scheme where health insurers are required to make financial transfers to reflect the differing costs of insurers arising from the differences between the profile of consumers' age or health.

In 1972, the General Medical Services (GMS) scheme replaced the GP dispensary system with eligible patients entitled to free GP care.[61] The advantage of the GMS scheme is that a patient can register with another GP who has a GMS contract in the area, which was not possible under the dispensary system. A GMS contracted GP provides full-time cover for a maximum 2,000 patients. GPs must work a minimum of 40 h a week and provide full cover for out-of-hours services. Many GPs with GMS contracts employ other GPs in their practices to provide out-of-hours service. A GMS contract can only be terminated if a GP is removed from the medical register, is physically or mentally incapacitated or reaches mandatory

---

[56] Ibid, p. 268.

[57] Ibid, pp. 276–277.

[58] Ibid, p. 269.

[59] Wren 2003, p. 57.

[60] See: www.hia.ie/.

[61] Adshead and Millar 2003, pp. 13–14.

retirement age of 70.[62] The Irish Medical Organisation (IMO), doctor's trade union established in 1839, has strong lobbying power. The agreement of the IMO must be obtained for any change to the GMS contract.[63] GMS contract terms and conditions are found in over 70 letters and circulars issued by the Department of Health since 1972. There were differences in terms of access to GP care because some areas of Ireland had a limited number of GMS contracted GPs.[64] The state had difficulties in increasing the number of GMS contracts because the IMO is involved in regulating the number, location and allocation of GMS contracts with an IMO nominee sitting on the interview panel for every GMS contract.

Like the dispensary system, the GMS scheme cultivates a two-tier system where income rather than medical need dictates a patient's treatment because a GMS contracted GP is entitled to treat and charge private patients. GP income is derived from the GMS scheme and fees from private patients.[65] A substantial part of income comes from the GMS scheme. GPs receive a payment based on the number and profile of patients on their list, such as age, sex and the distance from their residence to the GP's surgery, regardless of the number of visits that a patient makes to the surgery. GPs receive superannuation benefits and ancillary benefits such as contributions towards hiring a *locum* to cover holidays, maternity leave, study leave and sick leave, secretarial and nursing support.[66] There are also fees for services, such as suturing and excisions. Additional payments are made to GPs in remote or rural areas where population densities do not support large practices. The GMS scheme subsidises private GP care, which has a deleterious impact on the availability and accessibility of affordable health care for public patients.

13.3.2 Impact of Economic Boom on Two-Tier Healthcare System

Government reports in 1987 and 1994 recognised the inequity of access to health caused by the two-tier health system.[67] Ireland's significant economic development provided the financial boon to end this inequity with a growth of 9.4 % per annum between 1995 and 2000 and 5.9 % per annum between 2001 and 2008. In 2002, CESCR found that Ireland had no economic impediment to vindicating the Covenant rights, including the right to health care.[68] Successive governments had the financial means to eliminate the two-tier system.

---

[62] Competition Authority 2010, p. 52.

[63] Ibid, p. 54.

[64] Ibid, p.18.

[65] Ibid, p. 25.

[66] Ibid, p. 23.

[67] Department of Health 1987, 1994.

[68] CESCR 2002, para 11.

In 2001, the government published a health strategy grounded on the four principles of equity, people-centeredness, quality and accountability. The strategy also had four goals which are better health for everyone, fair access that targets health inequalities, people are treated fairly according to need, responsive and appropriate care delivery and high performance.[69] These principles and goals were to be achieved through one hundred and twenty one action items with each item having a deliverable, target date and organisation responsible for the item. The strategy promised that private practice would not be at the expense of fair access for public patients.[70] There would be a revised contract for consultants and clarification of the rules of access to health for public patients. However, the strategy's fundamental flaw was that it did not replace the two-tier health system. Indeed, government actions re-enforced the two-tier system with increases in GP and consultant salaries, purchase of private healthcare services to reduce public hospital waiting lists and facilitating the development of private health facilities. The CESCR criticised this strategy for omitting a human rights framework encompassing, *inter alia*, the principles of non-discrimination and equal access to health facilities and services and recommended such a framework.[71]

GPs received an average of €220,000 under the GMS scheme in 2008.[72] 69 per cent of a GP's income arises from capitation and fees for services provided to patients, 24 per cent is for practice support allowances and 5 per cent for the GP's superannuation. The GMS scheme subsidies private GP care with GPs receiving an average of €65 for every visit made by a public patient whilst the average fee charged to private patients was €51 in 2010.[73] The establishment of a private-only practice is not attractive because the financial benefits under the GMS make it difficult for private-only GPs to compete on price.[74] The percentage of GPs in private practice fell from 11 per cent in 1982 to just 4 per cent in 2005, with most of the fall occurring in the period after 1992.[75]

In 1999, the CESCR expressed concern at the length of hospital waiting lists.[76] The government's response to the CESCR's concern was to reduce hospital waiting times to a maximum of three months by increasing the number of public beds and purchasing treatment in private hospitals located in Ireland and the United Kingdom.[77] The national average median waiting times for surgical procedures fell to 3.2 months by 2008. A common waiting list for public and private

---

[69] Department of Health and Children 2001.

[70] Considine and Dukelow 2009, p. 284.

[71] CESCR 2002, paras 22 and 35.

[72] Competition Authority 2010, p. 25.

[73] Ibid, p. 53.

[74] Ibid, p. 55.

[75] Ibid, p. 23.

[76] CESCR 1999, para 21.

[77] Considine and Dukelow 2009, p. 278.

patients based on need rather than income recommended by the CESCR would have been a more progressive step to tackle inequity of access.[78]

The public health system's subsidisation of the private system continued unabated during the economic boom from 2000 to 2008. The number of private hospitals increased with the introduction of building tax relief in 2000.[79] In 2006, there was tax relief for a 'co-location' scheme with private hospitals being built on the grounds of public hospitals.[80] In 2007, the government charged private health insurers 50 and 60 per cent of the cost of a private bed in a public hospital. These incentives increased the number of private beds to satisfy the public hospital bed shortage but private hospitals target elective treatments with no interest in expensive treatment such as emergency medicine. In 2008, the new consultant contract system supported the two-tier health system. Consultants now work a slightly longer working week and at weekends which are crucial to satisfy the accessibility objective of General Comment No 14. There were 2571 consultants employed at the end of June 2012. 15.8 per cent of consultants opted to remain on their existing contract which allowed 70–30 per cent public/private patient mix. There are three types of consultant contract with the new consultant contract system. The first contract involves a consultant working exclusively in the public system and receiving a higher salary for doing so. 22.2 per cent chose this contract. The majority of these consultants worked in specialisms with little or no opportunity for private practice with 65.8 per cent in psychiatry and 12.1 per cent in emergency medicine. The second contract involves consultants working to 80–20 per cent public/private patient mix in public and co-located hospitals. 77.8 per cent opted for this contract. The third contract allowed consultants to treat private patients outside the public hospital system. These contracts were to be offered on an exceptional basis and none have been offered to date. The new system contains the first monitoring mechanism to ensure consultants adhere to the public/private patient mix. In 2011, the HSE engaged with 32 consultants whose private practice accounted for more than 50 per cent of their activity. Two consultants had their right to private practice suspended. The HSE is currently engaging with 49 consultants who exceeded their specified public/private mix.

Despite improvements in the efficiency of the public health system during the economic boom, subscribers to health insurance continued to increase with 50.9 per cent of the population with private health insurance at the end of 2008. During the boom, increases in the average income of employees negatively impacted on access to health.[81] In 2003, the rise in incomes rendered 25 per cent of the population ineligible for free public health services and unable to afford health insurance. These patients paid for every GP visit and received free hospital care for a nightly 'bed fee'. These patients had a considerably lower number of GP visits

---

[78] CESCR 2002, para 35.

[79] Colombo and Tapay 2004, p. 18.

[80] Considine and Dukelow 2009, pp. 280–281.

[81] Adshead and Millar 2003, p. 15.

13 The Challenges to Realising the Right to Health in Ireland 387

than patients who receive free or subsidised GP care.[82] These patients relied on accident and emergency services because the cost of such services was less than that for a GP visit.[83]

13.3.3 Impact of Financial Crisis on Ireland's Healthcare System

The financial crisis has resulted in drastic cuts in health expenditure by the state. Hospital consultant and GP salaries have been reduced. Since 2013, the government is seeking to reduce the costs of medicines by requiring dispensing of generic medicines and reference pricing.[84] Generic substitution allows pharmacists to substitute a cheaper generic equivalent, at the patient's request, when a more expensive product has been prescribed. Reference pricing involves setting a common reimbursement price for selected groups of medicines.

Many actions items listed in the 2001 health strategy have been delayed indefinitely. The treatment purchase fund has been wound up resulting in increased waiting times for public patients. Thus, the number of patients waiting for their *first* outpatient appointment had increased to 385,462 by October 2012. 185,000 have been waiting for an appointment for more than 6 months, with 115,000 waiting more than 12 months. 11,805 patients have been waiting for more than 4 years. Three factors have increased the detrimental impact of the public health expenditure cuts. First, many patients cannot afford to renew their health insurance. The number of insured patients dropped below 46 per cent in March 2013. Second, the government is seeking to end the public system's subsidisation of the private healthcare system. The accident and emergency charge for private patients was increased significantly in 2008. In January 2012, the government levied the full economic cost on a private patient occupying a private bed in a public hospital. In 2013, the Minister for Health announced legislative changes necessary to levy the full economic cost of private patients occupying public beds. This charge will be phased in over time to mitigate the impact on the private health insurance market. Insurers will have to augment their premium and those currently struggling to pay existing premiums will abandon insurance for an already overstretched public health system. Third, the government must propose a new risk equalisation scheme for the private health insurance companies because the Supreme Court found that the HIA's scheme was illegal for distorting competition in 2008.[85] This new scheme may affect the principles of open enrolment, community rating and lifetime cover allowing anyone to subscribe to insurance

---

[82] Competition Authority 2010, p. 26.

[83] Ibid, p. 11.

[84] Health (Pricing and Supply of Medical Goods) Act 2013.

[85] *Bupa Ireland Ltd v. Health Insurance Authority*, unreported, Supreme Court, 16th July 2008.

regardless of age or health status and pay the same premium Patients may be ineligible for insurance under this scheme and will be dependent on the public system.[86]

13.3.4 Conclusions on Availability and Accessibility Objectives

One would expect a government managing the worst recession in Irish history to avoid any political commitment to a new model for organising and funding the healthcare system. However, the current government has committed itself to a social health insurance model for hospital care and a NHS model for GP care. The government will introduce universal health insurance (UHI).[87] Access to health care will be determined by medical need and paying for healthcare services will be determined by ability to pay. UHI will be a statutory system of health insurance guaranteed by the state and would not be subject to competition law. Insurance with a public or private insurer is compulsory. The state will pay insurance premia for people on low incomes and subsidise premia for people on middle incomes. Everyone will have a choice between competing insurers. State funding for hospital care will be placed into a Hospital Insurance Fund which will subsidise or pay insurance premia for those who qualify for subsidy. Insurers must offer the same package of services to all and will be prohibited from selling insurance to provide faster access to procedures covered by the UHI package. In addition, a statutory right to free universal primary care will be introduced on a phased basis. Primary care teams, including GPs and other professionals, are capable of meeting 90–95 per cent of health needs. Primary care teams and centres should reduce demands on the hospital system. In 2012, the government started dismantling restrictive aspects of the GMS scheme by legislating to permit any qualified and trained GP to establish a practice and treat public patients in the location of their choice.[88] The viability of existing GP practices in an area is no longer a factor in awarding GMS contracts. The social health insurance and NHS model proposals will eliminate the two-tier health system. The challenge lies in paying for these models with the number of subscribers to private health insurance continuing to fall due to the recession and proposals to charge the full cost of private patients using the public health system. The government cannot afford to pay for a social health insurance model for hospital care and a NHS model for GP care unless there are significant cuts in healthcare costs such as salary of clinicians. The government may be on a collision path with healthcare trade unions that have exercised influence in the past to frustrate reforms of the health system.

---

[86] Considine and Dukelow 2009, p. 282.

[87] Department of Health and Children 2013.

[88] Health (Provision of General Practitioner Services) Act 2012.

13.4 Acceptability of Healthcare Delivery in Ireland

The acceptability objective of General Comment No 14 requires that state funded health care is respectful of medical ethics and culturally appropriate.[89] The acceptability objective is a significant challenge for Ireland for two reasons. Firstly, the population is overwhelmingly Catholic with 84.2 per cent of the population identifying themselves as such in the 2011 census.[90] Secondly, the Catholic Church (church) was a state within a state providing essential social services on behalf of the state such as education and health. All voluntary and public hospitals bar one subscribe to this church's ethos.[91] Many hospitals are also teaching hospitals where medical students receive their training in accordance with the church's ethos. Healthcare institutions and units within institutions are named after Catholic saints with displays of Catholic statutes and iconography.

The moral teaching and ethos of the church had a dominant influence on ethics and the practice of medicine, particularly at the beginning of and end of life. The church's ethos comes into conflict with right to health encompassing access to contraception and family planning. Successive governments have failed to reduce the impact of the church's ethos, which was reflected in the tragic case of Savita Halappanavar which made international headlines. In October 2012, Savita, a Hindu and Indian citizen, requested a termination of her pregnancy as she was suffering a miscarriage. A midwife informed Savita that a termination was unavailable because Ireland is a 'Catholic country'. A consultant obstetrician informed Savita and her husband that a termination of her pregnancy is lawful when a pregnancy poses a risk to a mother's life, not her health. Savita died from multi-organ failure caused by septic shock and *E. coli*, four days after she delivered her dead baby. Noting the global impact of the midwife's remark, the coroner inquiring into the cause of Savita's death claimed that Irish hospitals do not follow any religious dogma.[92] The coroner's claim satisfies the acceptability objective by respecting the culture of individuals, minorities, peoples and communities. However, the substance of the coroner's claim must be assessed.

---

[89] General Comment No 14: The Right to the Highest Attainable Standard of Health (Article 12 of the Covenant), para 12.

[90] Central Statistics Office 2012, p. 6.

[91] The Adelaide Hospital adhered to a Protestant religious ethos which is protected in the structure and management of the Tallaght hospital which also incorporates two catholic hospitals.

[92] See: HSE 2013.

13.4.1 Dominant Influence of Catholic Church on Family Planning Regulation

The church strenuously lobbied to ensure that legal and ethical regulation of family planning reflected its ethos. Catholic dogma, legal and ethical regulation of family planning sang from the same hymn sheet for 50 years. In 1935, the government acceded to the church's request to criminalise the importation, distribution, advertising and sale of contraceptives.[93] It has been a criminal offence for a woman and clinician to terminate a pregnancy since 1861.[94] Any state attempt to interfere in the church's domain in family planning was met with fierce resistance. In 1951, the church attacked a proposal to provide free maternity care for mothers and health for children up to the age of 16. The church claimed that this proposal was a precursor to the introduction of contraception and abortion. The issue was so politically divisive that the coalition government that made the proposal fell. Attempts by individual parliamentarians to repeal the criminal prohibition on access to contraception were easily defeated in the early 1970s.[95] The first divergence between the ethos of the church and the law occurred when the Supreme Court decided that the criminal prohibition on contraception was unconstitutional in 1973. A married woman, Mrs McGee, established that her life was at risk if she became pregnant and this criminal prohibition prevented her accessing contraceptives.[96] The Supreme Court found that the criminal prohibition breached her right to marital privacy. The Irish Supreme Court was conscious of the US Supreme Court decision of *Roe v. Wade*[97] where that court decided that a woman's right to privacy extended to a right to terminate her pregnancy. Members of the Irish Supreme Court stated that the Irish constitutional right to marital privacy did not extend to termination of a pregnancy.[98]

A consequence of the *McGee* decision was the need to legislate for access to contraceptives. However, the church's ethos checked the political will to legislate for even a limited right of access to contraceptives. Indeed, the Prime Minister and one Minister voted against their own government's proposal to regulate family planning in 1974. The first planning family legislation was finally introduced in 1979. The Minister for Health described this proposal as 'an Irish solution to an Irish problem'. Married couples were entitled to access contraceptives with a doctor's prescription for '*bona fide*' family planning or medical reasons under this

---

[93] Criminal Law Amendment Act 1935, s 17.

[94] Offences against the Person Act 1861, s 58.

[95] Criminal Law Amendment Bill 1971, Criminal Law Amendment Bill 1972 and Family Planning Bill 1973.

[96] *McGee v. Attorney General* 1974 IR 284.

[97] 410 US 113 1973.

[98] *McGee v. Attorney General* 1974 IR 284 at pp. 312–313 *per* J Walsh and at p. 335 *per* J Griffin.

13 The Challenges to Realising the Right to Health in Ireland

law.[99] A healthcare professional could conscientiously object to providing contraception under this law.[100] A patient had no ability to identify a professional with no conscientious objection so access to contraception varied from region to region. The church opposed the extremely restrictive legislative proposal on family planning by establishing hospital ethics committees in 1978 to preserve its ethos in family planning within hospitals.

In 1979, the Medical Council (Council) was established and one of its responsibilities is to provide ethical guidance to doctors. The Council fulfils this responsibility by issuing an ethics guide every 5 years. The first edition of the guide was issued in 1981 and each subsequent edition is longer than its predecessor providing enhanced guidance on ethical issues. The guide is primarily ethical and is not a legal code. However, a doctor may be sanctioned by the Council for breaching the guide including removal from the medical register which prevents a doctor from practising. There has been a very gradual divergence between the teaching of the church on contraceptives and state regulation of family planning to prevent pregnancy. Condoms have only been readily available to the public since 1992 and the morning after pill was made available through pharmacies without a prescription in 2011.[101]

13.4.2 Preserving Prohibition on Abortion

The church focussed on safeguarding the legal and ethical prohibition on abortion. In 1983, the church was instrumental in garnishing support for a constitutional amendment that prevented abortion by guaranteeing an equal right to life for a pregnant mother and her unborn child.[102] The Irish Supreme Court issued an injunction preventing disclosure of information about abortion in other states, on the basis of this amendment.[103] The ECtHR found that this injunction was a disproportionate restriction on the right to receive and impart information.[104]

In 1992, the litmus test of the 1983 amendment arose when a 14-year-old girl sought an abortion in England because she was suicidal after being raped by a family friend. In the X case, the High Court granted an injunction preventing the girl from travelling to England. The Supreme Court decided that an abortion is lawful when there is a 'real and substantial risk' to a mother's life, including the

---

[99] Health (Family Planning) Act 1979, s 4(2).

[100] Health (Family Planning) Act 1979, s 11.

[101] Health (Family Planning)(Amendment) Act 1992 and Health (Family Planning) (Amendment) Act 1993.

[102] Constitution of Ireland 1937, Art. 40.3.3.

[103] *Attorney General (SPUC) v. Open Door Counselling Ltd* 1988 IR 593.

[104] *Open Door and Dublin Well Woman v. Ireland (Application nos 14234/88; 14235/88)*, 29th October 1992.

risk of suicide, but not her health.[105] The government proposed three constitutional amendments shortly after the *X* case.[106] Two amendments were passed conferring a right to information on abortion services in other states and a right to travel for an abortion to another state. The remaining amendment that sought to remove the risk of suicide as a ground for aborting a pregnancy was not passed.

The Council's ethical guide failed to reflect the divergence between the law and ethics on abortion following the *X* decision. The 1994 version of the guide reaffirmed the ethical position that abortion was professional misconduct. Thus, a doctor ran the risk of being sanctioned for performing an abortion that was simultaneously lawful and unethical. In 1996, the Constitution Review Group recommended clarification as to when an abortion was lawful. Despite this recommendation, legal proceedings were required to vindicate the rights of pregnant adolescents in state care.[107] A 2002 referendum to remove the risk of suicide as a ground for aborting a pregnancy was defeated by a mere 10,500 votes. The legal and ethical positions on abortion did not come into alignment until the issuing of the 2004 version of the ethical guide.

There was political procrastination in legislating for the extremely limited circumstances for a lawful abortion.[108] In 2010, the ECtHR found that Ireland breached a woman's right to respect for her private life when she could not discover if an abortion were permissible to eliminate the risk of her cancer returning.[109] In 2012, the government's expert group recommended legislation and regulations. During parliamentary hearings to consider this expert report, it was disclosed for the first time that ten to twenty abortions are performed every year in order to save a woman's life. In 2013, the Irish Parliament passed the Protection of Life During Pregnancy Act, which adheres to the *X* case test in that an abortion is permitted where there is a real and substantial risk to the mother's life either because of an emergency, physical illness or suicide risk. The restrictive approach of the 2013 Act for the grounds under which an abortion is permitted is similar to the restrictive approach to accessing contraceptives under Ireland's early family planning laws. The 2013 Act requires that an obstetrician and another doctor must jointly agree and certify that an abortion is necessary to avoid a real and substantial risk to the mother's life arising from a physical illness. An obstetrician and two psychiatrists must agree and certify that an abortion is necessary to avoid a real and substantial risk to the mother's life arising from a risk of suicide. The 2013 Act allows one doctor to perform an abortion in an emergency. There is a review process if a woman is refused an abortion. The woman must apply in writing for a review. There

---

[105] *Attorney General v. X* 1992 1 IR 1 at pp. 53–54 *per C.J. Finlay.*

[106] Twelfth, thirteenth and fourteenth amendments to the Irish Constitution.

[107] *A and B v. Eastern Health Board* 1998 1 IR 464 and *D (A Minor) v. District Judge Brennan and Health Services Executive,* unreported, High Court, *J. McKechnie,* 9th May 2007.

[108] Regulation of Information (Services Outside the State For Termination of Pregnancies) Act 1995.

[109] *A, B and C v. Ireland (Application no 25579/051),* 6th December 2010.

13 The Challenges to Realising the Right to Health in Ireland

may be a hearing which the woman may attend or have representation. A review involves the same number of doctors with the relevant qualifications for a physical illness or risk of suicide. A review requires all doctors to agree to a termination. A review must be completed within seven days.[110] There is no legal or medical provision to assist a woman to present her case during a review. Ireland's review mechanism may not satisfy the requirements set down by the ECtHR in *Tysiąc* which decided that any review mechanism must be accessible to a woman, effective and timely in order to limit or prevent damage to a woman's health.[111]

The legislative scheme adopts a new approach to a clinician's conscientious objection to abortion. The law protected the clinician's objection previously by preventing a clinician from being forced to perform or assist in the performance of a lawful abortion. However, the law provided no means through which a patient could identify a clinician who did not have a similar objection. The 2013 Act provides that a clinician with a conscientious objection must make necessary arrangements for the transfer of pregnant woman's care to enable this woman to avail of a lawful abortion.[112]

13.4.3 Lingering Impact of Church Ethos on Access to Lawful Treatment

The church has relinquished day-to-day management of many healthcare institutions over the past two decades.[113] The church has sold facilities to the state with a requirement that the state preserves the church's ethos. This ethos continues to permeate formalised and institutional ethical decision-making processes, such as ethics committees and professional bodies. In 2005 Dublin's Mater Hospital ethics committee refused clinical trial approval for a cancer drug because participants were required to use contraception. In 2010, Cork University Hospital's ethics forum refused to authorise an abortion for a woman who became pregnant during cancer treatment. The ethics forum decided that this woman's life was not under 'immediate threat'. The woman's condition worsened and she required assistance to travel abroad for an abortion.[114] The woman died in November 2011. The ethos is also impacting on the regulation of assisted human reproduction services such as in vitro fertilisation and the use of donated gametes or embryos.

The church's ethos was also evident regarding legal and ethical issues concerning the end of life. In 1996, the High and Supreme courts decided that

---

[110] Protection of Life During Pregnancy Act 2013, s 13(1).

[111] *Tysiąc v. Poland (Application no 5410/03)*, 20th March 2007, paras 118 and 124.

[112] Protection of Life During Pregnancy Act 2013, s 17(3).

[113] Barrington 2003, pp. 161–162.

[114] See: *Woman with cancer forced to travel for abortion* (www.irishhealth.com/article.html?id=18394).

withdrawal of treatment from an incompetent patient was lawful even though withdrawal would result in the patient's death.[115] The courts did not order staff or institution caring for this patient to withdraw treatment because such an order would violate their conscientious objections and ethical views.[116] The Council and Nursing Board (Board) issued statements indicating that participation in withdrawal of this patient's treatment could breach their ethical guides. A clinician ran the risk of suspension or removal from the professional register if the clinician assisted the family in carrying out a lawful order. These statements hampered the ability of the patient's family to source an institution and identify clinicians willing to withdraw treatment in accordance with the Supreme Court order. There was speculation that the patient would have to be transported to a clinic in the United Kingdom to withdraw treatment, however, a number of Irish clinicians contacted the family and treatment withdrawal was performed at the family home.

13.4.4 Conclusions on Acceptability Objective

One cannot measure the lingering impact of the dominant church ethos on the private and confidential interaction between a patient and individual clinician. Therefore, it is impossible to validate the claim of the coroner inquiring into the death of Savita that religious dogma does not impinge on the delivery of health care sufficiently to satisfy the acceptability objective of General Comment No 14. The acceptability objective requires that state funded health care is respectful of medical ethics and culturally appropriate. Thus, a state can fund healthcare institutions with a religious ethos, provided that a state funds other institutions that provide health care that respect other religions and cultures. Ireland is failing to satisfy the acceptability objective by funding so many institutions with a Catholic ethos when there has been a growth in non-practising Catholic patients, patients of other Christian faiths, patients of non-Christian faiths and patients with no faith.

13.5 Quality of Health Care in the Irish System

The quality objective of General Comment No 14 provides that health facilities, goods and services must be scientifically and medically appropriate and of good quality.[117] A state must have proactive and reactive approaches to quality.

---

[115] *In Re A Ward of Court (withholding medical treatment)(No 2)* 1996 2 IR 79.

[116] *In Re A Ward of Court (withholding medical treatment)(No 2)* 1996 2 IR 79, p. 99 *per J. Lynch* and p. 110 *per C.J. Hamilton.*

[117] General Comment No 14: The Right to the Highest Attainable Standard of Health (Article 12 of the Covenant), para 12.

However, Ireland's approach to quality was reactive until the end of the twentieth century. The reactive approach required patients to complain against a clinician for being guilty of 'professional misconduct' to the professional body with which a clinician must register in order to practice.[118] Clinicians dominated these professional bodies, for example, the Council had twenty-five members with a paltry four members who could not be doctors appointed to represent the public interest. The quality of care was rarely considered in complaints to the Council because the courts defined 'professional misconduct' as 'infamous' or 'disgraceful' involving 'some degree of moral turpitude, fraud or dishonesty'.[119] The professional bodies addressed the deficiency by amending the professional misconduct definition in their professional and ethical guides to include omissions and conduct that fell 'seriously' short, of the standards of conduct expected among clinicians—the 'expected standards test'.[120] However, a clinician's negligence could not constitute professional misconduct because a clinician had to fall 'seriously' short of the expected standards test.[121] A reactive approach favours clinicians over patients. The regulatory system was also deficient as there was no legal duty on clinicians to maintain their professional competence or any statutory power on the Council to monitor clinical competence once a clinician was registered. This is not to suggest that clinicians did not take it upon themselves to maintain their clinical competence. An injured patient may also sue a clinician for negligence in the civil courts. There were three reasons that such a decision was not lightly taken. First, Ireland has an adversarial and fault based compensation system. Second, a patient must prove that his injuries were caused by a clinician breaching a standard of care, which can be described as a professional friendly standard.[122] Third, a patient is liable for substantial legal costs if the patient loses his or her negligence action.

13.5.1 Improving Quality Assurance After Healthcare Scandals

The quality of health care became a priority for politicians, clinicians and patients due to serious health failures at the end of the twentieth century, such as the Hepatitis C scandal.[123] In 1994, the Blood Transfusion Services Board revealed it had been providing contaminated Anti-D to pregnant women for over a decade and infected these women with hepatitis C. Two inquiries established that more than

---

[118] Medical Practitioners Act 1978, Nurses Act 1985 and Dentists Act 1985.

[119] See: *O'Laoire v. Medical Council*, unreported, High Court, *J. Keane*, 27th January 1995.

[120] See: *Prendiville v. Medical Council* 2008 3 IR 122 and *Brennan v. An Bord Altranais*, unreported, High Court, *J. Dunne*, 20th May 2010.

[121] *Brennan v. An Bord Altranais*, unreported, High Court, *J. Dunne*, 20th May 2010.

[122] See: *Dunne v. National Maternity Hospital* 1989 IR 91 at p. 109 *per C.J. Finlay*.

[123] See: Government of Ireland 1997.

1,600 women had been infected with hepatitis C, while haemophiliacs were infected with hepatitis C and HIV. The death toll has nearly reached 100 patients. Hepatitis C victims require regular treatment, including liver transplants. The state paid hundreds of millions of euro in compensation. The state response to these public health failures was to improve the reactive approach and supplement it with a proactive approach to quality of health care.

In 2007, the Council was conferred with the statutory duty of monitoring doctor's clinical competence and continuing professional development. Since 2011, doctors are legally obliged to maintain their professional competence. Each doctor is expected to complete 50 h of continuing professional development and one clinical audit per year. There is a similar duty for nurses but this duty has yet to become operative.[124] Thirteen of the 25 Council members are not medical practitioners.[125] Regulatory bodies were conferred with the power to take action for poor professional performance which arises from a failure to meet the standards of competence that can reasonably be expected of a clinician practising the same type of medicine.[126] Statutory registration and regulation was extended to twelve existing healthcare professions with ministerial power to extend registration and regulation to other professions.[127] Two of the twelve regulatory bodies have been established.[128] These bodies have power to investigate complaints but the investigating committees have yet to be established. The legislation unfortunately did not impose a duty on these bodies to monitor competence or duty on members of these professions to maintain competence. In 2007, the state also improved the public healthcare complaint system by bestowing a statutory right to complain to a staff member/service manager or a complaints officer in that body rather than to the Ombudsman. The complaints officer can issue a recommendation. Patients can request that Ombudsman undertake an independent review of the complaint.

In 2007, the Health Information and Quality Authority[129] (HIQA) was established to regulate quality of public health care by developing standards, monitoring adherence to these standards and undertaking investigations. The Mental Health Commission is responsible for the quality of mental health services. HIQA has no responsibility for private health organisations apart from nursing homes. There are proposals to expand HIQA's remit to other private health organisations.

---

[124] Nursing and Midwives Act 2011, part 11.

[125] Medical Practitioners Act 2007, s 17(1).

[126] Medical Practitioners Act 2007, s 2 and 57(1) and Nursing and Midwives Act 2011, s 2 and 55(1).

[127] Health and Social Care Professionals Act 2005, s 4(1) applies to clinical biochemists, medical scientists, psychologists, chiropodists/podiatrists, dieticians, orthoptists, physiotherapists, radiographers, speech and language therapists, occupational therapists, social care workers and social workers.

[128] Social Workers and Radiographers.

[129] www.hiqa.ie/.

HIQA's quality and safety standards are based on the best and most recent national and international evidence. HIQA consults with service users, healthcare professionals and general public when developing standards. HIQA develops specific standards, such as prevention and control of health care associated infections and general standards, such as the National Standards for Safer Better Healthcare issued in June 2012. These national standards are grounded on eight themes, which unintentionally reflect and address the AAAQ objectives of General Comment No 14. HIQA is responsible for monitoring adherence to standards in order that organisations maintain and strive to improve quality and safety. HIQA can investigate safety, quality and standard of healthcare services, where there is a serious risk to service users' health and welfare. The Minister for Health can require HIQA to undertake such an investigation.

13.5.2 Conclusions on Quality Objective

Ireland's decision to improve the existing reactive approach to quality and adopt a proactive approach is to be welcomed. The ability to satisfy the proactive approach depends on sufficient investment in human and other resources for HIQA's monitoring capacity. HIQA's monitoring task is daunting when one considers that HSE organisations employ more than 67,000 employees directly with a further 35,000 employed by agencies in receipt of HSE funding. HIQA employs a mere 170 staff to achieve every one of its functions including monitoring. HIQA applies a risk assessment approach when deciding which standards are monitored; many organisations are not monitored even applying this standard. It is not surprising to discover that organisations must initially self-assess to ensure adherence to the national standards. In addition, it is unclear how HIQA's standards address the quality of health care in Ireland's two-tiered health system.[130] We do know that consultants treat private patients because consultants receive a fee for each patient. Consultants provide consultant-led care to public patients because they receive a salary. Consultant-led care involves junior doctors treating public patients while these doctors are still in training. There is a risk that public patients receive substandard care due to the inexperience of junior doctors who may be unwilling to seek advice from senior doctors and consultants.

13.6 Conclusions

This chapter has demonstrated stakeholders in health care can hamper achieving the AAAQ objectives of General Comment No 14 where there is no enforceable legal right to health. The church and medical profession in Ireland have

---

[130] Considine and Dukelow 2009, p. 268.

significantly hindered the vindication of the AAAQ objectives for decades by adopting the same or similar positions on issues. The church and medical profession were so powerful that the state acted as a mere rubber stamp for the position of these stakeholders on certain issues. Indeed, the positions of the church and the medical profession on the issues became embedded aspects of Irish health policy. Irish governments were unwilling to remove or challenge these embedded aspects of Irish health policy. One consequence of the economic health policy has become a contested space, despite the continued absence of a legal right to health. The strength and attitude of the church and medical profession have weakened over the past couple of decades. The church transferred ownership and day-to-day management of healthcare institutions to the state. A consequence of this transfer has been that the church is restricted to lobbying on policy issues affecting its ethos in terms of healthcare delivery. However, the medical profession and health insurers remain strong stakeholders in terms of the availability and accessibility objectives of General Comment No 14. The current government has thrown down the gauntlet to these stakeholders with its proposal of universal health insurance. Furthermore, the government is emboldened by the terms of Ireland's EU-IMF bailout, which require fundamental changes to the Irish health system. These changes will achieve some but not all the availability and accessibility objectives of General Comment No 14. The state is failing to meet the acceptability objective of General Comment No 14 because of the prevalence of Catholicism and the lingering impact of church ethos on healthcare delivery in Ireland. The greatest strides have been made in terms of the quality objective because healthcare professionals and their representative bodies are also demanding improvements in quality. Ireland must strive to ensure that stakeholders should not dictate Ireland's health policy and organisation of healthcare system to the detriment of the AAAQ objectives of Comment No 14.

References

Literature

Adshead M, Millar M (2003) Ireland as Catholic corporatist state: a historical institutional analysis of healthcare in Ireland. Limerick Papers in Politics and Public Administration, pp 1–19. http://ulir.ul.ie/bitstream/handle/10344/477/MA_Ireland.pdf?sequence=2

Backman G, Acurio Páez D, Hunt P, Armijos Pineda M, Farcasanu D, Frisancho A, Khosla R, Jaramillo-Strouss C, Mekuria Fikre B, Motlagh M, Pevalin D, Rumble C, Tarco D, Vladescu C (2008) Health systems and the right to health: an assessment of 194 countries. Lancet 372:2047–2085

Barrington R (2003) Catholic influence on the health services 1830–2000. In: Mackay JP, McDonagh E (eds) Religion and politics in Ireland at the turn of the millennium. Columba Press, Dublin, pp 152–165

Barry J, Allwright S, Darker C, O'Dowd T, Thomas D (2010) Primary medical care in Irish prisons. BMC Health Serv Res 10:74. http://www.biomedcentral.com/1472-6963/10/74

Bhagwati PN (1985) Judicial activism and public interest litigation. Columbia J Transnatl Law 23:561–578

Cassels J (1989) Judicial activism and public interest litigation in India: attempting the impossible? Am J Comp Law 37:495–519

CESCR (1999) Committee on Economic, Social and Cultural Rights 1999, Concluding observations E/C.12/1/Add.35 14th May 1999

CESCR (2002) Committee on Economic, Social and Cultural Rights 2002, Concluding observations E/C.12/1/Add.77 5th June 2002

Colombo F, Tapay N (2004) Private health insurance in OECD countries: The benefits and costs for individuals and health systems. OECD working papers no 15. www.oecd.org/els/healthpoliciesanddata/33698043.pdf

Considine M, Dukelow F (2009) Irish social policy: a critical introduction. Gill and Macmillan, Dublin

Constitution Review Group (1996) Report of the Constitution Review Group. Stationary Office, Dublin 1996

General Comment No 14: The right to the highest attainable standard of health (Art 12 of the covenant) (E/C.12/2000/4)

Government of Ireland (1997) Report of the tribunal of inquiry into the blood transfusion service board, Pn 3695

Gwynn Morgan D (2002) A judgment too far? judicial activism and the constitution. Cork University Press, Cork

Hardiman A (2004) The role of the supreme court in our democracy. In: Mulholland J (ed) Political choice and democratic freedom in Ireland. Lead Irish Thinkers 40:32–44

Hogan G (2001) Directive principles, socio-economic rights and the constitution. Irish Jurist 36:174–198

HSE (2013) Investigation of Incident 50278 from time of patient's self-referral to hospital on the 21st October to the patient's death on the 28th October 2012

Irish Times (2001a) Woman applies to court over hospital's deferral of cancer treatment, Irish Times, p 326, June 2001

Irish Times (2001b) Cancer patient assured of private bed after taking hospital to court, Irish Times, p 4, 28 June 2001

Kinney E, Clark B (2004) Provisions for health and health care in the constitutions of the countries of the world. Cornell Int Law J 37:285–355

Palmer A, Fernandes K, Ford N, Guyatt G, Joffres M, Lima V, Mills E, Montaner J, Phung C, Tomkinson J, Zeng L (2009) Does ratification of human-rights treaties have effects on population health? Lancet 373:1987–1992

Regulation of Information (Services outside the state for termination of pregnancies) Act 1995

Rossa Phelan D (1994) The concept of social rights. Dublin Univ Law J 16:105–146

Toth F (2013) The choice of healthcare models: how much does politics matter. Int Polit Sci Rev 34:159–172

Wren M (2003) Unhealthy state: anatomy of a sick society. New Island Books, Dublin, Ireland

Documents

Central Statistics Office (2012) Profile 7 religion, ethnicity and Irish travellers

Competition Authority (2010) Competition in professional services: general medical practitioners

Constitution of Ireland 1937

Criminal Law Amendment Act 1935

Criminal Law Amendment Bill 1971

Criminal Law Amendment Bill 1972

Dentists Act 1985

Department of Health (1947) Outline of proposals for the improvement of the health service

Department of Health (1987) Health the wider dimensions

Department of Health (1994) Shaping a healthier future—a strategy for effective health care in the 1990s

Department of Health and Children (2001) Quality and fairness: a health system for you health strategy

Department of Health and Children (2013) The path to universal healthcare

European Convention for the Prevention of Torture and Inhuman or Degrading Treatment or Punishment 1987

European Convention for the Protection of Human Rights and Fundamental Freedoms 1950

European Social Charter 1961

Family Planning Bill 1973

Health and Social Care Professionals Act 2005

Health (Family Planning) Act 1979

Health (Family Planning) (Amendment) Act 1992

Health (Family Planning) (Amendment) Act 1993

Health (Pricing and Supply of Medical Goods) Act 2013

Health (Provision of General Practitioner Services) Act 2012

International Covenant on Civil and Political Rights 1966

International Covenant on Economic, Social and Cultural Rights 1966

International Convention on the Elimination of All Forms of Racial Discrimination 1966

Medical Practitioners Act 1978

Medical Practitioners Act 2007

Nurses Act 1985

Nursing and Midwives Act 2011

Offences against the Person Act 1861

Protection of Life During Pregnancy Act 2013

United Nations Convention against Torture and Other Cruel, Inhuman or Degrading Treatment or Punishment 1984

United Nations Convention on the Elimination of All Forms of Discrimination against Women 1979

United Nations Convention on the Rights of the Child 1989

United Nations Convention on the Rights of Persons with Disabilities 2006

Cases

A and B v. *Eastern Health Board* (1998) 1 IR 464

A, B and C v. *Ireland* (Application no 25579/051), 6th December 2010

Application of Woods (1970) IR 154

Attorney General (SPUC) v. *Open Door Counselling Ltd* (1988) IR 593

Attorney General v. *X* (1992) 1 IR 1

Brennan v. *An Bord Altranais*, unreported, High Court, Dunne J, 20th May 2010

Bupa Ireland Ltd v. *Health Insurance Authority*, unreported, Supreme Court, 16th July 2008

CK v. *Northern Area Health Authority* (2002) 2 IR 545

D (A Minor) v. *District Judge Brennan and Health Services Executive,* unreported, High Court, McKechnie J, 9th May 2007

Dunne v. *National Maternity Hospital* (1989) IR 91

E v. *E* (1982) ILRM 497

Eastern Health Board v. *An Bord Uchtála* (1994) 3 IR 207

FN v. *Minister for Education* (1995) 1 IR 409

In Re A Ward of Court (withholding medical treatment) (No 2) (1996) 2 IR 79

In Re Health (Amendment) (No 2) Bill 2004 (2005) 1 IR 105

In Re Ó Laighléis (1960) IR 93

13 The Challenges to Realising the Right to Health in Ireland

Jazvinský v. *Slovakia* (Application nos 33088/96, 52236/99, 52451/99, 52453/99, 52455/99, 52457/99 and 52459/99), 7th September 2000

Kavanagh v. *Ireland* (1996) 1 IR 321

Kennedy v. *Ireland* (1987) IR 587

Kudła v. *Poland* (Application no 30210/96), 26th October 2000

McDonagh v. *Frawley* (1978) IR 131

McGee v. *Attorney General* (1974) IR 284

McMenamin v. *Governor of Wheatfield Prison*, unreported, High Court, Hanna J, 29th June 2012

Nitecki v. *Poland* (Application no 65653/01), 21st March 2002

O'Laoire v. *Medical Council*, unreported, High Court, Keane J, 27th January 1995

O'Reilly v. *Governor of Wheatfield Prison*, unreported, High Court, Hanna J, 22nd June 2007

O'Reilly and Others v *Limerick Corporation* (1989) ILRM 181

Open Door and Dublin Well Woman v. *Ireland* (Application nos 14234/88; 14235/88), 29th October 1992

Prendiville v. *Medical Council* (2008) 3 IR 122

Roe v. *Wade* 410 US 113 (1973)

Ryan v *Attorney General* (1965) IR 294

TD v. *Minister for Education* (2001) 4 IR 259

The State (C) v. *Frawley* (1976) IR 365

The State (Richardson) v. *Governor of Mountjoy Prison* (1980) ILRM 82

Tysiąc v. *Poland*, (Application no 5410/03), 20th March 2007

Chapter 14
Dutch Realities: Evaluating Health Care Reform in the Netherlands from a Human Rights Perspective

Brigit Toebes and Maite San Giorgi

Abstract In light of the rising costs of health care, the Netherlands has introduced regulated competition into its health care system from 2006 onwards. In addition, it is trying to contain the costs with the gradual introduction of a number of austerity measures. This chapter looks at these developments from the perspective of the internationally guaranteed human right to health, thereby paying particular attention to the dimension of 'access to health care' under the right to health. An assessment is made of the legal entitlements to health care, and the recognition of the right to health care in the Netherlands. Subsequently, the Dutch health care system is analysed in light of an important component of the human right to health, i.e. the 'AAAQ' requirements, which stipulate that health care services have to be available, accessible, acceptable and of good quality. This will be followed by an analysis of the governmental 'obligation to protect', in the light of which attention will be paid to accountability mechanisms for addressing possible failures to realise the right to health (care) in the Netherlands. The overall aim of this chapter is to illustrate how from the perspective of the right to health a developed country like the Netherlands tries to cope with a number of serious challenges in the health sector. Our main findings are that while the international right to health is not given much recognition in the Netherlands, the notions underpinning this right are embedded in Dutch law, policies and practice. In terms of health outcomes, issues of concern are the rising socio-economic health inequalities, which raise the

---

Brigit Toebes: Associate Professor and Rosalind Franklin Fellow, Faculty of Law, the University of Groningen. Maite San Giorgi: Secretary of the Board of Medical Specialists at the Onze Lieve Vrouwe Gasthuis hospital in Amsterdam. The authors wish to thank Aart Hendriks and Milan Markovic for their useful comments, and Zlatka Koleva and Marlon Steine for editorial support. All mistakes are the responsibility of the authors.

B. Toebes (✉)
University of Groningen, Groningen, The Netherlands
e-mail: b.c.a.toebes@rug.nl

M. San Giorgi
Onze Lieve Vrouwe Gasthuis, Amsterdam, The Netherlands

B. Toebes et al. (eds.), *The Right to Health*, DOI: 10.1007/978-94-6265-014-5_14,   403
© T.M.C. ASSER PRESS and the authors 2014

question of how such inequalities can best be tackled, for example by improving the living conditions of disadvantaged groups within the population and by placing more emphasis on prevention. Furthermore, health care privatisation and the recent cuts in health care expenditure raise some issues with regard to the 'AAAQ', for example in terms of geographic accessibility and affordability of care. When it comes to accountability and participation in the Dutch health care system, the problems are not so much a lack of mechanisms, but rather a lack of coordination and efficiency.

Contents

14.1 Introduction 404
14.2 The Human Rights Framework 406
     14.2.1 The Definition of Health and Health Care as a Human Right 406
     14.2.2 The 'AAAQ' Classification 407
14.3 Accountability and the 'Obligation to Protect' 410
14.4 Health, Health Care and Human Rights in The Netherlands 413
     14.4.1 Health Outcomes, Health Care Performances and Health Care Spending 413
     14.4.2 Legal Recognition of the Human Right to Health and Health
             Care in The Netherlands 414
     14.4.3 Legal Entitlements to Health Care and the Dutch Health Care System 415
14.5 The Netherlands and the 'AAAQ' 416
     14.5.1 Effects of the Introduction of Regulated Competition 417
     14.5.2 Effect of Austerity Measures 419
14.6 Accountability and the Obligation to Protect 421
     14.6.1 Legislation 421
     14.6.2 Monitoring Mechanisms 422
     14.6.3 Accountability Mechanisms: Legal Enforceability of the Right to Health 424
     14.6.4 Accountability Mechanisms: Quasi-Judicial Enforceability 426
     14.6.5 Accountability Mechanisms: Domestic Complaint Bodies 427
     14.6.6 Participatory Mechanisms 428
     14.6.7 Non-State Actors in Dutch Health Care 430
14.7 Conclusions 431
References 433

14.1 Introduction

According to a recent report of the OECD, health care spending in Europe has risen dramatically over the past thirty years.[1] Cost increases are generally due to a variety of factors, including technological advancements, population growth and an overall ageing population.[2] To address these rising costs, health care reform has

---

[1] OECD 2010 (Executive Summary).

[2] Eg. Weale 1998, p. 138.

found its way to the top of many policy agendas. Most of the measures governments are taking focus on economic reforms in which market-oriented and cost-benefit approaches are expected to resolve the problems health care systems are facing.

The human rights perspective, however, is largely absent from the debate on health care reforms and implementation of measures.[3] Human rights experts claim that the implementation of such measures in health care systems in practice adversely affects the accessibility and affordability of health care and can lead to arbitrary discrimination against certain groups. This in turn may constitute a violation of the right to health.[4]

This contribution looks at the trend of introducing market-oriented and cost-benefit measures by conducting a case study on the effects of these measures within the Dutch health care system. As will be explained further below, the Netherlands has recently reorganised its health care system by introducing a de-centralised health insurance system with regulated competition. A private health insurance market has been created, in which all (now private) health insurance companies are to compete with each other and to exert pressure on health care providers to improve efficiency and keep costs down. To guarantee solidarity, affordability and accessibility of health care, restrictive governmental regulation limits the possibilities of insurance companies to, for example, refuse customers on the basis of their health status. At the same time, being confronted with an economic crisis, the hardly manageable rising health care costs are being fought by several austerity measures, including cuts in the basic health care package.

From a human rights perspective, two important questions arise: what does this market-oriented health care reform mean for patients individually and for the public in general? And what are the effects of the austerity measures taken in addressing the rising costs of health care? Taken together, do these developments in the Dutch health care system pose a threat to the availability, accessibility, acceptability and quality of health care services? The framework used in this analysis concerns the right to health framework as set forth in several human rights standards. The overall aim of this chapter is to inform human rights scholars, public health specialists, civil society actors and others about the challenges posed by the rising costs of health care in a health care system which has introduced a system with market-oriented and cost-benefit measures in combination with austerity measures.

---

[3] San Giorgi 2012, p. 3; Chapman 1994, p. vi; Leary 1994b, p. 94; and Naderi and Meier 2010.

[4] San Giorgi 2012, p. 3; Leary 1994b, p. 92, 96; Mackintosh and Koivusalo 2005, p. 8; Gómez Isa 2005, p. 15; Toebes 2008; Den Exter 2010.

14.2 The Human Rights Framework

14.2.1 The Definition of Health and Health Care as a Human Right

With the adoption of the Constitution of the World Health Organization (WHO) in 1946 and subsequent human rights treaties, the international community recognised that the 'enjoyment of the highest attainable standard of health' is a human right.[5] Generally, it is referred to as 'the right to health'.[6] The right to health is firmly embedded in a substantial number of international United Nations and regional Council of Europe human rights instruments which have been supplemented and clarified through additional instruments and through the practice of monitoring bodies.[7]

In this analysis of the Dutch health care system this broad set of human rights standards is used as a framework of which in particular the right to health as defined in Article 12 of the International Covenant on Economic, Social and Cultural Rights (ICESCR), and its related General Comment No. 14 (hereinafter referred to as 'General Comment 14'), are being applied. Article 12 ICESCR prescribes that State Parties have to take all steps necessary to achieve the full realisation of the right to health. In addition, the Committee on Economic, Social and Cultural Rights (CESCR), which is the independent expert monitoring body overseeing the implementation of the ICESCR, has developed further guidance on the full realisation of the right to health in its General Comment 14.[8] This document, which was adopted in 2000, is strictly speaking not legally binding and can be characterised as a so-called 'soft law' instrument. Nevertheless, as with other General Comments of the CESCR, it remains frequently quoted and it is frequently used, also by other (judicial) human rights bodies as a framework for assessing compliance with international human rights regulation.[9]Altogether, General

---

[5] Adopted by the International Health Conference held in New York from 19 June to 22 July 1946, signed on 22 July 1946 by the representatives of 61 States (Off. Rec. Wld Hlth Org., 2, 100), and entered into force on 7 April 1948; Leary 1994a, p. 25.

[6] San Giorgi 2012, p. 9; Leary 1994a, p. 26; Hendriks 1998, pp. 389–408.

[7] San Giorgi 2012, p. 9.

[8] General Comment 14, 2000.

[9] Two examples: in Complaint No. 41/2007, Mental Disability Advocacy Center (MDAC) v. Bulgaria, para 37, the European Committee of Social Rights applied the criteria set out in General Comment No. 13 (UN doc. E/C.12/1999/10, General Comment 13 (1999), 8 December 1999, The right to education, para 6) and held that all education provided by States must fulfil the criteria of availability, accessibility, acceptability and adaptability; the European Court of Human Rights designated the ICESCR and its corresponding General Comment No. 12 (UN Doc. E/C.12/GC/20, General Comment 20 (2009), 2 July 2009, Non-discrimination in economic, social and cultural rights (Article 2, para 2 ICESCR)) as relevant legal frameworks for its case law in Demir and Baykara v. Turkey, Application No. 34503/97, 12 November 2008, paras 41, 99; Kiyutin v. Russia, Application No. 2700/10, 10 March 2011, para 30.

14 Dutch Realities: Evaluating Health Care

Comment 14 gives an authoritative explanation of the meaning and implications of Article 12 ICESCR. Moreover, it offers a comprehensive framework for assessing the effects of health care systems and introduced measures, in order to ascertain whether this right to health is enjoyed in practice.

As confirmed by Article 12 ICESCR and General Comment 14, the right to health is not a right to be healthy.[10] The right to health comprises the right to health care and other underlying determinants such as nutrition, safe and potable water, adequate sanitation, safe and healthy occupational conditions, a healthy environment, and access to health-related education and information.[11] This approach underscores that not only health care, but also other determinants are essential to people's health. Furthermore, this is not exclusively an issue in developing countries; it is now widely recognised that living conditions, also in Western societies, are of decisive influence to people's state of health.[12] People's socio-economic circumstances or 'social determinants' can be crucial and a decisive factor for their health.[13]

Nonetheless, as the focus in our analysis is on the Dutch *health care* system and the effects of the current health insurance system, we will focus in particular on the right to health care, as an important component of the broader right to health. As such, particular attention will be paid to access to health care as an important component of the overall scope of the right to health. However, where relevant, other underlying determinants will be included in the discussion.

14.2.2 The 'AAAQ' Classification

In General Comment 14 on Article 12 ICESCR, the CESCR adopted a four-fold classification of guidelines that inter alia describe how the right to health is to be fulfilled.[14] This classification also offers a comprehensive framework for assessing the effects of health care systems and introduced measures. As set out in General Comment 14, health care facilities, goods and services must be available, accessible, acceptable and of good quality.

Availability means that health care services have to be available in a sufficient quantity to service the entire population within a State.[15] This includes e.g. hospitals, clinics and other health-related buildings, medical and professional

---

[10] General Comment 14, para 8.

[11] General Comment 14, para 11.

[12] WHO 2008.

[13] '(...) the fundamental structures of social hierarchy and socially determined conditions that determine how people live, work, are raised and educated, which subsequently determine people's state of health' (...). WHO 2008; Marmot et al. 2008; see also Fair Society Healthy Lives (Marmot Review, 2010).

[14] General Comment 14, para 12.

[15] General Comment 14, para 12.

personnel, drugs and other equipment. Criteria adopted by the CESCR for the assessment of the availability of health care comprise for example the amount of resources allocated to health care, and the length of waiting time for admission to health care services. Another criterion is the number of hospital beds and health care providers per inhabitant.[16] Although these criteria are applied as indicators to evaluate the available health care in a specific State, such assessments remain dependent on various factors, amongst which the developmental level of a State and the demand for health care within that State.[17]

Accessibility implies non-discrimination, financial accessibility (affordability), and physical accessibility.[18] According to the principle of non-discrimination, there should be no discrimination in access to health care which has the intention or effect of nullifying or impairing the equal enjoyment or exercise of the right to health care.[19] Unequal enjoyment of the right to health care is at stake when an apparently equal treatment in obtaining access to health care results in unequal access to health care. This can for example be the case when the personal characteristics of a patient or group of patients, such as health care needs and financial possibilities, are not sufficiently taken into account, i.e. they are treated the same as others.

All persons should have equal access to health care throughout their complete life cycle, which is adapted to the various accessibility needs.[20] Consequently, health care organisations should be responsive to the needs of the recipients and be appropriate to the demand, as otherwise this could result in a discriminatory effect on health due to the recipients' health status.[21]

This criterion of non-discrimination is considered of great importance by various human rights committees, institutions and organisations. In addition to the CESCR, the Parliamentary Assembly of the Council of Europe argued in its recommendation 'The reform of health care systems in Europe: reconciling equity, quality and efficiency' that:

> ...[T]he main criterion for judging the success of health system reforms should be effective access to health care for all without discrimination, which is a basic human right. This also has the consequence of improving the general standard of health and welfare of the entire population.[22]

---

[16] San Giorgi 2012, p. 52.

[17] General Comment 14, para 12.

[18] It also mentions information accessibility. This is an underlying determinant of the right to health, and not specific to the right to health care. It is therefore not included in this paragraph. San Giorgi, p. 54.

[19] Concluding Observations of the CESCR with regard to India, UN Doc. E/C.12/IND/CO/5, para 52; E/CN.4/2003/58, 13 February 2003. Report *The right of everyone to the enjoyment of the highest attainable standard of physical and mental health,* Report of the Special Rapporteur, Paul Hunt, submitted in accordance with Commission Resolution 2002/31, para 61.

[20] Chinkin 2006, p. 56.

[21] Lie 2004, p. 4.

[22] Recommendation 1626 (2003) of the Parliamentary Assembly of the Council of Europe on "The Reform of Health Care Systems in Europe: Reconciling Equity, Quality and Efficiency", para 4.

14 Dutch Realities: Evaluating Health Care

Therefore, the pursuit of cost containment and maximising efficiency should not go at the expense of equality in access to health care.[23] Financial accessibility requires that health care, including drugs, should be affordable for everyone.[24] The costs of health care should therefore not place an excessive financial burden on individuals as access to health care should be based on need and not on ability to pay.[25] If necessary, steps must therefore be taken to reduce the financial burden on patients.[26]

Finally, physical accessibility implies that health care has to be within safe reach and physically accessible for everyone.[27] Also part of the criterion of physical accessibility to health care is access for specific groups of patients in a literal sense. For example, older persons and persons with disabilities should have adequate access to buildings and other public areas where health care is provided.[28] Timely accessibility is also an important component of the right to health. General Comment 14 stresses in paragraph 17 that the right to health facilities, goods and services includes timely access to basic preventive, curative or rehabilitative health services.

According to General Comment 14 acceptable health care signifies that it must be 'culturally appropriate, i.e. respectful of the culture of individuals, minorities, peoples and communities, sensitive to gender and life-cycle requirements'.[29] This means that the cultural tradition of persons may have to be respected. Examples are the refusal of blood transfusions by Jehovah witnesses, the refusal of protestant christians to vaccinate their children, the use of traditional preventive care, healing practices and medicines by various indigenous groups and the use of alternative medicines and medical treatments.[30]

Lastly, quality requires that health services are scientifically and medically appropriate and of good quality.[31] This requires scientifically approved and unexpired drugs and up-to-date hospital equipment and an adequate training of health care personnel, including as regards health and human rights.[32] Other elements that are of importance in order to obtain an impression of the level of quality of the health care provided and of the health care system, is life expectancy, infant

---

[23] Recommendation 1626 (2003), paras 2 and 5.

[24] General Comment 14, para 12(b) and Economic and Social Council 2009, paras 56(b) and 57(f).

[25] Digest of case law of the European Committee of Social Rights, September 2008, p. 83.

[26] San Giorgi 2012, p. 57.

[27] General Comment 14, para 12(b); and Economic and Social Council 2009, para 56(a).

[28] General Comment 14, para 12(b); and Economic and Social Council 2009, para 56(a).

[29] General Comment 14, para 12(c); This paragraph also deals with medical ethics as part of the appropriateness of health and health care. This is not discussed in this Chapter as it stretches beyond the subject and purpose of the present study.

[30] General Comment 14, para 27. Alternative medicines include for example homeopathy, acupuncture and herbalism.

[31] General Comment 14, para 12 (d).

[32] General Comment 14, para 12(d); and Economic and Social Council 2009, para 56(c) and 56(d).

mortality rates, the number of health care professionals with secondary or higher education, waiting lists and waiting times.[33]

14.3 Accountability and the 'Obligation to Protect'

As the entities that have ratified the human rights treaties, States Parties including the Netherlands carry primary duties under human rights law. To clarify the duties that fall upon them, in human rights doctrine a typology of States' obligations has been developed, which is frequently quoted and applied, in particular with respect to economic, social and cultural rights. This so-called 'tri-partite typology of State obligations' implies that human rights impose three levels of obligations on States Parties: the obligation to respect, the obligation to protect and the obligation to fulfil human rights.[34] According to General Comment 14, the obligation to *respect* is a negative State obligation and requires States to refrain from interfering directly or indirectly with the enjoyment of the right to health. The obligations to *protect* and to *fulfil* are positive State obligations.

The obligation to *respect* requires States to refrain from interfering directly or indirectly with the enjoyment of the right to health. The obligation to protect requires States to take measures that prevent third parties from interfering with Article 12 ICESCR guarantees.[35] This entails that the State should ascertain that individuals can freely realise their rights and freedoms.[36] The second obligation, the obligation to protect, requires States to actually take measures, e.g. by legislation and the implementation of effective measures to prevent the State, its agents or other individuals from violating individual fundamental rights.[37] The third obligation, the obligation to fulfil, implies that States have a positive duty to make health-related services accessible to all residents. They should create conditions to enable and assist individuals and communities to enjoy their right to health. Such conditions can include the adoption of appropriate legislative, administrative, budgetary, judicial, promotional and other measures towards the full realisation of the right to health. Consequently, States must recognise the right to health in their national health policies and legal systems and they have to ensure that a national health system is in place that meets with the obligations imposed. Health insurance

---

[33] San Giorgi 2012, p. 60; Council of Europe Committee of Ministers, Recommendation No. R (99)21 on criteria for the management of waiting lists and waiting times in health care, September 1999, para 3; Waiting lists and waiting times are also accessibility issues.

[34] Asbjørn Eide 1983. Asbjørn Eide (at the time UN Rapporteur on the Right to Food) developed this typology, which was based on the proposal of Shue (1980) which states that for every basic rights there are three types of correlative State obligations: 'to avoid depriving', 'to protect from deprivation', and 'to aid the deprived'; Shue 1980.

[35] General Comment 14, para 33.

[36] San Giorgi 2012, p. 44.

[37] San Giorgi 2012, p. 44.

14 Dutch Realities: Evaluating Health Care

systems play a crucial role in such systems.[38] Moreover, in case an individual or a group of individuals is unable, for reasons beyond their control, to realise their right to health themselves by the means at their disposal, States actually have to provide them with health care needed.[39]

The obligations of States Parties according to this tripartite typology of State obligations are not static. For example, when health care systems are reformed, the obligations of States can shift from fulfil to protect. Most of the measures governments are currently taking in reforming health care systems, focus on economic reforms in which market-oriented and cost-benefit approaches are considered to resolve the problems health care systems are facing. Commonly taken measures within such reforms are privatisation of the health insurance sector, privatisation of health care provision and cross-border investment in health care by multinational corporations.[40] Privatisation of health care systems does not discharge States from their obligations in relation to health care. States can never be relieved from their obligations in the field of health care.[41] When a State privatises certain elements of its health care system, as is the case with the privatisation of Dutch health insurers, there is a shift from the State's obligation to fulfil to the State's obligation to protect.[42] In this regard, the State is in fact no longer the provider of health care, but the protector of a fundamental right. Consequently, in the health sector, where many non-State actors engage with each other in multiple opaque relationships, it is of the utmost importance that all these actors are supervised closely by the State. This requires the implementation of sufficient and adequate accountability mechanisms.

General Comment 14 does not specifically refer to the notion of accountability. Nevertheless, the importance of ensuring accountability is increasingly emphasised in the context of economic, social and cultural rights.[43] A useful analysis of this important yet complex feature under human rights law is set out by Potts, who defines accountability for the right to health as:

> (...) the process that requires government to show, explain and justify how it has discharged its obligations regarding the right to the highest attainable standard of health.[44]

Newel and Wheeler identify two dimensions to effective accountability mechanisms: *answerability*, meaning that there should be possibilities to make claims and rights to demand a response, and *enforceability*, which implies that there should be mechanisms for imposing accountability.[45] Along similar lines,

---

[38] San Giorgi 2012, p. 48.

[39] General Comment 14, paras 34–35.

[40] Toebes 2008, p. 442.

[41] San Giorgi 2012, p. 46.

[42] De Feyter and Gómez Isa 2005, p. 3.

[43] General Comment 14, para 59, which focuses mostly on legal accountability. For accountability see, inter alia, Brinkerhof 2003, Newel and Wheeler 2006, and Potts 2008a.

[44] Potts 2008a, p. 13.

[45] Newel and Wheeler 2006, p. 13.

Potts holds that an effective accountability process comprises the following essential elements: monitoring, accountability mechanisms, remedies, and participation. Monitoring means consistently analysing and overseeing the process towards the realisation of health-related rights. Accountability mechanisms ensure that the State is held to account for a failure to realise these health-related rights. Several types of accountability mechanisms can be distinguished; ex ante mechanisms, such as human rights impact assessments that intend to regulate the duty bearer's obligations in advance, and ex post mechanisms which enable rights-holders to hold duty bearers to account if they fail to meet their obligations.[46] This is delineated as judicial accountability. Furthermore, remedies are means of redress when rights have been violated. Remedies can roughly speaking take three forms: restitution, compensation or rehabilitation. Lastly, an important element in this entire process is the participation of the public in the decision-making process over issues that involve their health-related rights (see below).[47]

The State obligation to ensure 'accountability' is closely connected to the above-mentioned State's 'obligation to protect'. We assert that the obligation to protect falls into a number of interlinked duties on the part of the State. Firstly, as also asserted by General Comment 14, the duty to protect embraces a duty to adopt legislation regulating all the actors in the health sector. In addition, monitoring and accountability mechanisms aimed at regulating the behaviour of States, as well as accountability mechanisms for holding them accountable, are required. Lastly, it is of crucial importance that participatory mechanisms are established to enable the public to participate in health care decision-making. All in all, based on the obligation to protect, we suggest the following typology of obligations:[48]

1. The adoption of *legislation* to regulate all the actors in the health sector;
2. The adoption of *monitoring mechanisms* aimed at regulating the behaviour of insurance companies, health care providers, and pharmaceutical industry;
3. The creation of (judicial and other) *accountability mechanisms* for individuals to complain about failures or malpractices by the actors in the health care sector, which should be followed by means of redress;
4. The establishment of *participatory mechanisms* in health care decision taking.

We assert that these measures should not only be taken as regards health care systems that are fully or partially privatised. As with the obligation to respect and the obligation to fulfil, the obligation to protect applies regardless of the type and organisation of the health care system concerned. Consequently, the measures as set out above have to be taken to ensure that all actors in the health sector, whether public or private, respect the right to health.[49] In Sect. 14.5 we will explain how the Netherlands discharges itself from these obligations.

---

[46] Newell 2006, p. 46.

[47] Potts 2008b.

[48] As also suggested in Toebes 2008, p. 451.

[49] San Giorgi 2012, p. 44.

14 Dutch Realities: Evaluating Health Care

14.4 Health, Health Care and Human Rights in The Netherlands

14.4.1 Health Outcomes, Health Care Performances and Health Care Spending

The Netherlands is a country with an overall high level of health. Life expectancy at birth has risen dramatically between 1970 and 2012: from 73.6 to 80.9 years.[50] While the infant mortality rate has also dropped during that period, perinatal mortality is still a point of concern.[51] As to the most common diseases, there has been an important shift: while in 1970 diseases of the circulatory system were the main cause of death, in 2007 most deaths were caused by cancer. Furthermore, the health status of people with a low socio-economic status is relatively low compared to people with a higher socio-economic status. Furthermore, among immigrants, often with a lower socio-economic status, the burden of disease is higher than among the native Dutch.[52] Lastly, while an important risk factor in the Netherlands is smoking, almost half of the Dutch population is reported to be overweight.[53]

As to costs, health care expenditure in the Netherlands corresponds to 11.9 % of the gross domestic product (GDP).[54] This makes the Netherlands the country with the second highest percentage in the world after the United States, but the difference with a number of other European countries is small, and there is some variety as regards the degree to which long-term care is included in the statistics.[55] The Netherlands also ranks relatively high when it comes to health costs per capita: in 2012 it was fourth highest among OECD countries (behind the USA, Norway and Switzerland).[56] When it comes to type of funding of health care, in 2010 85.7 % of current health expenditure in the Netherlands was funded by public sources, which is above the average of 72.2 % in OECD countries.[57] All in all, compared to other European countries, while overall health care expenditure is rather high, the Dutch spend a relatively low percentage of their income on health.

---

[50] Schäfer et al. 2010.

[51] Schäfer et al. 2010, p. 6.

[52] Schäfer et al. 2010, pp. 6–7.

[53] Schäfer et al. 2010, pp. 6–7. See also OECD Health data 2012.

[54] Statistics Netherlands and OECD Health Data 2012, Nederlandse Vereniging van Ziekenhuizen 2012.

[55] Statistics Netherlands and OED Health Data 2012.

[56] OECD Health data 2012.

[57] OECD Health Data 2012.

14.4.2 Legal Recognition of the Human Right to Health and Health Care in The Netherlands

The Netherlands is a party to most of the international human rights treaties that guarantee a right to health care, including the ICESCR, the Convention on the Elimination of Discrimination against Women (CEDAW), the Convention on the Rights of the Child (CRC), and the European Social Charter (ESC).[58] In Sect. 14.5 we will pay attention to the implementation of these provisions in the Dutch legal order (under 'redress').

In addition to the international treaty provisions, the Dutch Constitution stipulates the State's responsibilities with respect to the protection of health in Article 22 (1): 'The authorities shall take steps to promote the health of the population.'[59] As such the Dutch Constitution does not recognise an individual 'right' or entitlement to health. Rather, this provision entails a general promotional obligation on the part of the government which in principle leaves the authorities with a wide margin of discretion. However, this does not mean that the Dutch authorities operate in a vacuum. An elaborate body of health-related legislation is in place in the Netherlands, regulating various features of the health care system, varying from preventive health care, to health care financing and provision (see also Sect. 14.5). In the contexts of these laws, and also in health policy and practice, the most important notions and principles underpinning the right to health are frequently mentioned and applied. Notions of accessibility, availability and quality, core notions under the right to health, are often referred to in these contexts, and their implications are taken into account with the adoption of new laws and policies. To quote from the explanatory memorandum of the Dutch Health Insurance Act (Zvw), which will be further discussed below:

> The Constitution of the Netherlands and international treaties require that the Dutch government establishes a health care system that provides the Dutch population with access to necessary and good quality medical services.[60]

Below we will give an assessment of how notions of a right to health are embedded in the Dutch health care system.

---

[58] Up till September 2013, the Netherlands had not ratified the UN Disability Convention.

[59] Article 22(1) of the Constitution of the Netherlands, available at. http://www.wipo.int/wipolex/en/text.jsp?file_id=191759, accessed April 2013.

[60] Memorie van Toelichting Zorgverzekeringswet [Explanatory Memorandum to the Health Insurance Act], Kamerstukken II 2003–2004, 29 763, p. 2, available at http://www.st-ab.nl/wetzvwmvt.html, accessed November 2012.

14.4.3 Legal Entitlements to Health Care and the Dutch Health Care System

The former Dutch health care system can be classified as a Bismarckian system in which non-profit health care providers provided health care services. Two-thirds of the population, i.e. those with lower incomes, was covered by a social health insurance system with multiple public health insurers. The remainder of the population was covered by private insurance.[61] Over the years, adaptations to the system were made, followed by a far-reaching health care reform when a new health insurance system was introduced in 2006.[62] With the new insurance system, regulated competition was introduced into the Dutch health care system. On the basis of this new system, the public health insurance scheme and the private insurance scheme were united and turned into one private insurance system, operated by privatised health insurers. This health care insurance system is primarily regulated by the Health Insurance Act (*Zorgverzekeringswet*, Zvw), which entered into force in January 2006.

Health insurers now compete with each other in favour of the consumer, they make profit, and play a central role in the health care purchasing market when contracting with health care providers. Health insurers are to exert pressure on health care providers to improve efficiency and to keep the costs down. In turn, health care providers will to a certain extent compete with each other in favour of health insurers and the patient. In addition, restrictive governmental regulation strives to guarantee solidarity, affordability and accessibility of health care. Based on the Zvw, each person is, regardless of income, legally required to take out a basic health insurance provided by a private insurance company of his or her own choice.[63] Moreover, health insurers have to accept any new applicants for their basic health insurance and are not allowed to differentiate the premium for the basic health insurance package according to the risk profiles of the applicants. However, this premium will vary between the various health insurers. In addition to this basic premium, employees

---

[61] Schäfer et al. 2010, p. 13; Euro Health Consumer Index 2012, p. 10; The National Health Service covered employees with income below a certain level, people entitled to a social benefit, and self-employed individuals up to a specified income level. People with a higher income could choose either to take out private health insurance or to remain uninsured. See also Toebes 2006, p. 109.

[62] Similar to the Swiss system, which was introduced in 1996 (Civitas 2011). The system is also said to be inspired by the American scholar Alain Enthoven, also called the 'father of managed competition'. See also http://healthpolicy.stanford.edu/people/Alain_C_Enthoven accessed March 2013.

[63] Roughly speaking, this covers the following services: medical care, including care provided by general practitioners, medical specialists and obstetricians; hospital treatment; medication; dental care up to the age of 18; postnatal care; limited physiotherapy, exercise therapy, speech therapy, occupational therapy and dietary advice; and help to stop smoking. See website of the Government of the Netherlands at http://www.government.nl/issues/health-issues/health-insurance, accessed October 2012.

pay an income-related contribution towards health insurance costs, which is partly reimbursed by their employers. Children under 18 do not pay premiums for health insurance cover. Instead, the State pays a contribution to the insurance company. The proper functioning of the new health care insurance system that introduced regulated competition, is supervised by independent bodies such as the Dutch Health Authority (*Nederlandse Zorgautoriteit*, NZa) (see Sect. 14.5).

The basic health insurance, regulated by the Zvw, covers essential curative care. In addition, there is the Exceptional Medical Expenses Act (*Algemene Wet Bijzondere Ziektekosten*, AWBZ), which regulates a compulsory social State insurance for costs of long-term chronic and mental health care.[64] It provides treatment, support, nursing, personal care, and accommodation. Almost everyone who lives or works in the Netherlands is automatically insured according to the AWBZ and pays a mandatory income-related contribution. Receiving AWBZ-care may involve cost-sharing, i.e. payment of a personal contribution. Given the rise of AWBZ expenditure, the government is looking into possibilities for restricting some of the conditions of the AWBZ and to increase payments by means of a personal contribution. As a result of these measures, many elderly and patients with chronic diseases are confronted with increased out-of-pocket payments.

In addition to the health care covered by the Zvw and the AWBZ, a supplementary insurance can be purchased for additional coverage. Contrary to the basic health care insurance, regulated by the Zvw, in case of these supplementary insurances health care insurers are under no obligation to accept new applicants, nor are they restricted in differentiating the premiums according to the risk profile of the applicants. A supplementary health care insurance is a non-mandatory, private health care insurance.

Preventive health care does not form part of the Zvw or the AWBZ. It is mainly financed through general taxation.[65] Lastly, the Social Support Act (WMO) has made municipalities responsible for certain forms of home care. It includes services like domestic aid, adapted housing, provision of wheelchairs and transport facilities for persons with physical limitations due to health problems, ageing or disabilities. The WMO provides municipalities with a considerable freedom as to how they organise these services, which means there are variations in the level of services provided by the various municipalities.[66]

14.5 The Netherlands and the 'AAAQ'

As explained above, with the reorganisation of the Dutch health care system, a decentralised health insurance system with regulated competition was introduced. Health care insurers were turned into private entities, which compete with each

---

[64] Algemene Wet Bijzondere Ziektekosten, see also Schäfer et al. 2010, p. xiii.

[65] Schäfer et al. 2010, p. xxiii.

[66] Schäfer et al. 2010, p. 23, 29 and 36.

other and exert pressure on health care providers to improve efficiency and keep the costs down. At the same time, being confronted with an economic crisis, the State battles to keep already hardly manageable health care costs in check by implementing various austerity measures. When considering the effects of the Dutch health care system reform, two intertwined developments appear to be of decisive importance: the effects of the introduction of regulated competition on the one hand and the effects generated by the austerity measures, on the other. The first effects mentioned relate to the part of the health care system regulated by the Zvw. The austerity measures affect both the care covered by Zvw and the care covered by the AWBZ.

14.5.1 Effects of the Introduction of Regulated Competition

Since the latest reform of the health care system, health care insurers are obtaining a more prominent and powerful position. It is their task to selectively contract with health care providers. Selective contracting implies that health care insurers do not contract with every health care provider in the market. Instead, they contract with health care providers that comply with their conditions, i.e. to provide health care at a certain price and under certain conditions. The rationale is that health care insurers, who occupy a key position in the health sector, will only contract with those health care services that meet the needs of their clients.

During the first phase of the introduction of the health care reform, selective contracting did not take place that often; health care insurers contracted with almost all existing health care providers (e.g. hospitals and general practitioners). However, over the course of the years, health care insurers contract more and more selectively. An effect of this manner of contracting is that health care providers are trying to distinguish themselves in order to get contracted. They do so by attempting to differentiate themselves from other health care providers with the treatments they offer and the prices they ask. In addition to offering regular forms of health care, health care providers have also started offering certain types of additional health care; non-essential treatments that make them more attractive to patients. An example is a therapy and treatment offered in certain hospitals for people who snore. Moreover, at the request of health care insurers, some health care providers have prioritised clients of such insurers to avoid waiting lists. This included special contracts, such as for cataract operations performed during night hours.[67]

Another effect of the steering role health care insurers have been assigned with, is that health care providers, and especially hospitals, are gradually merging into larger-scale organisations. The rationale for this approach is to increase efficiency and to create a more powerful position in relationship to health care insurers by forming a significant player in the contracting health care market. Moreover,

---

[67] San Giorgi 2008, p. 9.

quality requirements prompt scaling-up and that can be obtained by e.g. mergers. In the Dutch health care system, organisations such as the Dutch Health Care Inspectorate (*Inspectie voor de Gezondheidszorg*, IGZ), the NZa, and scientific societies of medical specialists take important and increasing notice of quality outcomes of health care. They determine quality standards, specify the number of treatments or operations a doctor should perform on a yearly basis in order to meet quality requirements, and evaluate and control the level of health care provided.[68] Besides, since the reform of the Dutch health care system, in addition to factors such as cost or meeting certain specific criteria, there is a tendency among health care insurers to take into account the quality of the health care provided when contracting with health care providers for their clients. Nevertheless, to provide evidence of the quality of care given is difficult, not only for health care providers, but also for health care insurers. Therefore, certain types of health care providers, for example hospitals, are required to obtain prescribed quality labels, attributed by independent quality institutes, in order to be eligible for contracting.

The question arises, how these trends relate to the human rights framework and in particular, to the right to health framework under General Comment 14. Neither the human rights framework in general and General Comment 14 in particular, nor the outcomes of the supervising role of international human rights bodies such as the CESCR stipulate how States should draw up a health care and health insurance system. General Comment. 14 only denotes that one of the State's obligations includes the provision of a public, private or mixed health insurance system which is affordable for all.[69] Considering this, market-oriented elements of the Dutch health insurance system, including the instrument of selective contracting that health care insurers have at their disposal, does in itself not create tension with the human rights framework. Moreover, the fact that the Dutch authorities, scientific societies of medical specialists and health care insurers pay more and more attention to the quality of health care provided, can be considered to meet the requirement of States' responsibility to guarantee the quality of health facilities, goods and services.

However, when looking at the effects of these market-oriented elements from the perspective of the other criteria enshrined in General Comment 14, it can be concluded that the criterion of geographic accessibility requires some attention. This can be illustrated with the following example: in the north of the Netherlands, which is a remote area with a low population density, several hospitals were closed down and health care providers have stopped offering health care services. Two of the most paramount grounds for this were the effects of selective contracting and quality and quantity requirements. Consequently, patients in this remote area now have to travel further or have less of a choice in selecting their health care provider. The risk of having no or no timely access to health care is counteracted partly by the legal obligation for health care insurers to contract health care in such

---

[68] Inter alia Soncos 2012.

[69] General Comment 14, para 36.

14 Dutch Realities: Evaluating Health Care

a way that emergency care is accessible to their clients within a 45 min' drive by ambulance.[70] Nevertheless, for women in labour or someone having a heart attack this may still constitute a problem.[71] From a human rights perspective, this could cause a dilemma, especially if this should be the case in more remote areas.

The second point of concern is accessible health care without discrimination as one of the components of 'accessibility' under the AAAQ in General Comment 14. In light of this principle it requires special attention that some health care providers have prioritised clients of certain health care insurers. This has led to much commotion in the media. In light of the principle of accessible health care without discrimination as one of the AAAQ criteria, this could be a questionable development in the Dutch health care system. As set out in Sect. 14.2.2 and as stipulated by General Comment 14, health care must be accessible to all without discrimination.[72] In this case, discrimination could arise by making a difference in treatment, i.e. providing access to health care based on the type of health care insurance of a specific group of patients. In such cases, when health status is no longer decisive in prioritising and providing health care treatment, this could imply that the effect of such a difference in treatment leads to unequal access to health care when considering health status and health care needs.

As human rights institutions and experts have pointed out, the pursuit of cost containment and maximising efficiency should not come at the expense of equality in access to health care. The order in which patients are treated or placed on waiting lists should only be governed by medical criteria. This must never be based on discriminatory grounds, such as the ability of individuals to pay or their health status, as this could lead to a denial of or delay in access to health care for a particular group or part of the population.[73]

14.5.2 Effect of Austerity Measures

The Netherlands is confronted with ever rising health care costs. In 2012 nearly 12 % of the Gross Domestic Product (GDP) was spent on health care.[74] Due to an increasing life expectancy and progress in medical science and technological advancements, the expectation is that health care expenditure will continue to rise up to 31 % of GDP health care spending in 2040.[75]

---

[70] Nederlandse Zorgauthoriteit 2012, p. 50.

[71] Weeda 2012.

[72] General Comment 14, paras 12, 18, 19.

[73] San Giorgi 2012, p. 56.

[74] Statistics Netherlands and OECD Health Data 2012, Nederlandse Vereniging van Ziekenhuizen 2012.

[75] CPB 2011.

It is held that this increasing health care expenditure, and therefore the manner in which the health care system is now financed, is untenable and that radical measures have to be taken. Being confronted with these hardly manageable costs of health care, the Dutch government is effectively gradually introducing a variety of austerity measures. Two of the most important measures taken include limiting the basic health insurance package and the long-term health care covered by the AWBZ, and increasing excess payments for health care used.[76] As a result of the first measure, ongoing limitation of the basic health insurance package or the health care covered by the AWBZ, patients themselves are more and more paying for the costs of medical services or can purchase supplementary health insurance for these services. However, contrary to the basic health care insurance, there rests no obligation on health care insurers to accept new applicants for supplementary care insurance and they are free to differentiate their premiums according to the patients' risk profiles. Consequently, those needing additional health care, such as the chronically ill, disabled, elderly and psychiatric patients, thereby falling into the so-called 'high risk groups', and who choose to purchase supplementary health care insurance, can expect to be confronted with higher premiums. Consequently, access for these groups of patients can be diminished due to affordability problems. Several patient organisations and prominent medical associations have expressed concern that these measures will seriously threaten the affordability of health care for those groups of patients they represent.[77]

In line with the effects of the austerity measures taken by the Dutch government to face the increasing health care costs, there is a trend that probably will even further influence the decline in solidarity in the current, relatively egalitarian health care system of the Netherlands. Various independent advisory bodies provide the Dutch government with results of research and advise on how to develop policies for the current health care system.[78] Recent reports of these bodies emphasise that due to the fact that health care spending will eat up an increasing part of the budget of the Dutch population, and due to the economic crisis, there is a limit to the solidarity which characterises the Dutch health care system, and therefore a reduced willingness among people to contribute to this solidarity. Moreover, as shown by research included in these reports, high income groups contribute relatively more to the health care system, while they consume relatively less.[79]

Seen from the perspective of the human rights criterion of financial accessibility (affordability), it is essential that the Dutch government takes measures to ensure that health care remains affordable for all. The payments for health care have to be based on the principles of equity, ensuring that these services, whether privately or

---

[76] CPB and RVZ 2013.

[77] Among others, see statement by the patients' organisation NCPF, at http://www.npcf.nl/?option=com_content&view=article&id=5007&catid=2:nieuws&Itemid=26, accessed August 2013.

[78] CPB and RVZ 2013.

[79] CPB 2011.

14 Dutch Realities: Evaluating Health Care   421

publicly provided, are affordable to all, including socially disadvantaged groups. As defined by the CESCR, 'equity demands that poorer households should not be disproportionately burdened with health expenses as compared to richer households'.[80] As inappropriate health resource allocation can lead to discrimination, even if not overtly, this will be in conflict with the criterion of access to health care without discrimination.[81]

14.6 Accountability and the Obligation to Protect

Earlier in this chapter it was set out that the obligation to protect, as one of the tripartite State obligations, implies that States have to take measures that prevent third parties from interfering with the right to health enshrined in Article 12 ICESCR. As part of this obligation, sufficient and adequate accountability mechanisms have to be in place. Four interlinked duties were distinguished to meet this requirement: (1) the adoption of legislation to regulate the health sector; (2) the adoption of monitoring ('accountability') mechanisms aimed at regulating the behaviour of (private) insurance companies and (private) health care providers; (3) the creation of possibilities for individuals to complain about failures or malpractices by the (private) actors in the health care sector (redress; remedies); and (4) the establishment of participatory mechanisms to enhance the participation of the public in the decision-making process concerning the health sector.[82]

In this section an overview is provided of the accountability mechanisms and processes available in the Netherlands to hold the Dutch government and other actors in the health care sector to account for possible failures to realise the right to health. The efficiency and effectiveness of these mechanisms will be discussed in order to evaluate how the Dutch government realises its obligation to create accountability for the right to health. The four duties set out above will be adopted in this assessment. Although the supervision of the Dutch health care system was not designed in light of human rights law, it is nonetheless assessed whether the system is in compliance with this human rights framework.

14.6.1 Legislation

In The Netherlands, the legislation regulating the health care system is rather comprehensively designed. A substantial body of regulation is in place governing the position and activities of the various actors in health care. An example is the

---

[80] Economic and Social Council 1993.

[81] General Comment 14, para 19.

[82] As also suggested in Toebes, 2008, p. 451.

Zorgverzekeringswet (Zvw) which was discussed extensively in Sect. 14.4.3. As mentioned, the Zvw regulates the behaviour of private insurance companies. An important component of this law is the obligation it imposes on health care insurers to accept all new applicants.[83] Moreover, health care insurers are forbidden to differentiate their premiums in accordance with the risk profiles of their clients, such as health status, use of medication, and age.[84] These measures regulated by the Zvw constitute clear examples of organising a health care system where the financial accessibility of health care services, as an important component of the 'AAAQ' criteria, may be guaranteed.

Another illustration thereof is the complex of legislation that regulates the quality of health care provided. A legal framework for quality assurance has been laid down in the Quality of Health Facilities Act (*Kwaliteitswet Zorginstellingen*, KZi), the Individual Health Care Profession Act (*Wet op de beroepen in de individuele gezondheiszorg*, BIG) and the Medical Treatment Agreement Act (*Wet geneeskundige behandelingsovereenkomst*, WGBO).[85] The latter is important as it regulates a wide variety of well-embedded patients' rights, including the notion of informed consent, i.e. the patient's authorization or agreement to undergo a specific medical intervention.[86]

14.6.2 Monitoring Mechanisms

Where it comes to monitoring mechanisms, a distinction can be made between external and internal (institutional) mechanisms. External governmental regulation of the Dutch health care system is carried out by three main regulatory bodies: the Health Care Inspectorate (*Inspectie voor de Gezondheidszorg*, IGZ), the Dutch Health Care Authority (*Nederlandse* Zorgautoriteit, NZa),[87] and the Netherlands Authority for Consumers and Markets (*Autoriteit Consument & Markt*, ACM).[88] For the purpose of this chapter, we mainly focus on the Health Care Inspectorate (IGZ), as its mandate is most closely connected to the realisation of the right to health. An important advisory body is the Health Care Insurance Board (*College voor Zorgverzekeringen*, CVZ), which plays an important role with regard to the safeguarding of the quality of the health care insurance system by regulating the

---

[83] Zvw, Article 3.

[84] Zvw, Article 14(1).

[85] Schäfer et al. 2010, p. 41.

[86] WGBO, Articles 446–454.

[87] Supervisory body for all different sectors of the health care market in the Netherlands. Website: http://www.nza.nl/organisatie/sitewide/english, accessed April 2013.

[88] This organisation aims to enhance fair trade between businesses and consumers (up till 1 April 2013 the Netherlands Competition Authority was the relevant body (NMa)); for website ACM see https://www.acm.nl/en/about-acm/mission-vision-strategy/our-mission, accessed April 2013.

14 Dutch Realities: Evaluating Health Care

nature, contents and scope of the compulsory health care insurance.[89] As the health insurance companies are the key actors in the health sector, and therefore of huge influence on the realisation of the right to health, some attention is paid to this body hereafter.

The overall mandate of the IGZ is to promote public health by overseeing the quality of health services. Based on the Public Health Act, the main tasks assigned to the IGZ are to conduct research into the general state of health in the Netherlands and its determinants as well as to promote its improvement; to exercise supervision on the detection of offences; and to advise the Minister of Health, Welfare and Sports in this field.[90] As such, it has a wide mandate and its activities range from supervising health care providers as well as combating and preventing illness, and promoting health and mental health care.[91] It advises the responsible ministers and applies various measures, including advice, encouragement, pressure and coercion, to ensure that health care providers offer only 'responsible' care.[92] Supervision by the Inspectorate is based on legislation and regulations, so-called 'field norms' set by health care providers and professional groups, as well as its own supervisory norms.[93] Four forms of supervision can be identified: phased supervision, incident-based supervision, theme-based supervision and detection of criminal offences.[94] It has various measures at its disposal, varying from corrective or coercive measures, to disciplinary or criminal proceedings in the most serious cases.[95] According to Hout et al., the Inspectorate does not use the more formal legal instruments very often.[96] Based on an investigation of the activities of the Inspectorate, Hout et al. conclude that most of the IGZ's work consists of consultations and giving encouragement and advice.[97]

Recently, the IGZ has been criticised for failing to take the complaints of patients seriously and for responding too slowly to medical malpractices (also by the National Ombudsman, see below).[98] Hout et al. explain that since the second half of the 1990s politicians and the public at large expect the Inspectorate to respond more stringently to cases of sub-standard care and serious events in the sector'.[99] Health care providers, in turn, 'often see the regulator as being too severe

---

[89] See Article 58–76 Zvw, in particular Article 64.

[90] Gezondheidswet [Public Health Act], Articles 36 and 37.

[91] Schäfer et al. 2010, p. 348.

[92] IGZ (Health Care Inspectorate), see http://www.igz.nl/english, accessed February 2013.

[93] For its own supervisory norms, see IGZ 2008.

[94] IGZ 2008, p. 7. See also Hout et al. 2010, p. 350.

[95] IGZ (Health Care Inspectorate), see http://www.igz.nl/english/, accessed February 2013.

[96] See also Hout et al. 2010, p. 357.

[97] See also Hout et al. 2010, p. 358.

[98] De Volkskrant 2012. National Ombudsman of the Netherlands 2009.

[99] Hout et al. 2010, p. 359 (referring to a report of the Dutch Ministry of Health of 2009 entitled Ruimte en rekenschap voor zorg en ondersteuning).

and too quick to impose formal remedies (...)'.[100] This has led to a debate as to whether it is indeed the IGZ's role and responsibility to analyse such incidences, or whether its supervisory role should be mere 'systemic' in nature, in the sense that it is expected to supervise the overall functioning of the health care system.

As mentioned the Health Care Insurance Board (CVZ) aims to regulate the nature, contents and scope of the health care insurance.[101] Its responsibility is to take a critical look at whether the basic health care insurance package provides care that is necessary, accessible and affordable for the entire Dutch population.[102] This includes providing advice on the contents of the basic health care insurance package (package management), dividing the contribution funds among insurers in such a way that they can insure everyone (risk adjustment to create risk solidarity), and providing regulations for citizens in danger of being excluded from the health insurance system or for those who decline to take out insurance (regulations for special groups).[103] Given that this body is responsible for advice on the contents of the health care package, it has been criticised by several stakeholders for advising against the inclusion of certain treatments in the basic health care package (e.g. psychiatric care).[104]

14.6.3 Accountability Mechanisms: Legal Enforceability of the Right to Health

In light of the obligation to provide remedies for violations of the right to health, the first question that arises is to what extent the right to health as an international norm is applied by the Dutch courts. Due to a 'monist' system when it comes to the interpretation of international treaties, once ratified, international treaties automatically form part of the domestic legal order. This means that the right to health does not have to be transformed into national law before it can be applied; it automatically has 'internal effect'. However, this does not imply that the right to health is 'justiciable' per se, or in other words, that it has so-called 'direct effect' and is as such enforceable before the Dutch courts.

When it comes to the direct effect of international human rights standards, we may observe a difference between civil and political rights and economic, social and cultural rights. Generally, the Dutch courts consider that internationally

---

[100] Hout et al. 2010, p. 359.

[101] See Article 58–76 Zvw, in particular Article 64.

[102] College van Zorgverzekeringen (CVZ), general website http://www.cvz.nl/en/cvz, accessed July 2012.

[103] College van Zorgverzekeringen (CVZ), general website http://www.cvz.nl/en/cvz, accessed July 2012.

[104] Inter alia Zorgvisie, 22 January 2013.

guaranteed economic, social and cultural rights do not have direct effect.[105] For example, with respect to several provisions in the Convention on the Rights of the Child (CRC), including the right to health in Article 24, the Court of first instance of The Hague took the following position:

> With respect to the complaints based on Articles 3, 23, 24 and 27 of the CRC the Court is of the opinion that these treaty provisions do not contain norms which are susceptible to judicial enforcement by the court; given their wording, character and scope these provisions do not have direct effect.[106]

We may conclude that given its general character and given its programmatic duties, the right to health, as set forth in international treaties, is up to this point not justiciable in the Netherlands.

Furthermore, the right to health is also contained in Article 22(1) of the Constitution of the Netherlands, but here too, its justiciability proves problematic. Firstly, due to the supremacy of statutes in the Dutch legal system, the courts cannot review the constitutionality of domestic legislation.[107] As a result, domestic health legislation, as opposed to health regulations and decisions of the lower authorities, cannot be tested against the right to health as contained in Article 22(1) of the Dutch Constitution. A further hurdle is that when it comes to the enforceability of the social rights in the Constitution, justiciability issues arise similar to those of the international economic, social and cultural rights. The drafters of the various social rights in the Dutch Constitution were of the opinion that conceivably only in theory a situation could arise where a court would rule that a decision of the public authorities would violate a social right.[108] In practice, justiciability of the constitutional social rights before the Dutch courts is indeed very limited. All in all, we may conclude that human rights and constitutional provisions do not provide much chance of redress in case of failures to realise the right to health in the Dutch health care system.

A promising development for the domestic enforceability of the right to health in the Netherlands, and across Europe more in general, concerns the development of case law of the European Committee of Social Rights (ECSR), the treaty-monitoring body of the (Revised) European Social Charter (ESC). The case law of this mechanism, which allows for collective complaints, gives evidence of justiciability of economic and social rights before an international court. As such, it can create important precedents for national judicial and quasi-judicial bodies. Several

---

[105] For an elaborate assessment of case law of the 1990s see Toebes 1999, p. 195. It seems that this attitude of the Dutch courts has not changed substantially, as illustrated by the decision of 2012.

[106] Court of first instance The Hague, 2 March 2010, LJN: BM2383, Rechtbank 's-Gravenhage, AWB 09/39970 and AWB 09/39971, available at www.rechtspraak.nl, accessed 30 October 2012. Author's translation.

[107] Article 120 of the Constitution of the Netherlands reads: 'The constitutionality of Acts of Parliament and treaties shall not be reviewed by the courts'.

[108] General Revision of the Constitution of the Netherlands, Part 1a Basic Rights, The Hague, 1979, p. 7. *Tweede Kamer* 1975–1976, 13 873, No. 3, p. 258.

of its (non-binding) decisions involved the right to protection of health, as stipulated in Article 11 ESC.[109] Up to this point, the right to protection of health as contained in Article 11 ESC has not been addressed by the ECSR vis à vis the Netherlands. However, there has been an interesting case addressing the housing conditions of undocumented children residing in The Netherlands. In *DCI v. the Netherlands*, the ECSR decided that the denial of entitlements to shelter to children unlawfully present in the Netherlands constituted a violation of the right to housing and the right to protection against poverty and social exclusion in the ESC.[110] This case has created an important precedent for Dutch court cases addressing similar matters.[111]

14.6.4 Accountability Mechanisms: Quasi-Judicial Enforceability

A further complaint option is provided by the Dutch National Ombudsman who can investigate complaints brought to him by members of the public and can launch investigations on his own initiative. This entity offers a fall-back position: it can only deal with a complaint if the administrative authority and the complainant have failed to settle the matter together.[112] While the Ombudsman's decisions, recommendations and reports are not legally binding, the Ombudsman has extensive investigative powers. By law, both administrative authorities and witnesses have to cooperate with his investigations.[113]

---

[109] European Committee of Social Rights, *Maragopoulous Foundation for Human Rights (MFHR)* v. *Greece*, No. 30/2005, 6 February 2007, *INTERIGHTS* v. *Croatia*, No. 45/2007, 30 March 2009, *European Roma Rights Centre (ERRC)* v. *Bulgaria*, No. 46/2007, 3 December 2008, *FIDH* v. *Greece (72/2011)*, admissibility decision 7 December 2011, cases available at http://www.coe.int/t/dghl/monitoring/socialcharter/Complaints/Complaints_en.asp, accessed April 2013.

[110] *DCI v. the Netherlands*, complaint no. 47/2008, 20 October 2009.

[111] Based on an email interview with Fischer Advocaten, Haarlem, the Netherlands, website see http://www.fischeradvocaten.nl, accessed April 2013. It is also worth mentioning that at the beginning of 2013 an organisation named the Conference of European Churches submitted a collective complaint to the ECSR alleging that the Dutch authorities have violated the rights to social and medical assistance and to shelter by failing to ensure these rights to undocumented migrants. Conference of European Churches v. The Netherlands, Complaint No. 90/2013, 21 January 2013. available at http://hudoc.esc.coe.int/esc2008/query.asp?language=en, accessed April 2013.

[112] Article 12(1) of the National Ombudsman Act stipulates that the complaint can only be submitted 1 year after the date on which the court gives a judgment against which there is no appeal, or after the proceedings have ended in some other way. http://www.anticorruption.bg/ombudsman/eng/readnews.php?id=4104&lang=en&t_style=tex&l_style=default, accessed May 2013.

[113] Website of the Dutch National Ombudsman at http://www.nationaleombudsman.nl/english, accessed April 2013.

14 Dutch Realities: Evaluating Health Care

The Ombudsman's office comprises eight different investigation teams, one of which is the Team Health Care. As mentioned above, the current Ombudsman has on several occasions criticised the role of the above-mentioned Health Care Inspectorate (IGZ). He has argued that based on European and international human rights law there is a duty to investigate individual cases rather than to conduct a mere 'systemic supervision'.[114] In his reports, the Ombudsman explicitly refers to the internationally recognised right to health as an important norm against which the Dutch health care supervision needs to be assessed:

> The right to health is a human right. Based on this human right the Government is expected to guarantee the availability, (geographic) accessibility and quality of health care services, to the maximum of its available resources. (…) The Dutch Government has the duty to respect, protect and fulfil the right to health. If health care is privatised, the Government should focus mostly on the duty to protect. As a governmental supervisory body, the Dutch Health Care Inspectorate should place emphasis on the protection of the quality of health care.[115]

This debate illustrates how a national monitoring mechanism (Ombudsman) uses international human rights law as a framework to hold a supervisory body in the health care system (Health Care Inspectorate) to account. We observe that this approach forms an exception to the somewhat reticent attitude towards the right to health of other institutions and bodies in The Netherlands.

14.6.5 Accountability Mechanisms: Domestic Complaint Bodies

Several possibilities are open to patients to file complaints with judicial and quasi-judicial bodies. There is in fact a range of parallel possibilities for patients to file their complaints about health care performance in the Dutch health care system. The options vary from complaining directly to the health care provider to filing a complaint with a complaints committee, or a disciplinary board, while there are some additional possibilities under Dutch national law and professional codes of conduct.[116]

When it comes to the first (quasi-judicial) option, i.e. the complaint to a health care provider, the Clients' Right of Complaint Act (*Wet klachtrecht cliënten zorgsector*, WKCZ) requires every health care institution or provider to set up or to join a complaints committee.[117] One of the objectives of this law is to reduce the number of complaints filed in formal (judicial) procedures. An important formal

---

[114] National Ombudsman of the Netherlands (Alex Brenninkmeijer) 2009.

[115] National Ombudsman of the Netherlands (Alex Brenninkmeijer) 2009, p. V. Translation: the authors.

[116] Schäfer et al. 2010, p. 44.

[117] Alhafaji et al. 2011, p. 129.

(judicial) procedure is offered by the Medical Disciplinary Tribunals, as regulated by the above-mentioned Individual Health Care Professions Act of 1997 (Wet BIG).[118] This complaint mechanism consists of five regional disciplinary tribunals, and an appeal body (Central Disciplinary Body). If the tribunal finds the complaint to be justified, it can take various binding decisions, varying from the imposition of a warning, reprimand or fine, to temporary suspension or striking off from the Register.[119] Lastly, in the most serious cases, the Public Prosecution Service may initiate proceedings against a health care provider.

It is clear from the above that a serious attempt is made in the Dutch health care system to realise accountability in the Dutch health care system. Several complaint options are open, and it is also worth observing that patients wanting to lodge a complaint do not have to follow a specific pathway: rather, they can choose the mechanism that suits them best.[120] However, given the many possibilities for lodging complaints, the question arises as to how often situations occur in which one and the same treatment by a provider results in various different complaints procedures being instigated. Alhafaji et al. 2011, who have analysed the cases that were published between 1997 and 2007, found that concurrence between complaints procedures occurred in 42 cases, and that such concurrence is generally on the rise.[121] They conclude that a certain amount of concurrence is perhaps unavoidable, but may nonetheless give rise to legal questions and may also constitute an improper use of public money.[122] They suggest that good reasons have to be given for two procedures being instigated at the same time, and that the Government should play a role in regulating this.[123]

14.6.6 Participatory Mechanisms

Lastly, the question arises how the notion of 'participation' is embedded in the Dutch health care system. In general, two levels of participation in health care systems can be identified: (1) patients' rights and thereby the ability of patients to have a say in the patient-doctor-relationship; and (2) the ability of patients and the public at large to participate in the decision-making process with respect to decisions affecting national health care policy. This includes for example the treatment of diseases, the availability of medical services and medicines, and the reorganisation of the health care sector and system.[124]

---

[118] See also Alhafaji et al. 2011, p. 129.

[119] See also Alhafaji et al. 2011, p. 130.

[120] Schäfer et al. 2010, p. 44.

[121] Alhafaji et al. 2011, p. 127.

[122] Alhafaji et al. 2011, p. 148.

[123] Alhafaji et al. 2011, p. 148.

[124] For a useful analysis of the notion of participation in the health decision-making process see Potts 2008b.

14 Dutch Realities: Evaluating Health Care

During the 1980s and 1990s there was a strong focus on patients' rights. This culminated in the adoption of an extensive body of regulations with respect to the protection of patients and their rights in the health care system in the second half of the 1990s. A key regulation in this respect is the above-mentioned Medical Treatment Agreement Act (*Wet geneeskundige behandelingsovereenkomst*, WGBO) which, among other issues, requires health care providers to obtain 'informed consent' from their patients.

Furthermore, based on the Client Representation Act (*Wet medezeggenschap cliënten zorginstelling*, WMCZ), patients can also seek to influence the policies of health care institutions. They can make recommendations with regards to, inter alia, the budget, annual accounts and important changes in the organisation. The client councils that have been established based on this law, have however been criticised for failing to meet these goals.[125] Van der Voet asserts that participation as prescribed under the WMCZ is not an effective or efficient way to strengthen the collective legal position of the clients, nor to improve the match between supply and demand of care. [126] According to Van der Voet, the legislator also did not succeed in striking the right balance in the WMCZ between the matters that need to be regulated by law and those that can be left to self-regulation.[127]

In addition to this mechanism to influence health care institutions, other mechanisms have been established for patients to influence health insurers. Based on the Health Insurance Act (Zvw) health insurers are required to involve patients in the decision-making process over purchases in health care.[128] This is an important possibility, given that health insurers have become responsible for contracting health care providers since the reorganisation of the Dutch health care sector in 2006.

The marketization of health care has added an extra dimension to the position of the patient. Schäfer et al. observe that since 2000 the emphasis is much more on the patient as a consumer, who increasingly makes independent and rational choices.[129] This has caused a shift towards enhancing the patient's range of choice, rather than focusing on the mere supply of services.[130]

All in all, over the past decennia the Dutch health care system has placed much more emphasis on the demand-side. Trappenburg asserts that the possibilities for participation in the Dutch health care system have increased considerably, even to the extent that the range of options has grown out of proportion.[131] Van de Bovenkamp et al. observe that the extensive possibilities for participation in the Dutch health care system are not always efficient and effective. It is not always

---

[125] Schäfer et al. 2010, p. 43.

[126] Van der Voet 2005.

[127] Van der Voet 2005.

[128] Schäfer et al. 2010, p. 43.

[129] Schäfer et al. 2010, p. 36 and 43.

[130] Schäfer et al. 2010, p. 36 and 43.

[131] Trappenburg 2008a, b.

easy for patients to understand how to participate in the formal participatory structures, while health care providers still struggle to establish an open and equal dialogue with the patient.[132]

14.6.7 Non-State Actors in Dutch Health Care

As States have ratified the human rights treaties, they carry the primary legal responsibility to realise the rights set forth in the treaties. However, at the same time the question arises whether non-State actors in the health care sector also carry responsibilities under human rights law. General Comment 14 stresses the responsibilities of non-State actors with respect to the realisation of the right to health and the right to health care:

> (...) all members of society—individuals, including health professionals, families, local communities, intergovernmental and non-governmental organisations, civil society organisations, as well as the private business sector—have responsibilities regarding the realisation of the right to health (...)[133]

Whether there is strictly speaking a legal obligation or not, this statement would imply that all actors in the health care sector, varying from (public and private) health care providers, insurance companies, and the pharmaceutical industry have responsibilities regarding the realisation of the right to health. In an era of privatisation, this notion is all the more important, as private non-State actors attain an increasing power and influence over the way in which patients can access the health care system.

Applying this notion to the Netherlands, the question arises how human rights can best be safeguarded in the partly privatised Dutch health care system? As mentioned above, while there is a duty on the part of the government to oversee the actors in the health sector, arguably non-State actors are also bound by the human rights standards. Based on this assumption, all actors in the health sector have responsibilities to guarantee the availability, accessibility, acceptability and quality of the health-related services they provide.

In this respect it is worth devoting some attention to the realisation of quality by health institutions as one of the components of the AAAQ. An important piece of legislation is the Quality of Health Facilities Act (*Kwaliteitswet Zorinsinstellingen*, KZi), which was introduced in 1996 and takes as a starting point the self-regulation of health institutions. Based on this law, public and private health care providers need to meet a number of quality standards. They are, however, free to choose the way in which to meet these standards. A critical report of the Netherlands Court of Audit (*Algemene Rekenkamer*) has established that self-regulation in the Dutch health care sector, as based on the KZi, has failed to achieve the

---

[132] Bovenkamp et al. 2008, p. 4.

[133] General Comment 14, para 42.

14 Dutch Realities: Evaluating Health Care

desired result.[134] Health care providers, insurers and patients failed to define a 'shared vision' with respect to what is meant by 'responsible health care'. Furthermore, according to this report, the implementation of this new law has not resulted in the adoption of adequately functioning quality systems by the health care providers.[135]

This example raises the question to what extent the realisation of the 'AAAQ' can be left to the health sector, and/or to what extent governments should remain involved. While there is a shared responsibility, governments retain ultimate and overall responsibility for the realisation of the right to health.

14.7 Conclusions

This contribution has assessed the Dutch health care system, the current health reform and its effects in the light of the internationally guaranteed right to health. It has applied the framework of General Comment 14, and in particular the so-called 'AAAQ' and the notion of the State 'obligation to protect'. This concluding section presents a reflection on the implementation of the current health care system and its effects.

When it comes to health status and health indicators, it may be concluded that the overall health of the Dutch population is of a high standard. While the focus in this chapter has been on accessing health care services, it is important to note that there are increasing health inequalities in the Netherlands and that improving and enhancing the socio-economic determinants of health are also important human rights concerns.[136]

Like most countries, the Netherlands is struggling to cope with the rising costs of health care. With the reform of the Dutch health care system and the introduction of regulated competition in 2006, the Dutch government has partly privatised its health care system. While the insurance companies have become private entities, they are still heavily regulated. The Dutch government has an important role in ensuring the availability, accessibility and quality of health care services. This way the Dutch health care system seeks to address such difficulties as scarcity of resources or inefficiency in the health sector, whilst still ensuring universal access.

Nevertheless, in light of the 'AAAQ' criteria of General Comment 14, some points of concern can be raised. Overall, as an effect of the current system, an increasing pressure from the health insurance companies on health care providers can be observed, which may have negative consequences for the realisation of the 'AAAQ criteria'. In this regard we have first pointed at a growing trend of

---

[134] Algemene Rekenkamer (Netherlands Court of Audit) 2009.

[135] Algemene Rekenkamer 2009, p. 12.

[136] Toebes et al. 2012, Chap. 7.

selective contracting by health care insurers. As a result of this selective contracting, health care providers seek to differentiate themselves, which on occasion may lead to health care providers offering unnecessary care. There are also examples of health care providers trying to convince health insurers by prioritising the patients of that insurer in case of waiting lists. Another effect of the increased steering role of health care insurers is the growing trend of mergers between hospitals and/or other health care facilities. When looking at these developments from a human rights perspective, one perceives the possible friction between the principle of 'geographic accessibility' and the merging of hospitals into large-scale organisations. There is a risk that patients have to travel too far for necessary care. Furthermore, the prioritisation of patients raises concern in light of the principle of non-discrimination, as one of the components of 'accessibility' under the AAAQ. As mentioned, when health status is no longer the decisive factor in prioritising patients and providing health care, there may constitute unequal access to health care.

The Dutch government is furthermore taking a number of austerity measures that may have consequences for the realisation of the 'AAAQ criteria' of General Comment 14 as well. Compared to other Europeans, the Dutch spend a relatively small amount of their overall budget on health care. Nonetheless, the growing trend of reducing the basic health insurance package and package of long-term AWBZ-care, and increasing excess payments for health care, are issues of concern in light of the 'financial accessibility' of health care services. This may in particular affect the so-called 'high risk' groups, as they need more care than others.

Subsequently, we have looked at the 'obligation to protect' of the Dutch government, as a State's duty flowing from the right to health. We have identified four components of this obligation: the adoption of *legislation* and of *monitoring mechanisms*, the creation of (judicial and other) *accountability mechanisms*, and the establishment of *participatory mechanisms* in health decision-making. When it comes to legislation, we have concluded in general that there is a comprehensive body of regulations governing all actors in the Dutch health care sector. Furthermore, notions underpinning the 'AAAQ' are firmly embedded in the Dutch health care system and in Dutch health care policy and legislation. When it comes to monitoring mechanisms, we have observed that since the 1990s there is growing pressure from the Dutch population on the public authorities to address substandard care, which has led to a discussion about the adequacy of the functioning of the Dutch Health Care Inspectorate. When it comes to accountability mechanisms, we have first looked at the *judicial enforcement* of the right to health ('justicability'). We have observed that while the Netherlands is party to a wide range of human rights treaties that include a right to health, the internationally recognised human right to health does not play a significant role in judicial procedures. There is still significant reluctance on the part of courts and quasi-judicial bodies to adjudicate cases on the basis of these norms. When it comes to other accountability mechanisms, we have observed that there are many options in the Dutch health care sector to complain about malpractices, but that these are not in any way streamlined, thus resulting in the same complaint being submitted to more

14 Dutch Realities: Evaluating Health Care

than one complaints body. Similarly, when it comes to the participation of the public in the health decision-making process, a number of mechanisms is available, but they are not always effective or easy to access.

Finally, we have briefly touched on the responsibilities of non-State actors for the realisation of the right to health. While many non-State actors, including for example the food and pharmaceutical industries, arguably carry an important responsibility for protecting the health of the population, we have focused in particular on non-State actors responsible for the provision and financing of health care. We have referred to research pointing out that the self-regulation of health institutions in the Netherlands has not functioned adequately, which leads to the question of how the balance should be tilted when it comes to carrying the responsibility for providing adequate health care. Based on General Comment 14 we have suggested that although there is a shared responsibility for all actors in the health sector to realise the right to health, governments cannot absolve themselves from their ultimate responsibility for realising the right to health.

All in all, this chapter has illustrated how a developed country seeks to implement a number of important perceptions underpinning the right to health. Despite the high level of health in the Netherlands, the Dutch Government is grappling with a number of difficult and costly realities, including socio-economic health inequalities, the ageing of the population and the resulting rising costs of health care. In its attempt to enhance and to protect health in general as well as guaranteeing access to health care, the Dutch Government barely looks at the right to health as an international norm. Nonetheless, notions like accessibility, accountability and participation are still firmly embedded in the Dutch health care sector.

References

Algemene Rekenkamer (2009) (Netherlands Court of Audit), Implementatie Kwaliteitswet Zorginstellingen [implementation of the Quality of Health Facilities Act]. http://www.rekenkamer.nl/Publicaties/Onderzoeksrapporten/Introducties/2009/06/Implementatie_Kwaliteitswet_zorginstellingen. Accessed April 2013
Alhafaji FY, Frederiks BJM, Leegemaate J (2011) Concurrence between complaints procedures in the Dutch health care system. Eur J Health Law 18:127–148
Brinkerhoff D (2003) Accountability and health systems: overview, framework, and strategies. Partners for Health Reform Plus, Maryland
Bovenkamp H van de, Grit K, Bal R (2008) Inventarisatie patientenparticipatie in onderzoek, kwaliteit en beleid [Inventory of patient participation in research, quality and policy], Erasmus Medical Center Rotterdam. http://oldwww.bmg.eur.nl/personal/r.bal/vd%20Bovenkamp%20et%20al%20-%202008%20-%20inventarisatie%20patientenparticipatie.pdf. Accessed April 2013
Centraal Planburo (CPB) (2011) Trends in gezondheid en zorg [trends in health and care]. http://www.cpb.nl/publicatie/trends-in-gezondheid-en-zorg. Accessed April 2013
Centraal Planburo (CPB) and Raad voor de Volksgezondheid en Zorg (RVZ) (2013) Het belang van wederkerigheid. Solidariteit gaat niet vanzelf [the importance of reciprocity—solidarity is not self-evident]. https://vpn.olvg.nl/+CSCO+00756767633A2F2F6A6A6A2E65696D2E617267++/uploads/docs/Advies_Het_belang_van_wederkerigheid.pdf. Accessed April 2013

Chapman AR (1994) Preface. In: Chapman AR (ed) Health care reform: a human rights approach. Georgetown University Press, Washington, DC, pp vii–x

Chinkin C (2006) Health and human rights. Publ Health Suppl: 52–60

Civitas (updates by Claire Daley and James Gubb) (2011) Health care systems: Switzerland. http://www.civitas.org.uk/nhs/download/switzerland.pdf. Accessed Mar 2013

College voor Zorgverzekeringen (CVZ) General website. http://www.cvz.nl/en/cvz. Accessed July 2013

Cosmo G (2005) Human rights and the privatisation of public utilities and essential services. In: De Feyter K, Gómez Isa FG (eds) Privatisation and human rights. Intersentia, Antwerp-Oxford, pp 33–56

De Feyter K, Gómez Isa F (eds) (2005) Privatisation and human rights in the age of globalisation. Intersentia, Antwerp-Oxford

De Volkskrant, Massale kritiek op 'falende' Inspectie voor de Gezondheidszorg, 31 March 2012. www.volkskrant.nl. Accessed April 2013

Den Exter A (2010) Health system reforms in The Netherlands: from public to private and its effects on equal access to health care. Eur J Health Law 17(3):223–233

Economic and Social Council, UN Doc. E./C12/2008/2 (2009) Guidelines on treaty-specific documents to be submitted by State parties under Articles 16 and 17 of the international covenant on economic, social and cultural rights. www.ohchr.org. Accessed April 2013

Eide A (1983) The new international economic order and the promotion of human rights. Report on the right to adequate food as a human right, united nations commission on human rights 1983, UN Doc. E/CN.4/RES/1983/16. http://www.refworld.org/cgi-bin/texis/vtx/rwmain?page=topic&tocid=4565c22529&toid=458aa9e72&publisher=&type=RESOLUTION&coi=&docid=3b00f0ea3c&skip=0. Accessed Mar 2013

Euro Health Consumer Index (2012) http://www.healthpowerhouse.com/index.php?Itemid=55. Accessed Mar 2013

Fair Society Healthy Lives (Marmot Review) (2010), UCL Institute of Health Equity. http://www.instituteofhealthequity.org/projects/fair-society-healthy-lives-the-marmot-review. Accessed Sep 2013

Hendriks AC (1998) The right to health in national and international Jurisprudence. Eur J Health Law 5(4):389–408

Hout FAG, Nienhuis ED, Robben PBM, Frederiks BJM, Leegemaate J (2010) Supervision by the Dutch health care inspectorate. Eur J Health Law 17(4):347–360

Inspectie voor de Gezondheidszorg (IGZ) (2008) Richtlijn voor transparante handhaving [Enforcement framework for the Inspectorate], The Hague, Health Care Inspectorate. http://www.rijksoverheid.nl/documenten-en-publicaties/kamerstukken/2008/12/23/handhavingskader-igz.html. Accessed July 2013

Leary VA (1994a) The right to health in international human rights law. Health Hum Rights Fall 1(1):24–56

Leary VA (1994b) Defining the right to health care. In: Chapman AR (ed) Health care reform. A human rights approach. Georgetown University Press, Washington, DC, pp 87–105

Lie RK (2004) Health, human rights and mobilization of resources for health. BMC Int Health Hum Rights 4(4):1–8

Mackintosh M, Koivusalo M (2005) Commercialization of health care: global and local dynamics and policy responses. Palgrave Macmillan, Basingstoke

Marmot M, Friel S, Bell R, Houweling TA, Taylor S (2008) Commission on social determinants of health. Closing the gap in a generation: health equity through action on the social determinants of health. Lancet 372:1661

Naderi PSD, Meier BD (2010) Privatisation within the Dutch context: a comparison of the health insurance systems of the Netherlands and the United States. Health 14(6):603–618

National Ombudsman of the Netherlands (3 December 2009) De Inspectie voor de Gezondheidszorg: een papieren tijger? [Dutch health Care Inspectorate: a Paper Tiger?] Report No. 2009/250. http://www.nationaleombudsman.nl/sites/default/files/rapport2009-250_1.pdf. Accessed April 2013

14 Dutch Realities: Evaluating Health Care

Nederlandse Zorgautoriteit (NZa) (2012) http://www.nza.nl/organisatie/sitewide/english/. Accessed July 2012

Nederlandse Zorgautoriteit (NZa) (2012) Beleidsregel TH/BR-005, Toezichtkader zorgplicht zorgverzekeraars (Zvw) De reikwijdte van de zorgplicht in begrippen, verantwoordelijkheden en normen [the scope of the duty of care in concepts, responsibilities and norms], 2012, p 50. http://www.nza.nl/137706/406031/TH_ BR-001-Toezichtskader-zorgplicht-zorgverzekeraars-(Zvw).pdf. Accessed April 2013

Newell P (2006) Taking accountability into account: the debate so far. In: Newell P, Wheeler J (eds) Rights, resources and the politics of accountability. Zed Book, New York, pp 37–58

Newell P, Wheeler J (2006) Rights, resources and the politics of accountability. Zed Books, New York

OECD Health at a glance: Europe (2010) http://www.oecd.org/berlin/46607585.pdf. Accessed March 2013.

OECD Health Data (2012) http://www.oecd.org/health/health-systems/oecdhealthdata2012.htm. Accessed Mar 2013

Potts H (2008b) Participation and the right to the highest attainable standard of health, and accountability and the right to the highest attainable standard of health. University of Essex Human Rights Centre/Open Society Institute. http://www.essex.ac.uk/human_rights_centre/research/rth/projects.aspx. Accessed April 2013

Potts, Helen (2008a) Accountability and the right to the highest attainable standard of health. University of Essex Human Rights Centre/Open Society Institute. http://www.essex.ac.uk/human_rights_centre/research/rth/docs/HRC_Accountability_Mar08.pdf. Accessed May 2013

San Giorgi M (2008) Voorkruipzorg logisch gevolg van marktwerking [Priority care is a natural result of the marketisation of health care]Trouw, 24 November 2008. www.trouw.nl. Accessed Sep 2013

San Giorgi M (2012) The human right to equal access to health care. School of human rights research, vol 53. Intersentia, Antwerp

Schäfer W, Kroneman M, Boerma W, Berg M van den, Westert G, Devillé W, Ginneken E Van (2010) The Netherlands: health system review (European observatory on health systems and policies/nivel). health systems in transition (2010) 12(1):1–229. http://www.euro.who.int/__data/assets/pdf_file/0008/85391/E93667.pdf. Accessed Mar 2013

Shue H (1980) Basic rights, subsistence, affluence and US foreign policy. Princeton University Press, Princeton

Soncos, Multidisciplinaire normering oncologische zorg Nederland (2012) [multi-disciplinary norms for oncological care the Netherlands]. www.soncos.org/soncos. Accessed April 2013

Statistics Netherlands (CBS), Gezondheidszorg in cijfers [health care in statistics], 2012. http://www.cbs.nl/en-GB/menu/home/default.htm?Languageswitch=on. Accessed Mar 2013

Tamminga M (2012) Hoeveel ziekenhuizen kunnen nog overleven' [How many hospitals can still survive], NRC Handelsblad, 21 December 2012. www.nrc.nl. Accessed April 2013

Toebes B (1999) The right to health as a human right in international law. School of human rights research, vol 1. Intersentia/Hart, Antwerp

Toebes B (2006) The right to health and the privatisation of health care: a case study of the Netherlands. Health Hum Rights 9(1):102–127

Toebes B (2008) Taking a human rights approach to health care commercialization. In: Cholewka PA, Motlag MM (eds) Health capital and sustainable socioeconomic development. Taylor and Francis, Philadelphia, pp 441–458

Toebes B, Hartlev M, Hendriks A, Rothmar H (eds) (2012) Health and human rights in Europe. Intersentia, Antwerp–Oxford

Trappenburg M (2008a), Genoeg is genoeg. Over de grenzen van de patiëntenparticipatie [Enough is enough, about the limits to patient participation], De Balie, Amsterdam, 26 September 2008. http://www.margotrappenburg.nl/lezingen/lezingenbestanden/Genoeg%20is%20genoeg%20balie.pdf. Accessed April 2013

Trappenburg M (2008b) Genoeg is genoeg. Over gezondheidszorg en democratie [Enough is enough, about health care and democracy]. Amsterdam University Press, Amsterdam

Trappenburg M (2011), Dankzij markwerking in de zorg worden patienten verwend met cappuccino en dure onderzoekjes en de armen betalen het gelag [Thanks to the marketization of health care patients are being spoilt with cappuccino and expensive tests while it is the poor who pay the price]. NRC Handelsblad (Opinie), Saturday 11 June 2011, p. 40. www.nrc.nl. Accessed April 2013

UN Committee on Economic, Social and Cultural Rights (CESCR) (2013a) General comment 14 on the right to the highest attainable standard of health, UN Doc. E/C.12/2000/4, August 11, 2000. www.unhchr.ch. Accessed July 2013

UN Committee on Economic, Social and Cultural Rights (CESCR) (2013b) General comment 20, Non-discrimination in economic, social and cultural rights, UN Doc. E/C.12/GC/20, June 10, 2009. www.unhchr.ch. Accessed March 2013

Vaillancourt Rosenau P, Lako CJ (2008) An experiment with regulated competition and individual mandates for universal health care: the new Dutch health insurance system. J Health Polit Policy Law 33(6):1032–1055

Van der Gaag RJ (Interview), in ZorgEthiek.Nu. http://zorgethiek.nu/interview-met-professor-rutger-jan-van-der-gaag-voorzitter-nederlandse-vereniging-voor-psychiatrie/. Accessed April 2013

Van der Voet GW (2005) De kwaliteit van de WMCZ als Medezeggenschapswet [the quality of the WMCZ as a participatory act], Erasmus School of Law. Rotterdam, The Netherlands

Weale A (1998) Ethical issues in social insurance for health. In: Sorell T (ed) Health care: ethics and insurance, London, pp 138–150

Weeda F (2012) Je kunt erop wachten dat een kind langs de weg wordt geboren [we can wait until a baby is born on the road] NRC Handelsblad, Monday 17 December 2012. www.nrc.nl. Accessed April 2013

World Health Organization (WHO), webpage on the Social determinants of health. http://www.who.int/social_determinants/en/. Accessed Jan 2013

World Health Organization (WHO)/Commission on the Social Determinants of Health (CSDH) (2008) Closing the gap in a generation: health equity through action on the social determinants of health. Final report of the commission on social determinants of health. http://www.who.int/social_determinants/thecommission/finalreport/en/index.html. Accessed Mar 2013

Zorgvisie (2013) CVZ wil helft GGZ schrappen uit pakket [Health Care Insurance Board wants to cut half of the mental health care budget]. http://www.zorgvisie.nl/Kwaliteit/Nieuws/2013/1/CVZ-wil-helft-ggz-schrappen-uit-pakket-1152907W/. Accessed April 2013

Part VI
Conclusions

Chapter 15
Conclusions

Rhonda Ferguson, Obiajulu Nnamuchi and Milan M. Markovic

Abstract This book has presented a survey of intersections between geographies and health issues that help to uncover the possibilities and limits of the international framework for the human right to health in national and regional contexts. Many of the countries and regions profiled in this book have integrated aspects of the right to health into policies and programs already. Some have formally recognized the right to health in their laws and constitutions, and a few have used the normative content of the right to inform public health strategies. Despite increasing recognition and acceptance of the right to health, some of its most basic elements remain unattainable for large numbers of people, with particular subpopulations bearing disproportionate disease burdens.

Contents

References.. 444

R. Ferguson (✉)
Irish Centre for Human Rights, National University of Ireland Galway, University Road, Galway, Ireland
e-mail: r.ferguson1@nuigalway.ie

O. Nnamuchi
University of Nigeria, Enugu, Nigeria
e-mail: obi.nnamuchi@yahoo.com

M. M. Markovic
Institute of Social Sciences, Kraljice Natalije, Belgrade, Serbia
e-mail: mmarkovic@idn.org.rs

M. M. Markovic
Institute of International Law, University of Graz, Graz, Austria

B. Toebes et al. (eds.), *The Right to Health*, DOI: 10.1007/978-94-6265-014-5_15, 439
© T.M.C. ASSER PRESS and the authors 2014

Why use an international right to health framework?

The human right to health provides a lens through which health challenges can be understood and progressive steps encouraged. Branches of medical inquiry such as epidemiology provide invaluable information on the "what" and the "how" of disease patterns. However, looking at health through a human rights lens tells us something about the nature of illness that epidemiology and biology cannot: it encourages us to consider to what extent illness is unjust. It also frames illness and disease within the political, social, cultural, and economic conditions that surround it; considers the power dynamics that perpetuate illness and disease; and focuses the attention on marginalized and vulnerable groups that may exist outside of medical research priorities or beyond the target demographics of political decisions, at greatest risk of becoming invisible. Worse still, history has shown us that in extreme situations medical professionals can be used as tools of the state to cover up or even inflict abuse. Considering the complex relationship between justice and health, using the international framework for the right to health offers the possibility of mitigating some of the effects of deeply embedded inequalities and discrimination and promoting environments in which anyone can achieve their highest level of health.

What are the limitations of this framework?

Considering that most countries have recognized the right to health and related obligations by ratifying the International Covenant on Economic, Social and Cultural Rights, why do significant *gaps* in health between groups of people persist in developed and developing countries alike? Convergences of factors hinder the emergence of enabling environments for health. As outlined in the chapters of this book, resource and capacity constraints, economic austerity, poverty, conflict, corruption, deeply embedded inequalities and discrimination, and lack of enforcement mechanisms contribute to health inequality. However, in many cases, it is the failure of states to comply with even their core obligations that stifle the potential of the framework to guide health-related decisions and improve health status. Although each country faces unique challenges, the following themes reappear throughout many chapters in this book.

Political will

Political will is central to operationalizing the right to health. The most basic application of political will involves adhering to core obligations set out by the Committee on Economic, Social and Cultural Rights in General Comment 14, which asserts that States must "ensure equitable distribution of all health facilities, goods and services."[1] Therefore, regardless of the level of development of a state, whatever health resources are available must be accessible by all people in that state equally. In some cases, actualizing the equitable distribution of health resources may require little more than the removal of discriminatory barriers.

---

[1] UN Committee on Economic, Social, and Cultural Rights 2000.

The right to health framework is particularly useful for prioritizing the needs and participation of vulnerable groups in health-related decisions. However, there is little incentive for governments and decision-makers to seek input from marginalized groups who may find themselves excluded from the political sphere. Too often, the needs and voices of women, the elderly, indigenous peoples, and people who are imprisoned, living in poverty, living with disabilities or stigmatized illnesses, working in precarious conditions, and residing illegally are unheard. Government commitment to "take steps" toward the realization of the right to health can begin with the formal guarantee of the right through a country's constitution or laws, in addition to the removal of barriers. These actions initiate the process of empowerment for health by offering an avenue for effective remedies when needs are unmet. However, they are only the *first steps* in the creation of an environment that enables individuals to achieve their highest attainable standard of health.

Lack of policy cohesion: Mainstreaming the right to health throughout multiple sectors

While only states have legal obligations in regard to human rights, the responsibility for reducing barriers and creating an enabling environment extends beyond health ministries and national governments. Because health is determined not only by access to health care, but social and biological factors as well, all actors involved in decision-making that impact health and health-supporting goods and services must consider how their actions serve to advance or impair the objectives of the right to health.

General Comment 14 lists underlying determinants such as safe drinking water, nutritiously safe food, adequate housing, a healthy environment, and sanitation among the factors necessary for people to achieve their highest standard of health.[2] Additionally, the broader social determinants of health—that is, the "conditions in which people are born, grow, live, work and age"[3]—which are closely linked to realization of the right to health, are impacted by a wide range of actors in public and private sectors. Actors responsible for matters pertaining to education, employment, agriculture, infrastructure, housing, social security, and child welfare among others must take into account how their decisions impact health and the determinants of health.

Lack of concrete obligations for non-state actors

Corporate entities, international agencies, and individuals can all play a role in creating or preventing enabling environments for health, though they occupy an indeterminate legal space in terms of human rights obligations. The absence of

---

[2] Ibid.
[3] World Health Organization 2013.

concrete legal obligations for nonstate or private actors means that it is difficult to ensure their actions comply with norms. It can be equally difficult to hold nonstate actors accountable for their impacts on health. Certain types of nonstate actors are particularly relevant to this discussion: Agriculture and mining companies, for example, can play a role in promoting the right to health by providing employment, improving living conditions, providing access to nutritious foods. On the other hand, they can contribute to ill health through unsafe labor conditions, environmental destruction, and complicity in various human rights abuses.

Pharmaceutical corporations play a key role in determining the accessibility of essential medicines. The research and development, marketing, and price setting decisions affect what diseases are researched and who can afford them. When responsibilities and obligations in regard to the right to health and overarching human rights principles are mainstreamed throughout private sector activities, it will likely result in greater opportunities for people to exercise healthy decision-making and access the determinants of health. Healthcare insurers too have a role in ensuring the accessibility of health care that is acceptable and of good quality.

When healthcare decisions are influenced by nonstate actors including corporations and nongovernmental organizations, the AAAQ dimensions of health care must be monitored closely. It is not enough to rely on governments to protect the right to health from infringement by nonstate actors; nonstate actors themselves must adhere to the objectives of international human rights treaties and the national laws that support them. The motivations of nonstate actors such as religious groups and corporations may or may not be compatible with all elements of the right to health, particularly as they regard vulnerable populations.

Lack of international cooperation and acceptance of collective/extra territorial obligations

In addition to a state's obligations to respect, protect, and fulfill the right to health for people residing within its jurisdiction, it has obligations to promote the enjoyment of the right to health for those existing outside of its borders as well.[4] States have obligations to act collectively to provide "disaster relief and humanitarian assistance in times of emergency, including assistance to refugees and internally displaced persons."[5] The needs of the most vulnerable populations, for example refugees and people living in conflict situations, are to be given particular consideration. Therefore, the responsibility to ensure protections for refugees rests not only with hosting governments, or with other governments in the same region, but also with the international community, and particularly developed states with greater resources and capacities.[6]

---

[4] UN Committee on Economic, Social, and Cultural Rights 2000, at 39.

[5] UN Committee on Economic, Social, and Cultural Rights 2000, at 40.

[6] Ibid.

15 Conclusions

Furthermore, states acting collectively through international agencies and organizations—health, development, financial, or otherwise—must not abdicate their individual responsibilities in such contexts. In order to reduce the health gaps between countries, collective decision-making bodies must ensure that consideration of human rights norms are mainstreamed throughout processes and policies.

Particularizing the plight and needs of vulnerable populations

It is obvious that vulnerable populations represent a key constituent of the right to health framework. This is evident in General Comment No. 14 which uses the term "vulnerable" and/or "marginalized" population at least 11 times to emphasize the importance human rights attach to the needs of these populations.[7] The emphasis recognizes the circumstances which subject this segment of the society to disproportionate burden of diseases, illnesses, poverty, and so forth as unjustifiable infringements on their rights to health. Although vulnerability arises in different forms and contexts, there is always a common denominator—unjustifiable suffering engendered by the operation of socioeconomic and political forces over which those that live on the fringes of society lack control.

Poor health outcomes and even death that inevitably result from the interplay of these forces invoke the remedial powers of human rights—an obligation not only to eliminate access difficulties but also efface other factors that irrepressibly stifle health and wellbeing. By presenting women, indigenous people, refugees, poor people, and other marginalized populations as disproportionately impacted by access difficulties and negative health outcomes, this book has aligned itself with this catechism. It is alignment that calls for greater action on the part of national authorities and the global community. Like liberation theology, human rights is most productive when the plight of the most marginalized amongst us is particularized and their needs prioritized. This prioritization involves soliciting the views of the poor and integrating them into national and international health policy frameworks. It also requires education on the forces sustaining vulnerability, the actors that set the forces in motion and how to reverse the status quo.

Rising costs of health care

The sustainability of AAAQ health care is increasingly threatened by new and greater financial demands on health care. While advancements in medicine are welcomed and necessary, such as the availability of new diagnostic equipment, medicines, and other goods, they also contribute to the rising costs of health care. Because technological and pharmacological advancements are not enjoyed by all countries equally, they can actually serve to widen the gap between healthcare availability in developing and developed countries.

---

[7] Para(s) 12(b)(i), 12(b)(ii), 18, 35, 37, 40, 43 (a), 43(f), 52, 62, 65.

Emerging threats to health, such as the increasing prevalence of chronic and noncommunicable diseases, which often require treatment over long periods of time and lead to a variety of health complications throughout a patient's life, put additional strain on health budgets. Demands on the healthcare system will only increase as the world population expands and countries may be faced with decisions on how to reduce costs and reallocate resources. However, these decisions will have to be made without introducing retrogressive measures or disproportionately impacting vulnerable populations.

Failure to address challenges surrounding the determinants of health

Progress toward realizing the right to health in any context is not only dependent on resource availability and government action in regard to specific health matters; it is also highly dependent on ensuring access to the determinants of health. This is especially true in countries wherein a large gap in health status exists between the subpopulations. Social and biological factors comprise the determinants of health: For example, education, gainful employment, safe working conditions, sex and gender, safe drinking water, and access to nutritionally safe foods, are among some of the determinants of health. Addressing poverty requires collaborative effort across all sectors to ensure that needs are met, particularly for vulnerable groups.

Looking forward

Our hope is that the contents of this book will serve to inform the activities of actors engaged in health policy and healthcare delivery—from research to service provision. Similarly, we hope that actors involved in activities within the scope of the social determinants of health are reminded of how human rights can inform their work and keep them engaged in efforts to improve health and wellbeing for all. When assessing national and regional implementation of the right to health around the world, findings must be contextualized by the realities of the locations examined. The particular needs, resource and capacity limits, and challenges of a country must be kept in mind. But these considerations also call into question what progressive realization looks like on a global scale. The objective here has not been to compare countries, yet glaring inequalities exist in global health and development; looking forward, it will be useful to consider how we define progress and the successful adoption of the right to health framework in various contexts. These are questions the authors of this book will continue to explore.

References

UN Committee on Economic, Social, and Cultural Rights (2000) The right to the highest attainable standard of health E/C.12/2000/4. http://www.unhchr.ch/tbs/doc.nsf/%28symbol %29/E.C.12.2000.4.En. Accessed 28 Nov 2013
World Health Organization (2013) Social determinants of health. http://www.who.int/social_determinants/sdh_definition/en/index.html. Accessed 28 Nov 2013

About the Authors

Aline Albuquerque (PhD) holds a post-doctorate in Human Rights from the Emory University, Atlanta, (2011) and a Doctor's degree in Health Science from the University of Brasilia (2010). Ms. Albuquerque is a Justice Department Attorney at the Human Rights Secretariat at the Presidency of the Republic; she is a Professor, Associate Researcher and Advisor at the post-graduate course in Bioethics at the University of Brasilia and in the UNESCO Chair in Bioethics and Human Rights at the University of Brasilia; and a Human Rights Professor at the Centro de Ensino Universitário de Brasília. She currently develops research in: Human Rights Indicators System within the international research; the right to health: a multi-country study of law, policy and practice, coordinated by Brigit Toebes from the University of Aberdeen, and in the area of Bioethics and Human Rights at the University of Brasilia, and coordinates the Clinic of Human Rights at the Centro de Ensino Universitário de Brasília. Ms. Albuquerque has two published books: one is about Criminal Law and Genetics and the other is about Bioethics and Human Rights. She has a vast experience in Law with emphasis in Bioethics, mainly working with the following themes: bioethics and human rights; and human right to health.

Marco Barboza is a lawyer specialised in Human Rights & Health, Gender, Sexuality and Public Policy. He has experience in systems analysis and social security legislation; as well as in the advocacy and protection of health rights, in the Ministry of Health and the office of the Ombudsman. His research area includes social security, law and policy on sexual and reproductive rights, HIV/AIDS, mental health and health promotion. He served as consultant for the National Multisectoral Commission for Health (CONAMUSA), the Pan-American Health Organization (PAHO), the Peruvian Ministry of Health and FLACSO–Mexico.

Dabney P. Evans is Executive Director of the Emory University Institute of Human Rights. She received her Doctoral degree in 2010 in law from the University of Aberdeen (United Kingdom) and her Master of Public Health degree in 1998. Currently, an Assistant Professor in the Hubert Department of Global Health at the Rollins School of Public Health at Emory University Evans teaches

B. Toebes et al. (eds.), *The Right to Health*, DOI: 10.1007/978-94-6265-014-5,
© T.M.C. ASSER PRESS and the authors 2014

courses in 'Interdisciplinary Perspectives in Human Rights' and 'Health and Human Rights'. Evans has previously published her dissertation research, 'The Synergistic Approach' and a curriculum based on the HBO documentary film Sergio, a biography of former UN High Commissioner for Human Rights Sergio Viera de Mello. She is co-editor of 'Rights Based Approaches to Public Health' and outgoing chair of the International Human Rights Committee of the American Public Health Association. Evans is an avid capoeira practitioner with the group Passo A Frente and fluent in Portuguese.

Rhonda Ferguson is a Ph.D. candidate at the Irish Centre for Human Rights, National University of Ireland Galway. She has expertise in economic, social and cultural rights, particularly as they pertain to health, food, international development and gender equality. Most recently, she was a Doctoral fellow with the Irish Centre for Human Rights in Ireland. In the past, Ferguson has conducted qualitative and quantitative research with non-governmental organisations in Canada and Thailand and completed an internship with the Office of the United Nations High Commissioner for Human Rights in Switzerland. She has taught on the subjects of health and human rights in universities in Canada and Ireland and has presented at numerous academic and professional conferences in North America and Europe.

Sondus Hassounah (Ph.D) is a researcher in the WHO Collaborating Centre for Public Health Education and Training at the Department of Primary Care & Public Health, Imperial College London. She is actively involved in health system strengthening research, assessing and building health leadership capacity with particular focus on low-middle income countries, health systems in transition and post-conflict countries. Dr. Hassounah's Background is in clinical practise. She graduated from the Faculty of Medicine-Cairo University where she received her MBBS and worked as a Doctor. She then moved onto Public Health, working in harm reduction for HIV prone communities, predominantly Injecting Drug Users (IDU's), and People Living with HIV (PLHA). Prior to that, Dr. Hassounah worked in the TB department at the Eastern Mediterranean Regional Office for the World Health Organization (EMRO), where she gained ample experience liaising with local government and International partners on capacity building, research and project management in the region. Coming to Imperial College London, and after being awarded a MPH (Masters in Public Health), her main research focus has been geared towards Universal Health Coverage and equity in health. She also leads on building local health-workforce capacity through training and education. Dr. Hassounah's vested interest is in marrying up public health research and field work, bringing evidence-based best practises to ground-root sustainable implementation.

Ruth Iguiñiz-Romero is Executive coordinator of the International Association for the Studies of Sexuality, Culture and Society-IASSCS and researcher at the School of Public Health and Administration 'Carlos Vidal Layseca', Universidad

About the Authors

Peruana Cayetano Heredia. Her specialist areas are reproductive health policy, women's rights and gender and health. She has a Master in Philosophy in Urban and Public Policy and a Master of Arts in Anthropology from the New School University. She has been a Associate Researcher at the University of Deusto with the support of the Marie Curie Program of the European Union, and serves on the Editorial board of the Spanish version of the journal Reproductive Health Matters/ Temas en Salud Reproductiva.

Milan M. Markovic is a research fellow with Institute of Social Sciences in Belgrade, a doctoral candidate at the Institute for International Law and International Relations, University of Graz, and a legal advisor with Mental Disability Rights Initiative MDRI-S (Disability Rights International). He is a Secretary General of the Serbian Association of Lawyers for Medical and Health Law. His main research interests include the right to health, human rights, disability rights, health law and international law, and he has published internationally. He was a visiting fellow with Max Planck Institute in Heidelberg, Centre of Excellence in International Courts University of Copenhagen and University of Vienna. Markovic has been engaged in several research projects within the FP7 and IPA EU frameworks, as a national expert. He has served as an advisor to the National Preventive Mechanism against Torture in Serbia.

Adam McAuley is a Law lecturer at the School of Law and Government at Dublin City University in Ireland. One of his research areas is role of law, ethics and politics in health. He was recently appointed to the Department of Health and Children's National Advisory Committee on Bioethics.

Getahun A. Mosissa (LL.M) is a Ph.D Candidate at the Faculty of Law of the University of Groningen and Lecturer at School of Law of Jimma University (Ethiopia). Previously, he was a Judge at Oromia National Regional State. Getahun obtained Batchlor of Laws from Addis Ababa University, Ethiopia; LL.M in International Law and Laws of International Organisations (with specialisation in human rights) from the University of Groningen where he graduated with 'cum laude'. His Ph.D research focuses on the investigation of the theories and practices of Economic, Social and Cultural Rights. His research interest includes international human rights law, constitutional law and social justice.

Tokuko Munesue (Ph.D) is an Associate Professor at the Faculty of Law of Kanazawa University in Japan. Her specialist areas are social security law and international human rights law, in particular health and human rights. Her research focuses on the normative content and obligations of the right to health; 'Policy Approach' of human rights and use human rights indicators and benchmarks mainly in relation to economic, social and cultural rights; universal coverage and national health systems; cancer control and patients' rights; and support systems for sexual assault victims and sexual and reproductive rights.

Obiajulu Nnamuchi (Ph.D) is an Assistant Professor of law at the University of Nigeria as well as President and Chief Consultant at the Centre for Health, Bioethics and Human Rights, Enugu, Nigeria. His expertise lies in human rights, bioethics, moral philosophy and, health law and policy. A formally trained ethicist, he teaches clinical and research ethics to students as well as health professionals throughout the world. Prior to assuming his current position, Dr. Nnamuchi was a researcher at the Beazley Institute for Health Law and Policy, an affiliate of Loyola University Chicago Law School. His scholarship focuses mainly on the intersection of health and human rights; health governance and financing; human rights and culture controversies; law and ethics of medical practice; gender and minority issues; critical legal theory; and development issues, especially as they relate to health and delivery of health care—areas on which he has written extensively.

Nancy Palomino is a Professor and a Coordinator of Sexuality and Reproductive Health Unit of the School of Public Health and Administration, Universidad Peruana Cayetano Heredia. She has a Master Degree in Public Health and studies on Anthropology and Political Philosophy. Her specialist areas include gender and health, violence against women, and reproductive and sexual rights. She is Chief Editor of Journal Reproductive Health Matters in Spanish/Temas en Salud Reproductiva.

Natalya Pestova recently completed her Ph.D in law at the Irish Center for Human Rights, National University of Ireland, Galway. Her doctoral research addressed perspectives of application of the human rights-based approaches at the level of local government. She holds LL.M. in International Human Rights Law from the National University of Ireland, Galway, and LL.M in Jurisprudence from the Moscow State Law Academy. Previously, she worked as a Practicing Lawyer in private and public sector and as a law lecturer at the Vyatka State University of Humanities, Russia. Currently, Natalya is coordinating integration work with migrant communities in the West of Ireland with the local NGO. Her academic interests are economic, social and cultural rights of disadvantaged groups and challenges of their implementation through the interdisciplinary perspectives of governance, development and management of natural resources.

Shengnan Qiu (Ph.D) did her first degree in Law at the Northwest University of Politics and Law in China. She also did an LLM (general) at the University of Southampton and an LLM (human rights) at the University of Nottingham. She completed her Ph.D in Law at the University of Essex in 2012. Her Ph.D thesis examined the extent to which the right to health is realised in China with a particular focus on equality and accountability. Now she is a project-based researcher. Her research interests focus on the right to health, economic, social and cultural rights, international law, human rights and China.

About the Authors

Salman Rawaf is the Director of the WHO Collaborating Centre, and a Professor of Public Health in the Department of Primary Care and Public Health at Imperial College, London. He acquired his qualification in Medicine, with training in paediatrics and public health, and spent the breadth of his career in the NHS; including 26 years as an Executive Director (County Medical Adviser) and a Medical Director. In the latter 23 years of his service in the NHS, Professor Rawaf served as the Director of Public Health in South-West London, from which he then moved to Imperial College as a Professor of Public Health, and the Director of the WHO Collaborating Centre for Public Health Education and Training, which supports several WHO Regions and their Member States. Professor Rawaf is globally recognised for his international work and contribution to global public health, primary care in research and service delivery. His work is well documented in supporting countries to strengthen their health systems and service development; including Bahrain, Brazil, Iran, the Kingdom of Saudi Arabia, the State of Kuwait, Libya, Malaysia, Maldives, Malta, Oman, Poland, Tunisia, Uzbekistan, Iraq, Palestine, Qatar and Yemen.

Maite San Giorgi (Ph.D) is Secretary of the Board of Medical Specialists at the Onze Lieve Vrouwe Gasthuis hospital in Amsterdam (the Netherlands) and member of the Patient Council at the Diakonessenhuis hospital in Utrecht (the Netherlands). In 2012, she successfully defended her dissertation The Human Right to Equal Access to Health Care (Intersentia Publishing, 2012) at the Erasmus University of Rotterdam (the Netherlands). Alongside her Ph.D research, Maite has been an active member of various working groups at the Netherlands School of Human Rights Research. She has taught various courses on health law and health sciences. Maite has given seminars and presentations on her Ph.D research and has followed various courses on human rights at the Erasmus University, as well as courses on philosophy at the University of Amsterdam and the Catholic University of Leuven.

Thamer Sartawi is a Medical Doctor and an independent researcher from Jordan. He is a holder of an M.Sc in Health inequalities and Public Policy form the Global Public health unit at the University of Edinburgh. He practices medicine in a hospital and in the Syrian refugee camp of Al-Za'atari. His research interest lies in addressing health inequalities in the Eastern Mediterranean region, with specific focus on the relationship between poverty and health. His focus on realising the rights of most vulnerable populations in Jordan has lead him to be involved in research projects regarding refugee rights in Jordan.

Brigit Toebes (Ph.D) is an Associate Professor and Rosalind Franklin Fellow at the Faculty of Law of the University of Groningen (the Netherlands) where she teaches public international law, international humanitarian law and human rights law. Her specialist areas are human rights law, in particular economic, social and cultural rights, the definition of health as a right, the interfaces between health and human rights, as well as (international) health law, medical ethics, and international humanitarian law. She has written widely in these areas, including books with Intersentia Publising (The Right to Health as a Human Right in International Law, 1999; Health and Human Rights in Europe, 2012), and articles in leading human rights and health law journals. She is an editor of the Netherlands Quarterly of Human Rights and a Board Member of the International Federation of Health and Human Rights Organizations (IFHHRO).

Lara Walker (Ph.D) is a Lecturer in law at the University of Sussex where she teaches European law and family law. Her specialist area is cross-border family law, particularly the civil aspects of child abduction and the recovery of maintenance and child support. Her research takes account of regional and international developments in this area. In the context of child abduction she is particularly interested in the discourse between the case law of the Court of Justice of the European Union and the European Court of Human Rights. She has also carried out empirical research on the recovery of maintenance in the EU as part of a project funded by the European Commission.

Index

A

AAAQ (Availability, Accessibility, Acceptability and Quality), 127, 144, 207, 215, 346–347, 407, 416

Aboriginal
  Aboriginal Healing and Wellness Strategy, 303
  Aboriginal health, 283–284
  Aboriginal-specific health initiatives, 283–284, 293, 300, 303
  Indian Act, 288, 298–303
  Indian Registry, 298, 300
  National Aboriginal Health Organization (NAHO), 285, 291
  Non-Insured Health Benefits (NIHB), 283, 298, 300–302
  Residential schools, 301

Abortion, unsafe, 355–356, 366

Abuse, 106
  alcohol abuse, 138
  sexual abuse, 319
  substance abuse, 138, 301, 304, 363

Access
  to health care/healthcare, 89, 97–98, 108–109, 143, 155, 158
  to justice, 48, 56, 63–66, 89, 267, 272

Accident(s), 274, 365, 387
  nuclear accidents, 129–130

Accountability, Ex ante mechanisms, 412

Adult mortality rate, 345

Affordability, 208, 405, 408, 415, 420

African Charter on Human and People's Rights, 29, 34, 77–80

African Commission, 34, 59, 89

African Human Development Report, 68

African Union (AU), 12, 31, 43–44, 47–49, 50, 56, 61, 69, 71, 80, 83, 86, 89

Affordable Care Act (ACA), 233, 235, 239, 244, 245, 246, 248, 251, 253

Aging (of the population), 124–127, 128

AIDS, 107, 313, 316, 319–320, 322, 323, 325, 344, 347, 358, 361–363
  See also HIV/AIDS

Ambulatory system, 365

American Convention on Human Rights, 314
  Article 11, 316
  See also Pact of San Jose; Costa Rica

American dream; the, 236, 241, 246, 249

Alma-Ata Conference, 16, 61, 66

Answerability, 411

Anti-retroviral treatment, 322, 325, 358, 362, 364, 367

Arab world, 135, 138–139, 146, 218

African Union (AU)
  Social Policy Framework, 47, 67–71
  Executive Council, 86

Austerity, Measures, 405, 417, 419–420, 432

B

Banjul Charter, 73, 82

Barriers, 105–107, 207–208, 217, 291–293, 440

Basic health entitlements, 46, 59, 61–63, 66, 70, 74

Biological characteristics, 344

Blood transfusion, 395, 409

Breast cancer, 126

C

Cairo Declaration on Human Rights in Islam, 172

Canada Health Act, 296

Cancer, 126, 376, 392–393, 413

Catholic Church, 389–390

Chronic disease(s), 128, 208, 215–216, 327, 416

Civil society, 32–33, 35, 261, 271–273
  actors, 323, 405

B. Toebes et al. (eds.), *The Right to Health*, DOI: 10.1007/978-94-6265-014-5,
© T.M.C. ASSER PRESS and the authors 2014

451

452   Index

organizations (CSO), 33–35, 37, 86–87, 270, 326
Colonization, 294–295
Commercialized service model, 108
Commission on the Social Determinants of Health (CSDH), 55, 183
Committee on Economic; Social and Cultural Rights (CESCR), 59, 85, 87, 101, 129, 343, 345, 354, 356
Communicable disease, 138, 207, 316, 321, 334, 358, 444
    non-communicable, 350
Competition, 108, 383, 387–388, 415–417
Communist party, 109
Condom(s), 319, 326, 391
Confidentiality, 175–176, 180, 330–332
Constitution, 141–143
    of China, 103–105
    of Ireland, 375–376, 379, 390
    of Japan, 122–123
    of the Netherlands, 414, 425
    of Nigeria, 20
    of the Russian Federation, 351–352
Constitutional enactment (of the right to health), 138
Constitutional justice, 63–65, 72, 84
Constitutional rights, 106, 375–376, 380
Consultant(s), 381, 353, 355–357, 397
Contraceptives (contraception), 60, 179–181, 248, 354–355, 366, 390–392, 389
Convention of Belem do Para
    See Inter-American Convention on the Prevention; Punishment and Eradication of Violence against Women
Convention on the Elimination of All Forms of Discrimination Against Women (CEDAW), 101–103, 122, 168, 170–172, 174–176, 180–181, 184–185, 189, 345, 351, 354
    Article 5, 189
    Article 12, 101–102, 174–177, 189
    General Recommendation 24, 177, 180, 264
Convention on the Rights of Persons with Disabilities (CRPD)
    Article 25, 345
Convention on the Rights of the Child (CRC), 171, 345, 357
    Article 24, 188, 357, 425
Corruption, 18–21, 69, 87, 350
Culturally appropriate health care, 283, 285–286, 298, 300, 304–306, 347, 389, 409
Cultural practices, 168, 181, 185

Cultural responsibility, 284
Cultural safety, 285, 305
Curative model, 138, 416

D
Darfur case, 79–80
Declaration of the Rights of the Child, 315
Deng Xiaoping, 108
Dentistry, 160–162
Development
    Development Research Centre of the State Council (the DRCSC) of China, 108
    economic development, 67, 99, 113–114, 115–117, 246, 384
    equal development/unequal development, 108
Diabetes, 126, 128, 182, 215, 289, 360
Diarrhea, 28
Disabled persons; persons with a disability; disability, 75, 110, 250, 253, 275, 420, 261, 345
    Law on the Protection of Disabled Persons of the People's Republic of China, 106
Direct effect, 424–425
Disadvantaged communities, 347
Disaggregated data, 261, 290
    See also indicators
Discrimination
    direct discrimination, 98, 107–108, 118
    discriminatory policies, 97
Disease burden, 10, 14, 15, 17, 18, 21, 31, 45, 67, 138, 283, 289
Doctors (physicians), per 1000 population, 10, 116, 125, 139, 158–159
Domestic
    law, 123, 198, 368, 379
    legal system, 123, 352, 368
    legislation, 198, 352, 362, 425
    workers, 169, 184–188
(Re)Distribution of wealth, 100, 116, 202, 210, 217, 440
DRC case, 78, 80
Drug(s)
    clinic, 364
    users, 343, 361, 362–364, 367–369
Dworkin (Ronald), 104

E
European Social Charter, 351, 414, 425
    Article 11, 426
Earthquake, 129
E. coli, 389

Index

Economic
  expansion, 118
  independence, 106
  reforms, 98, 100, 108, 110, 113, 115, 117
Economic; social and cultural rights, 7, 29, 54, 80, 101, 171–172, 196, 200, 238–239, 253, 260–263, 265–266, 410–411, 424–425
Economy
  centrally-planned economy, 98, 113, 115, 117
  market economy, 99, 115
Education, 7, 23, 31, 80, 99, 107, 168, 172, 179, 180, 189, 210, 216, 218, 220, 237–238, 292, 307, 315, 318, 320, 354, 358, 362–363, 375, 389
Elderly, 107, 197, 250, 255, 275, 344, 416, 420
Emergency, 14, 130, 176, 179, 189, 206, 292, 386, 392, 419, 442
Employment, 54, 100, 105, 107, 114, 169, 183, 208, 217, 292, 352
Enforceability, 411, 424–426
Epidemic, 32, 316–319, 323–329, 333, 350, 361–363, 368
Equality
  Chinese concepts of equality, 103
  formal equality, 98, 100, 101, 103, 107
  substantive equality, 98, 100, 101–103, 107
Equity, 9, 30, 55, 118, 217, 244, 287, 384–386, 420–421
Essential medicines, 9, 11, 12, 61, 139, 146, 155–157, 222
European Court of Human Rights (ECtHR), 360, 379–380, 391–393
Exercise, 138, 182, 189

F

Family planning, 31, 60, 177, 180, 354, 355, 366, 390–391
Financial crisis, 387
Foreign workers, 166
  See also migrant workers
Freedom of choice, 48, 58, 59–61, 65–66, 74

G

Gender (discrimination), 175
General Comment 14, 85, 98, 101, 136, 201–202, 235, 283, 344, 348, 365, 406–407, 409–412, 418–419
General Practitioner (GP), 381, 383–388, 417
Generic medicines, 139, 145, 155–157, 387
Geographic accessibility, 418, 427, 432

Government Medical Insurance Scheme (the GMIS), 111–112
Gross Domestic Product (GDP), 20, 124, 137–138, 141, 196, 352, 413, 419
Guidelines on State Reporting (Reporting Guidelines), 82
Gynaecological complications, 356, 366

H

Harmful traditional practices, 354
Health
  budget, 14, 17, 112, 444
  expenditure, 47, 99, 112, 126, 138, 197, 254, 352, 370, 387, 413
  outcomes, 9, 18, 29, 147, 242, 245–247, 353, 413
  (related) legislation, 414, 425
  resources, 108, 115–116, 440
  sector, 14, 67, 109, 319–320, 352, 368, 411–412, 421, 423, 430
  system (operation), 147
  workforce, 10, 139, 146, 160, 446
Health care
  Inspectorate, 418, 422, 427, 432
  models, 242
  performance(s), 126, 413, 427
  reform, 109, 403, 405, 415, 417
  schemes, 109, 110, 244, 292, 301
  spending, 243, 244, 246, 413, 419, 420
  See also Universal Health Care
Health insurance
  act, 123, 414, 415, 429
  public/private, 118, 415, 99, 109, 183, 184, 186, 190, 248, 282, 386–388, 405
Heart disease, 125, 182
Hepatitis B, 107
Hepatitis C, 395–396
High blood pressure, 182, 353
HIV/AIDS, 327, 333
  HIV-positive drug users, 364, 369
  people/persons living with HIV/AIDS (PLWHA), 320–323, 325–334
Hospital(s)
  beds, 139, 144, 155–157, 350, 382, 386, 408
  private beds, 377, 382–383, 386–387
Hukou system, 108, 112, 114
Human dignity, 49–53, 55–57, 61, 74, 335
Humanitarian crisis, 59, 73, 76, 80, 81, 89, 200, 211, 220
Human rights-based approach, 313, 364, 369
Human rights indicators, 262–273
Human rights mechanisms, 47, 348

454 Index

Human Rights Watch, 182, 186, 216, 362, 364
Hunt (Paul), 66, 178, 196, 202, 210, 217, 235, 254, 268–269, 329, 360

I

Immunization, 14, 31, 207, 208, 219, 266, 358
International Covenant on Civil and Political Rights (ICCPR), 23, 35, 103, 122–123, 171, 175, 189, 197, 360
  Article 6, 360
Immediate obligation, 58, 101, 123
Indicator(s)
  attributes, 273–275
  disaggregation, 265, 268–269, 272, 275
  measuring progress, 203, 263, 265, 324
  National Human Rights Indicator System, 269
  progress indicators, 261, 263, 265
  result indicators, 262–267, 272, 274, 276
  structure indicators, 264
Inhuman(e) and degrading treatment, 74, 77, 79, 80, 122, 379–380
Insurance
  mandatory insurance, 245
  market, 383, 387, 405
  premiums, 110, 197, 245, 252, 382
Infant mortality rate, 125, 179, 242, 268, 273, 289, 357, 413
  See also under five mortality rate
Inter-American Commission on Human Rights, 261, 262, 265, 327
Inter-American Convention on the Prevention, Punishment and Eradication of Violence against Women, 314, 315
International Covenant on Economic, Social and Cultural Rights (ICESCR), 15, 23, 29, 38, 53, 101, 129, 171, 175, 199–201, 235, 245, 254, 255, 262, 264–265, 345, 357, 406, 407, 421
  Article 12, 129, 136, 195, 199, 234, 255, 262, 264–270, 343, 357, 374, 406–407
International Labour Organization (ILO), 351
  Convention No. 169, 295
Internet, 118
Islamic law, 170, 171, 175

J

Judicial enforcement, 425, 432

K

Kafala (sponsorship system), 184

L

Labour
  contracts, 107
  laws, 169, 184, 185, 188
  Urban Labour Medical Insurance Scheme (ULMIS), 109
Leisure, facilities, 183, 185
Life expectancy, 27–28, 125, 173, 195, 196, 243, 246, 289, 353, 365, 367, 409, 413, 419
Lifestyle, 31, 138, 275, 289, 344, 350, 353, 367
  factors, 138
Live birth(s), 8, 11, 46, 178, 179, 357
Local government, 17–18, 109

M

Marginalised (groups/communities), 343–349
Market
  economy, 99, 115
  oriented, 405, 411, 418
Maternal mortality rate, 6, 178, 179, 182, 196, 207 274
Medical
  disciplinary tribunals, 428
  industry, 116
  register, 383, 391
  treatment, 37, 359, 360, 376, 378, 380, 409
Medically appropriate, 347, 394, 404
Medicines, 12, 298, 301–303, 387, 409
Middle East, 137, 211
Middle East and Northern Africa (MENA), 137
Midwife(s), 10, 11, 125, 389
Migrant(s) workers, 114, 169, 178–179, 183–188
Ministry of Health, 28, 38, 128, 196, 273–274, 320, 328
Minorities, 55, 201, 283, 343, 348, 389, 409
Morning after pill, 391
Muslim(s), 171
Malawi Africa Association, 77, 80, 85
Market economy
  See economy
Marketization, 429
Marriage, 107, 113, 138
Medical facilities, 128, 293
Medical technology(ies), 115, 117
Medicines, 12, 155–157, 286, 297–298, 301–303, 386–387, 409
Migrant workers, 114, 169, 178–179, 183–188

Index 455

Mikhail Trepashkin, 360
Millennium Development Goals (MDGs), 9, 46, 355
Monitoring mechanisms, 432
Mortality (rate), 17, 46, 125, 177, 207, 242, 265, 289, 327, 367, 410, 413
Morbidity (rate), 17, 126, 207, 290

N

New Rural Cooperative Medical Insurance Scheme (NRCMIS), 111, 114
National Health Service (NHS), 27, 381, 388
Non-communicable diseases (NCDs), 138, 207
Non-discrimination, 54, 82, 101–103, 174–175, 189, 324, 345, 349, 352, 369, 408
Non-governmental organisations NGO(s), 15, 86, 216, 221, 318, 323, 325, 326
Non-state actor, 199, 430
Nurses, 10, 116, 396
    per 1000 population, 10, 116, 125, 139, 158–159

O

Obesity, 182
Organization for Economic Cooperation and Development (OECD), 11, 126, 404
Ogoni, 34, 78
Office of the High Commissioner for Human Rights (OHCHR), 131, 260
Obligations
    core obligations, 199, 349, 440
    international obligations, 78
    to respect; protect and fulfil, 59, 176, 253, 348, 427
    tripartite typology, 251, 411
Ombudsman, 396, 423
Opioid, 363
Obstetrician, 389
Out-of-pocket (payment/expenditure) (OOP), 12, 107, 144, 197, 241, 302, 352, 416
Outpatient, 16, 110, 208, 350, 387
Overconsumption (of fatty and salty foods), 138

P

Pact of San Jose; Costa Rica
    See American Convention on Human Rights
Participation, 23, 53, 102, 129, 167, 217, 266, 307, 328, 394, 412

Participatory mechanisms, 428
Patient-doctor relationship, 428
Payments, Formal/informal, 352
Penitentiary system, 361
People/persons living with HIV/AIDS (PLWHA)
    See HIV/AIDS
Pharmaceutics/Pharmaceuticals, 13, 352
Physical accessibility, 263, 308, 347, 408
Physicians (doctors), 10, 76, 128, 159, 292
Planned economy, 97
Political procrastination, 392
Post-natal care, 106
Potts (Helen), 65–66, 411–412
Pregnancy, 22, 46, 181, 329, 355, 389
Pregnant woman/women, 393, 178, 197, 313, 361, 395
Prescription, 16, 143, 248, 292, 390
Pricing, 387
Primary health care, 15, 61, 113, 143, 173, 209, 306
Prison(s), overcrowding, 359
Privacy, 185, 313, 330, 367
Private expenditure (on health), 139, 352
Private-owned enterprises, 99
Progressive realization, 58, 101, 200, 245, 282, 444
Prostate cancer, 126
Protocol of San Salvador, Article 10, 19, 260
Public good, 64, 108, 237
Public health system, 215, 259, 350, 386

R

Radioactive material, 129
Rawls, 104
Regulated competition, 415
Refugees, 194, 347, 441
Remedies, 64, 118, 412
Reproductive (health) rights, 325
Resource constraints, 15, 47, 101, 177, 253
Risk-taking behaviour, 138, 353
Roe v. Wade, 390
Roma Communities, 333
Rural
    rural areas, 46, 99, 355, 384
    rural population, 46, 99
    See also New Rural Cooperative Medical Insurance Scheme (NRCMIS)

S

School curricula, 354
Seat belts, 138

Sen (Amartya), 104
SERAC, 34, 78
Sex education, 318, 354, 179
Sexual health, 315
Sexual orientation, 315
Sex workers, 315
Sharia, 170
Smoking, 60, 138, 413
Social benefits, 104
Social justice, 49, 117
Social sector, 109
Socio-economic health inequalities, 433
Solidarity, 53, 382, 405
Soviet healthcare policy, 350
Special mechanisms, 81
Special Rapporteur, 130, 235, 268, 360
Sport, 149, 182, 330
State-owned enterprises, 100
Substantive inequalities, 101
Suicide, 275, 329, 358, 392
Substance (abuse)
    See abuse
Supreme Court
    of Canada, 297
    of Ireland, 376
    of the United States, 235
Syphilis, 317
Systemic right, 58

T
TEPCO (Tokyo Electric Power Company),
    129
Tokyo District Court, 123
Tradition
    traditional healers, 302
    Traditional Healer travel fund, 283
    traditional medicine, 303
    traditional values, 167
Transparency, 82, 129, 202, 252, 265
Transportation, 115, 251, 292
Two-tier hospital system, 392
Tuberculosis, 43, 289, 328, 365

U
Under five mortality rate, 6, 46
    See also infant mortality rate
Underlying determinants of health, 27, 61,
    102, 136, 315, 345
United Nations Committee on the Rights of the
    Child (UNCRC), 357–358
United Nations High Commissioner for Refu-
    gees (UNHCR), 186, 196
Universal Declaration of Human Rights
    (UDHR), 23, 53, 264
Universal Health Care, 243, 291
Universal Health Coverage (UHC), 109, 136,
    243
Universal Periodic Review, 261
Urban
    labourers, 109
    residents, 110
    Urban Labour Medical Insurance Scheme
        (ULMIS), 109
    Urban Resident Medical Insurance Scheme
        (the URMIS), 110

V
Vienna Declaration and Programme of Action,
    37, 265
Vulnerability, 45, 211, 291, 321, 344
Vulnerable groups, 109, 174, 253, 323, 343

W
Waiting
    list(s), 382, 432
    time(s), 385
Water, 27, 407
Wheelchair, 347, 416
World Health Organization (WHO), 7, 67, 117
Women, 46, 102, 167, 247, 290, 317, 353
    Law on the Protection of Women of the
        People's Republic of China, 106
World Bank, 17, 173, 349
World Health Report, 9, 46